D0077397

COURSE Bank

To register, use the URL provided by your instructor

If your instructor has not assigned CourseBank, visit https://coursebank.net
to register for self-study

Scratch here for your access code

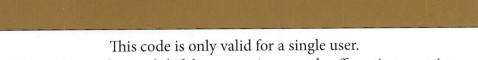

This code is only valid for a single user.
This code may be invalid if the protective scratch-off coating covering
the code has been removed and redeemed by the book's previous owner.

For instructors:

- A turnkey solution for your online sections.
- Auto-graded assignments and quizzes, whether your course is online or lecture-based.
- Integrates with Blackboard, Canvas, and other LMSs for single sign-in and single gradebook.
- Detailed diagnostic tools to assess class and individual student performance.

For students:

- Self-study and practice.
- Immediate feedback from quizzes and assignments, if enabled by your instructor.

Assets:

- Narrated and animated chapter overview
- Videos
- Lecture PowerPoints
- Confidence-based flash cards
- Quizzes
- Exercises
- Discussion boards with chapter-specific prompts

Human Resource MANAGEMENT

edition 2

Jean M. Phillips
Pennsylvania State University

Stanley M. Gully
Pennsylvania State University

CHICAGO
BUSINESS PRESS

CHICAGO
BUSINESS PRESS

For product information or assistance visit: www.chicagobusinesspress.com

Paperback ISBN-13: 978-0-9988140-1-8
Paperback ISBN-10: 0-9988140-1-6
Loose-leaf ISBN-13: 978-0-9988140-2-5
Loose-leaf ISBN-10: 0-9988140-2-4
ebook ISBN-13: 978-0-9988140-5-6
ebook ISBN-10: 0-9988140-5-9

Brief Table of Contents

Table of Contents

2   The Role of Human Resource Management in Business   32

3   The Legal Context of HRM   64

5   Sourcing and Recruiting   136

6   Selection and Hiring   168

PART THREE
Training and Performance Management   205

8   Performance Management   240

PART FOUR
Managing Total Rewards   279

9   Base Compensation   280

13 Creating Positive Employee–Management Relations   396

Preface

Approach

Although some students will go on to become managers requiring a working knowledge of human resource management (HRM), all students will eventually use this knowledge in some way. This book has been written to prepare both, through personal development to help them all understand HRM in order to optimize the benefit that derives from it. And to make the subject engaging while developing long-lasting impact, we focus on developing both *skill* and *knowledge* so students learn how to *take action* in addition to learning about HRM.

HRM Is Critical to Success

By helping to successfully acquire, deploy, and motivate the right talent, HRM is critical to every manager's and organization's success. The central theme of our book is helping you understand how to use HRM to hire, develop, motivate, and retain the right people and bring out the best in employees to execute the company's business strategy and secure a competitive advantage. Our book is intended for those who are or who might become a manager or an HRM professional. We discuss the roles of HRM professionals, managers, and employees in the design and implementation of effective HRM systems, and include many current examples of how HRM is executed in organizations.

Flexibility Is Necessary in HRM

Because there is rarely a single best way to implement HRM, every chapter has an **HR Flexiblity** feature that highlights how HR needs to be flexible to best meet the needs of different situations. The **Global Issues** feature in each chapter discusses how HRM practices differ around the world and how HRM needs to be adapted to best meet the demands of different global and cultural contexts.

Developing HRM Skills to Become More Effective Managers

Each chapter's **Develop Your Skills** feature focuses on improving a specific skill related to that chapter's topic. By developing your competence and confidence in using important HRM skills, this book will help you become a more effective manager through the better use of HRM tools and practices. The importance of the context of HRM, including laws, ethics, and globalization, is woven throughout the book. How organizations are using various technologies to improve and facilitate the execution of HRM is also described.

Each chapter opens with a **Real World Challenge**, describing an actual HRM situation faced by a company or manager to highlight the business importance of the chapter's topic and to prompt reflective reading. The chapters conclude with the **Real World Response**, which describes how the organization or manager handled the situation to show how the chapter concepts were applied. In addition to the case study contained in each chapter, the **Real World Challenge** is designed to improve analytical and problem-solving skills.

We wrote this book to be very experiential and to cultivate skill development. Rather than just learning *about* HRM, we also want you to become better *at* HRM. Developing your

HRM skills will make you a more effective manager and will make your job easier no matter what field you are in. A **book-long integrated project, case studies, videos, and numerous exercises** develop readers' personal skills and provide some experience in applying various HR concepts. **The Happy Time Toys videos** written and filmed exclusively for this book reinforce the relevance of the textbook material and enhance decision-making, analytical, and HRM skills.

Engaging by Example

We wrote the book to be engaging to read. We include **many practical examples**, and focus on teaching **HRM as it is done today**. We also provide many opportunities to develop your HRM-related skills, and we hope that you find these activities to be both developmental and enjoyable. If you have any questions, comments, or suggestions about the book please feel free to contact us at phillipsgully@gmail.com.

This book clearly communicates the importance of effective talent management to individual and firm performance. By focusing on the importance of flexibility in applying different HRM methods to find, keep, and motivate the right employees for the company and job, and on the importance of developing HRM skills, this book will prepare readers to effectively use HRM to be better managers and more effective leaders.

Features for Applying What You've Read

Real World Challenge

Each chapter starts with a close-up look at an HRM problem or challenge faced by an actual company or manager. This highlights the business importance of the chapter's topic. As you read the chapter, you will discover concepts that apply to that problem.

Real World Response

Each chapter ends with a close-up look at how the company or manager addressed its HRM problem or challenge. Here, you come full circle and learn how the featured company or manager applied the chapter concepts.

Strategic Impact ●●●●●●●●●●●●●●●●●●●●●●●●●●●●

Highlights the business impact of HRM in an actual company.

 Strategic Impact
Aligning Mattel's HRM Strategy

Toy company Mattel developed a better integrated HRM strategy to support its new strategic objectives of improving productivity, globalizing and extending the firm's brand name, and creating new brands. Mattel wanted to better align its HRM functions to motivate employees to work together, improve their skills, and improve retention. To support these goals, it created employee development programs, established metrics to better understand how the workforce was performing, and created a systematic succession strategy to increase the retention of the valuable talent it developed.[17] Mattel's staffing, performance measurement, and training programs now support each other and reinforce the firm's corporate goals.

🔴 HR Flexibility
Human Resource Management in Small Organizations

Smaller firms with fewer than 500 workers make up more than 99 percent of the business establishments that exist, employing nearly 50 percent of the total workforce.[18] However, small organizations often lack the budget for a dedicated human resource management function. Unfortunately, managers in small organizations often lack training in HRM and do not recognize generally accepted HRM practices as necessary for improving productivity.[19] This lack of understanding of HRM issues and their importance in the operation of a successful business has negatively impacted many small firms. Inadequate and inefficient management of human resources often result in low productivity and high employee dissatisfaction and turnover.[20] At least one study has found HRM practices to be the leading cause of small firms' failures,[21] and numerous studies have indicated that recruitment and training are two of the most important management problems facing small businesses.[22]

Even small organizations can effectively use HRM to improve their performance. Organizations of all sizes share a need to identify and hire the right people, motivate them to perform their best, develop their skills, and retain them. Investing in HRM improves productivity and profitability of smaller as well as larger organizations.[23] Although HRM practices obviously increase a company's talent-related costs, they should be seen as an investment in the company's performance rather than solely as an expense.

HR Flexibility ●●●●●●●●●●●●●

The HR Flexiblity feature highlights how HRM needs to be flexible to best meet the needs of different situations.

💼 Develop Your Skills
Careers in HRM

A career in human resource management can be rewarding both personally and financially. Occupational forecasts suggest that the income and opportunity prospects in HRM are favorable for at least the next decade or two. In fact, the Occupational Outlook Handbook provided by the U.S. government's Bureau of Labor Statistics states that, "Employment is expected to grow much faster than the average for all human resources, training, and labor relations managers and specialist occupations. College graduates and those who have earned certification should have the best job opportunities."[60]

Some of the job titles in the area of HRM include director of human resources, recruitment specialist, compensation analyst, employee benefits manager, work-life manager, training and development specialist, international human resource manager, diversity and inclusion specialist, and human resource generalist. Different skills are needed in the different areas of HRM. For example, strong quantitative and analytical skills are helpful in compensation, and good communication skills are critical in recruiting and training.

You can learn more about career opportunities in HRM by entering HRM-related search terms in the Occupational Outlook Handbook at http://www.bls.gov, or by using O*NET www.online.onetcenter.org.

Develop Your Skills ●●●●●●●●●●●●●●●●●●●●●●●●

Develop Your Skills focuses on improving a specific skill related to that chapter's topic.

🌐 Global Issues
Managing Global Volunteers

Managing talent in for-profit organizations can be challenging enough. The challenges are further increased in not-for-profit organizations and nongovernmental organizations (NGOs), including global humanitarian and relief organizations. In these types of organizations, some of the employees are volunteers or unpaid staff who work in non-native countries. There are no reward systems and no ability to use financial incentives to motivate volunteer performance. In addition, nonproductive volunteers may linger in the organization, diverting resources and other workers from accomplishing the organization's mission.[40]

One of the key challenges in managing global NGOs is managing diversity and conflict. Language and cultural barriers exist, as well as differences in work styles and priorities. Another key challenge in any NGO is assigning volunteers to roles that they are motivated to do and that they are capable of doing well. Because so much of volunteers' motivation comes from intangible rather than from tangible rewards, managers must meet the needs of each individual volunteer. Flexibility in motivating and rewarding the performance of each volunteer, clear goal setting and training in the ways tasks are to be carried out, and regular performance feedback and appreciation are important in meeting these needs. The California State Railroad Museum gives each paid supervisor 200 thank you cards at the beginning of the year that must all be used to thank volunteers by the end of the year.[41] These techniques are also effective in managing paid employees but are particularly critical when managing volunteers.

Global Issues ●●●●●●●●●●●

The Global Issues feature discusses how HRM practices differ around the world and how HRM policies and practices need to be adapted to best meet the demands of different global and cultural contexts.

CASE STUDY: HR Transformation at IBM

Multinational technology and consulting firm IBM transformed itself from a strong multinational business to a globally integrated enterprise. As Barbara Brickmeier, vice president of HR, services delivery, and HR delivery says, "We want to be able to focus on getting the right talent at the right time, in the right place. Because if we don't, someone else is right behind us."[53] Now operating in more than 170 countries and with 62 percent of its business service based, IBM knows how important it is to capitalize on talent worldwide.[54] IBM now locates its business functions around the world based on the right mix of costs and skills.

To support its new strategy, IBM's human resources function separated core HR roles, including designing HRM policies and internal business consulting, from more administrative tasks such as payroll, relocation, performance management, and data entry. This allowed IBM's HRM professionals to focus on strategic and employee needs as well as streamline services and reduce costs while improving flexibility and service quality.

IBM employees are now supported by country and regional HR line managers. HRM subject matter experts focus on key functions such as payroll and designing programs relevant to business goals. Standardized administrative roles are centralized in cost-effective global employee service centers that provide payroll processing, travel and expense processing, and employee records management.

IBM relies on repeatable technology-enabled, cost-effective processes, such as a proprietary system for processing travel expenses that provides faster, more accurate employee reimbursements. Brickmeier states, "If we had to do those administrative tasks, and deal with technology, we wouldn't be able to do the things that help push the business forward, like hiring people, upskilling, leadership development and getting the right talent in place. . . .This gives us time to devote to talent management, compensation, developing skills and expertise, and helping the business grow."[55]

IBM also changed its annual performance review to one that allows employee goals to change during the year and that provides more frequent feedback.[56] The system now gives employees feedback at teachable moments throughout the year rather than only once a year during the annual perofrmance review, and it allows all employees to give feedback to each other regardless of rank.[57]

Questions:
1. How does separating core HRM roles from administrative HRM roles help IBM better execute its business strategy?
2. How has technology helped IBM implement its new HRM configuration?
3. How would getting feedback more than once a year and from employees other than your supervisor help you to perform better at work?

Case Study ●●●●●●●●●●●●●●●●●●●●●●●●●●●●●●

These cases present how real companies responded to events and challenges. By reading this brief case study and answering the questions, you will improve your analytical and problem-solving skills and gain practical insights about how businesses function.

So What?

These items are brief explanations in the margin explaining why and how an HRM concept is important in the day-to-day productive functioning of a company.   · · · · · · · · · · · · · · ·

so what?

Understanding HRM and developing HRM skills can help you succeed both personally and professionally.

Takeaway Points

1. HRM influences organizational performance through its influence on what employees *should* do, what employees *can* do, and what employees *will* do. HRM creates the system that acquires, motivates, develops, and retains the talent that determines the organization's success. Because employee costs are a large part of an organization's operating budget, it is essential to properly manage the investments a company makes in its people.
2. The six primary HRM functions are staffing, performance management, training and development, rewards and benefits, health and safety, and employee-management relations.
3. If even a single HRM functional area reinforces goals that are in conflict with the other functional areas, influencing employee behaviors in desired ways and executing the company's strategy will be much more difficult. For example, the performance-enhancing potential of reward and incentive programs will not be fully leveraged if the training and development and staffing functions do not acquire and develop the right skills. The alignment of these separate functions creates an integrated human resource management system supporting the execution of the business strategy, guided by the talent philosophy of the organization.

Takeaway Points

A numbered list of the key points of the chapter, linked to the chapter's Learning Objectives..

Discussion Questions

Application and reflection questions posed from the perspective of both an employee and an employer.

Discussion Questions

1. Which aspects of HRM discussed in this chapter are illustrated in these videos? Explain your answer.
2. How could a company's investment in HRM help or undermine its success and its execution of its business strategy? Explain your answer
3. How else might you answer the question of whether Happy Time Toys should continue to invest money in HRM or reallocate some of it to sales or R&D?

Personal Development Exercise: Managing Ethical Issues in HRM

As you learned in this chapter, there are a variety of ethical issues that exist in HRM. Working in a group of three to five people, brainstorm at least five ethical issues that can exist in HRM. For example, a very productive manager bullies his subordinates and treats them in ways inconsistent with the corporate culture. Then identify how a company can use HRM to handle these ethical challenges. Be prepared to share two of your issues and HRM solutions with the class.

· · · · · · · · · · · · · · · · **Personal Development Exercises**

These are exercises that students can use to gain personal experience applying HRM concepts.

Strategic HRM Exercises

These are exercises requiring the strategic application of chapter concepts to illustrate HRM's impact on business outcomes.

Strategic HRM Exercises

Exercise: Culture Choice at Amazing Apps

Form groups of three to five students. Imagine that you started a company called Amaz Apps to develop applications for the iPad. You've had some good early success, but you n to hire more people to more quickly develop new products and get them up on the Apple St You know that the creativity and programming talent of the people you hire is going to critical to your company's future success, and you know that your HRM system will be to hiring and motivating the right talent. Be prepared to share your answers to the follow questions with the class.

1. Describe the type of culture you would like to create in your company.
2. How would you use HRM to reinforce this culture?
3. What would be the biggest threats to establishing your intended culture, and how could you overcome them?

Integrative Project

Introduced at the end of the first chapter, this project is continued through the book at the end of all the succeeding chapters. Here, you will develop your HRM skills and gain experience in applying various HRM concepts as you continue to build and apply your HRM knowledge in addressing various HRM challenges facing a real or fictitious company of your choosing.

Integrative Project

In the last chapter, you identified a company and an industry to focus on for this project. You also described the business strategy, competitive advantage, and talent philosophy you would use to create a competitive advantage for your business. Your assignment for this chapter is to think about and formalize your company's position on social responsibility and ethics. Record your company's formal statement about each. Feel free to research other companies' statements online for insight into how to craft your own. Then describe the culture you would create at your company, explain why it is best suited to your company's needs, and explain how it will contribute to its success.

Video Case with Discussion Questions

Featuring the Happy Time Toys company, these video cases were written and filmed exclusively for this book. The cases reinforce the relevance of each chapter's material and enhance decision-making, analytical, and HRM skills by demonstrating the results of more and less effective HRM policies and practices.

Video Case

Imagine having HR responsibilities at Happy Time Toys, a company that designs and manufactures novelty toys. While chatting with two of your coworkers you all realize how busy you all are and how much money the company is investing in HRM. One of the coworkers asks if it might be worth scaling back HR and putting more money and time into some other areas of the company, such as research and development or sales. *What do you say or do?* Go to this book's video case, watch the challenge video for this chapter, and choose the best video response. Be sure to also view the outcomes of the two responses you didn't choose.

Changes to This Edition:

- All the chapter-opening Real World Challenges were updated or replaced with a current organizational challenge or opportunity.

- New sections were added on a number of topics, including the following:
  - HRM systems (Chapter 1)
  - Global HRM (Chapter 2)
  - The role of HRM in risk management (Chapter 3)
  - Succession management (Chapter 6)
  - Informal learning (Chapter 7)
  - The gamification of training (Chapter 7)
  - Predicting deviance (Chapter 8)
  - The performance review process and continuous performance management (Chapter 8)
  - Efficiency wages (Chapter 9)
  - Worker centers (Chapter 13)

- New features and case studies were added on topics including the following:
  - The U.S. air traffic controller shortage
  - Adaptive learning
  - Improving collaboration through performance management
  - The role of pay in the home health care worker shortage
  - How Patagonia uses benefits to retain employees
  - Engaging employees at REI

- New end-of-chapter exercises were added on a number of topics, including the following:
  - The role of HRM in risk management
  - What is it like to work for the Central Intelligence Agency (CIA)?
  - Gamified training

- Posters and statistics were updated.
- Video links were checked and updated.
- Approximately 50 new company examples were added throughout the book.

Supplements

Videos

Each chapter is supported by a video case that presents a problem or challenge in a hypothetical company called Happy Time Toys. The video case is an excellent tool for sparking discussion and debate about the appropriate course of action. For each case, we provide three response videos that demonstrate decision making from a manager's perspective and show the outcome of the three decisions. One of the responses is better than the other two, and all the responses illustrate the consequences of different HRM-related decisions. Use the videos in class to prompt discussion on the situation that all students see in the video, or assign them within CourseBank, our homework management and online course system.

Select end of chapter exercises provide questions to use with a collection of company-specific videos available on YouTube for students to view and study. The links to these videos are also available within CourseBank.

Instructor's Manual

A comprehensive instructor's manual supports every chapter with the following:

- Chapter Overview
- Learning Objectives
- Detailed Chapter Outline
- Additional comments regarding the Real World Challenge and Real World Response at the beginning and end of each chapter
- In-depth explanation of chapter concepts
- Expanded coverage of the HR Flexibility, Global Issues, Develop Your Skills, Strategic Impact, and Case Study features
- Answers to end-of-chapter questions and exercises
- Occasional additional exercises, including an Ivey job offer negotiation exercise that students may use for free when this book is assigned for the current class

Test Bank

A test bank has been carefully developed to cover every learning objective and term for each chapter. It presents multiple-choice and true/false questions that are compatible with any learning management system. Knowledge questions and application questions are included at a variety of difficulty levels. Multiple essay questions and answers are also provided for each chapter.

PowerPoint Slides

A Microsoft PowerPoint deck of slides for each chapter provides robust coverage of the key chapter topics, along with text figures, tables, So What? items, and end-of-chapter questions and exercises.

CourseBank for Homework Management and Online Sections

This book is available with **CourseBank**, a system that allows instructors to easily assign and automatically grade activities. **CourseBank** provides a comprehensive and flexible bank of media, assignments, and quizzes. Use it to assign homework that results in students coming to class better prepared, or use it as a turnkey solution for your online section, sparing the time and effort of creating an online course from scratch.

CourseBank works with Blackboard, Canvas, D2L, or any other popular learning management system for single sign-on and gradebook integration. Or, if you prefer, use it stand-alone.

eBook and Loose-Leaf Options

To provide students with lower-cost options, this edition is also available in loose-leaf and digital formats. The loose-leaf edition may be ordered through your campus bookstore, just like any other textbook. Students may also purchase it directly from our website, www.chicagobusinesspress.com.

We also offer a value-priced ebook directly from your bookstore, our website, RedShelf, or VitalSource. The price and usage terms are the same regardless of which source you prefer for ebooks.

Acknowledgments

We would like to thank the many reviewers and book users whose feedback strengthened the book. Their comments were invaluable. The following dedicated instructors provided specific advice about the improvements we made in this edition:

Steven Abraham, *Oswego, State University of New York*

D. Apryl Brodersen, *Metropolitan State University of Denver*

Callie Burnley, *California State Polytechnic University, Pomona*

Elizabeth Cooper, *University of Rhode Island*

Richard Gianni, *North Greenville University*

Teri Huggins, *Kansas City Kansas Community College*

Samira Hussein, *Johnson County Community College*

Edward Kaplan, *Trident University*

Joni A. Koegel, *Cazenovia College*

Ashley Lesko, *Central Piedmont Community College*

Cynthia Simerly, *Lakeland Community College*

Susan Stewart, *Western Illinois University*

Dennis Veit, *University of Texas, Arlington*

Lowell Woodcock, *Dutchess Community College, State University of New York*

Mary Ann Zylka, *Buffalo State, State University of New York*

We would also like to acknowledge Paul Ducham for his support and vision for this book. Jane Ducham was also wonderful in managing the production process and book layout and helping us refine and execute our vision.

And finally, we would like to thank all of the people who made the Happy Time Toys videos possible: Hébert Peck, J. Allen Suddeth, John Keller, Tom Sanitate, Pete Troost, Steve Barcy, Greg Bryant, Dave Preston, Jon Celiberti, Danielle DiTaranto, Mike Barnhart, Alex Fahan, Bob Paquette, Deb Andriano, Maddy Schlesinger, Diane Thorn, Kate Villanova, Sarah Sirota, Brandon Rubin, Alejandro Baena, Katie Lydic, J. Alex Cordaro, David Dean Hastings, and Chelsea Spack.

About the Authors

JEAN PHILLIPS is a professor of Human Resource Management in the School of Labor and Employment Relations at Penn State University. Jean earned her PhD from Michigan State University in Business Management and Organizational Behavior. Her interests focus on recruitment, staffing, and the processes that lead to employee and organizational success. Jean was among the top 5 percent of published authors in *Journal of Applied Psychology* and *Personnel Psychology* during the 1990s, and she received the 2004 Cummings Scholar Award from the Organizational Behavior Division of the Academy of Management. Jean is also a Fellow of the Society for Industrial and Organizational Psychology.

    Jean has published more than fifty research articles, chapters, and books, including *Strategic Staffing* (3e, 2014), *Organizational Behavior* (12e, 2016), *Human Resource Management* (2013), *Managing Now* (2008), and the five-book *Staffing Strategically* (2012) series for the Society for Human Resource Management (SHRM). Jean was also the founding coeditor of the *Organizational Behavior/Human Resource Management* series for Business Expert Press. Her applied work includes leveraging employee surveys to enhance strategic execution and business performance, developing leadership and teamwork skills, and creating and evaluating strategic recruitment and staffing programs. Jean has taught online and traditional courses in Human Resource Management and Organizational behavior in the United States, Iceland, and Singapore.

STAN GULLY was a professor of HRM in the School of Labor and Employment Relations at Penn State University. Stan held M.A. and PhD degrees in industrial/organizational psychology from Michigan State University and was a fellow of the Society for Industrial and Organizational Psychology. He has authored, coauthored, edited, or presented numerous papers, books, and book chapters on a variety of topics, including motivation, leadership, team effectiveness, strategic staffing and recruitment, and training. He was a coauthor of SHRM's *Staffing Strategically* series and a founding coeditor of the Organizational Behavior/ Human Resource collection of Business Expert Press. Stan won awards for his teaching, research, and service.

    Stan taught courses at the undergraduate, master's, executive, and PhD levels covering a wide range of topics, including team effectiveness, leadership, organizational learning and innovation, staffing, HRM, talent management, training, and statistics. He taught using traditional and hybrid technologies in the United States, Iceland, Singapore, and Indonesia. His applied work included, but was not limited to, designing leadership training programs, implementing team communication interventions, delivering interviewing skill workshops for HRM managers, implementing a strategic workforce planning intervention, creating a multisource feedback system, and working in management at UPS. Sadly, Stan Gully passed away in the fall of 2017.

PART 1

The Importance and Context of Human Resource Management

chapter 1

Strategic Human Resource Management

Learning Objectives

AFTER STUDYING THIS CHAPTER, YOU SHOULD BE ABLE TO:

1 Describe why HRM (human resource management) is important to a company's performance.

2 List the six primary HRM functions.

3 Describe why it is important to align the HRM functions in support of common goals and objectives.

4 Explain why HRM is important for smaller as well as larger organizations.

5 Explain why HRM is important to every manager's career.

Real World Challenge

The Role of Human Resource Management in Google's Success

Internet search and advertising giant Google is known for its unique approach to business, including how it hires, develops, and motivates its talent. Because Google's People Operations team (what Google calls its human resource management team) lives by the mantra "find them, grow them, keep them," it invests in staffing, employee development, and maintaining a distinct and inclusive culture.[1]

Google also recognizes the importance of making shareholders aware of talent management's role in the company's success. Google clearly states the direct connection between talent management and company success in its Securities and Exchange Commission legal filings, stating that, "We believe that our approach to hiring has significantly contributed to our success to date."[2] It also included this important statement in the "risks" section: "If we do not succeed in attracting excellent personnel or retaining or motivating existing personnel, we may be unable to grow effectively."[3] Google understands that it is in constant competition with other Internet companies to attract and retain the industry's best technology and software engineering talent, and that if it does not succeed, the company's performance will suffer.

Given the importance of human resource management, which it calls "people operations," to its success and to its stock price, what ideas do you have to help Google most effectively attract, hire, develop, motivate, and retain its employees? After reading this chapter, you should have some good insights.

competitive advantage
doing something differently from the competition that leads to outperformance and success

Effectively managing employees is critical to organizational success. If you disagree, then fire all of your current employees, replace them with the next people you see, put them on the job with no training, and pay them a low wage. Few successful managers would accept this challenge because they know that who they hire and how they motivate and treat their employees are essential to their performance and survival. A company has a **competitive advantage** when it does something differently from its competition that allows it to outperform them and succeed in its industry.

Competitive advantages can come from factors, including better technology, more innovative products or services, better locations, lower costs, or outstanding customer service, but these advantages don't happen by themselves. It is always the organization's employees who create, implement, or sustain a competitive advantage. Research has found that acquiring, nurturing, and retaining the best talent available is essential to firms' performance and viability, particularly for knowledge-based firms.[4] As Wade Burgess, VP of Talent Solutions for LinkedIn said, "Traditionally, what separated an average company from a great company had been technology. We're in the middle of a transformation. Today, what differentiates an average company from a great company is talent."[5]

So how do people make such a difference to an organization's success? At companies such as Google, featured in this chapter's opening Real World Challenge, successful products and services are created and delivered by the company's talent. Employees at Activision, Apple Computer, and Nike create, manufacture, and sell new and innovative product lines. Employees are responsible for creating the supply chains and manufacturing systems that produce low-cost, high-quality automobiles at Tata Motors and Hyundai. Finally, the high-caliber customer service at L.L. Bean, Marriott Hotels, and Zappos starts with quality employee-customer interactions. None of these companies would be as successful without the talents and efforts of their employees. By making employees more effective at their jobs and the company better at executing its strategy, HRM can create substantial value within an organization if it is done strategically.[6]

In the first section of this book, The Importance and Context of Human Resource Management, we discuss the important role the management of human resources plays in organizations. This chapter gives an overview of how human resource management (abbreviated HRM throughout the book) influences organizational performance and business strategy execution, as well as how effective HRM can create a competitive advantage. The importance of flexibly applying HRM in different organizations and among different employees (functions, and performance levels) is also discussed. After reading this chapter, you will understand the role HRM plays in a firm and how it adds value. Because HRM policies are created by the company but are executed by managers and supervisors, we also discuss managers' roles in executing HRM strategies and policies. After reading this chapter, you will understand the role HR plays in a firm and how it adds value.

What Is HRM?

human resource management
the organizational function responsible for attracting, hiring, developing, rewarding, and retaining talent

Human resource management is the organizational function responsible for attracting, hiring, developing, rewarding, and retaining talent. HRM is responsible for people-related issues as well as employment-related legal compliance. Effective HRM is critical to all organizations because it both manages risk and creates the system that acquires, motivates, manages, and retains the talent that determines the organization's success. In higher-performing companies, talent issues are a common focus of top leadership. Because employee costs are one of the largest components of an organization's operating budget, it is essential to properly manage the investments a company makes in its people. No organization will maximize its effectiveness without the acquisition, development, deployment, and retention of the right talent.[7]

HRM is also important to attend to as an employee or as a potential employee. Would you perform as well or be as satisfied in a company that invests in your development, gives you clear goals, rewards you for good performance, and gives you regular feedback about your performance as you would in one that does not? Most people wouldn't be able to perform as well and wouldn't stay very long in a company that doesn't motivate, develop, and fairly reward them. Companies differ widely in the rewards, training, and development opportunities they offer to employees. If you value developing your skills and advancing in your field, it is wise to choose an employer with HRM practices that will help you do this.

Our goal in writing this book is to help you to understand how to effectively use HRM tools to be a better manager and bring out the excellence in each of your employees. Effectively managing others is as important in marketing and accounting as it is in nursing, computer programming, construction, and every other field. We also want you to better understand how to leverage HRM to enhance your personal career success. Understanding how HRM policies and practices work can help you better identify a job or an organization you will enjoy working in, increase the chances of getting the job you want, and help you to be a more successful manager once you are there. An organization's HRM choices reflect a lot about its values and about what it is like to work there, and the better you understand HRM policies and choices, the better you'll be able to find a company that matches your values and motivations. The *Develop Your Skills* feature in each chapter will help you to develop more specific HRM skills by providing a variety of tools and materials related to different HRM topics. Investing in developing your HRM skills will prepare you to be a more effective employee and manager.

Table 1.1 illustrates how HRM affects the work processes that lead to competitive advantage, value creation, and organizational performance through strategic execution, the creation and maintenance of a positive work environment, and engaged employees. This model also illustrates the flow of this book.

Essentially, HRM influences organizational performance through its influence on three key areas:

1. Influencing what employees *should* do.
2. Influencing what employees *can* do.
3. Influencing what employees *will* do.

so what?

Understanding HRM and developing HRM skills can help you succeed both personally and professionally.

table **1.1**

How HRM Influences Organizational Performance

What Employees *Should* Do	What Employees *Can* Do	What Employees *Will* Do
• Planning • Laws and Regulations	• Staffing • Training	• Compensation • Performance Management

Effective Work Processes
- Strategic Execution
- Positive Work Environment
- Engaged Employees

Competitive Advantage

Organizational Performance

These three forces lead in turn to effective work processes, including a positive work environment, engaged employees, and strategic execution that create a competitive advantage for the organization. This competitive advantage then positively influences organizational performance.

What Employees Should Do

Factors including organizational strategy, competitive environment, and legal requirements all influence what an organization's employees *should* do. After establishing a business strategy, managers identify the resources, skills, and quantity and quality of talent that will be needed to execute it. HR planning is an important HRM activity that involves designing work for optimum efficiency and performance as well as identifying the amount and types of talents the company will need to execute the business strategy. Because this aligns the HRM strategy, policies, and activities with the business strategy, it is essential to effective HRM. If a manager wants to grow the business, wouldn't it be helpful to know what skills and competencies employees need to possess and have enough time to develop them before they are needed? Analyzing work and human resource planning are covered in Chapter 4.

There are also many laws and regulations that affect HRM practices and the employment relationship. Failure to follow them can be costly both financially and to your organization's reputation and future business success. Many of these laws are necessary because of past employment discrimination in the United States. Diversity, equal employment opportunity, and relevant employment laws are discussed in greater detail in Chapter 3.

What Employees Can Do

Influencing what employees *can* do is another way HRM influences organizational outcomes. By finding, attracting, and hiring the right talent, recruiting and staffing acquire the motivation and the abilities from which the company can draw. The HRM function of training and development influences the capabilities of an organization's employees by developing employees' skills to meet changing business needs. Imagine that you are a nurse trying to use a complex new machine without proper training. Would you expect to perform well? Even if you had the best intentions, if the company didn't develop your skills, it's unlikely that you would succeed on the job.

Similarly, if you were required to work in interdependent teams, but the company didn't attend to teamwork skills in the hiring process, would your teammates work as effectively as they would if job candidates were evaluated and hired based in part on their ability to work effectively in teams? Because staffing and development activities are responsible for an organization's skills base, they are the foundation of effective HRM. Even having a generous incentive plan won't matter if employees lack the basic ability to get their jobs done in the way the organization needs them done.

What Employees Will Do

Influencing what employees *will* do is the third way HRM influences organizational performance. By setting clear goals aligned with the business strategy, giving employees feedback on their performance toward those goals, and rewarding them for good performance, performance management and compensation influence employee motivation, effort, and persistence. If you were told to give customers high-quality service but were rewarded for the average number of customers you help in an hour, what would you focus on? Because people do what they're rewarded for doing, it is essential that rewards are aligned with desired behaviors and outcomes. Rewards include compensation (pay) but also praise, recognition, time off, or anything valued by the employee.

Compensation issues are often a contributing factor in unethical employee behavior. The bigger the potential reward, the greater the temptation for employees to cheat or even break the law, especially if they are close to earning the reward. One of the causes of the subprime mortgage crisis was the large incentive bonuses paid to mortgage brokers and loan officers for selling loans that carried higher interest rates than the borrowers were qualified for.[8] Sometimes people's jobs are even on the line if they don't hit the unrealistic performance targets, putting them in a difficult ethical position. Wells Fargo fired over 5,000 employees in 2016 for opening fake customer accounts to meet the sales quotas required to keep their jobs. Opening these fake accounts never benefitted Wells Fargo, which lost money on the dormant accounts, lost customer trust, and lost shareholder value when the news got out that this happened, and it faces large regulatory fines.[9] Thinking through possible unintended consequences of different compensation and incentive plans is clearly a good idea.

When what employees should do, can do, and will do are aligned in support of each other and are part of an organization's goals, work processes are most effective. Positive work environments help to generate engaged, committed employees who give the organization a competitive advantage through their increased effort and performance. Imagine what would happen if Google or Starbucks stopped investing in and rewarding their employees and creating a positive work environment. Do you think they would be as successful? Probably not. HRM creates value for an organization in a variety of ways, including reducing HR-related costs (e.g., turnover and lawsuits), improving customer service, creating stronger client relationships, and improving the cost and quality of the organization's products and services.

so what**?**

Aligning what employees should do, can do, and will do makes work processes most effective, maximizes employee motivation and performance, and gives the organization a competitive advantage.

What Does HRM Do?

In a sentence, HRM creates the system that acquires, motivates, develops, and retains talent and is a key source of competitive advantage. The core of HRM is designing systems that maximize the efficiency and effectiveness of an organization's use of its talent in accomplishing organizational goals. As shown in Figure 1.1, the main functions within HRM are staffing, performance management, training and development, rewards and benefits, health

figure **1.1**

Main Functions within HRM

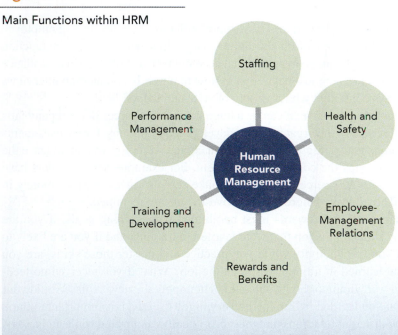

and safety, and employee-management relations. We next describe the role of each of these HRM functions and will be covering each topic in greater detail in later chapters.

Staffing

? so what

By bringing in the talent with the right ability and motivation to execute the organization's strategy, staffing provides the foundation for an organization's effectiveness and competitive advantage.

There are millions of employers in the United States, employing anywhere from one to tens of thousands of people. Millions of employees are hired or separated every month, making staffing a multibillion-dollar activity across the country. Staffing is the process of planning, acquiring, deploying, and retaining employees that enables the organization to meet its talent needs and execute its business strategy. This process supports the movement of talent into, through, and out of the organization in a way that enables it to compete successfully in its marketplace. Because an organization's people are central to its development of a competitive advantage and to the execution of its business strategy, strategic recruitment and staffing activities are cornerstones of organizational effectiveness. If you don't get the right people into the organization, no training or compensation program can make up for these initial talent deficiencies.

Effective staffing supports the organization's mission and objectives as well as its business strategy. After the nature and the requirements of the open job are identified, sourcing identifies potential recruits likely to meet or exceed the job's minimum personal and technical requirements. Recruiting then focuses on attracting these people to apply, retaining qualified applicants in the candidate pool while they are evaluated, and finally on enticing the chosen candidates to ultimately accept job offers. Once hired, efforts are made to retain successful employees and move them throughout the organization as needed. Separations due to poor performance, layoffs, or restructuring as well as employees quitting are also part of the staffing function.

Staffing practices can have a tremendous impact on a company's bottom line. Caribou Coffee discovered that the most important district manager competency was his or her ability to effectively staff the store manager position. When a district manager took the time to find the best replacement for a store manager instead of automatically promoting the shift supervisor with the most tenure, the results had a strong impact on revenue.[10] Recruitment is discussed in Chapter 5, and selection and hiring are covered in Chapter 6.

Training and Development

Training and development is an important HRM function focused on developing employee capabilities through both formal and informal activities. The training and development function is also responsible for career planning, organizational development, and often legal compliance as well. For example, supervisors must be trained in how to properly conduct job interviews and terminations in ways consistent with a variety of state and federal laws.

Because training is often expensive, it can be a huge waste of resources if a company fails to hire people able to succeed in the organization's development programs. Large investments in training and development also might not be the right choice if employees tend to leave the organization before it recoups the cost of training them. For example, some retailers have turnover rates approaching 200 percent. It doesn't make sense to invest a lot of money in employees who are likely to leave before training investments are recouped.

Performance management and rewards must be aligned with training goals. If you are not rewarded for using skills on the job that were learned in training, and if you are likely to experience a drop in your productivity while you practice and master those skills, are you likely to use what you learned in training while on the job? What if you received no feedback on how well you were doing or how you could better apply the new skills? Would your motivation to use what you learned in training be very high? Clearly, it is important to think of HRM as a system of different functions that must be mutually reinforcing while at the same time supporting the organization's goals and strategies.

Any organization's future success depends on its next generation of leaders. Unfortunately, CEO succession planning tends to be an overlooked governance risk, and most firms lack succession plans for their top leaders.[11] Because Citigroup's directors didn't start identifying a possible new CEO until after CEO Charles Prince stepped down, the company was left directionless at a time when it had already fallen behind rivals and was facing huge mortgage-related losses. Starbucks, on the other hand, planned for its CEO succession and took the time to prepare its incoming CEO for the role. The company announced in December 2016 that the current Starbucks president, Kevin Johnson, would be taking over the CEO role from Howard Schultz in April 2017, after Johnson had been on the Starbucks board of directors since 2009 and on its management team since 2015.[12] Succession planning and career development activities can help ensure that an organization has people ready to assume leadership positions as soon as they become available. Training and development are discussed in Chapter 7.

so what?

Training is essential for preparing employees to both be and stay effective in their jobs and to eventually become organizational leaders.

Performance Management

Performance management involves aligning individual employees' goals and behaviors with organizational goals and strategies, appraising and evaluating past and current behaviors and performance, and providing suggestions for improvement. Staffing influences the effectiveness of a performance management system by providing the raw talent that the system will manage. Even the best performance management system cannot replace important capabilities that employees must have to do their jobs well. Similarly, development programs are necessary to improve the skills identified in the performance management process. It doesn't do much good to let an employee know that she needs to improve her leadership skills if no opportunities for improving them are made available. Organizations also frequently tie compensation to performance management ratings. How would you feel if your bonus was determined by a supervisor's biased evaluation of skills and behaviors that weren't really related to your job performance? The authors know that this type of system wouldn't do much to motivate us!

so what?

Specific goals and frequent feedback are important to performance because they tell employees what they should be trying to do and whether or not they are doing it.

Without performance goals, employees do not know what aspects of their jobs to focus on or what performance level is expected of them. As a result, they will tend to underperform, and some will quit or need to be replaced, potentially bogging down the staffing system. Without feedback, employees cannot adjust their behavior when necessary to reach their goals. Even if highly talented employees are hired, they can't perform at their best if they get no feedback or inaccurate performance feedback. If they perceive the feedback they've been given about their performance is unfair, they will not be motivated to contribute as much as they could. Performance feedback is also important to maintaining ethical behavior and communicating organizational expectations. You will learn more about performance management in Chapter 8.

total rewards
the sum of all of the rewards employees receive in exchange for their time, efforts, and performance

direct financial compensation
compensation received in the form of salary, wages, commissions, stock options, or bonuses

indirect financial compensation
all the tangible and financially valued rewards that are not included in direct compensation, including free meals, vacation time, and health insurance

Rewards and Benefits

Compensation and benefits perceived as both adequate and equitable that reward employees for their contributions to organizational goal attainment are important to employee motivation, performance, and retention. As shown in Figure 1.2, **total rewards** refers to the sum of all of the rewards employees receive in exchange for their time, efforts, and performance. Total rewards are comprised of:

- **Direct financial compensation**: Compensation received in the form of salary, wages, commissions, stock options, or bonuses
- **Indirect financial compensation** (benefits): Any and all financial rewards not considered direct financial compensation, including health insurance, wellness benefits, paid vacations, and free meals
- **Nonfinancial compensation**: Rewards and incentives given to employees that are not financial in nature, including intrinsic rewards received from the job itself or from the physical or psychological work environment (e.g., feeling successful or appreciated)

nonfinancial compensation
rewards and incentives given to employees that are not financial in nature including intrinsic rewards received from the job itself or from the work environment

figure **1.2**

Total Rewards

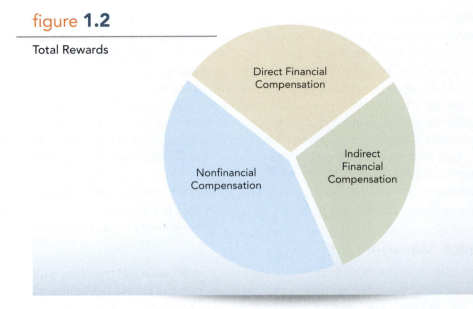

When evaluating an employer's job offer, it is important to consider the total rewards package, not just the salary level. When the value of other rewards including retirement contributions, continuing training and development, health and dental care, wellness programs, vacation time, and bonus programs are considered, a lower salaried job might be worth much more than one with a higher base salary.

The level of pay and total rewards an organization is willing and able to invest in employees can both determine and be determined by its ability to hire people with the necessary qualifications. If an organization is willing to pay premium wages, then its staffing effort can focus on identifying and attracting the most qualified candidates. If an organization would like to pay lower wages but is unable to hire the candidates it would like at its preferred salary levels, it may be forced to raise its salaries to be competitive in the labor market or make investments in training and development.

The success of incentive pay programs that reward employees for individual, group, or organizational performance is influenced by performance management systems. Clear and accurate performance feedback lets employees know how they are performing. Also, the performance-enhancing potential of reward and incentive programs will not be fully leveraged if employees' skills are lacking. Performance incentives are only effective if the individuals have the potential to perform well in the first place. Staffing and training must therefore be aligned with the behaviors and performance motivated by the incentive pay programs.

It should also be noted that paying top dollar to hire the highest quality candidates is not always the best strategy if the company doesn't really need top talent to meet its needs. In other words, sometimes the greater productivity of the most talented applicants fails to offset their higher salaries. For example, does every marketing employee really need an MBA? On the other hand, high pay can create a competitive advantage. Warehouse retailer Costco relies on its loyal customer base, high-quality supply chain, and engaged employees to give it a competitive advantage. Although Costco pays its employees twice the market rate and higher than its closest competitor, Sam's Club, Costco's lower turnover and higher employee productivity results in similar financial returns on its labor costs.[13] This, in turn, leads to a higher quality customer experience and a competitive advantage.

Direct financial compensation is discussed in Chapter 9, incentives and bonuses are discussed in Chapter 10, and nonfinancial benefits are discussed in Chapter 11.

Health and Safety

Workplace health and safety includes topics ranging from wellness, fire and food safety, ergonomics, injury management, disaster preparedness, industrial hygiene, and even bullying and workplace violence. Workplace accidents such as the Iowa pipeline leak of nearly 140,000 gallons of diesel fuel in 2017[14] and workplace violence incidents often make headlines. Workplace safety involves protecting employees from work-related toxins, accidents, and injuries. Workplace health refers to employees' physical and mental health. Reduced job stability and increased workload demands can increase stress and increase employees' risk for physical and mental illness. More than 83 percent of businesses in the United States with 200 or more employees have some form of wellness program, including exercise, stop-smoking classes, and stress management.[15]

Patrizio Martorana/Shutterstock

Employees' work environments can be dangerous. It is important to protect employees from work-related toxins as well as from accidents and injuries. Providing appropriate clothing and equipment, training employees in how to properly use them, and then holding them accountable for following the organization's safety rules all help keep employees healthy and safe.

A healthy and safe work environment is not only ethical, but it benefits organizations by increasing employee productivity, lowering health care and workers' compensation insurance premiums, and decreasing health-related lost work time. Societal pressures for healthy and safe work environments have led to federal and state legislation covering many aspects of health and safety. Creating a healthy work environment is discussed in Chapter 12.

so what?

Improving employees' health and safety is ethical, helps improve employees' quality of life, improves organizational performance, and decreases costs.

Employee-Management Relations

At its core, employee-management relations reflect societal beliefs about the relationship between employees and the capital owners of the organization. Employee-management relations ultimately determine the employment rights of both employers and employees. Labor participation programs, employee surveys, and other tools are used in managing employee-management relations. Positive employee-management relations improves communication, problem solving, and performance in both unionized and nonunionized organizations.

The field of employment relations (or industrial relations) focuses on unionized employment situations. By law, if employees want a union to represent them, then the company must recognize the union and bargain with it in good faith. The company and the union negotiate collective bargaining agreements that cover the terms and conditions of the employment relationship. In 2017, 34.4 percent of workers in the public sector belonged to a union, whereas only 6.4 percent of private sector employees were union members.[16] Labor unions and unionization rates have been declining for years, but they are still common enough that it is important to know about them and their influence on the practice of HRM. Creating positive employee-management relations is discussed in Chapter 13.

so what?

Maintaining positive employee-management relations is important for both unionized and nonunionized companies because it improves communication, problem solving, and performance.

Alignment of the HR Functions

As the numerous examples above illustrate, if HRM functional areas' goals conflict, then influencing employee behaviors and organizational goals in desired ways will be much more difficult. Each of the functional areas of HRM must be consistent in what they reinforce, and care must be taken to ensure that they do not undermine each other. This chapter's Strategic Impact feature discusses how toy maker Mattel aligned its HRM strategy.

Understanding how to implement various HRM practices to match different situations is essential to maximizing organizational effectiveness. No matter what the challenge, there are HRM tools that will help. The HR Flexibility feature in each chapter will help you to recognize how to best apply HR policies and tools in different ways depending on the situation. This chapter's HR Flexibility feature describes HRM in smaller organizations.

so what?

Organizations of all sizes can use HRM to improve their performance.

♞ Strategic Impact

Aligning Mattel's HRM Strategy

Toy company Mattel developed a better integrated HRM strategy to support its new strategic objectives of improving productivity, globalizing and extending the firm's brand name, and creating new brands. Mattel wanted to better align its HRM functions to motivate employees to work together, improve their skills, and improve retention. To support these goals, it created employee development programs, established metrics to better understand how the workforce was performing, and created a systematic succession strategy to increase the retention of the valuable talent it developed.[17] Mattel's staffing, performance measurement, and training programs now support each other and reinforce the firm's corporate goals.

💬 HR Flexibility

Human Resource Management in Small Organizations

Smaller firms with fewer than 500 workers make up more than 99 percent of the business establishments that exist, employing nearly 50 percent of the total workforce.[18] However, small organizations often lack the budget for a dedicated human resource management function. Unfortunately, managers in small organizations often lack training in HRM and do not recognize generally accepted HRM practices as necessary for improving productivity.[19] This lack of understanding of HRM issues and their importance in the operation of a successful business has negatively impacted many small firms. Inadequate and inefficient management of human resources often result in low productivity and high employee dissatisfaction and turnover.[20] At least one study has found HRM practices to be the leading cause of small firms' failures,[21] and numerous studies have indicated that recruitment and training are two of the most important management problems facing small businesses.[22]

Even small organizations can effectively use HRM to improve their performance. Organizations of all sizes share a need to identify and hire the right people, motivate them to perform their best, develop their skills, and retain them. Investing in HRM improves productivity and profitability of smaller as well as larger organizations.[23] Although HRM practices obviously increase a company's talent-related costs, they should be seen as an investment in the company's performance rather than solely as an expense.

We now turn our attention to better understanding how HRM influences organizational performance.

How Does HRM Influence Organizational Performance?

Human resource management policies and practices add value to organizations and influence organizational performance by either improving efficiency or contributing to revenue growth.[24] Because strategic interest in HRM is relatively new, it is a source of competitive

table 1.2

What Effective HRM Systems Do

- Improve organizational efficiency.
- Contribute to revenue growth.
- Increase employees' understanding of their responsibilities and how they relate to the organization's mission, business strategy, and goals.
- Develop and enhance employee capabilities and talents to enable strategic execution and goal attainment.
- Equitably link rewards to responsibility level and performance.
- Promote the efficient and effective utilization of employees' skills and knowledge.
- Increase employee engagement, effort, and performance.
- Increase the organization's ability to manage change.
- Decrease an organization's legal liability for compliance with employment laws.

advantage that many firms have yet to fully leverage. As shown in Table 1.2, effective HRM systems increase the organization's ability to meet its goals, enhance the organization's ability to grow and manage change, and increase employee engagement, effort, and performance.

Workforce issues can impact a company's revenue and earnings. Managing human resources strategically helps organizations manage four primary types of risk:[25]

1. *Strategic risk*: HRM initiatives can affect business strategy through the overall talent strategy, company culture, ethics, investments in people, and the implementation of change initiatives.
2. *Operational risk*: HRM affects the speed and the effectiveness of talent acquisition as well as the development of employees' skills and the identification and retention of top performers. These and other HRM activities can directly influence the organization's success or failure.
3. *Financial risk*: HRM performance affects the organization's workforce costs and productivity directly through compensation, benefits, turnover, overtime, and time-to-hire and indirectly through errors, accidents, delays, and lost production.
4. *Compliance risk*: Every employment-related decision can have legal ramifications, particularly in the areas of diversity, health and safety, union relations, whistleblowers, and harassment. SEC regulations mandate the board of directors' responsibility for oversight of risk management policies. Boards must make known any material risks with the potential to affect company earnings. Because the acquisition, retention, and performance of talent have the potential to affect company earnings, it is essential that organizations identify and manage these risks through effective HRM.

HRM practices also influence the interest rate a company must pay to borrow money. Moody's is an internationally known corporate bond rating service whose bond rating can dramatically impact a company's cost of credit. After making a direct connection between companies' financial performance and their success in the areas of recruiting, retention, leadership development, and training, these types of HRM factors now influence Moody's bond ratings and subsequent corporate interest rates.[26]

Consulting firm Watson Wyatt found that good people practices can increase a company's value by as much as 30 percent. Russell Investments reports that firms on the Fortune 100 Best Companies to Work For list outperform the S&P 500 and the Russell 3000 by as much as 10 percent.[27] Finding and keeping talent is often named as one of the biggest obstacles to achieving the growth global companies are hoping to achieve.[28]

so what

Using solid data and re-
search to develop HRM
systems improves their
effectiveness.

The most effective HRM systems are based on solid research, identifying and implementing best practices, and aligning the HRM system with organizational goals and environmental realities. HRM strategies have the biggest influence on organizational performance when they are aligned not only with the business strategy but with each other. We discuss the role of HRM in business in greater detail in Chapter 2.

The Role of HRM in Executing Business Strategy

business strategy
defines how the firm will
compete in its marketplace

A company's **business strategy** defines how the firm will compete in its marketplace. A business strategy should reflect what the organization's customers want, what the firm wants, and what the firm can cost-effectively deliver. Business strategies are likely to differ across business units in a diversified corporation. Frito-Lay, Johnson & Johnson, and Colgate-Palmolive take different strategic approaches to ensure the success of their various business lines.

Developing a business strategy involves making choices about which products and services to offer and which strategies to pursue to gain a competitive advantage. Both choices depend on a company's competitive capabilities, strengths, and weaknesses. In other words, for a company to execute its business strategy, not only must its HRM policies and practices fit with its strategy, but its business strategy must also align with the competitive environment and the immediate business conditions.[29]

Business strategies are created to leverage the firm's resources and capabilities in ways that result in superior value creation compared to their competitors. Competitive advantage results from the ability to leverage resources and capabilities that derive in part from its talent. How a company positions itself to compete in the marketplace determines the competitive advantage it needs to create and the HRM strategies it needs to pursue to acquire, develop, motivate, and retain the appropriate talent.

talent philosophy
a system of beliefs about
how its employees should
be treated

An organization's **talent philosophy** is a system of beliefs about how its employees should be treated, including:

- The value placed on diversity;
- Ethics;
- Whether the firm would like employees to stay for a limited time or for their entire careers; and
- Whether employees are viewed as assets to be managed or as investors choosing where to allocate their time and effort.

Typically shaped by company founders, the talent philosophy reflects how an organization thinks about its employees. For example, some organizations view employees as partners and important stakeholders in the company, whereas others view employees as easily replaceable. Some firms plan to develop and retain employees for their entire careers, whereas others encourage more frequent employee "churn" to reduce training costs, and some firms place a higher value on treating employees ethically and fairly than do other companies.

A company's business strategy can also influence how a company interacts with its employees, which then affects how it decides to manage the movement of people into, through, and out of the company. Reflecting this, Goldman Sachs states, "Our people are our greatest asset—we say it often and with good reason. It is only with the determination and dedication of our people that we can serve our clients, generate long-term value for our shareholders and contribute to the broader public. At the crux of our effort is a focus on cultivating and sustaining a diverse work environment and workforce, which is critical to meeting the unique needs of our diverse client base and the communities in which we operate."[30]

**human resource
strategy**
links the entire human
resource function with the
firm's business strategy

A firm's **human resource strategy** links the entire human resource function with the firm's business strategy. Strategic human resource management aligns a company's values and goals with the behaviors, values, and goals of employees and influences the strategies of each of the firm's human resource functions, including staffing, performance management, training and development, and compensation. The alignment of these separate functions creates an integrated human resource management system supporting the execution of the business strategy, guided by the talent philosophy of the organization.

Global Issues

Effective HRM requires flexibility in matching HRM practices to the business strategy, internal and external labor market, and an appreciation that people's expectations and values differ around the world. The more an organization is able to tailor its HRM efforts to the different values and needs of its employees around the world, the more effectively it will attract, hire, motivate, and retain the talent it needs. Kevin Martin, the Chief Research Officer of human capital research and data firm Institute for Corporate Productivity believes that the business case to develop leaders with global competencies is very clear. "Business skills and acumen remain critical but are now table stakes. It's the ability to influence and drive collaboration across cultures, boundaries, and borders that has the greater variability on global leadership effectiveness and can make the biggest difference."[31]

A **global mindset** is a set of individual attributes that enable you to influence individuals, groups, and organizations from diverse socio/cultural/institutional systems.[32] Because global mindset is learned, experiences can influence it in a positive or negative manner.[33] Every year, the financial services giant HSBC sends promising new hires and managers into long-term international business experiences to build a cohort of international officers. To make a career at HSBC, managers must perform these international missions in Western countries as well as in Saudi Arabia, Indonesia, and Mexico. This enables HSBC to develop a continuous supply of globally competent managers. Other multinationals pursue similar approaches to enable them to transfer expertise and know-how around the globe.[34]

Although good pay and interesting work are motivating to most people,[35] people from different cultures have different traditions, are often motivated by different things, and communicate in different ways.[36] For example, some cultures communicate directly, and others are more reserved. Some cultures put a high value on family life, whereas others stress the importance of work. As Kofi Annan, former Secretary-General of the United Nations put it, "Tolerance, intercultural dialogue, and respect for diversity are more essential than ever in a world where peoples are becoming more and more closely interconnected."[37] Motivating employees in a multinational organization can be particularly challenging, and it requires some degree of flexibility.

global mindset
a set of individual attributes that enable you to influence individuals, groups, and organizations from diverse socio/cultural/institutional systems

> *"Tolerance, intercultural dialogue and respect for diversity are more essential than ever in a world where peoples are becoming more and more closely interconnected."*
>
> **—Kofi Annan, former Secretary-General of the United Nations**

The effectiveness of HRM policies and practices is influenced by the role expectations, norms, and traditions in that society.[38] For example, countries including the United States, Sweden, and Germany have small variation in the distribution of power across supervisors and employees, whereas others such as Japan and Mexico have a large power difference. Research has found that managers in paternalistic and high power-distance cultures tend not to provide job enrichment and empowerment to employees.[39] If supervisors feel that large power differences are legitimate and appropriate, they may be uncomfortable implementing HRM policies promoting employee development and autonomy.

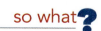

Because expectations, norms, and traditions in different cultures influence the effectiveness of HRM practices, it is important to match HRM practices with the societal culture.

 ## Global Issues

Managing Global Volunteers

Managing talent in for-profit organizations can be challenging enough. The challenges are further increased in not-for-profit organizations and nongovernmental organizations (NGOs), including global humanitarian and relief organizations. In these types of organizations, some of the employees are volunteers or unpaid staff who work in non-native countries. There are no reward systems and no ability to use financial incentives to motivate volunteer performance. In addition, nonproductive volunteers may linger in the organization, diverting resources and other workers from accomplishing the organization's mission.[40]

One of the key challenges in managing global NGOs is managing diversity and conflict. Language and cultural barriers exist, as well as differences in work styles and priorities. Another key challenge in any NGO is assigning volunteers to roles that they are motivated to do and that they are capable of doing well. Because so much of volunteers' motivation comes from intangible rather than from tangible rewards, managers must meet the needs of each individual volunteer. Flexibility in motivating and rewarding the performance of each volunteer, clear goal setting and training in the ways tasks are to be carried out, and regular performance feedback and appreciation are important in meeting these needs. The California State Railroad Museum gives each paid supervisor 200 thank you cards at the beginning of the year that must all be used to thank volunteers by the end of the year.[41] These techniques are also effective in managing paid employees but are particularly critical when managing volunteers.

Each chapter in this book contains a *Global Issues* feature that highlights how HRM practices are affected by globalization, culture differences, or other global issues. The *Global Issues* feature in each chapter will highlight how the practice of HRM differs in different countries and cultures. This is not only important when doing business internationally, but it can also explain how employees from different cultures react differently to different HRM practices. This chapter's Global Issues feature discusses issues that can arise when managing global volunteers.

Gaining a Competitive Advantage Through HRM

All organizations can benefit from effective HRM. Imagine the difference between a company with skilled, motivated employees with clear goals aligned with the business strategy and one with unhappy employees who lack the ability to do their jobs safely and well, and who are unclear about what they need to do. As NASCAR Senior Vice President and CMO Steve Phelps says, "It ends up being about people. . . . Give them the opportunity to be excellent. Each individual is an important part of the whole."[42]

> *"It ends up being about people. . . . Give them the opportunity to be excellent. Each individual is an important part of the whole."*
>
> **—Steve Phelps, NASCAR Senior Vice President and CMO**

According to Michael Porter, to have a competitive advantage, a company must ultimately be able to give customers *superior value for their money* (a combination of quality, service, and acceptable price). This could be due to providing either a better product that is worth a premium price or a good product at a lower price.[43] Different competitive advantages require different approaches to HRM. Operationally excellent organizations operate with tight margins and rely more on teamwork than individual performance. They are typically not able to provide high pay or benefits, and they need to attract and retain employees willing to follow consistent procedures and control costs.

A competitive advantage based on product innovation requires employees to continually develop new products and services to create an advantage in the market. This strategy is common in technology and pharmaceutical companies. Apple, Nintendo, and 3M are good examples of organizations whose competitive advantage is based on product innovation. To protect their entrepreneurial environment, HRM must develop and reinforce an innovative culture. Instead of hiring based only on candidates' related job experience, it is important to assess whether a candidate can work cooperatively in teams and whether she or he is analytical and creative.[44] HRM in innovative companies also motivates employees to persist and overcome challenges.[45]

A competitive advantage based on delivering unique and customizable products or services requires tailoring the company's offerings to meet the demands of different market niches. Employees must be able and willing to combine detailed knowledge about their customers with operational flexibility so they can respond quickly to almost any customer need, from customizing a product to fulfilling special requests. Consulting, retail, and banking organizations often adopt this approach.

Starbucks is able to command a high price for a cup of coffee because it focuses on customer relationships. Imagine if Starbucks reduced its HRM investment, cut back on its employee benefits, and began to hire cheaper labor, including people who don't enjoy interacting with customers. Starbucks' competitive advantage would quickly erode, and its performance would suffer. Starbucks would have to reduce its prices to keep customers coming back, which would further hurt profits. Talent is often considered to be the most critical element in building a customer-oriented company.[46] Hiring active learners with good customer relations skills and emotional resilience under pressure helps to ensure that an organization continually enhances its ability to deliver on promises to customers.[47]

Pursuing a growth strategy requires the development of current talent and the acquisition of additional talent. For example, growth-oriented chains such as Chipotle Mexican Grill and Panera Bread regularly open new stores that require additional management, employees, and even product distribution staff. The success of a growth strategy depends on the firm's ability to find and retain the right number and types of employees to sustain its intended growth. Growth can be *organic*, happening as the organization expands from within by opening new factories or stores. If it is, it requires an investment in recruiting, selecting, and training the right people to expand the company's operations. Firms can also pursue growth strategies through *mergers and acquisitions*. Mergers and acquisitions have been a common way for organizations to achieve growth, expand internationally, and respond to industry deregulation. In addition to expanding the organization's business, mergers and acquisitions can also be a way for an organization to acquire the quality and amount of talent it needs to execute its business strategy.

It is important to consider the match between the two organizations' cultures, values, and organizational structures when using mergers and acquisitions as a way to implement a growth strategy. Mismatches between merged or acquired organizations can result in underperformance and the loss of talented employees. Mergers and acquisitions often fail because of culture issues rather than technical or financial issues.[48] The failed DaimlerChrysler, HP and Compaq, and AOL-Time Warner mergers are just a few prominent examples.

Retaining high-performing employees and keeping employees engaged helps to create and maintain any type of competitive advantage. Southwest Airlines' high employee engagement and fun culture contribute to low employee turnover, great customer service, and high company performance.[49] Software provider SAS created an award-winning work environment that makes the company a challenging, employee-friendly, and fun place to work. A casual dress code,

so what?

Different HRM practices are needed to support different business strategies and competitive advantages.

training and career advancement opportunities, fitness center, flexible work schedule, and excellent health benefits help to keep SAS's turnover rate low and its employees productive.[50] Managing employee engagement and turnover is discussed in greater detail in Chapter 14.

Who is Responsible for HRM?

Although larger organizations often have an organized HRM department, many smaller organizations do not. Some of the more administrative HRM tasks, including benefits management and payroll, are increasingly being outsourced for cost savings to allow the HRM function to focus on more strategic business issues. Technology is also making it easier for organizations to require supervising managers to perform more HRM activities, thus increasing the effectiveness and efficiency of various HRM activities. From global positioning systems to cloud computing, technology has influenced the way firms conduct business. Human resource management has also been influenced by technology. Technology can be a training aid, a feedback and communication system such as instant messaging or e-mail, or a tool for sourcing and recruiting potential employees. Automated performance feedback, career portals, and online benefits and wellness management systems are just a few modern HRM tools made possible by technology. Throughout this book, we highlight ways technology is being used by organizations to execute various HRM activities, and we give you tips to use it most effectively.

?so what

Many different types of employees share the HRM responsibilities with HRM professionals.

HRM activities are performed by HRM professionals, managers, individual employees, shared service centers, outside vendors, and professional employer organizations. Let's take a look at the various functions and roles that are responsible for HRM, beginning with HRM professionals.

HRM Professionals

HRM professionals are not the organization's police. Their role, along with the HRM function, is to align the talent philosophy and HRM strategy with the business strategy and company values, develop supervisors' skills in managing and using HRM effectively, and serve as a resource for supervisors' questions and ongoing needs. Although focused on the "people" side of the business, HRM professionals are responsible for the effective running of the business and need appropriate business acumen. HR professionals must understand how their business makes money and understand the company's economic and financial capabilities to make sound business decisions. The HRM department is also the warehouse of the firm's expertise in all areas of HRM, including employment law, staffing, compensation, benefits, teamwork, communication, performance management, and employee development.

HRM professionals are also responsible for managing organizational change, including business expansion, restructuring, and downsizing. This requires good communication and influence skills as well as problem-solving and leadership competencies. The Society for Human Resource Management (SHRM) is the world's largest professional association devoted to HRM. SHRM's Code of Ethical and Professional Standards in Human Resource Management is available on its website and in Table 1.3.

nd3000/Shutterstock

As a manager, it is important to meet your job and HRM responsibilities and help your employees reach their personal career goals as well. Supervisors who help their employees advance often enjoy high performing and motivated employees.

The Manager

HRM is the responsibility of every supervising manager. In fact, the effectiveness of HRM systems often depends on the ability and the willingness of managers to execute HRM

table **1.3**

The SHRM Code of Ethical and Professional Standards in Human Resource Management[51]

The Society for Human Resource Management
CODE PROVISIONS

PROFESSIONAL RESPONSIBILITY

Core Principle

As HR professionals, we are responsible for adding value to the organizations we serve and contributing to the ethical success of those organizations. We accept professional responsibility for our individual decisions and actions. We are also advocates for the profession by engaging in activities that enhance its credibility and value.

Intent

- To build respect, credibility and strategic importance for the HR profession within our organizations, the business community, and the communities in which we work.
- To assist the organizations we serve in achieving their objectives and goals.
- To inform and educate current and future practitioners, the organizations we serve, and the general public about principles and practices that help the profession.
- To positively influence workplace and recruitment practices.
- To encourage professional decision-making and responsibility.
- To encourage social responsibility.

Guidelines

1. Adhere to the highest standards of ethical and professional behavior.
2. Measure the effectiveness of HR in contributing to or achieving organizational goals.
3. Comply with the law.
4. Work consistent with the values of the profession.
5. Strive to achieve the highest levels of service, performance, and social responsibility.
6. Advocate for the appropriate use and appreciation of human beings as employees.
7. Advocate openly and within the established forums for debate in order to influence decision-making and results.

PROFESSIONAL DEVELOPMENT

Core Principle

As professionals, we must strive to meet the highest standards of competence and commit to strengthen our competencies on a continuous basis.

Intent

- To expand our knowledge of human resource management to further our understanding of how our organizations function.
- To advance our understanding of how organizations work ("the business of the business").

Guidelines

1. Pursue formal academic opportunities.
2. Commit to continuous learning, skills development, and application of new knowledge related to both human resource management and the organizations we serve.
3. Contribute to the body of knowledge, the evolution of the profession, and the growth of individuals through teaching, research, and dissemination of knowledge.

Continued

4. Pursue certification where available, or comparable measures of competencies and knowledge.

ETHICAL LEADERSHIP

Core Principle

HR professionals are expected to exhibit individual leadership as a role model for maintaining the highest standards of ethical conduct.

Intent

- To set the standard and be an example for others.
- To earn individual respect and increase our credibility with those we serve.

Guidelines

1. Be ethical; act ethically in every professional interaction.
2. Question pending individual and group actions when necessary to ensure that decisions are ethical and are implemented in an ethical manner.
3. Seek expert guidance if ever in doubt about the ethical propriety of a situation.
4. Through teaching and mentoring, champion the development of others as ethical leaders in the profession and in organizations.

FAIRNESS AND JUSTICE

Core Principle

As human resource professionals, we are ethically responsible for promoting and fostering fairness and justice for all employees and their organizations.

Intent

To create and sustain an environment that encourages all individuals and the organization to reach their fullest potential in a positive and productive manner.

Guidelines

1. Respect the uniqueness and intrinsic worth of every individual.
2. Treat people with dignity, respect, and compassion to foster a trusting work environment free of harassment, intimidation, and unlawful discrimination.
3. Ensure that everyone has the opportunity to develop their skills and new competencies.
4. Assure an environment of inclusiveness and a commitment to diversity in the organizations we serve.
5. Develop, administer, and advocate policies and procedures that foster fair, consistent, and equitable treatment for all.
6. Regardless of personal interests, support decisions made by our organizations that are both ethical and legal.
7. Act in a responsible manner and practice sound management in the country(ies) in which the organizations we serve operate.

CONFLICTS OF INTEREST

Core Principle

As HR professionals, we must maintain a high level of trust with our stakeholders. We must protect the interests of our stakeholders as well as our professional integrity and should not engage in activities that create actual, apparent, or potential conflicts of interest.

Continued

Intent

To avoid activities that are in conflict or may appear to be in conflict with any of the provisions of this Code of Ethical and Professional Standards in Human Resource Management or with one's responsibilities and duties as a member of the human resource profession and/or as an employee of any organization.

Guidelines

1. Adhere to and advocate the use of published policies on conflicts of interest within your organization.

2. Refrain from using your position for personal, material, or financial gain or the appearance of such.

3. Refrain from giving or seeking preferential treatment in the human resources processes.

4. Prioritize your obligations to identify conflicts of interest or the appearance thereof; when conflicts arise, disclose them to relevant stakeholders.

USE OF INFORMATION

Core Principle

HR professionals consider and protect the rights of individuals, especially in the acquisition and dissemination of information, while ensuring truthful communications and facilitating informed decision-making.

Intent

To build trust among all organization constituents by maximizing the open exchange of information, while eliminating anxieties about inappropriate and/or inaccurate acquisition and sharing of information

Guidelines

1. Acquire and disseminate information through ethical and responsible means.

2. Ensure only appropriate information is used in decisions affecting the employment relationship.

3. Investigate the accuracy and source of information before allowing it to be used in employment-related decisions.

4. Maintain current and accurate HR information.

5. Safeguard restricted or confidential information.

6. Take appropriate steps to ensure the accuracy and completeness of all communicated information about HR policies and practices.

7. Take appropriate steps to ensure the accuracy and completeness of all communicated information used in HR-related training.

tasks and responsibilities. The HRM department is a support function that gives managers the tools needed to execute the firm's HRM strategy and helps them develop the skills in using these tools. For example, the HRM department might develop structured interview guides or performance management forms, but if the managers do not use these tools properly, their potential value to the organization will not be realized. Because HRM policies are created by the company but are executed by managers, the role of supervisors as well as the HRM department in executing HRM strategies and policies is important to understand.

so what?

The most effective supervisors are skilled in using HRM.

The Employee

Employees are increasingly being held at least somewhat responsible for taking the lead in their own development and career management. It is always best to have your own career development plan and continually develop your skills to meet your career goals. Employees are also sometimes held jointly responsible for keeping the HRM system accurate and current with regard to their skills and certifications.

employee handbooks
print or online materials that document the organization's HRM policies and procedures

Communication and feedback between HR and employees are extremely important. Most employees' knowledge of HRM and associated legal issues is minimal, and it is up to the employer to ensure that employees have the HR knowledge they need. **Employee handbooks** document the organization's HRM policies and procedures, and they are very important in helping employees learn about the company's HRM policies. Further, handbooks allow employees to easily research topics they need more information on later. Many organizations have put their HRM handbooks online, making it easy for employees to quickly find the information they need.

Shared Service Centers

shared service center
centralizes routine, transaction-based HRM activities

A **shared service center** centralizes the routine, transaction-based HRM activities, including payroll, benefits administration, and employee exit surveys. A shared service center can prevent redundancies and save money, as well as improve the consistency and the efficiency with which these tasks are done. This can provide an alternative to outsourcing these tasks, and it can free up HR professionals' time to focus on more strategic issues. Some companies, such as Home Depot, are creating call centers to handle HR questions directly from both employees and managers throughout the company.[52]

Outside Vendors

outsourcing
hiring an external vendor to do work rather than doing it internally

Outsourcing is the hiring of an external vendor to do work rather than doing it internally. When another company or provider can perform a task or service better, cheaper, or more efficiently, it can make sense to outsource work. Payroll processing, time and attendance records, and benefits management are some of the more frequently outsourced HRM tasks. A company can outsource one or many HRM tasks.

? so what

Not all HRM activities need to be provided by units within an organization to be effective—outsourcing some HRM activities is a good choice for many firms.

Outsourcing some HRM activities is particularly attractive to smaller companies. HR functions including payroll, benefits administration, and new hire relocation require special knowledge, and full-time employees may not be worth the expense to smaller firms. Because they specialize in human resources, outsourcing companies often know how to get employees the best HR services, including health benefits and retirement plans. They may also be able to provide rewards programs to your company for less than you would pay on your own. Also, if your company needs any kind of HR support in issues such as worker's compensation, outside vendors have this expertise and can also help you stay current on the most recent state and federal regulations to help your company stay compliant. It is critical to develop a strong relationship with external vendors to ensure they strongly support your organization's goals, strategies, culture, and philosophies.

This chapter's case study discusses how IBM separated its administrative from its strategic HRM activities to better focus on strategic needs and reduce costs while improving HRM service quality.

CASE STUDY: HR Transformation at IBM

Multinational technology and consulting firm IBM transformed itself from a strong multinational business to a globally integrated enterprise. As Barbara Brickmeier, vice president of HR, services delivery, and HR delivery says, "We want to be able to focus on getting the right talent at the right time, in the right place. Because if we don't, someone else is right behind us."[53] Now operating in more than 170 countries and with 62 percent of its business service based, IBM knows how important it is to capitalize on talent worldwide.[54] IBM now locates its business functions around the world based on the right mix of costs and skills.

To support its new strategy, IBM's human resources function separated core HR roles, including designing HRM policies and internal business consulting, from more administrative tasks such as payroll, relocation, performance management, and data entry. This allowed IBM's HRM professionals to focus on strategic and employee needs as well as streamline services and reduce costs while improving flexibility and service quality.

IBM employees are now supported by country and regional HR line managers. HRM subject matter experts focus on key functions such as payroll and designing programs relevant to business goals. Standardized administrative roles are centralized in cost-effective global employee service centers that provide payroll processing, travel and expense processing, and employee records management.

IBM relies on repeatable technology-enabled, cost-effective processes, such as a proprietary system for processing travel expenses that provides faster, more accurate employee reimbursements. Brickmeier states, "If we had to do those administrative tasks, and deal with technology, we wouldn't be able to do the things that help push the business forward, like hiring people, upskilling, leadership development and getting the right talent in place. . . .This gives us time to devote to talent management, compensation, developing skills and expertise, and helping the business grow." [55]

IBM also changed its annual performance review to one that allows employee goals to change during the year and that provides more frequent feedback.[56] The system now gives employees feedback at teachable moments throughout the year rather than only once a year during the annual perofrmance review, and it allows all employees to give feedback to each other regardless of rank.[57]

Questions:

1. How does separating core HRM roles from administrative HRM roles help IBM better execute its business strategy?
2. How has technology helped IBM implement its new HRM configuration?
3. How would getting feedback more than once a year and from employees other than your supervisor help you to perform better at work?

Professional Employer Organizations

A **professional employer organization** (PEO) is a company that leases workers to companies that need them for a fee, ranging from 2 to 7 percent of the worker's gross wages.[58] The PEO is technically the employer of these workers, and it manages their administrative needs, including training, discipline, payroll, and benefits. Leasing workers helps companies

professional employer organization
a company that leases employees to companies that need them

acquire talent they may not be able to hire on their own, and it increases their flexibility. Instead of hiring permanent employees who may have to be let go in a business downturn, leased employees give the organization the option of not renewing the lease if the worker is no longer needed.

Human Resource Management Systems

Employee data must be kept accurate, current, and private. Organizations used to rely on Excel spreadsheets to maintain this information, but the evolution of technology has created a better way. Human resource management systems (HRMS) are technology-based platforms that help human resource management professionals securely house sensitive employee records, including benefits and payroll information; monitor the performance of the recruiting and staffing process; conduct analytics, and more. They can be cloud-based, such as Workday or Cornerstone OnDemand, or they can be maintained by the company.

Some organizations create secure private portals that allow employees to upload confidential information, and others allow for extensive analytics to be run. The HRMS platforms available today can have varying degrees of specialization, with some optimized for the management of a lot of hourly workers and others emphasizing specific talent management areas such as recruiting, compensation, or benefits. Because there are so many features and tools available, it is important that how a company will actually use its HRMS be identified and drive its HRMS selection decision. If employees and managers need to use the system as well as the HRM department for open enrollment or to approve time sheets, it is important that the system be easy for them to use as well.

HRMS platforms are increasingly able to integrate a variety of applications and conduct analytics and produce reports that have more relevant and deeper insights than ever before. The technology is also increasingly able to support continuous performance feedback programs rather than annual performance reviews.[59]

 # Develop Your Skills

Careers in HRM

A career in human resource management can be rewarding both personally and financially. Occupational forecasts suggest that the income and opportunity prospects in HRM are favorable for at least the next decade or two. In fact, the Occupational Outlook Handbook provided by the U.S. government's Bureau of Labor Statistics states that, "Employment is expected to grow much faster than the average for all human resources, training, and labor relations managers and specialist occupations. College graduates and those who have earned certification should have the best job opportunities."[60]

Some of the job titles in the area of HRM include director of human resources, recruitment specialist, compensation analyst, employee benefits manager, work-life manager, training and development specialist, international human resource manager, diversity and inclusion specialist, and human resource generalist. Different skills are needed in the different areas of HRM. For example, strong quantitative and analytical skills are helpful in compensation, and good communication skills are critical in recruiting and training.

You can learn more about career opportunities in HRM by entering HRM-related search terms in the Occupational Outlook Handbook at http://www.bls.gov, or by using O*NET www.online.onetcenter.org.

Why Is HRM Important to Your Career?

so what**?**

HRM can help you be a more effective manager in any field.

Knowing how to design maximally productive and mutually rewarding work relationships with employees is important to every manager's success, even if your profession is something other than HRM. If you are unable to hire effectively, motivate employees, or retain your best performers, then your job performance will suffer. Hiring the right people, motivating and developing them, and ensuring that they are engaged in their work and committed to the company are some of the skills that define great managers. Knowledge of HRM and skills in practicing it will give you a competitive advantage in your own career, even if you are not going into the field of HRM.

If you are interested in learning more about HRM as a career field, this chapter's Develop Your Skills feature gives you more information about careers in HRM. This book isn't written solely for HRM majors—every future manager will benefit greatly from learning and applying the knowledge in this book.

Summary and Application

Why is it that some organizations perform better than others in the same industry? The answer is that it is not the buildings, chairs, or technology that make a company successful. It is the organization's *people* that really make a difference in how an organization performs. By acquiring the talent that is the foundation of any organization's performance, by developing the skills and teamwork needed to execute its strategies, and by motivating and rewarding employees for accomplishing company goals, HRM is critical in converting potential employee performance to actual performance and to strategic execution. Effective HR systems positively influence what people should do, can do, and will do for the organization.

Business strategies are intended to leverage the firm's resources and capabilities in ways that result in superior value creation compared to competitors. A competitive advantage depends on an organization's ability to leverage the resources and capabilities that derive from its talent. How an organization positions itself to compete determines the competitive advantage it needs to create and the HRM strategies it needs to pursue to acquire, motivate, and retain the appropriate talent. By influencing what employees should do, can do, and will do, effective and strategic human resource management aligns employees' talents, goals, and motivation with what the organization needs. Each of the HRM functional areas, including staffing, training, compensation, and performance management, must be consistent in what they reinforce, and care must be taken to ensure that they do not undermine each other. Human resource management systems help organizations leverage technology to make HRM processes more efficient and enable analytics that generate accurate and relevant insights into what can be done to enable higher individual, team, and organizational success and enhance strategic execution.

As we said at the beginning of this chapter, understanding human resource management can help you succeed in whatever career you pursue. Studying this book can help you better understand how organizations differ, understand the role of human resource management in your own job performance, and improve your HRM skills. By studying the chapters and putting some thought into how you can use various the concepts in different situations, you are taking an important step in advancing your career.

Real World Response

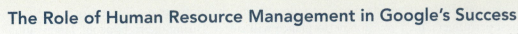

The Role of Human Resource Management in Google's Success

Its employees are the backbone of Google's success. Google designed itself on the idea that work should be challenging and fun, and it has an overarching philosophy to "create the happiest, most productive workplace in the world."[61] Google recognizes that its employees' needs vary across countries, and it offers benefits, policies, and perks that reflect the local environment and make their lives easier. Because its employees are highly analytical, Google's team also uses data to change opinions and persuade its managers and employees to commit to changes.[62]

Google calculated that exceptional technologists outperform average technologists by as much as 300 times, allowing it to convince executives to provide the resources necessary to invest in hiring, retaining, and developing truly extraordinary talent. Google's people operations professionals consistently make a strong business case for new initiatives, which is an important reason why they receive such extraordinary executive support.[63]

To ensure it hires the best talent, Google is extremely selective. Its recruiting machine regularly identifies people who may not currently be looking for a job but who it believes would be high-quality job candidates. The hiring process is lengthy and thorough, focused on finding smart, analytical, entrepreneurial people who can help Google achieve its vision of changing the world. Employees are also given quarterly performance reviews around core job competencies to ensure they know how they're doing and how to enhance their performance.

The goal of Google's People Operations group is to remove everything that might get in employees' way. In addition to buildings that foster teamwork and creativity, Google offers employees free gourmet meals and snacks, exercise facilities, game rooms, a laundry service, and even an on-site medical staff. Google also allows its software engineers to devote up to 20 percent of their time to noncore initiatives of their own choosing toward its vision of "changing the world." These extensive benefits may seem generous, and they certainly are, but every one of them exists for the purpose of enhancing Google's business results and was implemented and is retained based on data and analytics.

Google motivates its talent through its "learn fast, fail fast" approach to experimentation. Its engineers can try something new with few managerial sign-offs, but their ideas must generate positive feedback from colleagues if they are to be given significant resources for their initiatives. The ideas that get the most positive feedback tend to be those most likely to eventually attract millions of users.

Google also developed a mathematical algorithm to proactively identify employees at risk of quitting, allowing management to personalize retention solutions and act before it is too late.[64] It also created an incubator called Area 120 that Google teams can apply to join full-time for several months by pitching a business plan and possibly establish a new company with Google as an investor.[65]

Motivating employees to "change the world" and find the next big success is further enhanced through multimillion dollar stock grants called "Founders Awards" that are given to individuals or teams that make particular contributions to Google's success. So far, Google's approach to motivating its engineers has worked, with noncore projects regularly leading to successful new product launches.[66] Google's investment in attracting, hiring, developing, rewarding, and retaining talented people has paid off in the company's success and its stock market performance.

Takeaway Points

1. HRM influences organizational performance through its influence on what employees *should* do, what employees *can* do, and what employees *will* do. HRM creates the system that acquires, motivates, develops, and retains the talent that determines the organization's success. Because employee costs are a large part of an organization's operating budget, it is essential to properly manage the investments a company makes in its people.

2. The six primary HRM functions are staffing, performance management, training and development, rewards and benefits, health and safety, and employee-management relations.

3. If even a single HRM functional area reinforces goals that are in conflict with the other functional areas, influencing employee behaviors in desired ways and executing the company's strategy will be much more difficult. For example, the performance-enhancing potential of reward and incentive programs will not be fully leveraged if the training and development and staffing functions do not acquire and develop the right skills. The alignment of these separate functions creates an integrated human resource management system supporting the execution of the business strategy, guided by the talent philosophy of the organization.

4. Even small organizations can effectively use HRM to improve their performance. Organizations of all sizes share a need to identify and hire the right people, motivate them to perform their best, develop their skills, and retain them. Investing in HRM improves productivity and profitability of smaller as well as larger organizations.

5. Knowing how to design maximally productive and mutually rewarding work relationships with employees is important to every manager's success. The job performance of someone unable to hire effectively, motivate employees, or retain top performers will suffer.

Discussion Questions

1. Describe some good and bad experiences you have had with HRM as a job candidate or as an employee. How could the bad experiences have been avoided?

2. Would an organization's HRM practices influence your decision to apply for a job or accept a job offer? Why or why not?

3. How would you prioritize what workers can do, what they should do, and what they will do in terms of their importance to the employer? Why did you rank them as you did?

4. If you worked in a small organization, how would you convince the CEO to invest more in HRM?

5. Which aspects of HRM do you feel are most important for the employee, supervisor, and HRM professional to be responsible for? Why?

6. How can HRM help you advance and succeed in your career?

Personal Development Exercise: What HRM Career Is Right for You?

Go to O*NET at www.online.onetcenter.org, and enter different HRM keywords in the "Occupation Search" box (e.g., training, recruiting, and human resource manager). Click on one of the resulting job titles, and read the information provided about the job tasks, tools and technology used, and characteristics needed for successful job performance. Also read the information about the education, interests, work styles, and work values to learn about your potential fit with that position. Do this again for at least two other HR-related positions. Be sure to choose your state from the drop-down menu at the bottom of each job's O*NET page to see more information about the jobs and possibly view a short video further describing the job.

Choose your favorite of the jobs you explore, then research the wage and employment trends information about it. This information is available on the job's O*NET page, and you can get state-specific information by choosing a state from the drop-down menu near the bottom of the page. Write a one-page paper describing your chosen position, why you chose it, and the employment outlook in the location you hope to live. Evaluate your current capabilities and identify areas you might need to strengthen to increase your chances of acquiring this job in the future.

Strategic HRM Exercises

Exercise: Competitive Advantage Through HRM

Form small groups of three to five people. Vote on a spokesperson, and discuss the following questions to share with the class after 10 to 15 minutes. Be sure to record your ideas.

1. What companies do you think make the best use of HRM in creating a competitive advantage? Why?
2. What companies do you think could do a better job leveraging HRM to enhance their performance? Why?

Exercise: How HRM Influences Organizational Performance

We would like to thank Professor Daniel Montez of South Texas College for this exercise idea.

Divide the class into three groups of three to five students. The first group will discuss what employees *should* do. The second group will discuss what employees *can* do. The third group will discuss the topic of what employees *will* do. Students should share personal experiences about their own work experiences as well as what they know from friends and family and what they know from reading this chapter. Be prepared to share your group's five favorite ideas with the class.

Exercise: Did You Know?

Watch the video, "Did You Know, in 2028. . ." (3:15). After watching the video, answer the following questions:

1. What information did you find the most surprising?
2. What will these trends mean for employers?
3. What will these trends mean for you and for your career? What can you do to best position yourself for success in the future?

Exercise: Informational Interviews

We would like to thank Professor Barbara Rau of the University of Wisconsin-Oshkosh for this exercise idea.

Conduct e-mail, phone, or in-person informational interviews with two to three different HRM professionals at different types of companies. Identify three to five questions you would like to ask each person about HRM or how HRM is used in his or her organization. Write a one- to two-page report summarizing your interview results.

Exercise: Why We Hate HR

We would like to thank Professor Barbara Rau of the University of Wisconsin-Oshkosh for this exercise idea.

Use your favorite browser to find the article, "Why We Hate HR" by Keith Hammonds (published in Fast Company magazine on August 1, 2005). Write a one-page response to the author's criticisms of HR. The article can be found at: https://www.fastcompany.com/53319/why-we-hate-hr.

Integrative Project

Identify an industry in which you are interested in someday working, and create a name for a fictitious company that you will be working on all semester for this case study. If you want to use a current or past employer, you may do that instead. If you haven't already thought about a preferred industry, take the time to research several options to identify one that best meets your preferences for growth, financial performance, ethics, and environmental sustainability. Choosing an industry is as important as choosing an employer and a specific job—it influences how much flexibility you will have in your job (for example, some industries are more regulated than others), your promotion opportunities (faster growing industries provide greater opportunity for advancement), and your compensation (industries with higher profit margins can afford to pay employees more than industries without high profits).

Your first task is to read as much as you can about the industry, its top performing companies, its growth outlook, and its current challenges and opportunities to be able to make decisions in setting up a human resource management function for your company. Describe what your company's business strategy, competitive advantage, and talent philosophy will be—how will you position yourself to successfully compete in this industry? Assume that your company will be of any size and located anywhere that you would like; just be consistent throughout the case.

Video Case

Imagine having HR responsibilities at Happy Time Toys, a company that designs and manufactures novelty toys. While chatting with two of your coworkers you all realize how busy you all are and how much money the company is investing in HRM. One of the coworkers asks if it might be worth scaling back HR and putting more money and time into some other areas of the company, such as research and development or sales. *What do you say or do?* Go to this book's video case, watch the challenge video for this chapter, and choose the best video response. Be sure to also view the outcomes of the two responses you didn't choose.

Discussion Questions

1. Which aspects of HRM discussed in this chapter are illustrated in these videos? Explain your answer.
2. How could a company's investment in HRM help or undermine its success and its execution of its business strategy? Explain your answer
3. How else might you answer the question of whether Happy Time Toys should continue to invest money in HRM or reallocate some of it to sales or R&D?

Endnotes

1. Google. People. Retrieved January 28, 2017, from https://careers.google.com/fields-of-work/people/
2. Sullivan, J. (2010, November 22). Game-changing: Financial analysts begin assessing talent management effectiveness. ERE.net. Retrieved January 5, 2017, from http://www.ere.net/2010/11/22/15900/
3. *Ibid.*
4. Crook, T. R., Todd, S. Y., Combs, J. G., Woehr, D. J., & Ketchen, D. J. Jr. (2011). Does human capital matter? A meta-analysis of the relationship between human capital and firm performance. *Journal of Applied Psychology, 96*, 773–456.
5. Audrerie, J. B. (2016). 20 quotes about digital economy, talents, and skills. *Futurs Talents*, January 25. Retrieved January 14, 2017, from http://futurstalents.com/transformation-digitale/intelligence-digitale/20-quotes-about-digital-economy-talents-and-skills/9/
6. Saridakis, G., Lai, Y., & Cooper, C. L. (2017). Exploring the relationship between HRM and firm performance: A meta-analysis of longitudinal studies. *Human Resource Management Review, 27*, 87–96.
7. Saridakis, G., Lai, Y., & Cooper, C. L. (2017). Exploring the relationship between HRM and firm performance: A meta-analysis of longitudinal studies. *Human Resource Management Review, 27*, 87–96.
8. Reckard, E. S. (2010). Senate votes to ban certain bonuses for mortgage brokers, loan officers. *Los Angeles Times*, May 12. Retrieved January 5, 2017, from http://articles.latimes.com/2010/may/12/business/la-fi-mortgage-bill-20100513
9. Clements, N. (2016). The Wells Fargo reminder: Incentives can be dangerous. *Forbes*, September 27. Accessed January 21, 2017, from http://www.forbes.com/sites/nickclements/2016/09/27/the-wells-fargo-reminder-incentives-can-be-dangerous/#1349af14c49a
10. Heide, C., & Sevy, B. (2010). The key to competency success at Caribou. *Talent Management Magazine*, March, 38.
11. Orsagh, M. (2016). CorpGov roundup: CEO succession planning is in dismal state, global report finds. *CFA Institute*, June 8. Retrieved January 22, 2017, from https://blogs.cfainstitute.org/marketintegrity/2016/06/08/corpgov-roundup-ceo-succession-planning-is-in-dismal-state-global-report-finds/
12. Bishop, T. (2016). Starbucks CEO Howard Schultz stepping down, to be replaced by tech vet Kevin Johnson. *GeekWire*, December 1. Retrieved February 1, 2017, from http://www.geekwire.com/2016/starbucks-ceo-howard-schultz-stepping-replaced-tech-vet-kevin-johnson/
13. Campeau, M. (2014). 'A stick and a carrot at the same time': Why Costco pays twice the market rate. *Financial Post*, October 30. Retrieved January 4, 2017, from http://www.businessweek.com/magazine/content/04_15/b3878084_mz021.htm
14. Hersher, R. (2017). 'It's a big one': Iowa pipeline leaks nearly 140,000 gallons of diesel. *NPR*, January 26. Accessed February 4, 2017, from http://www.npr.org/sections/thetwo-way/2017/01/26/511636325/its-a-big-one-iowa-pipeline-leaks-nearly-140-000-gallons-of-diesel
15. The Henry J. Kaiser Family Foundation. (2016). 2016 employer health benefits survey. Retrieved January 6, 2017, from http://kff.org/report-section/ehbs-2016-summary-of-findings/
16. Bureau of Labor Statistics. (2017, January 26). Union members summary. Retrieved February 5, 2017, from https://www.bls.gov/news.release/union2.nr0.htm
17. Ruiz, G. (2006). Shaking up the toy shop. *Workforce Management*, June 26, 26–34.
18. U.S. Census Bureau. (2015, February). Statistics of U.S. businesses employment and payroll summary: 2012. Retrieved February 1, 2017, from https://www.census.gov/content/dam/Census/library/publications/2015/econ/g12-susb.pdf
19. Amba-Rao, S. C., & Pendse, D. (1985). Human resources compensation and maintenance practices. *American Journal of Small Business* (Fall), 19–29.
20. Mathis, R.L. & Jackson, J.H. (1991). *Personnel/Human Resource Management*, 6th ed. St. Paul, MN: West Publishing Company.
21. McEvoy, G. M. (1984). Small business personnel practices. *Journal of Small Business Management* (October), 1–8.
22. Julien, P.A. (Ed.). (1998). *The state of the art in small business and entrepreneurship.* Vermont: Ashgate Publishing Company.
23. Sels, L., DeWinne, S., Delmotte, J., Maes, J., Faems, D., & Forrier, A. (2006). Linking HRM and small business performance: An examination of the impact of HRM intensity on the productivity and financial performance of small businesses. *Small Business Economics, 26*, 83–101.
24. Becker, B., & Gerhart, B. (1996). The impact of human resource management on organizational performance: Progress and prospects. *Academy of Management Journal, 39*, 779–801.
25. For more information see ECO Trade and Development Bank. (2007). Operational and compliance risk management. Retrieved January 15, 2017, from http://www.etdb.org/content/operationalandcompliancriskmanagement; Goldberg, S., & Dyer, C. (2012). Reassessing HR risk management. *Human Resource Executive Online*, November 29. Retrieved January 11, 2017, from http://www.hreonline.com/HRE/view/story.jhtml?id=534354685; Lowers Risk Group. (2017). *Forces at work: Trends impacting HR's role in enterprise risk management.* Retrieved January 15, 2017, from http://www.lowersrisk.com/files/HR-ERM-Whitepaper.pdf
26. Sullivan, J. (2010, November 22). Game-changing: Financial analysts begin assessing talent management effectiveness. ERE.net. Retrieved January 4, 2017, from http://www.ere.net/2010/11/22/15900/
27. *Ibid.*
28. Stukel, P. (2015). Growth is the name of the game for middle market companies in 2015. *President & CEO*, January 1. Accessed February 1, 2017, from http://www.presidentandceomagazine.com/growth/66071-growth-is-the-name-of-the-game-for-middle-market-companies-in-2015.html
29. Olian, J. D., & Rynes, S. L. (1984). Organizational staffing: Integrating practice with strategy. *Industrial Relations, 23*(2), Spring, 170–183.
30. Goldman Sachs. (n.d.). People and culture. Retrieved February 2, 2017, from http://www.goldmansachs.com/who-we-are/people-and-culture/
31. Ellis, R. K. (2015). Want a global mindset? Integrate global skills into training for first-level leaders. *Association for Talent Development*, July 9. Retrieved February 2,

2017, from https://www.td.org/Publications/Blogs/Global-HRD-Blog/2015/07/Want-a-Global-Mindset

32. Javidan, M., Steers, R. M., Hitt, M. A. (2007). *The global mindset (advances in international management*, Vol. 19). New York: Elsevier.

33. Arora, A., Jaju, A., Kefalas, A. G., & Perenich, T. (2004). An exploratory analysis of global managerial mindsets: A case of U.S. textile and apparel industry. *Journal of International Management, 10*, 393–411.

34. Warren, K. (2009). *Developing employee talent to perform.* J. M. Phillips and S.M. Gully (Eds.). New York: Business Expert Press.

35. Harpaz, I. (1990). The importance of work goals: An international perspective. *Journal of International Business Studies, 21*, 75–93.

36. Forstenlechner, I., & Lettice, F. (2007). Cultural differences in motivating global knowledge workers. *Equal Opportunities International, 26*(8), 823–833.

37. UNFPA. (2004). Quotes on culture and culturally sensitive approaches. *United Nationas Poopulations Fund.* Retrieved May 7, 2017, from http://www.unfpa.org/resources/quotes-culture-and-culturally-sensitive-approaches

38. Fatehi, K. (2007). *Managing internationally: Succeeding in a culturally diverse world.* New York: Sage.

39. Aycan, Z.et al. (2000). Impact of culture on human resource management practices: A 10-country comparison. *Applied Psychology: An International Review, 49*, 192–221.

40. Alfes, K., Antunes, B., & Shantz, A. D. (2016). The management of volunteers—What can human resources do? A review and research agenda. *The International Journal of Human Resource Management*, October, 1–36.

41. McKee, T. W. (2010). How to motivate volunteers: The top motivation and retention winners, volunteer power. Retrieved January 3, 2017, from http://www.volunteerpower.com/articles/motivate.asp

42. Secrets of an undercover boss. *Fortune,* September 22, 2010. Retrieved January 5, 2017, from http://money.cnn.com/galleries/2010/pf/1009/gallery.undercover_boss.fortune/5.html

43. Porter, M. E. (1985). *Competitive advantage.* New York: Free Press.

44. Beatty, R. W., and Schneier, C. E. (1997). New HR roles to impact organizational performance: From 'partners' to 'players.,' *Human Resource Management, 36*, 29–37; Deloitte & Touche LLP. (2002). *Creating shareholder value through people: The human capital ROI study.* New York: Deloitte & Touche, LLP; and Treacy, M., & Wiersema, F. (1993). Customer intimacy and other value disciplines. *Harvard Business Review, 71*, 84–94.

45. Schuler, R., & Jackson, S. (1987). Linking competitive strategies and human resource management practices. *Academy of Management Executive, 1*, 207–219.

46. Kiger, P. J. (2002). Why customer satisfaction starts With HR. *Workforce*, May, 26–32.

47. Beatty, R. W., & Schneier, C. E. (1997). New HR roles to impact organizational performance: From 'partners' to 'players.' *Human Resource Management, 36*, 29–37; Deloitte & Touche LLP. (2002). *Creating shareholder value through people: The human capital ROI study.* New York: Deloitte & Touche, LLP; and Treacy, M., & Wiersema, F. (1993). Customer intimacy and other value disciplines. *Harvard Business Review, 71*, 84–94.

48. Weber, R. A., & Camerer, C. F. (2003). Cultural conflict and merger failure: An experimental approach. *Management Science, 49*(4), 400–415.

49. Russo, D. (2010). *17 rules successful companies use to attract and keep top talent: Why engaged employees are your greatest sustainable advantage.* New York: FT Press.

50. Life at SAS. (n.d.). SAS. Retrieved January 3, 2017, from https://www.sas.com/en_us/careers/life-at-sas.html

51. Code of ethics. (2014, November 21). Society for Human Resource Management. Retrieved May 9, 2017, from https://www.shrm.org/about-shrm/pages/code-of-ethics.aspx

52. Marquez, J. (2008). HR under remodel. *Workforce Management, 87*, 1–3.

53. IBM.com. (2010, May). IBM HR rises to the transformational challenge. Retrieved December 21, 2010, from http://www-01.ibm.com/software/success/cssdb.nsf/CS/JHUN-85W62F?OpenDocument&Site=corp&cty=en_us

54. Applegate, L. M., Austin, R., & Collins, E. (2009). *IBM's decade of transformation: Turnaround to growth.* Boston, MA: Harvard Business School.

55. IBM.com. (2010, May). IBM HR rises to the transformational challenge. Retrieved January 6, 2017, from http://www-935.ibm.com/services/au/gts/pdf/HR_transformational_challenge.PDF

56. Zillman, C. (2016, February 1). IBM is blowing up its annual performance review, *Fortune.* Retrieved January 20, 2017, from http://fortune.com/2016/02/01/ibm-employee-performance-reviews/

57. Gay, W. (2016, July 13). How IBM changed its feedback system to engage millenial employees. *Forbes.* Retrieved January 16, 2017, from http://www.forbes.com/sites/under30network/2016/07/13/how-ibm-changed-its-feedback-system-to-suit-millennial-employees/2/#701617e11a34

58. Davlin, L. (2007). Human resource solutions for the franchisee. *Franchising World, 39*, 27–28.

59. Foxall, D. (2017). Where is HRMS going in 2017? *HRMS World*, January 9. Retrieved February 4, 2017, from http://www.hrmsworld.com/where-is-hrms-going-in-2017.html

60. Bureau of Labor Statistics (2010). Job outlook, occupational outlook handbook, 2010–2011 edition. Retrieved December 22, 2010, from http://www.bls.gov/oco/ocos021.htm#outlook

61. Stewart, J. B. (2013, March 15). Looking for a lesson in Google's perks. *The New York Times.* Retrieved February 2, 2017, from http://www.nytimes.com/2013/03/16/business/at-google-a-place-to-work-and-play.html

62. Sullivan, J. (2013, February 25). How Google became the #3 most valuable firm by using people analytics to reinvent HR. *ERE.* Retrieved January 25, 2017, from https://www.eremedia.com/ere/how-google-became-the-3-most-valuable-firm-by-using-people-analytics-to-reinvent-hr/

63. *Ibid.*

64. *Ibid.*

65. Risen, T. (2016, April 25). Report: Google's Area 120 aims to retain startup talent. *U.S. News.* Retrieved January 12, 2017, from https://www.usnews.com/news/articles/2016-04-25/report-googles-area-120-aims-to-retain-startup-talent

66. Hamel, G., with Breen, B. (2007). *The future of management.* Boston, MA: Harvard Business School Press.

chapter 2

The Role of Human Resource Management in Business

Learning Objectives

1 Explain how human resource management (HRM) reinforces organizational culture.

2 Describe how HRM supports high-performance work systems.

3 Describe the five standards that help us decide if an action is unethical.

4 Explain how HRM influences ethics and corporate social responsibility.

5 Explain how HRM can support organizational change.

6 Describe Hofstede's five cultural dimensions and how they each might influence HRM in different cultures.

7 Describe how employees influence the success of a merger or acquisition and how HRM can create the foundation for the success of the combined company.

Real World Challenge

How Culture Reinforces Business Strategy at Marriott

Executive Chairman and Chairman of the Board J. W. Marriott, Jr. has led Marriot International, Inc. for almost 60 years.[1] After modest beginnings as his parents' family restaurant business, the global lodging company now has more than 5,700 lodging properties across 30 brands in over 110 countries and territories.[2]

J. W. Marriott's vision for the company is to be the world's lodging leader. To accomplish this goal, he focuses intensely on taking care of guests, developing a highly skilled and diverse workforce, and extensive operational knowledge. Through his hands-on management style, Marriott has built a strong culture that emphasizes the importance of the company's people and the value they bring to the organization.

Marriott International's "Spirit to Serve" culture focuses on executing fundamental ideals of service to associates, customers, and the community. Its fundamental ideals of service to its associates are:[3]

- The unshakeable conviction that our people are our most important asset.
- An environment that supports associate growth and personal development.
- A home-like atmosphere and friendly workplace relationships.
- A performance-reward system that recognizes the important contributions of both hourly and management associates.
- A reputation for employing caring, dependable associates who are ethical and trustworthy.
- Pride in the Marriott name, accomplishments, and record of success.
- A focus on growth—managed and franchised properties, owners, and investors.

Marriott asks you for your advice on how the company can use HRM to further enhance its "Spirit to Serve" culture. After reading this chapter, you should have some good ideas.

HRM affects the performance of any business. Although some industries and businesses are more dependent than others on their talent to create a competitive advantage, it is difficult and perhaps impossible to identify a business in which talent does not matter.[4] As Thomas J. Watson, Jr., founder of IBM once said, "I believe the real difference between success and failure in a corporation can be very often traced to the question of how well the organization brings out the great energies and talents of its people."[5] Understanding the role of HRM in business will help you to identify which investments in HRM are likely to matter most.

> *"I believe the real difference between success and failure in a corporation can be very often traced to the question of how well the organization brings out the great energies and talents of its people."*
>
> **—Thomas J. Watson, Jr., founder of IBM**

Data consistently shows that people are one of the highest costs of running an organization, and strategic HRM positively affects business outcomes. For example, the market value of companies that use HRM best practices including selective recruiting, training, and employment security is more than 50 percent higher than that of firms that do not.[6] Many organizations could dramatically improve their business outcomes by investing in the strategic use of HRM, including:[7]

- Creating an HRM strategy that is integrated with the business strategy
- Using effective HRM metrics and analytics
- Ensuring that HRM employees have high levels of business knowledge and skill
- Delivering HRM services effectively and efficiently.

HRM influences business in both direct and indirect ways. In addition to acquiring and developing the skills and the capabilities the organization needs, aligning employee and organizational goals, and motivating employees to perform their best, HRM also influences the environment in which work is done and how employees get their work done. Great companies often (and appropriately) credit their employees with their success. As Phil Knight, chairman of the board and co-founder of Nike explains, "It's not a single product model, nor a single manager, nor one ad, nor a single celebrity, not even a single innovation that is key to Nike. It is the people of Nike and their unique and creative way of working together."[8]

By reinforcing the values of the firm, HRM helps clarify for employees how they are to behave and make decisions. For example, why do you think employees in some companies act more socially responsible than do employees in other firms? Although certainly due in part to differences in the values of the employees, these differences are also driven by the expectations, rewards, goals, and feedback created by the HRM system through organizational culture. Hiring socially responsible people, rewarding employees for acting responsibly, and punishing or removing employees who do not support social responsibility strongly affects employees' socially responsible behavior and decision making.

In this chapter, we begin by discussing the importance of organizational culture and how HRM supports different types of cultures. These topics are part of effective work processes in our book's overall model of HRM. We then turn our attention to the importance of ethics and social responsibility and how HRM can reinforce both of these important values. We then discuss the role of HRM in creating high-performance work systems. These topics are part of effective work processes in our book's overall model of HRM. The chapter ends with a discussion of how HRM supports organizational change and success in mergers and acquisitions. After reading this chapter, you should have a good idea of the variety of ways HRM systems and activities contribute to organizational effectiveness.

Why Is Organizational Culture Important?

An organization's culture is like its personality. **Organizational culture** is made up of the norms, values, and assumptions of organizational members. A company's culture is reinforced by things such as logos, ceremonies, dress codes, and even office decorations and furniture placement. An organization's culture guides employees' attitudes and behaviors in the absence of formal policies or rules and creates the context for what they do. Culture is often defined more casually as "the way we see and do things around here" and is critical in aligning employees' goals with those of the organization.

organizational culture
The norms, values, and assumptions of organizational members that guide members' attitudes and behaviors.

When asked for tips on building a strong company, Fred Wilson of venture capital fund Union Square Ventures stated that, "You have to start with culture, values, and a commitment to creating a fantastic workplace. You can't fake these things. They have to come from the top. . . . They are everything."[9] Research has found that a firm's culture is positively related to important outcomes, including financial performance (Tobin's Q and revenue growth), employee attitudes, and analysts' stock recommendations.[10]

Business strategies can be reinforced or undermined by their fit with the firm's culture.[11] Isadore Sharp, founder, chairman, and CEO of the Four Seasons hotels, states, "Personal service is not something you can dictate as a policy. It comes from the culture. How you treat your employees is how you expect them to treat the customer."[12] Similarly, rigid, bureaucratic, rule-oriented cultures are much less likely to support creative new product innovation.

Four broad types of organizational culture are:[13]

so what?

To maximize strategic execution, build an organizational culture to reinforce the business strategy.

- *Entrepreneurial*: Emphasizes creativity, innovation, and risk taking. Electronic Arts and IDEO are examples of companies with entrepreneurial cultures.
- *Bureaucratic*: Emphasizes formal structures and the correct implementation of organizational procedures, norms, and rules. This type of culture is commonly associated with consistency and high ethical standards. Pharmacies and drug manufacturers such as GlaxoSmithKline and Merck often adopt bureaucratic cultures.
- *Consensual*: Emphasizes loyalty and tradition, and encourages employees to stay with the organization for a long time. Promotion is generally from within. Law firms and the military are good examples of this type of culture.
- *Competitive*: Emphasizes competitive advantage and market superiority. Brokerage and currency trading firms are consistent with this type of culture, which often produce a large amount of stress.

Organizations frequently possess a combination of these four types of culture but with an emphasis on one over the others.[14] Another aspect of culture that is particularly related to organizational effectiveness is the degree to which it is focused on high performance. A **performance culture** focuses on hiring, retaining, developing, motivating, and making work assignments based on performance data and results. Because all employees are focused on winning, performance permeates every aspect of the firm. Sports teams such as the New York Yankees and the Pittsburgh Steelers consistently excel because of their strong performance culture, as do restaurants that schedule their highest performing servers to their busiest shifts.

performance culture
performance culture: focuses on hiring, retaining, developing, motivating, and making work assignments based on performance data and results

Understanding the power of its strong positive culture, insurer Aflac uses its corporate culture on the corporate careers section of its website to attract recruits:

> Join a company that's been named to Fortune Magazine's "100 best Companies to Work For" 16 years in a row. As part of the Aflac team, you'll find yourself in a supportive work environment with an organizational culture that champions an open-door management philosophy, competitive salaries, excellent benefits, and more.[15]

The HRM system strongly influences employees' perceptions of the organization's culture. What type of culture do you think is reinforced by low pay, few benefits, little training, lots of rules, and fast punishment if you break them? Probably not Aflac's culture described above! Investing in establishing and maintaining a culture that supports the organization's goals and business strategy pays off. Customer satisfaction, customer service quality, financial performance, organizational effectiveness, and total quality management outcomes are influenced by employees' perceptions of culture.[16] 3M credits its success at regularly innovating new products to a culture "that stimulates ordinary people to produce extraordinary performances."[17]

Culture and HRM work together to influence employees' performance and behaviors. The HRM system has the most immediate effect on employees' behaviors because it formalizes the company's expectations through explicit goals and formal policies. It in situations where formal policies don't exist, the organizational culture takes over. By reinforcing the desirability of certain values or behaviors, the HRM system helps to reinforce the organizational culture. This emphasizes the importance of aligning the HRM system, the organizational culture, and the business strategy.

? so what

Because HRM formalizes an organization's expectations and guides employees when formal policies don't exist, the HRM system helps create and reinforce the organizational culture

A negative organizational culture can risk an organization's reputation and even its survival. When an Uber employee went public with reports of managers' misconduct, a movement started to delete their app, and their ability to recruit the top technology on which it is dependent likely decreased.[18] Because small culture failures ultimately lead to big culture crises, an important role of human resources is to monitor the culture and keep things in check. When the Uber employee reported her experience, she was told by both HR and upper management that "even though this was clearly sexual harassment, they wouldn't feel comfortable giving him anything other than a warning and a stern talking-to."[19] For her, HR was the only recourse she had to report managers' wrongdoings, and HR's failure to provide a safe environment in which she could report misconduct left her feeling unsupported and left with no choice but to either ignore the harassment or leave. Ultimately, Uber only addressed the issue because the employee went public with her story.[20] To many people, cultural issues of diversity, equity, and inclusion seem like "soft" issues, but it is becoming clear how important it is for companies to incorporate these issues into their culture, which ultimately creates an environment where success is possible.[21]

A study of new accounting employees found that new hires stayed an average of 14 months longer in companies with people-oriented cultures.[22] Starbucks is a good example of a people-oriented culture. Starbucks pays above minimum wage, offers health care and tuition reimbursement benefits to part-time as well as full-time employees, and provides additional benefits such as weekly free coffee. These policies help Starbucks benefit from a turnover rate lower than the industry average.[23] On the other hand, a bureaucratic culture that stifled innovation and risk taking is thought to have contributed to Nokia's declining market share.[24]

An organizational culture can have a strong influence on behavior when employees develop a shared interpretation of the organization's policies, practices, procedures, and goals and develop shared perceptions about what behaviors are expected and rewarded. The more HRM practices send strong signals about what strategic goals are most important and what employee behaviors are expected, supported, and rewarded relative to those goals, the more likely it is that those goals will be achieved.[25] Companies can advertise hotlines and encourage employees to report anything improper, but if the culture has too much fear and not enough trust, no one will call. In some cases, these fears are warranted. Some employees who called the Wells Fargo ethics hotline to report unethical sales practices were fired despite it being against the law to suppress whistleblowing.[26]

At Starbucks, customers pay a premium price for the culture as well as the coffee. By focusing on hiring customer-oriented employees, training them well, and then providing excellent pay and benefits including health care and tuition reimbursement, the company reduces turnover and motivates its employees to provide excellent products and customer service.

Hollywood animation hit factory Pixar's culture is as strong as its technology. Pixar communicates and instills its culture through Pixar University, a unique training complex in which all employees learn together. Randy Nelson, Dean of Pixar University, states, "Most companies eventually come around to the idea that people are the most important thing. It's fine to have wildly talented individuals. But the real trick, the higher degree of difficulty, is to get wildly talented people to make productive partnerships."[27] He concludes that for Pixar the most urgent question is, "How do you do art as a team sport?"[28] Pixar's answer has been to build a culture supported by HRM that encourages people to share their works-in-progress and support coworkers. Pixar's president, Ed Catmull, believes that his calling is to create a sustainable creative culture that will persist in the company for a long time.[29] He even comes to all new hires' orientation sessions to reinforce its culture.[30]

so what?

To enhance goal achievement, HRM practices should help employees prioritize their goals and know what they need to do to support their own goals and the organization's goals.

> *"Most companies eventually come around to the idea that people are the most important thing. It's fine to have wildly talented individuals. But the real trick, the higher degree of difficulty, is to get wildly talented people to make productive partnerships."*
>
> **—Randy Nelson, Dean of Pixar University**

A strong HRM system increases the chances that employees will perceive the organization similarly and identify the same culture.[31] A weak HRM system sends either mixed or ambiguous messages that are subject to individual interpretation. This leads to either variability in how the culture is interpreted or the interpretation of a culture other than the one the organization desires.[32] HRM influences organizational cultures by determining the type of person who is hired and fired, what is trained, what goals and expectations exist, what people are held accountable for, and who is rewarded. Volkswagen's "no failure" culture and climate of fear combined with the CEO's ambitious growth goals are blamed for its emissions-test scandal where it installed software to beat emissions tests by using phony data rather than fixing the problem.[33]

To maximize your satisfaction with your career, it is helpful to put as much thought into the industry and the organization in which you will work as you do into the work in which you will specialize. Some industries, including pharmaceuticals and chemical manufacturing, are inherently more formalized and bureaucratic due to extensive legal regulations. Other industries, including entertainment and advertising, are inherently more creative and informal.

Understanding your preferences for different cultural features can help you choose the best fit for you. Here are some of the characteristics you might consider:

- A focus on competition versus cooperation
- Formal versus flexible procedures
- A focus on company success versus the public good
- Individual versus team-based rewards
- Well-defined versus flexible career paths
- A formal versus informal atmosphere
- Centralized versus decentralized decision making
- Clearly defined responsibilities versus varied responsibilities.

so what

How well we fit with our industry's and our organization's culture influences how satisfied we are with our career.

Employee and organizational preferences for different types of cultures tend to vary across national cultures.[34] This chapter's global issues feature summarizes one study's assessment of organizational culture preferences in different regions of the world.

 Global Issues

Organizational Culture Preferences and Realities Around the World[35]

Organizational Culture Preferences		Asia	United States	Latin America	Europe
Focus	Company success	76%	72%	78%	77%
	Public good	24%	28%	22%	23%
	Total	100%	100%	100%	100%
Competition/ Cooperation	Internal competition	13%	10%	8%	10%
	Cooperative atmosphere	87%	90%	92%	90%
	Total	100%	100%	100%	100%
Career Path	Well-defined	31%	21%	24%	18%
	Flexible career opportunities	69%	79%	76%	82%
	Total	100%	100%	100%	100%
Atmosphere	Formal	23%	21%	23%	14%
	Informal	77%	79%	77%	86%
	Total	100%	100%	100%	100%
Responsibilities	Clearly defined	69%	47%	58%	54%
	Varied/fluid	31%	53%	42%	46%
	Total	100%	100%	100%	100%

This chapter's HR flexibility feature describes how different business strategies can be reinforced by different cultures, and how HRM can help to do this.

HR Flexibility

Using HRM to Reinforce Different Business Strategies Through Culture

Companies differ in the strategies they use to compete. Some firms, including Wal-Mart, work to keep their costs low in order to provide the lowest prices to customers. Others, such as Lexus or Tiffany's, strive to provide the best quality or service. Still other firms try to serve specific market niches or continually develop new and innovative products or services. The organizational cultures and HRM policies and activities that support each business strategy differ.

Think for a moment about what culture you would create and how you might use HRM to reinforce a low-cost business strategy. This doesn't necessarily mean paying low wages, only making sure that the return on wages is sufficiently high. Outsourcing services or activities that an external partner can provide as well or better than the company at a lower price would also reinforce a low-cost strategy. Creating a culture of thrift and frugality is another possibility, as well as training employees in the most efficient ways of getting their work done.

Now contrast those ideas with the culture you would create and how you might use HRM to reinforce an innovation strategy focused on developing new and innovative products. This strategy is often supported by a culture of teamwork and collaboration supported by extensive training, team development, and performance-based rewards.[36] Staffing might focus on acquiring creative, talented, entrepreneurial people (which is what Google does). When Charles Schwab and Company's performance slipped during the recession, it decided to move away from its long-standing culture of teamwork and start providing incentives for individual brokers. It claimed that the change was intended to improve client relationships and reward highly productive individuals working in underperforming branches who weren't being properly rewarded, but the new system sent mixed messages to its employees about whether the company now placed a greater value on individual performance or teamwork.[37]

It is important to remember that there is no "best" HRM system.[38] As you read this book and apply what you learn, recall that it is most critical to align HRM policies and practices with each other and with the business strategy. Also remember that using the "wrong" HRM tool or incorrectly using the right tool can both cause a lot of damage.

Because it guides employee attitudes and behaviors, organizational culture is essential to the establishment of corporate ethics and corporate social responsibility. We now turn our attention to how HRM can reinforce both values.

What Is the Role of HRM in High-Performance Work Systems?

Companies that implement **high-performance work systems** (HPWS) utilize a fundamentally different approach to managing than do more traditional hierarchical and bureaucratic organizations. HPWS, sometimes known as *high-involvement* or *high-commitment* organizations,

high-performance work systems
high involvement or high commitment organizations

enable high performance through employees. HPWS organizations should be structured so that individuals at the lowest level in the organization not only perform work but also are responsible or improving work methods and procedures, solving problems on the job, and coordinating their work with that of others. Employees also can and should be expected to operate without a controlling supervisor.[39]

In HPWS, workers are to a large degree self-controlled and self-managed. With the help of leaders who develop a clear vision, mission, and goals, HPWS workers are expected to adapt to changing circumstances. Because employees in HPWS identify with, are committed to, and fully participate in the organization, they give greater effort and are more effective than workers in control-oriented organizations.[40] Research has, in fact, found that using a wide variety of power-sharing, reward, information-sharing, and training practices has positive outcomes.[41] Noted management scholar Jeffrey Pfeffer concluded that, "Substantial gains, on the order of 40 percent or so in most of the studies reviewed, can be obtained by implementing high performance management practices."[42]

In his book *The Human Equation*,[43] Pfeffer identified seven elements of HPWS:

1. Employment security
2. Selective hiring of new talent
3. Self-managed teams and decentralization of decision making as the basic principles of organizational design
4. Comparatively high compensation contingent on organizational performance.
5. Extensive training
6. Reduced status distinctions and barriers, including dress, language, office arrangements, and wage differences across levels
7. Extensive sharing of financial and performance information throughout the organization.

? so what?

Although there is no one set of HRM practices that support a HPWS, whatever HRM practices are used must be internally consistent and reinforcing to be most effective.

The particular set of managerial and HRM practices supporting a HPWS varies across companies, but it must always be internally consistent and reinforcing.[44] Employees in a high-involvement organization feel responsible for its success because they know more, do more, and contribute more.[45] They have the power, information, knowledge, and rewards to perform at the highest level.[46] Among the successful companies making use of this approach are Men's Wearhouse, Southwest Airlines, and Virgin Atlantic Airways.[47]

Although some employees find the increased responsibility of HPWS to be stressful, many are motivated by it. The benefits of HPWS to employees and to the organization are summarized in Table 2.1.

Aligning HRM activities and policies with the goals and processes that support HPWS is particularly important because HPWSs require a heavy investment in employees that is lost if the firm cannot attract and retain quality people.[48] This is a core theme that runs throughout this book: the most effective HRM systems are *internally aligned* and are *targeted toward clear organizational objectives*.

The Role of HRM in Corporate Ethics and Social Responsibility

ethics

the standards of moral behavior that define socially accepted behaviors that are right as opposed to wrong

Ethics are the standards of moral behavior that define socially accepted behaviors that are right as opposed to wrong. Honesty, tolerance, and responsibility are basic moral values that guide ethical evaluations. Although it might seem intuitive that firms should behave ethically, a glance at the news headlines often suggests that unethical behavior is more common than you might think. Bernie Madoff's Ponzi scheme defrauded investors of tens of

table **2.1**

Benefits of HPWS

Employee Benefits
Greater personal development
Higher work engagement, satisfaction, and commitment
Greater involvement in organizational decisions
Higher quality of life
Higher self-esteem
Organization Benefits
Higher productivity
Greater flexibility and competitiveness
Higher customer satisfaction
Higher product quality
Lower turnover

billions of dollars and was called, "extraordinarily evil" by the judge handling the case.[49] Fertilizer producer Intrepid Potash's Chief Operating Officer Patrick L. Avery resigned after confirming that he didn't receive previously claimed degrees.[50] Corporate espionage by the Formula One racing team McLaren on rival Ferrari,[51] unsanitary manufacturing conditions in a ConAgra peanut manufacturing plant,[52] and the intentional contamination of baby formula and pet food with melamine[53] are just a few additional high-profile ethical lapses. When ethical lapses occur, as happened during the U.S. Secret Service agents' misconduct in Columbia, a "culture problem" is often blamed.[54] HRM professionals are uniquely positioned to build and reinforce an ethical culture because their role in hiring, training, evaluating, and rewarding employees allows them to influence ethical values and practices at all levels of an organization.[55]

It is important to remember that "unethical" is not always the same as "illegal." Some unethical behaviors can be acceptable under the law. This makes it critical that organizations proactively identify their ethical values and reinforce these values with their employees. As shown in Figure 2.1, ethical employee behavior results from ethical values, clear expectations, and rewards and punishments supporting ethical behavior.[56]

The challenge of managing workplace ethics is complicated by the diverse values of today's global workforce. Because some people feel that the business ethics message of "do the right thing" only states the obvious, they don't take business ethics seriously. For many others, ethical principles go right out the door when they are highly stressed.[57]

so what**?**

A behavior that is unethical may not be illegal.

figure **2.1**

A Formula for Ethical Behavior

utilitarian standard
the ethical action best balances good over harm

rights standard
the ethical action is the one that best respects and protects the moral rights of everyone affected by the action

fairness standard
the ethical action treats all people equally, or at least fairly, based on some defensible standard

common good standard
the ethical action shows respect and compassion for all others, especially the most vulnerable

virtue standard
the ethical action is consistent with certain ideal virtues including civility, compassion, benevolence, etc.

❓so what

A behavior can be considered ethical under one standard but unethical under a different standard.

How can we tell if an action is unethical? There are five different types of ethical standards that help us evaluate the ethics of an action:

1. The **utilitarian standard**: The ethical action best balances good over harm by doing the most good or doing the least harm. When Southwest Airlines cuts all employees' pay rather than laying anyone off, it is following a utilitarian standard.
2. The **rights standard**: The ethical action is the one that best respects and protects the moral rights of everyone affected by the action, including the right to privacy, to be told the truth, or to be safe. If a supervisor tells an employee to handle a toxic substance without appropriate protective gear, the employee has a right to refuse.
3. The **fairness standard**: The ethical action treats all people equally, or at least fairly, based on some defensible standard. The fairness standard is central in the debate over the appropriateness of CEO salaries and bonuses that are hundreds of times larger than the pay of the average employee.
4. The **common good standard**: The ethical action shows respect and compassion for everyone, especially the most vulnerable. Ensuring that suppliers do not employ child labor or provide unsafe working conditions is an example of applying the common good standard.
5. The **virtue standard**: The ethical action is consistent with certain ideal virtues including civility, compassion, and benevolence. This standard asks, "Is this action consistent with my behaving at my best?" A company valuing honesty quickly recalling products that might be defective or dangerous reflects the virtue standard.

These five different types of ethical standards sometimes suggest different actions in a given situation. Different people may even disagree on the execution of some of the approaches or support different ethical standards. Nonetheless, each ethical standard provides guidance in evaluating the ethics of a situation or decision.

Some unethical behaviors occur because some people are simply less ethical than others,[58] but the broader organizational context and systems are also relevant. Company leaders often give too little thought and time to developing and reinforcing an organizational culture in which people can and do act ethically. There are three types of systemic errors organizations often make that undermine their ethics efforts:[59]

1. *Omission errors*—a lack of written rules
2. *Remission errors*—pressure to make unethical choices
3. *Commission errors*—a failure to follow sound, established operational and ethical practices.

All three of these errors can have obvious negative consequences. One of the strongest predictors of unethical behavior is the employee's emphasis on self-gain. In fact, the factor most likely to cause an employee to compromise an organization's ethical standards is the pressure to meet unrealistic business objectives or deadlines.[60]

You are probably already familiar with the moral benefits of attending to ethics. Additional benefits from managing corporate ethics include:[61]

- Promoting a strong public image
- Substantially improving society
- Helping to manage change
- Cultivating teamwork and productivity
- Supporting employee growth
- Helping to ensure that policies are legal
- Helping to avoid criminal acts on the part of employees
- Helping to manage employee values associated with quality management, strategic planning and diversity management.

table 2.2

Common Ethical Issues in HRM

Privacy Issues: Keeping employees' and applicants' personal and medical information private; deciding on the appropriate use of employee surveillance (including via e-mail and video cameras); maintaining confidentiality.

Staffing: Handling pressure to hire a friend or family member; dealing with employees found to have faked their credentials during the hiring process; avoiding illegal discrimination.

Layoffs and Downsizings: Managing employee separations fairly and equitably.

Rewards: Responding to pressure to classify a person into a job grade higher than they deserve in order to give them a raise; responding to pressure to give executives more generous incentives or benefits than is necessary; paying fair wages.

Safety: Deciding how to handle bullying; creating and enforcing safety and health policies; managing work stress and employee wellness.

Performance Appraisal: Ensuring objectivity and fairness; avoiding the use of nonperformance factors in the performance evaluation.

Labor Practices: Using child labor; limiting working hours; exploiting workers; respecting human rights.

Ethical employee behavior determines short-term organizational performance and long-term organizational success. If employees do not consistently behave ethically, long-term sustainability is unlikely for any organization. As management experts Wayne Cascio and Peter Cappelli state, "Ethics, values, and strong organizational cultures are the very fabric of business."[62] Despite the obvious problems that can result from unethical employee behavior, most organizations do not have a comprehensive ethics and compliance program.

> *"Ethics, values, and strong organizational cultures are the very fabric of business."*
>
> **—Wayne Cascio and Peter Cappelli**

In addition to the ethical challenges facing all managers, HRM has its own ethical issues. Some common ethical issues in HRM are described in Table 2.2.

HRM promotes ethics by hiring ethical employees, setting clear goals for ethical behavior, training employees in recognizing ethics issues and properly handling ethical situations, and holding employees accountable for ethical behavior. To guide ethical behavior, organizations frequently adopt a code of conduct or a code of ethics to clarify what is and what is not acceptable.

so what?

HRM influences organizational ethics in a variety of ways, and has its own ethical challenges to manage.

Codes of Conduct and Codes of Ethics

Codes of conduct specify expected and prohibited actions in the workplace and give examples of appropriate behavior. A **code of ethics** is a decision-making guide that describes the highest values to which an organization aspires. It specifies the company's ethical rules regarding what employees should and should not do. Companies maintaining high-quality codes of conduct are more likely to be ranked higher on corporate citizenship, ethical behavior, sustainability, and public perception.[63]

Relying solely on a code of conduct to manage ethical behavior in the workplace is not enough. Companies must also treat employees fairly, align HRM systems to promote ethical

code of conduct
specifies expected and prohibited actions in the workplace and gives examples of appropriate behavior

code of ethics
a decision-making guide that describes the highest values to which an organization aspires

table **2.3**

How HRM Can Support Corporate Ethics

- Hire employees likely to behave ethically.
- Train employees how to recognize and handle different ethical situations.
- Implement a company code of conduct, and make all employees accountable for following it.
- Include ethics information in regular company communications to reinforce its importance.
- Promptly remove employees involved in unethical behavior or decision making.
- Create a reward program that reinforces ethical behavior.
- Develop a support system that helps employees make the right decisions and anonymously report others' unethical behavior.

behavior, and hire and promote ethical leaders at all levels of the company who reinforce the values behind the code. A clear system of reward and punishment is particularly important in establishing an ethical culture. Effective managers both reward ethical behavior and respond quickly to ethical violations. Table 2.3 highlights some of the ways HRM can support corporate ethics.

How Does HRM Influence Corporate Ethics?

According to the Federal Sentencing Guidelines for Organizations, six basic elements are important to a complete ethics and compliance program.[64] Note how many of these are the responsibility of the HRM function:

1. Written standards for ethical conduct
2. Ethics training
3. Providing a way for seeking ethics-related advice or information
4. Providing a mechanism for anonymously reporting misconduct
5. Disciplining employees who violate the law or the standards of the organization
6. Evaluating ethical behavior as part of an employee's regular performance appraisals.

We will regularly discuss the role of ethics in HRM throughout this book. This chapter's case study describes how ethical and social responsibility issues contributed to the Deepwater Horizon oil rig explosion and resulting environmental disaster.

CASE STUDY: The Deepwater Horizon Explosion

On April 20, 2010, BP's mobile offshore drilling rig the Deepwater Horizon exploded in the Gulf of Mexico, killing 11 employees and injuring 17 others. Approximately 206 million gallons of crude oil spilled into the ocean for months after the rig sank two days after the explosion, producing the largest offshore oil spill in U.S. history and creating an environmental disaster.[65]

The morning the Deepwater Horizon oil rig, owned by Transocean, exploded, a BP executive and a Transocean official had argued over the next procedure. The BP official

Continued

wanted heavy mud, used to keep the well's pressure at safe levels, replaced with lighter seawater to speed up a process that was costing BP an estimated $750,000 a day and already running five weeks late. Doug Brown, the rig's chief mechanic, says that the BP executive won the argument and "basically said, 'Well, this is how it's gonna be.'"[66] Because engineers were hurrying to reduce the delay and the expense, they had also cut corners on the well design, safety features, and safety tests.[67]

During the subsequent investigation of the explosion, in a letter to BP's then-CEO Tony Hayward, the House Energy and Commerce Committee wrote, "Time after time, it appears that BP made decisions that increased the risk of a blowout to save the company time and expense."[68] A *Fortune* magazine investigation determined that the disaster was, "the product of a corporate culture that venerated risk taking." [69]

One of the continuing questions about the disaster involves the lack of a whistleblower in the time leading up to the explosion. The blowout preventer, a key piece of safety equipment intended to be the last line of defense in the case of a well blowout, was damaged four weeks before the explosion. When pieces of the rubber gasket were found in the drilling fluid, the supervisor said, "Oh, it's no big deal."[70] Rig survivors reported that raising safety concerns that might delay drilling had previously led to some coworkers being fired, and retaliation against whistleblowers prevented many employees from speaking up.[71]

Questions:

1. What are some of the core ethical and social responsibility issues presented by BP's behavior?
2. If you were an employee of BP, would you have spoken up about the safety issues? Why or why not?
3. How can HRM improve the ethical and social responsibility culture at BP?

How Does HRM Influence Corporate Social Responsibility?

Corporate social responsibility happens when businesses show concern for the common good and value human dignity. This can include philanthropy and social initiatives such as giving employees paid time off to engage in community service projects. Corporate social responsibility can also involve hiring diverse employees, protecting employees on the job, protecting the environment, and making safe products.

corporate social responsibility
businesses showing concern for the common good and valuing human dignity

In the area of social responsibility, eco-friendly candle company Altered Seasons provides a meal to an American in need through Feeding America for every candle it sells.[72] Rather than offering money or prizes to survey takers, SurveyMonkey donates 50 cents per completed survey to the taker's charity of choice, including the Humane Society, Boys & Girls Club of America, and Teach for America.[73] Hotelier Marriott International, featured in this chapter's opening real-world challenge, replaced plastic and paper containers in its cafeteria with real plates and compostable, potato-based containers called SpudWare. Marriott employees also receive thermoses to eliminate paper cups and can trade in burnt-out regular light bulbs from home or work for compact fluorescents. Green ambassadors throughout the company spread the word on shutting off lights and electronics, printing double-sided, and forgoing paper whenever possible.[74]

Some organizations blend their social responsibility initiatives with employee development activities. Mars Chocolate's Mars Ambassador Program allows employees to spend up to six weeks on projects run by one of the company's partner organizations, such as the World Wildlife Federation, or on projects initiated in partnership with local sites and communities. The projects allow employees to share their professional or technical expertise to enhance their partners' capabilities and improve employees' understanding of the communities that support the business.[75]

How an employer treats its employees is an important part of corporate social responsibility.[76] Organizations are increasingly interested in balancing their financial performance with their employees' quality of life and improving the local community and broader society. One expert defined corporate social responsibility this way: "Regardless of how many people with whom you come in contact, every one of them should be better off for having known you and your company."[77]

Adopting a broader **stakeholder perspective** that considers the interests and opinions of all people, groups, organizations, or systems that affect or could be affected by the organization's actions supports social responsibility. The stakeholder perspective puts responsibility above shareholder value or profitability. Ethical behavior and social responsibility are increasingly seen as the appropriate ways of managing and conducting business. Environmental issues, ethics, employee and product safety, and corporate governance are the four primary categories that encompass corporate social responsibility.

Can socially responsible behavior also help a company? In fact, it can help a firm attract the best talent,[78] and customers are increasingly patronizing companies that do the right thing. As Walter J. Cleaver, President and CEO of the Human Resource Planning Society puts it, "Sustainability is not just looking at the short term; it's building for the long haul. A lot of companies are looking at the financial, social and environmental impact of what they do. Starbucks pays more for coffee beans because it donates a certain amount to the farmers and schools (of a foreign country) so they can keep a good supply source. A company's long-term existence is in many ways connected to how the public perceives it in terms of values."[79]

Socially responsible business practices are becoming a core part of how many organizations do business. Nonetheless, some people still believe that companies and their managers should focus solely on stockholders' interests. Others believe that because business is an influential element of society it has a duty to help solve public problems. Social responsibility supporters also believe that ethical and socially responsible behavior is more rational and more profitable, and, therefore, it is essential for organizational effectiveness.[80]

So how are organizations using HRM to support corporate social responsibility? Human rights are increasingly being incorporated into HR vision, mission, and values statements. Starbucks Coffee's Global Human Rights Statement states, "Starbucks Global Human Rights Policy emphasizes Starbucks commitment to basic human rights as a core component of the way Starbucks does business and how Starbucks engages its employees."[81] Corporate social responsibility is also increasingly included as a factor in performance evaluations and merit pay increases. Training in corporate social responsibility awareness and skills, training managers to report abuses, developing an ethical corporate culture, and ensuring that global contractors act in ethical and socially responsible ways are examples of other HRM initiatives that support social responsibility.

To be lasting, social responsibility efforts must be integrated into the culture of the organization. Accordingly, corporate social responsibility has the biggest impact when it is integrated with HRM. HRM's threefold role in corporate social responsibility includes making sure people management practices are ethical, giving employees the right support and training to embed corporate responsibility in their behaviors, and embedding ethics into the organizational culture.[82] Serving stockholders as well as the larger population of stakeholders, which includes workers, customers, the community, and even our planet, are not mutually exclusive.

Table 2.4 highlights some of the socially responsible HRM programs and policies being implemented by U.S. corporations.

Employee participation in social responsibility initiatives can motivate employees and generate some good ideas. When a printing company set a goal to reduce its waste by 20 percent over five years, its executive team naturally focused on streamlining its printing operations to reduce paper waste. A receptionist pointed out that the number of individual lunches delivered to the office every day created a significant amount of food packaging waste. By investing in

stakeholder perspective
considering the interests and opinions of all people, groups, organizations, or systems that affect or could be affected by the organization's actions

 **so what?**

When organizations adopt a stakeholder perspective, they develop a broader and longer-term perspective in their decision making.

so what?

Companies serious about corporate social responsibility make it part of the organizational culture and a business priority.

table 2.4

Examples of Socially Responsible HRM Practices

- Workplace diversity
- Favorable working conditions
- Nonexploitation of workers, including discrimination and harassment
- Work-life balance initiatives
- Community volunteerism and charitable giving programs

a small café and encouraging employees to eat a buffet-style lunch, the printer reduced twice as much waste as it did by streamlining its printing operations.[83]

The International Organization for Standardization (ISO), the world's largest developer and publisher of international standards,[84] has created a variety of standards that help organizations meet their environmental and social responsibility objectives. In addition to environmentally related standards such as sustainability and carbon emissions, the ISO publishes management standards including those for leadership, customer focus, involvement of people, and continual improvement.

Managers have a great deal of influence over the execution of corporate responsibility programs, and they need to be aware of any likely challenges to successful implementation. Some of the greatest obstacles to successful execution of corporate responsibility programs are:[85]

1. A focus on quarterly earnings or other short-term targets
2. The cost of implementation
3. Difficulty in measuring and quantifying return on investment
4. A nonsupportive corporate culture.

This chapter's Develop Your Skills feature will help you to evaluate how you view the role of ethics and social responsibility in business. This can help you determine how important it might be to you to work for an organization with similar values.

Develop Your Skills

The Perceived Importance of Ethics and Social Responsibility[86]

This series of questions will help you to better understand your beliefs about the role ethics and social responsibility should play in companies. Please use the following scale in responding to the 10 questions below. When you are finished, follow the scoring instructions at the bottom to calculate your score. Then read more about what your score means.

| Strongly | | | | Strongly |
Disagree	Disagree	Neutral	Agree	Agree
←------	---------------	---------------	---------------	--------------	------→
(1)	(2)	(3)	(4)	(5)

_____   1. If the stockholders are unhappy, nothing else matters.

_____   2. Being ethical and socially responsible is the most important thing a firm can do.

_____   3. Efficiency is much more important to a firm than whether the firm is seen as ethical or socially responsible.

_____   4. Business has a social responsibility beyond making a profit.

Continued

_____ 5. To remain competitive in a global environment, business firms have to disregard ethics and social responsibility.

_____ 6. Business ethics and social responsibility are critical to the survival of a business enterprise.

_____ 7. The ethics and social responsibility of a firm is essential to its long-term profitability.

_____ 8. The overall effectiveness of a business can be determined to a great extent by the degree to which it is ethical and socially responsible.

_____ 9. The most important concern for a firm is making a profit, even if it means bending or breaking the rules.

_____ 10. If the survival of a business enterprise is at stake, then you must forget about ethics and social responsibility.

Scoring:

For some questions, a higher number reflects lower perceived importance of ethics and social responsibility—reversing these scores will make a higher score on all questions reflective of greater perceived importance of ethics and social responsibility. *For questions 1, 3, 5, 9, and 10, subtract your rating from 6, which should change your score as follows: 1=5; 2=4; 3 = 3; 4=2; 5=1.* Cross out your old rating so you don't get confused. Now add up your responses to identify your perceived importance of ethics and social responsibility score.

Interpretation:

If your score is between 10 and 20, you tend to place a higher value on performance than on social responsibility and business ethics. This could present challenges for you in balancing what is right with what you feel you need to do to succeed. Following a company's code of conduct and code of ethics will be important to your future success. You may not be happiest working in an organization that places a high value on social responsibility and employee ethics.

If your score is *between 10 and 20*, you tend to place a higher value on performance than on social responsibility and business ethics. This could present challenges for you in balancing what is right with what you feel you need to do to succeed. Following a company's code of conduct and code of ethics will be important to your future success. You may not be happiest working in an organization that places a high value on social responsibility and employee ethics.

If your score is *between 21 and 35*, you tend to strike a balance between performance and social responsibility and business ethics. This is not inherently good or bad, but it is important for you to think about your ethical principles and fully evaluate the impacts of your decisions. You probably don't have a particularly strong need to work for a company that stresses social responsibility, but you likely wouldn't be unhappy in one either.

If your score is *between 36 and 50*, you realize that high moral and ethical standards are in the best long-run interest of profits and shareholders. It is important to realize that you may need to prepare yourself for handling pressure to lower your standards to meet short-term shareholder demands. You are likely to be happiest in an organization with strong ethics and social responsibility values.

How Does HRM Support Organizational Change?

Strategy implementation and strategic change often require large-scale organizational changes. Two of the largest changes are often the change to the new organizational culture and the installation of new employee behaviors. Some of the most common changes managed by HRM include:

1. New production processes
2. Opening a new location
3. Rolling out a new benefits program
4. Implementing a new human resource information system (HRIS) or upgrading the current HRIS system
5. Expanding international operations.

Depending on the nature of a strategic change, some employees are likely to lack the willingness or even the ability to support a new strategy. Targeting HRM efforts to develop, motivate, and retain the people who are critical to implementing a new strategy may expedite its adoption and ultimately improve the strategy's effectiveness. Employee participation can also be a positive tactic for change management, as it is ultimately the employees who need to adopt different behaviors and goals to support a change if it is to succeed.

Imagine an organization currently manufacturing semiconductor chips. The competitive environment requires the organization to compete on cost, so it focuses on operational efficiencies to control expenses. The culture reinforces strict adherence to operating rules to help achieve these low-cost goals. What do you think would change if the organization adopts a new business strategy of designing new and innovative computer chips and outsourcing their production? The organization's focus would now change to innovation, problem solving, and collaboration. Managers would need to be trained and reinforced for doing less rule enforcement and more leading, motivating, and communicating. Intel went through this type of transformation in the early 1970s when it moved from being a producer of semiconductor memory chips to programmable microprocessor chips.

The HRM system supporting organizational change necessarily varies depending on the nature of the change.[87] It is essential to first identify the key goals of the change initiative and focus on these in developing new HRM practices and redesigning the HRM system. A variety of HRM initiatives are possible to support change. Lockheed Martin designed a cultural change management program around its core competencies of candid and open communication, taking personal action to remove obstacles to effective performance, and acting when a need exists rather than ignoring issues.[88] This chapter's Strategic Impact feature discusses some methods Hewlett-Packard (HP) used to change its culture.

One of the most important factors in successfully creating organizational change is the creation of a culture of trust.[90] There is a great deal of uncertainty before and during a change effort. Trust is the glue that keeps employees committed to the organization and focused on making the change effort successful. Because resistance to change is common when behavioral patterns need to be changed, clear communication and training, goals, feedback, and rewards linked to the new behaviors align employees' goals and behaviors with the new goals and needs of the organization. When quick, radical change is necessary, it may be appropriate to use coercion, but whenever possible, it is best to use more collaboration and consultation to promote engagement and commitment to the change.[91]

so what?

Because employees need to change their behaviors and goals for an organizational change effort to succeed, involving employees in a change management effort can improve their commitment to the change.

♞ Strategic Impact

Culture Change at HP

When problems prompted HP to change its culture, it began requiring staff to formulate three personal and three professional goals each year. Employees and managers are encouraged to cheer those who meet their goals, such as getting away early to be with family. After two years, HP found no loss in productivity despite staff working shorter hours, and the staff retention rate improved.[89]

Global HRM

Cultural differences can influence the appropriateness and the effectiveness of different HRM practices. Noted scholar Geert Hofstede performed thousands of interviews and substantial research on over 40 countries, ultimately identifying five dimensions that tend to distinguish cultures across countries.[92] Here is a description of each dimension and how it might affect HRM practices in different cultures:

power distance
how much inequality exists and is accepted among people with and without power

1. *Power Distance*: **Power distance** is the amount of inequality that exists and that is accepted among people with and without power; higher power distance (e.g., Philippines, Guatemala, and Malaysia) is associated with more hierarchical companies that have large gaps in authority and compensation, while lower power distance (e.g., Austria, Israel, and Denmark) is reflected in flatter organizations in which employees and supervisors are considered and treated more equally.

individualism
the strength of the ties people have with others in their community—high individualism reflects looser ties with others

2. *Individualism*: **Individualism** refers to the strength of the ties people have with others in their community. Higher individualism (e.g., United States, Australia, and New Zealand) is reflected in greater valuation of people's time and need for freedom with an emphasis on individual and extrinsic rewards, whereas lower individualism (e.g. Guatemala, Ecuador, and Bangladesh), is reflected in placing a high value on harmony rather than honesty with an emphasis on intrinsic and collective rewards.

masculinity
the degree to which a society values and exhibits traditional male and female roles—in highly masculine cultures, men are expected to be more assertive and to be the sole provider for the family

3. *Masculinity*: **Masculinity** refers to how much a society values and exhibits traditional male and female roles. In highly masculine cultures, men are expected to be assertive and be the sole provider for the family. Higher masculinity (e.g., Japan, Hungary, and Slovakia) is reflected in a distinction between men's work and women's work, while lower masculinity (e.g., Denmark, Sweden, and Norway) is reflected in equal employment opportunity, often supported with legislation.

uncertainty avoidance
the degree of anxiety felt in uncertain or unfamiliar situations

4. *Uncertainty Avoidance*: **Uncertainty avoidance** reflects the degree of anxiety felt in uncertain or unfamiliar situations. Higher uncertainty avoidance (e.g., Greece, Portugal, and Uruguay) is associated with a need for structure and very formal and rule-driven business conduct, whereas lower uncertainty avoidance (e.g., Singapore, Jamaica, and Hong Kong) is associated with an informal business culture, greater acceptance of risk, and more concern with long-term performance than with daily events.

long-term orientation
reflects a focus on long term planning, delivering on social obligations, and avoiding "losing face"

5. *Long-Term Orientation*: **Long-term orientation** reflects a focus on long-term planning, delivering on social obligations, and avoiding "losing face." A longer-term orientation (e.g., China and Taiwan) is reflected in a strong work ethic and placing high value on education and training, whereas a shorter-term orientation (e.g., West

Africa and Canada) is characterized by higher individualism, creativity, and equality.

Understanding a society's culture can help you design more effective HRM systems. The desire to apply best practices from an organization's home country must be balanced with the need to adopt local HRM practices. Business locations in high uncertainty avoidance cultures may benefit from more detailed policies and plans, and HRM managers' leadership style may need to be more independent and achievement-oriented in more masculine cultures and more collaborative in more feminine cultures. Incentives should be individual or group based, depending on the local culture, and the time frame for incentives may need to be adjusted to match each culture's long- or short-term orientation.[93] In cultures with a shorter-term orientation, you can introduce changes more quickly and expect employees to be more innovative.[94]

It is important to remember that belonging to a particular culture or being from a particular country does not ensure that the culture describes a particular individual. Individuals from the same area or culture are not all the same, and cultural values can change over time

One common stimulus to organizational change is a merger or acquisition. Let's briefly discuss the role of HRM during these events.

When organizations expand into other countries it is important to understand the local culture and how it is likely to affect the implementation of the company's human resource management practices. To be most effective, it is usually necessary to balance some of the best HRM practices from the organization's home country with some HRM practices that better fit the local culture.

HRM During Mergers and Acquisitions

Corporate mergers and acquisitions such as the one between Delta and Northwest Airlines or acquisitions such as Facebook's acquisitions of LiveRail and Oculus VR frequently make business headlines. Unfortunately, as many as 85 percent of mergers fail to accomplish their objectives, and the cost of failure can be enormous.[95] Culture mismatch is often blamed as a cause of the failure,[96] as was the case in the Daimler-Chrysler merger, as well as conflicts between managers coming from each firm.

Different HRM activities become important during different stages of a merger or acquisition.[97] During the due diligence phase, the cultures of both organizations need to be evaluated to determine their compatibility. Focusing on talent planning and retention efforts early in this phase is also a good idea. During the integration phase, deciding which employees will be retained and which will be separated and developing retention strategies for key employees becomes critical as well as the establishment of a common culture for the combined organization. During the post-close phase, stakeholder satisfaction is addressed, the new culture is strengthened, and employee development plans are developed and implemented.

Because cultural issues are a frequent reason for derailed mergers, it is important that HR managers assure that cultural issues are recognized and addressed before, during, and after the merger.[98] Through their behaviors and decisions to stay or leave the merged company, employees have an enormous impact on the ultimate success or failure of a merger or acquisition. In some cases, companies are acquired because the acquiring company needs the talent and skills of the other company. If those key employees leave after the acquisition, the effort is futile.

Communication is critical to the success of a merger or acquisition,[99] and HRM must carefully manage the treatment of and impact on employees who are let go and on those who survive.

HR can and should act as both a facilitator and a coach during the process.[100] In addition to deciding what skills and competencies the combined organization needs, HRM is also typically responsible for identifying which employees, if any, will be let go. It is important to identify and try to retain key performers at the acquired company. When Oracle launched its hostile takeover of PeopleSoft, many top executives and other employees left PeopleSoft.[101] Employee retention plans during a hostile takeover can include cash bonuses, raises, and promotions.

Let's next discuss how to assess different aspects of HRM.

?so what?

It is important to treat both departing and surviving employees fairly and respectfully during a merger or acquisition to maximize its success.

HRM Metrics

Metrics and measurements are essential in identifying where the HRM system can be improved and helping HRM best meet the needs of the organization and its stakeholders, including its employees.[102] Without meaningful data, it is difficult to make sound decisions in support of the business and strategic execution. Table 2.5 highlights some standard metrics organizations use to measure HRM performance.

table 2.5

Common HRM Metrics

Metric	Definition
Absence rate	Number of employee absences/(average number of employees during the period X the number of workdays)
Cost per hire	Recruitment costs/(cost of compensation + benefits)
Customer service ratings	Average customer ratings of employee customer service performance
Engagement	Level of employee satisfaction or engagement with the company
Healthcare cost per employee	Total cost of employee health care/number of covered employees
Innovation	Percent of sales coming from products introduced in the last five years
Job offer acceptance rate	Number of job offers accepted/number of job offers extended
Percent of performance goals met or exceeded	Number of individual or group performance goals met or exceeded/total number of performance goals
Profit per employee	Profit/total number of employees
Return on investment (ROI)	[(value of a program or intervention's benefits - total cost)/total cost] X 100
Revenue per employee	Revenue/total number of employees
Tenure	Average years of service at the organization
Time to fill	Days to fill a position
Turnover rate	Number of employees leaving/average number of employees during the same period
Workers' compensation cost per employee	Total annual workers' compensation cost/average number of employees

It is not practical or necessary to measure every HRM activity. It is most important to identify and measure the HRM activities that contribute to business strategy execution and the organization's financial performance. Software exists to facilitate the data collection and calculation of HR metrics, including OrcaEyes' SonarVision and IBM's Cognos. By carefully mapping metrics to business goals and objectives, organizations can better identify their best recruiting sources and performers, select the best incentive systems, and align workforce skills with business objectives.

To be most effective, metrics should be tied to business goals, drive employee behaviors, and be tied to rewards. Metrics must be based on accurate data and should be used to guide decision making. Organizations pursuing a product differentiation strategy might track innovation indicators, whereas organizations pursuing a low-cost strategy might focus on efficiency indicators.[103]

so what?

Tying metrics to business goals helps HRM influence the right employee behaviors.

Summary and Application

Clearly, HRM can have a large influence on business performance and strategy execution through its effects on culture, ethics, and social responsibility. HRM activities play a strong role in high-performance work systems and in organizational change initiatives including mergers and acquisitions. Understanding a society's culture is important in designing effective HRM systems. Best practices from an organization's home country may not work in other cultures and must be balanced with the need to adopt local HRM practices.

Although it is rarely practical or necessary to measure every HRM activity or outcome, sound metrics and accurate data are essential to understanding where the HRM system can be improved. Without meaningful and accurate data, making sound HRM decisions is difficult to impossible

In this chapter, you have learned how HRM influences organizations in both direct and indirect ways. In addition to acquiring and developing the appropriate talent, aligning employee and organizational goals, and motivating employees to perform their best, HRM influences the organizational culture and environment in which work is done. By reinforcing the values of the firm, HRM helps clarify for employees how they are to behave and make decisions.

Understanding the best fit between your ethics and social responsibility preferences and that of a potential employer, as well as understanding the fit between its culture and your values and preferred work styles, is critical in choosing a job and organization you will succeed in and enjoy. Because HRM systems create and reinforce these organizational characteristics, understanding your preferences can help you better manage your own career.

Real World Response

How Culture Reinforces Business Strategy at Marriott

Marriott International is well known as a great place to work, consistently being named on *Fortune's* lists of best places to work, top companies for minorities, and most admired companies. The company is also strongly committed to diversity, social responsibility, and community engagement. J. W. Marriott Jr. believes that, "if employees are content, confident, and generally happy with themselves and the job, their positive attitude will be felt in everything they do."[104] Accordingly, the company has established a strong HRM system reinforcing its strategic goals. The company's core values are:[105]

- We Put People First: Take care of associates, and they will take care of the customers.
- We Pursue Excellence: Our dedication to the customer shows in everything we do.
- We Embrace Change: Innovation has always been part of the Marriott story.
- We Act with Integrity: How we do business is as important as the business we do.
- We Serve Our World: Our "spirit to serve" makes our company stronger.

Marriott makes a point of "hiring friendly" and "training technical" to ensure that it hires people with the "Spirit to Serve" who it can then train to do the work. Marriott also promotes from within, allowing associates to advance in the company as far as their abilities allow. It also focuses on retaining and inspiring employees in jobs they truly enjoy and who possess the "spirit to serve." Employees with good financial performance who do not embrace the employees-first philosophy are let go.[106]

Marriott also offers a total rewards package composed of competitive compensation, profit sharing, and a great workplace. Marriott invests millions of dollars a year in training to reinforce its culture of hands-on management and attention to detail to promote retention. It invested $2 million just in a jobs training program with the goal of training and placing Washington, DC, residents in jobs in its newly opened Marriott Marquis.[107] Employees who wrote to founder J.W. Marriott to bring a problem or complaint to his attention always got a response. Current CEO Bill Marriott's blog (online at: http://www.blogs.marriott.com/) recognizes individual employees' successes and helps keep employees informed of happenings around the company.

The annual Award of Excellence was established in 1987 as a lasting tribute to company founder J. Willard Marriott's ideals of achievement, character, dedication, effort, and perseverance. It is presented to a select few who demonstrate these ideals through providing outstanding service, consistently exceeding expectations, leading by example, and enhancing the lives of their coworkers, customers, and neighbors with their commitment to service excellence. Each year, the J.W. Marriott Award for Diversity Excellence recognizes a Marriott business unit and its team of associates that demonstrates excellence in promoting diversity and unity.[108]

For more than 70 years, Marriott has lived by a simple motto: "Take care of associates, and they'll take care of your customers."[109] This is a strategy rather than merely a sentiment—the company knows that retaining and strategically managing its talent drives economic value for Marriott.

Takeaway Points

1. By reinforcing the desirability of certain values or behaviors, the HRM system helps to reinforce the organizational culture.

2. HRM supports high-performance work systems through goals and processes that support employee participation, commitment, and identification with the organization. HRM practices promoting power-sharing, information-sharing, and training tend to best support HPWS.

3. There are five standards that help us evaluate the ethics of an action: Utilitarian, rights, fairness, common good, and virtue. The utilitarian standard strikes the best balance of good over harm. The rights standard best respects and protects the moral rights of everyone affected by the action. The fairness standard promotes the equal or at least fair treatment of everyone. The common good standard promotes respect and compassion for everyone. The virtue standard promotes consistency with ideal virtues including civility, compassion, and benevolence.

4. By setting direct expectations of employees and through their influence on corporate culture, HRM policies and practices promote both ethics and corporate social responsibility.

5. HRM supports organizational change by creating a culture of trust, managing employee resistance to change, and aligning employees' goals and behaviors with the new goals and needs of the organization.

6. Hofstede's five cultural dimensions are power distance, which reflects how much inequality exists and is accepted and influences preferences for hierarchy and how equally employees are treated; individualism, which reflects the strength of the ties people have with others in their community and influences whether individual or collective rewards are preferred; masculinity, which is the degree to which a society values and exhibits traditional male and female roles and affects equal employment opportunity; uncertainty avoidance, which involves the anxiety felt in uncertain or unfamiliar situations and is associated with culture formality, risk acceptance, and concern with long-term versus short-term performance; and long-term orientation, which reflects a focus on long-term planning, delivering on social obligations, and avoiding "losing face" and influences work ethic, the value placed on training and education, and creativity.

7. Through their behaviors and decisions to stay or leave the merged company, employees affect the success or failure of a merger or acquisition. To promote success, HR must carefully manage the treatment of and impact on employees who are let go and on those who survive. HR should act as both a facilitator and a coach during the merger process and objectively identify which employees, if any, need to be let go based on the combined organization's needs.

Discussion Questions

1. What type of culture do you find most desirable as a potential employee? What HRM clues can you identify that might let you know the degree to which a prospective employer has this culture?

2. How can HRM support a performance culture? How could HRM undermine a performance culture?

3. Why do you think some employees act unethically? How could you use HRM to help address these causes and encourage more ethical behavior?

4. Do you consider ethics or social responsibility in evaluating prospective employers? What do you look for?
5. What type of business strategy do you think is most compatible with a high-performance work system? Why?
6. What type of business strategy do you think would be a poor fit with a high-performance work system? Why?
7. If you were assigned to work in another culture, how would you use Hofstede's cultural dimensions to be a more effective manager?
8. If your company was about to be acquired by another, how would you want to be treated by HRM? What are some of the biggest mistakes you feel HRM could make during the acquisition process?

Personal Development Exercise: Managing Ethical Issues in HRM

As you learned in this chapter, there are a variety of ethical issues that exist in HRM. Working in a group of three to five people, brainstorm at least five ethical issues that can exist in HRM. For example, a very productive manager bullies his subordinates and treats them in ways inconsistent with the corporate culture. Then identify how a company can use HRM to handle these ethical challenges. Be prepared to share two of your issues and HRM solutions with the class.

Strategic HRM Exercises

Exercise: Culture Choice at Amazing Apps

Form groups of three to five students. Imagine that you started a company called Amazing Apps to develop applications for the iPad. You've had some good early success, but you need to hire more people to more quickly develop new products and get them up on the Apple Store. You know that the creativity and programming talent of the people you hire is going to be critical to your company's future success, and you know that your HRM system will be key to hiring and motivating the right talent. Be prepared to share your answers to the following questions with the class.

1. Describe the type of culture you would like to create in your company.
2. How would you use HRM to reinforce this culture?
3. What would be the biggest threats to establishing your intended culture, and how could you overcome them?

Exercise: What Would You Do?

We would like to thank Professor Nancy Zimmerman of the Community College of Baltimore County for this exercise idea

Form groups of three to five students, and discuss what you would do in each of the following situations. Be prepared to share your ideas with the class.

1. Imagine you just joined the leadership team of a large financial services company that wants to improve its financial performance. The rest of the leadership team wants to reduce the company's workforce through outsourcing or selling some business units and then hire back some of the former employees as contract labor so it can pay them less and not provide benefits. Essentially, they want to find ways to pay people

less for doing the same work without benefits and with fewer legal obligations. What would you recommend?

2. Imagine your CEO recently read about another company focusing its training and compensation resources on the highest-performing 10 percent of its employees and asks for your opinion.

3. Imagine you are starting a new online marketing company and are trying to establish the compensation system for your employees. In percentages, how much more would you pay the highest paid employee than the lowest paid employee?

Exercise: Creating a High-Performance Work System

We would like to thank Professor Gery Markova of Wichita State University for this exercise idea

Divide the class into teams of three to five students. Half of the teams are to imagine that they are owners of a high-end local restaurant. The restaurant's business strategy is to provide high customer service and a premium-quality product. You use recipes that have been in your family for generations and use only the highest quality ingredients. Employee turnover is low, and you pay above-average wages. You want to invest in a high-performance work system because you believe it will enable you to best execute your strategy and obtain a competitive advantage. How would you utilize various HRM functions and activities in designing a high-performance work system that would best accomplish your goals?

The other half of the teams are to imagine that they are owners of a local fast food restaurant. The business strategy is to be a low-cost provider of quality food. The restaurant is competing with many other fast food restaurants, and you want to invest in a high-performance work system because you believe it will enable you to best execute your strategy and obtain a competitive advantage. Turnover is fairly high, and you are only able to pay market wages. How would you utilize various HRM functions and activities in designing a high-performance work system that would best accomplish your goals?

All teams should be prepared to share their ideas with the class after a 20-minute discussion.

Exercise: Ethics

We would like to thank Professor Gery Markova of Wichita State University for this exercise idea.

Divide the class into teams of three to five students. Each team has 20 minutes to identify HRM behaviors representing different functional areas that fit in one of the four quadrants in the matrix below, identifying work behaviors and decisions that are:

1. Legal and ethical
2. Legal and unethical
3. Illegal and ethical
4. Illegal and unethical.

Be prepared to share your ideas with the class.

	Unethical	Ethical
Illegal		
Legal		

Exercise: Ethics Codes

We would like to thank Professor Bobbie Knoblauch of Wichita State University for this exercise idea.

Use the Internet to research the ethics codes (also called a "code of ethics") for at least three organizations. Write a one-page paper comparing and contrasting them. Be sure to include your thoughts about what an organization's ethical code should contain.

Exercise: Applying the Five Ethical Perspectives

We would like to thank Professor Barbara Rau of the University of Wisconsin-Oshkosh for this exercise idea.

You are responsible for cutting the cost of your sales force by at least $100,000 within one month. Each of the company's six sales people is described below. In addition to an individual commission of up to $10,000 per year, the company currently has a bonus plan that can increase pay by up to 20 percent if the department's sales goals are met. Apply the five ethical standards to your decision. How might your decision differ depending on which ethical standard you are applying?

1. R.P. has been with the company for six years and earns $60,000 per year. R.P.'s performance has been high, and R.P. has unique industry knowledge that helps the company create its annual sales strategy.
2. T.J. has been with the company for eight years and earns $58,000 per year. T.J.'s performance has been high, and T.J.'s spouse is having difficulty finding a job since becoming unemployed six months ago.
3. A.I. has been with the company for one year and earns $50,000 per year. A.I.'s performance has been about average. A.I.'s performance has increased over the past year, and the company expects A.I.'s performance to continue to improve with more experience.
4. W.N. has been with the company for two years and earns $53,000 per year. W.N.'s performance has been average. W.N. took on a lot of debt to help a family member, and is afraid that job loss will result in bankruptcy.
5. S.G. has been with the company for five years and earns $56,000 per year. S.G.'s performance has been slipping, and this year's sales performance was the lowest in the company. S.G. has been taking classes at night, hoping to eventually switch careers.
6. L.K. has been with the company for four years and earns $50,000 per year. L.K.'s performance has never been great, although the company has continued to invest in training to help L.K. improve. L.K. is an enthusiastic employee and a great fit with the company's culture.

Exercise: How HRM Helps SAS Succeed

After reading this chapter, you should have a good understanding of how HRM contributes to organizational performance. In 2010, business analytics software and services company SAS was rated number 1 on *Fortune* magazine's list of the "100 Best Companies to Work For." Go to SAS's company page at http://www.sas.com and its careers page at https://www.sas.com/en_us/careers.html to read about how the company presents itself to potential employees. Explore the website and learn more about working at SAS, then answer the following questions:

1. Identify three topics from this chapter that relate to SAS.
2. How are corporate social responsibility, ethics, and diversity valued by SAS?

3. Based on what you learned from its website, does SAS seem like a company you would enjoy working for? Why or why not?

Exercise: The Role of Corporate Culture at Zappos

View the two videos "Life at Zappos" (1:37) and "Zappos: Where Company Culture is #1" (3:29) to learn about online shoe retailer Zappos' corporate culture and how its CEO views the role of culture at the company. After watching the video, answer the following questions:

1. Why does Zappos' CEO Tony Hsieh feel that culture is so important to Zappos?
2. How does Zappos reinforce its culture through HRM?
3. Is Zappos' culture one in which you would enjoy working? Why or why not?

Integrative Project

In the last chapter, you identified a company and an industry to focus on for this project. You also described the business strategy, competitive advantage, and talent philosophy you would use to create a competitive advantage for your business. Your assignment for this chapter is to think about and formalize your company's position on social responsibility and ethics. Record your company's formal statement about each. Feel free to research other companies' statements online for insight into how to craft your own. Then describe the culture you would create at your company, explain why it is best suited to your company's needs, and explain how it will contribute to its success.

Video Case

Imagine a coworker at Happy Time Toys asks you if you think it would be alright if the company used the peer feedback it acquired for developmental purposes for pay raises as well. *What do you say or do?* Go to this book's video case, watch the challenge video for this chapter, and choose the best video response. Be sure to also view the outcomes of the two responses you didn't choose.

Discussion Questions

1. What are the ethical issues involved in using peer feedback solicited for developmental purposes for determining pay raises as well?
2. If your coworkers gave you constructive feedback to help you improve, and then the feedback negatively impacted your pay raise, would you think that was fair? Why or why not?
3. What do you think would be the best information to use in determining pay raises? What is the best way to collect this information?

Endnotes

1. Marriott (2017). J. W. Marriott, Jr. Retrieved February 7, 2017, from http://www.marriott.com/culture-and-values/jw-marriott-jr.mi

2. Marriott (2016). Our story. Retrieved February 7, 2017, from http://www.marriott.com/about/culture-and-values/history.mi#lookingahead

3. Marriott. (n.d.). Core values and culture. Retrieved February 7, 2017, from http://www.catererglobal.com/minisites/marriott-middle-east-and-africa/core-values-and-culture/

3. Saridakis, G., Lai, Y., & Cooper, C. L. (2017). Exploring the relationship between HRM and firm performance: A meta-analysis of longitudinal studies. *Human Resource Management Review*, 27(1): 87–96.

4. Greulich, P. E. (2017). Tom Watson, Jr., like his father, was focused on the 'how' not the 'shat' at IBM. Retrieved February 7, 2017, from http://mbiconcepts.com/blog/tom-watson-jr-like-his-father-was-focused-on-the-how-not-the-what-at-ibm

5. Ulrich, D., & Creelman, D. (2006). In touch with intangibles. *Workforce Management*, May 8, 39–42.

6. Lawler III, E., & Boudreau, J. W. (2012). *Effective human resource management: A global analysis*. Stanford, CA: Stanford University Press.

7. Careers, Nike.com. Retrieved March 9, 2012, from http://www.nikebiz.com/careers/

8. Wilson, F. (2012). Viewpoints: A strong foundation. *Inc.*, April, 27.

9. O'Reilly III, C. A., Caldwell, D. F., Chatman, J. A., & Doerr, B. (2014). The promise and problems of organizational culture: CEO personality, culture, and firm performance. *Group & Organization Management*, 39(6): 595–625.

10. Hartnell, C. A., Ou, A. Y., & Kinicki, A. (2011). Organizational culture and organizational effectiveness: A meta-analytic investigation of the competing values framework's theoretical suppositions. *Journal of Applied Psychology*, 96: 677–694; Naranjo-Valencia, J. C., Jiménez-Jiménez, D., & Sanz-Valle, R. (2011). Innovation or imitation? The role of organizational culture. *Management Decision*, 49: 55–72.

11. O'Brien, J. M. (2008). A perfect season. *Fortune*, February 1. Retrieved February 18, 2017, from http://money.cnn.com/2008/01/18/news/companies/fourseasons.fortune/index.htm?postversion=2008020111

12. Deshpandé, R., & Farley, J. (1999). Executive insights: Corporate culture and market orientation: Comparing Indian and Japanese firms. *Journal of International Marketing*, 7: 111–127.

13. Denison, D. (1990). *Corporate culture and organizational effectiveness*. New York: Wiley.

14. Aflac.com (2011). Life at Aflac. Retrieved February 7, 2017, from https://www.aflac.com/careers/life-at-aflac/default.aspx

15. Borucki, C. C., & Burke, M. J. (1999). An examination of service-related antecedents to retail store performance. *Journal of Organizational Behavior*, 20: 943–962; Johnson, J. W. (1996). Linking employee perceptions of service climate to customer satisfaction," *Personnel Psychology*, 49: 831–85; Ostroff, C., & Schmitt, N. (1993). Configurations of organizational effectiveness and efficiency. *Academy of Management Journal*, 36: 1345–1361.

16. Bartlett, C. A., & Mohammed, A. (1995). 3M: Profile of an innovating company. Harvard Business School, #9-395-016.

17. Huston, C. (2017). Uber harassment scandal will hurt but not in same way as #DeleteUber campaign. *MarketWatch*, February 23. Retrieved February 27, 2017, from http://www.marketwatch.com/story/uber-harassment-scandal-will-hurt-but-not-in-same-way-as-deleteuber-campaign-2017-02-22

18. Weissman, C. G. (2017). This is what caused Uber's broken company culture. *Fast Company*, February 27. Retrieved February 27, 2017, from https://www.fastcompany.com/3068475/pov/this-is-what-caused-ubers-broken-company-culture

19. Zipkin, N. (2017). Uber CEO Travis Kalanick launches investigation into sexual harassment claims. *Entrepreneur*, February 21. Retrieved February 27, 2017, from https://www.entrepreneur.com/article/289555

20. Weissman, C. G. (2017). "This is what caused Uber's broken company culture. *Fast Company*, February 27. Retrieved February 27, 2017, from https://www.fastcompany.com/3068475/pov/this-is-what-caused-ubers-broken-company-culture

21. Sheridan, J. (1992). Organizational culture and employee retention. *Academy of Management Journal*, 35: 1036–1056.

22. Weber, G. (2005). Preserving the counter culture. *Workforce Management*, 84: 28–34.

23. O'Brien, K. J. (2010). Nokia's new chief faces culture of complacency. *The New York Times*, September 26. Retrieved January 24, 2017, from http://www.nytimes.com/2010/09/27/technology/27nokia.html

24. Schneider, B. (1990). The climate for service: An application of the climate construct. In B. Schneider (Ed.), *Organizational climate and culture*, (pp. 383–412). San Francisco, CA: Jossey-Bass; Bowen, D. E., & Ostroff, C. (2004). Understanding HRM-firm performance linkages: The role of the 'strength' of the HRM system. *Academy of Management Review*, 29: 203–221.

25. Egan, M. (2016). I called the Wells Fargo ethics line and was fired. *CNN*, September 21. Retrieved February 7, 2017, from http://money.cnn.com/2016/09/21/investing/wells-fargo-fired-workers-retaliation-fake-accounts/index.html; Egan, M. (2017). Wells Fargo admits to signs of worker retaliation. *CNN*, January 24. Retrieved February 7, 2017, from http://money.cnn.com/2017/01/23/investing/wells-fargo-retaliation-ethics-line/index.html

26. Taylor, W. (2010). Why we (shouldn't) hate HR. *Harvard Business Review*, June 10. Retrieved February 7, 2017, from https://hbr.org/2010/06/why-we-shouldnt-hate-hr

27. *Ibid.*

28. Stallard, M. L. (2014). 3 ways Pixar gains competitive advantage from its culture. *Fox Business*, May 23. Retrieved February 19, 2017, from http://www.foxbusiness.com/features/2014/05/23/3-ways-pixar-gains-competitive-advantage-from-its-culture.html

29. Catmull, E. (2008). How Pixar fosters collective creativity. *Harvard Business Review*, 86: 64–72.

30. Ostroff, C., & Bowen, D. E. (2016). Reflections on the 2014 decade award: Is there strength in the construct of HR system strength? *Academy of Management Review*, 41(2): 196–214.

31. Bowen, D. E., & Ostroff, C. (2004). Understanding HRM-firm performance linkages: The role of the 'strength' of the HRM system. *Academy of Management Review, 29*: 203–221.

32. Glazer, B. (2016). The biggest lesson from Volkswagen," *Entrepreneur*, January 8. Retrieved February 18, 2017, from https://www.entrepreneur.com/article/254178

33. Leung, K., Bhagat, R., Buchan, N., Erez, M., & Gibson, C. (2005). Culture and international business: Recent advances and their implications for future research. *Journal of International Business Studies, 36*: 370; Edgington, R., & Bruce, G. (2006). Organizational culture: Preferences and realities. GMAC Research Report RR-06-11, June 7.

34. Edgington, R., & Bruce, G. (2006). Organizational culture: Preferences and realities. GMAC Research Report RR-06-11, June 7.

35. Lau, C.M., & Ngo, H. Y. (2004). The HR system, organizational culture, and product innovation. *International Business Review, 13*: 685–703; Shipton, H., West, M. A., Dawson, J., Birdi, K., & Patterson, M. (2006). HRM as a predictor of innovation. *Human Resource Management Journal, 16*: 3–27; DeLeede, J., & Looise, J. K. (2005). Innovation and HRM: Towards an integrated framework. *Creativity and Innovation Management, 14*: 108–117.

36. Lee, L. (2002). A singular sensation for Schwab brokers. *Bloomberg*, January 24. Retrieved February 7, 2017, from https://www.bloomberg.com/news/articles/2002-01-23/a-singular-sensation-for-schwab-brokers

37. Lazarova, M., Peretz, H., & Fried, Y. (2017). Locals know best? Subsidiary HR autonomy and subsidiary performance. *Journal of World Business, 52:* 83–96.

38. Lawler, E. E. (1992). *The ultimate advantage: Creating the high involvement organization*. San Francisco, CA: Jossey-Bass, 30.

39. Gong, Y., Chang, S., & Cheung, S.Y. (2010). High performance work system and collective OCB: A collective social exchange perspective. *Human Resource Management Journal, 20*: 119–137.

40. Lawler, E. E., Mohrman, S. A., & Ledford, G. E. (1995). *Creating high performance organizations: Practices and results of employee involvement and total quality management in Fortune 1000 companies*. San Francisco, CA: Jossey-Bass, 74.

41. Pfeffer, J. (1998). *The human equation: Building profits by putting people first*. Boston, MA: Harvard Business School Press, 32.

42. *Ibid.*

43. Saridakis, G., Lai, Y., & Cooper, C. L. (2017). Exploring the relationship between HRM and firm performance: A meta-analysis of longitudinal studies. *Human Resource Management Review, 27*: 87–96.

44. Lawler, E. E. (1992). *The ultimate advantage: Creating the high involvement organization*. San Francisco, CA: Jossey-Bass.

45. Lawler, E. E., Mohrman, S. A., & Ledford, G. E. (1995). *Creating high performance organizations: Practices and results of employee involvement and total quality management in Fortune 1000 companies*. San Francisco, CA: Jossey-Bass.

46. Pfeffer, J. (1998). *The human equation: Building profits by putting people first*. Boston, MA: Harvard Business School Press, 293–296.

47. Orlando, R., & Johnson, N. B. (2004). High performance work practices and human resource management effectiveness: Substitutes or compliments? *Journal of Business Strategies, 21*: 133–148.

48. Frank, R., & Efrati, A. (2009). 'Evil' Madoff gets 150 years in epic fraud. *Wall Street Journal Online*, June 30. Retrieved February 7, 2017, from http://online.wsj.com/article/SB124604151653862301.html

49. CBS MoneyWatch (2009, February 17). President and COO lies about degrees, resigns. Retrieved February 7, 2017, from http://www.cbsnews.com/news/president-and-coo-lies-about-degrees-resigns/

50. Lemkin, R. (2008, February 1). Dirty little secrets: Corporate espionage. *BBC News*. Retrieved February 7, 2017, from http://news.bbc.co.uk/2/hi/business/7220063.stm

51. Turner, H. (2007, May 1). Roaches and a rat found at ConAgra peanut butter plant. *LawyersandSettlements.com*. Retrieved February 7, 2017, from http://www.lawyersandsettlements.com/features/peanut-butter-roaches-rats.html

52. Weise, E. (2008, September 15). FDA: Melamine found in baby formula made in China," *USA Today*. Retrieved February 7, 2017, from http://www.usatoday.com/news/health/2008-09-11-tainted-formula_N.htm

53. McVeigh, K. (2012, April 20). Secret Service scandal in Colombia has agency's culture under a microscope. *The Guardian*. Retrieved February 7, 2017, from http://www.guardian.co.uk/world/2012/apr/20/secret-service-scandal-columbia-agency?newsfeed=true.

54. Meinert, D. (2014, April 1). Creating an ethical workplace. *Society for Human Resource Management*. Retrieved February 8, 2017, from https://www.shrm.org/hr-today/news/hr-magazine/pages/0414-ethical-workplace-culture.aspx

55. Phillips, J. M., & Gully, S. M. (2012). *Organizational behavior*. Mason, OH: South-Western/Cengage Learning.

56. Knutson, J. (2001). *Project management for business professionals*. New York: John Wiley & Sons.

57. Giacalone, R. A., Jurkiewicz, C. L., & Promislo, M. (2016). Ethics and well-being: The paradoxical implications of individual differences in ethical orientation. *Journal of Business Ethics, 137*(3), 491–506.

58. *Ibid.*

59. Marquez, J. (2006, May 22). Rebalancing Putnam. *Workforce Management*, pp. 1, 18–22. Retrieved February 7, 2017, from http://www.workforce.com/archive/feature/hr-management/rebalancing-putnam/index.php

60. Knutson, J. (2001). *Project management for business professionals*. New York: John Wiley & Sons.

61. Cascio, W. F. & Cappelli, P. (2009). Mesh values, incentives, and behavior. *HR Magazine*, January, 47–50.

62. Erwin, P. M. (2010). Corporate codes of conduct: The effects of code content and quality on ethical performance. *Journal of Business Ethics, 99*, 535–548.

63. U.S. Sentencing Commission. (2015). Chapter eight—Sentencing of organizations. Retrieved February 15, 2017, from http://www.ussc.gov/guidelines/2015-guidelines-manual/2015-chapter-8

64. Elkind, P., & Whitford, D. (2011, January 24). BP: 'An accident waiting to happen.' *Fortune*. Retrieved February 7, 2017, from http://features.blogs.fortune.cnn.com/2011/01/24/bp-an-accident-waiting-to-happen/

65. Bronstein, S., & Drash, W. (2010, June 9). Rig survivors: BP ordered shortcut on day of blast. *CNN.com*. Retrieved

February 17, 2017, from http://www.cnn.com/2010/US/06/08/oil.rig.warning.signs/index.html?iid=EL

66. Moynihan, C. (2010, June 19). BP: Creaky ethics in the Gulf oil spill. *Spero News*. Retrieved February 7, 2017, from http://www.speroforum.com/a/35142/BP-creaky-ethics-in-the-Gulf-oil-spill#.WJoqek2Qzj0

67. *Ibid*.

68. Elkind, P., & Whitford, D. (2011, January 24). BP: 'An accident waiting to happen.' *Fortune*. Retrieved February 7, 2017, from http://features.blogs.fortune.cnn.com/2011/01/24/bp-an-accident-waiting-to-happen/

69. Granatstein, S., & Messick, G. (2010, May 16). Blowout: The Deepwater Horizon disaster. *60 Minutes*. Retrieved February 7, 2017, from http://www.cbsnews.com/stories/2010/05/16/60minutes/main6490197.shtml

70. Bloxham, E. (2010, June 22). What BP was missing on Deepwater Horizon: A whistleblower. *Fortune*. Retrieved February, 7, 2017, from http://money.cnn.com/2010/06/22/news/companies/bp_horizon_macondo_whistleblower.fortune/index.htm

71. Taylor, N. F. (2015, July 1). 22 great examples of socially responsible businesses. *Business News Daily*. Retrieved February 17, 2017, from http://www.businessnewsdaily.com/5499-examples-socially-responsible-businesses.html

72. *Ibid*.

73. Conlin, M. (2008, February 18). Working life. *BusinessWeek*, p. 60.

74. Moss, D. (2016). One sweet job. *HR Magazine*, October, 43–45.

75. Barrena-Martinez, J., Lopez-Fernandez, M., & Romero-Fernandez, P. M. (2011). Research proposal on the relationship between corporate social responsibility and strategic human resource management. *International Journal of Management and Enterprise,10*(2-3), 173–187.

76. Sanders, T. (2008). *Saving the world at work*. New York: Doubleday Business.

77. Duarte, A. P., Gomes, D. R., & Das Neves, J. G. (2014). Tell me your socially responsible practices, I will tell you how attractive for recruitment you are! The impact of perceived CSR on organizational attractiveness. *Tékhne*, *12*, 22–29.

78. Workforce Management (2006). 5 questions for Walter J. Cleaver, president and CEO of the Human Resource Planning Society. *Workforce Management*, July 31, p. 7.

79. Etheridge, J. M. (1999). The perceived role of ethics and social responsibility: An alternative scale structure. *Journal of Business Ethics*, *18*(1), 51–64.

80. Starbucks Coffee. (2017). Global human rights statement. Retrieved January 29, 2017, from https://globalassets.starbucks.com/assets/1d7de46ff5f845d89c01a81bebdbdb59.pdf

81. Higginbottom, K. (2014, January 6). Why HR needs to take a leadership role in CSR. *Forbes*. Retrieved February 11, 2017, from http://www.forbes.com/sites/karenhigginbottom/2014/01/06/why-hr-needs-to-take-a-leadership-role-in-csr/#44c2c37f2e69

82. McClellan, J. (n.d.). Get your employees excited about sustainability. *Society for Human Resource Management*, June 27. Retrieved February 11, 2017, from https://www.shrm.org/resourcesandtools/hr-topics/behavioral-competencies/ethical-practice/pages/employeesandsustainability.aspx

83. See http://www.iso.org/iso/about.htm.

84. CIPS. (2013). *Effective CSR implementation*. Retrieved February 17, 2017, from https://www.cips.org/Documents/Knowledge/Procurement-Topics-and-Skills/4-Sustainability-CSR-Ethics/Corporate-Social-Responsibility/Effective_CSR_implementation.pdf; Yuen, K. F., & Lim, J. M. (2016). Barriers to the implementation of strategic corporate social responsibility in shipping. *The Asian Journal of Shipping and Logistics, 32*: 49–57.

85. Etheridge, J. M. (1999). The perceived role of ethics and social responsibility: An alternative scale structure. *Journal of Business Ethics*, *18*(1), 51–64.

86. Rees, C. J., & Johari, H. (2010). Senior managers' perceptions of the HRM function during times of strategic organizational change: Case study evidence from a public sector banking institution in Malaysia. *Journal of Organizational Change Management*, *23*, 517–536.

87. Carter, L., Ulrich, D., & Goldsmith, M. (2005). *Best practices in leadership development and organizational change: How the best companies ensure meaningful change and sustainable leadership*. San Francisco, CA: Pfeiffer.

88. El-Nadi, F. (2011). Examples of strong corporate cultures. Evancharmichael.com. Retrieved February 11, 2017, from http://www.evancarmichael.com/Human-Resources/840/Examples-Of-Strong-Corporate-Cultures.html

89. Argyris, C. (1993). *Knowledge for action: A guide to overcoming barriers to organizational change*. San Francisco, CA: Jossey Bass.

90. Dunphy, D., & Stace, D. (1990). *Under new management: Australian organizations in transition*. Sydney: McGraw Hill.

91. Hofstede, G. (2003). Culture's consequences: Comparing values, beliefs, behaviors, institutions, and organizations across nations. Thousand Oaks, CA: Sage Publications; Hofstede, G., & Hofstede, G. J. (2005). Cultures and organizations: Software of the mind. New York: McGraw-Hill; Hofstede, G. (1984). Culture's consequences: International differences in work-related values, Vol. 5. Newbury Park, CA: Sage.

92. Friedman, B. A. (2007). Globalization implications for human resource management roles. *Employee Responsibilities and Rights Journal*, *19*, 157–171.

93. Based on Hofstede, G. (2003). Culture's consequences: Comparing values, beliefs, behaviors, institutions, and organizations across nations. Thousand Oaks, CA: Sage Publications; Hofstede, G., & Hofstede, G. J. (2005). Cultures and organizations: Software of the mind. New York: McGraw-Hill; Hofstede, G. (1984). Culture's consequences: International differences in work-related values, Vol. 5. Newbury Park, CA: Sage.

94. Heffernan, M. (2012, April 24). Why mergers fail. *CBS MoneyWatch*. Retrieved February 14, 2017, from http://www.cbsnews.com/news/why-mergers-fail/

95. Marks, M. L., & Mirvis, P. H. (2011). A framework for the human resources role in managing culture in mergers and acquisitions. *Human Resource Management*, *50*, 859–877.

96. See EY. (2017). Human capital and merger and acquisitions: How to integrate the global mobility and talent management function of differing cultures. Retrieved February 19, 2017, from http://www.ey.com/Publication/vwLUAssets/EY_Human_capital_and_merger_and_acquisitions/$FILE/EY-HC_and_MA_talent_management.pdf; Talent retention: Make or break the deal. *PWC*, January 12. Retrieved February 19, 2017, from http://usblogs.pwc.com/deals/merger-talent-retention-make-or-break-the-deal/; Jackson, S. E., & Schuler, R. S. (2001). HR issues and activities in mergers and acquisitions. *European Management Journal*, *19*, 239–253 for more information.

97. Weber, Y., Rachman-Moore, D., & Tarba, S. Y. (2011). HR practices during post-merger conflict and merger performance. *International Journal of Cross Cultural Management*. Published online November 8, 2011. doi: 10.1177/1470595811413111

98. Siegenthaler, P. J. (2011). What role for HR during mergers and acquisitions? *Human Resource Management International Digest*, *19*, 4–6.

99. Weber, Y., & Tarba, S. Y. (2010). Human resource practices and performance of mergers and acquisitions in Israel. *Human Resource Management Review*, *20*, 203–211.

100. Gilbert, A. (2004). Besieged PeopleSoft suffers exodus of execs. *CNET*, March 15. Retrieved February 7, 2017, from http://news.cnet.com/2100-1022 -5173018.html

101. Porter, T. H., & Norris, S. E. (2012). Human resource metrics: A contemporary approach to managing human capital. In W. J. Rothwell (Ed.). *The encyclopedia of human resource management, Vol. 2, human resources and employment forms*, 129–136.

102. Gates, S., & Langevin, P. (2010). Human capital measures, strategy, and performance: HR managers' perceptions. *Accounting, Auditing & Accountability Journal*, *23*, 111–132.

103. Marriott, J. W., & Brown, K. A. (1997). *The spirit to serve: Marriott's way*. New York: HarperCollins, 36.

104. Marriott. (n.d.). Core values & heritage. Retrieved February 7, 2017, from http://www.marriott.com/culture-and-values/core -values.mi

105. Marriott, J. W., & Brown, K. A. (1997). *The spirit to serve: Marriott's way*. New York: HarperCollins.

106. Bhattarai, A. (2015). Nearly a year in, Marriott Marquis says job training program has worked. *The Washington Post*, March 20. Retrieved February 6, 2017, from https://www.washingtonpost.com/business/capitalbusiness/nearly-as-year-in-marriott-marquis-says-job-training-program-has-worked/2015/03/19/7417c056-ccb4-11e4-8c54-ffb5ba6f2f69_story.html?utm_term=.2a03289eeb4f

107. Marriott.com. (2016, May 11). Marriott International celebrates 30 years of honoring associates. Retrieved February 6, 2017, from http://news.marriott.com/2016/05/marriott-international-celebrates-30-years-honoring-associates/

108. Marriott.com, (2017). J. Willard Marriott. Retrieved February 6, 2017, from http://www.marriott.com/culture-and-values/j -willard-marriott.mi

chapter 3

The Legal Context of HRM

Learning Objectives

1 Explain human resource management's (HRM) role in risk management.

2 Explain why diversity and inclusion are important to organizational performance.

3 Describe a bona fide occupational qualification.

4 Define affirmative action.

5 Explain the difference between adverse impact and disparate treatment.

6 Describe four human biases that can create barriers to equal employment opportunity.

Real World Challenge

Merck's Commitment to Diversity and Inclusion

Global pharmaceutical company Merck knows that diverse, engaged, and talented employees are critical to its success. The company values the participation and ideas of its minorities, women, veterans, LGBT, and disabled employees and believes that its diversity has been essential to its global success.[1] Celeste Warren, leader of Merck's Global Diversity and Inclusion Center of Excellence and vice president of human resources of Merck's manufacturing division, says, "I firmly believe that diversity and inclusion aren't simply 'nice' virtues for a company to have or boxes for us to check — they create success both in our bottom line as well as in fostering a happy, healthy, and invested workforce."[2]

Merck strives to ensure that diversity and inclusion is woven into the fabric of its business to create a competitive advantage for the company. Merck would like HRM to further reinforce the company's commitment to diversity and inclusion. Imagine that the company asks you for ideas. After studying this chapter, you should have some good ideas.

In addition to being ethical, complying with employment laws is also good for business. Besides avoiding the negative publicity and legal expenses that accompany litigation, compliance can improve organizational performance. Legal compliance focuses on treating employees fairly and making employment decisions based on job-relevant information, performance, and merit rather than on protected characteristics including gender, disability, or race. Organizations that truly value diversity and are respectful and inclusive of all employees are better able to hire and retain quality people from all segments of the labor force and motivate employees to perform better.

Proactive firms often go beyond legal compliance in recruiting, managing, and retaining diverse employees. Reinforcing the importance of both diversity values and ethical standards, one study found that turnover intentions were lowest among workers perceiving both a pro-diversity and highly ethical climate.[3] Apple recognizes that diversity supports innovation. They state, "At Apple, we take a holistic view of diversity that looks beyond the usual measurements. A view that includes the varied perspectives of our employees as well as app developers, suppliers, and anyone who aspires to a future in tech. Because we know new ideas come from diverse ways of seeing things."[4]

U.S. employment laws cover issues including hiring, termination, safety and health, medical issues, sexual harassment, and union relations. Federal, state, and local laws and court interpretations of these laws create a dynamic legal environment that requires HRM professionals to stay abreast of current federal and state level legal issues and keep managers' legal knowledge current. This chapter cannot give legal advice and does not substitute for the advice of a qualified labor and employment attorney. Although there are many legal issues you should be able to deal with alone, this chapter should give you sufficient knowledge to understand when to consult a qualified lawyer. Diversity and the legal context influence what employees *should* do in our book's overall model of HRM.

In this chapter, we will first briefly explain the importance of HRM to risk management. We then discuss the importance of employment laws and of employee diversity and provide an overview of some of the key laws and legal issues surrounding the employment relationship. A discussion of different types of lawsuits and emerging legal issues is then followed by a description of the federal enforcement agencies. The chapter concludes with a discussion of some common barriers to legal compliance. After reading this chapter, you should have a good understanding of the legal context of HRM and of some of the barriers to legal compliance in organizations. Additional employment laws and legal issues will be discussed throughout the book.

The Role of HRM in Risk Management

risk management
identifying, assessing, and resolving risks before they become serious threats

The goal of **risk management** is to identify, assess, and resolve risks before they become serious threats to the organization. Although risk management departments have traditionally focused on risks such as natural disasters, risk managers are becoming increasingly aware that an organization's employees and talent-related issues often pose great risk, particularly in uncertain times.[5]

Importantly, Section 409 of Sarbanes-Oxley, an act passed by U.S. Congress in 2002 to improve corporate financial disclosures and protect investors from fraudulent corporate accounting, requires real-time public disclosure of financial or operational changes that might have a material impact on a company's bottom line. This includes the departure of top executives, government fines or penalties, employee turnover, employment lawsuits, revision of benefits programs, and new labor contracts.[6] Because poorly designed, documented, or executed HRM processes can lead to noncompliance with Section 409 as well as increase both legal and financial risks under federal and state employment laws, HRM risk management has taken on new importance in organizations. The fact that Sarbanes-Oxley places increased responsibility and potential liability on management and requires that senior executives take individual responsibility for the accuracy and completeness of corporate financial reports has increased many companies' awareness of the role HRM plays in risk management.[7]

Risk management attention is typically paid to short- and long-term risks to project schedules and costs; the quality and timeliness of project deliverables; and the overall monitoring necessary to minimize re-work, schedule and cost overruns, and production and quality problems. Other potential areas of risk management for HRM include employee turnover, low morale, potential litigation from misunderstandings arising between staff and management, and negative publicity resulting from these or other employee issues.[8]

Risk management consists of two primary types of activities: Risk assessment and risk control.[9] **Risk assessment** consists of identifying, analyzing, and prioritizing risks. Identifying risks involves identifying factors or events (perhaps changes in employment laws or talent shortages) that might have some type of negative and significant impact on the organization. Risk identification checklists, employee surveys, exit interviews, and contingency planning are some of the tools used to identify risks. Risk analysis relies on tools and processes including decision analysis, cost risk analysis, schedule analysis, and other techniques to analyze the identified risks. Risks are then prioritized by ranking them based on their likelihood of occurring and their impact if they were to occur.[10]

risk assessment
identifying, analyzing, and prioritizing risks

Risk control involves risk management planning and monitoring and resolving risks. Risk management planning involves acquiring information, avoiding risk, transferring risk, and reducing risk. Resolution techniques for common HRM risks include employing appropriate assessment and screening tools, sourcing talent ahead of actual demand, leadership succession planning, hiring manager training in bias reduction and employment laws, and legal compliance audits. Many HRM risks can be avoided altogether by better managing the talent side of the corporate equation through interventions, including adequate hiring practices, succession planning, adequate severance and outplacement, and executive coaching and development.[11]

risk control
risk management planning and monitoring and resolving risks

Risk monitoring enables responsible risk management and timely risk resolution. It incorporates techniques such as tracking top risks and regularly reassessing known risks.[12] Risk management plans, like all human resources initiatives, should be regularly updated as new risks are identified and addressed.

Some of the top risks in HRM are:

- Succession planning and the company's leadership pipeline;
- Compliance and regulation violations;
- Ethics and corporate culture;
- A shortage of necessary skills in the company's workforce;
- A shortage of necessary skills in the labor market;
- A gap between current employee capabilities and the capabilities needed to execute the business strategy; and
- Mergers and acquisitions risks.

Once risks have been identified and assessed, all techniques to manage the risk fall into one or more of these four major categories:[13]

1. *Avoidance*: Eliminate, withdraw from, or do not become involved in the situation leading to the risk (e.g., decide not to acquire a company because of poor cultural fit).
2. *Reduction*: Mitigate or reduce the risk (e.g., conduct contingency and succession planning and employee development activities to improve the depth of the company's leadership pipeline or train all hiring managers and recruiters in common hiring biases, relevant employment laws, and the organization's interview process).
3. *Sharing*: Transfer the risk by outsourcing or insuring against it (e.g., decide to outsource employee background checks to a qualified vendor).
4. *Retention*: Accept and budget for the risk (e.g., set aside funds to cover equal employment opportunity (EEO) fines, employee severance payments, or lawsuit settlements).

The Importance of Employment Laws

Employment laws and regulations exist because organizations typically have more power than do employees in the employment relationship. Because employers determine employees' pay, promotions, and working conditions, employment laws help to limit the employer's power, reduce unfair discrimination, and provide equal employment opportunities for everyone.

Unfair discrimination occurs when employment-related decisions and actions are not job-related, objective, or merit-based. **Fair discrimination** is when only objective, merit-based, and job-related characteristics are used to determine employment-related decisions.

JeffG/Alamy

Just having diverse employees isn't enough to realize the potential benefits of a diverse workforce. Employees must also have a positive attitude toward working with people different from themselves in a variety of ways.

Unlawful employment practices are those that violate a federal, state, or local employment law, for example by unfairly discriminating against people with legally protected characteristics including pregnancy, religion, or age. An employment decision can be unfair without being unlawful. For example, if a manager's favorite sports team loses, and he goes to work the next day and fires anyone wearing the opposing team's colors, the manager has not broken any laws (as long as he has not disproportionately fired employees in any protected group), although this is obviously unfair and not strategic. This actually happened when a salesperson was fired for wearing a Green Bay Packers tie to work after the Packers won an NFC title game against the Chicago Bears.[14]

Workforce barriers based on characteristics including race, gender, age, ethnicity, religion, and disabilities exist. Employment laws discourage this type of discrimination and promote diversity and equal employment opportunity. **Equal employment opportunity** (EEO) means that employment

unfair discrimination
when employment decisions and actions are not job-related, objective, or merit-based

fair discrimination
when only objective, merit-based, and job-related characteristics are used to determine employment related decisions

unlawful employment practices
violate a federal, state, or local employment law

equal employment opportunity
a firm's employment practices must be designed and used in a manner that treats employees and applicants consistently regardless of their protected characteristics, such as their sex and race

practices must be designed and used in a manner that treats employees and applicants consistently regardless of their protected characteristics. Because laws alone do not provide the tools to recognize and break down discrimination barriers, proactively managing diversity is also important.[15]

Employment laws define what is expected and required of employers, and they clarify what is not allowable. They also promote more strategic HRM by focusing on job-related qualifications and merit rather than superficial characteristics. This enhances the quality of the firm's workforce and, thus, its performance. Avoiding unfair discrimination helps companies better execute their strategies and reach their goals by:

- Enhancing the quality of an organization's talent pool;
- Promoting the perception of fairness and trust among employees and job candidates, which increases motivation and engagement;
- Reducing the negative public relations that can result when employees feel they are being discriminated against and tell others about their experience;
- Reinforcing a company's ethical culture and commitment to inclusion and diversity;
- Reducing turnover by improving employee motivation and perceptions of fairness; and
- Promoting diversity, which can enhance a company's ability to appeal to a broader customer base.

The Equal Employment Opportunity Commission website (http://www.eeoc.gov/) is an excellent resource for more information about EEOC laws.

The Importance of Diversity and Inclusion to Business Performance

Other than staying out of legal trouble, why should we care about diversity? Because the better you are able to work with all types of people, the more effective you will be in your job. Diversity awareness enables you to hire, retain, and motivate the best talent, which helps maximize your and your organization's performance. Consumer markets for people of diverse backgrounds are in the trillions of dollars and growing annually.

Diversity also fosters creativity and innovation. As L'Oreal's chief executive officer Frédéric Rozé put it, "Diversity fosters creativity. We need to generate the best ideas from our people in all levels of the company and incorporate them into our business practices."[16] Additionally, the business context is becoming increasingly globalized. Employees are much more likely to work with diverse employees or deal with customers from many different countries and backgrounds.

> *"Diversity fosters creativity. We need to generate the best ideas from our people in all levels of the company and incorporate them into our business practices."*
>
> — **Frédéric Rozé, chief executive officer of L'Oreal**

so what?

Listening to and respecting everyone in the organization improves organizational performance.

Employment discrimination laws are rooted in fairness and equal access to employment. Employment laws are also helpful in promoting workplace diversity, but this diversity is not always leveraged to increase organizational performance. **Inclusion** means that everyone feels respected and listened to, and everyone contributes to their fullest potential.[17]

Inclusion
everyone feels respected and listened to, and everyone contributes to their fullest potential

Just employing diverse people is not enough. Realizing the potential positive effects of diversity depends on employees' attitudes toward diversity. Firm performance increases when employees have more positive attitudes toward diversity.[18] A positive diversity climate has been found to be positively related to customer satisfaction.[19]

The Coca-Cola Company includes its global diversity mission on its website, "The Coca-Cola Company's global diversity mission is to mirror the rich diversity of the marketplace we serve and be recognized for our leadership in Diversity, Inclusion and Fairness in all aspects of our business, including Workplace, Marketplace, Supplier and Community, enhancing the Company's social license to operate."[20]

Laws and Definitions

Federal and state employment legislation, including wage and hour laws, safety and health laws, and equal employment opportunity legislation, often result from social pressures. Constitutional law supersedes all other laws and regulations and applies particularly to the due process rights of public employees. **Common law** is the body of case-by-case court decisions that determines what is legal and what remedies are appropriate. Individual states develop their own common law in response to federal and state legislation and the specific cases brought before state courts. Over time, these court decisions establish the permissibility of various employment practices and appropriate remedies for impermissible practices. For example, a **workplace tort**, a civil wrong in which an employer violates a duty owed to its customers or employees, is handled at the state level. An example of a tort is when an employee agrees to let a company use her photo in an employee newsletter, but the employer later uses it in a public advertisement without her permission. Because case law differs across states, companies must be familiar with the case law in all states in which they operate.

common law
the body of case-by-case court decisions that determines what is legal and what remedies are appropriate

workplace tort
a civil wrong in which an employer violates a duty owed to its customers or employees

Most employment discrimination lawsuits are brought under federal statutes, although state laws can be even more restrictive. A state's attorney general's office and website provide information about that state's fair employment practice laws. Some state laws extend protection to employers who are not covered by a federal statute. Other statutes protect groups not covered by federal acts and individuals who are performing civil or family duties outside of their normal employment. For example, New York protects workers from discrimination based on parental status.[21]

? so what

Because state laws can extend the protection of federal statutes, it is important to be familiar with the relevant laws in the states in which a company operates.

To interpret, administer, and enforce specific laws, local, state, and federal legislative bodies create agencies such as the Department of Labor and the Equal Employment Opportunity Commission. Because state laws differ and change over time, it is important to update your knowledge and regularly consult legal counsel to ensure compliance with current local, state, and federal regulations. The Society for Human Resource Management (SHRM), an association of HRM professionals, offers legal information and updates to its members.[22] Because some of the statutes and regulations that the U.S. Department of Labor enforces require employers to place notices in the workplace, the Department of Labor provides free electronic copies of the required posters on its website.[23]

Major Federal Employment Laws

There are several major federal laws that broadly apply to the employment relationship, summarized in Table 3.1. Let's take a closer chronological look at them.

table **3.1**

Chronological Summary of Major Employment Related Executive Orders and Federal Laws

	Description
National Labor Relations Act of 1935	Prohibits retaliation against employees seeking to unionize.
Fair Labor Standards Act (FLSA) of 1938	Establishes both a national minimum wage and overtime rules.
Equal Pay Act of 1963	Prohibits wage discrimination on the basis of sex.
Title VII of the Civil Rights Act of 1964	Prohibits employment discrimination based on race, color, religion, sex, or national origin.
Age Discrimination in Employment Act (ADEA) of 1967	Protects people 40 years of age or older.
Rehabilitation Act of 1973	Prohibits discrimination against qualified individuals with a disability.
Vietnam Era Veterans' Readjustment Assistance Act of 1974 (VEVRAA) (Amended in 2002 by the Jobs for Veterans Act)	Prohibits discrimination against and requires affirmative action for disabled veterans as well as other categories of veterans.
Pregnancy Discrimination Act of 1978	Prohibits discrimination for all employment-related purposes on the basis of pregnancy, childbirth, or related medical conditions.
Consolidated Omnibus Budget Reconciliation Act (COBRA) of 1986	Employers with group health plans and 20 or more employees in the prior year must offer continued health and dental insurance coverage to terminated employees for limited periods of time.
Immigration Reform and Control Act of 1986	Employers with at least four employees must verify the employment eligibility of everyone hired; only U.S. citizens, nationals of the United States, and aliens authorized to work in the United States are eligible for employment.
Worker Adjustment and Retraining Notification Act (WARN) of 1988	Employers with at least 100 employees must give at least 60 days' notice to workers of plant closings or mass layoffs of 50 or more people (excluding part-time workers).
Americans with Disabilities Act of 1990 (Amended in 2008)	Prohibits discrimination of a qualified individual with or perceived as having a disability; focus on fair treatment and reasonable accommodation.
Family and Medical Leave Act of 1993	Requires leave and job-return for personal or family medical reasons and for the care of newborn or newly adopted children.
The Uniformed Services Employment and Reemployment Rights Act (USERRA) of 1994	Ensures that members of the uniformed services are entitled to return to their civilian employment after their service.
Genetic Information Nondiscrimination Act of 2008	Prohibits employers from discriminating against individuals based on the results of genetic testing when making hiring, firing, job placement, or promotion decisions.

National Labor Relations Act of 1935.   Congress enacted the National Labor Relations Act (NLRA) to protect employee and employer rights and to encourage collective bargaining between labor unions and employers. The NLRA was also created to end certain private sector labor and management practices that can harm the general welfare of workers, businesses, and the U.S. economy "by depressing wage rates and the purchasing power of wage earners in industry and by preventing the stabilization of competitive wage rates and working conditions within and between industries."[24] The NLRA prohibits retaliation against employees seeking to unionize. In addition to giving workers the right to join unions and bargain collectively, it created a system to arbitrate disputes between unions and employers and prohibits employers from interfering in union activities.

Fair Labor Standards Act (FLSA) of 1938.   The Fair Labor Standards Act establishes a national minimum wage, overtime rules, recordkeeping requirements, and youth employment standards.[25] It covers employees in the private sector and in federal, state, and local governments. The FLSA excludes some jobs from FLSA coverage, making some employees, including commissioned salespeople, farm workers, and salaried executives, exempt from the overtime pay and minimum wage provisions.

Equal Pay Act of 1963.   To promote equal pay for equal work, the Equal Pay Act of 1963 prohibits discrimination in pay, benefits, and pensions based on an employee's gender. It covers most government employees and employers that engage in interstate commerce. Jobs are considered "equal" when they require substantially the same effort, skill, and responsibility under similar working conditions and in the same establishment. Employers in an industry can pay employees different wages for doing the same job, but male and female employees working in the same job in the same company must be paid the same.

Title VII of the Civil Rights Act of 1964.   Title VII of the Civil Rights Act[26] prohibits employment discrimination based on race, color, religion, sex, or national origin and provides monetary damages in cases of intentional employment discrimination. Title VII prohibits not only intentional discrimination but also practices that have the effect of discriminating against individuals because of their race, color, national origin, religion, or sex.

> Under Title VII, it is an unlawful employment practice for an employer:[27]
>
> "To fail or refuse to hire or to discharge any individual, or otherwise to discriminate against any individual with respect to his compensation, terms, conditions, or privileges of employment, because of such individual's race, color, religion, sex, or national origin;" or
>
> "To limit, segregate, or classify his employees or applicants for employment in any way which would deprive or tend to deprive any individual of employment opportunities or otherwise adversely affect his status as an employee, because of such individual's race, color, religion, sex, or national origin."

Intentional discrimination is established "when a complaining party demonstrates that race, color, religion, sex or national origin was a motivating factor for any employment practice, even though other factors also motivated the practice."[28] Either direct or specific and substantial circumstantial evidence can be used to create a reasonable inference that a protected characteristic was a determining factor in an adverse employment decision. For example, e-mail evidence that an employee had been subjected to sexual harassment before being terminated for alleged performance reasons may be sufficient to prove that sex was a motivating factor in her dismissal. The Civil Rights Act of 1991 is enforced by the Equal Employment Opportunity Commission.

There are limited situations in which a protected characteristic can be considered a **bona fide occupational qualification** (BFOQ) under Title VII and be legally used to make employment

bona fide occupational qualification (BFOQ)
a characteristic that is essential to the successful performance of a relevant job function

decisions. A BFOQ is a characteristic that is essential to the successful performance of a relevant job function, and the essence of the business operation would be undermined by including or excluding members with a protected characteristic.[29] Only a qualification that affects an employee's ability to perform the job can be considered a BFOQ. For example, corrections facilities with gender segregated wards usually require at least one staff member of the same gender as the inmates to always be on duty.

BFOQs do not apply to all jobs, and race and color can never be considered BFOQs.[30] Customer preference is also insufficient to justify a BFOQ defense. BFOQs must be based only on the actual inability of individuals with some protected characteristic (for example, their sex) to perform job duties, not on stereotyped characterizations.

It is not a violation of the Equal Pay Act if wage differences between male and female employees occur due to seniority systems, quality or quantity of work, or merit. Also, employers in violation of the act are not allowed to lower the wages of one gender to comply with the law—they must raise the wages of the underpaid gender.

The Age Discrimination in Employment Act (ADEA) of 1967.   The Age Discrimination in Employment Act[31] (ADEA) prohibits employers from discriminating against any worker with respect to compensation or the terms, conditions, or privileges of employment because he or she is age 40 or older. Some states have expanded the ages protected from employment discrimination. In New Jersey, it is illegal to discriminate against employees between the ages of 18 and 70.[32]

As age discrimination claims became more common, some companies including IBM gave employees losing their job a list of other colleagues being fired along with their positions, departments, ages, and other data. Employees could use this information to decide if they wanted to waive age discrimination claims in exchange for a severance package.[33]

The Rehabilitation Act of 1973.   The Rehabilitation Act of 1973[34] requires employers to engage in affirmative action to promote the hiring of individuals with a disability. Qualified individuals with disabilities are people who, with reasonable accommodation, can perform the essential functions of the job for which they have applied or have been hired to perform. **Reasonable accommodation** means an employer is required to take reasonable steps to accommodate a disability unless it would cause the employer undue hardship.[35]

Section 503 of the Rehabilitation Act regulations established a nationwide 7 percent goal for federal contractors to employ qualified individuals with disabilities. Federal contractors with over 100 employees must apply this goal to each job group, whereas contractors with 100 or fewer employees may apply the goal to their entire workforce. Because the OFCCP recognizes that the availability of qualified disabled individuals for some jobs in some locations may be less than 7 percent, a failure to meet the goal will not, in and of itself, result in a violation or a finding of discrimination.[36]

Vietnam Era Veterans' Readjustment Assistance Act of 1974 (VEVRAA) (Amended in 2002 by the Jobs for Veterans Act).   The Vietnam Era Veterans' Readjustment Assistance Act[37] (VEVRAA) prohibits discrimination against protected veterans and requires federal government contractors and subcontractors with a contract of $25,000 or more with the federal government to take affirmative action to employ and promote protected veterans.

The Pregnancy Discrimination Act of 1978.   The Pregnancy Discrimination Act of 1978[38] amended Title VII of the Civil Rights Act to prohibit sex discrimination on the basis of pregnancy. Pregnancy, childbirth, and related medical conditions must be treated the same way as other temporary illnesses or conditions.[39] This means that it is illegal to decide not to hire or promote someone simply because they are pregnant. The U.S. Supreme Court ruled that a former UPS truck driver could sue shipping company UPS for pregnancy discrimination after

reasonable accommodation

an employer is required to take reasonable steps to accommodate a disability unless it would cause the employer undue hardship the company refused to give her a less demanding shift after a medical professional ordered her to not lift heavy items while pregnant.[40]

Consolidated Omnibus Budget Reconciliation Act (COBRA) of 1986. The Consolidated Omnibus Budget Reconciliation Act (COBRA) gives workers and their families who lose their health benefits the right to choose to continue group health plan benefits. Benefits can be continued for limited periods of time under circumstances, including voluntary or involuntary job loss, reduction in the hours worked, transition between jobs, death, divorce, or another life event.[41] COBRA applies to group health plans sponsored by employers with 20 or more employees in the prior year.

The Immigration Reform and Control Act of 1986. Under the Immigration Reform and Control Act, employers must use an I-9 verification form to verify the employability status of every new employee within three days of hiring. This form requires documentation verifying the new hire's eligibility, identity, and authorization to work in the United States. To avoid the appearance of discrimination on the basis of national origin, it is a good idea to make the job offer contingent on proof of employment eligibility.

For privacy reasons, I-9s must be kept in a folder where managers cannot see them, and recruiters and hiring managers should be trained on I-9 compliance. The internet-based E-Verify system operated by the Department of Homeland Security in partnership with the Social Security Administration can help employers determine a person's eligibility to work in the United States.[42] An I-9 audit at restaurant chain Chipotle Mexican Grill's Minnesota restaurants forced it to fire hundreds of allegedly illegal workers, perhaps more than half of its staff at the time.[43]

Rather than conducting workplace raids to pick up undocumented workers, Immigration and Customs Enforcement policy has shifted to the criminal prosecution of businesses for workplace immigration law violations. Immigration and Customs Enforcement is increasingly making worksite criminal arrests of corporate officers, managers, and contractors. Because enforcement has been increased in recent years, it is a good idea to keep I-9 records updated, accurate, and regularly conduct internal I-9 workforce audits to identify and correct any problems.[44]

The Worker Adjustment and Retraining Notification Act (WARN) of 1988. The WARN Act is a federal law requiring employers of 100 or more full-time workers who have worked at least six of the last 12 months and an average of 20 hours or more per week to give employees 60 days' advance notice of closing or major layoffs.[45] WARN requires that notice be given to all hourly, salaried, managerial, and supervisory employees, but business partners, workers participating in strike actions, and contract employees are not covered. More details about what is covered are available on the Department of Labor's website.[46]

Some states have passed their own WARN-type Acts expanding this coverage. Illinois extends coverage to employers with as few as 75 full-time employees, and New Jersey increased the federal penalties for infractions.

The Americans with Disabilities Act (ADA) of 1990. The Americans with Disabilities Act (ADA) and the Americans with Disabilities Act Amendments Act that became effective on January 1, 2009, guarantee equal opportunity for individuals with disabilities or perceived as having disabilities. Similar protections to those provided on the basis of race, color, sex, national origin, age, and religion are also provided.[47]

Under the ADA, a person is to be considered disabled regardless of whether or not any form of treatment or corrective device (other than contact lenses or glasses) is used to ameliorate or control the condition. The ADA prohibits an employer from asking applicants about their disabilities or medical history before offering employment. The ADA and its amendment require employers to reasonably accommodate employee and applicant disabilities during the hiring process as well as during the employment relationship.

Home improvement retailer Lowe's was required to pay $8.6 million to settle an EEOC disability discrimination suit after it failed to provide reasonable accommodations and fired employees who were regarded as disabled, had a record of disability, or were associated with someone who had a disability when their medical leaves of absence exceeded the company's leave policy.[48]

Family and Medical Leave Act of 1993.   The Family and Medical Leave Act (FMLA) of 1993 (amended by the Family and Medical Leave Act and National Defense Authorization Act of 2008) requires eligible employees at worksites with at least 50 employees to take unpaid, job-protected leave for specified family and medical reasons with continuation of group health insurance coverage under the same terms and conditions as if the employee had not taken leave. In a single 12-month period, eligible employees are entitled to:[49]

- Twelve workweeks of leave for:
  - the birth of a child and to care for the newborn child within one year of birth;
  - the placement with the employee of a child for adoption or foster care and to care for the newly placed child within one year of placement;
  - the caring of the employee's spouse, child, or parent who has a serious health condition;
  - a serious health condition that makes the employee unable to perform the essential functions of his or her job;
  - any qualifying exigency arising out of the fact that the employee's spouse, son, daughter, or parent is a covered military member on "covered active duty;" **or**
- Twenty-six workweeks of leave to care for a covered military service member with a serious injury or illness who is the spouse, son, daughter, parent, or next of kin to the employee (military caregiver leave).

?so what
_____

Because managers can be held personally accountable for violating the Family and Medical Leave act, it is important for managers to understand the law to avoid personal liability.

Managers may be held personally liable for disputes involving hiring and firing decisions for the Family and Medical Leave Act.[50] In the case of *Narodetsky v. Cardone Industries*, a terminated employee sued three HRM executives who had allegedly conspired to find cause to fire him after he requested FMLA time off.[51] The judge ruled that "Each of the defendants exercised control over" the employee when terminating him in reaction to his FMLA request.[52] This ruling means that executives and managers can be held personally accountable for damages under the FMLA, and that it may be possible to hold managers personally liable for a broader range of employee decisions. It is clearly important for all managers to make hiring and termination decisions with the greatest fairness and objectivity to avoid personal liability.

The Uniformed Services Employment and Reemployment Rights Act (USERRA) of 1994.   The Uniformed Services Employment and Reemployment Rights Act of 1994[53] (significantly updated in 1996 and 1998) prohibits employers from discriminating against job applicants who may be called into military service or who volunteer for military service. The act also seeks to ensure that members of the uniformed services are entitled to return to their civilian employment upon completion of their service with the seniority, status, and rate of pay they would have obtained had they remained continuously employed by their civilian employer. The law also protects individuals from discrimination in hiring, promotion, and retention on the basis of present and future membership in the armed services.

Target Corporation lost a USERRA case after a production controller at a distribution center was demoted and later fired due to his service in the National Guard.[54] The jury awarded the plaintiff $17,950 in economic damages, $67,000 in noneconomic damages, and $900,000 in punitive damages.

The Genetic Information Nondiscrimination Act of 2008 (GINA).   The Genetic Information Nondiscrimination Act prohibits employers from discriminating against individuals based on the results of genetic testing when making hiring, firing, job placement, or promotion decisions. Genetic testing can identify people genetically susceptible to certain diseases that could result from workplace exposure to toxic substances such as chemicals or radiation. Genetic tests can't reliably predict whether a particular condition will develop because most diseases are not solely due to genetics but to a combination of factors including stress, diet, and environmental pollutants.

Because GINA makes even acquiring genetic information illegal, and because the term "genetic information" is broadly defined to include even family members' medical conditions, it is important to use HRM practices that don't intentionally or accidentally reveal genetic information. For example, job applications should not contain questions that can discriminate based on genetic makeup, and policies should be developed governing the use of social networking sites including Facebook that could inadvertently reveal protected information (for example, a job candidate's post that his father was just diagnosed with cancer).

No employment decisions should be made based on genetic information. Recruiters and hiring managers must be trained to not ask about genetic information or family health issues while making any employment decisions. Employee handbooks should also be updated to reflect this law. Any genetic information acquired by an employer should be placed in a confidential medical file separated from the employee's personnel file.[55]

Although asking a question in an employment interview may not be illegal in itself, it is illegal to discriminate on the basis of the information learned by asking such questions. As one expert explains, "Simply being asked a question does not make someone a victim of employment discrimination. Discrimination laws require someone to suffer a concrete harm, such as not getting a job, getting passed up for a promotion, or even being harassed."[56] Table 3.2 gives you the chance to decide if certain interview questions have the potential to solicit information about a protected characteristic based on the laws you just learned about. The answers are at the end of the chapter.

Global Differences.   Employment laws also vary across countries. Some countries make it much more difficult to terminate an employee than in the United States, and others give different legal rights to blue- and white-collar employees. This chapter's Global Issues feature describes the importance of understanding the employment laws of the countries in which an organization operates.

Affirmative Action

Affirmative action refers to proactive efforts to eliminate discrimination and its past effects. Concerned that ending formal discrimination would not eliminate racism by employers, President Johnson issued Executive Order 11246 in September 1965, requiring employers receiving federal contracts to take proactive steps—affirmative action—to integrate their workforces. Executive Order 11246 requires contractors with federal contracts of at least $50,000 and 50 or more employees to have a formal affirmative action plan.

The goal of affirmative action is to provide employment opportunities to **protected classes,** or groups underrepresented in employment—particularly blacks, Native Americans, Asian Americans, Hispanic Americans, and women. Affirmative action is also required for handicapped persons, disabled veterans, and Vietnam War veterans. Although Executive Order 11246 requires federal contractors to set goals for hiring minorities and females, there are no laws requiring goals for hiring other protected classes.

An **affirmative action plan** describes in detail the actions to be taken, procedures to be followed, and standards to be met when establishing an affirmative action program. Affirmative action plans can include, but are not limited to, provisions for nondiscriminatory

so what**?**

Do not make any employment decision on the basis of genetic information.

so what**?**

No interview question is itself illegal, but using information about any protected characteristic obtained from an interview response in making an employment decision is illegal.

affirmative action
proactive efforts to eliminate discrimination and its past effects

protected classes
groups underrepresented in employment

affirmative action plan
describes in detail the actions to be taken, procedures to be followed, and standards to be met when establishing an affirmative action program

table **3.2**

Are These Interview Questions Potential Legal Trouble?

Question	Trouble? Y/N	Reason
1 Do you rent or own your home?		
2 How far is your commute?		
3 How long have you lived here?		
4 What is your current address, and how long have you lived there?		
5 What is your date of birth?		
6 What school did you attend?		
7 Are you married or single?		
8 Where were you born?		
9 What was your military discharge?		
10 Have you served in the U.S. armed forces?		
11 Do you prefer to be called Miss, Mrs. or Ms.?		
12 Are you a U.S. citizen?		
13 What is the name and address of a relative to be notified in an emergency?		
14 What is your height and weight?		
15 Can you work on Christmas?		

 # Global Issues

Global Differences in Employment Law

U.S. multinational companies operating in other countries must also comply with the employment laws of their host countries. This is complicated by the fact that employment laws can vary widely across countries. Most employment contracts in France are for an open term, and a major legal distinction exists between top managers and lower-level workers. Unlike U.S. workers, Mexican workers enjoy a right to severance pay and benefit from laws that give them absolute caps on the number of hours they can work, paid vacations at premium-pay rates, paid weekends, annual profit-sharing bonuses, and annual 13th-month pay bonuses.[57]

In Iceland, special government permission must be obtained before performing workforce reductions involving four or more employees. In Switzerland, after probationary periods of up to three months, dismissal is normally lawful only for either gross misconduct or serious economic reasons, and working on Sundays is only possible with a special permit from government authorities. In Russia, terminating a contract of employment with pregnant workers and female workers with children of up to three years of age, as well as with single mothers having children of up to 14 years of age, is not allowed. Clearly, it is important to educate yourself on the local employment laws before operating in other countries.

recruitment, training, and promotion. Procedures for internal record keeping and internal compliance auditing to measure the plan's success are often included. Employers adhere to affirmative action plans because they want to, because a court orders them to, because they are federal contractors and they have to, or because they agree to them as a remedy for past discrimination.

Preferential treatment, or employment preference given to a member of a protected group, can temporarily be given to qualified applicants from underrepresented protected groups only in cases settled by a court of law—a company cannot legally decide on its own to give a protected group preferential treatment. Numerical benchmarks are usually established based on the availability of qualified applicants in the job market or qualified candidates in the employer's workforce. These numerical goals do not create quotas for specific groups mandating that certain numbers of people with certain protected characteristics be hired or guarantee proportional representation or equal results. In most cases, affirmative action plans identify voluntary goals and timetables for integrating workers from underrepresented groups into the workplace. In other words, the plans give employers a framework to use as they develop their recruiting, hiring, and promotion strategies. An employer's failure to attain its goals is not in and of itself an affirmative action violation—failing to make a good faith effort to attain the goals is. Affirmative action plans should be formally stated in writing and discontinued when the goals are met.

preferential treatment
employment preference given to a member of a protected group

Although they tend to be controversial, since the establishment of affirmative action programs, women and minorities have experienced significant employment gains. In the first 25 years after the government's affirmative action efforts, the participation by blacks in the workforce increased 50 percent, and there was a 500 percent increase in the percentage of blacks holding managerial positions.[58] But the result has been far from perfect. For example, in 2017, only 27 of the S&P 500 CEOs were women.[59]

There are several key factors that determine the legal defensibility of an affirmative action plan, particularly if it requires giving preferential treatment to any subgroup. Several federal court decisions have helped to clarify some of the factors that are important in determining whether an affirmative action plan that involves preferential treatment is in violation of Title VII.[60] Affirmative action plans should:[61]

- *Be remedial.* Employers that have not been found guilty of discrimination but that do have an imbalanced workforce may be able to justify an affirmative action plan to remedy the imbalance. An employer whose workforce is representative of the available workforce will have a difficult time justifying an affirmative action plan.
- *Include nonminorities.* An affirmative action plan that excludes all members of a nonminority group would likely be found to be illegal.
- *Be temporary.* A plan should be discontinued after meeting its goals.
- *Be formalized and in writing.* Actions taken under informal affirmative action plans (those lacking formal goals or a formal statement of the actions to be taken under the plan) have been found to be discriminatory.

Rather than giving any protected group preferential treatment, it may be better for employers to identify the specific business-related characteristic they are seeking (for example, a goal to hire people with knowledge of and influence in the Hispanic community) and use it in making hiring decisions rather than using the protected characteristic itself.

All recruitment communications should include an equal opportunity/affirmative action statement or phrases or acronyms such as *EOE/AA* (Equal Opportunity Employer/Affirmative Action), *Equal Opportunity Employer*, or *An Equal Opportunity/Affirmative Action Institution*. If these statements fail to recruit the quality and range of applicants desired, a more explicit and proactive statement can be used, such as, "Applicants from underrepresented groups are strongly encouraged to apply." An excellent sample affirmative action program has been created by the Equal Employment Opportunity Commission and is available at https://www.dol.gov/ofccp/regs/compliance/AAPs/Sample_AAP_final_JRF_QA_508c.pdf.

Independent Contractors

An **independent contractor** is an individual or business that provides services to another individual or business that controls or directs only the *result* of the work. Anyone who performs services for a company is legally an employee if the company controls *what is done and how it is done*. Whether a worker is an employee or an independent contractor with respect to the company determines the legal obligations the company has to the worker.

Independent contractors must make their own Social Security contributions, pay various employment taxes, and report their income to state and federal authorities. If an employee is incorrectly classified as an independent contractor instead of an employee, the company can be liable for employment taxes for that worker, plus a penalty.[62]

The Internal Revenue Service gives the example of Vera Elm, an electrician, who submits a job estimate to a housing complex for 400 hours of electrical work at $16 per hour. Elm is to receive $1,280 every 2 weeks for the next 10 weeks, which is not an hourly payment. No matter how long it takes her to complete the work, Vera will receive $6,400. She also performs additional electrical installations for other companies under contracts that she obtained through advertisements. The IRS classifies Vera as an independent contractor.[63]

Companies can strategically use independent contractors to help control costs and quickly and temporarily increase capabilities. Independent contractors often receive higher pay than do regular employees but can still be cost-effective because they do not receive benefits. Because independent contractors are often highly skilled, they may prefer to work on a project basis for many firms rather than be a single company's employee. Independent contractors also have greater control over the work they take on and the hours they work, which can enable people to work despite responsibilities preventing them from working traditional hours.

Some organizations try to save money by wrongly classifying regular employees as independent contractors, but federal and state officials, many facing record budget deficits exacerbated by the lost unemployment insurance and workers' compensation insurance revenue resulting from this misclassification, are aggressively pursuing these companies.[64] A home improvement company was fined $328,500 in penalties by the Illinois Department of Labor for misclassifying 18 workers after pressuring them to incorporate as separate business entities.[65]

Types of Employment Lawsuits

Employers can violate employment laws at every stage of the employment relationship from recruiting to terminating. Let's now turn our attention to exploring several different types of employment lawsuits.

Sexual Harassment

Sexual harassment refers to unwelcome sexual advances, requests for favors, and other verbal or physical conduct of a sexual nature. The victim and harasser can be of the same sex or of different sexes. When made a term or condition of employment or as a basis for employment and/or advancement decisions, the EEOC recognizes **quid pro quo harassment**. If an employee is demoted because she refuses a date with her supervisor, the supervisor's conduct is clearly illegal.

When the harassment creates a hostile, intimidating, or otherwise offensive working environment, the victim can make a claim for **hostile environment harassment**. A victim of hostile environment harassment, who may or may not be the target of the harassment, may feel fearful, demeaned, or belittled. Just being sufficiently bothered by the hostile environment created by behavior, including whistling, lewd jokes, foul language, pictures, or e-mails, can fuel a successful lawsuit. Even making offensive comments to a female employee about women in general is illegal.

Both men and women are victims of sexual harassment, although over 80 percent of the charges are filed by women. What matters to the court is the conduct of the individuals involved, not their sex or the presence or absence of sexual desire. Simple teasing, offhand comments, and isolated incidents that are not very serious are not prohibited, but when it is so frequent or severe that it creates a hostile or offensive work environment or results in an adverse employment decision (such as the victim being fired), then the harassment is illegal.[66]

The harasser can be the victim's coworker, direct supervisor, a supervisor in another area, or even a client or a customer. The victim does not need to suffer economic injury for the harassment to be illegal. The employer is always responsible for harassment by a supervisor that culminates in a tangible employment action. If the harassment did not lead to a tangible employment action, the employer is liable unless it proves that: (1) it exercised reasonable care to prevent and promptly correct any harassment; and (2) the employee unreasonably failed to complain to management or to avoid harm otherwise.[67] The victim does not need to be the person harassed—anyone affected by the offensive conduct can file a charge. Retaliation for harassment complaints is also illegal.

Victims can receive both punitive and compensatory damages, including back pay, reinstatement, payment of lost benefits, and attorney's fees. If the sexual harassment included physical conduct, criminal charges may be made, and damages may be assessed against the offending individual and the employer.

The best tool to prevent sexual harassment at work is prevention. Clearly communicate to employees what sexual harassment is and that it will not be tolerated. Establishing an effective grievance or complaint process and taking immediate and appropriate action in response to employee complaints is also recommended. Some companies give employees a sexual harassment questionnaire as part of a sexual harassment audit to determine what employees do and do not know about what is allowed. The best harassment prevention courses go beyond the law. Many things are not illegal but are not respectful or appropriate either. The EEOC recommends that companies supplement harassment prevention training with initiatives that emphasize broader topics including civility and respect.[68] This chapter's case study describes how to develop an effective and legally compliant sexual harassment policy.

so what?

Because both men and women can be victims of harassment, everyone should be trained on how to prevent sexual harassment.

CASE STUDY: Developing a Sexual Harassment Policy

Sexual harassment is not only illegal, it's bad for business. In addition to the risk of sizable jury awards, sexual harassment can lower employee morale and productivity, increase turnover and absenteeism, and increase the risk of negative publicity. Sexual harassment is best dealt with proactively by developing and adhering to a zero-tolerance sexual harassment policy and training employees on what sexual harassment is and how to report it. If an organization never provided a sexual harassment policy and training to employees, it can be held liable even if it didn't know the harassment was occurring.

A sexual harassment policy should:

1. Clearly define what will not be tolerated.
2. Describe how to report incidents.
3. Describe how a subsequent investigation will be performed.

Continued

Annual training on what sexual harassment is, how to avoid it, and what to do when and if it occurs is also advised. Additional supervisor training can ensure that they understand the policies and procedures and their role in handling complaints. It is helpful to cover every type of harassment and require employees to pass a quiz proving that they understand the policy and know what behaviors are not acceptable. Keeping accurate records of when employees received the training and that they passed the evaluation will help show a court that you made a good effort to prevent sexual harassment in your workplace.

Regularly auditing the organization for the presence of sexual harassment is also a good idea. Uncovering inappropriate workplace behaviors and proactively addressing them helps to prevent harassment and minimize any associated liability. Anonymous employee surveys can help to do this, and communicate to all employees that the company takes sexual harassment seriously.

Questions:

1. How do you think sexual harassment policies are best communicated to employees?
2. What type of training do you think would be most effective in communicating what isn't allowable?
3. What do you feel is an appropriate punishment for a first-time sexual harassment offense? What about a second offense?

Disparate Treatment

disparate treatment
intentional discrimination based on a person's protected characteristic

Title VII prohibits employers from treating applicants or employees differently because of their membership in a protected group. **Disparate treatment** is intentional discrimination based on a protected characteristic. Disparate treatment occurs if an employment decision would change if the applicant's race, religion, national origin, color, sex, disability, or age were different. The consistent administration of HRM practices is thought to create an equal opportunity for everyone, not just members of protected classes.

Disparate treatment can be inferred from situational factors. To establish this type of case of discrimination, the plaintiff must show:[69]

1. That he or she belongs to a group protected from discrimination (race or gender).
2. That he or she applied for the job and was qualified for the job for which the employer was seeking applicants.
3. That despite being qualified, he or she was rejected. (The plaintiff does not need to prove that he or she was rejected because of his or her protected status, only that despite his or her qualifications, he or she was rejected.)
4. That after being rejected, the position remained open, and the employer continued to seek applicants whose qualifications were similar to those of the plaintiff.

Once these four aspects are established, the burden shifts to the company to show that the hiring decision was the result of a BFOQ based on business necessity. Demonstrable evidence of a business necessity is required. A company can offer as evidence statistical reports, validation studies, expert testimony, prior successful experience, and other evidence to that effect.

If the company is successful in establishing a BFOQ defense, the plaintiff then has the opportunity to present evidence showing that the company's stated reason for the rejection was false and merely a pretext. To establish a case allowed to go to court, the plaintiff need not prove that discrimination was the motivating factor in the hiring or promotion decision, only raise an inference that such misconduct occurred.

One of the best ways to reduce the chances of being sued is to reduce an individual's desire to file a lawsuit. If a company proactively and genuinely tries to generate applicants from diverse groups and treats all employees fairly and with respect, legal action is less likely. Alternatively, if no effort is made to recruit from diverse groups, or employees are treated unfairly or with disrespect, applicants and employees may be more motivated to take legal action. Care must also be taken to ensure that records on protected characteristics are not easily accessible during the selection process so that charges of discrimination cannot easily be made. If a hiring manager never learned of a job candidate's veteran status, it cannot have been used against him in the decision to not hire him.

Adverse Impact

Adverse impact (also called disparate impact) occurs when an employment practice has a disproportionate effect on a protected group, regardless of its intent. Employment practices that are facially neutral in their treatment of different groups but that have a significantly adverse effect on a protected group can be legally challenged. The only defense for adverse impact is when it can be justified as job related and consistent with business necessity. A job-related assessment method predicts performance in the job for which it is used.

The seminal adverse impact case is the Supreme Court's 1971 decision in *Griggs v. Duke Power Co.* The day after the Civil Rights Act of 1964 was passed, Duke Power Company changed its policy of only allowing African American workers to be laborers to instead require a high school diploma and a passing score on an "aptitude test" for promotion beyond laborer. Because this requirement disproportionately affected blacks, Willie Griggs and 12 other black employees sued under Title VII of the Civil Rights Act. The Court held that due to the difference in pass rates for white and minorities, if the Duke Power Company could not show a business necessity for requiring applicants to possess a high school diploma or pass off-the-shelf intelligence tests, the employer would be in violation of Title VII. Examples of practices that may be subject to an adverse impact challenge include written tests, educational requirements, and height and weight requirements. In larger organizations, the probability of adverse impact is greater because the larger numbers of jobs increase the chances that it will occur somewhere.

Assessment scores cannot be altered or changed to reduce the adverse impact on protected groups. According to the Civil Rights Act of 1991, it is unlawful "to adjust the scores of, use different cutoff scores for, or otherwise alter the results of employment related tests on the basis of race, color, religion, sex, or national origin." This means that **race norming**, or comparing an applicant's scores only to members of his or her own racial subgroup and setting separate passing or cutoff scores for each subgroup, is unlawful.

There are several methods of measuring adverse impact. One method is the four-fifths rule, which requires calculating if members of a protected class are selected at a rate less than four-fifths (80 percent) of that of another group. For example, imagine that 50 percent of Hispanic applicants receive a passing score on a test, but only 30 percent of African Americans pass. In this case, the target ratio would be four-fifths of the 50 percent of Hispanic applicants, or 40 percent (0.8 x 50 percent = 40 percent). Blacks were hired at a rate of 30 percent, which is less than 40 percent, violating the 80 percent rule. The 80 percent rule is not a formal legal rule and is used as more of a guide for administrative convenience. The courts also look at whether the difference between the number of members of the protected class selected and the number that would be anticipated in a random selection system is more than two or three standard deviations.

In the 2009 case of *Ricci v. DeStefano*,[70] the U.S. Supreme Court ruled that the results of assessment tests cannot be ignored simply because they have an adverse impact on a protected group. A group of white firefighters argued that the city of New Haven, Connecticut, discriminated against them by throwing out a test that white firefighters passed at a 50 percent

adverse impact (also called disparate impact)
an employment practice has a disproportionate effect on a protected group, regardless of its intent

Because adverse impact can happen accidentally, it is important to monitor for its occurrence.

race norming
comparing an applicant's scores only to members of his or her own racial subgroup and setting separate passing or cutoff scores for each subgroup

table 3.3

Disparate Treatment and Adverse Impact

Disparate Treatment	Adverse (or Disparate) Impact
Intentional discrimination	Unintentional discrimination.
Different standards for people from different protected groups	Same standards for everyone resulting in different consequences for members of at least one protected group.
Unequal treatment based on a protected characteristic	Unequal employment-related consequences for people with a protected characteristic.
Discriminatory actions or policies	Facially neutral actions or policies.

greater rate than blacks. Because test performance determined who was promoted, none of the black candidates would have advanced if the test results were allowed to stand. The court ruled that once valid selection or promotion process and selection criteria have been established, invalidating assessment results is counter to the Title VII goal of a workplace where individuals are guaranteed equal employment opportunity. This makes it critical to use high-quality job-related assessments and to apply the most valid and unbiased criteria when evaluating job candidates. Table 3.3 highlights the differences between disparate treatment and adverse impact.

Fraudulent Recruitment

fraudulent recruitment (or truth in hiring) misrepresenting the job or organization to a recruit

Fraudulent recruitment or *truth in hiring* involves misrepresenting the job or the organization to a recruit. It is important to realize that oral statements can be considered a binding contract. During periods of low unemployment among people with desired skills, employers may be tempted to exaggerate the benefits of their jobs or make unrealistic promises to attract top candidates. Doing so risks being hit with a tort lawsuit based on a theory of fraudulent inducement to hire. A tort involves a claim that someone was harmed by another party's wrongful but not necessarily criminal act and does not require the existence of a contract. Damages must generally exceed job loss in order for a plaintiff to make a successful claim. Employment fraud cases are not easy to prove, but they are becoming more frequent. In

♞ Strategic Impact

Creating a False Impression During Recruitment

The Colorado Court of Appeals upheld a $250,000 jury award against a company for hiding information from a candidate during the recruitment process. The company presented a positive picture of itself and of the plaintiff's future with it and hid its financial losses and the substantial risk that the plaintiff could soon be laid off. The court ruled that an organization may not have to divulge its financial condition to every applicant, but full disclosure is required if statements are made to an applicant that would create a "false impression" about the employer's outlook and the applicant's future employment prospects.[72]

addition to sizable jury awards, the damage to a company's reputation as an employer could undermine its future recruiting efforts.[71] This chapter's Strategic Impact feature discusses the consequences of creating a false impression during recruitment.

Statements made to convince a job applicant to accept a position can be legally binding, even when no employment contracts are involved, or if the contract states that no employment promises have been made.[73] Any actions that adversely affect a recently hired employee's compensation or status can make it look like the company acted in bad faith and potentially give rise to a fraudulent recruitment claim. In its defense, the company would have to show that unexpected events or circumstances after the person was hired justified the action.

To win a case involving an allegation of fraudulent recruitment and hiring, the plaintiff must prove five things:[74]

1. That the employer made a false representation of a material fact;
2. That the employer knew or believed the representation was false or that there was an insufficient basis for asserting that it was true;
3. That the employer intended the employee to rely on the representation;
4. That the employee justifiably relied on the representation; and
5. That the employee suffered damages as a result of doing so, such as costs related to relocating, resigning from the firm, or rejecting other offers.

It is important that all company representatives avoid making any statements about the company or the job that they know are false and avoid making any promises that the individual or company does not intend to keep.[75] Although it is only natural to want to present the job in a positive light, it is best to qualify such statements so they are not taken as guarantees.

Negligent Hiring

Negligent hiring is a tort claim based on the common law concept that an employer has a general obligation not to hire an applicant it knows or should have known could harm a third party. Essentially, a company is considered responsible for an employee's damaging actions if it failed to exercise reasonable care in hiring the employee. These issues are particularly important when the employee will have a lot of contact with the public, customers, or children, or when hiring employees whose jobs would give them access to homes and apartments—installers, delivery drivers, and the like.

A company can be found legally liable for negligent hiring if it fails to uncover a job applicant's incompetence or unfitness by checking their references, criminal records, or general background. For a customer, employee, or other third party to win a negligent hiring suit, the following must generally be shown:[76]

1. The existence of an employment relationship between the company and the worker;
2. The employee's unfitness;
3. The company's actual or constructive knowledge of the employee's unfitness (failing to investigate an employee's background can lead to a finding of constructive knowledge);
4. The employee's act or omission caused the third party's injuries; and
5. That the company's negligence in hiring the employee was the most likely cause of the plaintiff's injuries.

To reduce a company's negligent hiring risk, applicants should be required to explain any gaps in their employment histories. This chapter's HR Flexibility feature explores three of the most common employment issues facing smaller organizations.

so what?

Lying to a candidate to persuade them to join your organization can result in a lawsuit.

negligent hiring
a company is considered responsible for the damaging actions of its employees if it failed to exercise reasonable care in hiring the employee who caused the harm

so what?

Negligent hiring risks are minimized by doing a thorough assessment of job candidates, asking candidates to explain gaps in their employment histories, and conducting reference and background checks.

HR Flexibility

Employment Law Issues Facing Smaller Organizations

Although some employment laws do not apply to businesses employing less than a certain number of workers, companies of all sizes need to be aware of and comply with employment laws. Companies with as few as 14 employees are subject to at least 15 federal employment laws. Once it reaches 50 employees, an organization can be covered by at least 20 federal employment laws, not to mention any relevant state and local employment laws.

Here are some common legal errors made by small businesses:

1. *Poor documentation*: Not having the proper process and documentation in place to support a termination can lead to expensive lawsuits.
2. *Not understanding BFOQs*: Smaller organizations may be unfamiliar with or uncomfortable with using assessment methods shown to predict job performance. Not only can poor hires cost a company money by negatively affecting the quality and quantity of what it does or makes, but using nonjob-related hiring criteria can also lead to costly lawsuits if it results in adverse impact.
3. *Not training supervisors in relevant laws*: As organizations exceed 40 to 50 employees, the responsibility for HRM issues including hiring, compensation, performance evaluation, and termination often moves to the supervisors. Without appropriate training in the relevant employment laws, the chances of illegal employment practices leading to litigation increases.

Retaliation

As the Equal Employment Opportunity Commission (EEOC) explains, "A person who files a complaint or participates in an investigation of an EEO [equal employment opportunity] complaint, or who opposes an employment practice made illegal under any of the statutes enforced by EEOC, is protected from retaliation.[77] The EEOC also explains that, "Retaliation occurs when an employer, government agency, or labor organization takes an adverse action against a covered individual because he or she engaged in a protected activity."[78]

Protected activities include complaining to a supervisor about unlawful discrimination or overtime, threatening to file an employment discrimination charge, and testifying against the employer in court. Employees, applicants, and former employees are all protected from retaliation if the employer employs more than 15 to 20 people (depending on the laws used to support the claim).

The employer must have retaliated in a way that would be harmful enough to dissuade a reasonable employee from exercising a protected right against the employer. Adverse actions include refusing to give a reference, excluding the individual from meetings or training, giving a smaller raise than other employees, and giving an undeserved negative performance review. Adverse actions do not include annoyances and petty slights, such as a negative comment in an otherwise positive or neutral evaluation or not being invited to lunch. Retaliation claims are rapidly increasing. Damages can include punitive awards in the case of economic or emotional distress, wage differences if demoted, and the wages that would have been paid if terminated.[79]

? so what

If an employee engages in a protected action, it is important to ensure that they are not retaliated against to prevent legal liability.

Enforcement Agencies

Legislative bodies at the local, state, and federal levels have the power to create, amend, and eliminate laws and regulations, including those pertaining to employment. Legislative bodies also create agencies for the purposes of interpreting, administering, and enforcing these laws. The two most important federal agencies for HRM are the Equal Employment Opportunity Commission (EEOC) and the Department of Labor's Office of Federal Contract Compliance Programs.

The Equal Employment Opportunity Commission (EEOC)

The EEOC was established by Title VII of the Civil Rights Act of 1964. Its original responsibility was to receive and investigate charges of unlawful employment practices and, for those charges found to be of "reasonable cause," to try to resolve the disputes. New legislation expanded the agency's responsibilities, and in 1972, the commission was also given the power to enforce certain laws. The EEOC currently enforces the following federal statutes:

- Title VII of the Civil Rights Act
- The Age Discrimination in Employment Act (ADEA)
- The Americans with Disabilities Act (ADA)
- The Rehabilitation Act
- The Civil Rights Act
- The Equal Pay Act

Workplace discrimination complaints have been increasing. In fiscal year 2016, the EEOC resolved 97,443 private-sector workplace discrimination charges and secured over $482 million for discrimination victims.[80] The EEOC attributed the surge in charges to several factors, including economic conditions, employees' greater awareness of the law, increased diversity and demographic shifts in the labor force, improvements in the EEOC's intake practices and consumer service, and greater public accessibility. E-RACE, a summary of significant private and federal EEOC race and color cases, is available on the EEOC's website at http://www.eeoc.gov/eeoc/initiatives/e-race/caselist.cfm.

One lawsuit by the EEOC against the owner and management company for a Columbus, Texas, Roadhouse restaurant resulted in the payment of $1.4 million for victimizing a group of female employees as young as 17 years old by subjecting them to sexual harassment and then retaliating against them for complaining.[81]

In addition to enforcing equal employment laws, the EEOC encourages and facilitates voluntary compliance via tailored programs that meet the needs of employers, including small business and federal sector employers; and via programs to educate the public on EEO laws. Another good reason to ensure that recruiters and hiring managers rely on objective standards and comply with antidiscrimination laws is that the EEOC is pursuing more systemic discrimination cases, which can generate judicial damage awards that run into hundreds of millions of dollars.

EEOC remedies for intentional or unintentional employment discrimination include:

- Hiring, promotion, or job reinstatement;
- Back pay, or the pay a plaintiff is entitled to up to the time the court rendered its judgment;
- Front pay, or pay a plaintiff is entitled to between the time the judgment is reached and the time the worker returns to the place of employment;
- Reasonable accommodation; and
- Other actions that will make an individual "whole" or in the condition he or she would have been if not for the discrimination.

so what?

Workplace discrimination complaints have been increasing, and the EEOC has increased its pursuit of cases that could generate large financial awards to plaintiffs.

When the EEOC finds intentional discrimination, it can award compensatory damages for victims' actual past and future monetary losses as well as damages for mental anguish and inconvenience. Punitive damages can be awarded as a deterrent or a punishment if an employer is found to have acted with malice or reckless indifference (although not against federal, state, or local government employers). The EEOC can also require an employer to take corrective or preventive actions to cure the source of the discrimination and minimize the chance of its recurrence. The EEOC's compliance manual can be found at https://www .eeoc.gov/laws/guidance/compliance.cfm.

The EEOC requires all employers with at least 15 employees to keep employment records. Some large employers are also required to file an annual EEO-1 report depending on the number of employees and federal contracts they have.[82]

The Office of Federal Contract Compliance Programs (OFCCP)

The Office of Federal Contract Compliance Programs (OFCCP) is part of the U.S. Department of Labor.[83] The OFCCP administers and enforces three equal employment opportunity programs that apply to federal contractors and subcontractors:

1. Executive Order 11246 (later expanded by Executive Order 11375);
2. Section 503 of the Rehabilitation Act of 1973; and
3. The affirmative action provisions of the Vietnam Era Veteran's Readjustment Assistance Act of 1974.

The primary mission of the OFCCP is to ensure that federal contractors with 50 or more employees who receive $50,000 or more in grants, goods, and services from the federal government take affirmative action to promote equal employment opportunity. Covered employers must annually file appropriate affirmative action plans with the agency. The OFCCP systemically reviews employers' employment practices to make sure firms are complying with U.S. discrimination laws. Although the OFCCP conducts formal compliance evaluations, the office focuses to a greater extent on class-action discrimination.

The OFCCP undertakes compliance reviews for contractors identified by a software program as having below average female or minority employment rates. The OFCCP also reviews randomly selected contractors and those identified through complaints. The OFCCP tries to reconcile violations of affirmative action or antidiscrimination requirements with the contractor before referring the case for formal administrative enforcement. The OFCCP gives Exemplary Voluntary Efforts (EVE) and Opportunity 2000 awards to companies that demonstrate significant achievement in terms of their equal opportunity and affirmative action. Although a contractor in violation of Executive Order 11246 may have its federal contracts terminated or suspended, this is uncommon, and the contractor gets sufficient due process before this happens.

Legal Compliance Obstacles

Responding strategically to an organization's legal employment context requires leveraging laws and guidelines to employ, motivate, and retain employees who will best help the firm perform well and execute its business strategy. In addition to obeying relevant laws, organizations must also identify and reduce barriers to fairness and diversity and provide equal employment opportunities for everyone.

EEOC Identified Barriers to Equal Employment Opportunity

Many barriers to equal employment opportunity exist. In Table 3.4, we summarize some of the more common structural barriers to equal employment opportunity in a variety of HRM areas identified by the U.S. Equal Employment Opportunity Commission.[84]

table **3.4**

Barriers to Equal Employment Opportunity Identified by the EEOC[85]

Recruiting Barriers:

- Failing to advertise widely in order to attract diverse applicants.
- Recruiting practices that overlook or fail to seek all qualified individuals.
- Over-relying on informal networks for recruitment (such as employee referrals).
- Having no formal recruiting systems.

Advancement and Promotion Barriers:

- Deficient feedback, performance evaluation, and promotion processes.
- A lack of universal employee access to informal employee networks.
- Different performance standards for different classes of employees.
- Unequal access to work assignments that provide skill development, visibility, and interaction with senior managers.

Barriers in the Terms and Conditions of Employment:

- Unequal pay.
- Counterproductive behavior and harassment in the workplace.
- Employer policies that are not family friendly.
- Inflexible working hours and working conditions.
- Failure to provide reasonable accommodation to qualified individuals with disabilities.

Termination and Downsizing Barriers:

- Using unfair standards in making downsizing decisions
- Giving different types of benefits to different employees.
- Inadequate layoff planning.
- Failing to provide counseling, job placement assistance, and training to laid-off employees.

Human Biases that Create Barriers to Equal Employment Opportunity

Understanding and proactively addressing equal employment opportunity barriers can minimize their impact and reduce the chances that an organization is discriminating unintentionally or intentionally in its employment practices. Some of the most common types of human biases that contribute to discrimination are summarized in Table 3.5 and discussed in more detail next.

 so what**?**

Because employment discrimination is sometimes the result of human biases, understanding them and training employees in how to reduce their impact can promote equal employment opportunity.

table **3.5**

Human Biases that Create Obstacles to Equal Employment Opportunity

Stereotypes: Believing that everyone in a particular group shares certain characteristics or abilities or will behave in the same way.

Prejudice: Outright bigotry.

Perception of possible personal loss: Believing one will "lose out" on future employment opportunities by hiring more diverse people.

Ignorance: Being unaware of all requirements of employment law.

People are sometimes stereotyped because they have a disability, and the stereotype is often negative. The fact is that most disabilities can be easily and cheaply accommodated in the workplace, and these stereotypes can easily cause a company to overlook high quality talent. Stereotypes like this also often lead to illegal discrimination and costly lawsuits.

Stereotypes.   A stereotype is a belief that everyone in a group shares certain characteristics or will behave in the same way. For example, "all young people are lazy" and "everyone who comes to work early is a high performer" are examples of stereotypes. Stereotypes are harmful because they judge an individual based solely on his or her being part of a particular group, regardless of his or her unique identity, and are often wrong.

People may stereotype others based on their race, color, religion, national origin, sex, disability, or age. Stereotypes are often negative and, thus, adversely affect the targeted individuals by breeding subtle racism, sexism, prejudice, and discomfort. Supervisors' stereotypes of what makes a good employee can obviously adversely affect people's equal employment opportunities.

Stereotyping often occurs in rejecting an applicant as "overqualified." Assuming a highly experienced candidate will be uninterested in staying long in a lower-paying position might be true, but case law says that someone who is overqualified is, by definition, qualified and cannot be rejected on that basis. It is more appropriate to ask why the candidate is interested in the position—it may be to change careers or secure a job with less responsibility. If there is additional evidence that the individual tends to job-hop, the interviewer is no longer speculating about whether the person will stay long and has a more solid basis for the rejection.[86]

This chapter's Develop Your Skills feature will help you learn how to avoid stereotyping others.

stereotype
believing that everyone in a particular group shares certain characteristics or abilities or will behave in the same way

Prejudice.   Outright bigotry still occurs despite Title VII now having been in existence for over 40 years.[87] Even if an organization has a strong commitment to equal employment opportunity, it is possible that the beliefs and the actions of the firm's individual employees are

 Develop Your Skills

How to Avoid Stereotyping Others

Stereotypes are a natural human bias. Putting people into categories speeds up our ability to understand how to relate to new people and what to expect from new situations. Nonetheless, stereotypes are often inaccurate, harmful, and can lead to a variety of employment law violations. Here are some tips to avoid stereotyping others:

1. *Try to identify when you are likely to stereotype others.* Look around your classroom. Do you find yourself jumping to conclusions faster about some people than about others? Try to identify what characteristics about these people are causing you to stereotype them.
2. *Think about your own characteristics and how you are seen by other people.* Do you think that what others tend to believe about you is accurate? Reminding yourself of this can help you take more time to form opinions about someone until you know them better.
3. *Try to get to know people with characteristics that are less familiar to you.* It could be people with disabilities, people of different ethnicities, or even people of different ages. Take the time to talk to a wide variety of people to learn about the range of people who share any particular characteristic.
4. *Become more aware of when you are stereotyping*, and consciously avoid jumping to conclusions. When you catch yourself making a generalization about someone, make a point to gather more information about them first.

inconsistent with the organization's policies and values. Organizations can help to reduce prejudice by carefully selecting and training employees, evaluating their performance in the area of diversity and inclusion, and tracking the diversity of the candidates recruited and hired by different managers to identify possible discriminatory trends that warrant further attention.

The Perception of Possible Personal Loss.   Individuals of advantaged groups who traditionally have dominated a company's workforce may feel threatened by diversity initiatives, believing they will "lose out" on future employment opportunities. Some employees may feel that they need to protect their own career prospects by impeding others.[88] This can influence employees' willingness to refer or objectively evaluate diverse job candidates, train new hires, and develop diverse employees for advancement in the company.

These issues can be minimized when employees become aware of them and consciously try to avoid them. Thoroughly understanding the company's focus on objectivity and equal employment opportunity rather than preferential treatment for anyone can also help.

Ignorance.   Some employers, particularly smaller organizations, are not aware of all requirements of employment law and discriminate against people out of ignorance. Although it is an ineffective legal defense, organizations may not know how the law applies to them because they have received poor or inaccurate advice. Even large employers may have individual managers who are not well versed in employment laws. As noted by the EEOC, to a large degree, stereotyping feeds on ignorance, but the repercussions of ignorance go much farther than stereotyping.[89]

Many supervisors lack an understanding of employment laws and may be unaware of the antidiscrimination laws with which they need to comply. In one successful discrimination case, the U.S. Court of Appeals for the Seventh Circuit found that a car dealership's hiring managers had never been trained concerning bias laws. The court wrote, "Leaving managers with hiring authority in ignorance of the basic features of the discrimination laws is an 'extraordinary mistake' for a company to make."[90] Training supervisors in employment law compliance is an important HRM responsibility.

> *"Leaving managers with hiring authority in ignorance of the basic features of the discrimination laws is an 'extraordinary mistake' for a company to make."*
>
> —**U.S. Court of Appeals for the Seventh Circuit**

The U.S. Department of Labor has created online interactive e-tools called e-laws to provide understandable information about a variety of federal employment laws. This information is found at http://www.dol.gov/elaws/ and can be useful to HRM professionals as well as hiring and supervisory managers. It is particularly useful to small business owners who may not have the resources for a full-time HRM professional.

Summary and Application

Many employment laws were created to promote equal access to employment opportunities and fair treatment of employees. Diversity and inclusion are important to avoid legal issues and costly lawsuits but can contribute to an organization's performance as well. The federal laws reviewed in this chapter should give you a good overview of some of the most relevant employment legislation.

Some state and local laws extend similar protection as provided by federal laws to employers who are not already covered by them (often smaller companies or nongovernment contractors). Other states protect groups not covered by the federal acts or individuals who are performing civil or family duties outside of their employment. Because laws change and differ from state to state, and they evolve over time, you should always consult legal counsel to ensure compliance with current local, state, and federal regulations.

It is important to take proactive steps to promote the diversity and inclusion of all employees. In addition to educating employees on their legal responsibilities, addressing the natural biases and barriers that often exist to the accomplishment of these goals is also very helpful in accomplishing these goals.

Real World Response

Merck's Commitment to Diversity and Inclusion

Merck understands how critical diverse, dedicated, and talented employees are to its continued global success. Not only does it look for talent from diverse backgrounds, it fosters an inclusive culture that welcomes all employees' perspectives. Merck wants every employee to feel valued and never have to hide who they are.[91] The CEO communicates Merck's commitment to diversity and inclusion by sponsoring national advocacy and health organizations, participating in diversity leadership events, and giving public keynote speeches.[92]

Merck views diversity as integral to its business practices and begins by hiring diverse people with diverse backgrounds and perspectives who can collaboratively address problems from multiple viewpoints.[93] Merck engages in numerous recruiting and outreach initiatives to attract diverse job candidates, including making a $20 million commitment to the United Negro College Fund to provide biomedical research scholarships, an Alliance/Merck Hispanic Scholars program promoting science education among Hispanic students, and partnering with Hire Heroes, U.S.A. to hire disabled veterans.[94] Every employee at Merck also has the opportunity to participate in development programs that emphasize the value of diversity and inclusion to Merck.[95]

Merck also has three major resources that support its diversity strategy. First, the Global Diversity and Inclusion Center of Excellence is charged with overseeing diversity and inclusion across all of Merck's business practices. Second, Employee Business Resource Groups represent the diverse constituencies that comprise Merck's internal and external stakeholders, including its differently able, minority, interfaith, and veteran employees, and third, Merck supports Employee Resource Groups to help interested millennial, LGBT, minority, and other employees find informal mentors, work in teams that provide business insights, and serve as educational resources inside the company.[96]

Merck's diversity and inclusion efforts have been widely recognized. Merck has been named to DiversityInc Top 50 Companies for Diversity list for over 10 years,[97] named a top 50 employer by CAREERS & the disABLED Magazine,[98] and named a best place to work by Human Rights Campaign.[99] For seven consecutive years, AT&T also earned the highest score of 100 percent on the Human Rights Campaign Corporate Equality Index.[100]

Takeaway Points

1. HRM helps to control organizational risks through risk assessment and risk control. Poorly designed, documented, or executed HRM processes can create noncompliance with Section 409 of Sarbanes-Oxley as well as legal and financial risks under federal employment laws.

2. Diversity fosters creativity and innovation, and it allows a company to hire, retain, and engage the best talent. Inclusion leverages the potential of diversity by helping everyone contribute to their fullest potential.

3. A bona fide occupational qualification is a characteristic that is essential to the successful performance of a relevant job function. Under Title VII, a BFOQ can be used legally to make employment decisions, even if it results in discrimination.

4. Affirmative action involves proactive efforts to eliminate discrimination and its past effects. The goal of affirmative action is to provide employment opportunities to protected classes.

5. Disparate treatment is intentional discrimination based on a protected characteristic. Adverse impact occurs when an employment practice results in unintentional discrimination.

6. There are four common biases to equal employment opportunity. The first is stereotyping or generalizing that everyone in a certain group shares certain characteristics or behaves in the same way. The second is prejudice—outright bigotry still exists. The third is the perception of possible personal loss if a member of a previously advantaged group feels that diversity initiatives will hurt their own career prospects. The fourth is ignorance. Unless trained in them, managers and employees often do not know or understand the requirements of employment law.

Discussion Questions

1. What do you think are the biggest types of organizational risk that an effective human resource management function can help minimize? Why?

2. How would you determine that there is a particular group that needs legal protection in employment relationships? What criteria would you use to evaluate whether a particular group needs protection?

3. How can diversity improve a company's performance?

4. Why is inclusion important to leveraging the potential of diversity?

5. Do you feel that it is helpful or hurtful to have so many employment laws? Why?

6. What would you do if an employer asked you an interview question that you knew was illegal?

7. What would you do if your employer asked you to ask job candidates interview questions that you know have the potential to be used illegally?

8. Is affirmative action appropriate? Why or why not?

9. What human bias to equal employment opportunity do you feel is the most difficult to overcome? How can organizations best address this bias?

Personal Development Exercise: The Implicit Associations Bias Test

This exercise will take 15 to 20 minutes to complete. Go to Project Implicit's website at: https://implicit.harvard.edu/implicit/demo/takeatest.html. Read the preliminary information, then click on "I wish to proceed." The next page presents a menu of possible tests. Start with the Race IAT by clicking on its blue button. You will need to complete a brief survey before receiving the results of your test. After reading your results, answer the following questions.

1. Do you agree with the results of your test? Why or why not?

2. How else do you think that people can become more aware of their biases?

3. Describe three ideas to help people overcome racial bias in the workplace.

Strategic HRM Exercises

Exercise: Risk Management for Software Engineers

Nearly 75 percent of Silicon Valley computer and mathematical employees ages 35 to 44 are foreign-born.[101] Many technology companies face the risk of losing an important part of their workforce if these employees leave the United States due to political or economic changes, or if they become bored with their work. Some of the other reasons these employees might consider leaving include the ability to earn higher Western-style salaries, be near their families, and raise their children in their home cultures.[102]

Questions:

1. How would you address this risk?
2. What would you do to monitor the success of your interventions?

Exercise: Diversity Is Good for Business at EY

Global professional services firm Ernst & Young considers diversity to be essential to every part of its business and a driver of both innovation and its global brand image. The company believes that becoming an industry leader requires a flexible, inclusive environment that respects all employees and everything that they bring to the table.[103] EY believes that by celebrating their differences, talented employees from all backgrounds can make more meaningful contributions to its clients and its culture.[104]

EY invests in developing employees' cross-cultural competencies and inclusive leadership skills using tools including a Diversity & Inclusion microsite, formal learning programs, and experiential learning programs.[105] These efforts can be difficult and, at times, expensive, but the company is convinced they're worth it.[106] Leaders throughout the company are held accountable for diversity and inclusion activities and outcomes including mentoring and sponsoring and advancing diverse talent.[107]

Questions:

1. How is diversity a competitive advantage for EY?
2. How can EY use HRM to further enhance its diversity goals?

Exercise: Troublesome Interview Questions

Complete the "Are These Interview Questions Potential Legal Trouble" activity in chapter Table 3-2 on p. 76. When you've evaluated all 15 questions, review the answers in Table 3-6 below. Now choose three of the questions that could be used illegally, and reword them so that they focus on BFOQs rather than protected characteristics.

Exercise: Has Disparate Impact Occurred?

The table shows the percentage of applicants from various protected groups who were ultimately hired over the past year. Use the four-fifths rule to determine whether or not disparate impact has occurred against any protected group.

Group	Percentage of Applicants Hired
Men	21%
Women	30%
Blacks	20%
Whites	15%
Hispanics	19%
Asians	13%

Exercise: Diversity and Inclusion

View the video "BASF Diversity + Inclusion: Everyone Counts" (5:07). After watching the video, answer the following questions:

1. Why do organizations pursue diversity?
2. How do you describe the relationship between diversity and inclusion?
3. How can a commitment to diversity and inclusion improve an organization's performance?

Integrative Project

Building on what you have done so far, identify how diversity and inclusion can help your organization execute its business strategy. Think about how different types of diversity can help you better create new products and attract and serve a wider variety of customers.

Write a statement explaining your company's approach to diversity and inclusion. Then identify how you will use different HR policies, media, and technologies to communicate and reinforce your approach with your employees. Be sure to include a few metrics for evaluating the success of your ideas (e.g., the percent of new products introduced or the percentage of employees representing different groups).

table 3.6

ANSWERS: Are These Interview Questions Potential Legal Trouble?

	Question	Trouble? Y/N	Reason
1	Do you rent or own your home?	N	Not job relevant, potential adverse impact against certain groups.
2	How far is your commute?	N	Possible sex or race discrimination; instead ask if they can arrive by "start time."
3	How long have you lived here?	N	Possible discrimination based on race or ethnic background.
4	What is your current address, and how long have you lived there?	Y	Contact information, potentially job relevant.

	Question	Trouble? Y/N	Reason
5	What is your date of birth?	N	Age discrimination.
6	What school did you attend?	Y	Okay, if education is job relevant.
7	Are you married or single?	Y	You can ask this *only* after hiring for tax purposes.
8	Where were you born?	N	Possible discrimination on race, ethnic background; you can ask for a birth certificate for documentation *after* hiring.
9	What was your military discharge?	N	Discrimination against veterans; you can ask for discharge papers after hiring.
10	Have you served in the U.S. armed forces?	Y	Allowable only if military experience is a job qualification.
11	Do you prefer to be called Miss, Mrs. or Ms.?	N	Sex discrimination.
12	Are you a U.S. citizen?	N	Discrimination on race or ethnic background. You can ask if they can legally work in the United States.
13	What is the name and address of a relative to be notified in an emergency?	N	Potential discrimination based on race or ethnic background.
14	What is your height and weight?	N	Potential discrimination based on several protected characteristics (e.g., sex).
15	Can you work on Christmas?	N	Religious discrimination; instead you can ask what days can you work? Can you work our required schedule?

Video Case

Imagine overhearing one of your subordinates at Happy Time Toys make some inappropriate comments to another subordinate about her attractiveness. *What do you say or do?* Go to this book's video case, watch the challenge video for this chapter, and choose the best video response. Be sure to also view the outcomes of the two responses you didn't choose.

Discussion Questions

1. What type of harassment is Emily experiencing? Explain your answer.
2. What would you do if you overheard this type of comment between two subordinates?
3. As a CEO, how could you decrease this type of behavior in your organization? Explain your answer.

Endnotes

1. Employee Diversity. (n.d.). Merck. Retrieved February 15, 2017, from http://www.merck.com/about/how-we-operate/diversity/employee-diversity.html

2. Warren, C. (2017). Diversity and inclusion: Good for business. Merck. Retrieved February 15, 2017, from http://www.merck.com/about/featured-stories/celeste-warren.html

3. Stewart, R. W. (2010). You support diversity, but are you ethical? Examining the interactive effects of diversity and ethical climate perceptions on turnover intentions. *Journal of Business Ethics*, *99*, 453–465.

4. Apple. (2017). Inclusion & diversity. Apple.com. Retrieved February 2017, from http://www.apple.com/diversity/

5. Goldberg, S., & Dyer, C. (2012, November 29). Reassessing HR risk management. *Human Resource Executive Online*. Retrieved February 2, 2017, from http://www.hreonline.com/HRE/view/story.jhtml?id=534354685; Boselie, P., Paauwe, J., & Farndale, E. (2013). The contribution of HRM to fairness, social legitimacy and public value: Human resource governance and risk management in seven leading multinational companies. In P. Leisink, P. Boselie, D. M. Hosking, & M. van Bottenburg (Eds.) *Managing social issues: A public values perspective*, 238–257.

6. *Ibid.*

7. The Bureau of National Affairs. (2006). *Sarbanes-Oxley Act: HR's role in ensuring compliance and driving cultural change*. Washington, DC: The Bureau of National Affairs. Retrieved from February 22, 2017, from http://www.section404.org/UserFiles/File/research/28_HRs_Role_In_SOX.pdf

8. Frederickson, V., & Flett, M. (2017). Risk management and the HR executive. *Innovative Employee Solutions*. Retrieved January 27, 2017, from https://www.innovativeemployeesolutions.com/articles/risk-management-and-the-hr-executive/

9. *Ibid.*

10. *Ibid.*

11. *Ibid.*

12. Frederickson, V., & Flett, M. (2017). Risk management and the HR executive. *Innovative Employee Solutions*. Retrieved January 27, 2017, from https://www.innovativeemployeesolutions.com/articles/risk-management-and-the-hr-executive/

13. Dorfman, M. S. (2012). *Introduction to risk management and insurance* (10 ed.). Englewood Cliffs, NJ: Prentice Hall.

14. Leahy, S. (2011, January 25). Chicago car salesman fired for wearing Packers tie at work. *USA Today*. Retrieved February 25, 2017, from http://content.usatoday.com/communities/thehuddle/post/2011/01/chicago-car-salesman-fired-for-wearing-packers-tie-at-work/1?loc=interstitialskip

15. Phillips, J. M., & Gully, S. M. (2009). *Strategic staffing* (1st ed.). Upper Saddle River, NJ: Prentice Hall.

16. Forbes. (2017). *Global diversity and inclusion: Fostering innovation through a diverse workforce*, p. 11. Retrieved February 18, 2017, from http://images.forbes.com/forbesinsights/StudyPDFs/Innovation_Through_Diversity.pdf

17. Olsen, J. E., & Martins, L. L. (2012, February 28). Understanding organizational diversity management programs: A theoretical framework and directions for future research. *Journal of Organizational Behavior*. Published online. doi: 10.1002/job.1792

18. McKay, P. F., Avery, D. R., & Morris, M. A. (2008). Mean racial–ethnic differences in employee sales performance: The moderating role of diversity climate. *Personnel Psychology*, *61*, 349–374.

19. McKay, P. F., Avery, D. R., Liao, H., & Morris, M. A. (2011). Does diversity climate lead to customer satisfaction? It depends on the service climate and business unit demography. *Organization Science*, *22*, 788–803.

20. The Coca-Cola Company. (2017). Global diversity mission. Retrieved February 19, 2017, from http://www.coca-colacompany.com/our-company/diversity/global-diversity-mission

21. New York State Division of Human Rights. (2017). Guidance on familial status discrimination for employers in New York State. Retrieved November 12, 2016, from https://dhr.ny.gov/sites/default/files/pdf/guidance-familial-status-employers.pdf

22. For more information, see https://www.shrm.org/resourcesandtools/legal-and-compliance/employment-law/pages/default.aspx. Retrieved February 17, 2017.

23. See https://www.dol.gov/general/topics/posters

24. National Labor Relations Act. (2011). National Labor Relations Board. Retrieved February 11, 2017, from http://www.nlrb.gov/about_us/overview/national_labor_relations_act.aspx

25. U.S. Department of Labor. (2017). Compliance Assistance—Fair Labor Standards Act (FLSA). Retrieved February 12, 2017, from http://www.dol.gov/whd/flsa/

26. For more information, see http://www.eeoc.gov/facts/qanda.html, http://www.dol.gov/oasam/regs/statutes/2000e-16.htm and http://www.eeoc.gov/eeoc/history/35th/1990s/civilrights.html

27. See Sec. 2000e-2. [Section 703] of the Civil Rights Act of 1964. Retrieved February 11, 2017, from www.eeoc.gov/policy/vii.html

28. Sec. 703 (m) of Title VII.

29. Massengill, D. (2007). Gender as BFOQ. *Employee Relations Law Journal*, *32*, 52–65.

30. EEOC Compliance Manual Directives Transmittal. (2006, April 19). EEOC. Retrieved February 12, 2017, from http://www.eeoc.gov/policy/docs/race-color.html

31. For more information, see http://www.eeoc.gov/laws/types/age.cfm

32. See http://www.state.nj.us/lps/dcr/downloads/fact-Age-Discrimination.pdf

33. Cao, J. (2017, January 30). IBM's big jobs dodge. *Bloomberg Businessweek*, 30.

34. See http://www.eeoc.gov/laws/types/disability.cfm

35. U.S. Equal Employment Opportunity Commission. (2002). *Enforcement guidance: Reasonable accommodation and undue hardship under the Americans with Disabilities Act*. Retrieved February 12, 2017, from https://www.eeoc.gov/policy/docs/accommodation.html

36. Smith, A. (2013). OFCCP softens disabilities hiring goal. *HR Magazine*, October, 8.

37. For more information, see https://www.dol.gov/ofccp/regs/compliance/vevraa.htm and https://adata.org/factsheet/VEVRAA. Retrieved February 12, 2017.

38. Facts About Pregnancy Discrimination Equal Employment Opportunity Commission. (2008). Retrieved February 11, 2017, from www.eeoc.gov/facts/fs-preg.html

39. Equal Employment Opportunity Commission. (2009). Federal laws prohibiting job discrimination questions and answers.

Retrieved February 13, 2017, from www.eeoc.gov/facts/qanda
.html

40. Zillman, C. (2015, March 25). UPS loses Supreme Court pregnancy discrimination case. *Fortune*. Retrieved February 12, 2017, from http://fortune.com/2015/03/25/ups-pregnancy -discrimination/

41. U.S. Department of Labor. (2017). FAQs about COBRA continuation health coverage. Retrieved February 12, 2017, from https://www.dol.gov/ebsa/faqs/faq-consumer-cobra .html?links=false

42. See https://www.uscis.gov/e-verify for more information about E-Verify.

43. Kurzban, Kurzban, Weinger, Tetzeli & Pratt, PA. (2012). More federal inquiry for Chipotle in wake of I-9 raid. Retrieved February 13, 2017, from http://www.kkwtlaw.com/blog/2012/05 /more-federal-inquiry-for-chipotle-in-wake-of-i-9-raid.shtml

44. Parker, S. C., & Photopulos, T. P. (2017, February 13). Increased enforcement highlights the need for employers to have immigration compliance programs. Butler Snow LLP Retrieved February 19, 2017, from http://www.butlersnow.com/2017/02 /increased-enforcement-highlights-need-employers-immigration -compliance-programs/

45. U.S. Department of Labor. (n.d.). The Worker Adjustment and Retraining Notification Act, U.S. Department of Labor employment and training administration fact sheet. Retrieved February 18, 2017, from http://www.doleta.gov/programs /factsht/warn.htm

46. See http://www.doleta.gov/programs/factsht/warn.htm

47. For more information, see http://www.eeoc.gov/laws/types /disability.cfm, www.usdoj.gov/crt/ada/ and www.eeoc.gov/ada /amendments_notice.html

48. U.S. Equal Employment Opportunity Commission. (2016, May 13). Lowe's to pay $8.6 million to settle EEOC disability discrimination suit. Retrieved February 11, 2017, from https:// www.eeoc.gov/eeoc/newsroom/release/5-13-16.cfm

49. U.S. Department of Labor. (n.d.). Family and Medical Leave Act (2011). Retrieved February 19, 2017, from http://www.dol.gov /whd/fmla/

50. Schappel, C. (2017, March 22). Turns out HR pros & manager can be liable (personally) for FMLA violations. *HR Morning*. Retrieved March 23, 2017, from http://www.hrmorning.com /hr-managers-personally-liable-fmla-violation/?pulb=1

51. Gould, T. (2010, April 9). New exposure for HR pros under FMLA. Retrieved January 20, 2017, from http://www .hrmorning.com/new-exposure-for-hr-pros-under-fmla/

52. Elliott, R. (2010). HR managers named personally in Family Medical Leave Act (FMLA) claim get new trial. Retrieved February 18, 2017, from http://blog.reduceyourworkerscomp .com/2010/04/hr-managers-named-personally-in-family-medical -leave-act-fmla-claim-get-new-trial/#axzz102gOMUM7

53. For more information, see www.dol.gov/elaws/userra.htm

54. *Patton v. Target Corp.*, 2007 U.S. Dist. LEXIS 20712 (District of Oregon February 19, 2017).

55. Gordon, P. L. (2010, November 29). 10 tips for avoiding GINA violations. *Workplace Privacy Council* Retrieved January 26, 2011, from http://privacyblog.littler.com/2010/11/articles /genetic-information/10-tips-for-avoiding-gina-violations/; Risey, S. (2014, March 6). Do not ask! Tips for avoiding GINA claims. *Frilot, LLC*. Gordon, P. L. (2010, November 29). 10 tips for avoiding GINA violations. *Workplace Privacy Council*. Retrieved February 21, 2017, from http://privacyblog.littler. com/2010/11/articles/genetic-information/10-tips-for-avoiding -gina-violations/

56. Lucas, S. (2012, February 29). When illegal interview questions are legal. *CBS MoneyWatch*. Retrieved April 12, 2012, from http://www.cbsnews.com/8301-505125_162-57387286 /when-illegal-interview-questions-are-legal/

57. Dowling, D. C., Jr. (2004). HR is going global. *National Law Journal*, *26*, S1.

58. Andre, C., Velasquez, M., & Mazur, T. (1992). Affirmative action: Twenty-five years of controversy. *Issues in Ethics* 5, 2 (Summer 1992). Retrieved January 22, 2011, from www .scu.edu/ethics/publications/iie/v5n2/affirmative.html

59. Catalyst. (2017, February 21). Women CEOs of the S&P 500. *Catalyst*. Retrieved February 21, 2017, from http://www.catalyst. org/knowledge/women-ceos-sp-500

60. For example, *Steelworkers v. Weber*, 443 U.S. 193 (1979); *Wygant v. Jackson Board of Education*, 476 U.S. 267 (1986).

61. Based on Breaugh, J. A. (1992). *Recruitment: Science and practice*. Boston, MA: PWS-Kent Publishing Company.

62. Internal Revenue Service. (2016). Independent contractor (self-employed) or employee? Retrieved February 21, 2017, from https://www.irs.gov/businesses/small-businesses-self-employed /independent-contractor-self-employed-or-employee

63. IRS. (2016, November 7). Exempt organizations: Who is an independent contractor. *IRS*. Retrieved February 21, 2017, from https://www.irs.gov/charities-non-profits/exempt -organizations-who-is-an-independent-contractor

64. Greenhouse, S. (2010, February 18). U.S. cracks down on 'contractors' as a tax dodge. *The New York Times*, A1.

65. *Ibid*.

66. U.S. Equal Employment Opportunity Commission. (2011). Sexual harassment. Retrieved February 19, 2017, from http:// www.eeoc.gov/laws/types/sexual_harassment.cfm

67. U.S. Equal Employment Opportunity Commission. (2010). Questions and answers for small employers on employer liability for harassment by supervisors. Retrieved February 19, 2017, from https://www.eeoc.gov/policy/docs/harassment-facts.html

68. Suddath, C. (2016, November 28). Compliance videos don't stop sexual harassment. *Bloomberg Businessweek* 42–49.

69. This is known as a McDonnell "Douglas Analysis." See *McDonnell Douglas v. Green*, 411 U.S. 792, 802 (1973).

70. http://www.supremecourt.gov/

71. Breaugh, J. A. (1992). *Recruitment: Science and practice*. Boston, MA: PWS-Kent.

72. Geyelin, M., & Green, W. (1990, April 20). Companies must disclose shaky finances to some applicants. *Wall Street Journal*, B8.

73. *Agosta v. Astor,* 120 Cal. App. 4th 596 (July 12, 2004).

74. LeWitter, J. (2017). Tell the truth or face the consequences: Misrepresentations in employment law. Siegel, LeWitter, & Malkani. Retrieved February 21, 2017, from https://www.sl -employmentlaw.com/tell-the-truth-or-face-the-consequences -misrepresentations-in-em.html

75. *Ibid*.

76. Kleiman, L. S., & Kass, D. (2014). Employer liability for hiring and retaining unfit workers: How employers can minimize their risks. *Employment Relations Today*, *41*, 33–41.

77. U.S. Equal Employment Opportunity Commission. (2017). Facts about retaliation. Retrieved February 22, 2017, from https:// www.eeoc.gov/laws/types/facts-retal.cfm

78. *Ibid*.

79. *Ibid*; Deskin Law Firm. (2011). Retaliation by your employer after making an employment complaint or for whistleblowing. Retrieved February 22, 2017, from http://deskinlawfirm.com /retaliation_by_your_employer_after_making_an_employment _complaint_or_for_whistleblowing

80. U.S. Equal Employment Opportunity Commission. (2016, November 16). EEOC issues fiscal year 2016 performance report. Retrieved February 22, 2017, from https://www1 .eeoc.gov/eeoc/newsroom/release/11-16-16.cfm

81. U.S. Equal Employment Opportunity Commission. (2016, September 21). Texas Roadhouse Restaurant, management company to pay $1.4 million to settle EEOC sexual harassment and retaliation suit. Retrieved February 22, 2017, from https:// www.eeoc.gov/eeoc/newsroom/release/9-21-16b.cfm

82. U.S. Equal Employment Opportunity Commission. (2016). 2016 EEO-1 survey. Retrieved February 21, 2017, from https://www .eeoc.gov/employers/eeo1survey/

83. The OFCCP can be found online at https://www.dol.gov/ofccp/

84. U.S. Equal Employment Opportunity Commission. (1997). Best practices of private sector employers. Retrieved February 21, 2017, from https://www.eeoc.gov/eeoc/task_reports/best _practices.cfm

85. *Ibid.*

86. Hansen, F. (2006, May 23). Recruiting on the right side of the law. *Workforce*. Retrieved February 22, 2017, from http:// www.workforce.com/2006/05/23/recruiting-on-the-right-side -of-the-law/

87. U.S. Department of Labor. (1995, March). Federal glass ceiling commission, good for business: Making full use of the nation's human capital. Available online at http://www.dol.gov/oasam /programs/history/reich/reports/ceiling.htm

88. *Ibid.*

89. U.S. Equal Employment Opportunity Commission. (1997). Best practices of private sector employers. Retrieved February 21, 2017, from https://www1.eeoc.gov//eeoc/task_reports/best _practices.cfm?renderforprint=1

90. *Mathis v. Phillips Chevrolet Inc.*, 269 F.3d 771, U.S. App. (7th Cir. 2001), No. 00-1892.

91. Warren, C. (2017). Diversity and inclusion: Good for business. Merck. Retrieved February 15, 2017, from http://www.merck .com/about/featured-stories/celeste-warren.html

92. Global diversity & inclusion. (2017). Merck. Retrieved February 15, 2017, from http://www.msdresponsibility.com/employees /global-diversity-inclusion/

93. Diversity at Merck. (2017). Merck. Retrieved February 15, 2017, from http://www.merck.com/careers/diversity-at-merck.html

94. Programs and partnerships. (2017). Merck. Retrieved February 15, 2017, from http://www.merck.com/about/how-we-operate /diversity/programs-and-partnerships.html

95. *Ibid.*

96. Employee diversity. (2017). Merck. Retrieved February 15, 2017, from http://www.merck.com/about/how-we-operate /diversity/employee-diversity.html

97. No. 17 Merck & Co. (2017). Diversity Inc. Top 50. Retrieved February 15, 2017, from http://www.diversityinc.com/merck-co/

98. Diversity at Merck. (2017). Merck. Retrieved February 15, 2017, from http://www.merck.com/careers/diversity-at-merck.html

99. Best places to work 2016. (2016). *Human Rights Campaign*. Retrieved February 5, 2017, from http://www.hrc.org/resources /best-places-to-work-2016

100. Marsh, J. (2011, July 19). The facts that matter on jobs and diversity. AT&T Public Policy Blog. Retrieved April 22, 2012, from http://attpublicpolicy.com/wireless/the-facts-that-matter -on-jobs-and-diversity/

101. Giaritelli, A. (2016, February 12). 37 percent of Silicon Valley foreign-born. *Washington Examiner*. Retrieved February 18, 2017, from http://www.washingtonexaminer. com/37-percent-of-silicon-valley-foreign-born/article/2583195

102. Frederickson, V., & Flett, M. (2017). Risk management and the HR executive. *Innovative Employee Solutions*. Retrieved January 27, 2017, from https://www.innovativeemployeesolutions.com/ articles/risk-management-and-the-hr-executive/

103. Founded on inclusiveness. Strengthened by diversity. (2017). *EY*. Retrieved February 16, 2017, from http://exceptionaley.com /explore/diversity-and-inclusiveness

104. Founded on inclusiveness. Strengthened by diversity. (2017). *EY*. Retrieved February 16, 2017, from http://exceptionaley.com /explore/diversity-and-inclusiveness

105. No. 3 EY DiversityInc Top 50. (2017). *DiversityInc*. Retrieved February 25, 2017, from http://www.diversityinc.com/ey/

106. Donnelly, G. (2016, November 11). Global diversity officer at EY talks workplace inclusion post-election. *Fortune*. Retrieved February 16, 2017, from http://fortune.com /2016/11/11/global-diversity-officer-at-ey-talks-workplace -inclusion-post-election/

107. No. 3 EY DiversityInc Top 50. (2017). *DiversityInc*. Retrieved February 25, 2017, from http://www.diversityinc.com/ey/

PART 2

Planning and Staffing

chapter 4

Analyzing Work and Human Resource Planning

Learning Objectives

AFTER STUDYING THIS CHAPTER, YOU SHOULD BE ABLE TO:

1 Describe human resource planning.

2 Explain the difference between efficiency and motivational approaches to job design.

3 Describe what a job analysis is and why it is done.

4 Explain the purpose of an action plan.

5 Explain why an organization's structure is important to its performance.

6 Describe the difference between workflow analysis and business process reengineering.

Real World Challenge

Managing a Pilot Shortage at American Airlines

American Airlines, along with American Eagle and U.S. Airways Express, operates an average of nearly 6,700 flights every day to 339 destinations in 54 countries from its hubs.[1] After surviving industry consolidation, bankruptcies, and even terrorism, the largest U.S. airline is facing a new problem: It may start running out of pilots as soon as 2019.[2] Due to a variety of factors, including retirements, declining interest in the career, global aviation growth, expanded service to previously unserved cities and towns, and an increase in low-cost airlines worldwide, pilots are in short supply and high demand.[3]

Earning a pilot license can be difficult and expensive. In addition, regional airlines pay much less than their longer-haul peers despite accounting for half or more of all flying. Regional carriers are also important because they both provide a supply of pilots and feed the legacy carriers with customers on their networks.

Pilots are obviously critical to American Airlines' ability to serve its customers and safely and consistently deliver them to their destinations around the world. After reading this chapter, knowing that this pilot shortage is here and likely to worsen, what advice would you give American Airlines?

The first three chapters of this book described the importance and context of human resource management. In this section of the book, we discuss analyzing work and human resource planning. Organizational structure and workforce planning, the subject of this chapter, provides the foundation for human resource management (HRM) activities by identifying and addressing future challenges to an organization's ability to get the right talent in the right place at the right time. Proactive workforce planning ensures that the right people will be in place to successfully execute the business strategy both now and in the future.[4] In the context of our book's model, recruiting and staffing influence what employees *can* do.

The competition for talent is always fierce for smaller companies that have a more difficult time attracting candidates despite providing most new jobs in the United States.[5] In the coming years, talent challenges are expected to increase for all companies as developing countries experience lower birth rates at the same time baby boomers retire. Forecasting and planning tools help organizations manage their talent flows. By understanding their business needs, current talent, and the most promising pipelines for locating future talent, organizations can do a better job getting the right people located anywhere in the world in the right place at the right time.

Many companies do minimal forecasting and planning and simply try to fill job openings as they occur. This is obviously not ideal. As Jim Robbins, the former president and CEO of Cox Communications, explains, "We spend four months per year on the budget process, but we hardly spend any time talking about our talent, our strengths and how to leverage them, our talent needs and how to build them. Everyone is held accountable for their budget. But no one is held accountable for the strength of their talent pool. Isn't it the talent we have in each unit that drives our results? Aren't we missing something?"[6]

> *"Everyone is held accountable for their budget. But no one is held accountable for the strength of their talent pool. Isn't it the talent we have in each unit that drives our results? Aren't we missing something?"*
>
> —**Jim Robbins, former president and CEO, Cox Communications**

Strategic workforce planning helps organizations decide where to locate new plants and offices, how to invest in training, and whether to outsource certain work. It also gives HR a better understanding of workforce dynamics, enabling the proactive management of talent to ensure that business goals are met. The best performing companies focus their talent investments where they can have the biggest impact on company performance. For example, in the technology industry where software development is critical to business success, top performing companies ensure that they have star talent in their software development positions. In companies where brand management plays a more important role, top talent is concentrated there rather than evenly spread across all job types in the organization.[7]

Workforce planning can yield important results. Consider the impact of workforce planning on these companies:[8]

- Corning Inc. hired Taiwanese engineers to design and build nonproprietary portions of a multibillion-dollar plant instead of using its own more expensive U.S. engineers after an analysis indicated that offshoring would provide the greatest value.
- Chicago-based insurance company CNA Financial Corp. discovered that at its current turnover rate it would run short of underwriters in two years.
- Valero Energy secured the resources to build its talent pool in time to alleviate anticipated future talent shortages.

In this chapter, we discuss the strategic planning process and labor supply and demand forecasting. We then discuss efficiency and motivational approaches to job design, organizational structure, and workflow analysis. After reading this chapter, you will have a good understanding of how to analyze work and engage in strategic talent planning.

The Strategic Planning Process

HRM executives and corporate leaders are increasingly focusing on how to best use talent located around the world to accomplish strategic objectives. HR leaders are often involved in the strategic planning process rather than merely implementing the strategic plan after it has been developed by other organizational leaders. **Strategic planning** is a process for making decisions about an organization's long-term goals and how they are to be achieved. Without the right talent in place, most organizational goals cannot be accomplished. Given the critical role of talent in any organization's strategic execution and performance, HRM is an important part of any company's strategic plan.

Strategic plans focus on high-level decisions, including the organization's vision, mission, and core values, what businesses the organization will be in, how it will compete in those businesses, and how the organization will be structured. Some organizations choose a traditional brick-and-mortar structure, whereas other organizations are virtual, with employees interacting through technology and rarely if ever seeing each other.

An organization's **mission** is its basic purpose and the scope of its operations. Global beverage giant The Coca-Cola Company's three-part mission is:[9]

- To refresh the world;
- To inspire moments of optimism and happiness; and
- To create value and make a difference.

A company's **vision** identifies the company's long-term goals regarding what the organization wants to become and accomplish and describes its image of an ideal future. Beauty, fashion, and home product company Avon's vision is, "To be the company that best understands and satisfies the product, service and self-fulfillment needs of women—globally."[10]

An organization's **core values** are the enduring beliefs and principles that guide its decisions and goals, including corporate social responsibility and environmental sustainability. Grocer Whole Foods states that these core values are the soul of the company:[11]

- Selling the highest quality natural and organic products available;
- Satisfying, delighting, and nourishing our customers;
- Supporting team member excellence and happiness;
- Creating wealth through profits and growth;
- Serving and supporting our local and global communities;
- Practicing and advancing environmental stewardship;
- Creating ongoing win-win partnerships with our suppliers; and
- Promoting the health of our stakeholders through healthy eating education.

A company's mission, vision, and core values then inform the company's analysis of its business opportunities and threats. Analyzing the external environment, including economic conditions and competitive threats, helps any company best position itself to succeed. Organizations also analyze their internal environments to assess what they can do best and what they might be compromised at doing.

The organization then uses this information to craft its **business strategy** outlining how it will compete in a particular market. Global alcoholic beverages company Diageo's business strategy is "to deliver sustainable organic growth through the stewardship of our outstanding range of premium drink brands."[12]

so what**?**

Because of the critical role of HRM in executing any business strategy, HRM leaders should be involved in the business strategy planning process.

strategic planning
a process for making decisions about an organization's long-term goals and how they are to be achieved

mission
the organization's basic purpose and the scope of its operations

vision
long-term goals regarding what the organization wants to become and accomplish, describing its image of an ideal future

core values
the enduring beliefs and principles that guide an organization's decisions and goals

business strategy
how an organization will compete in a particular market

figure **4.1**

The Human Resource Planning Process

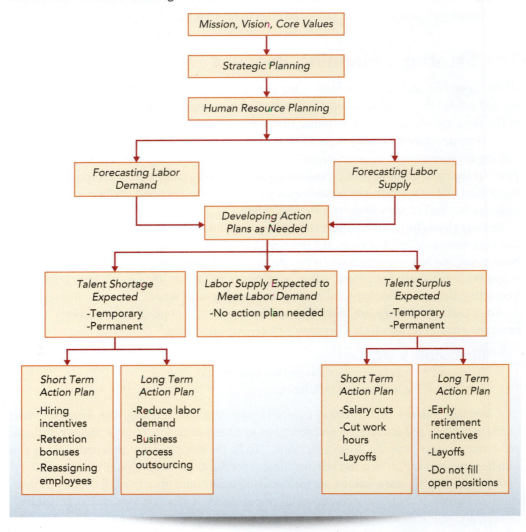

human resource planning
aligning the organization's human resources to effectively and efficiently accomplish the organization's strategic goals

After a company has identified its business strategy for competing in its marketplace, **human resource planning** aligns the organization's human resources to accomplish the organization's strategic goals. An organization's preferences and values about things such as promoting from within, retaining workers or allowing high turnover to keep payroll costs down, and treating employees as investors of their time and effort or as assets to be managed impact the nature of the firm's future labor supply and the type and number of employees it will need. The human resource planning process reconciles labor supply and demand gaps with action plans designed to help the organization manage anticipated talent surpluses or shortages. Figure 4.1 illustrates the human resource planning process.

As you can see in Figure 4.1, the human resource planning process includes four main steps:

1. *Strategic planning.* A company's strategic vision, mission, values, and strategy influence the type, quality, and quantity of skills and employees needed.
2. *Human resource planning.* Human resource planning aligns the organization's talent to effectively and efficiently accomplish the organization's strategic goals.
3. *Forecasting labor demand and labor supply.* Forecasting both expected labor demand and expected labor supply identifies any expected labor shortages or surpluses. It is also important to determine whether any gaps are expected to be short-term or long-term in duration. Online resources including the Bureau of Labor Statistics and the Department of Labor provide data and resources to assist in this type of forecasting.

4. *Developing and implementing action plans as needed*. Develop action plans to address any gaps between expected labor supply and demand. Action plans should be consistent with the firm's talent philosophy and values and include recruiting, retention, compensation, succession management, and training and development plans as needed. For example, addressing the issues related to a workforce lacking skills that will be needed in five years when the company plans to adopt a new technology might require an action plan focused on recruiting, training, and possibly compensation to motivate employees to learn the new skills.

Because forecasting is not an exact science, constructing forecasts as a range, including low, probable, and high estimates, is strongly advised. Recalculate estimates and revise action plans as the organization's talent needs and internal and external environments change. Even rapidly changing organizations will find planning to be valuable because it helps guide decisions even in the face of uncertainty.[13] Regularly evaluating the accuracy of previous forecasts helps to identify which forecasting tools to use.

At a minimum, workforce planning should be done for the jobs that add the most value to the organization and those that are critical for business strategy execution. For example, if innovation is the source of a firm's competitive advantage, then top researchers are essential. If customer service drives an organization's competitive advantage, the quality and performance of customer-facing employees is critical.[14] Workforce planning is also important for positions in which top performers significantly outperform average performers, such as sales. Ensuring that, at the very least, sufficient numbers of the right people are placed into these positions can positively impact a company's bottom line.

We next discuss labor demand and labor supply forecasting in greater detail, followed by action planning to address any forecasted gaps.

Forecasting Labor Demand

The biggest driver of an organization's need for workers is the demand for its products or services. When demand for an organization's products or services decreases, it usually needs fewer employees. If demand increases, its need for workers usually increases as well unless it outsources work or increases its use of automation. Although automation generally decreases the need for employees, it usually increases the demand for workers with the skills required to use and maintain the new technology. Nabors Industries, the world's largest onshore oil driller, expects automated drilling rigs to reduce the number of workers at each well site from 20 to 5.[15] Referring to drilling workers, Donald McLain, chairman of the industrial programs department at Victoria College in Texas, says, "It used to be you had a toolbox full of wrenches and tubing benders. Now your main tool is a laptop."[16]

Accurate forecasting requires identifying relevant and reliable predictors of business activity and quality sources of timely information for those predictors. For example, many suppliers of inputs to other companies (such as home builder suppliers or computer parts manufacturers) have methods to predict customers' orders to help them make more accurate projections about their own staffing needs. Let's turn our attention to sources of labor demand forecasting data and labor demand forecasting methods.

Sources for Forecasting Labor Demand

Firms can tap a wide variety of information to forecast the demand for what they do or make. Some predictors are specific to certain businesses or industries. For example, furniture companies might track the housing market as an indicator of future demand for home furnishings. Some of the most common types of information that can be used to evaluate general economic trends are summarized in Table 4.1.

so what?

Because point estimates are often incorrect and lack credibility, range forecasts of low, probable, and high estimates are more useful.

so what?

Focusing forecasting resources on the jobs that are the most important to business strategy execution or jobs in which high performers significantly outperform average performers is most strategic.

so what?

The demand for what an organization does or makes is the best predictor of future talent needs.

table **4.1**

Sources for Evaluating General Economic Trends

- ***Leading Economic Index***: The *Leading Economic Index*, a monthly composite economic index published by the Conference Board, is intended to signal peaks and troughs in the business cycle.

- ***Consumer Confidence Index***: The monthly Conference Board *Consumer Confidence Index* telephone survey asks 1,000 randomly selected adults questions about perceptions of job security and their willingness to spend money. This index of consumer sentiment can help predict future demand for a company's products and its resulting labor needs.

- ***Exchange rate trends***: Exchange rates reflect the cost of one country's currency in terms of another currency. By influencing the cost of raw materials, the price of the organization's exports, and the prices of competitors' imports, exchange rates influence product demand and subsequent demand for employees.

- ***Interest rate forecasts***: Interest rates reflect the cost of borrowing money. Higher interest rates make money more expensive to borrow. Accordingly, interest rates influence both consumer demand for a company's products and companies' willingness to borrow money to fund expansion plans.

Leading Economic Index.   The Conference Board's Leading Economic Index, a monthly composite economic index published by the Conference Board, is designed to signal peaks and troughs in the business cycle and forecast future economic activity.[17] When the index turns downward, it signals a coming recession. An expansion is signaled by an upward turn. The Leading Economic Index has 10 broad components, including average weekly manufacturing hours worked, stock prices, money supply, and an index of consumer expectations.

Consumer Confidence Index.   The monthly Conference Board Consumer Confidence Index measures consumer sentiment by asking randomly selected people questions about their perceptions of their job security and willingness to spend money. This index also can help predict future economic activity and thus demand for a company's products or services and associated labor needs.[18]

Exchange Rate Trends.   If a country's currency is strengthening against other currencies, it means that one unit of the country's currency translates into greater amounts of the foreign currency than when the country's currency was weaker. This means that the country's companies can import goods and materials more cheaply because one unit of the domestic currency buys more foreign goods than it used to. However, this also means that country's exported products are more expensive overseas, decreasing international demand. Competitors' imported products also become less expensive, decreasing domestic demand for the company's more expensive products. Conversely, as a country's currency weakens, the relative prices of its exported goods fall. This increases international demand for the country's products and the country's demand for workers to make them. Exchange rates can be volatile and difficult to predict in the long term. The more stable the exchange rate, the more accurate and useful product demand and labor forecasts will be.

Interest Rate Forecasts.   Higher interest rates make it more expensive for an organization to borrow money to expand and for its customers to borrow money to buy more of its products and services. Because product demand tends to decline when interest rates rise, rising interest rates generally suggest that the demand for labor will fall, and falling interest rates suggest that it will rise. For example, when interest rates rise, the demand for houses tends to decrease, decreasing the demand for skilled trade workers and mortgage specialists.

Additional Labor Demand Forecasting Sources and Metrics.   Additional economic indicators include gross domestic product (GDP), business inventories (reported by the Department of Commerce), and the monthly Purchasing Managers Index (reported by the Institute for Supply Management). Many industries, including the International Air Transport Association and the National Restaurant Association, provide their own annual industry forecasts.

Different metrics and forecasting methods work best for different industries and companies. To find the ones likely to work best, analyze past product demand with regard to various indicators to identify which best predicted actual changes in business activity. Then utilize these predictors to forecast future labor demand. Because predictors can change in how they are calculated and how well they predict, it is best to regularly reevaluate how useful different metrics are and to regularly test new ones. Appliance maker Whirlpool regularly recalculates the optimal size of its sales force to maximize profits.

The most important labor demand forecasts are for the positions and the skills that are central to the organization's future strategic execution. For example, if a retailer is consolidating its domestic bricks-and-mortar facilities but is expanding its increasingly successful online store or expanding overseas, its labor forecasts might indicate that its overall hiring will stay relatively flat. However, in light of the new strategic initiative, the company obviously will need fewer retail employees but more IT specialists and software writers. It will also need customer service employees who are technologically competent if its new Web-based initiative is likely to succeed.

so what**?**

There is no best metric or forecasting method for all companies.

Labor Demand Forecasting Methods

We next discuss three of the most common techniques used to forecast labor demand: Trend analysis, ratio analysis, and judgmental forecasting. These are summarized in Table 4.2.

Trend Analysis.   **Trend analysis** involves using relevant past employment patterns, including the employer's, the industry's, or even the nation's, to predict a company's future talent needs. For example, if a company has been growing 12 percent annually for the last eight years, it might assume that it will experience the same growth rate for the next few years. Any employment trend that is expected to continue can be useful in forecasting a firm's future labor demand.

trend analysis
using past employment patterns to predict a firm's future labor needs

Valero Energy Corporation did a trend analysis using five years of historical records to forecast its talent demand three years in advance. This enabled Valero to accurately predict turnover by location, position type, salary, employee tenure, and division.[19] So many factors can affect a company's labor demand, including its competition, the economic environment, and technology (automation might improve its productivity, for example), that trend analysis is difficult to use by itself.

Ratio Analysis.   A company's estimated level of business activity can be converted into the number of employees needed to attain this productivity level by using past **staffing ratios**. A staffing ratio is a mathematical method of calculating the number of employees needed by

staffing ratio
indexing headcount with a business metric

table **4.2**

Forecasting Labor Demand

Trend analysis: Using past patterns to predict a firm's future labor needs.

Ratio analysis: Using past relationships to forecast how many employees will be needed for different levels of business activity.

Judgmental forecasting: Relying on the expertise of people in the organization to predict a firm's future employment needs.

"indexing" headcount with a relevant business metric. For example, an accounting firm might index the number of accounting assistants to the number of accountants based on a staffing ratio of 5:3, meaning that the firm needs five assistants for every three accountants. If it plans to hire six new accountants, it will, therefore, need to hire 10 assistants.

A ratio analysis assumes a relatively fixed ratio between the number of employees needed and certain business metrics. Using actual historical patterns helps to establish a reasonable range for these ratios. The process can be used for either justifying new positions or demonstrating the need for downsizing.

This chapter's HR Flexibility feature can help you identify some of the best forecasting tools for your needs.

If the headcount–business metric ratio is expected to remain stable over the forecasting period, then simply applying the past ratio to the upcoming period can be sufficient. If the organization is experiencing a change in productivity per employee due to a new hiring system, training, or a new incentive plan, then the use of unadjusted past ratios is inappropriate. Because managers often have a good understanding of how estimates should be adjusted, their expertise should be incorporated into the process. When past ratios do not exist, the only way to generate a reasonable staffing forecast is to rely on managers' judgment.

Using Multiple Predictors.   Although ratio analyses are limited to one predictor of labor demand at a time (labor hours per unit produced, for example), more advanced statistical techniques can incorporate multiple predictors. For example, a regression analysis is a more advanced statistical technique that could use mall occupancy rates, mall traffic, and seasonal trends to forecast the number of employees needed in a retail store.

so what

Forecasting labor demand is more challenging in smaller organizations.

It is more difficult to forecast labor demand in small- and medium-size organizations because historical trends are likely to be more variable and because less historical information is typically available. Additionally, hiring a new employee in a 10-employee company means expanding the workforce by 10 percent, which may not match the growth rate of the business.

Financial services company Capital One develops three-year labor demand forecasts by anticipating business changes that will impact its talent needs. Proprietary forecast models then predict what the company's maximum sustainable size will be in each market. Capital One even does an employee zip code analysis to identify the optimum areas in which to locate to avoid poaching its own employees from existing locations.[20]

💬 HR Flexibility

Choosing a Forecasting Tool

Different forecasting tools are useful at different times and for different purposes. It is important to match the forecasting tool you use with the organization's business and to track it over time to make sure it works. Some of the ratios that can be used in estimating target head count levels include:

- Support staff per employee
- Managers to employees
- Revenue to employees
- Customers or calls per hour to employees
- Store size to employees
- Labor costs to all production costs

Judgmental Forecasting.   **Judgmental forecasting** relies on managers' expertise to predict a firm's future talent needs. Because managers are close to customers and can have a good understanding of market conditions, including their thoughts about their future staffing and employee skill levels can be very helpful.

Top-down judgmental forecasting relies on the organization's leaders and their experience and knowledge of their industry and company to make predictions about the firm's future talent needs. These estimates then become the talent goals for lower levels. In some cases, budgets may determine the firm's targeted headcount.

Bottom-up judgmental forecasting starts with lower-level managers' estimates of the firm's future talent needs. Each manager's estimates of the number and types of employees he or she will need are modified and consolidated as they move up the organization's hierarchy. Top managers then review and formalize the estimates.

Because historical trends and relationships can change, supplementing the more quantitative ratio, scatter plot, and trend forecasting methods with managerial judgment is often helpful. The quantitative methods are often used to generate initial estimates that are then adjusted based on managers' judgment.

judgmental forecasting
relies on managers' expertise to predict a firm's future employment needs

Forecasting Labor Supply

Understanding current and future skill and competency trends in the labor market helps organizations prepare to meet their future talent needs. The amount and quality of talent expected to be available when needed should be considered while formulating business strategy. Growing an Internet firm by 20 percent a year might not be possible if there aren't a sufficient number of qualified software engineers willing to work for salaries the firm is able to pay. A reasonable estimate of the projected availability of talent for key positions is important when developing a strategy that depends on a specific talent pool. This is especially true for small firms that have a harder time attracting candidates.

An organization's internal and external labor markets influence estimates of its future labor supply. We will next discuss each of these.

Forecasting the Internal Labor Market

As shown in Figure 4.2, to estimate a firm's internal talent supply at a future point in time, subtract the number of employees the firm anticipates losing (via promotions, transfers, retirements, demotions, and resignations) from the number of employees in the position at the beginning of the forecasting period. Then add the anticipated talent gains for the position (from transfers, promotions, and demotions) to this number to calculate the internal labor supply forecast. Supervising managers may also be able to estimate the percentage of their current workforce likely to be with the organization after some period of time.

figure **4.2**

Estimating Future Internal Talent Supply

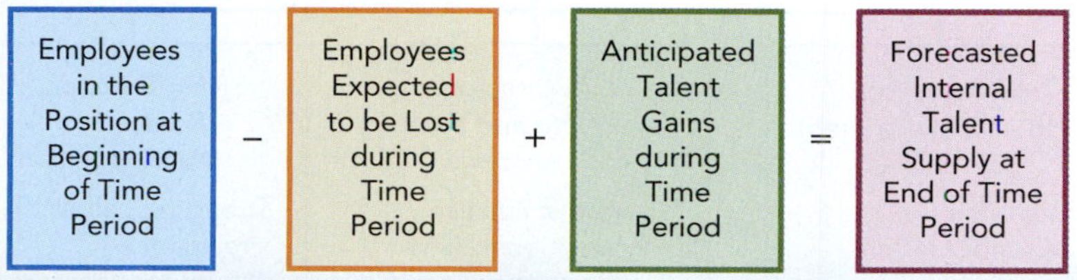

Talent inventories, replacement charts, and employee surveys are some of the methods that can be used to forecast internal talent resources, and will be explained next.

Talent inventories and replacement charts.   Forecasting a firm's future talent supply is only half of the picture. Identifying which current employees are likely to be qualified for the anticipated job openings is also important. This requires current, accurate information about employees' skills. Although identifying some internal candidates for a position might be easy, formal planning is essential to maximizing the size and quality of the internal talent pool.

Talent inventories are worksheets or databases that summarize each employee's competencies, qualifications, and anything else that can help the company understand how the employee can contribute. Talent inventories are helpful in getting the right talent in the right place as soon as it is needed.

Computerized human resource information systems can manage talent inventories and facilitate internal labor supply forecasting by matching employees' expertise with business needs and deploying talent such as a supply chain asset. IBM's Workforce Management Initiative software catalogs what employees do, their competencies, and their work history. Its computerized talent inventory then tracks the skills available to an organization and provides a minute-by-minute view of its labor supply chain.

Talent inventories are also used to create **replacement charts** to track the potential replacements for particular positions.[21] A replacement chart graphically shows current jobholders, possible successors, and each successor's readiness to assume the job, including their strengths, present performance, promotion readiness, and development needs. Figure 4.3 shows an example of a replacement chart. This tool is useful for **succession planning** or identifying, developing, and tracking employees to enable them to eventually assume higher level positions.

Employee surveys.   A company's future internal talent availability depends a great deal on retaining talent. Using employee surveys and other tools to monitor indicators of employee dissatisfaction, including employee absenteeism and complaints, can help forecast future turnover. Monitoring employees' attitudes can be critical for any company for which turnover is important to strategic execution. Many firms also conduct annual employee surveys of work attitudes, satisfaction, and engagement to identify any trends that suggest that turnover rates may rise. Google developed an algorithm that identifies which employees are most likely to quit based on performance reviews, pay histories, and promotions.[22]

The primary limitation of most forecasting techniques is their reliance on historical patterns, but if the environment changes, these past patterns may no longer be accurate. For example, an increasing unemployment rate might make employees less likely to leave the company than they were when it was easier to find another job, increasing retention and thus the internal labor supply.

talent inventories
worksheets or databases summarizing each employee's competencies, qualifications, and anything else that can help the company understand how the employee can contribute

replacement charts
graphically shows current jobholders, possible successors, and each successor's readiness to assume the job

succession planning
identifying, developing, and tracking employees to enable them to eventually assume higher level positions

? so what

Retaining talent is essential to future internal talent availability.

figure **4.3**

A Replacement Chart

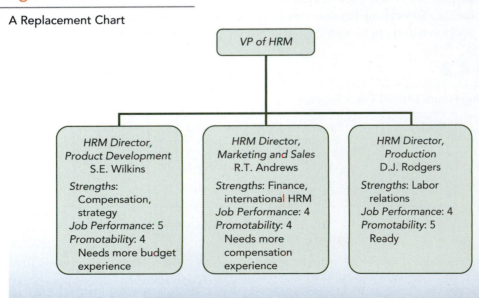

Forecasting the External Labor Market

At some point, all organizations must hire from the external labor market to either hire new employees or to replace those who leave. An organization can monitor its external labor markets in two ways. The first way is by monitoring its own experiences. For example, if the quality and quantity of applicants responding to job announcements is getting worse, this could signal a tighter labor market.

The second method of monitoring external labor markets is through the statistics generated by others. The U.S. Bureau of Labor Statistics (BLS) provides comprehensive, free data on the U.S. labor market. The BLS website (www.bls.gov) contains information on the nation's productivity, benefits, and unemployment. Its National Compensation Survey provides wage and benefit data for over 400 occupations in over 80 metropolitan and nonmetropolitan areas in the United States. This chapter's Develop Your Skills feature contains additional sources of external labor market information.

This chapter's Global Issues feature discusses some global labor market trends that could influence future economic growth.

Addressing Gaps Between the Firm's Labor Supply and Labor Demand Forecasts

Comparing the organization's forecasted labor demand with its forecasted labor supply is the next step in the workforce planning process. Also called a **gap analysis**, comparing labor and supply and demand forecasts identifies the firm's future talent needs. This information is critical to any company's future business strategy execution.

A firm could expect to have sufficient labor quantity and quality to meet its future needs, or it could forecast a talent surplus or shortage. Companies develop **action plans** to proactively address either a talent shortage or surplus. Action plans should reinforce the firm's business strategy, talent philosophy, and HR strategy. For example, if layoffs are required, they should focus on retaining the skills the company will need in the future. A company that values employees as investors of their time and talent rather than as assets to be managed might decrease everyone's work hours rather than conduct layoffs.

gap analysis
comparing labor supply and demand forecasts to identify future talent needs

action plan
a strategy for proactively addressing an expected talent shortage or surplus

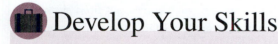 Develop Your Skills

External Labor Market Information Sources

There are many good sources of labor market information that will help you make your own labor supply and demand forecasts. Here are some of the most popular sources and their Web addresses.

- Labor Market Information by State: https://www.servicelocator.org/OWSLinks .asp
- U.S. Bureau of Labor Statistics: www.bls.gov
- U.S. Census Bureau: www.census.gov
- ISM Report on Business: http://www.ism.ws/ISMReport
- Manpower Employment Outlook Survey: http://press.manpower.com/
- Longitudinal Employer-Household Dynamics from the U.S. Census Bureau: http://lehd.did.census.gov/led
- Conference Board Data: http://www.conference-board.org/data/

🌐 Global Issues

Global Labor Market Trends

One factor in the future demand for a company's products or services is overall economic growth. An expanding global economy is generally good for business. Economic contraction suggests that overall business conditions are weakening and suggests greater potential for declining future business.

In 2016, nearly half of the workers in Southern Asia and nearly two-thirds of sub-Saharan African workers lived in extreme or moderate poverty (i.e., having less than $3.10 per day in purchasing power).[23] In 2016, global GDP growth was 3.1 percent, a six-year low. Although global unemployment levels and rates are expected to remain high in the short term, the global labor force continues to grow.[24] The U.N.'s Population Division forecasts a much slower growth in the world's labor force between now and 2030.[25] The greatest growth in the labor force is expected to occur in sub-Saharan Africa, which has the world's weakest record of long-term economic performance. Of the 2.4 billion new people forecast to be on the planet by 2050, 1.3 billion of them are expected to come from Africa.[26]

Although these trends suggest increasing pressures for slower global economic growth, improving educational opportunity and quality, improving health conditions, improving productivity, and encouraging older people to continue working may alleviate some of these pressures. Nonetheless, these global trends are worth watching.

This chapter's case study describes how a shortage of manufacturing workers in the United States is being managed through action plans.

CASE STUDY: Addressing a Shortage of U.S. Air Traffic Controllers

The Federal Aviation Administration (FAA) considers the United States to have the safest and most efficient airspace system in the world, but the U.S. air traffic control system now has the fewest certified professional controllers guiding flights in nearly 30 years. One veteran controller said, "There is an inherent risk to the system when you've got tired air traffic controllers. Overworked air traffic controllers. If they are not adequately staffed, they're working multiple shifts of overtime, ultimately what happens is mistakes are more likely to happen."[27] The controller shortage is also negatively impacting the staffing of TRACONS, the radar facilities responsible for controlling high-altitude flights.[28]

Part of the problem is due to a 2013 hiring freeze that resulted from a congressional budget fight that led to a funding cut.[29] Also, many of the thousands of controllers who were hired within a few years after President Reagan fired the nation's controller workforce in 1981 are expected to retire in the next decade.[30] These retirements have occurred at a faster rate than the FAA anticipated since the agency imposed a contract on controllers that froze their pay and lowered new hires' salaries.[31]

The FAA did not effectively plan for how many of these controllers would be retiring and from what facilities.[32] A recent wave of retirements without the hiring of replacement controllers has left fewer controllers to monitor increasing air traffic at towers and radar centers across the country.[33] Not only has the FAA missed its hiring goals for the last seven

Continued

years, the problem is likely to worsen as more controllers are currently eligible to retire than are in the pipeline to replace them.[34] Immediate actions are needed to address this gap.[35]

The FAA is aggressively seeking new applicants and is trying to hire more controllers than it needs to stay ahead of retirements and other anticipated departures, but training and certifying a new controller can take up to four years, and many new hires don't make it because the demands and stress of the job are so great.[36] The FAA predicts that 14 percent of new hires will leave in 2017, well above the 9 percent of new hires who quit in 2016.[37] The increased attrition rate of controllers in training not only undermines the FAA's efforts to increase its supply of controllers, but because it costs $78,000 to train each new controller, it also wastes a lot of money.[38]

Questions:

1. What might happen if the U.S. air traffic controller gap is not resolved?
2. What forecasting methods do you think would be most effective for forecasting air traffic controller supply and demand?
3. What suggestions do you have for closing the gap between air traffic controller supply and demand?

AT&T developed an action plan to increase the supply of potential future employees by investing $350 million in its Aspire program. The program provides grants to schools, researchers, and nonprofit organizations for initiatives targeting increasing the U.S. high school graduation rate.[39] To address the looming shortage of welders, the American Welding Society encouraged its 70,000 members to visit high schools to explain what welders do and use local media to get the word out about high-skilled, well-paid jobs in welding. They even bought a trailer with a virtual reality exhibit about welding that travels around the country to state fairs and other events. The effort is paying off, with almost twice as many kids completing welding courses two years after the effort began.[40]

It is important to try to assess whether any change in labor market conditions reflects a trend that is likely to continue or whether it is a shorter-term business cycle fluctuation. Different action plans are appropriate for each situation. If downsizing is needed, strategies that enable an organization to scale down gradually rather than abruptly through mass layoffs can help to minimize costs and retain top talent.

Talent gaps can occur quickly. When U.S. manufacturing jobs were increasingly outsourced to China and elsewhere, U.S. manufacturing labor supply outstripped demand. Increased costs in China have led to the repatriation of many of these manufacturing jobs. Now there is a shortage of U.S. talent able to operate the high-tech, productivity-enhancing robots that manufacturers are using to increase their global competitiveness. Community colleges and vocational programs are increasingly offering programs in these areas to address this gap.

Once an organization believes that it is able to secure the talent it will need to execute its business strategy and meet its growth needs, attention turns to how to design the actual jobs. This is the goal of job design, which we discuss next.

Because talent gaps can happen quickly, it is important to maintain current labor supply and demand forecasts, especially for critical jobs. Manufacturing jobs are a good example of this. Because of offshoring and the increased use of technology, the types of manufacturing skills needed in the U.S. changed in a relatively short time, leading to a shortage of workers.

Job Design

so what

Because people are motivated by different job design factors, it is helpful to be flexible in assigning people to the jobs that will best motivate them.

Different job characteristics motivate different employees. Managers who understand employees' different needs can design jobs to best fulfill those needs. For example, talented employees with a strong social need can be assigned to work with others, and those with a strong independence need can be assigned a job with more autonomy. The primary tradeoff in job design is choosing to focus on efficiency or on employee motivation.

Increasing Efficiency Through Job Design

Adam Smith's introduction of the division of labor increased interest in the best way to design jobs. In the 1890s, Frank and Lillian Gilbreth and Frederick Winslow Taylor studied the positive effects of precise instructions, goal setting, and rewards on employee motivation. Their ideas became known as **scientific management**. Scientific management breaks work down into its simplest elements and then systematically improves the worker's performance of each element.

scientific management breaks work down into its simplest elements and then systematically improves the worker's performance of each element

The foundation of scientific management is the belief that productivity is maximized when organizations are rationalized with precise sets of instructions based on time-and-motion studies. The four principles of Taylor's scientific management are:[41]

- Replace rule-of-thumb work methods with methods based on scientifically studying the tasks using time-and-motion studies;
- Scientifically select, train, and develop each worker rather than leaving them to passively train themselves;
- Managers provide detailed instructions and supervision to workers to ensure that they are following the scientifically developed methods; and
- Divide work nearly equally between workers and managers. Managers should apply scientific management principles to planning the work, and workers should perform the tasks.

so what

Focusing too much on maximizing efficiency through job design can decrease employee motivation.

Although scientific management improved productivity, it also increased the monotony of work. At its extreme, scientific management leaves no room for individual preferences or initiative, and it is not always accepted by workers. At one point, complaints that it was dehumanizing led to a congressional investigation.[42]

Increasing Motivation Through Job Design

Although pay is important to most employees, research has found only a modest relationship between pay and job satisfaction.[43] How can we improve employee motivation and job satisfaction through job design? Scholars J. Richard Hackman and Greg R. Oldham developed the job characteristics model to answer this question.

The Job Characteristics Model.   The focus of Hackman and Oldham's job characteristics model[44] is creating a good match between a person and his or her job. The **job characteristics model** proposes that objective characteristics of the job lead to job satisfaction. For example, perceiving that the work one is doing is important can improve motivation and performance.[45] If you are ever having a hard time motivating yourself to do a task, identifying how it contributes to a greater goal or how it is important in some way can increase your motivation and performance.

job characteristics model objective job characteristics including skill variety, task identity, task significance, autonomy, and task feedback, lead to job satisfaction for people with a high growth need strength

Hackman and Oldham[46] identified five characteristics on which jobs differ:

- *Skill variety*: The degree to which the job requires a variety of activities, enabling the worker to use different skills and talents.
- *Task identity*: The degree to which the job requires the worker to complete a whole and identifiable piece of work.
- *Task significance*: The degree to which job performance is important and affects the lives or work of others.

- *Autonomy*: The degree to which the job gives the worker freedom, discretion, and independence in scheduling the work and determining how to do the work.
- *Task feedback*: The degree to which carrying out the job's required activities results in the individual's obtaining direct and clear information about the effectiveness of his or her performance.

These five characteristics together determine a job's *motivating potential*.[47] But a job with a high motivating potential score is not necessarily more motivating for everyone. Not everyone wants more variety or responsibility. For people who just want to do their jobs without much thought or extra effort, stable jobs that are less complex and less demanding (i.e., jobs with a lower motivating potential score) would be more motivating.

Our *growth need strength*, derived from characteristics including our desire for advancement, reflects our desire to develop and improve ourselves. Comparing a job's motivating potential to our growth need strength score identifies our *job-person match*. Ideally, a job's motivating potential matches the employee's growth needs. Managers can improve this match through hiring the right people or by changing the motivating potential of the job.

Hackman and Oldham suggest that a good match between the needs of the person and the characteristics of the job generates three critical employee psychological states:

- Experienced meaningfulness of work;
- Experienced responsibility for work outcomes; and
- Knowledge of results of work activities.

According to Hackman and Oldham, these psychological states increase work motivation and job satisfaction. Figure 4.4 illustrates their model.

Although research has generally supported the existence of a positive relationship between the five job characteristics and job satisfaction and the role of growth need strength,[49] conceptual and methodological issues[50] in the research prevent firm conclusions from being

figure **4.4**

The Job Characteristics Model[48]

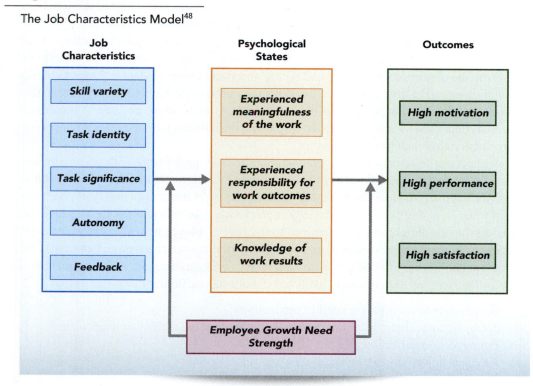

drawn.[51] Nonetheless, the job characteristics model highlights the need for managers to be aware of the role of job redesign in addressing worker motivation problems. For example, when a U.S. printing company in the Midwest organized workers into semiautonomous teams to increase worker autonomy, employees put in greater effort, used more skills, and did a better job solving problems.[52]

Recent research has highlighted the importance of interactions with the public as a key dimension of the social context of work.[53] These social interactions can enhance work motivation through positive mood and energy, decreased role ambiguity, greater social support, and performance feedback.[54]

Job Enrichment, Job Enlargement, and Job Rotation.

For many people, complex work tends to be more motivating than simple, repetitive work. Task variety, task significance, and autonomy, characteristics of motivating work proposed by the job characteristics model, are much more likely to exist when a task is complex than when it is simplified.[55] For many employees, enriching and enlarging jobs can increase employee motivation.

Job enrichment increases a job's complexity to give workers a greater sense of responsibility and achievement. Enriched jobs are usually expanded *vertically*—responsibilities previously performed by the supervisor are added to the enriched job. To enrich a job, a supervisor can introduce new or harder tasks, organize work in teams, or give employees more authority. Job enrichment gives employees more autonomy and feelings of control, and it can reduce the negative motivational effects of tasks that are repetitive or that require little autonomy.

For example, expanding a retail salesperson's job responsibilities to include managing inventory, previously done by the supervisor, enriches the job. Merely adding more tasks at the same level of responsibility and skill related to an employee's current position (*horizontal job expansion*) is considered **job enlargement**. When a secretary's job responsibilities of receiving visitors and answering phones expand to include typing letters and sorting mail, this enlarges the job. Job enlargement is not the same as job enrichment, although it can help to keep workers from getting bored.

Although performing a variety of tasks can be motivating, be careful not to put too much into any one job. When UPS discovered that the high turnover rate among its drivers was due to the exhausting task of loading packages onto the vehicle, it redesigned the job. Now separate workers handle vehicle loading, and drivers focus on making deliveries.[56]

Job rotation involves moving employees through a variety of jobs to increase their engagement and motivation. For example, a work group of three secretaries may take turns answering the phones, sorting mail, and typing and filing correspondence. **Cross-training** is usually required to give employees the skills they need to do multiple jobs. Because this enables employees to learn new skills, it can enhance motivation. Because it involves a horizontal rather than vertical expansion of job responsibilities, job rotation is a type of job enlargement rather than job enrichment.

It is important to remember that some workers actually prefer work with potentially low responsibility, autonomy, and variety over seemingly more stimulating jobs.[57] In addition to hiring workers likely to enjoy the work they will be doing, well-intentioned managers need to be careful when enriching or enlarging the jobs of people who like their jobs just the way they are.

Successful job enrichment interventions to improve employee motivation require an understanding of employee and management readiness for proposed changes, and an analysis of the job's suitability for enrichment. Although there is no guarantee that job enrichment will work as intended, job enrichment is likely to be more successful if:[58]

- Satisfaction is positively related to productivity;
- Job enrichment benefits will compensate for lower efficiencies due to decreased employee specialization;
- Changes in job content are not too expensive;

---

job enrichment
a job design approach that increases a job's complexity to give workers greater responsibility and opportunities to feel a sense of achievement

so what

Not everyone wants an enriched job.

job enlargement
adding more tasks at the same level of responsibility and skill related to an employee's current position

job rotation
workers are moved through a variety of jobs to increase their interest and motivation]]

cross-training
training employees in more than one job or in multiple skills to enable them to do different jobs

- Employees welcome changes in both job content and work relationships;
- Managers are knowledgeable about and experienced in implementing job enrichment; and
- Management understands that substantial payoffs from job enrichment usually take one to three years.

Job Analysis

Understanding what is required to perform a job well is the foundation of effective HRM. **Job analysis** is a systematic process used to identify and describe the important aspects of a job and the worker characteristics needed to succeed. Job analysis also identifies important tasks and working conditions as well as the tools and technologies used on the job. It involves making judgments about what an employee needs to do to perform a job well given the business strategy and organizational culture. Job analyses are used for multiple purposes, including:

- Determining hiring requirements
- Developing a recruiting plan
- Selecting job applicants for employment
- Creating employee training plans
- Designing compensation systems
- Developing performance evaluation tools

Research has shown that organizations that effectively utilize job analyses financially outperform their competitors.[59] This makes a lot of sense—unless you know how a job contributes to business strategy execution, it is impossible to consistently recruit and hire the talent best able to do the job, set the right performance goals, and reward the right behaviors. For example, a retail company may require store managers with specific educational and experiential backgrounds that make them best suited to contribute to the organization's specialized market niche (such as a medical devices store), but a retail company pursuing a low-cost strategy may focus on hiring efficiency minded people who are willing to work for a lower wage to keep costs down. Conduct thorough job analyses is the first step in designing effective staffing, training, performance management, and compensation systems.

Done properly, job analysis can strategically align job requirements with the company's business strategy and competitive advantage. If the job changes, new hires and employees should also be able to effectively perform the changed job. Imagine the job of marketing in the late 1990s, when the Internet was beginning to have business impact. If a company planned to soon begin using the Internet as a marketing tool, hiring someone unable to use the Internet and failing to train current employees in its use would be a poor strategic choice.

Because it objectively establishes the requirements of a job and of the person performing the job, job analysis is also the foundation of an effective legal defense against failure to hire and wrongful discharge lawsuits. Job analysis can also be helpful in designing or redesigning a job. After performing a job analysis on its sales force, General Electric learned that its salespeople were spending 80 percent of their time on bureaucratic tasks unrelated to sales. This insight allowed GE to better align its salespeople's activities with GE's goals.[60]

Sometimes the speed at which jobs change can make it difficult to cost-effectively maintain current job analyses. In this case, organizations should focus on key jobs to maximize the return on the investment.

Job Analysis Outcomes

Job analysis first identifies a job's required tasks and behaviors, and then it evaluates what is required to perform each one. Many job analysis techniques exist, most of which involve

job analysis
a systematic process used to identify and describe the important aspects of a job and the characteristics a worker needs to perform the job well

so what?

Job analysis is the foundation of HRM activities and helps improve a company's legal defensibility in certain types of lawsuits.

collecting information from job experts (typically experienced incumbents and supervisors). A job analyst then summarizes this information, and the job experts check the results for accuracy and thoroughness.

job description
written descriptions of the duties and the responsibilities of the job itself

Job Description.   The primary outcome of a job analysis is a **job description**, or a written description of the duties and the responsibilities of the job itself. Job descriptions usually include:

- Job title;
- Department;
- Salary range;
- Position grade or level;
- To whom the employee reports and for whom the employee is responsible;
- Summary of the main duties and responsibilities of the job;
- Summary of the occasional duties and responsibilities of the job;
- Any special equipment used on the job;
- Any special working conditions (e.g., weekend work or travel); and
- The statement, "Other duties as assigned" to accommodate job changes and special projects.

job task
an observable unit of work with a beginning and an end

task statements
identify in specific behavioral terms the regular duties and responsibilities of a position

A **job task** is an observable unit of work with a beginning and an end, such as sorting parts or completing a purchase order. In a job analysis, **task statements** identify in specific behavioral terms the regular duties and responsibilities of a position. Task statements are written after researching the job and interviewing multiple job experts, including incumbents, supervisors, and others with a thorough knowledge of the job.

Each task statement should describe a specific, identifiable aspect of the work performed on the target job and describe *what* the worker does, *how* the worker does it, and *for what purpose*. To comply with the Americans with Disabilities Act, task statements should focus on what needs to be done and not how it needs to be done. Try to avoid nondescriptive verbs such as "prepares" or "conducts" and be as specific as possible. Here is an example of a weak and a better task statement:

Weak: Accounts for all inventory at the end of each quarter.

Better: Accounts for all store inventory at the end of each quarter by counting the merchandise, visually comparing the amount with the accounting total, and identifying and correcting errors to balance the accounting books.

Task statements can describe a lot about a job, including:

- Physical working conditions
- Physical job requirements (e.g., how much lifting, stooping, and bending is conducted and under what conditions)
- Knowledge and skills used
- Amount of supervision authority
- Technology and tools used
- Need to work individually or as a team member.

Job descriptions are typically part of an organization's recruitment materials to inform potential candidates about the requirements and the responsibilities of the job. The most effective job descriptions capture the reader's attention and get potential recruits excited about their fit with the job and the company.

 so what

Because they also serve a recruiting function, job descriptions should be engaging and not just a list of job requirements.

Seafood restaurant chain Red Lobster feels that although job descriptions need to identify essential job functions to comply with federal laws, they don't have to be boring, so the company made its description of essential job functions engaging by incorporating the company's principles, values, and mission statement. Here is an excerpt from a Red

Lobster bartender job description: "Would you like to craft enticing drinks inspired by the sea? As a bartender at Red Lobster, you will help our guests celebrate by preparing Red Lobster signature beverages in a fun, friendly atmosphere. Responsibilities will include following recipes, upholding company specifications and standards, and keeping the bar stocked and clean."[61]

Here are some experts' tips to help you write more effective job descriptions:

- To meet the primary objective of "selling" the organization and the job to qualified candidates, provide enough information to attract their interest. Describe how the organization is unique by communicating its values, mission, and why employees enjoy working in the organization.[62]
- Include sufficient flexibility (including a statement similar to, "and any other tasks as assigned by the supervisor") so that workers are comfortable taking on new tasks when needed, helping coworkers, and proactively finding additional ways to contribute.[63]
- The job title is an important part of a job description—be sure it is as descriptive, accurate, and interesting as possible.[64]

Person Specification.   The second important outcome of a job analysis is a **person specification** based on the job description that summarizes the characteristics of someone able to perform the job. These characteristics should be as specific as possible, relate directly to the core job duties, and describe the minimum requirements essential to do the job effectively. These characteristics form the basis of the recruiting and selection strategy. A person specification helps to identify where and how to recruit and helps to identify relevant applicant assessment and screening criteria.

It is unreasonable for a person specification to describe the perfect employee who excels at every job requirement. Such people rarely exist. Prioritizing the characteristics most important to job success leads to more effective person specifications. Job holder characteristics vital to adequate job performance are called **essential criteria**, and should be used in recruiting and screening job candidates. Job holder characteristics that enhance job success but are not essential to adequate job performance are **desirable criteria** and are used to compare job candidates who possess the essential criteria.

Job-related worker characteristics are typically described in terms of knowledge (K), skills (S), abilities (A), other characteristics (O) (referred to as a group as KSAOs), and competencies. **Knowledge** is organized factual or procedural information that can be used to perform a task. Examples include knowledge of recruiting technologies and knowledge of labor law. Knowledge required for job performance should be stated as specifically as possible. Using a staffing specialist as an example, instead of "knowledge of hiring laws," it would be more appropriate to state "knowledge of Equal Employment Opportunity (EEO) and affirmative action guidelines and laws, such as The Family and Medical Leave Act." The possession of knowledge does not ensure that it will be used properly, but it can be a foundation for successful job performance. Examples of knowledge are:

- Knowledge of which vendors are best for different supplies;
- Knowledge of local building codes; and
- Knowledge of the Mandarin language.

A **skill** is the ability to use some sort of knowledge in performing a physical task. Skills often refer to psychomotor activities performed using body movements and vision, for example. A performance standard must be defined for effective job performance using any skill (e.g., 20/20 vision or folding two shirts per minute).

A person can have knowledge without skill. Imagine, for example, a child who knows about the function and use of a bicycle's pedals, handlebars, and brake but who is unable

---

person specification
summarizes the characteristics of someone able to perform the job

essential criteria
job holder characteristics that are vital to job performance

desirable criteria
job holder characteristics that may enhance job success but are not essential to adequate job performance

knowledge
organized factual or procedural information that can be applied to perform a task

so what**?**

Job candidates should first be compared on essential criteria, then on desirable criteria to ensure that the most important requirements of a job are met.

skill
the ability to use some sort of knowledge in performing a physical task; often refers to psychomotor activities

to actually ride a bike. This child would have bicycle riding knowledge but not skill. Other examples of skills are:

- Driving a truck
- Depth perception
- Manual dexterity

ability
a stable and enduring capability to perform a variety of tasks (e.g., verbal or mechanical ability

An **ability** is a stable and enduring capability to perform a variety of tasks. Abilities may be inherited, learned, or a combination of both. Abilities reflect more natural talents than do skills, including cognitive (e.g., analytical abilities), sensory (e.g., the ability to see particularly well), and physical capabilities (e.g., endurance). Some additional examples of abilities are:

- Running ability
- Quantitative ability
- Ability to repair small motors

other characteristics
a miscellaneous category for worker characteristics that are not knowledges, skills, or abilities, including personality traits, values, and work styles

Other characteristics is a miscellaneous category for worker characteristics that are not knowledges, skills, or abilities, including personality traits, values, and work styles. Examples of other characteristics are:

- Education
- Work experience
- Extroversion

It is important to identify whether each KSAO is something that new hires are expected to have or whether new hires will be trained on that dimension. If new hires will be trained on a particular KSAO, then the company only needs to hire people with the ability and the motivation to learn it, not people who already possess it.

Job Analysis Methods

Different job analysis methods vary in how they collect, analyze, document, and use job information. Some methods are better at describing the job, and some are better at describing the worker. Each method also requires different amounts of time, resources, and job expert involvement. Job analysts typically use multiple methods to best understand both job and worker requirements. It is best to think of each job analysis method as a tool that obtains different information about a job and its workers.

Two of the most important features of any job analysis method are that it be *reliable*, or replicable, and *valid*, or accurately measure what it was intended to measure. A reliable job analysis method produces the same results when it 1) is used by different job analysts for the same job; 2) uses different job experts; and 3) is done at a different time. A valid job analysis accurately captures the target job without omitting anything and without adding any irrelevant information.

We will next discuss five of the most common job analysis methods. Table 4.3 summarizes these five methods and their advantages and disadvantages.

critical incidents job analysis technique
job experts describe stories of good and poor performance to identify desirable and undesirable competencies or behaviors

Critical Incidents Technique.   The **critical incidents job analysis technique**[65] asks job experts to tell stories of good and poor performance to identify particularly desirable and undesirable competencies or behaviors. Because it focuses on extremely effective or extremely ineffective behaviors rather than typical work behaviors, the critical incidents method is typically not used by itself.

table 4.3

Summary of Five Job Analysis Methods

Job Analysis Method	Advantages	Disadvantages
Critical Incidents Technique: Job experts describe episodes of good, average, and poor performance.	• Provides examples of particularly effective or ineffective job behaviors. • The incidents are actual on-the-job behaviors and can often be crafted into interview questions.	• The narrative data (like stories) can be hard to use. • A fair amount of time and resources are necessary to gather enough incidents.
Job Elements Method: A group of job experts list and rate the important worker characteristics that influence success in the job, including knowledge, skills, abilities, and personal characteristics.	• Job experts feel more ownership because they are involved in every stage. • Efficient. • Results in well-organized documentation of both the job and the worker.	• Can be difficult to communicate the methodology.
Structured Interview Technique: Job experts supply information about the job and workers that distinguishes superior performance.	• Requires minimal time and resources.	• A job analysis professional is needed to reduce interviewer bias. • Interview data can be difficult to analyze.
Task Inventory Approach: Job experts generate a list of 50 to 200 tasks that are then grouped in categories reflecting major work functions.	• Objective. • Results in reliable description of job.	• May not identify important but infrequently displayed characteristics. • Does not identify the characteristics that distinguish superior workers.
Structured Questionnaires: Written questionnaires that assess information about worker inputs, work output, job context, and job characteristics.	• Fast and relatively cheap. • Can be used for almost any position. • Standardized so different jobs can be compared. • Produces quantitative estimates of a job's mental, perceptual, psychomotor, personality, and physical ability requirements.	• May require a high reading level. • Predetermined questions may miss unique aspects of the job or work context.

What is a critical incident? A critical incident is a story about someone's either extremely effective or ineffective work behavior.[66] For each incident, the critical incidents job analysis technique identifies:

1. The *circumstances* leading up to the event, or the context of the incident;
2. The *action* taken by the worker; and
3. The *consequences* of that action.

Critical incidents can be collected through interviews with incumbents or supervisors or by reviewing written records of job events, such as safety logs (these are usually more effective for collecting negative critical incidents). Job experts can focus on predetermined job duties or be encouraged to discuss any events they feel are significant examples of particularly effective or ineffective job performance.

The critical incidents technique is particularly useful for identifying infrequent but important work events that may be missed by other job analysis methods. It is relatively inexpensive and helps capture extreme job behaviors that help distinguish superior from average or barely acceptable workers. The collected stories of actual work events are useful for developing work sample tests and interview questions. The critical incidents job analysis technique also helps to defend against discrimination by identifying the capabilities to perform the job duties shown to be most critical to successful job performance.

job elements job analysis method
expert brainstorming sessions identify the characteristics of successful workers

Job Elements Method.   The **job elements job analysis method**[67] is used primarily with industrial occupations and lesser skilled jobs. A group of job experts brainstorms and rates the importance of various characteristics of workers successfully performing the job. The process involves:

1. Selecting a group of job experts.
2. Conducting brainstorming sessions to identify the characteristics (elements) of at least minimally successful workers.
3. Assigning weights to each element based on the following criteria:
   a. The proportion of barely acceptable workers who have the characteristic;
   b. The effectiveness of the element in selecting a superior worker;
   c. Any problems likely to occur if the element is not considered; and
   d. Practicality, or the effect that using the job element will have on the organization's ability to fill job openings.
4. Analyzing the data to identify important job elements.

structured interview technique
job experts provide information about the job during a structured interview

Structured Interview Technique.   The **structured interview technique** asks job experts to provide information about the job during a structured interview. This method can be effective when only a small number of job experts are able to participate in the job analysis, or if time is limited. Because this technique collects a relatively small amount of information, a job analysis professional should conduct the interviews to reduce the risk of interviewer bias and ensure a focus on identifying characteristics that distinguish superior workers. Possible questions that would be asked during a structured job analysis interview are, "What are the main duties and responsibilities of your position?" "How long do they take?" "How do you do them?"

task inventory approach
job experts generate a list of 50 to 200 tasks that are grouped in categories capturing major work functions

Task Inventory Approach.   The **task inventory approach** relies on job experts to generate a list of tasks (typically 50 to 200) that are subsequently grouped in categories capturing major work functions. The information is typically collected via a survey. Because the focus is on identifying typical job tasks, this technique may not identify important but infrequently displayed worker characteristics or those that distinguish superior workers. Combining the task inventory approach with other approaches can help overcome these limitations.

structured job analysis questionnaire
a list of pre-identified questions designed to analyze a job

Position Analysis Questionnaire
a copyrighted, standardized structured job analysis questionnaire

Structured Questionnaires.   A **structured job analysis questionnaire** is a list of pre-identified questions designed to analyze a job. The **Position Analysis Questionnaire**[68] (PAQ) is a copyrighted, standardized structured questionnaire designed to be used for just about any job. It assesses the information input, mental processes, work output, job context, and other job characteristics associated with a position. Because the PAQ report includes estimates of the job's requirements for mental, perceptual, psychomotor, and physical abilities, as well as the usefulness of certain personality characteristics and interests, it is very useful for designing selection systems.

The advantages of using structured questionnaires for job analysis include their speed, low cost, and the ease of objectively comparing different jobs. The disadvantages include the fact that it may be written at a high reading level, and the predetermined questions may miss unique aspects of the job or work context.

Combining Job Analytic Methods.   Job analysis methods are often combined to address the limitations in any single approach. Because of the expense, many smaller organizations opt to purchase collections of generic job descriptions or adapt job descriptions found online instead of doing their own job analyses. In addition to not providing an adequate legal defense, these options obviously do an inferior job of integrating the organization's business strategy with its talent needs.

Adequately investing in and planning a job analysis makes the results more accurate, useful, and faster to complete. The process can get complex, but it is essential that the information collected be as accurate as possible. Important professional and legal guidelines for conducting a job analysis are in the Uniform Guidelines on Employee Selection Procedures, available online.[69]

Because job analysis results influence how employees are evaluated, promoted, and rewarded, they can become politicized as participants try to influence the interpretation of the job to suit their personal goals. For example, an incumbent good at the interpersonal part of a sales position

Because no single job analysis method is perfect, different methods are usually combined to derive the most accurate understanding of the job possible given time and resource constraints.

might play up the importance of the job's interpersonal aspects, while another incumbent who excels at the administrative part of the job might play up the job's recordkeeping requirements. Identifying job experts' conflicting motivations helps the job analyst accurately interpret the job information they provide. When job experts know that multiple sources will be used to collect job information, they are often more honest.

Considering the organization's culture and business strategy and how the job fits into the organization's work flow can help identify appropriate job experts and frame how the job contributes to strategy execution and to the company's competitive advantage. Another helpful source of job information is O*NET, the government's online job classification system.[70] O*NET contains information about a wide variety of jobs. Although the job analysis information contained in O*NET must usually be modified and supplemented to fit a particular job and organization, it is a great place to begin gathering background job analysis information and identifying a job's requirements. The online resource Job Analysis[71] can also be useful resources.

Competency Modeling.   **Competency modeling**[72] is a job analysis method that identifies the worker competencies characteristic of high performance. **Competencies** are broadly defined worker characteristics that underlie successful performance or behavior on the job. Competencies can encompass multiple knowledges, skills, and attitudes. Competencies can serve the additional purpose of reinforcing an organization's culture, while KSAO statements are derived mostly by job analysts in the context of the job itself.

Because competency modeling may not identify infrequently displayed but important worker characteristics, it often supplements other job analysis methods. A competency-based job description enhances a manager's flexibility in assigning work, lengthens the life of a job description, and can allow firms to group jobs requiring similar competencies under a single job description. Table 4.4 describes some examples of competencies and jobs often requiring them.

The first step in competency modeling is identifying the organization's strategy, vision, and values. Job experts then identify the characteristics that enable an incumbent to best execute the strategy and consistently practice the company's values. If an organization's strategy requires employees to continually learn new technologies, adaptability and the ability to learn quickly can be more important than specific skills. A strategy with a large customer service component requires employees committed to integrity and customer service. The most important competencies often vary across business units and departments. The competencies required by a company's sales department, for example, are likely to differ from those required by its supply chain or finance departments.

It is generally best to keep the list of key competencies between six and 12 to facilitate using them. Accomplishing this goal may require the generation of a longer competency list at first,

so what

Job analysis experts can have conflicting motivations or unique views of a job that need to be taken into account when using the information they provide.

competency modeling identifies the worker competencies characteristic of high performance

competencies broad worker characteristics that underlie successful job performance

so what?

Using too many competencies makes it difficult to focus on what is most important to job success.

table 4.4

Competencies Related to Specific Job Environments

Competency	Job Requirement
Results focus: Ability to stay focused on and attain outcomes and results.	Complex or dynamic jobs (e.g., executives, researchers).
Customer Service: Meeting the needs of internal and external customers.	Jobs involving customer interaction (e.g., sales, cashiers, call center staff).
Leadership: Building motivation, skills, and a sense of shared purpose.	Jobs requiring supervising or influencing others (e.g., supervisory roles, team settings).
Emotional Intelligence: Ability to recognize and control one's emotions, understand others' emotions, and relate effectively to others.	Jobs requiring interpersonal interaction, negotiation, and influence (e.g., salespeople, customer service, management roles).
Interpersonal Communication: Developing and maintaining positive relationships and constructively exchanging ideas.	Jobs requiring interaction with others (e.g., most jobs).
Teamwork: Collaborating and cooperating effectively with others.	Jobs requiring employees to work in a team.

then evaluating which make the most difference to job and organizational performance. The identified competencies must be truly meaningful to job performance—there is no substitute for taking a data-driven look at which competencies influence organizational outcomes.

The greater simplicity and flexibility of competency analysis appeals to companies with rapidly changing jobs as well as to smaller firms for which traditional job analysis methods are too expensive. Because the level of rigor and documentation is less than traditional job analysis methods, it is also unclear how well the approach will withstand legal challenges.[74] Until it has withstood greater legal scrutiny, competency modeling should be combined with more traditional job analytic techniques.

Both job analysis and competency modeling techniques can be used for jobs that are changing or that do not yet exist. In these situations, the job or subject matter experts are interviewed and asked to identify the future KSAOs and competencies likely to be critical for effective performance.

 Strategic Impact

Linking Core Competencies to Job Descriptions at Dell Computer

Dell Computer Corporation does a good job linking core competencies, values, and experiences to job descriptions. Dell believes that it can teach its new executives the nuances of the computer industry, but it cannot teach them how to be effective in its dynamic environment. After reviewing data on the performance ratings and compensation levels of Dell Vice Presidents and Directors and interviewing the superiors of executives who had left or not advanced, Dell learned who had been successful and why. Their research resulted in the identification of five core competencies for executive hires: The ability to learn fast; to thrive in a changing environment; to deliver results; to solve problems; and to build teams.[73]

Job Rewards Analysis

Another type of job analysis is called **job rewards analysis**. Job rewards analysis is a job analysis technique that analyzes a job's nonmonetary **intrinsic rewards** derived from the work itself, and its **extrinsic rewards** with monetary value. Intrinsic rewards can include working with friendly colleagues and helping others. Extrinsic rewards include base pay, performance bonuses, and benefits. Intrinsic and extrinsic rewards combined are a job's **total rewards**.

Job rewards information can be used in candidate assessment to match worker motivations to the rewards offered by the job. It can also be a strategic recruiting tool. After learning what motivates a job candidate, a recruiter can focus on the job rewards most appealing to the candidate. For example, a job candidate motivated by money can be told extensively about the company's pay, benefits, and bonus system, and a job candidate motivated by developing his or her skills can be told more about the company's training, development, and continuing education programs. Global bank Barclays has this information in the benefits and rewards section of its website:

> We know what it takes to attract the best people, and that the chance to work alongside experts in the field and develop your own expertise in a multimillion-dollar facility is just part of the reward. The pace of change alone means that there's no shortage of opportunities to progress, and our commitment to training means you're always equipped for the next big move.[75]

We next turn our attention to the importance of organizational structure and workflow analysis in HRM planning.

Organizational Structure

The process of selecting and managing aspects of organizational structure to facilitate organizational goal accomplishment is called **organizational design**. Designing and redesigning the organization in response to internal and external changes is important to many firms' survival and performance.

Organizational structure is the organization's formal system of task, power, and reporting relationships. Organizational structure coordinates, controls, and motivates employees to cooperate in attaining organizational goals. Aligning the organizational structure with organizational needs generates greater efficiencies and less conflict.

Organizational structures influence employee behavior by enabling or restricting communication, teamwork, and cooperation as well as inter-group relationships. Imagine the difference between working in an organization comprised of independent work teams given the authority to make their own decisions compared to a highly centralized, bureaucratic organization in which decisions are made solely by the CEO. Your autonomy, influence, and work variety would differ greatly in each firm. Each type of structure can be effective depending on the nature of the organization and its environment, but each creates very different patterns of communication and levels of individual responsibility. A company's structure should be designed to support the behaviors, communication patterns, and teamwork required for business strategy execution. To be most satisfied in your own career, organizational structure is also something you should take into account in deciding where to pursue employment.

The Organizational Chart

Imagine that you start a business selling smartphone applications. You start by working alone but soon realize that you need help developing your ideas and getting them to market quickly, so you hire people to help you make and market your apps. When your new hires report for their first day of work, what do you do? You organize them to get the work done in the way you

---

job rewards analysis
job analysis technique that identifies the intrinsic and extrinsic rewards of a job

intrinsic rewards
are nonmonetary and derived from the work itself

extrinsic rewards
rewards with monetary value

total rewards
the combined intrinsic and extrinsic rewards of a job

so what?
Job rewards information can be useful in recruitment by providing information about how well a candidate matches the rewards offered by a job.

organizational design
selecting and managing aspects of organizational structure to facilitate organizational goal accomplishment

organizational structure
the organization's formal system of task, power, and reporting relationships

so what?
Because organizational structures influence employee behavior, communication, and teamwork, it is important to link the structure to business strategy execution needs.

figure **4.5**

Organizational Chart

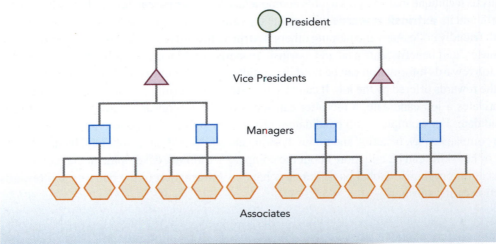

organizational chart
diagram illustrating the chain of command and reporting relationships in a company

want and need it done. You may even create an **organizational chart** such as the one shown in Figure 4.5 to illustrate the chain of command and reporting relationships in your company. Higher levels in an organizational chart supervise and are responsible for the activities and performance of the levels beneath them. HR may also play a major role in compensating the board of directors, to whom the CEO at the top of the organizational chart reports.

It is a common mistake to believe that a job's location in the organizational chart reflects its importance to the company. What matters most is what each person contributes, and people at all levels of an organization can make meaningful contributions. Think of the servers at your favorite restaurant. They may be low on the organizational chart, but imagine what would happen to the restaurant's performance if its servers were poorly trained, poorly motivated, and poorly managed. Servers have a huge impact on a restaurant's performance despite their low position on the organizational chart. As an executive vice president for global shipper FedEx said about the company's drivers, "If I don't come to work, we're OK. If they don't come to work, we're . . . out of luck."[76]

> *"If I don't come to work, we're OK. If they don't come to work, we're . . . out of luck."*
>
> **—Executive Vice President, FedEx**

Characteristics of Organizational Structure

Organizational structures reflect the company's division of labor, span of control, hierarchy, and centralization. Different structures have different levels of each of these characteristics, generating different strengths and weaknesses. Table 4.5 summarizes these characteristics.

formalization
the degree to which organizational rules, procedures, and communications are documented

Formalization.   **Formalization** reflects the degree to which organizational rules, procedures, and communications are documented.[77] In highly formalized companies, little decision-making flexibility exists, and both procedures and rewards follow explicit rules. Formalization is not necessary for high performance, but because formalization increases job and role clarity, it can increase employee commitment.[78] Motivation is increased when employees perceive that rewards are consistently allocated based on formal rules and procedures.

table **4.5**

Characteristics of Organization Structure

> **Formalization**: To what extent are organizational rules, procedures, and communications written down?
>
> **Centralization**: To what degree are power and decision-making authority concentrated at higher levels of the organization rather than distributed?
>
> **Division of labor**: Do employees specialize or generalize?
>
> **Span of control**: How many people report directly to an individual?
>
> **Hierarchy**: How much formal authority do some employees have over others?

Centralization.   When organizations are first formed, they are typically very **centralized**, concentrating power and decision-making authority at higher levels. Centralization is most effective in noncomplex, stable environments. The two subcomponents of centralization are participation in decision-making and hierarchy of authority.[79] When a company is started, the founder (or founders) typically makes all the decisions and perform a variety of tasks and roles. As employees are added, centralization creates clear lines of communication and responsibility, facilitating decision-making.

Whereas centralized organizations concentrate authority at higher levels, decentralized organizations give lower levels more authority and decision-making autonomy.[80] Because employees' greater autonomy decreases the need for middle management, decentralized organizations tend to have flatter structures with fewer organizational levels than centralized organizations. Flatter structures promote innovation and decision-making speed, and fewer management layers can save money. Decentralization is best when nonroutine tasks are performed in complex environments because the managers closest to the environment are empowered to make and quickly implement decisions.

Giving employees appropriate information and empowering them to make decisions through decentralization often benefits both the organization and its employees.[81] Employee involvement and participation increase organizational effectiveness and positive employee attitudes.[82] Decentralization also enhances organizational commitment through greater involvement and increased identification with the organization's mission and values.[83]

Organizations are rarely fully centralized or fully decentralized. Centralization is a continuum, and different functions often have different levels of centralization. When Lou Gerstner led IBM's turnaround, he said, "Let's decentralize decision-making wherever possible, but . . . we must balance decentralized decision-making with central strategy and common customer focus."[84]

Division of Labor.   Organizational charts show the company's **division of labor**, or the degree to which employees specialize. Companies with a high division of labor have more specialists who perform a well-defined set of tasks (HRM, finance, or maintenance). In general, jobs at lower organizational levels tend to be more specialized than higher levels. The division of labor is reflected in the number of job titles in an organization[85] and the extent to which specialist roles exist within each function.[86]

Division of labor increases work efficiency.[87] Specialized employees often learn their jobs faster and with less training. Specialists' expertise makes them more efficient and able to act autonomously, increasing the company's flexibility and ability to quickly adjust to environmental changes. Because division of labor tends to isolate employees, it can be more difficult for different divisions in the company to understand each other's priorities and needs. This can increase the potential for conflict.

Generalists are Often Less Expensive than Specialists.   However, because generalists are not experts, they often need more time to make decisions because they must to do additional research.

---

centralized organizations concentrate power and decision-making authority at higher levels of the organization

division of labor the degree to which employees specialize

span of control
the number of people reporting directly to an individual

Span of Control.   A manager's **span of control** is the number of people who report directly to him or her. Narrow spans of control are costlier, but they provide closer supervision, more coaching, and are necessary for novel and complex tasks. Wider spans of control are more efficient, give employees greater autonomy and self-management responsibility, and are best for routine, predictable, production-type work.

Although there is no ideal span of control, more than nine direct reports are generally considered too many to effectively manage. Technology (such as an assembly line or computerized call center management technology) that substitutes for close supervision, subordinates who need less supervision, and supervising similar jobs enable wider spans of control.

hierarchy
the degree to which some employees have formal authority over others

Hierarchy.   A **hierarchy** defines authority and supervisory relationships. Hierarchy establishes the tallness or the flatness of an organizational chart—more layers in an organization reflects greater hierarchy. Hewlett-Packard is considered to have minimal hierarchy with eight organizational levels coordinating its tens of thousands of employees.[88]

Organizations should have only as many hierarchical levels as are necessary. Too many levels create unnecessary expense and slow decision-making. Having too few levels can also cause problems—middle management layers facilitate work processes requiring control and coordination. Hierarchy also increases the risk of unethical behavior by giving too much power to a few people at the top of the organization.

Understanding the type of organizational structure you work best in can help you choose the best organization for you. If you enjoy predictability and formalized rules, you will be happier in a bureaucracy. If you enjoy innovating and want a more flexible and dynamic work environment, looking for an organization with less formalization and centralization is likely to better meet your needs.

Workflow Analysis

workflow
how work is organized to meet the organization's goals

workflow analysis
investigates how work moves through an organization to identify changes to increase efficiency and better meet customers' needs

business process reengineering
a more radical rethinking and redesign of workflow and business processes to achieve large improvements in speed, service, cost, or quality

An organization's processes have a large impact on its effectiveness. **Workflow** describes how work is organized to meet the organization's goals. Analyzing workflow is important to understanding how work creates value to a business. **Workflow analysis** investigates how work moves through an organization.

Workflow analysis starts with the customer request or order that creates a need for work to get done, to the employees whose value creation moves the product or service through the organization completing the work, to the point where the delivered order closes the loop on the work flow cycle. Workflow analysis identifies steps or jobs that can be eliminated, simplified, or even combined to increase efficiency and better meet customers' needs.

Business process reengineering is a more radical rethinking and redesigning of workflow and business processes to achieve large improvements in speed, service, cost, or quality.[89] Unlike workflow analysis, which focuses on incremental changes to existing processes, business process reengineering starts with a clean slate in identifying the best workflow for the company's needs, which may look nothing like what it is currently doing.

Although morale and productivity can be threatened during a business process reengineering, it can improve business outcomes. When Taco Bell reengineered itself to prepare the raw ingredients in central locations outside of the restaurants and utilizing restaurant employees to assemble the ingredients for each order, employee morale and product quality increased, accidents and injuries decreased, and the company decreased its costs.[90]

Because business process reengineering puts the customer at the center, it helps improve strategic execution as well as improve efficiencies. The adoption of new technology often makes the more radical process changes from business process reengineering appropriate. Because business process reengineering often results in large layoffs, and because business processes are not always the reason for a company's underperformance, caution should be taken to avoid exaggerated expectations. Business process reengineering requires a

 so what

Regularly conducting a workflow analysis maximizes efficiency and customer satisfaction.

long-term perspective and should be strategically aligned with business goals. The focus on efficiency and technology should not disregard the importance of the organization's people.[91]

Summary and Application

Carefully planning an organization's workflow and structure and forecasting labor supply and demand provide the foundation for any organization's HRM activities. Not only are efficiencies maximized, taking the time to forecast and plan helps the organization stay flexible and able to manage environmental changes.

Real World Response

Managing a Pilot Shortage at American Airlines

American Airlines is addressing its pilot shortage by increasing new pilot pay, which helps to make pilot training costs more affordable. American Airlines is also giving pilots incremental pay raises over a five-year period.[92] Although raising pay doesn't solve the industry's pilot shortage problem, it could temporarily help American Airlines' subsidiaries attract pilots from other air carriers.[93] This would move pilot shortages to lower paying airlines, however, and not remedy the industry shortage.

The effect of the increased competition on the movement of current pilots can be seen in Alaska, a state with six times more pilots per capita as the rest of the country. Competition for Alaskan pilots is pushing up salaries and luring pilots and mechanics to jobs in the lower 48 states.[94] To compete for pilots, other airlines are starting to offer signing bonuses and retention bonuses after the first year.[95] To broaden its candidate pool, Jet Blue Airways created a program called Gateway Select in which inexperienced recruits who pass a series of screenings can pay $125,000 to enter an intense four-year pilot training program, after which successful graduates get a job offer.[96]

The U.S. Air Force also faced a shortage of 750 fighter pilots at the end of 2016, up from 511 in 2015. The Air Force attributes a lot of their problem to increased hiring by commercial airlines that can offer bigger paychecks. The Air Force is addressing this deficit by reducing fighter pilot requirements, boosting retention, and increasing the number of new pilots.[97]

Takeaway Points

1. Human resource planning aligns the organization's human resources to effectively and efficiently accomplish the organization's strategic goals by reconciling labor demand and labor supply forecasts.
2. The difference between efficiency and motivational approaches to job design is that efficiency approaches focus on the most efficient way to do a job, whereas motivational approaches focus on how to make a job the most engaging for the employee.
3. A job analysis is a systematic analysis of a job and the characteristics needed by a worker to do the job well. The two primary outcomes of a job analysis are a job description that describes the duties and the responsibilities of the job and a person specification that summarizes the characteristics of someone able to perform the job.
4. An action plan proactively addresses an expected talent shortage or surplus to help the organization get the right talent in the right place at the right time.

5. Organizational structures are formal systems of task, power, and reporting relationships. A firm's organizational structure influences its employees' behavior by enabling or restricting communication, teamwork, and cooperation as well as intergroup relationships.

6. Workflow analysis investigates how work moves through an organization to enable incremental changes in efficiency and customer satisfaction. Business process reengineering has similar goals, but it is focused on more radical rethinking and redesign of business processes and may completely change what the company does.

Discussion Questions

1. Why do you think organizations might skip workforce planning? How would you overcome these obstacles if you were a manager who understood the value of doing it?

2. How would you forecast labor demand for a retail store in a local shopping mall? What sources would you use and why?

3. How would you forecast labor supply for a retail store in a local shopping mall? What sources would you use and why?

4. If you forecasted a shortage of workers for a retail store in a local shopping mall, what type of action plan would you suggest? How can that type of store find more workers?

5. Do you think it is important for employees to be familiar with their employer's organizational chart? Why or why not?

6. If you wanted to enhance the engagement and motivation of your workforce, what organizational structure characteristics would you use? How much formalization, centralization, division of labor, span of control, and hierarchy would you recommend?

7. When would you suggest that an organization engage in workflow analysis?

Personal Development Exercises

Exercise: Using O*Net

Visit https://www.onetcenter.org/, and type an occupation you would like to pursue in the Occupation Quick Search box in the top right corner (it does not need to be an HRM job). Review the job tasks, tools and technology used, and KSAOs. Also review the education, experience, and training requirements needed for the position. Also consider your fit with the work styles and values offered by this type of career. Look through the information about the position to learn more about what it takes to qualify for and succeed at that type of job.

When you get to the bottom of the summary page, you will see a section called, "Wages & Employment Trends." Click on a state of your choice to learn about the labor demand forecast for that state. If a video is provided for the position, spend a few minutes watching it. Then look through the state and national trends table to learn more about the outlook for that job in your chosen state. The employment trends information will help you to identify if job opportunities in this field are expected to increase or decrease.

When you have finished exploring your chosen job on O*NET, write a one-page report summarizing the position, its outlook, and what you feel you will need to do in the next three years to best prepare yourself for success in this career. Now set some short-term goals for how to get started in the next six months pursuing your dream career!

Exercise: Writing an Appealing Job Advertisement for an Animal Shelter Supervisor

Using the following job analysis information, create a job advertisement that makes the position sound as attractive (yet realistic) as possible to potential recruits. The goal is not to mislead candidates but rather to make the job appealing to recruits who would be a good fit. You can use pictures and create a larger job ad, or just words and create a posting that might appear on an online job board. You can use the Internet to research the wording of other job ads if you would like.

Summary

Responsible for the operation of the City's Animal Shelter, including kennel operations, health care, support services for animal care issues, and administration. Responsibilities include supervising professional, technical, and clerical personnel and volunteers.

Duties:

- Overseeing the daily operation of the city's animal care and sheltering, including animal care staff and volunteers.
- Assuring proper and humane handling of all animals with attention to their comfort, stress, and special needs.
- Assisting with front counter operations, including adoptions and customer service. Providing adoption counseling.
- Establishing and promoting a team approach with staff and direct weekly staff meetings.
- Overseeing the administration of vaccines and drugs.
- Networking with other shelters and rescue organizations to ensure the placement of all adoptable animals.
- Performing canine temperament evaluations and training other staff to perform them.
- Performing related duties as assigned.

KSAOs:

- Reading, analyzing, and interpreting common scientific and technical journals.
- Understanding dosage of chemicals, including chlorine, insecticides, and halothane.
- Applying mathematical concepts such as fractions, percentages, and ratios to practical situations.
- Defining problems, collecting data, establishing facts, and drawing valid conclusions.
- Communicating effectively both verbally and in writing.
- Establishing and maintaining effective work relationships.

Education and Experience

Education equivalent to graduation from high school. Related college course work desirable. Two years of experience in animal shelter administration, animal health care management, or animal hospital office management; this includes supervision of staff.

Strategic HRM Exercise

Exercise: Strategic Job Descriptions

Think of two companies in the same industry that pursue different business strategies and have different competitive advantages (McDonalds and Red Robin, Dunkin' Donuts and Starbucks, Neiman Marcus and Target, Wal-Mart and Tiffany). Now think of a single job that would be important to both of those companies (cashier, buyer, or customer service representative). Write a job description for each company that would be attractive to the type of person who would help the company best execute their strategy.

Exercise: The Impact of Global Trends on HRM

View the video, "Did you Know 2016" (6:56). After watching the video, answer the following questions:

1. Choose two of the trends discussed in the video and discuss how each will influence the future of jobs in HRM.
2. Which trend did you find most surprising? Why?
3. Which trend do you think will have the greatest impact on labor supply or demand? Why?

Integrative Project

Building on what you have done so far, think about a job that is critical for your chosen organization's success. Do a mini competency analysis on the position, considering the company's business strategy and competitive advantage. Do some research online to learn how similar companies are presenting their job opportunities in this area. Now write a job description that would be likely to attract a job seeker who would be a great fit with that position.

Video Case

Imagine learning that Happy Time Toys is having difficulty finding skilled manufacturing workers. If the company can't hire these workers soon, it will adversely affect the company's production schedule and profits. *What do you say or do?* Go to this book's video case, watch the challenge video for this chapter, and choose the best video response. Be sure to also view the outcomes of the two responses you didn't choose.

Discussion Questions

1. How could Happy Time Toys have better anticipated the talent shortage?
2. Which aspects of HRM discussed in this chapter are illustrated in these videos? Explain your answer.
3. How else would you handle this situation? Explain your answer

Endnotes

1. American Airlines. (2017). Investor relations. American Airlines. Retrieved February 28, 2017, from http://phx .corporate-ir.net/phoenix.zhtml?c=117098&p=irol-IRHome

2. Schlangenstein, M., & Sasso, M. (2016, June 29). Shrinking pool of future pilots keeps major airlines on edge. *Bloomberg*. Retrieved February 28, 2017, from https://www.bloomberg.com /news/articles/2016-06-29/shrinking-pool-of-future-pilots-keeps -major-airlines-on-edge

3. Pilot Career Centre, (2017). Pilot shortage 2016 and beyond. *Pilot Career Centre*. Retrieved February 28, 2017, from https://www.pilotcareercentre.com/global-pilot-shortage

4. Butler, J. E., Ferris, G. R., & Napier, N. K. (1991). *Strategy and human resources management*. Cincinnati, OH: South-Western.

5. Johnson, W. B., & Packer, A. E. (1987). *Workforce 2000: Work and workers for the 21st century*. Indianapolis, IN: Hudson Institute, Inc.

6. Handfield-Jones, H., Michaels, E., & Axelrod, B. (2001). Talent management: A critical part of every leader's job. *Ivey Business Journal* (November/December), 6.

7. Mankins, M. (2017, February 3). The best companies don't have more stars—They cluster them together. *Harvard Business Review*. Retrieved February 12, 2017, from https://hbr .org/2017/02/the-best-companies-dont-have-more-stars -they-cluster-them-together?utm_medium=email&utm _source=newsletter_weekly&utm_campaign=insider& referral=03405

8. Hirschman, C. (2007). Putting forecasting in focus. *HR Magazine*, 52, 44.

9. Mission, vision, and values. (n.d.). The Coca Cola Company. Retrieved March 1, 2017, from http://www.coca-colacompany .com/our-company/mission-vision-values

10. About Avon. (2017). Avon. Retrieved March 1, 2017, from http://avoncompany.com/aboutavon/index.html

11. Our core values. (n.d.). Whole Foods. Retrieved March 1, 2017, from http://www.wholefoodsmarket.com/company/corevalues.php

12. Our strategy. (n.d.). Diageo. Retrieved March 1, 2017, from http://www.diageo.com/en-row/ourbusiness/aboutus/Pages/our-strategy.aspx

13. Bechet, T. P., & Walker, L. W. (1993). Aligning staffing with business strategy. *Human Resource Planning*, *16*, 1–16.

14. Agrawal, V., Manyika, J. M., & Richards, J. E. (2003). Matching people to jobs. *McKinsey Quarterly,* 2.

15. Wethe, D. (2017, January 30). Drilling is back. What about the workers?" *Bloomberg Businessweek*, 14–15.

16. *Ibid.*

17. The Conference Board. (2017, February 17). Global business cycle indicators. Retrieved March 1, 2017, from http://www.conference-board.org/data/bcicountry.cfm?cid=1

18. The Conference Board. (2017, February 28). Consumer confidence survey. Retrieved February 28, 2017, from http://www.conference-board.org/data/consumerconfidence.cfm

19. Schneider, C. (2006, February 15). The new human-capital metrics. *CFO Magazine*. Retrieved March 1, 2017, from www.cfo.com/article.cfm/5491043/1/c_2984284?f=archives

20. Arend, M. (2001, July). Campus culture. *Site Selection Magazine*. Retrieved June 21, 2017, from http://siteselection.com/issues/2001/jul/p460/

21. Werther, W. B., Jr., & Davis, K. (2005). *Human resources and personnel management* (5th ed.), New York: McGraw-Hill.

22. Morrison, S. (2009, May 19). Google searches for staffing answers. *Wall Street Journal Online*. Retrieved March 1, 2017, from http://online.wsj.com/article/SB124269038041932531.html.

23. International Labour Organization. (2017). *World employment social outlook*, 2017. Geneva: International Labour Office. Retrieved March 1, 2017, from http://www.ilo.org/wcmsp5/groups/public/---dgreports/---dcomm/---publ/documents/publication/wcms_541211.pdf

24. International Labour Organization. (2017). *World employment social outlook*, 2017. Geneva: International Labour Office. Retrieved March 1, 2017, from http://www.ilo.org/wcmsp5/groups/public/---dgreports/---dcomm/---publ/documents/publication/wcms_541211.pdf

25. United Nations. (2015). Population 2030. Retrieved March 1, 2017, from http://www.un.org/en/development/desa/population/publications/pdf/trends/Population2030.pdf

26. Mohammed, O. (2015, November 13). Africa has the world's fastest-growing labor force but needs jobs growth to catch up. *Quartz*. Retrieved March 1, 2017, from https://qz.com/547929/africa-has-the-worlds-fastest-growing-labor-force-but-needs-jobs-growth-to-catch-up/

27. Stock, S., Carroll, J., & Nious, K. (2016, August 21). Crisis in air traffic control towers. *NBC Bay Area*. Retrieved March 11, 2017, from http://www.nbcbayarea.com/news/local/Crisis-in-Control-Towers-390763982.html

28. Stock, S., Carroll, J., & Nious, K. (2016, August 21). Crisis in air traffic control towers. *NBC Bay Area*. Retrieved March 11, 2017, from http://www.nbcbayarea.com/news/local/Crisis-in-Control-Towers-390763982.html

29. Isidore, C. (2016, June 15). Air traffic controller shortage could mean more flight delays. *CNN Money*. Retrieved March 11, 2017, from http://money.cnn.com/2016/06/15/news/air-traffic-controller-shortage/

30. Levin, A. (2017, March 14). Attrition rate of new air traffic controllers more than doubles. *ABC News*. Retrieved March 14, 2017, from http://abcnews.go.com/Travel/story?id=5051340&page=1

31. Levin, A. (2017, March 14). Attrition rate of new air traffic controllers more than doubles. *ABC News*. Retrieved March 14, 2017, from http://abcnews.go.com/Travel/story?id=5051340&page=1

32. Isidore, C. (2016, June 15). Air traffic controller shortage could mean more flightdDelays. *CNN Money*. Retrieved March 11, 2017, from http://money.cnn.com/2016/06/15/news/air-traffic-controller-shortage/

33. Gilbert, T. (2016, June 15). Air traffic control staffing shortage must be addressed. *The Hill*. Retrieved March 11, 2017, from http://thehill.com/blogs/congress-blog/technology/283328-air-traffic-control-staffing-shortage-must-be-addressed

34. Stock, S., Carroll, J., & Nious, K. (2016, August 21). Crisis in air traffic control towers. *NBC Bay Area*. Retrieved March 11, 2017, from http://www.nbcbayarea.com/news/local/Crisis-in-Control-Towers-390763982.html

35. Gilbert, T. (2016, June 15). Air traffic control staffing shortage must be addressed. *The Hill*. Retrieved March 11, 2017, from http://thehill.com/blogs/congress-blog/technology/283328-air-traffic-control-staffing-shortage-must-be-addressed

36. Stock, S., Carroll, J., & Nious, K. (2016, August 21). Crisis in air traffic control towers. *NBC Bay Area*. Retrieved March 11, 2017, from http://www.nbcbayarea.com/news/local/Crisis-in-Control-Towers-390763982.html

37. Levin, A. (2017, March 14). Attrition rate of new air traffic controllers more than doubles. *ABC News*. Retrieved March 14, 2017, from http://abcnews.go.com/Travel/story?id=5051340&page=1

38. Levin, A. (2017, March 14). Attrition rate of new air traffic controllers more than doubles. *ABC News*. Retrieved March 14, 2017, from http://abcnews.go.com/Travel/story?id=5051340&page=1

39. Goldman, D. (2012, April 16). AT&T's $350 million plan to groom new U.S. workers. *CNNMoney*. Retrieved March 1, 2017, from http://money.cnn.com/2012/04/16/technology/att-aspire/index.htm?iid=Lead

40. Murphy, C. (2014). Where have all the workers gone? Inc., April, 54–60.

41. Taylor, F. W. (1911). *The principles of scientific management*. New York: Harper & Brothers.

42. Spender, J. C., & Kijne, H. (1996). *Scientific management: Frederick Winslow Taylor's gift to the world*? Boston, MA: Kluwer.

43. Judge, T. A., Piccolo, R. F., Podsakoff, N. P., Shaw, J. C., & Rich, B. L. (2010). The relationship between pay and job satisfaction: A meta-analysis of the literature. *Journal of Vocational Behavior*, *77*, 157–167.

44. Hackman, J. R., & Lawler, E. E. (1971). Employee reactions to job characteristics. *Journal of Applied Psychology Monograph*, *55*, 259–286; Hackman, J. R., & Oldham, G. R. (1975). Development of the job diagnostic survey. *Journal of Applied Psychology*, *60*, 159–170; Hackman, J. R., & Oldham, G. R. (1976). Motivation through the design of work: A test of a theory. *Organizational Behavior and Human Performance*, *16*, 250–279; and Hackman, J. R., & Oldham, G. R. (1980). *Work redesign*. Reading, MA: Addison-Wesley.

45. Grant, A. M. (2008). The significance of task significance: Job performance effects, relational mechanisms, and boundary conditions. *Journal of Applied Psychology*, *93*, 108–124.

46. Hackman, J. R., & Oldham, G. R. (1975). Development of the job diagnostic survey. *Journal of Applied Psychology*, *60*, 159–170.

47. Hackman, J. R., & Oldham, G. R. (1980). *Work redesign*. Reading, MA: Addison-Wesley

48. Adapted from Hackman, J. R., & Oldham, G. R. (1975). Development of the job diagnostic survey. *Journal of Applied Psychology, 60,* 159–170.

49. Loher, B. T., Noe, R. A., Moeller, N. L., & Fitzgerald, M. P. (1985). A meta-analysis of the relation of job characteristics to job satisfaction. *Journal of Applied Psychology, 70,* 280–289.

50. Loher, B. T., Noe, R. A., Moeller, N. L., & Fitzgerald, M. P. (1985). A meta-analysis of the relation of job characteristics to job satisfaction. *Journal of Applied Psychology, 70,* 280–289; Renn, R. W., & Vandenberg, R. J. (1995). The critical psychological states: An underrepresented component in job characteristics model research. *Journal of Management, 21,* 279–303; Roberts, K. H., & Glick, W. (1981). The job characteristics approach to task design: A critical review. *Journal of Applied Psychology, 66,* 193–217; Pierce, J. L., & Dunham, R. B. (1978). The measurement of perceived job characteristics: The diagnostic survey vs. the job characteristics inventory. *Academy of Management Journal, 21,* 123–128.

51. Kanfer, R. (1990). Motivation theory and industrial and organizational psychology. In M. D. Dunnette & L. M. Hough (Eds.), *Handbook of industrial and organizational psychology,* 2nd ed., Vol. 1. Palo Alto, CA: Consulting Psychologists Press, pp. 75–170; Renn, R. W., & Vandenberg, R. J. (1995). The critical psychological states: An underrepresented component in job characteristics model research. *Journal of Management, 21,* 279–303.

52. Morgeson, F. P., Johnson, M. D., Campion, M. A., Medsker, G. J., & Mumford, T. V. (2006). Understanding reactions to job redesign: A quasi-experimental investigation of the moderating effects of organizational context on perceptions of performance behavior. *Personnel Psychology, 59,* 333–363.

53. Humphrey, S. E., Nahrgang, J. D., & Morgeson, F. P. (2007). Integrating motivational, social, and contextual work design features: A meta-analytic summary and theoretical extension of the work design literature. *Journal of Applied Psychology, 92,* 1332–1356.

54. Grandey, A. A., & Diamond, J. A. (2010). Interactions with the public: Bridging job design and emotional labor perspectives. *Journal of Organizational Behavior, 31,* 338–350.

55. Melamed, S., Ben-Avi, I., Luz, J., & Green, M. S. (1995). Objective and subjective work monotony: Effects on job satisfaction, psychological distress, and absenteeism in blue-collar workers. *Journal of Applied Psychology, 80,* 29–42.

56. Cappelli, P. (2000). A market-driven approach to retaining talent. *Harvard Business Review, 78,* 103–111.

57. Molstad, C. (1986). Choosing and coping with boring work. *Urban Life, 15,* 215–236; Forbes, J. B., & Barrett, G. V. (1978). Individual abilities and task demands in relation to performance and satisfaction on two repetitive monitoring tasks. *Journal of Applied Psychology, 63,* 188–196; Phillips, C. R., Bedeian, A. G., & Molstad, C. (1991). Repetitive work: Contrast and conflict. *The Journal of Socio-Economics, 20,* 73–82.

58. Herbert, T. T. (1976). *Organizational behavior: Readings and cases,* pp. 344–345. New York: Macmillan Publishing Co., Inc.

59. Huselid, M. A. (1995). The impact of human resource management practices on turnover, productivity, and corporate financial performance. *Academy of Management Journal, 38,* 635–672.

60. SkillsNet.com. (2007). General Electric. Retrieved April 1, 2011, from http://www.skillsnet.com/Customers.aspx

61. Red Lobster. (2017). Bartender. Retrieved March 12, 2017, from https://www.linkedin.com/jobs/view/295455015/

62. The Society for Industrial and Organizational Psychology. (n.d.). Tips for writing job descriptions. Retrieved March 1, 2017, from http://www.siop.org/Placement/TipsforWritingJobDescriptions.pdf

63. Callaway, P. (2015, March 1). Perform 'other duties as assigned' clause: Benefits and limitations. *LinkedIn.* Retrieved March 13, 2017, from https://www.linkedin.com/pulse/perform-other-duties-assigned-clause-benefits-callaway-phd-

64. Deering, S. (2017). 7 tips to writing an effective job description. *Undercover Recruiter.* Retrieved March 11, 2017, from http://theundercoverrecruiter.com/write-effective-job-description/

65. Flanagan, J. C. (1954). The critical incident technique. *Psychological Bulletin, 51,* 327–359.

66. *Ibid.*

67. Primoff, E. S. (1975). How to prepare and conduct job element examinations. Washington, DC: U.S. Government Printing Office (GPO No. 006-000-00893-3).

68. McCormick, E. J., Jeanneret, P. R., & Mecham, R. C. (1972). A study of job characteristics and job dimensions as based on the position analysis questionnaire. *Journal of Applied Psychology, 56,* 347–368; PAQ Services, Inc. (n.d.). Job Analysis Questionnaire. Retrieved March 2, 2017, from http://www.paq.com/index.cfm?FuseAction=bulletins.job-analysis-questionnaire

69. Uniform Guidelines on Employee Selection Procedures. (1978, August 25). Federal Register, *43*(166).

70. See www.onetcenter.org

71. See http://www.job-analysis.net/

72. Several good references for competency modeling are available, including: Cooper, K. C. (2000). *Effective competency modeling and reporting: A step-by-step guide for improving individual and organizational performance.* New York: American Management Association; Shippmann, J. S. et al. (2000). The practice of competency modeling. *Personnel Psychology, 53,* 703–740; and Green, P. C. (1999). *Building robust competencies: Linking human resource systems to organizational strategies.* New York: Jossey-Bass.

73. Salter, C. (2001). Talent – Andy Esparza. *Fast Company, 30,* 216–221.

74. Shippmann, J. S. et al. (2000). The practice of competency modeling. *Personnel Psychology, 53,* 703–740.

75. Barclays. (n.d.). Life in technology: Benefits and rewards. Retrieved March 2, 2017, from http://www.lifeintechnology.co.uk/working-for-us/the-benefits/

76. Katz, J. (2010). The soul of Memphis. *Smithsonian, 71.*

77. Pugh, D. S., Hickson, D. J., Hinings, C. R., & Turner, C. (1969). Dimensions of organizational structure. *Administrative Science Quarterly, 13,* 65–105.

78. Morris, J. H., & Steers, R. M. (1980). Structural influences on organizational commitment. *Journal of Vocational Behavior, 17,* 50–57.

79. Hage, J., & Aiken, M. (1969). Routine technology, social structure, and organizational goals. *Administrative Science Quarterly, 14,* 366–376.

80. Pugh, D. S., Hickson, D. J., Hinings, C. R., & Turner, C. (1968). Dimensions of organizational structure. *Administrative Science Quarterly, 13,* 65–105.

81. Glew, D. J., O'Leary-Kelly, A. M., Griffin, R. W., & Van Fleet, D. D. (1995). Participation in organizations: A preview of the issues and proposed framework for future analysis. *Journal of Management, 21,* 395–421.

82. Shadur, M. A., Kienzle, R., & Rodwell, J. J. (1999). The relationship between organizational climate and employee

perceptions of involvement. *Group & Organization Management, 24,* 479–503.

83. Meyer, J., & Allen, N. (1991). A three-component conceptualization of organizational commitment. *Human Resource Management Review, 1,* 69–89; Herscovitch, L., & Meyer, J. P. (2002). Commitment to organizational change: Extension of a three component model. *Journal of Applied Psychology, 87,* 474–487.

84. Gerstner, L. V., Jr. (2002). Who says elephants can't dance? Inside IBM's historic turnaround, 22. New York: Harper Business.

85. Blau, P. M., & Schoenherr, R. A. (1971). *The structure of organizations.* New York: Basic Books.

86. Pugh, D. S., Hickson, D. J., Hinings, C. R., & Turner, C. (1969). Dimensions of organizational structure. *Administrative Science Quarterly, 13,* 65–105.

87. Campion, M. A. (1989). Ability requirement implications of job design: An interdisciplinary perspective. *Personnel Psychology, 42,* 1–24.

88. Lashinsky, A., Burker, D., & Kaufman, S. (2006, April 17). The Hurd way. *Fortune,* 92.

89. Hammer, M., & Champy, J. (1993). Reengineering the corporation: A manifesto for business revolution. London: Harper Collins.

90. Luenendonk, M. (2014, May 20). Making your business more competitive with business process reengineering (BPR). *Cleverism.* Retrieved March 13, 2017, from https://www.cleverism.com/business-competitive-business-process-reengineering-bpr/

91. White, J. B. (1996, November 26). Next big thing: Re-engineering gurus take steps to remodel their stalling vehicles. *Wall Street Journal,* A1.

92. Schmidt, A. (2017, January 30). What are airlines doing to solve the pilot shortage? *Market Realist.* Retrieved February 28, 2017, from http://marketrealist.com/2017/01/what-are-airlines-doing-to-solve-the-pilot-shortage/

93. Schmidt, A. (2016, October 6). How is American Airlines trying to cope with the pilot shortage? *Market Realist.* Retrieved February 28, 2017, from http://marketrealist.com/2016/10/how-is-american-airlines-trying-to-cope-with-the-pilot-shortage/

94. Johnson, K. (2016, December 29). Alaska, reliant on air transit, faces pilot shortage. Are drones an answer? *The New York Times.* Retrieved February 28, 2017, from https://www.nytimes.com/2016/12/29/us/alaska-pilot-shortage.html?_r=0

95. Page, V. (2016, September 16). American Airlines combats pilot shortage. *Investopedia.* Retrieved February 28, 2017, from http://www.investopedia.com/news/american-airlines-combats-pilot-shortage-aal/

96. Schlangenstein, M. & Sasso, M. (2016, July 4). Flights are full. Pilot ranks, not so much. *Bloomberg BusinessWeek* 16–17.

97. Bogan, R. (2017, February 21). Air Force faces pilot shortage, but training is a challenge. *Fox News.* Retrieved February 28, 2017, from http://www.foxnews.com/us/2017/02/21/air-force-faces-pilot-shortage-but-training-is-challenge.html

chapter 5

Sourcing and Recruiting

Learning Objectives

AFTER STUDYING THIS CHAPTER, YOU SHOULD BE ABLE TO:

1 Explain the difference between sourcing and recruiting.

2 Describe the difference between active, semipassive, and passive job seekers, and explain how different recruiting sources are often needed to reach each group.

3 Describe recruitment spillover effects.

4 Describe realistic job previews.

5 Define employer image and employer brand, and explain how they influence recruiting outcomes.

Real World Challenge

Analyzing Recruiting Sources at Valero Energy

Valero Energy Corporation, a *Fortune* 50 company based in San Antonio, Texas, knows that talent is the key to its continued success.[1] Valero believes that it is essential to map recruitment planning to business objectives, and it wants to maximize the quality of its hires as well as the return on its recruiting investment. Valero would like to focus on its best recruiting sources to continue to find top recruits, but it does not have a good understanding of how its different talent sources are performing.

Valero wants to be able to continually evaluate the performance of its recruiting function to support Valero's growth strategy and position itself to hire the best talent in a tightening labor market.[2] Valero asks you for advice about how to evaluate the different recruiting sources it can tap for its different job openings. After reading this chapter, you should have some good ideas.

Not only is finding and recruiting the right talent critical to a firm's performance, great recruiting can also increase a company's value. Global consulting firm Watson Wyatt found that having an excellent recruiting function increased a firm's total market value (the dollar value of all its stock) over 18 percent.[3] If you reflect for a moment on the business impact of not being able to hire the right quality or quantity of employees, you can easily understand the importance of recruiting to organizational performance. As Jack Welch, former CEO of GE, said, "HR should be every company's "killer app." What could possibly be more important than who gets hired, developed, promoted, or moved out the door? Business is a game, and as with all games, the team that puts the best people on the field and gets them playing together wins. It's that simple."[4]

> *"HR should be every company's "killer app." What could possibly be more important than who gets hired, developed, promoted, or moved out the door? Business is a game, and as with all games, the team that puts the best people on the field and gets them playing together wins. It's that simple."*
>
> **—Jack Welch, former CEO of GE**

Because people must apply to an organization before they can become its employees, finding and recruiting the right talent is the foundation of an effective HRM function. Because recruiting determines future employees' characteristics, abilities, and motivations, it impacts everything from training success to the motivational impact of the company's compensation and performance management systems. Recruiting is also a source of sustainable competitive advantage. Rapidly growing companies and firms such as P&G and Enterprise Rent-A-Car, which promote almost entirely from within, are particularly dependent on a strong recruiting pipeline. As two experts stated, "the ultimate cost of failure to attract applicants may be organizational failure."[5]

Understanding how organizations find and recruit candidates can help you to be more competitive when looking for a job. By understanding what organizations do, you can best position yourself to be identified when they are seeking recruits.

Sourcing and recruiting are related but distinct activities. **Sourcing** is the process of identifying qualified individuals and labor markets from which to recruit. **Recruiting** refers to activities that affect either the number or the type of people willing to apply for and accept job offers. Sourcing uses analytical skills to generate recruiting leads. Recruiting relies on interpersonal and communication skills that convert those leads into applicants and new hires. Because they influence the capabilities available to an organization, sourcing and recruiting influence what employees *can* do.

Desirable recruits are those who fit both the job and company, and who are likely to accept job offers if they are extended. In this chapter, we first discuss sourcing techniques as well as strategies for applicant attraction. We begin the chapter by discussing sourcing and describing a variety of internal and external recruiting sources. We then discuss recruiting and the nature of the recruiting message. We end the chapter with a discussion of different strategies companies can use to attract applicants and various ethical issues in sourcing and recruiting. After studying this chapter, you should have a good understanding of the important role both sourcing and recruiting play in identifying and attracting quality applicants.

sourcing
identifying qualified individuals and labor markets from which to recruit

recruiting
activities that affect either the number or the type of people willing to apply for and accept job offers

Sourcing

The goal of marketing is to learn who is likely to be interested in purchasing a product and identify how to best reach them. The goal of sourcing is to do the same thing but with talent rather than products. Once a job analysis has identified the type of person best suited for a position, sourcing involves finding the sources of potential applicants who will best meet the firm's staffing goals. Consulting firm Booz Allen Hamilton created a sourcing department that is an integral part of its recruiting efforts. Some Booz Allen Hamilton sourcers only seek out the names of possible recruits to actively pursue, and others work on traditional job boards and more traditional sources of applicants. One team of sourcers even developed unique capabilities for finding candidates with hard-to-find skill sets.[6]

The optimal sourcing strategy often differs across jobs and types of recruits. Professional employees, including lawyers, scientists, and managers, are usually recruited differently than are mechanics, machine operators, or cashiers. Sourcing strategies also vary depending on whether or not targeted recruits are actively looking for a job. An **active job seeker** is actively on the job market and seeking information about job opportunities. This type of job seeker can often be reached through traditional job advertising methods.

Because active job seekers include those recently fired or laid off as well as frequent job changers, the overall quality of this group may not be the highest. College recruiting is the exception to this statement, as graduating college students are active job seekers and tend to be of higher than average quality. In poor economic times, displaced quality talent is also more actively seeking a new job.

A **semipassive job seeker** is at least somewhat interested in finding a new job but is not constantly looking for one. A semipassive job seeker may be comfortable in his or her current position but is also interested in finding a better job. More proactive and strategic recruiting efforts are required to reach this group because they are not regularly looking at traditional recruiting channels and may not see a posting on an online job board or on the company's website. With the exception of graduating college students, more high-quality candidates tend to be semipassive than active job seekers.

A **passive job seeker** is not actively seeking another job, but he or she could be tempted by the right opportunity. A passive job seeker may be happy in his or her current position but could be persuaded to leave for the right opportunity. Although many high-quality potential recruits are usually in this group, finding them and interesting them in other opportunities can be challenging. Because they are not looking for information about other jobs, identifying passive job seekers requires the most proactive and strategic sourcing and recruiting effort. Because they are happy in their current positions, it often takes more time and information to persuade passive job seekers to pursue a different job opportunity.

Table 5.1 summarizes these three types of job seekers.

Many firms find that if they continue relying on the same traditional job posting channels (such as newspaper ads and online job boards), over time they start seeing many active job seekers again and again. To maximize applicant quality, it is helpful to continually try to identify new quality sources of recruits. Microsoft's sourcers spend about 5 percent of their time on active talent identification and 95 percent of their time on passive talent identification.[7] Google similarly recruits heavily through targeted sourcing and recruiting to find passive and semipassive job seekers rather than relying heavily on the active job seekers who independently apply to the company. When global security technology company McAfee started focusing

active job seeker
someone actively looking for information about job opportunities

semipassive job seeker
someone at least somewhat interested in finding a new job, but who inconsistently looks for one

passive job seeker
someone not actively looking for a new job but who could be tempted by the right opportunity

so what**?**

Passive job seekers are often of high quality but are difficult to attract through conventional recruiting methods.

table **5.1**

Types of Job Seekers

Active job seeker: Someone actively looking for information about job opportunities.
Semipassive job seeker: Someone at least somewhat interested in finding a new job, but who inconsistently looks for one.
Passive job seeker: Someone not actively looking for a new job but who could be tempted by the right opportunity.

on engaging high-value prospects rather than on broad job marketing, it decreased time to fill from 35 days to 11 days for critical positions and reduced what it spent on search firms.[8]

Different recruiting sources are best at accomplishing different recruiting goals. Next, we discuss different recruiting sources and the strengths and limitations of each.

Recruiting Sources

Effective recruiting sources help a company meet its staffing goals for a position. Applicant quality is usually more important than applicant quantity, and some firms consider promotion rates an important staffing outcome, particularly if lower level positions are the primary source of the company's future leaders. It doesn't matter how many people apply for a job if none meet the hiring requirements. If the only applicant is a great fit, accepts the job offer at a reasonable salary, and performs well, then the recruiting effort was successful. It is best to recruit more people for a position than will ultimately be hired, assess them, and hire those who best fit the job and organization.

Recruiting sources have different strengths and weaknesses.[9] Some of the criteria companies use to evaluate recruiting source effectiveness are:

- Speed
- Cost
- Applicant diversity
- Applicant quality
- Applicant quantity
- Identifying people who fit the company's culture
- Job offer acceptance rates

internal recruiting source
locates talent currently working for the company that would be a good fit with another position

external recruiting source
targets people outside the organization

To maximize recruiting goals, it is best to be familiar with a variety of sourcing techniques. Recruiting sources can be either internal or external to the company. An **internal recruiting source** locates current employees who would be a good fit with another position. An **external recruiting source** targets people outside the organization.

Both internal and external recruiting sources have strengths and limitations. Many firms, particularly those with a philosophy of promoting from within, first try to fill positions internally. Relying exclusively on internal sourcing for higher level positions can limit the new insights available to the organization. External hires are sometimes better at leading change, but they usually take longer to hire. Research has found that external hires tend to perform lower for the first two years, have higher exit rates, and are paid 18 to 20 percent more than internal hires.[10] When strong existing knowledge of the corporate culture or business units is important, internal hires are best. This chapter's Strategic Impact feature discusses one company's analysis of the benefits of internal versus external sourcing.

 so what

Good job candidates can often be found both inside and outside the organization.

Research has yet to investigate how organizations can and do make systematic and effective applicant sourcing decisions. Targeting active job seekers through job advertisements online and in newspapers is often fastest, although it may not generate the highest quality hires. Organizations should have multiple sourcing methods in their arsenal from which to choose depending on the specific needs and goals of each hiring effort. This is something that Valero Energy, described in this chapter's opening Real World Challenge, does very effectively.

Let's turn our attention to how organizations recruit internally.

Internal Recruiting Sources

Succession management, talent inventories, and internal job posting systems are common internal recruiting sources. Let's discuss each in more detail.

succession management
the ongoing process of preparing employees to assume other positions in the organization

Succession Management.   Ideally, at least one employee is always available to assume the key positions in an organization. **Succession management** is the ongoing process of

♟ Strategic Impact

Internal or External Sourcing?

Executives at PNC Financial Services suspected that their tendency to hire experienced outsiders over internal candidates might be hurting the bank, so PNC's human resources (HR) team partnered with colleagues from the company's marketing analytics group to analyze several years' worth of sales performance. As they suspected, in several key job categories, internal candidates were significantly more productive in their first year than experienced external hires. In subsequent years, the outsiders narrowed—but never closed—the gap. The performance difference was worth millions of dollars to the company.[11]

preparing employees to assume other positions in the organization. The goal of succession management is to keep the firm's talent pipeline full to ensure a supply of qualified people, especially for key jobs. Succession management systems are based on the organization's long-term business strategy and goals, and they focus on preparing employees to assume leadership roles and other key positions.

Obviously, a company's inability to quickly replace key talent can compromise its ability to execute its business strategy and even to survive. Research has found that a delay in naming a successor after a CEO's death decreases the firm's future net income.[12] In general, firms choosing insider successors outperform those hiring a replacement from outside the organization.[13]

Recruiting, hiring, and training a replacement can take months or longer, particularly for higher level positions. The imminent retirement of baby boomers, fierce competition for talent, and efforts to increase upper management diversity have prompted many organizations to take succession management more seriously.

Employee development is a key component of succession management. Identifying which employees might have the potential to eventually assume other jobs isn't enough—proactively developing them to assume other jobs and roles in the firm is also important. Dow Chemical uses employee development activities, including mentoring, coaching, on-the-job learning, and both online and university-based training programs, to identify and develop promising internal talent. Eli Lilly uses individualized development plans, a formal mentoring program, 360-degree feedback, and job rotation to develop employees' skills and prepare them for other jobs.[14]

Talent Inventories. A **talent inventory** is a manual or computerized record of employees' relevant characteristics, experiences, and competencies. Both employees and their managers are often held responsible for ensuring the accuracy of talent inventories, which allow the company to identify employees qualified for other positions. Talent inventories can be a very effective way to quickly and cheaply source qualified internal candidates. However, if the talent inventories are inaccurate or incomplete, then some qualified internal candidates will be overlooked.

By tracking employees' performance in various development activities and updating employees' talent inventories with their new capabilities, it is possible to quickly identify which employees have the potential to fill various positions throughout the company. Searchable databases can expedite this process.

Internal Job Posting Systems. Many companies let employees apply for internal openings based on their interest in and perceived fit with other positions in the firm. **Internal job posting systems** communicate information about internal job openings to employees,

so what?

Not having a succession plan can compromise organizational performance.

talent inventory
manual or computerized records of employees' relevant characteristics, experiences, and competencies

internal job posting systems
communicate information about internal job openings to employees

?so what
Posting jobs internally helps qualified employees locate other positions in which they might be interested. Qualifications inventories helps the company reach out to qualified employees to let them know of other opportunities in the company.

often via a bulletin board or the company's intranet. Any interested employee can ask to be considered. HR then typically reviews each interested employee to confirm that he or she meets the requirements of the vacancy.

Because internal job posting systems allow employees to directly apply for positions in which they are interested, the possibility of overlooking qualified internal talent is reduced. Internal job posting systems are relatively fast and inexpensive but may overlook some qualified employees who do not look at them. Many firms use a combination of internal job postings and qualifications inventories to reduce the chances of missing a qualified internal candidate.

External Recruiting Sources

When internal recruiting is unable to fill openings, organizations must use external recruiting. Table 5.2 summarizes some of the most common external recruiting sources. Let's explore a variety of common external recruiting sources and how to use them most effectively.

careers site
the area of an organization's website devoted to jobs and careers with the company

Careers Sites.   A **careers site** is the area of an organization's website devoted to jobs and careers with the company. A link to the careers site is usually on every page of the company's website to help interested visitors easily learn about what it is like to work for the company, what job openings exist, and how to apply. To assemble a searchable database of all applicants and comply with EEO laws, some organizations use multiple recruiting sources but require that all applications be through their careers site.

Careers sites are very cost-effective, and can communicate a lot of information about a company's business, values, and job requirements. This allows potential applicants to decide if they are a good fit and whether or not to apply. Enterprise Rent-A-Car's career site (www .enterprisealive.com) is an excellent example of how career sites help to source recruits.

?so what
Because most job seekers will explore a company's careers site to learn more about them, it is strategic to make sure your company's careers site contains the information they are looking for and helps to recruit them.

 Creative Sourcing.   Some firms have utilized creative sourcing strategies, including "speed hiring" sessions modeled after speed dating, reading chat room postings and blogs to locate talented people, and holding talent competitions with job offers awarded to the winners. Google

table **5.2**

Commonly Used External Recruiting Sources

Careers sites
Creative sourcing
Employee referrals
Internet data mining
Job fairs
Military transition services
Non-U.S. citizens
Observation
Online job boards
Previous employees
Résumé databases
Schools
Search firms
State employment agencies
Walk-ins
Written advertisements

hosts a programming competition called Code Jam that presents multiple online rounds of algorithmic puzzles. The 26 finalists are invited to Google to compete for cash prizes and an opportunity for a job at Google.[15] Some firms even network with realtors to learn when people with needed skills might be moving into the area.

When Oath (formerly Yahoo!) was downsizing, executives from Internet voice and video company TokBox put a taco truck across the street, offering a free lunch and information about working for TokBox. The novelty of their efforts generated hundreds of thousands of dollars worth of free PR and employment advertising.[16]

The U.S. Army uses a highly successful recruiting game called America's Army[17] and created a multimillion-dollar U.S. Army Experience Center in Philadelphia where potential recruits explore different Army bases and occupations using video games.[18] IBM, KPMG, and other companies have used virtual job fairs, interviews, and tours to find and engage promising candidates.[19]

The important thing to remember about creative sourcing is that the goal is not to be creative for creativity's sake but to reach qualified candidates in novel ways, as a marketing professional would. Sometimes a creative sourcing campaign is only useful for a few months or is copied by competitors and stops being a competitive advantage.

so what**?**
Sourcing creativity should reinforce the goal of reaching qualified candidates in novel ways.

Employee Referrals.   Asking employees, particularly top performers, to recommend people they feel would be good performers can generate high-quality leads. Many firms make referrals one of their primary recruiting sources. Victor Settergren, Raytheon's missile systems director of global talent development, states, "Top-performing employees recommend top-performing recruits; average staff recommend average people. Referral programs are critical for recruiting 'A' players, and so is talking very transparently about wanting top talent."[20] Consulting firm Booz Allen hires more than 55 percent of its employees from referrals, and it encourages recruits to identify Booz Allen employees who might help to recruit them.[21] As many as 45 percent of all new hires come from employee referrals.[22]

> *"Top-performing employees recommend top-performing recruits; average staff recommend average people. Referral programs are critical for recruiting 'A' players, and so is talking very transparently about wanting top talent."*
>
> **— Victor Settergren, Raytheon's missile systems director of global talent development**

Employees generally provide accurate information about the people they refer, and referral bonuses are paid only if the person is hired.[23] Employees hired via referrals are also likely to have a more realistic picture of what working at the firm is like, increasing their retention.[24] Because employees sometimes receive rewards for referring employees, and because employee referrals often receive special recruiter attention, reaching out to current employees of companies in which you would like to work can be very helpful during your own job search.

If employees do not believe that their employer is a good place to work, they are unlikely to recommend it to others. Because people tend to refer people they know, which often means people who are demographically similar, employee referrals do not tend to increase diversity in currently homogeneous companies. In this case, demographically underrepresented groups (typically women and minorities) could be adversely affected by a heavy reliance on employee referrals.[25]

Employee referral programs tend to be relatively fast and inexpensive, although some organizations reward employees quite generously for making successful referrals. Employees who have been referred tend to have lower turnover soon after joining the company[26] and tend to be good performers.[27]

so what**?**
Employee referrals can generate quality recruits but can also perpetuate discrimination if employees lack diversity.

Internet data mining
proactively searching the internet to locate semipassive and passive job seekers with the characteristics and the qualifications needed for a position

job fairs
a place where multiple employers and recruits meet to discuss employment opportunities

Internet Data Mining.   Some companies have found that, over time, the same active job seekers often respond to newspaper ads, job postings on careers websites, and Internet job boards, decreasing their effectiveness. **Internet data mining** involves proactively searching the Internet to locate semipassive and passive job seekers with the characteristics and the qualifications needed for a position. Recruiters then try to convert these leads into applicants.

Linkedin.com has become one of the most popular sourcing tools for a variety of professional positions. If you are looking for a job, it is a good idea to upload a professional photo and keep your LinkedIn profile updated to help recruiters find you. This is especially important for people seeking jobs in communications, media and public relations, marketing and sales, and advertising as well as IT professionals, HRM staff, and executives.[28] Many companies, including global technology giant Siemens,[29] use LinkedIn to find passive and semipassive job candidates. The candidates generated by social networking sites are often passive or semipassive job seekers.

Job fairs are a common way organizations recruit at colleges and universities. They are efficient for both employers and job seekers and are a great way to explore your own career options.

Job Fairs.   At **job fairs** multiple employers and recruits meet to discuss employment opportunities. They are common at colleges and universities, and some cities even host them to help match residents with local jobs. Job fairs can be an effective way to source recruits, assuming the people attending the job fair are appropriately qualified. Some job fairs focus on transitioning military veterans or workers with disabilities.

Job fairs sometimes take place on the Internet, with multiple employers posting banner advertisements in a common area. Clicking on a banner sends the job seeker to the company's virtual area containing company information, descriptions of job openings, and electronic job applications.[30] Job fairs tend to be best for finding active and semipassive job seekers.

?so what

Because many companies use the Internet to identify promising recruits, it is a good idea to make sure your professional information is thorough and current so they can easily find you.

Military Transition Services.   Military transition services, such as GIjobs.com, help place separating professional and semiprofessional military members, veterans, and their family members. The service allows employers to advertise job vacancies ranging from skilled mechanics to junior executives. This can also be a good source of veterans with disabilities who are fully capable of performing difficult and hard-to-fill positions. This chapter's HR Flexibility feature describes how The Home Depot uses targeted recruitment to attract recruits from the military and elsewhere.

Non-U.S. Citizens.   Although recruiting globally can dramatically increase the talent available to a company, hiring foreign workers to work in the United States requires sponsoring an immigration visa for them. The most popular employment-based immigration program, the H-1B visa, requires that the visa application process be repeated if the employee wishes to leave the sponsoring organization. This hassle increases the likelihood that foreign workers will stay with the initial company for the duration of their visas, increasing employee stability and reducing turnover costs.[34] Only 85,000 H-1B visas were issued in 2017, and the application pool was closed in four days because there were so many applicants.[35] The visas are used most often by technology companies seeking computer specialists, and the Department of Homeland Security is working on measures to better deter and identify fraud and abuse in the program.[36]

The Immigration and Nationality Act allows companies to hire only eligible aliens specifically authorized to work in the United States. Legal immigrants must acquire a green card from the Immigration and Naturalization Service to become eligible for employment. Applicants

💬 HR Flexibility

Targeted Recruitment at The Home Depot

Home improvement retailer The Home Depot believes that workforce diversity is critical to its success. It believes that it must know its customers to best serve them, and to know its customers means that it must reflect their diversity. In recruiting employees, The Home Depot casts a wide net to attract quality, diverse people.

The Home Depot uses targeted recruitment to best attract high-quality, diverse applicants. The company partners with community organizations that support its diversity initiatives, including Catalyst, National Urban League, and the National Association of Asian Professionals.[31]

The Home Depot also collaborates with organizations in hiring partnerships to pursue diverse recruits. Its military partnership, called Operation Career Front, supports military job seekers including reservists, National Guard members, veterans, separating active duty service members, and military spouses.[32] The company has a portion of its website dedicated to military recruitment and even conducts interviews on military bases.[33] The Home Depot's recruiting methods have paid off in employee diversity and low employee turnover, which it feels enhances its customer service quality.

must complete an I-9 form to prove their U.S. employment eligibility. Employers must verify the employment eligibility of all new employees, and I-9 forms must be kept on file for at least three years after the applicant is hired or one year after employment ends, whichever is less.

Foreign professionals must be paid the prevailing U.S. wage in their field, and employers must demonstrate that they have unsuccessfully tried to hire U.S. citizens for seasonal work. Some workers, including nurses, must comply with the certification procedures set forth by the Department of Labor. Although the process can take up to two years, these programs can be worthwhile for companies seeking highly skilled workers. A regional Department of Labor certifying officer can grant a labor certification if the employer can show that qualified workers are not available, and the wages and working conditions offered will not adversely affect those of similarly employed U.S. workers.

An alternative to relocating foreign workers to the United States is **offshoring** by opening a location in another country or outsourcing work to an existing company abroad. Offshoring is discussed in more detail in this chapter's Global Issues feature.

Observation.   **Observation** is watching people working in similar jobs for other companies to evaluate their potential fit with your organization. If you are a retail manager, observing the employees at other retail stores can help you identify who you want to recruit for your own job openings.

Nucor Steel sources new steelworkers from the construction workers who build its plants. While monitoring the company's construction sites, Nucor's managers look for construction workers who demonstrate the work habits they value and then recruit them to join Nucor.[41] FirstMerit Bank sends recruiters to visit nonbank retail stores to identify good customer service performers. FirstMerit also sends recruiters to other banks to open bank accounts and note whether the employees follow up when they say they will.[42]

Observation can be an effective way to target all types of potential recruits, especially passive job seekers, but the ethics of engaging in behaviors that cost the other firm money (for example, the salesperson's or new account representative's time) must be carefully considered.

offshoring
opening a location in another country or outsourcing work to an existing company abroad

observation
watching people working in similar jobs for other companies to evaluate their potential fit with your organization

so what**?**

Observing other companies' employees can help identify talented recruits, but be sure to do it ethically.

Global Issues

Offshoring

Offshoring has become increasingly popular for many organizations seeking productivity gains. Some companies have reduced their labor costs by more than 70 percent by offshoring,[37] although increasing international labor and product transportation costs can decrease the savings. Offshoring is particularly well suited to projects or intermittent work, for example, updating software or developing new Web pages.

Reducing a firm's labor costs is one of the most obvious reasons for offshoring, but it also helps companies pursue top talent wherever it is located. Reliable and affordable communication technology has made offshoring possible for many jobs. Although not a fast solution to a hiring need, sourcing offshore labor can help acquire quality talent at an affordable price.

The risks involved with offshoring are primarily the result of conducting work in two countries having different cultures, different intellectual property laws, and conflicting legal systems. It is important to consider the nature of the other country's judicial system, local laws, and what would happen if the offshore company goes bankrupt and to ensure that a dispute resolution procedure is outlined in the outsourcing contract.[38] Offshore employees also must usually be trained in the company's culture and practices.

Because of the negative effects on U.S. jobs, there has been much debate over offshoring and how it is implemented. Bank of America received negative media attention when it required some of its laid off IT workers to train their Indian replacements. The company now gives its workers six to eight months' notice before offshoring their jobs, which usually gives them enough time to train for new assignments or find other jobs.[39] Firms must also balance the savings of moving some jobs to cheaper locations with the need to protect their business secrets. To prevent its technology from being stolen, Symantec, producer of Norton Antivirus, won't offshore or outsource its virus definitions or the engine that works with these definitions to prevent viruses.[40]

online job board
an Internet site that helps job seekers and employers find one another

Online Job Boards.   **Online job boards** are websites that allow job seekers to post résumés and employers to post jobs and use a search engine to find one another. Both general (including Indeed.com, ZipRecruiter.com, SimplyHired.com, HotJobs.com, CareerBuilder.com, and Monster.com) and specialty job boards (for example, Dice.com for technology jobs, Ecoemploy.com for green jobs, Cafepharma for pharmaceutical sales professional positions, and jobsinhr.org for HRM professionals) help employers source promising recruits by searching the résumés that potential applicants have posted. Some websites, including hirediversity.com and minorityjobs.net, specialize in diversity recruiting. USAJOBS.gov specializes in federal jobs. As mentioned earlier, many companies also use LinkedIn to find passive and semipassive job candidates as the site enables professional networking that assists in sourcing and recruiting as well as job searching.

Online classified ads can help source candidates just as their paper counterparts can. When skyrocketing demand for Silly Bandz, the fun-shaped silicone-rubber bracelets, increased the company's need for new employees, the company effectively used Craigslist job advertisements to quickly find people.[43]

Previous Employees.   An employee who voluntarily leaves may find that the new job is not what he or she expected, the new venture may not work out, or the person may decide that they miss working at your company. Rehiring these "boomerang" employees gives you talent that is already familiar with the job and organization, and you have a good idea of their talents and fit with the firm. They may have even enhanced their skills while they were gone.

Organizations are increasingly staying in touch with previous employees and are often willing to rehire them later.[44] Apple Computer did this when it rehired CEO Howard Schultz. Because it can't quickly train people with expertise in aircraft engine performance problems, the Navy keeps the addresses of retirees and other past employees in a database in case they are needed. IBM and KPMG have set up websites for their alumni networks to keep in touch with former employees.[45] Software that analyzes the dynamics of each alumnus's connections helped one accounting firm rehire 31 people through its alumni network.[46]

It is a good idea to make sure that potential rehires were previously good employees and to learn how they spent their time away from the company and how they feel about returning. If they previously felt mistreated, they may have low morale or an undesirable attitude.[47] If returning employees are given better positions than they had when they left, care must be taken to prevent other employees from concluding that the only way to get ahead is to leave the company and then return.

Résumé Databases. **Résumé databases** are searchable databases of prescreened résumés. Maintaining a database of unhired candidates who were finalists for other jobs can be a quality source of candidates. When Microsoft recruiters reached out to previous candidates who had declined job offers or interviews to see if they would like to discuss opportunities with the firm again, the initiative was so successful that it became one of Microsoft's core sourcing strategies.[48]

To help your résumé get noticed, this chapter's Develop Your Skills feature gives you some tips for writing an effective résumé.

so what**?**

Separated good performers can be an excellent source of future talent if they are interested in being rehired.

résumé database
a searchable database of prescreened résumés

 # Develop Your Skills

Résumé Tips

Here are some tips for writing your own résumé:

1. *Focus on your achievements:* State your experience as achievements rather than simply stating the title and requirements of past jobs. Be honest and specific, using numbers when you can.

Weak:
- Maintained inventory
- Responsible for energy use reduction
- Responsible for recruiting by a deadline

Strong:
- Worked directly with the plant manager to manage inventory and reduced shrinkage by 12 percent
- Reduced department energy use by 20 percent over six months
- Recruited 80 technical hires eight days before the deadline

2. *View your résumé as an advertisement:* Highlight your major accomplishments, strengths, and skills not covered in the company's online application, including any language skills, technical skills, or volunteer work relevant to the job. Using the job description, match your résumé to the company's needs, and describe how you can fill those needs to help them screen you into the candidate pool. Be sure to target your résumé to each job to which you apply—one résumé does not fit all jobs and organizations!

3. *Use keywords:* Many organizations get so many résumés that they need to use keyword searches to identify which applicants to consider further. Be sure your résumé contains as many keywords as possible that a company might use in finding someone to fit the job you're looking for. Add a section at the bottom of your résumé entitled "skills" or, even, "keywords" where you list as many keywords as possible. Be creative, but be accurate. Include the standard job titles for your current and previous jobs, particularly if a previous employer used nonstandard titles. Use the job description or job advertisement to identify additional keywords and abbreviations likely to be used to screen résumés for the position.

4. *Attend to the details:* Make sure your formatting and design are attractive and consistently applied. Make sure the content is recent, relevant, and significant. Avoid poor grammar and misspellings. Some companies, including Google, eliminate résumés that have even one error!

5. *Use action words:* Avoid passive tense and use high-impact words. Words such as accomplished, motivated, modernized, developed, enabled, and innovated better demonstrate your capabilities.

6. *Choose your email address carefully:* Don't use a goofy e-mail address (e.g., partygirl@gmail.com), or your message will probably not be taken seriously. Use the e-mail address as an opportunity to market and differentiate yourself—such as rphillip-chemist@aol.com or tjohn_engineer@aol.com

7. *Get to the point:* One to two pages is long enough. If you have an extensive work history, covering the most recent 15 years of your career is generally enough.

8. *Get feedback:* Have other people look at your résumé and provide feedback to you.

9. *Be positive:* Frame all experiences, skills, and positions in a positive tone. Avoid including negative experiences.

10. *Be honest:* Include realistic statements of talents, skills, accomplishments, experiences, and background. Don't try to be something that you are not.

Schools.   Colleges and universities are a common recruiting source for both internships and full-time positions. Companies often focus on a few universities for each job family, focusing on programs whose graduates best meet the firm's needs. Microsoft tracks the schools its best workers come from and adjusts its recruiting activities accordingly.[49]

To address labor shortages, companies are increasingly partnering with community colleges. Machinery and computer programs are constantly being upgraded, requiring more advanced skill sets than entry-level hires typically have. Community colleges are increasingly being asked to train people for specific skills and jobs that exist in the local area. In 2011, the federal government set aside more than $2 billion to support job training efforts at community colleges.[50]

Developing a relationship with university faculty can also give a company greater access to its students. Qualcomm has on-campus ambassadors and funds faculty research projects on targeted campuses. Some companies ask faculty members to refer students who would fit their needs. The National Association of Colleges and Employers' ethical guidelines for career service professionals and campus recruiters are available online.[51]

Internships give employers a good look at potential hires, and they give interns the opportunity to evaluate whether the company is a place they would like to work. Internships can be a very effective source of new hires. In fact, most new hires at J.P. Morgan and Goldman Sachs are previous interns.[52] A survey of more than 300 employers found that internship programs produce 30 percent of new college hires.[53] Merrill Lynch gives 75 percent of its summer interns a full-time job offer, sourcing them as early as their first year in college to build relationships and increase the probability that it will be able to hire them.[54]

Search Firms.   **Search firms** are independent companies that specialize in recruiting particular types of talent. Although they are not necessarily fast or cheap, often charging 50 percent of the employee's first year salary, search firms can be an effective way to source quality candidates. Researching a search firm's placement and retention rate and speaking with former clients of a search firm can help identify how to best utilize them.

A quality executive search firm is usually a member of the Association of Executive Search Consultants (AESC), a worldwide professional association for the retained executive search industry. If a search firm is not a member of the organization, ask if it is willing to abide by the AESC Code of Professional Practice and Standards of Excellence.[55]

Some search firms focus on finding people whose careers are limited at their current companies. Offering the number two or three person on a successful team a job with greater responsibility can be an effective way to source passive job seekers. Search firms often look for frustrated high performers by keeping files on firms' bench strength.[56] Their extensive networks and sometimes their relationships with potential recruits help search firms tap into a broader pool of talent than smaller or midsize firms can do on their own.

One drawback of search firms is the fact that they are often unable to source recruits from companies who are also clients of the search firm. When Coca-Cola Co. evaluated its hiring metrics, it found that senior employee turnover was twice as high among employees sourced by outside recruiting firms compared to those found by its own recruiters. Coca-Cola learned that this was because its own recruiters were better able to find people who are a good culture fit and because they could pursue high-quality talent from competing companies.[57]

State Employment Agencies.   State employment agencies serve both job seekers and employers. State employment agencies often provide interviewing, counseling, testing, and training services to better prepare job seekers for employment. They often offer specialized employment services for veterans, people with disabilities, and older workers.

Walk-Ins.   **Walk-ins** are people who apply for a job based on a "help wanted" sign in a window or on company property. It is helpful to include sufficient information on a help wanted sign to encourage people who are good fits to apply (e.g., the position and the work hours). Just putting "help wanted" in front of your building is only likely to attract active job seekers who may not even be good fits with the open position.

Some walk-ins occur even when no openings exist when a job seeker likes the company or its location and decides to inquire about employment opportunities. Walk-in applicants are usually asked to complete a job application and are sometimes given a quick interview to assess their qualifications.

Written Advertisements.   One of the oldest methods of recruiting external applicants is through written advertisements in newspapers, magazines, trade journals, or anything job seekers are likely to read. Although the help wanted section of the newspaper is best at recruiting active job seekers, some semipassive job seekers are also likely to see them. Placing ads near things passive or semipassive candidates are likely to read in trade journals, magazines, or in relevant sections of the newspaper can also help reach them. Many firms still rely heavily on written advertisements, particularly for lower level jobs.

search firm
an independent company that specializes in the recruitment of particular types of talent

walk-ins
people who apply for a job based on a sign on company property

recruiting

the set of practices and decisions that affect either the number or the types of individuals willing to apply for and accept job offers

recruitment spillover effects

the positive or negative unintended consequences of recruiting activities

As a final note on external recruitment sources, it is important to note that research has found that informal sources tend to outperform more formal sources.[58] In particular, employees recruited through informal sources, including employee referrals, tend to have the highest performance and job tenure.[59] If low turnover is a primary goal, formal recruiting methods such as advertising in print media and posting jobs on the Internet may, therefore, be less effective than informal methods such as rehiring previous employees and employee referrals.

Recruiting

Recruiting is the set of practices and decisions that affect either the number or the types of individuals willing to apply for and accept job offers.[60] This includes converting sourcing leads into job applicants, interesting targeted recruits in the company, retaining candidates throughout the hiring process, and persuading candidates to accept job offers. Sourcing differs from recruiting in that sourcing *identifies* the talent that recruiting then *attracts*.[61]

Until either the organization (or the applicant) removes an applicant from further consideration or the individual reports for work, recruiting keeps him or her interested in the opportunity. Recruiters should help candidates continually feel excited about the opportunity and ultimately accept a reasonable job offer. Because the purpose of recruiting is to generate a pipeline of talent to help the organization get the right people in the right place at the right time, it is essential to business strategy execution and obtaining a competitive advantage.

Outcomes of recruiting include sufficient applicant quantity and quality, applicant perceptions of the company, new hires' performance and tenure, and new hires' fit with the company, workgroup, supervisor, and job. One important recruiting outcome is leaving applicants with a positive feeling about the organization even if they are not hired. Job candidates can spend hundreds of dollars in clothes, lost work time, transportation, and other expenses to be interviewed and assessed. It is important to recognize their time and investments and always treat them with respect.

Recruitment spillover effects are the positive or negative unintended consequences of recruiting activities. When unhappy job candidates tell their friends about a bad recruiting experience, the negative spillover effects can reduce the organization's performance and its ability to recruit candidates effectively in the future. If you met with a late and unprepared interviewer, felt the selection process was unfair, or were made to feel like the decision to hire a different candidate had already been made before you interviewed, would you be as interested in shopping with the company or applying for another job with it in the future? Probably not. Now suppose you were greeted by name, treated respectfully, interviewed on time by a prepared and enthusiastic recruiter, and were evaluated on fair, job-related characteristics. Most applicants treated this way are likely to continue to do business with the company and even reapply for another job in the future, experiencing positive recruitment spillover effects.

When Valero Energy, featured in this chapter's opening Real World Challenge, began viewing every hiring prospect as a potential customer or lost customer, it started keeping applicants apprised of their status throughout the hiring process. It sends at least three automated and personalized e-mails to each candidate during the hiring process, starting at the point of application, and mails a postcard to all rejected candidates after a job is closed.[62] The company credits this automated communication as having transformed its candidate image. Because Valero knows that many rejected candidates have the potential to become great employees, it also encourages rejected candidates to apply for other positions with which they are a good fit.

Employment inquiries and job applications should always be treated with respect. Mistreating an applicant, even when there are no current job opportunities, could reduce the applicant's interest in future employment opportunities and in doing business with you. Although this may seem obvious, it can be difficult to execute, particularly when the firm is trying to hire a lot of people in a short period of time. Because he understands that just one bad candidate experience could create a negative impression that can influence many more potential candidates, particularly because millennials are so highly networked and likely to broadcast their experience, Victor Settergren, missile systems director of global talent development at Raytheon Co., believes, "If we truly want to attract and retain top talent, we must create a "brag-worthy" impression for every candidate and hire experience."[63]

> *"If we truly want to attract and retain top talent, we must create a 'brag-worthy' impression for every candidate and hire experience."*
>
> **— Victor Settergren, missile systems director of global talent development at Raytheon Co**

Although timeliness is positively related to applicant attraction,[64] responding to many applicants can be difficult or impossible without technology. The job of sorting through online applications can be enormous. Worse yet, if a large proportion of them don't meet the requirements of the positions posted, which is fairly common, the screening burden placed on the organization is increased. Résumé tracking and talent management software such as Oracle's Taleo and IBM's Kenexa can help to coordinate and expedite the hiring process.

Important Recruiter Characteristics

Nearly 80 percent of the variation in quality of hire is driven by recruiter characteristics, including their skills, experiences, and attitudes and how they are trained and managed.[65] Because a recruiter is usually the first person with whom potential applicants have contact, they are critical to the hiring process. One study showed that the recruiter was the primary reason a business or engineering graduate chose a particular company in over one-third of the cases.[66] At early phases of the hiring process, a potential applicant who is "turned off" by a recruiter might decide not to apply at all. Active job seekers might persist despite a negative encounter with a recruiter, but the most desirable semipassive and passive job seekers will be less likely to do so. Because front-line recruiters have the largest impact on a firm's hiring decisions by screening the most recruits, the negative spillover effects caused by lower-skilled front-line recruiters can cost firms a lot of money and lost talent acquisition opportunities.

Because outsiders usually have limited information about an organization and its jobs, they rely on the recruiter and the recruiter's behaviors as signals of broader organizational characteristics. The recruiter's professionalism, competence, timeliness, and so on all signal applicants about what it might be like to work for that company.[67] Recruiter demographics can also make a difference. For example, minority recruiters may better appeal to minority applicants. If an actual hiring manager or the CEO is involved in recruiting, this can signal that the company really values its talent. Signaling is reduced when job candidates have sufficient information about the organization, or if the recruiter is from HR rather than from the applicant's functional area.

Recruiters should be selected and trained to be knowledgeable about the job opening,[68] effectively communicate this information, be perceived by applicants as trustworthy, and positively reflect what it is like to work for the company. Just as a recruiting message should be customized to address the needs and concerns of each applicant, recruiters should be chosen based on their ability to communicate with and persuade a recruit to make the organization their employer of choice.[69]

Although using line managers as recruiters can work, it is often impractical to take employees out of their regular jobs to recruit. Effective recruiting also requires more than just technical job knowledge. Recruiters can usually be trained in how to explain a job to applicants, answer applicants' questions, and have a better understanding of legal issues. Recruiters are

so what?

The most important recruiter characteristics are that they be knowledgeable about the job opening and the company, able to communicate this to the applicant, and able to effectively persuade people to apply and to accept job offers.

also usually better able to answer broader questions about the organization's policies and careers and identify other positions in the organization for which recruits might be a good fit. Highly specialized positions, such as bioscience research, that require the recruiter to be well versed in appropriate jargon to fully communicate job requirements and screen candidates may require more hiring manager involvement. In this case, the recruiter should minimize the time the manager has to spend off the job recruiting.

Applicant Tracking Systems

applicant tracking system
software that helps manage the recruiting process

An **applicant tracking system** is software that helps manage the recruiting process. Applicant tracking systems can be scaled to fit any size organization, and they are used to process job applications, manage résumé data, track where applicants are in the hiring process, and even automate the recruitment process. A central database for an organization's recruiting efforts makes it easier to coordinate recruiting efforts and analyze data to improve future recruiting efforts. It is also possible to quickly run reports on cost per hire, time to fill, recruiting source effectiveness, and more. In addition, the recruiting process is usually faster and easier for applicants, increasing their interest in being considered for the position. Because applicant tracking systems store predominantly personal data, it is controlled by data protection legislation that prevents the data from being held offshore where identity theft is more likely.

Recruiting Metrics

efficiency-oriented recruiting metrics
track how efficiently a firm is hiring

strategic recruiting metrics
recruiting metrics that track recruiting processes and outcomes that influence the organization's performance, competitive advantage, or strategic execution

How does a firm know if it is recruiting effectively? **Efficiency-oriented recruiting metrics** track how efficiently a firm is hiring. Efficiency-oriented metrics include hiring speed (also called time to fill), number of applicants, number of hires, and the average cost per hire. Although these metrics can be useful, because they are not tied to the business strategy, they may not improve the organization's performance. Because the hiring cycle for senior software architects can exceed five years, recruiters at one major software company are not assessed on the number of jobs they fill as much as on the number of qualified individuals they identify and the relationships they build with them.[70]

Strategic recruiting metrics are those that track recruiting processes and outcomes that influence the organization's performance, competitive advantage, or strategic execution. The following is a list of strategic recruiting metrics one HR expert recommends tracking:[71]

- *Manager satisfaction:* Are the managers of employees in key jobs satisfied with the hiring process and the candidates sent to them?
- *New hire satisfaction:* Are applicants and new hires in key jobs satisfied with the hiring process?
- *Training success:* How well do new hires perform in training?
- *Time to productivity:* How long does it take for new hires to meet the firm's minimum output standards?
- *Job performance:* How well do new hires perform the job six to 12 months after hire?
- *Failure rate:* How many new hires in key jobs are terminated or asked to leave?
- *Voluntary turnover:* How many employees voluntarily quit within their first year?

? so what

Efficiency metrics can decrease costs but don't necessarily improve the organization's performance.

Tracking strategic recruitment metrics can help a firm improve its staffing results. If the best recruitment sources, messages, and recruiters can be identified, it can be possible to leverage this information when planning future recruiting initiatives.

It is important to note that metrics and feedback, although very helpful in aligning recruiters' goals and behaviors with organizational goals, are more impactful when rewards are aligned with goal accomplishment. Rewarding recruiters for recruiting quality talent that remains with the firm and performs well aligns the hiring goals of the organization with the recruiter's personal goals. T-Mobile recruiters' goals are drafted by recruiters and approved

? so what

Strategic recruitment metrics help organizations improve their staffing results by identifying and helping them leverage their most effective sources, messages, and recruiters.

by managers, and must support the firm's corporate-wide goals. T-Mobile then gives its recruiters quarterly bonuses based on their individual goal accomplishment.[72]

If recruiters are expected to work as a team, team members' rewards must be linked to behaviors that support the entire team. A balanced incentive plan should consider the organization's long-term and short-term strategic hiring goals to better motivate recruiters to do what the organization really needs done. Because any recruiter's performance can be compromised by a difficult hiring manager, sometimes firms make adjustments for this as well as other uncontrollable factors recruiters face, such as a tight labor market.[73]

Although recruiters are often very busy, unresponsive recruiters are often seen as incompetent rather than overworked, risking a negative recruitment spillover effect for the company. Next, we turn our attention to what makes recruiters effective.

The Recruiting Message

Organizations choose how much and what information to communicate to potential recruits. The primary goal of a recruiting message is to attract desirable recruits who would be a good fit with the job and the organization and persuade them to apply to the organization. Let's explore some considerations in crafting an effective recruiting message.

What Information to Include

Although there are relatively few studies on the best information to include when recruiting, research suggests that recruiting materials should be informative, address a range of job or organizational characteristics, and provide specific information about those characteristics.[74] Greater job posting detail can be helpful in "weeding out" unqualified applicants through self-selection, increasing the efficiency of the subsequent screening process.[75] Providing specific information about a job's location, job type and level, and salary range in the recruiting materials can save time in processing applications from people who would ultimately turn down job offers.

Also, the amount of information in the recruiting message influences whether or not job seekers will apply to an organization.[76] General ads that include limited job attributes may appeal to a wide variety of job seekers and generate a lot of applicants, but they also tend to increase the number of unqualified applicants and the expense of screening them. General ads can also be unappealing to job seekers who are highly focused in their job search strategies and don't want to take the time to research the missing information.[77] Table 5.3 summarizes some best recruitment practices based on research findings.[78]

One of the best ways to ensure that job seekers make accurate assessments of their fit with a job or organization is to give them a realistic job preview.

Realistic Job Previews

The realism of recruiting sources can influence job satisfaction, turnover, and absenteeism,[80] which could partially explain why informal recruiting sources tend to outperform more formal sources. Organizations choose how objective to be when communicating the nature of the work and the organization to recruits. Some organizations embellish the nature of the job and the organization to make the opportunity seem more positive and enjoyable than it really is. Inflating recruiting information can be detrimental to an organization.[81] Particularly in a strong labor market when employees can easily find another job if the job is not what they expected, misled employees are more likely to leave.[82]

Some organizations disclose as little potentially undesirable information as possible to applicants, believing that if applicants knew what it was really like to work there, they would not want the job. Trying to persuade candidates to accept job offers without them thoroughly understanding what they are committing to can be misguided. **Realistic job previews (RJPs)**

realistic job preview
presenting both positive and potentially negative information about a job in an objective way

table **5.3**

Recruiting Best Practices[79]

To improve their recruiting efforts, research suggests that organizations:
• Provide applicants with sufficient information about the job and the organization to allow them to assess their fit.
• Hire personable and trustworthy recruiters.
• Make initial recruiting activities (job postings or on-campus recruiting efforts) attractive to candidates.
• Provide clear, specific, and complete information in recruitment materials and messages to help candidates make accurate inferences.
• Create a positive organizational image in the minds of applicants, both before and during recruitment.
• Respond quickly to applications and inquiries.
• Treat candidates fairly and respectfully throughout the recruiting process.
• Train recruiters to explain the company's selection procedures, keep candidates informed, and avoid communication delays to enhance perceptions of fairness.

present both positive and potentially negative information about a job. Rather than trying to sell recruits on the job and the company by presenting the job opportunity in the most positive light, realistic job previews strive to objectively present an honest and accurate picture. If people decide not to apply because of the information, the loss is minimal, as they would have been poor fits anyway. Presenting objective information about a position and letting people self-select into it knowing what the job will really be like increases the likelihood that once employed they will stay and perform well.[83]

Companies are increasingly trying to help candidates understand the organization and the job before they even apply. Nationwide Insurance created a 10 multiple-choice question realistic job preview for its call center customer service role. Participants anonymously listen to different scenarios, select the best response from three multiple choice answers, and get feedback on their fit with the company.[84] Comcast created a YouTube channel with realistic job preview videos to provide more information to prospective recruits for a variety of jobs.[85] When you look for a job, it is a good idea to seek out this type of information to determine whether the opportunity and the company are right for you.

After finding that job candidates were spending less than 10 minutes on its website, global accounting firm PricewaterhouseCoopers' (PwC) Hungary location created a game called Multipoly to better educate recruits about its vision, services, and the skills needed for success.[86] The game has worked to improve candidate engagement and employee retention. The number of job candidates has increased 190 percent, and users have reported a 78 percent greater interest in learning more about working at PwC.[87] An additional benefit is that job candidates hired after playing Multipoly transitioned to the company more easily because they already had a feel for PwC's company culture from playing the game.[88]

The goal of an RJP is not to deter candidates by focusing on factors that might be perceived negatively but to provide accurate information about the job and the organization.[89] IBM's careers website has highly interactive multimedia including "day-in-the-life" videos, business-unit specific information, and information about the company's employer awards and recognition. Some companies even provide online video tours of their facilities.

The most common mistake made when initially developing a realistic recruiting message is a tendency to emphasize only the potentially negative features of a job. The goal, however, is to present a *realistic* picture of the job, including both potentially positive and potentially negative aspects, in as objective a way as possible to allow prospective applicants to self-select into or out of consideration. Job characteristics are by nature objective, and any positive or negative interpretation of them should be left to the applicant. For example, rather than stating that the organization has a high-pressure work environment, communicating that the job requires attention to detail and a sense of time urgency would be more appropriate.

Three functions are served by an RJP are:[90]

1. *Self-selection:* Providing a more balanced picture of the job and the organization allows applicants to drop out if the opportunity is not a good match for them.[91]
2. *Vaccination:* RJPs may "vaccinate" employees' expectations and allow them to develop coping mechanisms to deal with unpleasant features of the job. The employee is then better prepared and less negatively affected by the features.
3. *Commitment to the choice:* Learning about potential negative aspects of a job before accepting a job offer may increase job commitment because the employee knowingly accepted the offer.[92]

so what**?**

Realistic job previews are not intended to present the most negative picture of a job and turn off candidates. The goal is to present realistic, balanced information that allows candidates to assess their fit with the position.

Because RJPs are relatively inexpensive to develop and communicate, they may be useful for reducing turnover rates when departing employees say jobs were not what they expected when they accepted job offers.[93] Some companies also use RJPs to counter inaccurate employer images. McDonald's responded to critics in the United Kingdom who claim it is a poor employer by launching a campaign with the slogan "Not bad for a McJob," which describes the flexible hours and benefits the company offers.[94] Online shoe retailer Zappos even developed a music video to give job seekers more information about their unique, fun-loving culture.

Developing a realistic picture of the job does not have to be expensive or difficult. Focus on aspects of the work not likely to be known by an outsider—say, the fast pace, high-performance expectations, working conditions, and work hours— rather than things that are already visible or known to applicants. Research what the firm's current employees like and dislike about the job. A survey might indicate that they particularly like the pay and benefits, friendly culture, and supportive supervisors. Information collected from departing employees can also help a firm understand what might have been unexpected. All relevant information can then be included into a realistic recruiting message. The most effective RJP design for reducing turnover might be a post-hire RJP designed to signal organizational honesty and delivered orally or in writing.[95]

The best thing to do with a job that has potentially undesirable characteristics is to improve it as much as possible before recruiting candidates. Poor supervisors can be trained or separated, pay levels can be raised, or working conditions can be improved. Providing realistic job information about a bad job is no substitute for providing a better job.

This chapter's case study describes how one convenience store chain effectively used RJPs to reduce turnover.

Sheetz developed a series of Web-based realistic job preview videos to give potential applicants the ability to assess if a job is a good fit for them before they apply. The videos helped to reduce new hire turnover and saved the company hundreds of thousands of dollars in the first year alone.

CASE STUDY: Realistic Job Previews at Sheetz

Sheetz is one of the fastest growing family- and employee-owned convenience stores in the United States, with over $6 billion in sales, over 430 locations across six states, and over 14,500 employees.[96] After experiencing an average 49 percent turnover at its stores, it wanted to improve its recruiting and retention practices to reduce attrition by creating a more effective recruiting process.[97]

Continued

To give applicants a better understanding of the job requirements, personal appearance expectations, and pre-employment screening processes, it decided to develop a series of Web-based realistic job preview videos to help potential applicants assess if the job is right for them before applying. The first video is a pep talk from the Chairman of the Board, Steve Sheetz, about career opportunities and expectations at the company. Detailed video job profiles are then presented by a beverage host or hostess, sales associate, shift supervisor, assistant manager, and associate manager. Although each video cost about $45,000, including a job analysis, filming, editing and production,[98] they reduced new hire turnover 2 percent in the first year, saving $350,000 in manager time alone.[99]

Questions

1. Why do you think the RJP has been effective in reducing turnover at Sheetz's retail stores?
2. How could Sheetz improve the video to enhance its effectiveness?
3. What else might Sheetz do to reduce turnover among its retail employees?

Applicant Attraction Strategies

Having a great job opportunity does not guarantee sufficient numbers of quality applicants. Applicants must first be attracted to a job opportunity before they are willing to apply. One popular model of applicant attraction[100] suggests that job seekers research potential employers by gathering information about the types of rewards offered and whether their skills meet the requirements of any job openings. They also look for signals that help them assess the culture of the organization to assess their likely fit with the job and the company. When applicants are attracted to a firm, they are more likely to apply for jobs, accept job offers, and remain with the company over time.

Next, we discuss the role of a company's organizational and employer images in applicant attraction.

Employer Image

organizational image
people's general impression of an organization based on both feelings and facts

Because most applicants have a limited amount of information early in the job search process, their decisions to apply or not apply for different opportunities are largely based on general impressions of organizational attractiveness.[101] **Organizational image** is people's general impression of an organization based on both feelings and facts.[102] The first thoughts that come to mind when you think about a particular company reflect the company's image.

People usually have an image for an organization and its products whether the organization is proactive in establishing it or not, but these images are not always accurate. If a company known for poor management practices is acquired and the processes are improved, the company's negative image may persist. Many factors, including community involvement, ethics violations, environmental accidents, and corporate philanthropy, can affect an organization's image positively and negatively. Most of us prefer to be members of an organization that has a favorable image.[103]

An organization's image can:[104]

- Be positive or negative
- Be weak or strong
- Be clear or vague
- Vary from person to person
- Change over time

Organizational images have been found to differ across subgroups of individuals. Corporate executives and college undergraduates sometimes disagree in their corporate image ratings. In one study, executives' corporate images relied on economic performance indicators and detailed knowledge of the companies. College students' image assessments were influenced more strongly by familiarity with the organization (using its products, knowing an employee, and seeing company advertisements).[105] Exposure to a greater amount of positive organizational information enhanced the organization's image as an employer and increased undergraduates' job pursuit intentions with that company.[106]

An **employer image** is an organization's reputation as an employer. A positive employer image enhances an organization's attractiveness to job seekers. Because college undergraduates' employer images are malleable and independent of their assessments of the organization's corporate image, organizations that do not have high-profile corporate images may still be able to compete successfully for undergraduate students by using recruitment messages that establish a positive employer image for the organization.[107] Because different people base their employer image assessments on different factors, different methods are likely to have different success rates in influencing the organization's image among different groups. Providing different information about the organization to different types of recruits may maximize the organization's appeal.

An employer's reputation or image is valued differently by people from different cultures. One study found that job seekers from collectivist cultures placed greater importance on a firm's reputation or image than did job seekers from more individualistic cultures.[108]

Let's next explore employer branding and how it can influence a firm's employer image.

Employer Brand

A **brand** is a symbolic picture of all the information connected to a company or a product, including its image. Although images are created and held by individuals, organizations create their brands and often try to link their brands with their business strategies. For example, for many people Saks Fifth Avenue, Gucci, and Lexus conjure the intended images of luxury and quality. When you think of Wal-Mart and Old Navy, you probably think of low-cost products. These companies have created effective consumer brands that reinforce their business strategies. Brands are often represented by symbols such as logos, slogans, and designs. Brand recognition is affected by a person's experiences with the specific product or service and through the influence of communications, advertising, and media exposure.[109]

Firms often create **employer brands** to manage internal and external perceptions of what it is like to work there. An employer brand summarizes what an employer offers to employees and answers the question, "Why should I work here?" Employer brands influence people's intentions to apply for jobs.[110] Rich Floersch, McDonald's chief human resources officer, states, "I really believe that the strongest employment brand that you can have is one where employees say they are proud to work for their companies. Our goal is to continue to build that sense of pride."[111]

> *"I really believe that the strongest employment brand that you can have is one where employees say they are proud to work for their companies. Our goal is to continue to build that sense of pride."*
>
> **—Rich Floersch, Chief HR Officer, McDonald's**

The more favorable a company's image and brand are, the more people are likely to consider the organization attractive as an employer and respond to its recruiting advertisements.[112]

---

employer image
an organization's reputation as an employer

so what?
Crafting an employer image can increase an organization's appeal to potential recruits.

brand
a symbolic picture of all the information connected to a company or a product, including its image

employer brand
summary of what an employer offers to employees

This is why newer or lesser-known organizations with weak or nonexistent brands often have greater difficulty attracting applicants using passive recruitment sources, such as job board postings, than organizations that are favorably thought of and more widely known.

Oath (formerly Yahoo!) actively created an employer brand based on its corporate mission, brand, and values. Oath's employer brand enables it to best market itself to both technical and nontechnical talent. The recruitment brand is consistent, but it looks different depending on where it is being used, such as at colleges, at a technical conference, or for attracting marketing people.

An effective employer brand differentiates a firm from its talent competitors and appeals to targeted applicants. It is also critical that the company deliver on its employer brand promises. In the age of Glassdoor.com, Vault.com, and other Internet sites where employees share their insights and experiences with their employers, what a firm delivers to its employees will generally be widely known. If new hires expect that an employer holds certain values and will provide a certain type of employment experience, they are likely to leave if it does not meet their expectations.

Employer branding should not try to fool potential applicants—it should effectively communicate the firm's message of what it intends to provide as an employer.[113] As one employer branding expert said, "The purpose of the employer brand proposition is not to invent a further set of values but to help to ensure that the purpose and value statements that currently exist are translated into something relevant and meaningful to employees, and made consistent with the values the organization wishes to project externally."[114]

Table 5.4 contains some popular companies and their employer brand slogans.

It can be worthwhile for any organization to evaluate its brand among its targeted applicant pools and take steps to make it as strong and positive as possible before launching a recruiting campaign. Rather than have a one-size-fits-all marketing strategy, Allstate Insurance Co. customizes its marketing and employment offerings. Depending on a job candidate's age and situation, the company might emphasize its stability, growth opportunities, or specific benefits. Suzanne Sinclair, director of leadership talent acquisition, says, "When you look at different segments of the labor market, there are discernible differences in what [job candidates] want."[115] U.K. retailer Tesco explicitly divides its potential front-line recruits into three segments: Those joining straight from school, students looking for part-time work, and graduates. A separate section of the company's website is devoted to each group that contains recruiting materials tailored to that group.[116]

? so what

An effective employer brand both differentiates a company from its talent competitors and attracts targeted applicants.

"When you look at different segments of the labor market, there are discernible differences in what [job candidates] want."

—Suzanne Sinclair, Director of Leadership Talent Acquisition, Allstate

table **5.4**

Employer Brand Slogans

P&G: "A New Challenge Every Day"
Eli Lilly: "Innovation Has a Face: Our People"
Medtronic: "Careers with a Passion for Life"
Pepsi: "Performance with Purpose"
Southwest Airlines: "Not Just a Career, a Cause"

One way a company can distinguish itself is by focusing on its symbolic meaning as an employer[117]—for example, whether applicants think of the company as trendy, prestigious, or innovative and whether its jobs are thought of positively. Because repetition is powerful in marketing messages, recruiters and employees should be trained in how to consistently and clearly promote the employer's brand at every opportunity. Managers can be trained to present a brief pitch designed to attract talent that is concise, compelling, and answers questions including: How is the company different? What is its vision? Why should a talented person join?

Magazines and other publications and organizations periodically assess employers in terms of how good they are to work for. This can significantly enhance a firm's employer brand. *Fortune* magazine's annual lists of the "100 Best Companies to Work For" and the "Best Companies for Minorities," *Working Mother* magazine's annual list of the "100 Best Companies for Working Mothers," and the American Association of Retired Persons' list of the "Best Employers for Workers over 50" are good examples of such assessments. How an organization is reputed to treat its employees can greatly influence its attractiveness to applicants. This explains why many organizations are eager to appear on lists such as these.

Increased job seeker interest resulting from a positive brand increases the burden on the organization's selection system, and there is no guarantee that more applicants mean higher applicant quality. Once a company is on a "best companies to work for" list, it also risks negative reactions from existing employees if it later falls off the list. Although many employers try to be named to these lists, the competition for developing ever-creative and ever-increasing employee benefits might not be something to which every organization wants to commit.

so what?

Being an employer of choice can increase the volume of applications without necessarily improving applicant quality.

Ethical Issues

There are numerous ethical issues with sourcing and recruiting. Sharing only appropriate information, maintaining confidentiality, and providing timely information and feedback to candidates and hiring managers are essential. Poaching talent from competitors and misleading recruits about the nature of the job or about their chances of getting a job offer are other common ethical issues.

Some recruiters, particularly those in the military, are punished if they fail to meet recruiting quotas. This can increase unethical behavior by putting hiring numbers above all other goals. When *ABC News* put hidden cameras on a group of high school students posing as potential applicants and sent them into 10 Army recruiting stations in New York, New Jersey, and Connecticut, more than half of the recruiters were caught lying. One recruiter wrongly told the applicant that his chances of being deployed to Iraq or Afghanistan after basic training and job school were "slim to none," when deployment was likely. Another recruit was told he could quit the Army whenever he wanted to just by asking, which is not the case.[118]

Because there is no regulating agency that oversees sourcing and recruiting practices, ethical behavior begins by clearly defining expected recruiter behaviors when interacting with candidates and hiring managers. Creating an ethical code for sourcers and recruiters that emphasizes key values and provides ethical guidance can help. Ensuring that hiring agreements are in writing can help to resolve more complicated issues, as can providing a clear channel for recruiter questions and hiring issues.

so what?

Ethical codes and guidelines are essential in guiding sourcer and recruiter behaviors.

In addition to a decreased risk of lawsuits, there are numerous benefits to ethical sourcing and recruiting practices. High-quality passive candidates are often more reluctant to pursue job opportunities with recruiters they do not trust. Because recruiters often rely on referrals, more ethical recruiters will also be more trusted and will receive more leads. Applicant reactions are meaningfully related to how attractive they find the organization and various intentions, including their intentions to pursue the job, accept the job, and recommend the job to others. Applicant reactions also influence the acceptance of job offers and candidates' willingness to recommend the employer to others.[119] Ensuring that recruiting methods are perceived as fair and build trust enhances the effectiveness of both current and future recruiting efforts.

Summary and Application

Sourcing and recruiting lay the foundation for effective HRM and effective organizations. By identifying where quality recruits can be found, sourcing is the foundation of an organization's talent supply chain. By persuading the right people to apply and accept job offers, recruiting brings in the talent that creates an organization's competitive advantage and executes its business strategy. No training program can instill skills that employees are unable or unwilling to learn, and no compensation program can motivate employees to do things they are unable or unmotivated to do. Because different types of job candidates respond differently to different recruiting sources and attraction strategies, it is important to tailor recruiting strategies to the talent being targeted.

Real World Response

Analyzing Recruiting Sources at Valero Energy

Some of Valero Energy's sources of labor include succession management, employee referrals, outsourcing, niche websites, college hiring, and contract workers.[120] Valero uses a "talent pipeline model" to evaluate its recruiting sources and chooses those best suited for each job opening. This model lets Valero quickly change between various talent sources depending on which is likely to best meet it current business needs.

Valero began measuring every source of labor by speed, cost, and efficiency.[121] Valero also categorized its labor supply channels into four areas:

1. Full-time employees;
2. Temporary employees;
3. Business process outsourcing; and
4. Alternative sources.

Valero continually evaluates its recruiting sources to improve its recruiting function and best utilize each source. A weekly sourcing-channel report identifies the sources having a major impact on the firm's recruiting success based on cost, time, and quality. This helps Valero's recruiting managers identify possible problems and correct them early. To maximize results, sourcing outcomes are even tracked down to the individual recruiter level.[122]

To predict which recruiting sources will be most effective with a staffing need, Valero uses past employment, cost, and employee performance data. The data from these reports helped Valero reduce its hiring costs by 60 percent in just two years. By examining historical data, such as recruiting costs, where new hires were sourced, how long they stay, how well they fit in with Valero's culture, and their level of productivity, the company can identify the best recruiting sources for each hiring project both financially and strategically, or even whether it is best to outsource the work.[123]

Takeaway Points

1. Sourcing and recruiting are related but distinct activities. Sourcing is more analytical and identifies qualified individuals and labor markets from which to recruit. Recruiting is more interpersonal. Recruiting activities influence the number or type of people willing to apply for and accept job offers.
2. An active job seeker is actively on the job market and can be reached through traditional job advertising methods. A semipassive job seeker is somewhat interested

in finding a new job but is not constantly looking for one. More proactive and strategic recruiting efforts are required to reach semipassive than active job seekers because they are not regularly looking at traditional recruiting channels. A passive job seeker is not actively seeking another job but could be tempted by the right opportunity. Because they are happy in their current positions, it often takes more time and information to persuade passive job seekers to pursue a different job opportunity.

3. Recruitment spillover effects are the positive or negative unintended consequences of recruiting activities. Viewing every hiring prospect as a potential customer or lost customer and treating all applicants with respect promotes positive spillover effects.

4. Realistic job previews present both positive and potentially negative information about a job in as objective a way as possible to allow prospective applicants to self-select into or out of consideration. People who would have been poor fits can self-select themselves out of consideration or not apply, and those who accept job offers are more likely to stay because they do not feel misled about the job and better know what to expect.

5. An employer image is an organization's reputation as an employer. An employer brand is a summary of what a company offers to employees. Employer images are created and held by individuals, whereas organizations proactively create their brands. By increasing outsiders' understanding of what the company offers as an employer, employer brands increase a company's attractiveness as an employer.

Discussion Questions

1. Do you think that most job seekers are active, semipassive, or passive? What does this mean to organizations' recruiting efforts?
2. If you needed to hire researchers who are key to your company's competitive advantage, what recruitment outcomes would you focus on? If you were hiring cashiers for a low-cost retail store, what recruitment outcomes would you focus on? Why do your answers differ?
3. If an employer wanted to get a recruitment message to you, what recruitment sources would be most effective? Which would be least effective?
4. When do you think an organization should offshore work? When should it not offshore work?
5. Have you ever been particularly impressed or unimpressed with the way a company handled its recruiting of you? If so, were there any spillover effects?
6. What do you think are the most important recruiting metrics? Why?
7. What could a recruiter do that would make you more (or less) interested in pursuing a job opportunity?
8. Do employer images and employer brands influence your job search? If so, in what ways?

Personal Development Exercise: Develop Your Résumé

Using the tips in this chapter's Develop Your Skills feature, write (or revise) your résumé. Form a group with two to three other students, exchange résumés, and give each other developmental feedback about the strengths and the weaknesses of each one. Be sure to incorporate action verbs such as those found at http://jobmob.co.il/blog/positive-resume-action-verbs/.

Strategic HRM Exercises

Exercise: What is it Like to Work for the CIA?

It is obviously critical that an organization such as the U.S. Central Intelligence Agency (CIA) attract and hire the right people for its delicate and sometimes dangerous intelligence work. To give potential applicants a better perspective on what is involved in intelligence work and allow them some insight into whether their judgment and decision-making capabilities are likely to be a good fit with the demands of the job, they have created a job preview simulation.

For security reasons, CIA analysts cannot be approached by potential recruits and asked about their work. To help job seekers become familiar with these secretive career paths, the CIA created a crisis simulation competition that presents university teams with simulated intelligence traffic and gives them limited time to analyze the information with the help of a junior analyst. The teams then brief a senior analyst on their conclusions.[124] Events unfold rapidly, and participants learn at the end whether their analysis was correct.[125] The main job of a CIA analyst is to study and evaluate security information and make written and verbal reports of their assessments to U.S. policymakers.[126]

The CIA's regional recruiters hold about six of these simulation events per semester to educate college students about the CIA analyst job. Students are often interrupted while they were presenting their information with questions like "Why didn't we know about this sooner?" or "So what should we do?" to help students understand some of the realities for an analyst, which include critical thinking skills, concision, improvising, and working in groups.[127]

One participant commented, "The analysts are not just these intimidating people in suits. They are real people who are easy to talk to, and the insight I gained was not something that I could have experienced outside of this event."[128]

1. How does this simulation help the CIA recruit?
2. What are some limitations to this simulation?
3. How else can the CIA effectively source and recruit top quality talent?

Exercise: Targeted Sourcing

Think of two companies in an industry in which you are familiar that pursue different strategies. Maybe one focuses on low costs (e.g., Wal-Mart), and the other focuses on high-quality products or high customer service (e.g., Nordstrom). How would you source sales employees for each company? How and why do your recommended sourcing strategies differ for each organization?

Exercise: Internet Recruiting at Fizz

Imagine that you have just been hired as a recruitment specialist for Fizz, a fast-growing beverage company. The company has been finding it difficult to attract sufficient numbers of quality recruits. The leadership team has given you the responsibility for redesigning the website to improve the company's recruiting and hiring performance. The website has not been redesigned for several years and is in need of a pretty serious redesign.

Your boss would like a brief report on the following:

1. Analyze three competitor websites to identify their primary features and identify their strengths and weaknesses. What seems to work well on the competition's websites, and what should Fizz avoid doing on its own recruitment site?
2. Recommend five features that Fizz should include on its own recruitment page.

Exercise: Realistic Job Preview for FedEx Ground Package Handlers

View the video, "GroundWarehouseJobs Virtual Job Preview" (3:18). After watching the video, answer the following questions:

1. What type of recruit do you think would be turned off by this video?
2. What type of recruit do you think would be interested in working as a package handler for FedEx after watching this video?
3. What recommendations for improvement would you give FedEx about this video?

Exercise: Using HRM to Achieve Organizational Objectives

We would like to thank Professor Bobbie Knoblauch of Wichita State University for this exercise idea.

Assume that you are the human resources manager for BittyBots, a company that manufactures toy robots. You just received a request to hire five people from the manufacturing manager. List the pros and cons of two alternative responses:

1. "Will do"—we'll get right on it and let you know when your new hire will be starting.
2. "We need your involvement to effectively hire people"—let's discuss how HRM will partner with you to get this done most effectively.

Integrative Project

Using the same job you analyzed in the previous chapter, develop a sourcing and recruiting strategy to locate and attract high potential applicants. Identify three recruiting sources that you feel would be effective, and explain your reasoning. Then create a job posting that could appear on your careers site that would interest high-potential recruits in applying for the position. Be sure to incorporate realistic job preview information in your posting.

Video Case

Imagine that you are meeting with some coworkers at Happy Time Toys to discuss how to best hire five new sales managers. *What do you say or do?* Go to this book's video case, watch the challenge video for this chapter, and choose the best video response. Be sure to also view the outcomes of the two responses you didn't choose.

Discussion Questions

1. Which aspects of HRM discussed in this chapter are illustrated in these videos?
2. How would you determine the best recruiting approach? Explain your answer.
3. As a manager, what else might you suggest the company do? Explain your answer.

Endnotes

1. Schweyer, A., & LaMotta, S. (2005). From the basement to the boardroom at Valero Energy. *Human Capital Institute*, July. Retrieved March 9, 2017, from http://www.hci.org/files/field_content_file/hciLibraryPaper_17681.pdf

2. Sullivan, J. (2005, September 18). How a former CEO built a world-class recruiting department. Retrieved March 9, 2017, from http://www.drjohnsullivan.com/articles-mainmenu-27/recruiting-strategy-mainmenu

-36/92-how-a-former-ceo-built-a-world-class-recruiting -department

3. Watson Wyatt Worldwide (2005). *Maximizing the Return on your Human Capital Investment: The 2005 Watson Wyatt Human Capital Index Report.* Washington, DC: Watson Wyatt Worldwide.

4. Welch, J. (2014, March 24). So many leaders get this wrong. *LinkedIn.* Retrieved February 22, 2017, from https://www .linkedin.com/pulse/20140324053712-86541065-so-many -leaders-get-this-wrong

5. Barber, A. E., & Roehling, M. V. (1993). Job postings and the decision to interview: A verbal protocol analysis. *Journal of Applied Psychology*, *78*, 845.

6. Pyrillis, R. (2011). Who knows what talent lurks in the heart of the Web? *Workforce Management*, February 24.

7. McIntosh, R. (2005, October 27). Building creative and aggressive sourcing strategies. *ERE.net.* Retrieved March 11, 2017, from http://www.ere.net/2005/10/27/building-creative -and-aggressive-sourcing-strategies/

8. Weiss, D. (2012). McAfee: Building a community of talent. *Talent Management*, February, 22.

9. Blau, G. (1990). Exploring the mediating mechanisms affecting the relationship of recruitment source to employee performance. *Journal of Vocational Behavior*, *3*, 303–320; Griffeth, R. W., Hom, P. W., Fink, L. S., & Cohen, D. J. (1997). Comparative tests of multivariate models of recruiting sources effects. *Journal of Management*, *23*, 19–36.

10. Gardner, N., McGranahan, D., & Wolf, W. (2011). Question for your HR chief: Are we using our 'people data' to create value? *McKinsey Quarterly*, March. Retrieved March 23, 201, from https://www.mckinseyquarterly.com/PDFDownload .aspx?ar=2772

11. *Ibid.*

12. Behn, B., Dawley, D., Riley, R., & Yang, Y. (2006). Deaths of CEOs: Are delays in naming successors and insider/outsider succession associated with subsequent firm performance? *Journal of Managerial Issues*, *18*, 32–46.

13. *Ibid.*

14. Fulmer, R. M. (2002). Choose tomorrow's leaders today. *Graziadio Business Report*, Winter, Pepperdine University. Retrieved April 22, 2012, from http://gbr.pepperdine.edu/021 /succession.html

15. Code Jam. (2017). Retrieved March 12, 2017, from https://code .google.com/codejam/

16. Sullivan, J. (2008). Recruiting strategies—Proximity recruiting using a taco truck. *ERE Media.* Retrieved March 14, 2017, from https://www.eremedia.com/ere/recruiting-strategies-proximity -recruiting-using-a-taco-truck/

17. See https://www.americasarmy.com/

18. Wheeler, K. (2010, December 22). Serious recruiting games: 6 tips for using games and simulations for recruiting success. *ERE Media.* Retrieved March 17, 2017, from https://www.eremedia .com/ere/6-tips-on-using-games-and-simulations-for-recruiting -success/

19. *Ibid.*

20. Graber, J. (2016). Onboarding millennials. *Talent Management*, January/February 16.

21. Employee Referrals. (n.d.). Retrieved April 15, 2012, from http://www.boozallen.com/careers/find-your-job/employee -referrals

22. Designing and managing successful employee referral programs. (2016, December 20). *Society for Human Resource Management.* Retrieved March 12, 2017, from https://www .shrm.org/resourcesandtools/tools-and

-samples/toolkits/pages/tk-designingandmanagingsuccessfulemp loyeereferralprograms.aspx

23. Employee referrals improve hiring. (1997, March 13). *BNA Bulletin to Management*, 88.

24. Moser, K. (2005). Recruitment sources and post-hire outcomes: The mediating role of unmet expectations. *International Journal of Selection and Assessment*, *13*, 188–197.

25. Hill, R. E. (1970). New look at employee referrals as a recruitment channel. *Personnel Journal*, *49*, 144–148.

26. Weller, I., Holtom, B. C., Matiaske, W., & Mellewigt, T. (2009). Level and time effects of recruitment sources on early voluntary turnover. *Journal of Applied Psychology*, *94*, 1146–1162.

27. Taylor, M. S., & Collins, C. J. (2000). Organizational recruitment: Enhancing the intersection of research and practice. In C. L. Cooper & E. A. Locke (Eds.), *Industrial and organizational psychology: Linking theory with practice.* Oxford, UK: Blackwell, 304–330; Pesek, J., & McGee, C. (1988). Recruitment source as a factor affecting turnover & performance in hospitals. *Journal of Applied Business Research*, *4*, 167–172.

28. Schramm, J. (2015). Are you on #socialmedia? *HR Magazine*, December 2015.

29. Luhby, T. (2011, May 18). The secret life of a resume. *CNN Money.* Retrieved March 14, 2017, from http://money.cnn. com/2011/05/18/news/economy/filling_job_opening/index .htm?iid=HP_LN

30. The Home Depot. (2011). Embracing diversity, creating inclusion—One associate at a time. Retrieved May 3, 2012, from http://careers.homedepot.com.edgesuite.net/our-culture /diversity.html

31. The Home Depot, (2016). *2016 Responsibility Report.* Retrieved March 13, 2017, from https://corporate.homedepot.com /sites/default/files/image_gallery/PDFs/THD_0040 _2016%20Responsibility%20Report_Online.pdf

32. The Home Depot. (2011). Military partnership. Retrieved May 3, 2012, from https://careers.homedepot.com/cg/content .do?p=/military

33. The Home Depot. (n.d.). Military commitment. Retrieved March 13, 2017, from https://careers.homedepot.com /career-areas/military/

34. Based on West, L. A., Jr., & Bogumil, W. A., Jr. (2000). Foreign knowledge workers as a strategic staffing option. *Academy of Management Executive*, *14*, 71–83.

35. O'Brien, S. A. (2017, April 7). H-1B visa applications hit cap in 4 days. *CNN.* Retrieved May 7, 2017, from http://money.cnn.com /2017/04/07/technology/h1b-visa-cap/

36. Weise, E. (2017, April 4). 'Panic' as last-minute H1-B visa measures hit. *USA Today.* Retrieved May 7, 2017, from https: //www.usatoday.com/story/tech/news/2017/04/04/new-h-1b-visa -measures-employment/99992732/

37. Petershack, R. (2005, July 18). Consider the legal issues before outsourcing offshore. *WTN News.* Retrieved March 14, 2017, from http://wtnnews.com/articles/2007/

38. *Ibid.*

39. Lazarus, D. (2006, June 9). BofA: Train your replacement, or no severance pay for you. *SF Gate.* Retrieved March 11, 2017, from http://www.sfgate.com/business/article/BofA-Train-your -replacement-or-no-severance-pay-2517604.php

40. Lourie, S. (2004, August 27). An offshore conversation: Symantec's Dean Lane, part 2," *SearchCIO.com.* Retrieved March 13, 2017, from http://searchcio.techtarget.com/qna /0,289202,sid19_gci1002682,00.html

41. Carbonara P. (1996). Hire for attitude, train for skill. *Fast Company*, *4*, 73.

42. Sullivan, J. (2005, July 18). The best practices of the most aggressive recruiting department. *ERE Media*. Retrieved March 12, 2017, from https://www.eremedia.com/ere/the-best-practices-of-the-most-aggressive-recruiting-department/

43. Berfield, S. (2010). The man behind the Bandz. *Bloomberg Businessweek*, June 14–20, 64–67.

44. Hannon, K. (2015, September 7). Welcome back: Boomerang employees are on the rise," *Forbes*. Retrieved March 12, 2017, from https://www.forbes.com/sites/kerryhannon/2015/09/07/welcome-back-boomerang-employees-are-on-the-rise/#353bc7bc6eba

45. Baker, S. (2009, May 4). You're fired—But stay in touch. *BusinessWeek*, 54–55.

46. *Ibid.*

47. Hiring workers the second time around. (1997, January 30). *BNA Bulletin to Management*, 40.

48. McIntosh, R. (2005). Building creative and aggressive sourcing strategies. *ERE Media*. Retrieved March 13, 2017, from http://www.ere.net/2005/10/27/building-creative-and-aggressive-sourcing-strategies/

49. Baker, S. (2009, March 12). Data mining moves to human resources. *BusinessWeek*. Retrieved March 13, 2017, from http://www.businessweek.com/magazine/content/09_12/b4124046224092.htm?campaign_id=rss_daily

50. Luhby, T. (2011, August 1). Community colleges step in to fill 'skills gap'. *CNN Money*. Retrieved March 12, 2017, from http://money.cnn.com/2011/08/01/news/economy/community_colleges/index.htm

51. Available online at http://www.naceweb.org/principles/#careerservices

52. The Top 50. (2009. September 14). *BusinessWeek*, 40.

53. 2006 NACE experiential education survey. (2006). National Association of Colleges and Employers. Bethlehem, PA: NACE.

54. Leak, B. (2006, May 8). The draft picks get younger. *BusinessWeek*, 96.

55. Retrieved March 14, 2017, from https://www.aesc.org/excellence/code-professional-practice and https://www.aesc.org/excellence/aesc-standards-excellence

56. Kaihla, P. (2004, November 1). How to land your dream job. *Business 2.0*. Retrieved March 12, 2017, from http://money.cnn.com/magazines/business2/business2_archive/2004/11/01/8189350/index.htm

57. Gale, S. F. (2014). The recruiting numbers game. *Talent Management*, March, 16–19.

58. Barber, A. E. (1998). *Recruiting employees: Individual and organizational perspectives*. Thousand Oaks, CA: SAGE.

59. Wanous, J. P. (1992). *Organizational entry: Recruitment, selection, orientation, and socialization of newcomers* (2nd ed.). Reading, MA: Addison-Wesley.

60. Rynes, S. L. (1991). Recruitment, job choice, and post-hire consequences." In M. D. Dunnette & L. M. Hough (Eds.), *Handbook of industrial and organizational psychology* (2nd ed.), pp. 399–444. Palo Alto, CA: Consulting Psychologists Press.

61. Racz, S. (2000). Finding the right talent through sourcing and recruiting. *Strategic Finance*, *82*, 38–44.

62. Sullivan, J. (2005, October 2). Best recruiting practices from the world's most business-like recruiting function, part 3. Retrieved March 13, 2017, from http://www.drjohnsullivan.com/articles-mainmenu-27/recruiting-strategy-mainmenu-36/90-best-recruiting-practices-from-the-worlds-most-business-like-recruiting-function-part-3

63. Graber, J. (2016). Onboarding millennials. *Talent Management*, January/February, 16.

64. Carless, S. A., & Hetherington, K. (2011). Understanding the applicant recruitment experience: Does timeliness matter? *International Journal of Selection and Assessment*, *19*, 105–108.

65. Weiss, D. (2012). Avoid post and pray recruiting. *Talent Management*, February, 20–23.

66. Glueck, W. (1973). Recruiters and executives: How do they affect job choice? *Journal of College Placement*, *34*, 77–78.

67. Rynes, S., Bretz, R. D., & Gerhart, B. (1991). The importance of recruitment in job choice: A different way of looking. *Personnel Psychology*, *44*, 487–521.

68. Saks, A. M., & Uggerslev, K. L. (2010). Sequential and combined effects of recruitment information on applicant reactions. *Journal of Business and Psychology*, *25*, 351–365.

69. Connerley, M. L. (2013). Recruiter effects and recruitment outcomes. In K. Y. T Yu & D. M Cable (Eds.), *The Oxford handbook of recruitment*, pp. 21–34. New York: Oxford University Press.

70. Lefkow, D. (2006, December 13). Proactive recruiting metrics. *ERE.net*. Retrieved March 1, 2017, from http://www.ere.net/2006/12/13/proactive-recruiting-metrics/

71. Sullivan, J. (2003, September 29). The top strategic recruiting metrics. Retrieved May 3, 2012, from http://www.ere.net/2003/09/29/the-top-strategic-recruiting-metrics/

72. Hirschman, C. (2003). Incentives for recruiters? *HR Magazine*, November, 86–92.

73. Sullivan, J. (2003, October 27). The recruiter's scorecard: Assessing the effectiveness of individual recruiters. *ERE.net*. Retrieved March 12, 2017, from http://www.ere.net/2003/10/27/the-recruiters-scorecard-assessing-the-effectiveness-of-individual-recruiters/

74. Barber, A. E. (1998). *Recruiting employees: Individual and organizational perspectives*. Thousand Oaks, CA: SAGE.

75. Mason, N. A., & Belt, J. A. (1986). Effectiveness of specificity in recruitment advertising. *Journal of Management*, *12*, 425–432.

76. Barber, A. E., & Roehling, M. V. (1993). Job postings and the decision to interview: A verbal protocol analysis. *Journal of Applied Psychology*, *78*, 845–856.

77. Based on Chapman, D. S., Uggerslev, K. L., Carroll, S. A., Piasentin, K. A., & Jones, D. A. (1995). Applicant attraction to organization and job choice: A meta-analytic review of the correlates of recruiting outcomes. *Journal of Applied Psychology*, *90*, 928–944; Breaugh, J. A., & Starke, M. (2000). Research on employee recruitment: So many studies, so many remaining questions. *Journal of Management*, *26*, 405–434; Taylor, M. S., & Collins, C. J. (2000). Organizational recruitment: Enhancing the intersection of research and practice. In C. L. Cooper & E. A. Locke (Eds.), *Industrial and organizational psychology: Linking theory with practice*, pp. 304–330. Oxford, UK: Blackwell; Ryan, A. M., & Tippins, N. T. (2004). Attracting and selecting: What psychological research tells us. *Human Resource Management*, *43*(4), 305–318.

78. Based on Chapman, D. S., Uggerslev, K. L., Carroll, S. A., Piasentin, K. A., & Jones, D. A. (1995). Applicant attraction to organization and job choice: A meta-analytic review of the correlates of recruiting outcomes. *Journal of Applied Psychology*, *90*, 928–944; Breaugh, J. A., & Starke, M. (2000). Research on employee recruitment: So many studies, so many remaining questions. *Journal of Management*, *26*, 405–434; Taylor, M. S., & Collins, C. J. (2000). Organizational recruitment: Enhancing the intersection of research and practice. In C. L. Cooper & E. A. Locke (Eds.), *Industrial and organizational psychology: Linking theory with practice*, pp. 304–330. Oxford, UK: Blackwell.

79. *Ibid.*

80. Griffeth, R. W., Hom, P. W., Fink, L. S., & Cohen, D. J. (1997). Comparative tests of multivariate models of recruiting sources effects. *Journal of Management, 23*, 19–36.

81. Phillips, J. M. (1998). Effects of realistic job previews on multiple organizational outcomes: A meta-analysis. *Academy of Management Journal, 41*, 673–690.

82. Overman, S. (2010). Hiring candidates who will stay. *Staffing Management Magazine, 6*, 14–17.

83. Landis, R. S., Earnest, D. R., & Allen, D. G. (2013). Realistic job previews: Past, present. In K. Y. T Yu & D. M. Cable (Eds.), *The Oxford handbook of recruitment*, pp. 423–436. New York: Oxford University Press.

84. See https://clients.shl.com/nationwide/

85. See https://www.youtube.com/playlist?list=PLMWBWxMohtSbUWUn1CTsIjm_rUbbf9Jzd

86. See http://www.multipoly.hu/

87. Mak, H. W. (2015, September 21). PwC's Multipoly boosts employee recruitment and retention. *Gamification*. Retrieved March 15, 2017, from http://www.gamification.co/2015/09/21/pwcs-multipoly-boosts-employee-recruitment-and-retention/

88. Meister, J. (2015, March 30). Future of work: Using gamification for human resources. *Forbes*. Retrieved March 15, 2017, from https://www.forbes.com/sites/jeannemeister/2015/03/30/future-of-work-using-gamification-for-human-resources/#32f75da324b7

89. Phillips, J. M. (1998). Effects of realistic job previews on multiple organizational outcomes: A meta-analysis. *Academy of Management Journal, 41*, 673–690.

90. Wanous, J. P. (1980). *Organizational entry: Recruitment, selection, and socialization of newcomers*. Reading, MA: Addison-Wesley.

91. Phillips, J. M. (1998). Effects of realistic job previews on multiple organizational outcomes: A meta-analysis. *Academy of Management Journal, 41*, 673–690.

92. Salancik. G. R., & Pfeffer, J. (1978). A social information processing approach to job attitudes and task design. *Administrative Science Quarterly, 23*, 224–253.

93. Wanous, J. P. (1980). *Organizational entry: Recruitment, selection, and socialization of newcomers*. Reading, MA: Addison-Wesley.

94. McDonald's recruitment drive hits back at critics. (2006, April 21). *Personnel Today*. Retrieved April 23, 2012, from www.personneltoday.com/Articles/2006/04/21/34977/McDonald's+recruitment+drive+hits+back+at+critics.htm

95. Earnest, D. R., Allen, D. G., & Landis, R. S. (2011). Mechanisms linking realistic job previews with turnover: A meta-analytic path analysis. *Personnel Psychology, 64*, 865–897.

96. #55 Sheetz. (2015). *Forbes*. Retrieved March 12, 2017, from https://www.forbes.com/companies/sheetz/

97. Case study Sheetz realistic job preview. (2017). Five Star Development, Inc. Accessed June 21, 2017, from https://cdns3.trainingindustry.com/media/2628434/casestudy_sheetz_rjp.pdf

98. Tucker, M. A. (2012, January 1). Show and tell. *HR Magazine*. Retrieved March 13, 2017, from https://www.shrm.org/hr-today/news/hr-magazine/pages/0112tucker.aspx

99. Case study Sheetz realistic job preview. (2017). Five Star Development, Inc. Accessed June 21, 2017, from https://cdns3.trainingindustry.com/media/2628434/casestudy_sheetz_rjp.pdf

100. Rynes, S. L. (1991). Recruitment, job choice, and post-hire consequences. In M. D. Dunnette & L. M. Hough (Eds.), *Handbook of industrial and organizational psychology* (2nd ed.), pp. 399–444. Palo Alto, CA: Consulting Psychologists Press.

101. *Ibid.*

102. Barber, A. E. (1998). *Recruiting employees: Individual and organizational perspectives*. Thousand Oaks, CA: SAGE.

103. Tsai, W. C., & Yang, I. W. F. (2010). Does image matter to different job applicants? The influences of corporate image and applicant individual differences on organizational attractiveness. *International Journal of Selection and Assessment, 18*, 48–63; Tajfel, H., & Turner, J. C. (1985). The social identity theory of group behavior. In S. Worchel & W. G. Austin (Eds.), *Psychology of intergroup relations*, Vol. 2, pp. 7–24. Chicago, IL: Nelson-Hall.

104. Tom, V. R. (1971). The role of personality and organizational images in the recruiting process. *Organizational behavior and human decision processes, 6*, 573–592.

105. Gatewood, R. D., Gowan, M. A., & Lautenschlager, G. J. (1993). Corporate image, recruitment image, and initial job choice decisions. *Academy of Management Journal, 36*, 414–427.

106. *Ibid.*

107. *Ibid.*

108. Caligiuri, P., Colakoglu, S., Cerdin, J. L., & Kim, M. S. (2010). Examining cross-cultural and individual differences in predicting employer reputation as a driver of employer attraction. *International Journal of Cross-Cultural Management, 10*, 137–151.

109. Kotler, P., & Pfoertsch, W. (2006). *B2B Brand Management*. New York: Springer.

110. Lemmink, J., Schuijf, A., & Streukens, S. (2003). The role of corporate image and company employment image in explaining application intentions. *Journal of Economic Psychology, 24*, 1–15; Gatewood, R. (1993). Corporate image, recruitment image and initial job choice decisions. *Academy of Management Journal, 36*(2), 414.

111. Marquez, J. (2006). When brand alone isn't enough. *Workforce Management, 1*, 39–41. Retrieved March 15, 2017, from http://www.workforce.com/2006/03/13/when-brand-alone-isnt-enough-2/

112. Gatewood, R. D., Gowan, M. A., & Lautenschlager, G. J. (1993). Corporate image, recruitment image, and initial job choice decisions. *Academy of Management Journal, 36*, 414–427; Turban, D. B., & Greening, D. W. (1997). Corporate social performance and organizational attractiveness to prospective employees. *Academy of Management Journal, 40*, 658–672.

113. Barrow, S., & Mosley, R. (2005). *The employer brand*. New York: Wiley.

114. *Ibid.*

115. Light, J. (2011, May 16). In hiring, firms shine images. *The Wall Street Journal*. Retrieved March 12, 2017, from http://online.wsj.com/article/SB10001424052748704810504576307210092435484.html?mod=djem_jiewr_HR_domainid

116. Guthridge, M., Komm, A. B., & Lawson, E. (2008). Making talent a strategic priority. *McKinsey Quarterly, 1*, 48–59.

117. For further information about the role of instrumental functions and symbolic meanings associated with brands, and about image branding in general, see: Lievens, F., & Highhouse, S. (2003). The relation of instrumental and symbolic attributes to a company's attractiveness as an employer. *Personnel Psychology, 56*, 75–102; Gardner, B. B., & Levy, S. J. (1955). The product and the brand. *Harvard Business Review, 33*, 33–39; and Aaker, J. L. (1997). Dimensions of brand personality. *Journal of Marketing Research, 34*, 347–356.

118. Powers, R. (2008, January). Top 10 lies (some) recruiters tell. *About.Com*. Retrieved March 14, 2017, from http://usmilitary.about.com/od/joiningthemilitary/a/recruiterlies.htm

119. McCarthy, J. M., Bauer, T. N., Truxillo, D. M., Anderson, N. R., Costa, A. C., & Ahmed, S. M. (in press). Applicant perspectives

during selection: A review addressing "so what?" "what's new?" and "where to next?" *Journal of Management*. doi: 10.1177/0149206316681846

120. Sullivan, J. (2005, September 18). How a former CEO built a world-class recruiting department. Retrieved March 15, 2017, from http://www.drjohnsullivan.com/articles-mainmenu-27 /articles/recruiting-strategy-mainmenu-36/92-how-a-former-ceo -built-a-world-class-recruiting-department

121. Schneider, C. (2006, February 15). The new human-capital metrics. *CFO Magazine*. Retrieved March 14, 2017, from www .cfo.com/article.cfm/5491043/1/c_2984284?f=archives

122. *Ibid*.

123. Schneider, C. (2006, February 15). The new human-capital metrics. *CFO Magazine*. Retrieved March 12, 2017, from www.cfo.com/article.cfm/5491043/1/c_2984284?f=archives

124. CIA crisis simulation. (2014, December 16). *University of Richmond Newsroom*. Retrieved March 15, 2017, from http: //news.richmond.edu/features/article/-/12346/cia-crisis-simulation -competition--students-get-an-inside-look-at-the-cia-.html

125. CIA. (2013, April 30). CIA recruitment center exploring innovative outreach. Retrieved March 15, 2017, from https: //www.cia.gov/news-information/featured-story-archive/2012- featured-story-archive/innovative-outreach.html

126. Wilcox, A. (2015, March 16). CIA simulation, recruitment event provide insight into analyst job. *Daily Bruin*. Retrieved March 15, 2017, from http://dailybruin .com/2015/04/17/cia-simulation-recruitment-event-provide -insight-into-analyst-job/

127. Wilcox, A. (2015, March 16). CIA simulation, recruitment event provide insight into analyst job. *Daily Bruin*. Retrieved March 15, 2017, from http://dailybruin.com/2015/04/17/cia-simulation -recruitment-event-provide-insight-into-analyst-job/

128. CIA crisis simulation. (2014, December 16). *University of Richmond Newsroom*. Retrieved March 15, 2017, from http:// news.richmond.edu/features/article/-/12346/cia-crisis -simulation-competition--students-get-an-inside-look-at-the -cia-.html

chapter 6

Selection and Hiring

Learning Objectives

AFTER STUDYING THIS CHAPTER, YOU SHOULD BE ABLE TO:

1 Describe the three types of fit.

2 Explain the difference between screening, evaluative, and contingent assessment methods.

3 Describe the difference between structured, behavioral, and case interviews.

4 Describe the two ways of combining assessment scores.

5 Explain the factors that can influence the content of a job offer.

6 Explain the three types of fairness.

7 Describe the difference between implicit and explicit employment contracts.

8 Explain the role of succession management in organizations.

Real World Challenge

How Zappos Hires the Right People

Online shoe retailer Zappos' CEO Tony Hsieh firmly believes that the execution of his company's customer service strategy depends on its employees. Zappos invests heavily in building and maintaining a corporate culture that allows employees freedom and space.[1] Hsieh says, "If you get the culture right, then most of the other stuff, like great customer service or building a brand, will just happen naturally."[2]

Hsieh knows that hiring for ability is only part of what makes Zappos employees successful. To reinforce Zappos' business strategy of providing great customer service and a strong brand, Hsieh wants to ensure that it hires only passionate, customer-oriented people who fit its fun-loving culture. If Hsieh asked you for advice on how to make Zappos' culture fit a priority in hiring, what would you tell him? After reading this chapter, you should have some good ideas.

As former GE CEO Jack Welch once said, "Hiring good people is hard. Hiring great people is brutally hard. And yet nothing matters more in winning than in getting the right people on the field. All the clever strategies and advanced technologies in the world are nowhere near as effective without great people to put them to work." (Jack Welch, Winning, 2005, p. 81).

selection

the process of gathering and evaluating the information used for deciding which applicants will be hired

Once high-potential applicants have been recruited and formally apply for a job, the **selection** process gathers and evaluates the information that will be used to determine who will be hired. The lower the quality of the applicant pool, the better the assessment system must be to weed out any poor fits and identify the applicants most likely to succeed.

> *"Hiring good people is hard. Hiring great people is brutally hard. And yet nothing matters more in winning than in getting the right people on the field. All the clever strategies and advanced technologies in the world are nowhere near as effective without great people to put them to work."*
>
> —**Jack Welch, former CEO of GE**

Time Warner's talent analytics found that, on average, a customer service agent scoring in the top quartile on the pre-hire sales focus assessment generates as much as 71 percent more sales revenue than one scoring in the bottom quartile.[3] Apple Computer cofounder Steve Jobs believed the performance difference between the average programmer and a great one is at least 25 to 1, making it well worth the company's investment in finding and hiring the best talent. As Steve Jobs said, "The secret of my success is that we have gone to exceptional lengths to hire the best people in the world. And when you're in a field where the dynamic range is 25 to 1, boy, does it pay off."[4]

> *"The secret of my success is that we have gone to exceptional lengths to hire the best people in the world."*
>
> —**Steve Jobs, cofounder, Apple Computer**

Once collected, assessment information is combined and used to identify who will receive a job offer. Once the decision has been made to extend a job offer to a candidate, the contents of the job offer and employment contract are determined, and the job offer is negotiated. Because they influence organizational capabilities, selection and hiring influence what employees *can* do.

In this chapter, we describe the goals of candidate assessment and discuss a variety of assessment methods. We also discuss how to combine scores from multiple assessment methods and choose who will receive a job offer. We then cover elements of job offers and employment contracts as well as job offer negotiation tips. After reading this chapter, you should have a good idea how organizations evaluate job candidates, decide who to hire, and create and negotiate job offers.

Assessment Goals

The primary goal of assessment is to identify the people who best meet the organization's staffing goals, which usually include at a minimum high job performance and enhanced business strategy execution. It is also important to identify potentially bad hires because sometimes not hiring poor fits is even more valuable than hiring good performers. Think of the effect that one bad manager can have on a previously engaged and high-performing workgroup, or the effect that one unethical decision can have on an organization, and you'll understand why this is true. We discuss several other important assessment goals next.

Accuracy

It is important that the information used to screen candidates be accurate, both for usability and for legal reasons. The wider the range of talent in an applicant pool, the more important it is that the assessment system accurately weed out the bad fits and identify the good ones. Given the importance of all employees to firm performance, small businesses can be particularly hurt by poor hires.

There are four possible outcomes in selection, two successful and two unsuccessful. Job applicants would be either successful or unsuccessful job performers and are either hired or not hired. As shown in Figure 6.1, hiring successful performers results in *true positives*. Not hiring poor performers produces *true negatives*. These are both desirable outcomes. The two possible undesirable outcomes are not hiring people who would have succeeded, or *false negatives*, or hiring people who perform poorly, generating *false positives*. Perfect prediction is not a realistic goal, but assessment systems can do a good job generating high numbers of true positive and true negative assessment outcomes.

Sometimes one type of error is more important. For example, in high-risk jobs such as an air traffic controller or a surgeon, false positives are particularly problematic. False negatives are particularly damaging when losing out on good talent not only weakens a company's market position but also strengthens the competitor that does hire the person. When a top salesperson or researcher joins a competitor, not only does the company lose out on what that person could have contributed, but its competitor is also strengthened. False negatives are also expensive when a member of a protected class is not hired and wins a big settlement after filing a discrimination lawsuit.

Fit

Can you think of anyone you would not hire (or would like to fire) despite his or her high ability or performance? One possible reason for your answer is the fact that people need to fit the organization, workgroup, and job to be most successful. Let's explore each of these types of fit in more detail.

Person-job fit is the fit between a person's abilities and the job's demands and the fit between a person's needs and motivations and the job's attributes and rewards.[5] Because job performance is usually the most important staffing outcome, person-job fit is the primary focus of most assessment efforts.

Research suggests that person-job fit leads to higher job performance and satisfaction, as well as higher organizational commitment and intent to stay with the company.[6] Some companies customize jobs to maximize employee motivation and performance.[7] Deloitte's Mass Career Customization

person-job fit
the fit between a person's abilities and the job's demands and the fit between a person's desires and motivations and the job's attributes and rewards

Richard Levine/Alamy

When Deloitte started giving its employees some flexibility to fit their job to their personal and professional goals and needs, retention of high performers and employee satisfaction with career/life fit both improved.

figure **6.1**

Possible Selection Outcomes

	Unsuccessful	Successful
Not Hired	True Negative	False Negative
Hired	False Positive	True Positive

program lets employees increase or decrease their responsibilities or travel to fit their personal and professional goals and needs. After implementing the program, Deloitte's retention of high performers improved, and employee satisfaction with overall career/life fit increased 25 percent.[8]

In most jobs, working effectively with coworkers and the boss is also important. **Person-group fit**, or the match between the person and his or her workgroup and supervisor, is also important. Would you be as successful or satisfied in a situation in which you did not get along well with your supervisor and coworkers as you would in a situation in which you did? We know we wouldn't be. Person-group fit leads to improved job satisfaction, organizational commitment, and intent to stay with the company.[9]

Fitting with coworkers' communication styles, goals, and skills increases person-group fit. Person-group fit is particularly important when workers are interdependent, such as in smaller companies and team-oriented work environments.[10] Individual characteristics such as teamwork values, communication skills, and abilities that complement those of the rest of the members are particularly important to assess in environments in which work is done in groups.

Person-organization fit is the fit between an individual's values, attitudes, and personality and the organization's values, norms, and culture.[11] Zappos, featured in this chapter's opening real world challenge, believes that applicants who don't fit its culture won't be happy or successful there.[12]

Hilton Hotels receives over a million job applications and hires approximately 100,000 people each year. The first thing the company looks for is the applicant's fit with the brand and company culture. Hilton wants to hire people for whom hospitality is a calling and is then willing to train for more specific skills. Hilton looks for people who genuinely enjoy service and who are naturally warm, genuine, caring, and joyful. When interviewing housekeepers, one of the questions asked is, "Do you enjoy cleaning? What's your take on dirt?"[13]

Person-organization fit influences important organizational outcomes, including job satisfaction, performance, organizational commitment, and retention.[14] Integrity, compassion, and competitiveness influence person-organization fit. Research has found that person-organization fit has a strong positive relationship with job satisfaction, organizational commitment, and intention to stay and a moderate relationship with employee attitudes.[15] It also modestly impacts turnover, but it has little to no effect on meeting job requirements.[16] Table 6.1 summarizes these three types of fit.

person-group fit
match between an individual and his or her workgroup and supervisor

person-organization fit
fit between an individual's values, attitudes, and personality and the organization's values, norms, and culture

? so what

To maximize performance, retention, and engagement, it is important that employees fit the job, workgroup, and organization.

table **6.1**

Types of Fit

Type of Fit	Possible Dimensions of Fit
Person-Job Fit: The fit between a person's abilities and the job's demands and the fit between a person's desires and motivations and the job's attributes and rewards.	Education Job-related competencies Job knowledge Previous experience Personality characteristics relevant to performing job tasks
Person-Group Fit: Match between an individual and his or her workgroup and supervisor.	Expertise relative to other team members Conflict management style Teamwork values Communication skills Personality related to working effectively with others
Person-Organization Fit: Fit between an individual's values, attitudes, and personality and the organization's values, norms, and culture.	Integrity Compassion Competitiveness Values Goals

Remember that hiring for fit does not mean hiring those with whom we are most comfortable. This can lead to dysfunctional stereotyping against people different from us who may offer a great deal to the firm, and it could have legal ramifications resulting from illegal discrimination.

? so what

Hiring people we like or are comfortable with is not the same as hiring for fit.

Ethics

Ethics is an important issue in assessment. The entire selection process should be managed ethically, including explaining how assessment results will be used and how applicants' privacy will be protected. The ethics of using assessment methods that applicants might find invasive, including drug and integrity tests, should be considered. Assessment administration needs to be done by properly trained and appropriately qualified people, and confidentiality should be protected at all times. Information from rejected candidates should also be destroyed after an appropriate time.

Legal Compliance

Legally defensible hiring practices compare all applicants using the same fair, consistent, and objective information predictive of job success. Although rejecting someone based on subjective evaluations is not in itself illegal, because subjective evaluations are subject to stereotyping, they can create legal trouble if disparate impact occurs. Training is important whenever subjective assessments are used. Many state and federal laws and regulations govern staffing activities. Plaintiffs are often successful, winning court awards that often run into the hundreds of thousands of dollars.

The Uniform Guidelines on Employee Selection Procedures (UGESP) advises employers in legal compliance in candidate assessment and selection. The UGESP assists organizations in complying with the requirements of federal law prohibiting hiring practices from discriminating based on race, color, religion, sex, and national origin. Here are some sample guidelines from the UGESP, which is available online:[17]

- There should be a job analysis that includes an analysis of the important work behavior(s) required for successful performance and their relative importance and, if the behavior results in work product(s), an analysis of the work product(s).
- A requirement for or evaluation of specific prior training or experience. . . . including a specification of level or amount of training or experience, should be justified on the basis of the relationship between the content of the training or experience and the content of the job for which the training or experience is to be required or evaluated.
- Where cutoff scores are used, they should normally be set so as to be reasonable and consistent with normal expectations of acceptable proficiency within the work force.

The Standards for Educational and Psychological Testing[18] is a set of testing standards developed jointly by the American Educational Research Association, the American Psychological Association , and the National Council on Measurement in Education. The Principles for the Validation and Use of Personnel Selection Procedures[19] also provide guidelines for developing and using various assessment and selection methods, specifying principles of good practice in the choice, development, evaluation, and use of selection procedures and describing generally accepted professional practice in selection.

Positive Stakeholder Reactions

Meeting stakeholders' needs, including those of recruits, recruiters, and hiring managers, is another goal of the assessment process. For example, if taking two hours out of their busy day to interview each job candidate seems unreasonable to hiring managers, they may choose not to use the assessment. Recruiters may feel that scheduling four visits for each job applicant is too burdensome, and applicants may withdraw if they feel that they are being asked to complete an excessive number of assessments.

Applicant reactions are important to monitor because applicants are potential referral sources of future hires and are potential or current customers. Applicant reactions have strong effects on their attitudes toward the job and employer, application and job pursuit intentions, and actual job pursuit and job offer acceptance.[20] PNC Financial Services Group Inc. changed its recruiting practices when it realized that its slow response time to job board applicants was potentially hurting its brand. One company representative explains, "Someone who applies for a bank teller position might also be a customer or potential customer, and we were letting those applications fall into a black hole."[21] A company's employer image is reinforced with each contact with the organization, highlighting the importance of consistently reinforcing the firm's desired image at every opportunity.

Applicant reactions also have significant implications for the optimal design and implementation of selection tests.[22] Their reactions influence their performance on selection tests[23] and their ultimate job performance.[24] Applicants with higher test motivation[25] and higher self-efficacy[26] tend to score higher on selection tests, whereas applicants with higher levels of anxiety tend to score lower.[27] Higher levels of anxiety and lower levels of motivation create cognitive interference that lowers our ability to process performance-relevant information, which lowers test performance.[28] Ensuring that applicants believe that all assessments are fair and job-related and that their anxiety is reduced when taking the assessments can improve the accuracy and utility of all assessment methods.

so what

Because applicants are potential future hires, sources of future referrals, and potential or current customers, it is important to treat them ethically and respectfully.

Assessment Methods

The company's choice of assessment methods and the timing of each assessment should be based on the company's goals, timeline, and budget. Some firms use cheaper assessment methods first and more expensive methods later when fewer candidates are being considered. Using the lowest cost assessment methods first, or those assessing candidates' abilities to perform essential job functions, can quickly reduce large candidate pools to a more manageable size. Other strategies are to use the best predictors of job success first, or to first use the methods that promote candidate self-selection to encourage poor fits to opt out earlier to save time and resources. This chapter's appendix explains the role of reliability and validity in choosing candidate assessment methods.

Job candidate assessment is usually done in waves. When people first apply for a job, they are *job applicants* and are evaluated against the minimum acceptable criteria for the job, such as relevant education and experience. The purpose of **screening assessment methods** is to reduce the pool of job applicants to *job candidates*. Job candidates are then evaluated in more depth using **evaluative assessment methods** to identify whom to hire. Assessments typically get more rigorous as people move from being job applicants to job offer receivers.

Once the hiring decision has been made, job offers may be made contingent on the results of **contingent assessment methods**. If the contingent assessment (typically a background check, drug screen, or medical exam) is passed, then a formal job offer is extended.

Table 6.2 summarizes the general effectiveness of the assessment methods we discuss next in terms of applicant reactions, relative cost compared to other assessment methods, and ease of use, although these estimates vary across jobs and companies. The table is intended as a general guide—it is important to always assess how useful any predictor is in a specific job and organizational context before using it. Differences in job requirements, the degree of training assessment administrators receive, and how consistently the tool is used can all influence the costs and usefulness of any assessment method as well as applicant reactions

screening assessment methods
reduce the pool of job applicants to a group of job candidates

evaluative assessment methods
evaluate job candidates to identify whom to hire

contingent assessment methods
a job offer is made contingent on passing the assessment

table **6.2**

Commonly Used Assessment Methods

Assessment Method	Applicant Reactions[29]	Relative Costs[30]	Usability	Validity[31]*	Adverse Impact
Screening Assessment Methods					
Résumés and cover letters	Good	Low	Easy	n/a	Low
Job applications	Good	Low	Easy	n/a	Low
Telephone screens	Good	Low	Easy	n/a	Low
Evaluative Assessment Methods					
Cognitive ability tests	OK	Moderate	Easy	0.51	Moderate
Noncognitive ability tests	Good	Moderate	Easy	n/a	Low
Personality and values assessments	OK	Moderate	Easy	0-0.33	Low
Integrity tests	OK	Moderate	Easy	0.41	Low
Job knowledge tests	OK	Moderate	Easy	.048	Low
Structured interviews	Good	Moderate	Moderate	0.51–0.63	Moderate
Unstructured interviews	OK	Moderate	Easy	0.20–0.38	Moderate
Work samples	Good	High	Moderate	0.34	Low
Simulations	Good	High	Moderate	0.54	Low
Assessment centers	Good	High	Moderate	0.37	Low
Contingent Assessment Methods					
Reference checks	Good	Low	Moderate	0.26	Low
Medical and drug tests	OK	Moderate	Easy	n/a	Mixed
Background checks	OK	Moderate	Easy	n/a	Mixed

*Validity values closer to 1 reflect better prediction of job performance

to it. Validity reflects the method's effectiveness in predicting job performance. In Table 6.2, validity values closer to 1 reflect better prediction of job performance.

When choosing which assessment methods to use, it is important to match the assessment method to the characteristic or competency of interest. It is also helpful to consider the other assessment methods being used to see if they are redundant. Because no assessment method is perfect, it is best to use multiple methods when assessing applicants, particularly for the characteristics most important for job success. This chapter's Strategic Impact feature discusses how Cash America improved hiring quality, reduced turnover, and improved performance by changing its assessment practices.

Although the following external assessment methods are grouped into screening, evaluative, and contingent categories based on how they are typically used, it is possible to use any screening or evaluative assessment at any time during the hiring process. A contingent assessment should only be performed after a job offer contingent on passing the contingent assessment is extended.

Screening Assessment Methods

Résumés and Cover Letters.   Although little research exists on using résumés and cover letters as assessment methods, résumés and cover letters are a core part of the hiring process. Applicants typically submit a résumé summarizing their relevant education and experiences

so what?

The usefulness of an assessment method depends on the job, the skills of the assessor, and the consistency of its use.

so what?

It is best to use multiple assessment methods for the applicant characteristics most important to job success.

Strategic Impact

Tailoring Assessment Methods at Cash America

Using assessment methods tailored to the company and the job can create great value for any organization. When Cash America, a nationwide chain of over 900 loan and pawnshops in 20 states,[32] started evaluating applicants using personality and behavioral assessments benchmarked against its current employees, its turnover rate fell by 15 percent. Because its training programs must prepare employees for every potential financial transaction, Cash America's hiring and training costs are approximately $10,000 per manager and over $2,500 per customer service representative. The new assessment methods saved the company over $1 million by decreasing the number of replacement hires needing training.[33] Although improved hiring quality initially pushed up overall turnover because store managers realized that they no longer had to accept mediocre performance and, therefore, terminated subpar employees, revenue increased, and theft decreased because employee quality increased.[34]

---

along with a cover letter providing additional information about themselves and their fit with the position. Zappos even encourages applicants to submit creative "cover letter videos" when applying for a position.[35] Technology has facilitated the management of the large number of résumés companies often receive, and software has made it possible for firms to do a better and faster job evaluating them.

Résumé information is not always accurate. In 2016, 84 percent of surveyed employers uncovered falsehoods on applicant' résumés.[36] A CareerBuilder study found that lies related to skills and past work responsibilities were the most common.[37] Some CEOs, including Ross Levinsohn of Yahoo!, have even been fired or forced to resign after their companies discovered they inflated their educational credentials.[38] This illustrates the importance of confirming the accuracy of all self-reported information used to make hiring decisions. Requiring that applicants sign a statement that knowingly falsifying any information can result in immediate termination increases honesty.

Job Applications.   **Job applications** require applicants to provide the same written information about their skills, education, work experience, and other job relevant information, making it easier to evaluate and compare them. Although the application may replicate résumé information, applications help to check the accuracy of the information provided. By requiring a little more time and thought than just sending in a résumé, applications can also help to ensure that applicants have a genuine interest in the position and aren't just blindly applying to many employers. Job applications should contain a statement that providing inaccurate information is grounds for dismissal. Any applicant-provided information used for screening should also be verified.

Online applications help standardize the information collected from job applicants while minimizing costs and time. When job seekers apply at any The Fresh Market gourmet grocer, they first complete an online application. Within minutes of finishing, the hiring manger is emailed a three-page report summarizing the individual's biographical information, answers and an analysis of those answers, and a page of follow-up interview questions to use if the applicant passes the screening.[39] Online applications can greatly reduce the assessment burden placed on recruiters and hiring managers.

---

job applications
written information about skills and education, job experiences, and other job relevant information

so what

Online application systems save time and money and help standardize the information collected from each applicant.

In addition to work experience, education, and biographic information, online applications can include assessments of the behaviors and characteristics the company knows contribute to the applicant's work styles and culture preferences. When Mike's Carwash streamlined its application process to be entirely online and included pre-employment assessments of customer service focus, recruiters could spend more time developing relationships with high-quality candidates, which improved its quality of hire and reduced turnover.[40]

Online applications often ask candidates to provide information on protected characteristics, including age, gender, and race. This information is usually requested to collect data for the government showing that the organization is attempting to recruit and hire diverse people. If the online system is created correctly, recruiters should never see this information so that they can't use it to discriminate. Omitting this information will typically not negatively influence an applicant's chances of being considered for the position as the recruiter should not see it anyway, but providing it does help the organization comply with legal reporting requirements.

Telephone Screens.   Many firms use telephone screens to confirm résumé or application information and to assess applicants' availability, interests, and preliminary qualifications. Some recruiters also use phone screens to assess a job's fit with the applicant's noncompensatory screening factors (often salary, location, and travel) to prevent both parties from wasting time. The telephone screen can also help to identify other positions with which the applicant might be a good fit.[41] Siemens uses phone screens to confirm the information in a résumé or application, get examples of the person's on-the-job experience, and get a sense of whether they would be willing to relocate or travel. Siemens also uses phone screens to identify salary expectations and how the person would fit with its culture.[42]

Evaluative Assessment Methods

Evaluative assessment methods are usually more comprehensive in evaluating job candidates' fit with the job and organization. They are also often more expensive and time consuming but should be thought of as an investment in hiring the most successful employees. If a more expensive assessment method results in more good hires, fewer bad hires, and greater retention than a lower cost alternative, it can pay for itself many times over. When Time Warner Cable began using validated assessments for its customer service representative positions, first-year turnover fell 16 percent, performance went up, and the company estimated a cost savings of over $2.6 million.[43]

Cognitive Ability Tests.   China, which began using civil service exams 1,500 years ago, has long used tests to discover talent and determine status.[44] **Cognitive ability tests** typically use computerized or paper-and-pencil tests to assess general mental abilities, including reasoning, logic, and perceptual abilities. Individuals with higher levels of cognitive ability acquire new information faster and use it more effectively. Research suggests that cognitive ability influences job performance largely through its role in the acquisition and use of information about how to do the job.[45] Cognitive ability predicts success in virtually all jobs, but it is most important in complex jobs, when individuals are new to the job, and when changes require workers to learn new ways of performing.[46] Some companies, including Google, prefer to hire for intelligence rather than experience.[47] Apple also believes that raw intelligence and a passion for what you do are the best predictors of success.[48]

There are many different types of cognitive ability tests, including the Wonderlic Personnel Test, Raven's Progressive Matrices, the Kaufman Brief Intelligence Test, and the Wechsler Abbreviated Scale of Intelligence. Scores on these tests can predict someone's ability to learn in training or on the job,[49] be adaptable, solve problems, and tolerate routine. Table 6.3 contains some questions like those found on the Wonderlic Personnel Test.

cognitive ability tests
assess general mental abilities including reasoning, logic, and perceptual abilities

table **6.3**

Cognitive Ability Test Items

These questions are similar to those found on the Wonderlic Personnel Test measuring cognitive ability. The answers are at the bottom of the table.

1. Assume the first 2 statements are true. Is the final one true or false?

   The girl plays soccer.

   All soccer players wear cleats.

   The girl wears cleats.

2. Water sells for $2.50 per bottle. What will 5 bottles cost?

3. How many of the five pairs of items listed below are exact duplicates?

Swalter, A.B.	Neiman, R.E.
Rogers, D.R.	Neuman, P.E.
Holt, S.P.	Rodgers, D.R.
Krain, D.R.	Swalter, A.B.
Neiman, P.E.	Krane, D.R.

4. SATIATE SENTIENT—Do these words

   a. Have similar meanings

   b. Have contradictory meanings

   c. Mean neither the same nor opposite?

Answers: 1. True. 2. $12.50. 3. 1. 4. C.

so what

Although cognitive ability tests predict job performance well, they tend to result in disparate impact.

Because cognitive ability tests are subject to disparate impact against people with certain protected characteristics,[50] it is important to evaluate their effects before using them and to use them carefully and lawfully. Because cognitive ability tests can often be combined with other assessments to reduce adverse impact while retaining or improving the prediction of job success, and because alternative predictors with less adverse impact can predict job success similarly to cognitive ability tests alone, cognitive ability tests should not be used by themselves.[51] We stress that no assessment method is best used alone, but this is particularly true in the case of cognitive ability tests. Many organizations use cognitive ability tests, including the National Football League.[52] Applicants often dislike cognitive ability tests because they don't seem job related.[53]

Noncognitive Ability Tests.   Tests can also measure sensory and psychomotor abilities. **Sensory tests** assess visual, auditory, and speech perception. Speaking clearly, discriminating sounds, and seeing in low light are examples of sensory abilities. **Psychomotor tests** assess strength, physical dexterity, and coordination. Physical ability tests are used to ensure that employees can perform necessary physical tasks (e.g., package loaders must be able to safely lift heavy boxes).

Because psychomotor tests can result in adverse impact, it is important to ensure that the requirement is truly necessary for job performance. When carefully developed to assess relevant job requirements, noncognitive tests can be good predictors of job performance, are well received by applicants, and are relatively easy to use.

Personality and Values Assessments.   Because hundreds of different personality traits exist, personality researchers combined related personality traits into a few broad behavioral

sensory tests
assess visual, auditory, and speech perception

psychomotor tests
assess strength, physical dexterity, and coordination

traits that each encompasses many more specific traits. As a group, these Big Five factors of personality capture up to 75 percent of an individual's personality.[54] The Big Five factors are:

- *Extraversion*: Outgoing, assertive, upbeat, and talkative; predicts salesperson performance.[55]
- *Conscientiousness*: Planful, attentive to detail, willing to follow rules and exert effort; predicts performance across all occupations.[56]
- *Emotional Stability*: Calm, optimistic, well adjusted; predicts job performance in most occupations, particularly those involving interpersonal interactions and teamwork.[57]
- *Agreeableness*: Sympathetic, friendly, cooperative; predicts performance in jobs involving teamwork and interpersonal interactions.[58]
- *Openness to experience*: Imaginative, intellectually curious, open to change; predicts creativity and expatriate performance.[59]

Cognitive ability affects performance primarily through "can do" capabilities. Conscientiousness and emotional stability are both measures of trait-oriented work motivation and seem to affect performance through "will do" motivational components.[60]

Extraversion, agreeableness, and openness to experience predict performance only for specific occupations or criteria.[61] Extraversion is related to performance in jobs that involve interacting with others, influencing others, and obtaining status and power such as management and sales.[62] Agreeableness is best for jobs involving significant interpersonal interaction and jobs involving helping, cooperating, and nurturing others. Agreeableness may also be the single best personality predictor of working well in a team—employees who are argumentative, inflexible, uncooperative, uncaring, intolerant, and disagreeable are likely to be less effective at teamwork.[63] Openness to experience best predicts creativity and adaptability to change.[64]

Like all personality tests, the predictive ability of the Big Five is not high enough to recommend using them by themselves. However, it is often worth assessing the values and personality traits that are tied to job performance business strategy execution. Some companies have improved their effectiveness by actively matching employees' values to corporate culture.[65] Computerized or paper-and-pencil assessments of candidates' values exist, and some firms even watch groups of candidates interact on structured tasks and exercises. Lowe's and Circuit City use personality traits in evaluating job candidates. Wal-Mart prefers to hire applicants who disagree with the statement, "There is room in every corporation for a nonconformist."[66] This makes sense given its focus on following established high-efficiency procedures to maintain low costs.

It is important to note that the Big Five were not developed for work settings and are not necessarily the best personality assessments to use in making hiring decisions. The choice of which personality characteristics to assess should be based on the personal characteristics important to job success. For example, Machiavellianism, or the manipulation of others for one's own purposes, and having an external locus of control, or believing that the environment primarily determines one's experiences,[67] have been found to be related to greater unethical behavior.[68]

Both ethically and legally, applicants' scores on any psychological tests need to be protected.[69] It is a good idea to discuss the use of any psychological test with a qualified lawyer and to comply with relevant laws. If an assessment reveals anything about a mental impairment or a psychological condition, even if it is unintentional, the Americans with Disabilities Act may have been violated.[70] Applicant reactions to personality tests can be somewhat unfavorable as they often do not appear to be job related.[71]

Matching new hires' values and personality to the organizational culture and business strategy can improve performance. Apple evaluates whether senior level hires share the company's fundamental values.[72] Cirque du Soleil developed a creative and rigorous methodology for recruiting and evaluating new talent and is obsessed with making sure recruits understand and embrace Cirque's culture and processes.[73]

so what**?**

The personality characteristics assessed should be those most important to job success.

HR Flexibility

Personality Fit Differs Across Jobs

Different jobs require employees with different combinations of skills, abilities, and personality characteristics. Success as a salesperson is predicted by extraversion, conscientiousness, multitasking ability,[74] and achievement orientation.[75] Entrepreneurialism is predicted by emotional stability and independence.[76] Creativity tends to be predicted by strong symbolic interests, high aspirations, and independence.[77] Ethics, conscientiousness, resourcefulness, and sociability are related to managerial performance.[78] It is important to understand which abilities and characteristics are related to job success before assessing candidates using ability or personality.

This chapter's HR Flexibility feature discusses how different personality characteristics fit best with different types of jobs.

Integrity Tests.   Shoplifting and theft cost U.S. companies tens of billions of dollars every year. Hiring people less likely to steal or engage in other counterproductive behaviors can be particularly important for jobs requiring money handling, working in clients' homes, handling controlled substances, and working with valuable merchandise. **Integrity tests** assess candidates' attitudes and experiences related to their reliability, trustworthiness, honesty, and moral character.[79]

Because integrity tests do not tend to result in adverse impact and appear to be unrelated to cognitive ability, they can add value in predicting job performance and reduce the adverse impact of a cognitive ability test. Faking also does not appear to be a problem with integrity tests.[80]

Integrity tests are relatively inexpensive and can be administered any time during the hiring process. Because theft is not a problem for all companies, sometimes the cost of integrity testing and the small gains in reduced theft are outweighed by the costs of recruiting applicants to replace those screened out. Applicants' privacy rights need to be protected when administering integrity tests, as with any assessment method. Integrity tests can predict job performance, counterproductive work behaviors including absenteeism and disciplinary problems, and theft,[81] although applicants tend to react somewhat unfavorably to them.[82]

Job Knowledge Tests.   **Job knowledge tests** measure the job-related knowledge (often technical) required for success. These tests can assess either the candidate's knowledge of job duties or the candidate's knowledge about and level of experience with important job tasks, tools, and processes. An example is a test assessing a human resource job applicant's knowledge of human resources. Job knowledge tests usually result in minimal adverse impact and can be good predictors of performance, particularly for complex jobs.[83] One survey of 237 companies of all sizes, about half of which were in the United States, found that over half used skill and knowledge assessments in hiring.[84]

Interviews.   Interviews can assess a variety of characteristics, including interpersonal skills, decision-making style, and leadership style. Applicants typically like interviews, often rating them the most job-related selection procedure.[85] Interviews can also serve an important

integrity tests
assess attitudes and experiences related to reliability, trustworthiness, honesty, and moral character

job knowledge tests
measure the knowledge (often technical) required by a job

recruiting purpose and communicate information about the job and the organization to applicants, helping them self-select out if they are a poor fit.[86]

Lodging chain The Four Seasons interviews a high percentage of applicants because it is less concerned with experience than with a positive, helpful outlook, which only comes across in person. "I can teach anyone to be a waiter," says Isadore Sharp, founder, chairman, and CEO. "But you can't change an ingrained poor attitude. We look for people who say, 'I'd be proud to be a doorman.'"[87] Job candidates may face 10 interviews with Goldman Sachs Group before getting an offer.[88] And global beverage company AB InBev's vice president of people personally interviews every candidate for positions at and above the director level for North America because hiring top talent is such a focus for the company.[89]

> *"You can't change an ingrained poor attitude. We look for people who say, 'I'd be proud to be a doorman."*
>
> **—Isadore Sharp, founder, chairman, and CEO of The Four Seasons**

There are two types of employment interviews: Unstructured and structured. **Unstructured interviews** ask varying questions across interviews and usually lack standards for evaluating candidates' answers. The interviewer often relies on personal theories about what makes someone a good hire, such as appearance and nonverbal cues (e.g., confidence and making eye contact), and makes a global evaluation of the candidate when the interview has finished. Due to their lack of consistency, unstructured interviews are difficult to use in comparing job candidates and are not always good predictors of job performance. Given their expense and the legal risks associated with asking nonstandardized questions that have not been shown to be related to job success, unstructured interviews are not recommended.

Interview time is better spent conducting a **structured interview** using consistent, job-related questions.[90] A formal scoring system also helps compare candidates based on their answers. Structured interviews can assess a variety of skills and abilities including problem solving, leadership, and interpersonal skills. Because the questions are based on a job analysis, they are job related and usually well received by candidates. Structured interviews have three characteristics:

1. All applicants are asked the same questions.
2. Questions are systematically developed to assess specific job relevant qualifications.
3. A formal scoring system is used to consistently evaluate answers, and raters are trained in the use of the scoring system.

Structured interviews help reduce the effects of interviewer bias and unrelated factors such as physical attractiveness or fidgeting. Well-developed structured interviews are usually good predictors of job success. They can be moderately expensive to develop and require interviewer training.

There are two types of structured interviews: Behavioral and situational. **Behavioral interviews** are based on the idea that past behavior is a good predictor of future behavior, which is generally true.[91] In a behavioral interview, the candidate is asked to describe a specific problem or situation he or she has faced at work or any other relevant situation. The candidate then describes the action he or she took and the results. For example, to assess influence skills, a candidate can be asked to describe a decision he wanted to influence, what action he took, and what results he obtained. Table 6.4 shows an example of a behavioral interview question and scoring key.

Although interviewees rarely give the exact answers suggested in the scoring key, training helps interviewers consistently score an answer. Interviewers should present the questions in the same way to everyone. Skilled probing can help a candidate describe an appropriate

unstructured interview
varying questions are asked across interviews, and there are usually no standards for evaluating answers

structured interview
uses consistent, job-related questions with pre-determined scoring keys

so what**?**

Structured interviews are more job-related, consistent, and useful than are unstructured interviews.

behavioral interviews
uses information about what the applicant has done in the past to predict future behaviors

table 6.4

Behavioral Interview Question Assessing Customer Service Skills

Question: Tell me about a time when you had to deal with an unhappy customer. What did you do, and what was the result?

5—Excellent: I empathized and tried to find out exactly what was wrong. I found out what the customer needed to be happy and ensured that the customer was satisfied.

4

3—Marginal: I apologized and gave the person a refund.

2

1—Poor: I called my manager to deal with it.

situational interview
asks how the candidate might react to hypothetical situations

example. Behavioral interviews are most useful with candidates who have experience relevant to the questions being asked.

Companies including Southwest Airlines use **situational interviews**, asking people not about past behaviors but about how they might react to hypothetical situations.[92] Situational interviews also do a good job predicting job success.[93] Table 6.5 illustrates a behavioral interview rating scale that can be adapted for any type of structured interview.

table 6.5

Situational Interview Question Assessing Influence Skills

Question: Imagine that you are working on a project team and disagree with your teammates about an important decision. You are sure that your idea is best, but they are unconvinced. What would you do?

5—Excellent: Explain the idea and why it is better than the others without demeaning any of the other ideas. Give specific examples of why my option is the best for the team, and respond to my teammates' questions and concerns until they are also convinced.

4

3—Marginal: Insist that my idea is best and point out the flaws in the other ideas the team is considering.

2

1—Poor: Tell my supervisor about the idea since the team isn't listening.

The appropriateness of behavioral interview questions depends on whether job candidates can be reasonably expected to have had a relevant experience. For example, asking candidates for an entry-level position to relate stories of leadership experiences may not be as effective as asking behavioral questions involving customer service interactions. When interviewing people with limited work experience, situational ("What would you do if . . .") questions can generate more insightful answers than behavioral questions ("What did you do when . . ."). Both types of questions can be used during an interview. This chapter's case study describes how MITRE Corporation uses employment interviews and other assessment methods.

CASE STUDY: Hiring at MITRE Corporation

MITRE Corporation is a not-for profit organization chartered to work in the public interest in the areas of systems engineering and information technology, and it has its own research and development program that explores new technologies. MITRE has won awards for health and wellness and work-life balance, and it has been named to numerous "best places to work" lists.[94] MITRE employs over 7,500 scientists, engineers, and support specialists, most of whom have masters or PhD degrees.[95] The hiring process can take up to three months and is described in detail on the company's website.[96]

The first step of the hiring process is the review of résumés submitted for the position. All submitted résumés are acknowledged by e-mail, postcard, or onscreen if submitted at MITRE's career site. Because MITRE recruiters regularly search submitted résumés for other openings, applicants have the option of being considered for other jobs in the future. Phone screens are sometimes done to acquire additional information about the candidate's knowledge, interview availability, and salary expectations. Hiring managers review the prescreened résumés forwarded to them by a recruiter and select the candidates to be interviewed.[97]

Two to four individual interviews with department representatives are then done to evaluate the candidate and communicate information about MITRE and its work. Some candidates are asked in advance to prepare and deliver a brief presentation. Background checks covering employment history, references, and education are then done for candidates being considered for a job offer. An HR representative contacts selected candidates to present a job offer. Candidates are given a week to make a decision.

Questions

1. What elements of MITRE's hiring process do you find attractive? Which, if any would not appeal to you as a potential candidate? Explain your answers.
2. Do you think that MITRE's hiring process reinforces their image as a desirable employer? Why or why not?
3. How else do you think MITRE should assess candidates? Explain your answer.

In a **case interview**, the candidate is given a business situation, challenge, or problem and asked to present a well thought out solution. The applicant is allowed to ask questions to better understand the situation and gather the information needed to develop a recommendation. There is rarely a single "right" answer to a case. The process used to reach a recommendation is critical too, so be sure to think out loud when working through your answer. Case interviews are typically used to assess business, reasoning, presentation, and communication skills and are popular for management consulting and investment banking jobs. A list of case interview questions and answers for a wide variety of positions including HRM is available online at http://www.consultingcase101.com/.

case interview
the candidate is given a business situation, challenge, or problem and asked to present a well thought out solution

Work Samples.   **Work samples** evaluate the performance of actual or simulated work tasks. A work sample can be as simple as a situational judgment question asking, "What would you do in this situation?" or as comprehensive as an actual portfolio of the applicant's previous work.

A **simulation** is a type of work sample that gives candidates an actual job task to perform or simulates critical events that might occur to assess how well a candidate handles them. Candidates for a 9-1-1 emergency call center might be asked to handle hypothetical calls to assess how they respond, or sales representatives might be asked to communicate by phone with the evaluator and try to sell him or her something.

work samples
evaluate the performance of actual or simulated work tasks

simulation
a type of work sample that gives candidates an actual job task to perform or simulates critical events that might occur to assess how well a candidate handles them

Some companies use simulations and work samples to attract promising job applicants. VCA, an animal hospital chain, runs contests on Facebook to diagnose animal ailments, hoping to drive traffic to its Facebook careers pages and build a database of promising job candidates.[98]

Work samples have low adverse impact and are generally received well by applicants. Work samples are most useful for jobs and work tasks that can be completed in a short period and are less able to predict performance on jobs where tasks may take days or weeks to complete. The difficulty of faking job proficiency helps to increase the validity of work samples. Although they can be expensive to develop and administer, well-developed work samples tend to predict job performance with low adverse impact.

assessment center

puts candidates through a variety of simulations and assessments to evaluate their potential fit with and ability to do the job

Assessment Centers.   An **assessment center** put candidates through a variety of evaluation techniques to evaluate their potential fit with and ability to do the job. Common assessments used in assessment centers are:

- *In-basket exercises* asking the candidate to manage a hypothetical "in-basket" of memos, challenges, and job responsibilities in a set period of time.
- *Group discussions* to assess communication, leadership, and teamwork skills.
- *Simulations* of interactions with subordinates or clients.
- *Decision-making problems.*
- *Oral presentations.*
- *Written communications.*

Assessment centers typically involve approximately six participants and can last multiple days. As participants perform the assessments, they are observed by multiple assessors who are trained to observe and evaluate their behavior and knowledge level. Each assessor observes different participants in each simulation and takes notes on special evaluation forms. When the simulations have been completed, the assessors share their observations and make joint evaluations, incorporating any additional test and interview data. The assessors' final written assessment details each participant's strengths and development needs and evaluates his or her overall potential for success in the target position.[99]

? so what

Contingent assessment methods must be used after the decision to extend a job offer is made.

Contingent Assessment Methods

Contingent assessment methods are administered after the decision to extend a job offer is made. The job offer is then made contingent on the candidate passing the contingent assessment. Reference checks, medical and drug checks, and background checks are three of the most common contingent assessment methods.

Reference Checks.   Reference checks help companies learn about a candidate's past performance or confirm applicant-reported information. Individuals with previous experience with the job candidate, typically people identified by the job candidate, are asked to provide information about him or her. Although previous employers are often unwilling to provide extensive information about a candidate due to risks of a defamation lawsuit, references should still be contacted to reduce the risk of a negligent hiring lawsuit. Sometimes current employees who have worked with the candidate can provide useful information.

Instead of asking general questions, asking references for relevant information about the indicators of success that you have established for the job and asking about the types of situations and work environments in which the candidate would excel can generate useful information. For example:

- What kind of culture would be the best fit for John? Would he thrive in a more laid-back culture or a more structured environment with clear rules?
- Some people willingly assume responsibilities beyond their job description, whereas others focus on performing only their specific job duties. Where does Maggie fit on that continuum?
- Striking the ideal balance between quality and production is critical for us. If you had to choose whether Manuel favored one more than the other, would you say it is toward quality or quantity?

Reference checks have low adverse impact and are generally expected as a part of the hiring process. Many companies use reference checks late in the selection process, but contacting a person's references earlier in the assessment process can also be useful. One survey found that over half of 2,500 hiring managers surveyed have caught job candidates lying on their resumes, so it is a good idea to follow up on any unsubstantiated information used in making a hiring decision.[100]

so what?

Many organizations use reference checks to screen out job candidates, so be sure you provide the names of individuals likely to provide a good reference.

Medical and Drug Tests.   Because of legal compliance issues, medical tests, including drug tests, should be used with great care. Medical exams typically identify a job candidate's potential health risks and must assess only job-related factors consistent with business necessity.[101] Medical information should be consistently assessed for all entering employees in the same job, regardless of disability.[102] The Americans with Disabilities Act regulates the use of medical exams to prevent employers from screening out individuals with disabilities for reasons unrelated to job performance. The most common medical test used is drug testing, which is typically used to establish an applicant's ability to perform assigned job tasks. A survey by the National Safety Council found that over 70 percent of U.S. employers are experiencing a direct impact of prescription drug misuse in their workplaces.[103] Statistics suggest that approximately 10 percent of the workforce abuse alcohol and/or drugs, costing employers billions of dollars per year due in lost productivity, increased health problems, and workplace accidents.[104]

Any medical information obtained should be kept confidential and stored separately from other applicant and employee files.[105] Medical tests can be administered only after all other application components have been cleared and a job offer has been extended. Only by making the job offer contingent on passing the drug or other medical test is it possible to tell whether a rejection is due to insufficient qualifications rather than the test results. An applicant's medical information should be the last information collected after making a contingent job offer so that it cannot be accused of informing the hiring decision.

Although many state and local governments limit or prohibit workplace drug testing unless required by state or federal regulations for certain jobs, most private employers have the right to test for a wide variety of illegal substances. Familiarizing yourself with all relevant state and federal regulations is essential before designing a drug-testing program. Collective bargaining agreements can also impact drug testing policies.

A clear drug testing policy should be in place, and applicants should be informed of the policy before conducting the tests. Drug testing policies often include information about who will be tested, the consequences of a positive test, what substances will be tested for, when testing will be conducted, cutoff levels, safeguards, and confirmation procedures.

Background Checks.   **Background checks** assess factors including personal and credit characteristics, character, criminal history, and reputation. Pre-employment background checks for misdemeanor and felony convictions or other offenses are routine in many industries, including health care, childcare, eldercare, and financial services.

Many companies prefer to outsource background checks to qualified firms. Because criminal records are archived at the county level, criminal records must be searched in each county where the job candidate has lived. Because crimes committed post-hire could contribute to a negligent retention charge, some vendors send automated biweekly updates that alert a company to any new misdemeanor or felony convictions of any current employees.[106]

Organizations are also using online searches to learn about job candidates. Using a search engine such as Google.com to find information about a candidate can uncover additional information about them. Because much Internet content is archived, employers can access information about a candidate that goes back many years. Be sure that you don't post anything online about yourself that you wouldn't want a potential employer to see five or 10 years from now!

background checks
assess factors including personal and credit characteristics, character, lifestyle, criminal history, and reputation

Although roughly half of all employers use credit checks as part of the job application process, some legislators argue that this is unfair given how many people are experiencing economic hardship and not particularly useful, since credit history is irrelevant to many positions. The Fair Credit Reporting Act requires that applicants be provided a copy of their credit report and a written description of their rights under the Act, giving them the opportunity to address inconsistencies before any decisions are made based on the information.

Job candidates have even been denied job offers due to unprofessional content placed on social networking sites such as Facebook.[107] Many recruiters use their own social network to research candidates' Facebook sites. Some recruiters have asked candidates for their passwords so that they can login to their Facebook accounts directly. After a big public backlash, the Social Networking Online Protection Act was introduced that would make asking someone for access to a private account illegal. Facebook's privacy policies also prohibit the forced sharing of this information.

Unless a business is involved in national defense or security, background checks must be relevant to the nature of the job and job requirements. Employers must communicate that background checks will be conducted at the time of application, and applicants must give their written consent.[108] Fully document all background check efforts and any contact made with former employers, supervisors, and references. Although courts are increasingly challenging the use of background checks, consideration of criminal records may pass muster if an individualized approach is taken that considers the nature and the gravity of the offense, how long ago the conviction or completion of the sentence took place, and the nature of the job held or being sought.[109] A growing concern that criminal history checks disproportionately affect black and Hispanic individuals has prompted a "ban the box" movement preventing employers from asking about criminal history on employment applications. As of 2017, at least 24 states and 150 cities and counties have passed laws that require companies to wait until after a candidate has been found to meet the initial qualifications for a position to ask about the person's criminal background.[110]

If a background check uncovers negative information, the job applicant must be given an "adverse action notice," including the screening company's contact information and explaining that the applicant can dispute the information for accuracy or completeness. Applicants must be given a fair amount of time to contest the findings.

Job seekers can check the accuracy of and correct errors in their background reports and credit histories. MyBackgroundCheck.com and MyESRCHECK.com both allow you to perform background checks on yourself and even provide a certificate that verifies your degrees, credit, employment, and criminal history to potential employers. Doing this before you start a job search can ensure that accurate information is in the system and expedite the hiring process once you've found a job.

so what

Doing a background check on yourself can prevent mistakes from interfering with your job search.

An employer does not have to prove that background check results leading to an adverse employment decision are true as long as it conducts a proper investigation and acts in good faith on the information. Potential liability for negligent hiring can also be greatly reduced just by conducting a reasonable background check. Even if an employer is unable to obtain any information about a candidate from a previous place of work, going through the investigative process and documenting it well reduces liability. Background checks should include the accuracy of all stated academic credentials and other information provided by the applicant that is used in making a hiring decision.

Multiple Methods.   Can you imagine receiving a job offer after only a 15-minute interview or based only on your résumé? More extensive assessment reflects a sincere effort on the part of the company to match candidates with jobs at which they are likely to succeed. Don't neglect applicant reactions to assessment methods—applicants who hold positive perceptions about a company's selection processes and view them as fair are more likely to view the company favorably and report stronger intentions to recommend the employer to others and to accept job offers.[111]

Choosing Whom to Hire

Companies typically combine candidates' scores on a variety of assessment methods and compare these overall scores to determine whom to hire. We next discuss various ways of combining assessment scores to create an overall score to use to compare candidates and methods of choosing among the finalists.

Combining Scores

When using more than one assessment method, as is usually the case because using multiple predictors improves the prediction of job success, a candidate's scores on the different assessments must be meaningfully combined to derive an overall score that can be compared across candidates or to a minimum hiring standard. There are two ways of combining assessment scores: Multiple hurdles and compensatory approaches.

Multiple Hurdles.   Requiring candidates to perform at a satisfactory level on one assessment before being allowed to continue in the selection process is called a **multiple hurdles** approach. The FBI uses a multiple hurdles approach when hiring special agents. The FBI requires special agent applicants to first pass a cognitive ability test and a situational judgment test before advancing in the hiring process.[112]

The FBI uses a multiple hurdles selection approach when hiring special agents. Applicants must first pass a cognitive ability test and a situational judgment test before advancing in the hiring process.

Because multiple hurdles are costly and take more time, they are used when the cost of poor performance on a characteristic is high—for example, when safety is at risk. Firefighter applicants are usually required to pass a strength test (e.g., lifting 40 pounds) to ensure that candidates have the physical capabilities to perform the job. If they do not, there is no point in wasting time and resources evaluating them further because they cannot perform an essential job function.

Compensatory Approach.   When you reflect on the best teachers you have had, do you think that they are equally talented? Probably not—different constellations of talents can lead to success for teachers as well as many other jobs. A highly knowledgeable teacher may be an excellent instructor, while a less knowledgeable teacher could be equally effective because of his or her ability to challenge and inspire students. The **compensatory approach** allows high scores on some assessments to compensate for low scores on others. For example, work experience may be allowed to compensate for a lower GPA. This approach is less useful for talents that must exist at a minimum level, in which case the multiple hurdles approach is best.

Combining the Multiple Hurdles and Compensatory Approaches.   Often, some characteristics are considered essential to performing a job, but others can compensate for each other. A manufacturing hire may need to produce a certain number of units per minute on a simulation, which would establish minimum hurdles for productivity, but cognitive ability and personality may be compensatory factors. In this case, a simulation could be an initial hurdle to weed out candidates who do not meet the minimum productivity requirements. Cognitive ability and personality scores would then be combined in a compensatory manner and the highest scoring candidates offered jobs.

Making a Final Choice

Cut scores and rank ordering can be used to identify which finalists receive job offers. Using a **cut score** results in hiring only those who exceed a minimum score. Cut scores are often determined by job experts based on the job's requirements or by a statistical (regression)

---

multiple hurdles
candidates must receive a passing score on an assessment before being allowed to continue in the selection process

so what?

Multiple hurdles is a good choice when candidates must possess at least a minimum level of certain characteristics or talents.

compensatory approach
high scores on some assessments can compensate for low scores on other assessments

cut score
a minimum assessment score that must be met or exceeded to advance to the next assessment phase or to be eligible to receive a job offer

equation that identifies the minimum score on an assessment that is needed to obtain a predicted minimally acceptable level of job success. The FBI's special agent selection process applies cut scores for cognitive ability, a situational judgment test, a structured interview, and a written exercise.[113]

If a minimally acceptable competency level can be identified, then the cut score can be set at this level, and no candidates scoring below this level are considered further. If a company's talent strategy is to hire only the best, the cut score would be set at a high level. If a firm's talent philosophy is to focus on filling vacancies in the short term rather than hiring people for long-term careers, then a lower cut score may be more appropriate. If a company is pursuing a cost leadership strategy, lower cut scores may be necessary to hire people at the targeted salary level. A cut score is set at the level that best accomplishes the company's goals, including the number of hires needed and any affirmative action or EEO goals.

Another option is to **rank order** candidates from highest to lowest score. Although this method identifies the top-scoring candidates, it does not guarantee that any of them meet or exceed minimum hiring standards as cut scores do. Combining the two methods by extending job offers to the highest ranked candidates who exceed a cut score capitalizes on the strengths of both approaches and ensures that minimum hiring quality standards are met. Whenever possible, set cut scores high enough to ensure that new hires are likely to meet or exceed minimum performance standards.[114] It is also a good idea to identify at least one backup hire in case your first choice does not take the job.

Making the Job Offer

Given the importance of making good hires, and the time and money invested in the staffing process just to get to the point of making a job offer, it is surprising how little thought and effort many organizations put into the job offer process. At this stage, the focus shifts from evaluating to persuading the person to choose to work for your company. Thought should go into the content of the job offer, whether further negotiations will be allowed, and how the offer is presented. It is important to remember that financial compensation is not the only way to get top candidates to accept job offers. On the contrary, many of the most desirable employers, including Google and SAS, pay average salaries but provide employees other benefits such as free food, work-life balance, and a high-quality work environment.

Particularly for firms viewing employees as investors of their time and talents rather than as assets to be managed, the job offer should maximize the employee value proposition, or the set of intrinsic and extrinsic rewards an employee receives in exchange for his or her time and talents. The job offer should appeal to the finalist's needs and values and reflect the job rewards that are most important to the individual.

What to Offer

Assessing the likely reaction of the job offer recipient is important, and the offer should be created in a way that he or she will find maximally appealing. The type of job as well as organizational, finalist, external, and legal factors all influence the content of a job offer.

Job Type.   Job offers vary depending on whether the position is full- or part-time, exempt or nonexempt from overtime pay, and the level of the position. Job offers for lower level positions are often shorter and less detailed than job offers made to fill executive jobs.

Organizational Factors.   Organizational factors that can influence job offer content include formal policies, internal equity, how fast the company needs to hire, the content of union contracts, and business strategy. If a company has a policy of giving only standard job offers and standardizing new hire employment terms, then the choice of what to include in any individual job offer is constrained. Job offers must also be tied to the firm's compensation strategy. Some companies focus on preserving internal equity by ensuring that existing employees' employment terms are not exceeded by the terms of new hires' employment. Sometimes a candidate is given an enhanced job offer due to business necessity (the position must be filled immediately to complete an important project, and there is only one acceptable candidate). Although this may help staff the company in the short term, in the long run, it can be costly if current employees threaten to leave the company if their employment terms are not enhanced accordingly.

Union contracts dictate many of the terms and conditions of the employment relationship and can influence what must and what can be included in a job offer. Business strategy also affects job offer content. A firm pursuing a low-cost strategy may be less willing to enrich a job offer than a company pursuing an innovation strategy for which cost is less important and hiring top talent is a priority, but even companies pursuing low-cost strategies may be willing to enrich job offers for top talent in key positions.

Finalist Factors.   The finalist's compensation requirements, qualifications and experience, needs, and whether the finalist has other job offers can influence job offer content.

A finalist with a good job offer from another firm likely needs to be presented with an enticing job offer if the company is to have a chance at hiring him or her.

External Factors.   External factors including the tightness of the labor market, the cost of living, the risk of a coveted finalist being hired by a competitor, and the market level of rewards for the position can influence job offer content. If someone is the only person the organization wishes to hire, presenting a more generous offer can increase the likelihood of its acceptance. Job offer content can also differ based on where in the world the job is located. This chapter's Global Issues feature highlights some of ways job offer content differs in different parts of the world.

The cost of living and the market level of compensation and rewards can be determined through salary surveys, consulting with trade associations, and reading employment ads. Trade associations and trade magazines, employment agencies, and college placement offices can also provide helpful comparative salary information, as can the job offers finalists receive from other companies.

 # Global Issues

Global Influences on Job Offer Content

When presenting or receiving a job offer in another country, it is helpful to learn about the best way to receive compensation in that location. This is particularly true for employees in higher tax brackets. For example, transportation allowances are common in Singapore and Hong Kong. DHL Worldwide Express gives executives a $1,000 monthly transportation allowance. Some executives negotiate private school tuition for their children, cost of living adjustments, and housing subsidies as part of their pay.[115] In countries where the marginal combined tax rate is fairly high, a company might lease a residence or a car for an executive as part of the total pay package. Some executives also request that some of their salary be paid in the local currency. In less desirable destinations, perhaps because of safety issues or low quality of life, hardship allowances are sometimes paid.[116]

Legal Factors.   Equal employment opportunity and affirmative action goals are the two primary legal factors that influence the content of a job offer. If a firm has an affirmative action plan, or if it is actively pursuing diversity, its progress toward these goals might influence how high a job offer should be. If a company is having trouble getting some subgroups of finalists to accept job offers, enriched offers may be necessary.

Fairness Perceptions

Fairness perceptions are relevant to all aspects of the human resource management (HRM) system. Fairness perceptions influence candidates' willingness to accept job offers, recommendations of the company,[117] decisions to patronize the company, and intentions to file a discrimination or other lawsuit.[118] There are three types of fairness.[119] **Distributive fairness** is the perceived fairness of the outcomes received. Candidates receiving a job offer or a raise are more likely to feel that the hiring outcome is fair than those who do not. Given that most applicants for a position do not ultimately get the job, perceptions of distributive fairness are often low for most applicants.

Procedural fairness is the perceived fairness of the policies and the procedures used to determine the outcome. If someone believes that she was not given a fair chance at a promotion because the hiring manager had an implicit favorite and did not give her a chance to demonstrate her skills, she would perceive low procedural fairness. Selection procedures, particularly the perceived job relatedness of the selection method, the opportunity allowed by the method to demonstrate one's abilities, and the propriety of questions can influence procedural fairness outcomes.[120] The job relatedness (or face validity) of a selection method[121] and inappropriate or illegal questioning have also been found to increase applicant perceptions of unfairness.[122] Candidates also prefer selection methods that are definitive, not invasive of personal privacy, and validated.[123]

The third type of fairness, **interactional fairness**, reflects perceptions of the degree of respect and the quality of the interpersonal treatment received during the decision-making process. If interviewers are rude or unprepared, if interviews were canceled or rescheduled at the last minute, or if the person negotiating the employment contract is perceived as being unreasonable or unhelpful, interactional fairness perceptions can be low.

Applicant reactions are critical, and many job offer recipients use the job offer and negotiation process to further assess the organization's commitment to them and evaluate what it would be like to work at the company. Attending to procedural and interactional fairness perceptions can increase finalists' willingness to accept job offers and can help reduce the negative spillover effects among those applicants turned down for the job.

Negotiating Employment Contracts

Salaries and employment contracts are often negotiable, particularly for higher level jobs. The degree to which a job offer is negotiable depends on the job, the hiring manager, the organization, and the candidate's perceived value to the organization. Mid-level positions typically have negotiable salary ranges of between 10 and 20 percent (i.e., a job paying $50,000 a year may have a salary range between $40,000 and $60,000). Most state and federal government jobs have non-negotiable salary scales based on education and experience. In other organizations, negotiation typically occurs within the set salary range of the job's pay grade.

Managers' interests should be aligned with organizational goals to ensure that managers negotiate as desired.[124] Anyone negotiating on behalf of the organization should be held accountable for the results (completing the deal on time and obtaining desirable terms) through performance management and rewards.[125]

 so what

Because most people do not get hired, distributive justice perceptions are low for most applicants.

distributive fairness
the perceived fairness of the outcomes received

procedural fairness
the perceived fairness of the policies and the procedures used to determine the outcome

so what

Procedures that are perceived as fair can reduce the negative reactions to not getting hired or promoted.

interactional fairness
the degree of respect and the quality of the interpersonal treatment received during the decision-making process

so what

How people are treated during the hiring process influences their reactions to the organization and tendency to pursue a lawsuit.

table **6.6**

Negotiable Job Offer Elements

Salary
Sign-on bonuses
Nonsalary compensation: Performance bonuses, profit-sharing, and stock options
Relocation expenses: House-hunting, temporary living allowance, and travel expenses
Benefits: Personal days (number, amount paid, and timing), continuing education, professional memberships, product discounts, and short-term loans
Job-specific elements: Start date, timing of first performance review and raise, job title/role/duties, location, and work hours

The organization must identify which, if any, employment terms and conditions will be negotiable and what the lower and upper bounds for each will be. Most employee benefits are not negotiable, although vacation or personal leave days sometimes are. Flexible benefit packages allowing employees to choose among a variety of benefits, including health coverage, flexible work arrangements, and tuition reimbursement are becoming more common.

Table 6.6 summarizes some of the most commonly negotiated elements of a job offer.

To successfully negotiate a job offer, it is important to focus on the things that matter to the finalist. Money is important to many job seekers, but nonmonetary factors including development opportunities, the community's quality of life, career advancement, and flexible work hours are also important. Some people may be most excited about the opportunity to work with the latest technologies, and someone recently laid off may put job security at the top of the list. It is best to present and sell the opportunity based on the job rewards analysis results in the context of finalists' own values, needs, and desires.[126]

When you negotiate a job offer for yourself, it never hurts to ask for the things you most value and a slightly higher salary. Be reasonable and respectful, explain why you deserve the addition or why it will improve your productivity, and remember that if you don't ask for something at the time of hire, you probably won't get the opportunity to negotiate for it later. This chapter's Develop Your Skills feature gives you some tips on negotiating a job offer for yourself.

Once a job offer has been extended, it can be necessary to maintain the interest and enthusiasm of the other finalists until the hiring process is completed. Ensuring that both the hiring manager and the recruiter are in regular contact with the remaining finalists helps to maintain their interest in the position if the first job offer is declined.

Many women sacrifice more than $500,000 over the course of their professional lives by not negotiating their salaries. In a study of two graduating MBA classes, students who negotiated their job offer received 7 percent to 8 percent increases, but while 52 percent of the men negotiated, only 12 percent of women did. Women may also tend to negotiate lower salaries than do men because women value different outcomes (such as interpersonal relationships rather than more money),[129] or because women's performance may be devalued in comparison to men's performance.[130] Women also tend to use a more cooperative negotiation style than do men, although the difference is fairly small.[131] The fact that there can be gender differences in negotiation behaviors and outcomes[132] is important, particularly for female job seekers but also for companies. These differences in starting salaries can create gender-based wage disparities that can grow quite significant over time.

so what**?**

When negotiating a job offer, focus on the things that are important to the finalist.

so what**?**

Settling for a low salary at your first job can substantially decrease your lifetime earnings.

Develop Your Skills

Job Offer Negotiation Tips

Because employment is an ongoing relationship between the employee and the employer, it is important that negotiating happen in a positive and open manner that leads to greater understanding and win-win outcomes. Here are some experts' suggestions for being an effective negotiator from both sides of the table:[127]

- *Be appreciative and respectful.* Begin the negotiation by briefly expressing your appreciation for the initial offer. Cite specifics about your positive impressions, and reinforce your good fit with the job and company. Don't be greedy or unreasonable, and know when to quit bargaining. Over-negotiating can dampen a company's enthusiasm for hiring you.
- *Do not be competitive.* Negotiating is not about winning—focus on your goals and how both sides can come out ahead.
- *Be prepared.* Ask for what you want in one session. Introducing new requests over time risks appearing disorganized and can negatively influence the firm's expectations of you as an employee.
- *Identify what you can and cannot part with.* Identify the things most important to you (e.g., career development, desirable location) and those things that are less important (e.g., job title), and establish minimum requirements for your most important issues. Always be realistic—research your market value and typical salary ranges and benefits packages before you begin negotiating.
- *Identify and use leverage.* Anything that can help or hurt a party during bargaining is *leverage*. An employer who must hire quickly might be willing to negotiate a more favorable offer in exchange for an earlier start date. A competing job offer with more favorable terms can also increase your leverage.
- *Manage your emotions.* Negotiations can raise emotions. Constantly remind yourself of your goal to maintain an appropriate level of detachment to see the deal clearly.
- *Know your BATNA.* The acronym for "best alternative to a negotiated agreement" is BATNA. It is what you would do instead if you can't reach an agreement. If your needs cannot be better met by negotiating an agreement with this party, compared to this next best alternative, you are better off declining the offer.[128] If the offer is below your BATNA, letting the other side know that you're prepared to decline their job offer can help to loosen up the process.
- *Reference your skills and accomplishments.* Employers are more likely to meet a request if you can demonstrate why you need it for job performance.

The Employment Contract

explicit employment contract
a written or verbal employment contract

implicit employment contract:
an understanding that is not part of a written or verbal contract

In the absence of an **explicit employment contract** (written or verbal), an **implicit employment contract** or an understanding that is not part of a written or verbal contract, can still exist. Roughly half of the Fortune 500's CEOs work under implicit contracts.[133] Most small business employees are also hired without a formal written contract. Implicit employment contracts tend to be the norm for most positions in most organizations.

Although written contracts help to ensure that the employer and employee have shared expectations, establish that the employment relationship is at-will, and help to avoid future disputes about what was promised, few employers provide written contracts to the majority of their employees. If employees receive anything, it is often a letter of agreement that is less detailed and addresses more basic elements of the employment relationship, including job title and responsibilities, salary and benefits, and start date. Written contracts are more common for higher level positions.

A legally binding and enforceable employment contract requires an offer, acceptance of that offer, and sufficient "consideration" to make the contract valid. An *offer* contains the terms and conditions of employment as proposed by the employer and usually specific requirements for accepting the offer such as a signature and a deadline. A job offer's terms must be clear and allow the job candidate to reasonably expect that the business is willing to be bound by the offer on the proposed terms. Stating, "Come work for me next week," is too vague to be a valid job offer.

A clear expression of the accepting party's agreement to the terms of the offer is called *acceptance*. The offer must be accepted exactly as specified in the offer. If the offer requires signed acceptance by a certain date, the acceptance must beat the deadline and be in writing to be valid. Stating, "I'll accept the offer for an additional $10,000 per year" is a counteroffer and subject to negotiation.

Consideration is the bargained-for exchange between the contract parties—something of value must pass from one party to the other. Each party to the contract must gain some benefit from the agreement and incur some obligation in exchange for that benefit. Typically, the employer exchanges the promise of pay for the offer receiver's promise of labor.

Succession Management

An ancient Chinese proverb says, "A person who does not worry about the future will shortly have worries about the present." This lesson particularly resonates in the area of **succession management**, or the identification of critical jobs too important to be left vacant and creating a strategic plan to quickly fill them when they become available. Succession management is essential for top leadership roles or other key jobs that the business wouldn't be able to run without, and it is a problem for businesses of all sizes.[134] The Family Business Institute calculates that only 30 percent of family businesses survive into the second generation, 12 percent into the third generation and only 3 percent into the fourth, often due to a lack of succession management.[135]

> **succession management**
> the process of identifying critical jobs too important to be left vacant and creating a strategic plan to quickly fill them when they become available

> *"A person who does not worry about the future will*
> *shortly have worries about the present."*
>
> **—Ancient Chinese Proverb**

Every year 10 to 15 percent of corporations must appoint a new CEO because of executives' retirement, resignation, dismissal, or ill health.[136] The share price of United Kingdom insurance giant Legal and General plummeted after CEO Tim Breedon announced he was leaving but appeared to have no idea who would be replacing him.[137] Stephen Dando, former EVP and chief human resources officer at business data provider Thomson Reuters, states, "The absence of a succession plan means you raise the risk for your organisation significantly. Unplanned discontinuity can have serious consequences for the organisation—particularly with CEOs. Companies can immediately leave themselves open to hostile takeover if the CEO dies or leaves unexpectedly."[138]

British beverage multinational Diageo is an example of effective succession planning in action. After CEO Paul Walsh was in his position for 12 years, the company promoted an internal candidate to the newly created job of chief operating officer (COO). Walsh made clear that he would stay in his role for at least two more years and that the new COO role was intended to help prepare his successor. Diageo's successful management of its CEO transition resulted from succession planning being on its board's agenda and talent development for senior roles being a part of the company culture. Succession is taken so seriously in Diageo that a forum of regional leaders meets with the CEO, the COO, and other senior board members eight times a year to discuss company leadership.[139]

Qualified internal successors do not just appear overnight. Succession management involves assessing an employee's potential performance in various roles as much as his or her current performance. Effective succession management should be linked to long-term business strategy and involves cross training multiple generations of possible successors for key positions with a mix of on-the-job training, coaching, mentoring, and education. Job experiences are an important supplement to formal training to prepare employees for their future roles, which may be quite different from the roles that exist in the organization today.[140]

Summary and Application

The assessment and selection of job candidates is essential to getting the right talent in the right place at the right time. A wide variety of assessment methods exist—the choice of which to use should be based on the job analysis, business strategy, and an examination of what best predicts job success. Candidates are then compared to each other or to a minimum hiring standard. Once the decision is made to extend a job offer, the job offer strategy should be determined and negotiations undertaken to close the deal. An employment contract then details the terms and conditions of employment and formalizes the employment arrangement.

Real World Response

How Zappos Hires the Right People

Online shoe retailer Zappos believes that protecting the company's culture and adhering to its core values are essential to the execution of its customer service strategy. Zappos' CEO Tony Hsieh states, "There are a lot of experienced, smart, and talented people we interview that we know can make an immediate impact on our top or bottom line. But a lot of them are also really egotistical, so we end up not hiring them. At most companies, the hiring manager would probably argue that we should hire such a candidate because he or she will add a lot of value to the company, which is probably why most large corporations don't have great cultures."[141] Zappos will even fire people who are doing their job perfectly if they're bad for the culture.[142]

> *"There are a lot of experienced, smart, and talented people we interview that we know can make an immediate impact on our top or bottom line. But a lot of them are also really egotistical, so we end up not hiring them."*
>
> —Tony Hsieh, founder and CEO, Zappos

Because Zappos knows how important it is to hire employees who fit its unique culture, recruiters evaluate candidates for culture fit and a willingness to change and learn. They observe how applicants interact at lunch to see if they talk with other employees or focus only on the person who they think makes the hiring decision? Zappos even has its shuttle drivers tell the recruiting team what candidates say during the ride back to their hotels.

Zappos uses a two-step hiring process. It first evaluates applicants based on their skills and experience to ensure that they are a good fit with the job. It then interviews them again to assess the fit of their attitudes, values, and personality with Zappos' culture.[143] After a four-week paid training program that immerses all new hires in the company's strategy, culture, and customer obsession, Zappos offers its new hires a $2,000 bonus if they want to quit. Although this approach may sound crazy, Zappos believes that it is better for poor fits to leave earlier than later. About 10 percent of its call center employees take them up on the offer.[144]

All new hires must then work the phones for two weeks, regardless of their position, ensuring that all employees have interacted with Zappos' customers and understand the core business.[145] With strong financial performance and a very low annual call center turnover rate of 8 percent,[146] Zappos' hiring process seems to be working.

Appendix

This appendix describes reliability and validity and why each is important in choosing selection methods.

Reliability

Reliability refers to how consistently a measure assesses a particular characteristic. A scale that reported wildly different weights each time you stepped on it would probably not be very useful. The same principle applies to measures relevant to selection, such as job knowledge, intelligence, personality, and communication skills.

reliability
how consistently a measure assesses a particular characteristic

A measure that yields similar scores for a given person when it is administered multiple times is reliable. Reliability sets boundaries around the usefulness of a measure. A measure cannot be useful if it is not reliable, but even if it is reliable, it still might not be useful. For example, if a scale measures something other than what you intended, it doesn't matter how consistently it does it. Reliability is a critical component of any staffing measure, including candidate assessment. If a person completes an assessment twice, will he or she get a similar score or a much different score? If the scores radically change, then the measure isn't reliable. Why would a job candidate score differently when completing an assessment again, you might wonder? Think of why you might score differently on a personality assessment given on Monday morning and one given on Friday afternoon and you should have some insights.

The reliability of a measure is indicated by the reliability coefficient, which is expressed as a number ranging between 0 and 1, with 0 indicating no reliability (no correlation between the measure and the true score), and 1 indicating perfect reliability (perfect correlation between the measure and the true score). Like a correlation, we express reliability as a decimal, for example 0.83 or 0.95. The closer the reliability coefficient is to 1.0, the more reliable the scores are. Near perfect reliability is extremely rare. In general, reliabilities above 0.70 are considered acceptable, although reliabilities of 0.80 and above are preferred.

Validity

Validity is critical in selecting a measure. It refers to how well a measure assesses a given construct and the degree to which you can make specific conclusions or predictions based on observed scores. If you use assessment data to make decisions, then the data must relate in meaningful ways

validity
how well a measure assesses a given construct and the degree to which you can make specific conclusions or predictions based on observed scores

to desired job success outcomes. If an assessment is valid and helps you to identify high-quality talent, then it will give you a competitive edge over firms that do not use valid tests for selection.

It is important to understand the differences between reliability and validity. Reliability tells you how consistent scores from a measure will be; validity tells you how useful the measure is for a particular situation. You cannot draw valid conclusions unless a measure is reliable, but even when a measure is reliable, it might not be valid. For example, you might be able to measure a person's height reliably, but it probably won't be useful as a predictor of the person's job success. Any measure used in staffing needs to be both reliable and valid for the situation.

A bull's-eye image is commonly used to illustrate the relationship between reliability and validity. The center of the bull's-eye is whatever construct you are trying to measure, usually some aspect of job success. Each "shot" at the bull's-eye is a measurement for a single person. A bull's-eye means that your measure is perfectly assessing the person on the intended construct. Shots that are close together reflect higher reliability than the dots more spread out. Shots centered on the bull's-eye reflect higher validity than dots clustered away from the bull's-eye. You can easily picture how it is impossible for an unreliable measure (the shots are widely scattered) to be valid (on target). Our goal in assessment is using measures with shots that are consistently in the center of the target, reflecting both reliability and validity.

A measure's validity is established in reference to a specific purpose. Thus, a measure might not be valid for different purposes. For example, a measure you use to make valid predictions about someone's technical proficiency on the job may not be valid for predicting his or her leadership skills, job commitment, or teamwork effectiveness. Similarly, a measure's validity is established in reference to specific groups called reference groups. Thus, the same measure might not be valid for different groups. For example, a problem-solving skills measure designed to predict the performance of sales representatives might not be valid or useful for predicting the performance of clerical employees.

The user manuals that accompany assessment tools should describe the reference groups used to develop the measures. The manuals should also describe the groups for whom the measure is valid and how the scores for the individuals belonging to each of the groups were interpreted. You must then determine if the measure is appropriate for the particular type of people you want to assess. This group of people is called your target population.

Although your target population and the reference group might not match perfectly, they must be sufficiently similar so that the measure will yield meaningful scores for your group. For example, you will want to consider factors such as the occupations, reading levels, and cultural and language differences of the people in your target group. Use only assessment procedures and instruments demonstrated to be valid for your target group(s) and for your specific purpose. This is important because the Uniform Guidelines on Employee Selection Procedures[147] require that assessment tools have adequate supporting evidence for the conclusions reached with them in the event adverse impact occurs.

Takeaway Points

1. Person-job fit is the fit between a person's abilities and the job's demands and the fit between a person's desires and motivations and the job's attributes and rewards. Person-group fit is the match between an individual and his or her workgroup and supervisor. Person-organization fit is the fit between an individual's values, attitudes, and personality and the organization's values, norms, and culture.

2. Screening assessment methods reduce the pool of job applicants to a group of job candidates. Evaluative assessment methods evaluate job candidates to identify whom to hire. Contingent assessment methods are given after a hiring decision has been made. A job offer is made contingent on passing the assessment.

3. Behavioral interviews ask about actual experiences and situations. Situational interviews present hypothetical questions and ask candidates how they would respond to the situation. In a case interview, the candidate is given a business situation, challenge, or problem and asked to present a well thought out solution and explain how they arrived at it.

4. Multiple hurdles require candidates to receive a passing score on an assessment before being allowed to continue in the selection process. The compensatory approach allows high scores on some assessments to compensate for low scores on other assessments. The two approaches can also be combined such that candidates clearing the multiple hurdles are evaluated on the remaining characteristics using the compensatory approach.

5. Job type as well as organizational, finalist, external, and legal factors all influence the content of a job offer.

6. Distributive fairness is the perceived fairness of the outcomes received. Procedural fairness is the perceived fairness of the policies and procedures used to determine the outcome. Interactional fairness reflects perceptions of the degree of respect and the quality of the interpersonal treatment received during the decision-making process.

7. An explicit employment contract is a written or verbal employment contract. An implicit employment contract is an understanding that is not part of a written or verbal contract.

8. Succession management involves identifying critical jobs and creating a plan to fill them quickly should they become vacant. It should be linked to long-term business strategy and include preparing employees for their future roles in the company.

Discussion Questions

1. Which do you think is more important in hiring an instructor, avoiding false positives or avoiding false negatives? Why?
2. When you look for a job, how much relative focus to you put on person-job, person-group, and person-organization fit? Why?
3. Which evaluative assessment methods do you feel would be most appropriate to use in hiring a recruiter? Why?
4. Which evaluative assessment methods would you not want to be used in evaluating you for a position? Why?
5. What assessments might be appropriate to use in a multiple hurdles approach to hiring university instructors? Why?
6. How can organizations increase procedural and interactional fairness during the hiring process?
7. What can you do to negotiate a higher job offer? Do you have any experiences, qualifications, or other characteristics you might be able to use as leverage?

Personal Development Exercise: Job Offer Negotiation

Your instructor will assign you a partner and give you a role to play in a job offer negotiation exercise. One person will be the job offer recipient, and the other will be the organizational representative. Read through your role, and identify your target employment package. Take notes to help you negotiate most effectively. Think about what negotiation strategies will be most effective, and practice them during the negotiation. Remember, if you do not exceed your minimum point total, the job offer is not acceptable. Do not show your role sheet or payoff matrix to your negotiation partner.

Strategic HRM Exercises

Exercise: Selecting Servers

Imagine that you are the manager of Pizza Palace, a local pizzeria, and need to hire servers for your new location. You are pursuing a low-cost strategy but still want to hire the best servers possible to maximize revenue and keep customers coming back. What assessment methods would you use and in what order? How would you make a final hiring decision? What would be some of the key elements in your job offer?

Now imagine that you are the manager of Haute Cuisine, the fanciest restaurant in your nearest city. Your servers are career professionals and excel at what they do. Because they interact with your customers, they are essential to the execution of your customer service strategy. What assessment methods would you use to hire servers and in what order? How would you make a final hiring decision? What would be some of the key elements in your job offer?

Now compare and contrast your answers to the two settings. What elements are the same? Why? What elements are different? Why?

Exercise: Evaluating Personality Assessments

Point your favorite browser to the following pre-employment personality assessment providers:

- http://www.employment-testing.com/index.html
- http://www.shl.com/us/solutions/talent-acquisition/

Look around the websites to identify what they offer and understand how they are best used. Then answer the questions below.

1. What are the strengths and limitations of each?
2. How would each of the two vendors be best used in candidate assessment?
3. Think of a job you would like to someday hold. Drawing from these websites, if you wanted to assess personality when hiring for this position, what personality characteristics would you use?

Exercise: Practice Interview

(Optional: First view the video, "How to Communicate Your Strengths in a Job Interview" (2:17). Expand the text beneath the video to view more information about preparing for a job interview. Then watch the videos, "Job Interview Tips: Tell Me About Yourself. Example of a Bad Answer." (1:31) and "Interview Tips: Share a Conflict Resolution. A BAD answer/ example." (1:13).

Think about a job in a specific organization for which you would like to interview. Tell your interview partner about the job and the organization so that they can think of some good structured interview questions for you. They will tell you their chosen job and organization, and you will have 5 to 10 minutes to think of five structured interview questions for them. Try to come up with both behavioral and situational questions that will get at some of the key competencies required for success in that job and organization.

Try to think of questions that tap specific job-related characteristics important to that job and organization rather than "Tell me about yourself" or "Where do you see yourself in five years?"

Now take about 10 minutes to think about your skills and work experiences, and create a good summary of yourself, a statement of your personal brand, and how you would contribute in this role. Be sure to relate this information to the job and the organization you will be interviewing for with your partner.

Now conduct the interview while practicing good interview behaviors. Be professional, establish rapport, and use good communication behaviors. Monitor your nonverbal communication as well. When you have finished, switch roles. After each interview, give each other feedback about what went well and what could be improved.

Exercise: What Would You Do?

Watch the video, "Diversity Challenges—What Would You Do?" (7:01). After watching the video, answer the following questions.

1. Would you hire this candidate? Why or why not?
2. At what stage of the staffing process should attitudes toward diversity and inclusion be considered? Why?
3. If you did hire this candidate, what would you do to develop his attitudes toward diversity and inclusion? Why do you think your ideas would work?

Integrative Project

Develop a selection plan and job offer strategy for your chosen job. Explain which assessment methods you would use, how you would combine scores on the assessments into a final score, and how you would choose whom to hire. Then write a job offer letter to your chosen candidate that presents a valid job offer, reinforces your employer brand, and tries to persuade the finalist to accept your offer.

Video Case

Imagine meeting with some coworkers at Happy Time Toys to discuss the best approach to use for some upcoming hiring interviews that will be conducted by the hiring managers. You need to decide what type of interview format to use and how much discretion to give the hiring managers in conducting the interviews. *What do you say or do?* Go to this book's video case, watch the challenge video for this chapter, and choose the best video response. Be sure to also view the outcomes of the two responses you didn't choose.

Discussion Questions

1. Which aspects of HRM discussed in this chapter are illustrated in these videos? Explain your answer.
2. How much discretion do you think hiring managers should have in conducting their interviews? Explain your answer.
3. As a manager at Happy Time Toys, what other suggestions would you make about how to best manage the interview process?

Endnotes

1. Got talent? Competing to hire the best and motivate the rest. (2011, September 10). *The Economist*. Retrieved May 9, 2012, from http://www.economist.com/node/21528436

2. Stillman, J. (2009, February 11). Zappos' Hsieh: Hire and fire based on cultural fit. *BNET*. Retrieved May 6, 2012, from http://www.bnet.com/blog/bnet1/zappos-hsieh-hire-and-fire-based-on-cultural-fit/1026

3. Burke, E. (2013). Data insights at work at Time Warner Cable. *Talent Management*, November, 36.

4. Jobs, S. (2012). The payoff of a great employee. *Fast Company*, May, 79.

5. Adapted from Edwards, J. R. (1991). Person-job fit: A conceptual integration, literature review, and methodological critique. In C. L. Cooper & I. T. Robertson (Eds,), *International review of industrial and organizational psychology*, (Vol. 6), 283–357. New York: Wiley.

6. Kristof-Brown, A. L., Zimmerman, R. D., & Johnson, E. C. (2005). Consequences of individuals' fit at work: A meta-analysis of person-job, person-organization, person-group, and person-supervisor fit. *Personnel Psychology, 58*, 281–342.

7. Regeneron. (2011). Grow with us. Retrieved May 6, 2012, from http://www.regeneron.jobs/grow_with_us.html

8. Marquez, J. T. (2010). Tailor-made careers. *Workforce Management*, January, 16–21.

9. Kristof-Brown, A. L., Zimmerman, R. D., & Johnson, E. C. (2005). Consequences of individuals' fit at work: A meta-analysis of person-job, person-organization, person-group, and person-supervisor fit. *Personnel Psychology, 58*, 281–342.

10. Werbel, J. D., & Gilliland, S. W. (1999). Person-environment fit in the selection process. In G. R. Ferris (Ed.), *Research in personnel and human resource management*, Vol. 17, 209–243. Stamford, CT: JAI Press.

11. Kristof, A. L. (1996). Person-organization fit: An integrative review of its conceptualizations, measurement, and implications. *Personnel Psychology, 49*, 1–50.; Kristof, A. L. (2000). Perceived applicant fit: Distinguishing between recruiters' perceptions of person-job and person-organization fit. *Personnel Psychology, 53*, 643–671.

12. Cantoria, C. S. (2011, April 30). Landing a job at one of the best places to work. *Bright Hub*. Retrieved May 1, 2012, from http://www.brighthub.com/office/career-planning/articles/116161.aspx

13. Webb, W. (2016). CLO as brand ambassador. *Chief Learning Officer*, 18–21.

14. Chatman, J. (1989). Improving interactional organizational research: A model of person-organization fit. *Academy of Management Review, 14*, 333–349; Chatman, J. (1991). Matching people and organizations: Selection and socialization in public accounting firms. *Administrative Science Quarterly, 36*, 459–484; Vancouver, J. B., & Schmitt. N. W. (1991). An exploratory examination of person-organization fit: Organizational goal congruence. *Personnel Psychology, 44*, 333–352.

15. Kristof-Brown, A. L., Zimmerman, R. D., & Johnson, E. C. (2005). Consequences of individuals' fit at work: A meta-analysis of person-job, person-organization, person-group, and person-supervisor fit. *Personnel Psychology, 58*, 281–342.

16. Ibid.

17. Uniform Guideline 14C(4), 43 Fed. Reg. 38, 302 (1978). Retrieved April 12, 2012, from http://www.gpo.gov/fdsys/pkg/CFR-2011-title28-vol2/pdf/CFR-2011-title28-vol2-sec50-14.pdf

18. Available online at http://www.apa.org/science/programs/testing/standards.aspx

19. Available online at http://siop.org/_Principles/principlesdefault.aspx

20. McCarthy, J. M., Bauer, T. N., Truxillo, D. M., Anderson, N. R., Costa, A. C., & Ahmed, S. M. (in press). Applicant perspectives during selection: A review addressing "So what?" "What's new?" and "Where to next?" *Journal of Management*.

21. Light, J. (2011, January 18). Recruiters rethink online playbook. *The Wall Street Journal*. Retrieved May 7, 2012, from http://online.wsj.com/article/SB10001424052748704307404576080492613858846.html?mod=djem_jiewr_HR_domainid

22. Speer, A. B., King, B. S., & Grossenbacher, M. (2016). Applicant reactions as a function of test length. *Journal of Personnel Psychology, 15*–24.

23. McCarthy, J. M., Bauer, T. N., Truxillo, D. M., Anderson, N. R., Costa, A. C., & Ahmed, S. M. (in press). Applicant perspectives during selection: A review addressing "So what?" "What's new?" and "Where to next?" *Journal of Management*.

24. Konradt, U., Garbers, Y., Weber, M., Erdogan, B., & Bauer, T. N. (in press). Antecedents and consequences of procedural fairness perceptions in personnel selection: A 3-year longitudinal study. *Group & Organization Management*. doi:1059601115617665; McCarthy, J. M., Van Iddekinge, C. H., Lievens, F., Kung, M. C., Sinar, E. F., & Campion, M. A. (2013). Do candidate reactions relate to job performance or affect criterion related validity? A multistudy investigation of relations among reactions, selection test scores, and job performance. *Journal of Applied Psychology, 98*, 701–719.

25. McCarthy, J. M., Van Iddekinge, C. H., Lievens, F., Kung, M. C., Sinar, E. F., & Campion, M. A. (2013). Do candidate reactions relate to job performance or affect criterion related validity? A multistudy investigation of relations among reactions, selection test scores, and job performance. *Journal of Applied Psychology, 98*, 701–719.

26. Maertz, C. P., Jr., Bauer, T. N., Mosley, D. C., Jr., Posthuma, R. A., & Campion, M. A. (2005). Predictors of self-efficacy for cognitive ability employment testing. *Journal of Business Research, 58*, 160–167.

27. Karim, M. N., Kaminsky, S. E., & Behrend, T. S. (2014). Cheating, reactions, and performance in remotely proctored testing: An exploratory experimental study. *Journal of Business and Psychology, 29*, 555–572.

28. McCarthy, J. M., Van Iddekinge, C. H., Lievens, F., Kung, M. C., Sinar, E. F., & Campion, M. A. (2013). Do candidate reactions relate to job performance or affect criterion related validity? A multistudy investigation of relations among reactions, selection test scores, and job performance. *Journal of Applied Psychology, 98*, 701–719.

29. Based in part on Hausknecht, J. P., Day, D. V., & Thomas, S. C. (2004). Applicant reactions to selection procedures: An updated model and meta-analysis. *Personnel Psychology, 57*(3): 639–683; Coyne, I., & Bartram, D. (2002). Assessing the effectiveness of integrity tests: A review. *International Journal of Testing, 2*, 15–34.

30. Based in part on Ryan, A. M., & Tippins N. T., (2004). Attracting and selecting: What psychological research tells us. *Human Resource Management, 43*, 305–318.

31. Sources for validity coefficients: Schmidt, F. L., & Hunter, J. E. (1998). The validity and utility of selection methods in personnel

psychology: Practical and theoretical implications of 85 years of research findings. *Psychological Bulletin, 124*, 262–274; Ryan, A. M., & Tippins N. T., (2004). Attracting and selecting: What psychological research tells us. *Human Resource Management, 43*, 305–318; Situational judgment test validity is from McDaniel, M. A., Morgeson, F. P., Finnegan, E. B., Campion, M. A., & Braverman, E. P. (2001). Use of situational judgment tests to predict job performance: A clarification of the literature. *Journal of Applied Psychology, 86*, 730–740; Biodata validity is from Reilly, R. R., & Chao, G. T. (1982). Validity and fairness of some alternative employee selection procedures. *Personnel Psychology, 35*, 1–62; work sample validity is from Roth, P. L., Bobko, P., McFarland, L. A. (2005). A meta-analytic analysis of work sample test validity: Updating and integrating some classic literature. *Personnel Psychology, 58*(4), 1009–1037; for structured and unstructured interviews also from McDaniel, M. A., Whetzel, D. L., Schmidt, F. L., & Maurer, S. D. (1994). The validity of employment interviews: A comprehensive review and meta-analysis. *Journal of Applied Psychology, 79*, 599–616; Wiesner, W. H., & Cronshaw, S. F. (1988). A meta-analytic investigation of the impact of interview format and degree of structure on the validity of the employment interview. *Journal of Occupational Psychology, 61*, 275–290.

32. Cash America. (n.d.). About us. Retrieved March 16, 2017, from http://www.cashamerica.com/AboutUs.aspx

33. Cash America experiences a 43% reduction in employee turnover using PeopleAnswers. (2009, September 10). *Personnel Today.* Retrieved March 14, 2017, from http://www.personneltoday.com/hr/cash-america-experiences-a-43-reduction-in-employee-turnover-using-peopleanswers/

34. Zappe, J. (2011, May 20). Assessments can improve retention, save money. *ERE.net.* Retrieved May 2, 2012, from http://www.ere.net/2011/05/20/assessments-can-improve-retention-save-money/?utm_source=ERE+Media&utm_campaign=7bac865280-ERE-Daily-Assessment-Success&utm_medium=email

35. Zappos. (2011). Jobs.Zappos.com. Retrieved May 1, 2012, from http://about.zappos.com/jobs

36. HireRight. (2016). *2016 employment screening benchmark report.* Irvine, CA: HireRight.

37. Maurer, R. (2016). Making every check count. *HR Magazine,* October, 69–70.

38. Trumbull, M. (2012, May 14). Yahoo CEO's exit: Debacle for company and a warning for Resume padders. *The Christian Science Monitor.* Retrieved May 15, 2012, from http://www.csmonitor.com/Business/2012/0514/Yahoo-CEO-s-exit-debacle-for-company-and-a-warning-for-resume-padders

39. Martinez, M. (2004). Screening for quality on the Web. *Employment Management Today,* Winter, *9*(1). Retrieved May 2, 2012, from http://www.realestatesimulator.com/pdf/shrm_sept2004.pdf

40. Carlos, C., & Moreland, J. (2013). Cleaning up candidate screening. *Talent Management,* April, 44–46.

41. Frase-Blunt, M. (2005). Dialing for candidates. *HR Magazine,* April, 78–82.

42. Luhby, T. (2011, May 18). The secret life of a resume. *CNN Money.* Retrieved May 8, 2012, from http://money.cnn.com/2011/05/18/news/economy/filling_job_opening/index.htm?iid=HP_LN

43. Kuehner-Hebert, K. (2013). Assessments improve efficiency at Time Warner Cable. *Talent Management,* May, 54–55.

44. Golden, D. (2011). China's test prep juggernaut. *Bloomberg BusinessWeek,* May 9–15, 56–63.

45. Schmidt, F. L., & Hunter, J. E. (1981). Employment testing: Old theories and new research findings. *American Psychologist, 36*, 1128–1137; Schmidt, F. L., & Hunter, J. E. (1998). The validity and utility of selection methods in personnel psychology: Practical and theoretical implications of 85 years of research findings. *Psychological Bulletin, 124*, 262–274.

46. Hunter, J. E. (1986). Cognitive ability, cognitive aptitudes, job knowledge, and job performance. *Journal of Vocational Behavior, 29*(3), 340–362; Murphy, K. (1989). Is the relationship between cognitive ability and job performance stable over time? *Human Performance, 2*, 183–200; Ree, M. J., & Earles, J. A. (1992). Intelligence is the best predictor of job performance. *Current Directions in Psychological Science, 1*, 86–89.

47. Conlin, M. (2006). Champions of innovation. *IN,* June, 18–26.

48. Bryant, A. (2009). Connecting the dots isn't enough. *The New York Times,* July 19, BU2.

49. Gully, S. M., Payne, S. C., & Koles, K. L. K. (2002). The impact of error training and individual differences on training outcomes: An attribute-treatment interaction perspective. *Journal of Applied Psychology, 87*, 143–155.

50. Roth, P. L., Bevier, C. A., Bobko, P., Switzer, F. S., & Tyler, P. (2001). Ethnic group differences in cognitive ability in employment and educational settings: A meta-analysis. *Personnel Psychology, 54*(2), 297–330; Murphy, K. R. (2002). Can conflicting perspectives on the role of g in personnel selection be resolved? *Human Performance, 15*, 173–186; Murphy, K. R., Cronin, B. E., & Tam, A. P. (2003). Controversy and consensus regarding use of cognitive ability testing in organizations. *Journal of Applied Psychology, 88*, 660–671.

51. Outtz, J. L. (2002). The role of cognitive ability tests in employment selection. *Human Performance, 15*, 161–171.

52. Murphy, P. (2011, March 1). 2011 NFL Combine: Alabama QB Greg McElroy nearly aces Wonderlic test. *The Christian Science Monitor.* Retrieved May 3, 2012, from http://www.csmonitor.com/USA/Sports/2011/0301/2011-NFL-combine-Alabama-QB-Greg-McElroy-nearly-aces-Wonderlic-test

53. Smither, J. W., Reilly, R. R., Millsap, R. E., Pearlman, K., & Stoffey, R. W. (1993). Applicant reactions to selection procedures. *Personnel Psychology, 46*, 49–76.

54. Mount, M. K., & Barrick, M. R. (1995). The big five personality dimensions: Implications for research and practice in human resources management. in G. R. Ferris (Ed.), *Research in personnel and human resources management,* Vol. 13, pp. 153–200. Greenwich, CT: JAI Press.

55. Vinchur, A. J., Schippmann, J. S., Switzer, F. A., & Roth, P. L. (1998). A meta-analysis of the predictors of job performance for salespeople. *Journal of Applied Psychology, 83*, 586–597.

56. Barrick, M. R., & Mount, M. K. (1991). The big five personality dimensions and job performance: A meta-analysis. *Personnel Psychology, 44*, 1–26.

57. Mount, M. K., Barrick, M. R., & Stewart, G. L. (1998). Five-factor model of personality and performance in jobs involving interpersonal interactions. *Human Performance, 11*, 145–165.

58. *Ibid.*

59. Jordan, J., & Cartwright, S. (1998). Selecting expatriate managers: Key traits and competencies. *Leadership & Organization Development Journal,* April 19, 89–96.

60. Schmidt, F. L., & Hunter, J. E. (1998). The validity and utility of selection methods in personnel psychology: Practical and theoretical implications of 85 years of research findings. *Psychological Bulletin, 124*, 262–274.

61. Barrick, M. R., Mount, M. K., & Judge, T. A. (2001). The FFM personality dimensions and job performance: Meta-analysis of

meta-analyses.[Special issue], *International Journal of Selection and Assessment, 9*, 9–30.

62. *Ibid.*

63. Mount, M. K., Barrick, M. R., & Stewart, G. L. (1998). Personality predictors of performance in jobs involving interaction with others. [Special issue], *Human Performance, 11*, 145–166.

64. George, J. M., & Zhou, J. (2001). When openness to experience and conscientiousness are related to creative behavior: An interactional approach. *Journal of Applied Psychology, 86*, 513–524; LePine, J. A., Colquitt, J. A., & Erez, A. (2000). Adaptability to changing task contexts: Effects of general cognitive ability, conscientiousness, and openness to experience. *Personnel Psychology, 53*, 563–593; Barrick, M. R., & Mount, M. K. (2005). Yes, personality matters: Moving on to more important matters. *Human Performance, 18*(4), 359–372.

65. Pfeffer, J. (2005, December 1). Why resumes are just one piece of the puzzle. *Business 2.0.* Retrieved May 12, 2012, from http://money.cnn.com/magazines/business2/business2_archive/2005/12/01/8364603/index.htm

66. Ayres, I. (2007). *Super crunchers: Why thinking-by-numbers is the new way to be smart*, pp. 29. New York: Bantam Books.

67. Christie, R., & Geis, F. L. (1970). *Studies in Machiavellianism.* New York: Academic Press.

68. Kish-Gephart, J. J., Harrison, D. A., & Treviño, L. K. (2010). Bad apples, bad cases, and bad barrels: Meta-analytic evidence about sources of unethical decisions at work. *Journal of Applied Psychology, 95*, 1–31.

69. Richtel, M. (2000, February 6, pp. 1, 21). Online revolution's latest twist: Job interviews with a computer. *The New York Times National.*

70. See Ruiz, G. (2006, June). Staying out of legal hot water while conducting background checks. *Workforce Management Online.* Retrieved May 1, 2012, from http://www.workforce.com/archive/feature/news/staying-out-legal-hot-water-while-conducting-background/index.php

71. Rosse, J. G., Miller, J. L., & Ringer, R. C. (1996). The deterrent value of drug and integrity testing. *Journal of Business and Psychology, 10*(4), 477–485.

72. Bryant, A. (2009). Connecting the dots isn't enough. *The New York Times*, July 19, BU2.

73. Taylor, W. (2010, June 28). Why we (shouldn't) hate HR. *Fast Company.* Retrieved March 15, 2017, from https://www.fastcompany.com/1664723/why-we-shouldnt-hate-hr r

74. Conte, J. M., & Gintoft, J. N. (2005). Polychronicity, big five personality dimensions, and sales performance. *Human Performance, 18*, 427–444.

75. Warr, P., Bartram, D., & Martin, T. (2005). Personality and sales performance: Situational variation and interactions between traits. *International Journal of Selection and Assessment, 13*, 87–91.

76. Brandstatter, H. (1997). Becoming an entrepreneur—A question of personality structure? *Journal of Economic Psychology, 18*, 157–177.

77. Helson, R. (1996). In search of the creative personality. *Creativity Research Journal, 9*, 295–306.

78. Chatman, J. A., Caldwell, D. F., & O'Reilly, C. A. (1999). Managerial personality and performance: A semi-idiographic approach. *Journal of Research in Personality, 33*, 514–545.

79. See Sackett, P. R., & Wanek, J. E. (1996). New developments in the use of measures of honesty, integrity, conscientiousness, dependability, trustworthiness, and reliability for personnel selection. *Personnel Psychology, 49*, 787–829; Goldberg, J. R., Grenier, R. M., Guion, L. B., Sechrest, L. B., & Wing, H. (1991). *Questionnaires used in the prediction of trustworthiness in pre-employment selection decisions: An APA Task Force report.* Washington, DC: American Psychological Association.

80. See Ryan, A. M., & Sackett, P. R. (1987). Pre-employment honesty testing: Fakability, reactions of test takers, and company image. *Journal of Business and Psychology, 1*, 248–256; Cunningham, M. R., Wong, D. T., & Barbee, A. P. (1994). Self-presentation dynamics on overt integrity tests: Experimental studies of the Reid report. *Journal of Applied Psychology, 79*, 643–658.

81. Ones, D. S., Viswesvaran, C., & Schmidt, F. L. (1993). Comprehensive meta-analysis of integrity test validities: Findings and implications for personnel selection and theories of job performance. *Journal of Applied Psychology, 78*(4), 679–703.

82. Phillips, J. M., & Gully, S. M. (2002). Fairness reactions to personnel selection techniques in Singapore and the United States. *International Journal of Human Resource Management, 13*, 1186–1205; Steiner, D. D., & Gilliland, S. W. (1996). Fairness reactions to personnel selection techniques in France and the United States. *Journal of Applied Psychology, 81*, 134–141.

83. Dye, D. M., Reck, M., & McDaniel, M. A. (1993). The validity of job knowledge measures. *International Journal of Selection and Assessment, 1*, 153–157.

84. Roberts, B. (2014). Most likely to succeed. *HR Magazine*, April, 69–71.

85. Steiner, D. D., & Gilliland, S. W. (1996). Fairness reactions to personnel selection techniques in France and the United States. *Journal of Applied Psychology, 81*, 134–141; Phillips, J. M., & Gully, S. M. (2002). Fairness reactions to personnel selection techniques in Singapore and the United States. *International Journal of Human Resource Management, 13*, 1186–1205.

86. Barber, A. E., Hollenbeck, J. R., Tower, S. L., & Phillips, J. M. (1994). The effects of interview focus on recruitment effectiveness: A field experiment. *Journal of Applied Psychology, 79*, 886–896.

87. O'Brien, J. M. (2008, February 1). A perfect season. *Fortune.* Retrieved November 22, 2011, from http://money.cnn.com/2008/01/18/news/companies/fourseasons.fortune/index.htm?postversion=2008020111

88. Moore, T. (2011, March 9). Most admired for talent. *CNN Money.* Retrieved May 7, 2012, from http://money.cnn.com/galleries/2011/fortune/1103/gallery.most_admired_for_talent.fortune/index.html

89. Kalman, F. (2013). New brew: Anheuser-Busch InBev's Jim Brickey. *Talent Management*, November, 42–45.

90. Pursell, E. D., Campion, M. A., & Gaylord, S. R. (1980). Structured interviewing: Avoiding selection problems. *Personnel Journal, 59*, 907–912.

91. Fitzwater, T. L. (2000). *Behavior-based interviewing: Selecting the right person for the job.* Menlo Park, CA: Crisp Learning.

92. Pfeffer, J. (2005, December 1). Why resumes are just one piece of the puzzle. *Business 2.0.* Retrieved May 6, 2012, from http://money.cnn.com/magazines/business2/business2_archive/2005/12/01/8364603/index.htm

93. Taylor, P. J., & Small, B. (2002). Asking applicants what they *would do* versus what they *did do*: A meta-analytic comparison of situational and past behavior employment interview questions. *Journal of Occupational and Organizational Psychology, 75*, 277–294.

94. MITRE. (2017, March 16). Awards and recognition. Retrieved March 15, 2017, from https://www.mitre.org/about/awards-and-recognition

95. MITRE. (2017). Media resources. Retrieved March 17, 2017, from https://www.mitre.org/news/media-resources

96. MITRE. (2017). Our hiring process. Retrieved March 15, 2017, from https://www.mitre.org/careers/working-at-mitre/our-hiring-process

97. *Ibid.*

98. Raphael, T. (2011, May 19). Animal hospital testing Facebook contest for recruits. *ERE.net*. Retrieved May 2, 2012, from http://www.ere.net/2011/05/19/animal-hospital-testing-facebook-contest-for-recruits/?utm_source=ERE+Media&utm_campaign=601235666a-ERE-Daily-Facebook-Contest-Bulk-Hires&utm_medium=email#more-18996

99. *Ibid.*

100. White, M. C. (2015, August 13). You won't believe how many people lie on their resumes. *Time.com*. Retrieved March 16, 2017, from http://time.com/money/3995981/how-many-people-lie-resumes/

101. 42 U.S.C. § 12112(d)(4) (1994); 29 C.F.R. § 1630.14(c) (2000).

102. 42 U.S.C. § 12112(d) (1994); 29 C.F.R. § 1630.14 (1998).

103. 70% of employers say prescription drug abuse affects workplace. (2017, March 10). *Insurance Journal*. Retrieved March 17, 2017, from http://www.insurancejournal.com/news/national/2017/03/10/444117.htm

104. About us. (n.d.). National Drug-Free Workplace Alliance. Retrieved March 17, 2017, from http://www.ndwa.org/aboutus.php

105. 42 U.S.C. § 12112(d)(3) (1994); 29 C.F.R. § 1630.14(b)(1)-(2) (2000).

106. McGregor, J. (2006). Background checks that never end. *BusinessWeek*, March 20, 40.

107. Conlin, M. (2006). You are what you post. *BusinessWeek*, March 27, 52–53.

108. Frieswick, K. (2005). Background checks. *CFO Magazine*, August 1. Retrieved May 12, 2011, from http://www.cfo.com/article.cfm/4220232/1/c_4221579?f=insidecfo

109. Criminal background checks: 3 things to consider. (2016). *HR Magazine*, October, 16.

110. Scott, K. O., & Fraiolo, P. A., Jr. (2017). The increasing risks of background checks. *HR Magazine*, December 2016/January 2017, 66–67.

111. Hausknecht, J. P., Day, D. V., & Thomas, S. C. (2004). Applicant reactions to selection procedures: An updated model and meta-analysis. *Personnel Psychology*, *57*, 639–683.

112. Federal Bureau of Investigation. (1997, September). Phase I testing. Applicant Information Booklet.

113. USA IBP. (2011). *U.S. FBI Academy Handbook*. Washington, DC: International Business Publications; Federal Bureau of Investigation. (1997, September). Your guide to getting started. Applicant Information Booklet.

114. Cascio, R., Alexander, A., & Barrett, G. V. (1988). Setting cutoff scores: Legal, psychometric, and professional issues and guidelines. *Personnel Psychology*, *41*, 21–22.

115. Flagg, J. (2010). Updated: Leverage firms' willingness to negotiate, get the best expat package in Asia. Asia Legal Blog. Retrieved May 11, 2012, from http://asialegalblog.com/?p=1685

116. Expat's manual. (2011, May 10). Expat Info Desk. Retrieved May 11, 2012, from http://www.expatinfodesk.com/expat-guide/negotiating-your-contract/key-inclusions-in-an-expat-contract/

117. Hausknecht, J. P., Day, D. V., & Thomas, S. C. (2004). Applicant reactions to selection procedures: An updated model and meta-analysis. *Personnel Psychology*, *57*(3), 639–683.

118. Fodchuk, K. M., & Sidebotham, E. J. (2005). Procedural justice in the selection process: A review of research and suggestions for practical applications. *The Psychologist-Manager Journal*, *8*(2), 105–120; Truxillo, D. M., Steiner, D. D., & Gilliland, S. W. (2004). The importance of organizational justice in personnel selection: Defining when selection fairness really matters. *International Journal of Selection and Assessment*, *12*, 39–53; Truxillo, D. M., Bauer, T. N., Campion, M. A., & Paronto, M. E. (2002). Selection fairness information and applicant reactions: A longitudinal field study. *Journal of Applied Psychology*, *87*, 1020–1031.

119. Gilliland, S. W. (1994). Effects of procedural and distributive justice on reactions to a selection system. *Journal of Applied Psychology*, *79*, 691–701; Greenberg, J. (1990). Organizational justice: Yesterday, today, and tomorrow. *Journal of Management*, *16*, 399–432.

120. Gilliland, S. W. (1993). The perceived fairness of selection systems: An organizational justice perspective. *Academy of Management Review*, *18*, 694–734; Truxillo, D. M., Steiner, D. D., & Gilliland, S. W. (2004). The importance of organizational justice in personnel selection: Defining when selection fairness really matters. *International Journal of Selection and Assessment*, *12*, 39–53; Cropanzano, R., & Wright, T. A. (2003). Procedural justice and organizational staffing: A tale of two paradigms. *Human Resource Management Review*, *13*(1), 7–39.

121. Gilliland, S. W. (1994). Effects of procedural and distributive justice on reactions to a selection system. *Journal of Applied Psychology*, *79*, 691–701.

122. Bies, R. J., & Moag, J. S. (1986). Interactional justice: Communication criteria of fairness. *Research on Negotiation in Organizations*, *1*, 43–55.

123. Smither, J. W., Reilly, R. R., Millsap, R. E., Pearlman, K., & Stoffey, R. W. (1993). Applicant reactions to selection procedures. *Personnel Psychology*, *46*, 49–76.

124. Rau, B. L., & Feinauer, D. (2006). The role of internal agents in starting salary negotiations. *Human Resource Management Review*, *16*, 47–66.

125. *Ibid.*

126. Hirschman, C. (2002). Five mistakes to avoid. *HR Magazine*, April, 75.

127. Kaplan, M. (2005, May). How to negotiate anything. *Money*, *34*, 116–119; Berton, L. (2003, June 25). Eleven commandments for smart negotiating. *CFO Magazine*. Retrieved May 10, 2012, from http://www.cfo.com/article.cfm/3009720?f=singlepage; Johnson, R., & Schall, J. (2006). Pay up: Soft-sell strategies for negotiating a higher starting salary. *Graduatingengineer.com*. Retrieved May 10, 2012, from http://www.graduatingengineer.com/articles/feature/09-01-03g.html

128. Fisher, R., Ury, W. L. & Patton, B. (1991). *Getting to yes: Negotiating agreement without giving in*. New York: Penguin.

129. Major, B. (1987). Gender, justice, and the psychology of entitlement. In P. Shaver & C. Hendrick (Eds.), *Review of personality and social psychology: Sex and gender,* Vol. 7, pp. 124–148. Newbury Park, CA: SAGE; Tannen, D. (1990). *You just don't understand: Men and women in conversation*. New York: Ballantine Books.

130. Hansen, R. D., & O'Leary, V. E. (1985). Sex determined attributions. In V. E. O'Leary, R. K. Unger, & B. S. Wallston (Eds.), *Women, gender, and social psychology*, pp. 67–100. Hillsdale, NJ: Erlbaum; Nieva, V. F., & Gutek, B. A. (1981). *Women and work: A psychological perspective*. New York:

Praeger; Major, B., & Deaux, K. (1982). Individual differences in justice behavior. In J. Greenberg & R. I. Cohen (Eds.), *Equity and justice in social behavior*. New York: Academic Press.

131. Walters, A. E., Stuhlmacher, A. F., & Meyer, L. L. (1998). Gender and negotiator competitiveness: A meta-analysis. *Organizational Behavior and Human Decision Processes*, *76*, 1–29.

132. Stuhlmacher, A. F., & Walters, A. E. (1999). Gender differences in negotiation outcome: A meta-analysis. *Personnel Psychology*, *52*, 653–677

133. Gillan, S., Hartzell, J. C., & Parrino, R. (2006). Explicit vs. implicit contracts: Evidence from CEO employment agreements. American Finance Association Boston Meetings, March 30.

134. Talpoş ,M. F., Pop, I. G., Văduva, S., & Kovács, L. A. (2017). Talent management and the quest for effective succession management in the knowledge-based economy. In *Business ethics and leadership from an Eastern European, transdisciplinary context*, pp. 65–73. Springer International Publishing.

135. Schumpeter, J. (2016, February 4). Succession failure. *The Economist*. Retrieved March 16, 2017, from http://www .economist.com/news/business/21690027-family-businesses -arabian-gulf-need-address-problem-succession

136. Harrell, E. (2016, December). Succession planning: What the research says. *Harvard Business Review*. Retrieved March 16, 2017, from https://hbr.org/2016/12/succession-planning-what -the-research-says

137. Jacobs, K. (2012, November 19). HR's role in executive succession planning. *HR Magazine*. Retrieved February 11, 2017, from http://www.hrmagazine.co.uk/article-details/hrs -role-in-executive-succession-planning

138. Jacobs, K. (2012, November 19). HR's role in executive succession planning. *HR Magazine*. Retrieved February 11, 2017, from http://www.hrmagazine.co.uk/article-details/hrs-role -in-executive-succession-planning

139. *Ibid.*

140. Luby, V., & Stevenson, J. (2016, December 7). 7 tenets of a good CEO succession process. *Harvard Business Review*. Retrieved March 17, 2017, from https://hbr.org/2016/12/7-tenets-of-a -good-ceo-succession-process

141. Hsieh, T. (2010, May 24). How Zappos infuses culture using core values. *Harvard Business Review Blogs*. Retrieved May 13, 2012, from http://blogs.hbr.org/cs/2010/05/how_zappos_infuses _culture_using_core_values.html

142. Stillman, J. (2009, February 11). Zappos' Hsieh: Hire and fire based on cultural fit. *BNET*. Retrieved May 16, 2011, from http: //www.bnet.com/blog/bnet1/zappos-hsieh-hire-and-fire-based -on-cultural-fit/1026

143. Hsieh, T. (2010). *Delivering happiness: A path to profits, passion, and purpose*. New York: Business Plus.

144. Taylor, B. (2008, May 19). Why Zappos pays new employees to quit—And you should too. *Harvard Business Review Blogs*. Retrieved May 5, 2012, from http://blogs.hbr.org/taylor/2008/05 /why_zappos_pays_new_employees.html

145. Hsieh, T. (2010). *Delivering happiness: A path to profits, passion, and purpose*. New York: Business Plus.

146. Cantoria, C. S. (2011, April 30). Landing a job at one of the best places to work. *Bright Hub*. Retrieved May 16, 2011, from http: //www.brighthub.com/office/career-planning/articles/116161.aspx

147. Available online. Retrieved April 12, 2012, from http://www .gpo.gov/fdsys/pkg/CFR-2011-title28-vol2/pdf/CFR-2011 -title28-vol2-sec50-14.pdf

PART 3

Training
and Performance
Management

chapter 7

Training and Development

Learning Objectives

AFTER STUDYING THIS CHAPTER, YOU SHOULD BE ABLE TO:

1 List the five steps to effective training.

2 Describe the three types of learning objectives.

3 Describe five types of training methods.

4 Explain why learning style is important to training effectiveness.

5 Describe Kirkpatrick's four levels of training evaluation.

6 Describe three common training programs.

7 Explain what makes socialization more effective.

Real World Challenge

How Training Drives Performance at McDonald's

McDonald's pursues a low-cost business strategy but knows that consistency, good service, quality food, and cleanliness are essential to its success. It also knows that its employees are essential to providing this experience to its customers. Founder Ray Kroc once said, "If we are going to go anywhere, we've got to have talent. And, I'm going to put my money in talent."[1]

McDonald's wants its managers and franchisees to consistently represent the McDonald's brand. McDonald's training mission is, "To be the best talent developer of people with the most committed individuals to Quality, Service, Cleanliness and Value (QSC&V) in the world."[2] What advice would you give McDonald's to maximize the effectiveness of its management training programs and help it reach its goals? After reading this chapter, you should have some good ideas.

If you were better trained at your job, do you think you could be more productive, more efficient, or work more safely? If you took the time to train your subordinates well, do you think your job as a manager would be easier? Once the right people are hired, training helps ensure that they perform their best work. In this chapter, we turn our attention to the use of training and development to improve employees' and work groups' current performance and their preparation to assume future roles. **Training** refers to formal and informal activities intended to improve competencies relevant to an employee's or a workgroup's current job. **Development** focuses on developing competencies that an employee or a workgroup is expected to need in the future. A McKinsey survey found that building future capabilities was a top-10 priority for over 90 percent of responding organizations.[3] U.S. organizations with at least 100 employees regularly spend over $50 billion annually on training and development activities.[4] Training is equally important in smaller organizations.

Continuous investment in both training and development is essential for improving employees' performance and ensuring a pipeline of future leadership talent. Because Vanguard fills approximately 80 percent of its front-line leadership positions internally, it developed a Launch to Leadership program for high-performing employees. After passing a rigorous screening process, participants in the nine-week program have 34 hours of instruction by senior leaders and 17 hours of on-the-job enrichment activities with their supervisors. Almost half of the graduates have gone on to assume leadership roles.[5]

The Association for Talent Development (ATD) is the world's largest professional association for the training and development field. Local chapters provide professional development and networking opportunities for people interested training and development careers.[6] ATD's website is located at www. td.org.

This chapter focuses on how training can adapt employees' skills and capabilities to changing business needs. Because training and development influence the skills and the talents available to an organization, they influence what employees *can* do. We begin by discussing the importance of training to organizational performance. We then discuss the five steps to effective training, followed by the importance of reinforcing training back on the job. We then review three specific types of training programs as well as strategies for effective newcomer socialization.

training
formal and informal activities to improve competencies relevant to an employee's or a workgroup's current job

development
focuses on developing competencies that an employee or a workgroup is expected to need in the future

Developing a Competitive Advantage Through Training

Kzenon/Shutterstock

The only ways for an organization to get needed skills and competencies in its workforce are by hiring people who possess them or by training and developing its employees. Because job demands change over time, it is usually necessary for organizations to engage in some sort of employee training and development to ensure that its employees are able to perform well.

It is difficult to imagine an organization executing its business strategy or developing a competitive advantage without training. New employees and newly promoted employees need to learn the organization's expectations, work processes, and how to do their jobs. Managers must develop the interpersonal and feedback skills that lead to effective performance review sessions and ongoing employee coaching.[7] All employees need to understand the company's systems, work processes, and strategy and their role in executing the strategy. Company-specific resources, particularly knowledge resources, help to achieve a sustainable competitive advantage.[8]

In addition to the organization's performance, training is also essential to the performance of workgroups and individual employees. Can you imagine starting a job and receiving no training? How well would you expect to do in that position? Some jobs, including firefighter and power line maintenance worker, depend heavily on company training to enable employees to do their jobs. Training is also essential to safe work behaviors. If employees do not know the safest way to perform a task, how can they be expected to perform it in that way? Training also keeps employees' skills current and relevant for the organization's current and future business needs and enhances their ability to work effectively in teams.

Five Steps to Effective Training

As shown in Figure 7.1, effective training involves five steps:

1. Conduct a needs assessment to identify what needs to be accomplished;
2. Develop learning objectives that identify desired learning outcomes;
3. Design the training program;
4. Implement the training; and
5. Evaluate the training.

Training evaluation results are then included in the next needs assessment process in an ongoing cycle. Let's discuss each of these five steps in more detail.

Conduct a Needs Assessment

Needs assessment is the first step in establishing a training or development program. By identifying what should be accomplished, a needs assessment creates the foundation for effective training.[9] The primary outcome of a training needs assessment is the set of training objectives identifying the ultimate goals of the training program.

Needs assessments can address issues including performance, retention, business goals, and organizational change. The three levels of needs assessment are:

1. Organizational analysis
2. Task analysis
3. Person analysis

Organizational Analysis.   **Organizational needs analysis** identifies where in the organization development or improvement opportunities exist. Opportunities may exist in areas including competencies and behaviors relevant to business goal accomplishment, economic or technological changes, new laws, work process restructuring, or performance issues.

needs assessment
the process of identifying any gaps between what exists and what is needed in the future in terms of employee performance, competencies, and behaviors

organizational needs analysis
identifies where in the organization development or improvement opportunities exist

figure **7.1**

Training Process

Organizational level needs analysis information can be collected from a variety of sources including:

- Strategic plans
- Performance appraisals
- Customer surveys
- Employee surveys
- Restructuring plans
- Efficiency measures

When ADP wanted to improve its new hire training program for payroll client support associates, it conducted a needs analysis that included interviewing high-performing service associates and their leaders and observing and analyzing data from client calls to identify the most common reasons for client calls and their typical resolutions. ADP then redesigned the program to maximize the learning and business impact of the training via a shorter program that blends formal training modules with job immersion, in which new hires are paired with peer mentors. The program includes gamification elements including leaderboards, badges, real-time feedback, and social learning interaction. The new training program decreased call duration, improved client satisfaction, improved client issue resolution, and reduced training time and costs.[10]

task needs analysis
focuses on identifying which jobs, competencies, abilities, and behaviors the training effort should focus on

Task Analysis.   A **task needs analysis** focuses on identifying which jobs, competencies, abilities, and behaviors the training effort should focus on. Resources used in conducting a task analysis include:

- Job or competency analysis
- Observation
- Performance appraisals
- Quality control analysis

person needs analysis
evaluates how individual employees are doing in the training area and determines who needs what type of training

Person Analysis.   **Person needs analysis** evaluates how individual employees are doing in the training topic and determine who needs what type of training. Person level needs analysis information can be collected from sources including:

- Performance appraisals
- Customer surveys
- Individual assessments
- Performance issues
- Skill inventories

At banking company First Horizon National, executives set business goals every November that then cascade electronically through the company's talent management system in December. Business line learning managers then meet with their executives to review these business goals and identify training needs. A training summit is held in early January with top executives from across the organization to discuss the previous year's training performance and jointly prioritize training resources and projects based on business impact. After the summit, business learning managers and their executives meet weekly to establish goals, timelines, and priorities. The summit document is updated quarterly and reprioritized based on business changes.[11]

Needs assessments often identify multiple improvement opportunities that are then prioritized. Legal compliance issues and programs that will best help the organization execute its strategy or reach its most important goals are often given highest priority. It is important to remember that training is not always the best solution to an identified need—sometimes redesigning the job, providing better resources, or implementing staffing, performance management, or compensation solutions are more appropriate.

 so what

Training is not always the best solution to an identified need.

To best address performance problems, it is important to consider how the system is operating as a whole rather than focusing solely on individuals in isolation. Training is not always the correct solution to a performance problem. When a performance issue is identified, the cause may be with the person, the organizational system, or the materials with which the person is working. For example, if a manufacturing employee's performance starts to fall, rather than retraining them, the solution might be to replace the aging machine with which they work.

This chapter's Strategic Impact feature highlights how PNC Financial Services Group selects participants for one of its training programs.

Strategic Impact

Training for Results at PNC Financial Services

Regional managing directors at PNC Financial Services Group's asset management group select advisers to attend a three-month AdvisorTrac program that includes on-line courses, practice teleconferences, a two-day instructor-led training session, and an online final exam. After delivering a 45-minute mock client presentation, feed-back, video, and results are also given to each adviser. Graduates of the AdvisorTrac program outperform nonparticipants by $63,000.[12]

Develop Learning Objectives

Based on the needs assessment, **learning objectives** are created that identify desired learning outcomes. Learning objectives guide the development of the training content and delivery methods. Training assessment and evaluation later evaluate whether the learning objectives are met. The three types of learning objectives are:

learning objectives
identify desired learning outcomes

1. *Cognitive*: To increase some type of knowledge (e.g., knowledge of accounting practices).
2. *Affective*: To change an attitude, relationship, or appreciation (e.g., diversity and inclusion training).
3. *Psychomotor*: To build a physical skill (e.g., driver's education or dancing lessons).

Cognitive Objectives.   Bloom's taxonomy of cognitive objectives is often used to describe the action a learner takes in each level of learning.[13] The taxonomy organizes cognitive out-comes from lowest (remembering facts and definitions) to highest (putting materials together to create a unique product), as shown in Figure 7.2. As we begin learning something new, we begin at the bottom of the pyramid and work our way upward. An example of a cognitive learning objective is, "Given a description of a tool, the learner will be able to identify the tool verbally or in writing and describe the appropriate use(s) for that tool."

Affective Objectives.   Affective objectives seek to change the learner's attitude, choices, and relationships. Krathwohl and Bloom[14] created a popular taxonomy of affective outcomes from receiving or being aware of something (at the bottom of the pyramid) to acting consistently with the new value (indicating the greatest affect). This taxonomy is shown in Figure 7.3. An example of an affective learning objective is, "Motivates coworkers to consistently provide positive customer service."

Psychomotor Objectives.   Psychomotor objectives relate to progressive levels of behaviors from observing someone perform the physical skill to mastering the skill. A taxonomy of

figure **7.2**

Taxonomy of Cognitive Learning Objectives[15]

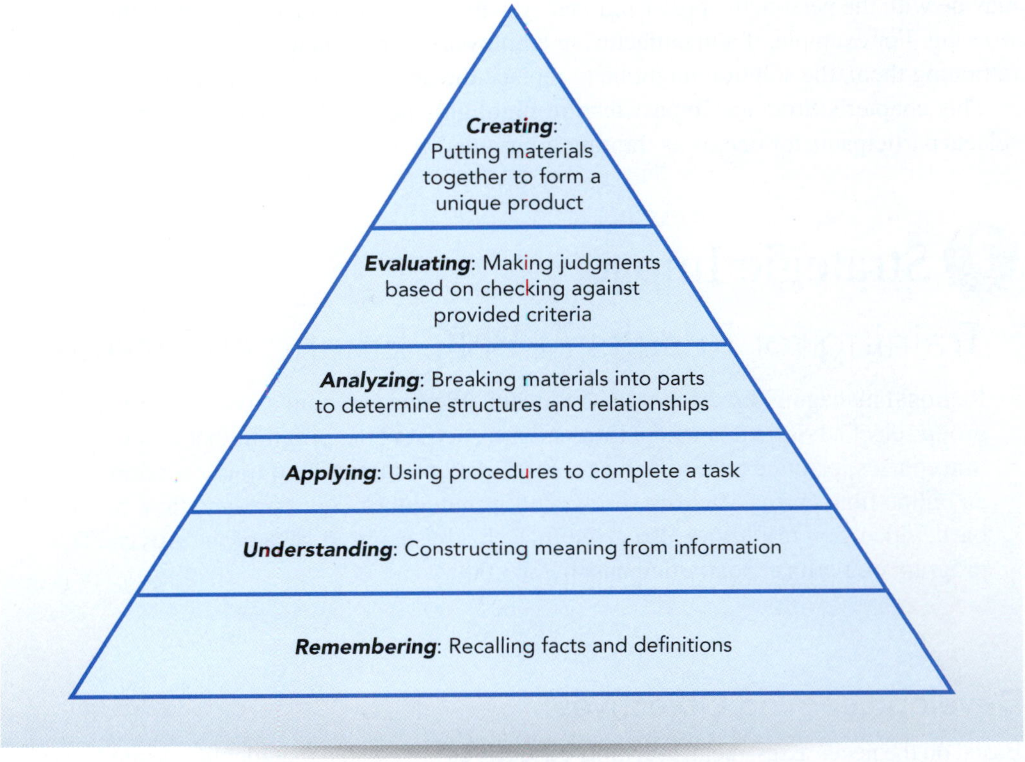

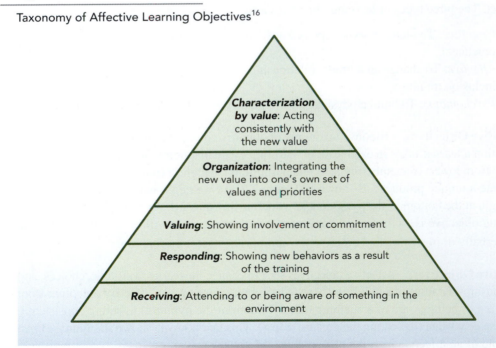

Creating: Putting materials together to form a unique product

Evaluating: Making judgments based on checking against provided criteria

Analyzing: Breaking materials into parts to determine structures and relationships

Applying: Using procedures to complete a task

Understanding: Constructing meaning from information

Remembering: Recalling facts and definitions

figure **7.3**

Taxonomy of Affective Learning Objectives[16]

Characterization by value: Acting consistently with the new value

Organization: Integrating the new value into one's own set of values and priorities

Valuing: Showing involvement or commitment

Responding: Showing new behaviors as a result of the training

Receiving: Attending to or being aware of something in the environment

psychomotor learning ranging from observing to originating new movements synthesized from several different taxonomies is shown in Figure 7.4. Again, as we begin learning something new, we begin at the bottom of the pyramid and work our way upward. An example of a psychomotor learning objective is, "Always wash hands before beginning to prepare food."

figure **7.4**

Taxonomy of Psychomotor Learning Objectives[17]

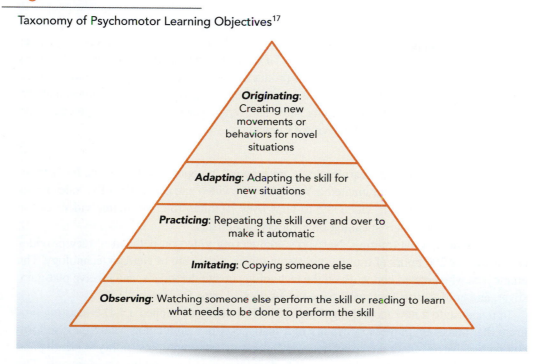

Originating: Creating new movements or behaviors for novel situations

Adapting: Adapting the skill for new situations

Practicing: Repeating the skill over and over to make it automatic

Imitating: Copying someone else

Observing: Watching someone else perform the skill or reading to learn what needs to be done to perform the skill

Design the Training Program

Training objectives inform the design of the training program. The training program developer, content, learning methods, materials, and setting need to be identified, and any instructors need to be identified and trained. We next discuss several of the most popular types of training methods.

Classroom Training.   Classroom training is conducted face-to-face with a trainer instructing an individual or a group of learners. Many of the country's top companies, including General Electric, Intel, and Dell, have their own large-scale corporate universities outlining the companies' core principles and important office protocols.

FedEx Express's 10-month Finance Leadership Exploration leadership development program for high-potential finance employees utilizes guest speakers, experiential and instructor-led workshops, assignments, and a one-on-one coaching session with a manager of each employee's choice. After the 10-month program, participants present their individual development plans to their vice presidents.[18] Tata Consultancy Services' seven-day training uses an unconventional mix of techniques including yoga, theater, and behavioral processes encouraging participants to reflect, introspect, and measure themselves against 12 leadership behavioral indicators. This helps employees create an individual development plan that is monitored for a year by supervisors and external coaches.[19]

On-the-Job Training.   On-the-job training occurs when an individual learns while performing the job. On-the-job training typically relies on both verbal and written instructions, observation, imitation, and practice. When a supervisor or coworker answers a question or gives feedback, on-the-job training has occurred.

One-the-job training can be *structured* and done formally by a supervisor or *unstructured* and done more casually through observation and asking questions. Unstructured on-the-job training is less thorough than structured training because different training methods and content may be used with different learners. Apprenticeships in which master craftsmen or skilled trade workers pass their knowledge and skills to others who work closely with

so what**?**

Even if structured on-the-job training is not provided, unstructured training happens informally when coworkers or supervisors provide feedback or answer questions.

them are an example of structured on-the-job training. High-end department store retailer Nordstrom provides little structured customer service training, expecting salespeople to learn on the job.[20]

Best Buy introduced an app-based training tool called Gravity that allows its employees to use any smart device to scan a product's UPC or QR code to view short training videos and learn key information on the scanned product. In less than 10 months, employees used Gravity more than 1.25 million times to educate themselves on Best Buy products and services. Products supported with Gravity show an average sales increase of 23 percent, with top-performing product sales improving 41 percent.[21]

Virtual Training.   Online learning tools are growing in popularity.[22] Paychex, Inc.'s training and development center created a YouTube-type video site called PayxTV. Sales teams remotely access the secure video site to view over 70 three- to eight-minute videos of top sales reps and key leaders speaking on a variety of subjects.[23]

For technical skills training, NetApp's engineering video-on-demand library provides access to over 200 hours of training videos on topics at the core of NetApp technology. The employees who created and work on the technology create the videos, and receive platinum, silver, and gold awards for creating the videos viewed most frequently.[24]

In response to a new federal regulation, BNSF Railway developed a 3-D e-learning program that places employees as avatars in a realistic virtual simulation where they perform comprehensive rail car brake inspections. The program tests employees' ability to identify and correct malfunctions that can be difficult to demonstrate in live training environments. The program incorporates all possible defects, reducing the safety risk that exists in live training environments. Throughout the class, instructors provide coaching and feedback. The new program has been extremely successful. Not only have all learners passed the knowledge and performance assessments, injuries fell 17 percent, and BNSF is considering pursuing a patent for the program after being approached by other railroads interested in purchasing the training program.[25]

Experiential Training.   Experiential training involves role plays, action learning, and other techniques designed to give learners experience doing the desired task or behaviors, rather than just learning about them. Giving teams or workgroups an actual problem and having them solve it as part of the training is also a type of experiential training. Some companies use adventure learning for teambuilding training and have employee teams complete structured outdoor activities such as ropes courses to build trust and camaraderie. IBM decided to make the vast majority of its training experiential, focusing on providing practical experiences through its training programs.[26]

Games.   Training games are growing in popularity[27] as technology is being increasingly leveraged to maximize training effectiveness. Cold Stone Creamery, after losing money because workers served too much ice cream, created an interactive video game that teaches employees how much should go into each scoop.[28] The U.S. Department of Defense uses a wide variety of video games for soldiers, sailors, and Marines that are also used by local emergency departments to simulate disaster scenarios.[29] Miller Brewing Company is developing a game called Tips on Tap that shows bartenders how to pour the perfect glass of beer. Trainees lose points if the mug hits the tap, risking contamination.[30]

One large study found that trainees who had used video games had an 11 percent higher factual knowledge level, a 14 percent higher skill-based knowledge level, and a 9 percent higher retention rate than trainees in comparison groups.[31] Training games work best when they engage the user, rather than instruct them passively.[32]

? so what

Because many people learn best by doing a task, experiential training and training games can enhance learning.

Workiva Inc. holds an annual "demOlympics" certification for its entire sales organization. Employees are engaged in a friendly week-long competition based on their technical skills and knowledge of the company's product. Throughout the competition, sales reps are given brief scenarios that they address in mock presentations. Employees with the highest scores receive prizes and advance to compete in the final round. The program builds team spirit and allows employees to grow their skills, encourages personal development, and helps identify employees who could benefit from additional training.[33]

Quicken Loans modeled its "Quicken's Got Talent" initiative off of the TV talent show *America's Got Talent* to improve mortgage banker phone skills, encourage the sharing of best practices, and spotlight and reward the company's top talent. Employees can electronically submit a recorded client conversation to be considered to win a $1,000 annual prize. One call a day is selected to be rated on a scale of 1 to 5 by Quicken's 1,200 mortgage bankers. The monthly winner receives a prize worth up to $200 and is spotlighted in a video with a panel of judges who determine whether or not the entry will move to the next round. The calls are also used for training and coaching throughout the year.[34]

Simulations.   Simulations can give employees hands-on experience with new skills and tasks with low risk. Aon, a risk and human resources services firm, uses an intense three-day simulation taught by its most senior leaders to teach its vice presidents how to advice CEOs.[35]

Lifelong Learning.   The skills and the knowledge needed by employees change as new technologies are used and as the company's strategy changes to stay competitive. Lifelong learning is a formal commitment to ensuring that employees have and develop the skills they need to be effective in their jobs today and in the future. Lifelong learning programs include in-house training in basic skills such as English, decision making, problem solving, and leadership. Lifelong learning can also include tuition reimbursement for relevant college-level coursework.

Goldman Sachs has made learning and development central to its culture. Carol Pledger, managing director of Goldman Sachs University, believes that, "Money is nice, but people want to feel like they are being challenged and that they are learning."[36] Goldman Sachs University is a core part of the company's operations, with trainers embedded in many of its divisions and an advisory board of 32 senior employees who monitor the company's business challenges and identify how to resolve them through training.[37]

> *"Money is nice, but people want to feel like they are being challenged and that they are learning."*
>
> **—Carol Pledger, managing director, Goldman Sachs University**

Because organizations must constantly adapt and change to succeed in an increasingly competitive and global business environment, and they need employees to learn new skills to meet these challenges, lifelong learning is important to organizational success. Lifelong learning can lead to productivity improvements, greater workforce flexibility, reduced material and capital costs, a better motivated workforce, and improved product quality.[38]

Learning Styles.   An **aptitude-treatment interaction** is the concept that some training strategies are more or less effective depending on a learner's particular abilities, personality traits, and other characteristics. Learning outcomes are optimized when the instruction methods are matched to the learner.

One of the most important learner characteristics influencing learning outcomes is learning style. **Learning style** refers to how people's information processing differs when problem solving or learning. Understanding how a learner best processes information helps maximize

---

lifelong learning
a formal commitment to ensuring that employees have and develop the skill they need to be effective in their jobs today and in the future

so what?

Training programs are not equally effective for all learners.

aptitude-treatment interaction
the concept that some training strategies are more or less effective depending on a learner's particular abilities, personality traits, and other characteristics

learning style
how people differ in how we process information when problem solving or learning

the fit between a learner and the training program[39] and improves training outcomes.[40] As one training executive at Farmers' Insurance says, "We're always mindful of the fact people learn differently. As a result, our key curricula are designed to reach people through multiple modalities. We develop thousands of participants annually through programs that integrate face-to-face, print, online, video, audio, virtual engagements, and coaching."[41]

> *"We're always mindful of the fact people learn differently. As a result, our key curricula are designed to reach people through multiple modalities."*
>
> **—Training executive, Farmers' Insurance**

sensory modality
a system that interacts with the environment through one of the basic senses

One way of thinking about learning styles is in terms of peoples' preferences for different sensory modalities. A **sensory modality** is a system that interacts with the environment through one of the basic senses.[42] The most important sensory modalities are:

- *Visual*: Learning by seeing.
- *Auditory*: Learning by hearing.
- *Tactile*: Learning by touching.
- *Kinesthetic*: Learning by doing.

About 20 to 30 percent of American students have a preference for auditory learning, about 40 percent prefer visual learning, and the remaining 30 to 40 percent are either tactual/kinesthetic, visual/tactual, or some combination of the major senses.[43]

Annette Towler and Robert Dipboye's[44] learning style orientation measure addresses some of the limitations of earlier inventories and identifies key learning preferences. They also demonstrated that learning style orientations predict preferences for instructional methods beyond personality. They identified five key learning preferences:

1. *Discovery learning*: A preference for exploration during learning. Discovery learners prefer subjective assessments, interactional activities, informational methods, and active-reflective activities.
2. *Experiential learning*: A desire for hands-on approaches to instruction. Experiential learners tend to prefer active learning activities.
3. *Observational learning*: A preference for external stimuli such as demonstrations and diagrams to help facilitate learning. Observational learners tend to prefer informational and active-reflective methods.
4. *Structured learning*: A preference for processing strategies such as taking notes, writing down task steps, and so forth. Structured learning is related to preferences for subjective assessments.
5. *Group learning*: A preference to work with others while learning. Group learning is related to preferences for action and interactional learning.

This chapter's HR Flexibility feature discusses how adaptive learning is being used to personalize educational material to match students' learning needs and improve the effectiveness of training.

Implement the Training

After the training design and instructional methods are finalized, the training program can be implemented. Sessions are scheduled, participants invited, instructors scheduled, materials prepared and delivered, and training conducted. Care should be taken to prevent information

HR Flexibility

Adaptive Learning

Adaptive learning uses computers, artificial intelligence, and analytics to adapt the presentation of educational material according to students' learning needs and even learning styles. If learners correctly respond to questions and tasks, they are moved more quickly through the learning module than learners whose incorrect responses indicate that they have yet to master the material being presented. Because it personalizes the training experience and more closely matches the way individuals learn, adaptive learning can be both highly efficient and more engaging for employee education and retraining.[45]

To be most effective, adaptive learning needs to help get every learner up to speed quickly. This requires adapting the material and the pace to each individual's learning needs.[46] Adaptive platforms also collect data to enable both the individual and the business to measure training impact. By flexibly teaching different learners the same content in different ways based on their learning styles and the methods they learn from the best, adaptive learning can improve the speed knowledge acquisition and mastery development.[47]

Adaptive learning has the potential to increase skills and build competencies at every level while accommodating employees' varied learning preferences, knowledge, and skills. With adaptive learning, courses can be adapted to each learner, from those who grasp the material easily and progress quickly to those who struggle. The system provides help as needed, as if each learner has a personal tutor.[48]

overload and provide trainees sufficient time to practice and learn the material. Breaking a long training session into multiple shorter sessions can enhance training effectiveness.

Methods to track trainees' progress should be built into the training program, including a series of training-related tasks or a knowledge test the employee must do correctly before leaving the training program. On-the-job materials should also be given to trainees' supervisors to promote transfer. For example, supervisors could be given a checklist of training behaviors to complete for each employee two weeks after they finish the training program.

Aetna trains sales representatives weekly, and sometimes daily, on healthcare reform by providing short "learning bites" that employees can access quickly with mobile devices or office computers. More than 70 percent of the 1,500-member sales force accesses the training in a mobile format, and participant satisfaction ratings have increased by 30 percent.[49]

Technology has made it easier to provide brief learning bites to employees via e-mail. Table 7.1 illustrates what learning bites can look like in the context of e-mail training. Training on the proper use of e-mail is something all organizations should provide. Employees should know better than to reply when feeling upset and to avoid inappropriate language.[50] Sending a subordinate glowing e-mails that are at odds with the content of performance reviews can also create legal issues.[51]

Evaluate the Training

Despite the significant amount of money spent training employees, many companies do not take the time to evaluate the success of their training efforts. **Training evaluation** means systematically collecting the information necessary to make effective decisions about adopting,

training evaluation
systematically collecting the information necessary to make effective decisions about adopting, improving, valuing, and continuing an instructional activity or set of activities

table 7.1

Email Training

Here is a primer on the proper use of e-mail in business settings. It is also an example of a learning bite that training organizations can periodically send to their employees to refresh their skills.

- Spelling, grammar, and punctuation matter. Use software or ask a trusted coworker to check your e-mail before sending it.

- Use consistent, professional formatting and an easily readable, black font.

- Never send Social Security numbers, credit card numbers, or other sensitive information in an e-mail.

- Try to limit the topics in an e-mail, and number or letter multiple points to help the reader thoroughly address all of them. Make it easy to read and understand your message on a small portable device.

- Use the subject line to summarize the important part of your message. Sometimes subject lines can replace e-mail content. For example, instead of the title "Meeting" use "Meeting Tuesday at 12 in my office."

- Only send an e-mail to people who really need to know the information you're sending. Assume that anything you send to one person will be read by the entire company and make sure that's okay before sending it.

- Avoid using caps lock—it means that you are screaming.

- Take great care in using "reply all." Unless everyone needs to know your message, it is best to respond selectively.

- Before forwarding an e-mail to someone else, make sure that nothing being forwarded is of a confidential or inappropriate nature.

- Include a professional signature and additional contact information such as a telephone number if appropriate.

? so what

Training evaluation helps organizations understand how to improve a training program and whether or not to continue using it.

improving, valuing, and continuing an instructional activity or set of activities. To realize the greatest business value from training, evaluating whether training objectives were met is essential. Without proper evaluation, an organization cannot know whether a training program should be improved or even continued. Training evaluation typically includes:

- Participant reactions
- Learning assessments
- Training transfer back to the job

Evaluation results are included in the next training needs assessment process. Assessing training results is an important part of the training process. How else will the organization know:

- If participants are actually learning?
- If participants are transferring what they learned back on the job?
- If cost and timeline goals are being met?
- If the training is generating a positive return on investment?
- If the intended business results are being achieved?
- How the training can be improved?

Pre- and post-tests are useful in measuring learning. To ensure the effectiveness of the training program and to continually improve it, surveys should also be administered after each segment of the training program and 60 or 90 days after training ends. These surveys should assess training outcomes, including trainee learning and retention and the perceived usefulness of the training as well as solicit suggestions for improving the program.

PricewaterhouseCoopers (PwC) continually evaluates, refines, and innovates to meet its constantly changing learning needs. Learner diagnostics, pre-course assessments, and training impact studies help it identify areas to improve. PwC tries to balance the efficiency offered by technology with opportunities to practice key skills, network, and satisfy employees' social learning needs. PwC uses technology to build, "better, more engaging and immersive experiences that help our people deliver their very best work."[52] For its leadership development programs, Aon evaluates participants' retention and engagement versus their nonparticipating peers, whether participants would recommend the program, and their direct program feedback.[53]

Kirkpatrick's Training Evaluation Model. The most well-known and frequently used model for assessing training effectiveness was developed by Donald Kirkpatrick. Kirkpatrick identified four levels of training and learning evaluation:[54]

1. *Reaction*: How did participants react to the program? Participant feedback forms are usually used to assess reactions.
2. *Learning*: What was the change in participants' knowledge, skills, or attitudes? Dunkin' Donuts training includes a final exam in which students must bake 140 dozen donuts in just eight hours. Six donuts are then randomly selected for evaluation.[55]
3. *Behavior*: What was the change in participants' on-the-job behavior due to the training? Verizon Wireless uses an automated scorecard for new customer service hires that displays performance by new hire training class in all core job performance metrics in the first 30, 60, and 90 days post-training. Verizon uses the results to drive improvements in curriculum, trainer delivery, and classroom management.[56]
4. *Results*: How did the organization benefit from the training? CarMax frequently evaluates whether the training, skills, and behaviors it thinks drive successful performance really do.[57]

As summarized in Table 7.2, each evaluation level addresses a different and important aspect of training program effectiveness. Each level provides information relevant for understanding outcomes at the next level. For example, if participants do not enjoy the training program (level 1), they are less likely to learn (level 2). If participants do not learn, they are unlikely to change their behaviors back on the job (level 3), and if participants do not change their on-the-job behaviors, the training is unlikely to have business impact (level 4).

Evaluation difficulty and cost increase through the levels. To be the most effective, training evaluation should be based on the initial goals for the training. For example, a retailer pursuing a customer service and sales growth strategy could have managers provide real-time coaching and role-model desired customer engagement behaviors. Instead of measuring the managers' time spent on training or employee satisfaction, it would be more strategic to assess the impact of the initiative on business metrics, including average sales and customer conversion rates. A manufacturer wanting to improve its plant operations by teaching supervisors lean manufacturing and coaching skills might track downtime, overall equipment effectiveness, or order completion times rather than how many managers have been trained.[58] Because it is possible for training to influence more than one outcome relevant to the organization, it is best to measure more than one possible training effect.[59]

Return on Investment. The most basic definition of percent return on investment, or ROI, is:

$$\text{ROI\%} = ((\text{Training Benefits} - \text{Training Costs})/\text{Training Costs}) \times 100$$

A positive ROI indicates that training benefits outweigh the costs and should be continued, although further improvement may also be possible. A negative ROI means the costs outweigh the benefits and suggests that the program should be changed or discontinued unless additional benefits exist that weren't considered (e.g., improved employee trust or morale).

table 7.2

Kirkpatrick's Training Evaluation Model

Level	What Is Assessed	Definition	Assessment Methodology	Usefulness
1	Reaction	How participants felt about the learning or training experience (like customer satisfaction).	• Feedback forms • Participant behaviors • Surveys	Fast, easy, inexpensive.
2	Learning	Change in participants' knowledge, skills, behavior, or attitudes due to the training.	• Pre and post training tests or assessments • Observation • Simulations • Interviews	Easier for more quantifiable and observable characteristics.
3	Behavior	The extent to which what is learned in training is used on the job.	• Long-term observation • Sustainability of new behaviors	Easy, less expensive if supervisors cooperate and support the effort.
4	Results	The business impact of the trainees' new knowledge and behaviors.	• Performance appraisal • ROI analysis	Supervisors can easily evaluate subordinates; business impact can be more difficult to assess due to greater number of factors influencing business units.

Consider this example. Assume that a new safety awareness program that cost $40,000 resulted in 15 percent fewer accidents. This translated into a first-year benefit of $200,000 in fewer lost workdays, lower workers' compensation costs, and less equipment damage. The ROI equation would be:

$$ROI = ((\$200,000\text{-}\$40,000)/\$40,000) \times 100 = 400\%$$

This means that for every $1 invested in the training program, the organization realized a return of 400%, or $4.

ROI can help trainers and management know whether training is beneficial to the organization and identify the financial return on the company's training investment. Telecommunications company PAETEC compares the cost of the trainer's time, employee work time lost during training, and travel costs to the financial outcome of the training program.[60]

Informal Learning

so what

Because most training occurs outside of formal training programs, it is important to be open to learning whenever the opportunity presents itself.

Not all learning occurs during formal training. We all learn new things almost every day. In fact, informal learning that occurs without a formal structure, curriculum, or professional trainer is probably the most common form of learning. When we learn through experience, or when a coworker answers a question or helps us do something for the first time, we are being informally trained. Because informal training is more casual and spontaneous than formal training, it is not formally planned and is less likely to be formally evaluated. Informal learning is essential to getting underperforming employees up to speed, and it is related to increased productivity.[61]

Gamification of Training

Training gamification involves the application of gaming designs and concepts to training to make it more engaging for the learner and increase learning and performance outcomes.[62] Gamification can involve utilizing games in instruction, such as creating virtual worlds or business simulations, that let the learner control the learning experience, or to the incorporation of "gaming mechanics" such as points or status bars to motivate or incentivize learners to participate in gaming or nongaming activities. Computer-based games can improve productivity and positively impact business results and are even being used to increase knowledge and loyalty among customers, channel partners, and other stakeholders. Because the millennial generation grew up playing computer and video games, they tend to enjoy learning experiences with game-like elements.[63] Gamification can also be used to personalize learning experiences by creating unique pathways through the content that best cater to each learner's needs.

When McDonald's was launching a new ordering system, it wanted to deliver an engaging and fun learning experience to its employees. They also wanted to create a safe learning environment in which employees could practice without frustrating customers. The online training game incorporated lifelines, bonuses, and other elements to engage the learner and reinforce the learning goals. Although using it was not made mandatory, the game had 145,000 visits in its first year and remains McDonald's most popular employee portal page ever launched. The game also resulted in significant improvements in customer experience, sales, and profit metrics.[64]

To ensure trainee engagement, Western Union added gamification tools including attendance points, completing e-learning courses, and participating in the online discussion platform. The company believes that the incentives combined with trainees' knowledge that they are being measured help to motivate its learners.[65] In Heineken's Capability Academy online training, as they progress through the activities, learners earn points, which pushes them up the leaderboard. Prizes are ultimately awarded to top scoring learners and teams.[66] The BBC Finance Game gives learners a challenge at each level and scores them on budget, staff satisfaction, and the quantity and quality of output based on the decision they make. Dynamic scoring allows for points to be lost and won across a range of skills.[67]

Reinforcing Training

Training is not an end in itself. Knowing something isn't the same as being willing or able to use it on the job. **Training transfer** refers to effectively using what is learned in training back on the job. One of the biggest training challenges is getting new skills and knowledge to transfer back to the work setting. Transferring **closed skills**, or near transfer, refers to getting trainees to apply skills performed similarly or exactly like they are taught in training (e.g., a telephone sales protocol). Transferring **open skills**, or far transfer, refers to getting trainees to transfer sets of principles that can be applied in many different ways (e.g., leadership skills) and in settings that differ from the one presented in the training program.[68]

The best predictors of whether someone will transfer what they learned in training back to the job are cognitive ability, conscientiousness, voluntarily participating in the training, and a work climate that facilitates transfer.[69] Strategies for increasing trainees' motivation prior to training and preparing coworkers and supervisors to support employees in transferring their learning to the job can also improve training transfer, as well as integrating learning into the organization's culture.[70] Making sure learners are confident in the use of their new skills is also an important precursor to training transfer.

Self-management strategies are a person's effort to control his or her motivation, emotions, and decision-making to enhance the application of learned capabilities to the job.[71] Goal setting helps learners consciously think about how they will use their new skills at work and how they will overcome anticipated obstacles to doing so.

training gamification
applying gaming designs and concepts to training to make it more engaging for the learner and increase learning and performance outcomes

training transfer
effectively using what is learned in training back on the job

closed skills
skills performed similarly or exactly like they are taught in training

open skills
sets of principles that can be applied in many different ways

self-management strategies
efforts to control one's motivation, emotions, and decision-making to enhance the application of learned capabilities to the job

? so what

Coworker, manager, and organizational support can promote or deter training transfer.

Support from coworkers, managers, and the organizational climate is essential for transfer to occur. It is also critical that the resources, opportunities, and tools necessary for training transfer be provided. For example, if an employee completes training on customer service interactions but when she returns to the job her supervisor tells her to do it the old way, she probably won't practice what she just learned in training for very long.

One organization created 3- to 9-minute podcasts of key training content to provide a quick refresher to participants, and every 2 weeks sent e-mail reminders of key things learners should be doing, watching for, or thinking about as well as links to the relevant podcasts. The company analyzed which e-mails and podcasts generated the most interest. An online discussion forum was created for learners to ask and answer questions and continue learning, and all training materials and references were placed in the forum for easy reference. Supervisors and trainers used the forums to identify transfer issues and to identify new training needs.[72] Organizations have also used e-mail reminders to highlight key things learners should be looking out for, thinking about, or doing. E-mail reminders can also include links to podcasts or discussion forums.

The transfer of what is learned during training is greatly facilitated by supportive managers and coworkers. If newly learned capabilities are not encouraged on the job, what is learned in training is not likely to be used and will probably be forgotten.

Reinforcement for performing learned behaviors also encourages the transfer of what is learned in training. Many behaviors can be controlled using different types of reinforcers.[73] **Reinforcers** are anything that makes a behavior more likely to happen again. Reinforcers work best when they are immediate, sincere, and specific to an activity. There are four types of reinforcers:

reinforcers
anything that makes a behavior more likely to happen again

- *Positive reinforcement*: Using rewards to increase the likelihood that a behavior will be repeated (such as a raise, bonus, or praise for applying the training).
- *Negative reinforcement*: Removing current or future unpleasant consequences to increase the likelihood that someone will repeat a behavior. The removal of something undesirable (such as not sending an employee to the training program again as long as his performance of the trained skills stays high) is motivating.
- *Punishment*: Creating negative outcomes to decrease the likelihood of a behavior (such as cutting the work hours of employees not using the training on the job).
- *Extinction*: Removal of any positive or negative reinforcement following the occurrence of the behavior to be extinguished decreases the likelihood of that behavior (such as no longer laughing at a coworker's efforts to not apply what was learned in training).

Training in Ethics, Global Leadership, and Diversity

Let's turn our attention to three popular types of training programs relevant for many different types of jobs: Ethics training, global leadership training, and diversity training.

Ethics Training

? so what

Ethics training helps prepare employees to deal effectively with the ethical issues they are likely to face in their jobs.

Having a code of ethics is not enough in itself to ensure ethical employee behavior. Enron Corporation's 64-page code of conduct did little to prevent unethical behavior, particularly by top management. A challenging economy also increases the need for ethics training, as employees are pressured to meet performance goals and cut budgets. Hiring ethical people, setting clear goals and standards regarding ethical behavior, providing methods for employees to report unethical behavior, and providing ethics training to all employees are also essential.

Although HR's greatest ethical impact may be in determining the ethical character of the employees a company hires and retains,[74] ethics training programs also help employees and managers understand their own ethical values and practice confronting ethical dilemmas.[75] Ethics training supporting the organization's code of ethics can provide a guiding framework, especially when it is revisited frequently, and all employees view ethics as an ongoing process.[76] Ethics training can be conducted through a variety of methods, including Internet-based training, simulations, and live training.

The Sarbanes-Oxley Act of 2002 was passed to hold accountable public and private companies registered with the Securities and Exchange Commission. Sarbanes-Oxley provides increased protection for whistleblowers, including the imposition of potential criminal penalties against individuals who retaliate against them.[77] Employees should be trained in their rights and responsibilities under this Act.

In addition, as published in the May 19, 2004, issue of *Federal Register*, the Federal Sentencing Guidelines require all employers to adopt formal and effective ethics and compliance programs and to train all employees on these programs.[78] The guidelines apply to corporations, partnerships, unions, trusts, associations, unincorporated organizations, nonprofit organizations, and the government, and they require training of high-level officials and employees in relevant legal standards and obligations. Some organizations are becoming creative with their ethics training, using interactive exercises and online games rather than a lecture-based approach.

Global Leadership Training

Globally competent leaders able to lead effectively across cultures and countries are critical to the success of multinational organizations.[79] The development of global leadership skills is essential for multinational firms' success. Collaborating with peers from multiple cultures, managing change, and cross-cultural employee engagement are important management skills that are lacking in many organizations.[80]

Without understanding our own cultural attributes, preferences, and characteristics, others' preferences may seem strange and perhaps unpleasant. These same differences influence both how leadership is perceived and different views of appropriate roles of followers, members of teams, department members, staff, and so on.[81] Global leadership training can help develop a variety of skills, including:

- Understanding cultural differences;
- Understanding the learner's personal cultural preferences;
- Knowing the cultural preferences of other countries and cultures;
- Understanding the implications of cultural differences to workplace effectiveness; and
- Effectively managing a multinational or multicultural workplace.

Although true in all types of training, people differentially benefit from intercultural training and experiences. Learners' knowledge, skills, abilities, and personality characteristics all influence global leadership training effectiveness. People who work successfully internationally tend to have high openness to experience, sociability, and emotional stability.[82] People higher in openness also tend to develop the most during developmental international assignments.[83] Offering employees with the requisite individual aptitudes global leadership development opportunities has the best chance of producing leaders who can effectively perform global leadership tasks and activities.[84]

Global beverage giant AB InBev receives thousands of applications every year from students from top universities, bringing in about 100 people for its global management training program. After a one-week induction session in which trainees work around the clock to learn about the company and complete a project, trainees are sent into the field to work for 10 months in different business functions. They also complete a capstone project at the end of the training program. Most of those hired after the program are then sent into the field for jobs in sales or production.[85]

Global leadership training methods include diversity training, cross-cultural training, and language training.[86] Whereas *culture-specific cross-cultural training* helps learners identify the most effective ways of working with people from a particular culture or country, *general*

so what**?**

Global leadership training can focus generally on how to work effectively with globally diverse people or specifically on how to work effectively with people from a specific culture.

 Global Issues

The Effect of Culture on Perceptions of Leadership[87]

A large 11-year study of global leadership effectiveness investigated the leadership beliefs of people in 62 different societal cultures to identify how middle managers worldwide distinguish between effective and ineffective leadership. The team identified many leader attributes universally seen as being at least somewhat responsible for a leader's effectiveness or ineffectiveness. They also identified many *culturally contingent* attributes, whose effects on leadership effectiveness differed across different cultures.

Some examples of universal *positive* leader attributes	Some examples of universal *negative* leader attributes	Some examples of *culturally contingent* leader attributes
Trustworthy	Irritable	Cunning
Dependable	Dictatorial	Sensitive
Excellence oriented	Uncooperative	Evasive
Honest	Ruthless	Risk taker
Motivating	Egocentric	Ruler

cross-cultural training can help individuals better manage the uncertainty of working with globally diverse people. Experiential opportunities, including mentoring, coaching, and immersion programs in foreign cultures tailored to the learner's strengths and needs, can also improve global leadership competence.[88]

Staffing and performance management are also important to the success of global leadership development programs. It is, therefore, important for organizations to approach global leadership development with a strategic and comprehensive approach.[89] Over 94 percent of U.S. Navy sailors and officers travel internationally and meet people from both adversarial and allied cultures. The Navy's Language, Regional Expertise, and Culture (LREC) program trains sailors in effectively interfacing with different cultures. The training includes mobile training teams, individual tutors, distance learning, and even mail-order delivery of learning materials.[90]

This chapter's Global Issues feature describes how cultural differences can impact leadership effectiveness.

Diversity Training

Diversity training promotes equality, fairness, and inclusiveness.[91] Not only does diversity training increase employees' awareness of diversity, but it also enhances trust, communication, and collaboration to help employees work together more effectively. Although it does not necessarily change participants' personal beliefs, by increasing awareness and promoting the acceptance and even leveraging of differences, successful diversity training can help create a positive work environment and decrease legal risks.

Appreciating the many types of diversity in the organization also helps to develop a confident and committed workforce. As KPMG's Associate Director for National Diversity and Corporate Responsibility Tori Carroll put it, "Diversity is about global competency. You should be able to work with anyone, anywhere, from any background."[92]

"Diversity is about global competency. You should be able to work with anyone, anywhere, from any background."

—**Tori Carroll, Associate Director for National Diversity and Corporate Responsibility, KPMG**

There are several reasons why diversity training programs fail. First, a diversity program will often fail unless the drive to create it comes from inside the organization rather than from legal compliance or another external reason. Also, off-the-shelf diversity programs not tailored to the organization's structure or culture are often ineffective at generating employee commitment. If employees do not see how the material is relevant to their job, many will see the training program as a waste of time. Finally, unless resources and support are provided to implement on-the-job changes, transfer is unlikely to occur.

The enthusiastic support and involvement of organizational leaders is the foundation of diversity training success. Organizational leaders must clearly communicate the importance of diversity as an organizational value and business goal. The diversity program should be clearly linked to the mission and objectives of the organization to maintain employees' interest and commitment to changing their behavior. In addition, mandatory attendance for all managers, long-term evaluation of training results, managerial rewards for increasing diversity, and a broad inclusionary definition of diversity in the organization enhance training success.[93] Calling the training "Inclusive Leadership" can also generate higher learner interest and engagement than calling it "Diversity Training."[94] Finally, the organization needs to conduct an adequate needs assessment to ensure the training material addresses diversity issues relevant to the organization.

so what?

Even the best diversity training program will fail to change employees' behaviors without sufficient organizational, leadership, and cultural support for diversity and inclusion.

Socialization

Most new hires need help getting up to speed. Learning a new job takes a mid-level manager an average of six months.[95] Even in restaurants and hotels, it can take about 90 days for a new employee to attain full productivity. On average, the time for new external hires to achieve full productivity is eight weeks for clerical jobs, 20 weeks for professionals, and more than 26 weeks for executives.[96]

Orientation is not the same as training. Training provides knowledge and skills relevant to job performance, whereas orientation is about learning to fit in as an organizational member. **Orientation**, or *onboarding*, involves processing employment-related paperwork, acquiring necessary passwords and identification cards, and establishing relevant technology such as e-mail and telephone numbers. Coworkers are introduced, and new hires are familiarized with their jobs and with the company's work policies and benefits. Orienting new employees also decreases the time it takes them to reach the break-even point at which they start generating a return on the company's investment in them.

Farmers Insurance's PowerUP! Program begins by sending new hires a letter confirming the offer and introducing the onboarding process. They then receive a welcome kit describing what will happen over the next six months, and they view five videos explaining Farmers' brand, values, facilities, and community engagement. Six online courses cover culture, company structure, products and distribution, work environment, and benefits. Business units participating in the PowerUP! Program experienced a 57 percent decrease in new hire turnover, saving the company $9 million.[97]

Socialization is a long-term process of planned and unplanned, formal and informal activities and experiences through which an individual acquires the attitudes, behaviors, and knowledge needed to successfully participate as an organizational member.[98] Without sufficient support and socialization, new hires are more likely to quit. Socialization helps new employees

orientation
training activities to help new hires fit in as organizational members

socialization
a long-term process of planned and unplanned, formal and informal activities and experiences through which an individual acquires the attitudes, behaviors, and knowledge needed to successfully participate as an organizational member

understand the organization's values, processes, and traditions[99] and prepares them to fit into the organization and establish productive work relationships.[100] Socialization is important for all employees, including part-time and temporary hires, and is important when employees move to new jobs in the company. When people are well socialized in their organizational roles, they tend to have a higher income, be more satisfied and more involved with their careers, and have a better sense of personal identity than those who are less well socialized.[101]

The purpose of socialization is to get new employees up to speed on their jobs and familiarize them with the organization's culture, which consists of the company's norms, values, behavior patterns, rituals, language, and traditions.[102] Because culture provides the framework through which employees interpret and understand everyday experiences, helping new hires understand and adjust to the organization's culture is one of the most important functions of socialization.

A successful socialization program helps to reduce newcomers' reality shock and facilitates adjustment and integration.[103] Well-socialized employees who are good fits with their job, workgroup, and organization and who share the firm's values are more engaged. Research studies have consistently shown that employee engagement is a driver of organizational success.[104]

? so what

Effective socialization decreases the time it takes to get new hires up to speed, enhances their commitment, and improves performance and retention.

Phases of Socialization

Socialization is an ongoing process that can last for a year as new hires form work relationships and become comfortable in the organization. The socialization process typically includes three phases:[105]

1. *Anticipatory socialization*: Before entering the organization, interacting with company representatives (e.g., recruiters or managers) develops new hires' expectations about the company and the job. The effectiveness of the anticipatory stage is enhanced when all employees who interact with recruits consistently reinforce the company's expectations of employees.
2. *Encounter*: When starting a new job, employees begin learning about the organization's culture, norms, and how to do the job. Higher quality work relationships are formed when managers help new employees understand their roles and how to cope with the stresses and issues that they are likely to experience. New hires at Google are called Nooglers (a combination of the words "new" and "Googler") and receive a baseball cap with a propeller on top to let others know to help welcome and socialize them.[106]
3. *Settling in*: When new hires start feeling comfortable with their job demands and work relationships, their attention turns to understanding the company's evaluation of their performance and possibly about future career opportunities within the company. At the end of their first year, participants in Microsoft's Academy for College Hires program participate in a one-and-a-half-day career planning workshop to map their path at the company.[107]

Financial services company Capital One's online orientation process helps new hires learn about the company, from its heritage to today's operations. It also provides comprehensive details about benefits options, allowing new hires time to study their options and discuss their choices with their families. A manager of similar rank from another department is also assigned to serve as an "assimilation buddy" to help the new manager get to know his or her peers and to answer questions. Six months after starting the job, the new leader receives a 360-degree review to identify where he or she can make additional progress in meeting goals and expectations and identify ongoing developmental goals and strategies.[108]

Socialization Options

Different newcomers have different socialization needs. A new hire with limited or no work experience needs a more extensive socialization experience than does an experienced hire or

table **7.3**

Socialization Options

One-time or staggered: Should the socialization be done in one long session or many smaller sessions?

Collective or individual: Should participants go through a common set of experiences as a group or be socialized one-on-one?

Formal or informal: Should socialization use specifically designed formal activities and materials away from the work setting or be done informally by coworkers on the job?

Sequential or random: Should participants complete a series of distinct steps to obtain full employee status or go through a random sequence of activities?

Fixed or variable: Should participants be given a fixed timetable associated with completing each stage in the transition or receive no consistent time frame and few cues as to when to expect the next stage?

Tournament or contest: Should each socialization stage be an "elimination tournament" where failure means that the participant is out of the organization or a "contest" in which new hires build up a track record and "batting average" over time?

Serial or disjunctive: Should experienced organizational members serve as role models or mentors who groom newcomers to follow in their footsteps, or should no role models be provided?

Investiture or divestiture: Should the organization take advantage of a participant's unique skills or try to deny or strip away personal characteristics?

What to include: What should be included in the socialization experience?

Whom to include: Who should be included in the socialization experience?

How to use technology: Should the socialization be virtual or in-person?

an employee receiving a promotion or transfer. The socialization experience should not overwhelm new hires with too much information, or it won't be remembered. There are multiple options when developing a socialization program, many of which also apply to other types of training programs. Table 7.3 summarizes these choices, which we discuss in more detail next.

One-Time or Staggered Approach.   Many organizations use a staggered approach to socialization to reduce the risk of information overload. Holding brief meetings over a few weeks can help participants process and remember the information presented better than in one long meeting. Although a one-time meeting can be cheaper, participants get a more thorough understanding of the organization if they need to attend meetings in different departments or different parts of the organization. Each activity or step can be given a time frame for completion or left open, and participants can be required to either complete socialization experiences in a set order or complete them in any order.

Collective or Individual Socialization.   Socialization can help reduce the uncertainty and the anxiety associated with the entry experience while helping newcomers adapt and acquire the necessary attitudes and behaviors.[109] **Collective socialization** puts new hires through a common set of experiences as a group. **Individual socialization** socializes newcomers individually as in an apprenticeship. Although it is more expensive, collective socialization increases newcomer embeddedness into the organization and reduces turnover.[110] Collective socialization is best when socialization content can be clearly specified, there are many people being socialized at the same time, and when the organization wants to build a collective sense of identity, solidarity, and loyalty within the cohort group being socialized.[111]

collective socialization
newcomers go through a common set of experiences as a group

individual socialization
newcomers are socialized individually as in an apprenticeship

formal socialization
structured socialization using specifically designed activities and materials that is done away from the work setting

informal socialization
unstructured, on-the-job socialization done by coworkers

sequential socialization
the degree to which socialization follows a specific sequence of steps

random socialization
socialization steps are ambiguous or changing

fixed socialization
new hires are informed in advance when their probationary status will end

variable socialization
employees do not know when to expect to pass to a different status level, and the timeline may be different across employees

tournament socialization
each stage of socialization is an "elimination round," and a new hire is out of the organization if he or she fails to pass

contest socialization
each socialization stage is a "contest" in which one builds up a performance record

serial socialization
accessible and supportive organizational members serve as role models and mentors

disjunctive socialization
newcomers are left alone to develop their own interpretations of the organization and situations they observe

investiture socialization
builds newcomers' self-confidence and reflects senior employees' valuing of newcomers' knowledge and personal characteristics

divestiture socialization
tries to deny and strip away certain personal characteristics

Formal or Informal Socialization.   **Formal socialization** is structured socialization done away from the work setting using specifically designed activities and materials. During the Naval Undersea Warfare Center Division's formal two-day face-to-face new hire orientation, 16 senior leaders give formal presentations on life at Division Newport.[112] **Informal socialization** is unstructured and done on-the-job by coworkers. More structured, formal socialization promotes proactive behavior, such as asking questions, seeking feedback, and building relationships, which increases job satisfaction and commitment.[113]

Sequential or Random.   **Sequential socialization** refers to the degree to which a specific sequence of socialization steps is followed. **Random socialization** occurs when the socialization steps are ambiguous or changing. Socialization for doctors is usually sequential, while socialization for managers is usually random. In random socialization, what newcomers learn first may be the things in which they are most interested rather than the things that are most important.

Fixed or Variable.   Whereas sequential and random socialization addresses the order of events, fixed and variable socialization address the temporal nature of the events. **Fixed socialization** processes inform new hires in advance when their probationary status will end. With **variable socialization**, employees do not know when to expect to pass to a different employee status level, and the timeline may be different across employees. Variable processes reduce the power of cohorts to remain cohesive over time.

Tournament or Contest.   **Tournament socialization**, treats each stage of socialization as an "elimination round," and a new hire is out of the organization if he or she fails to pass.[114] Many law firms use tournament socialization. If a manager is punished or fired because his or her performance is below target or because he or she fails to follow accepted norms, surviving employees quickly become risk averse to avoid a similar fate. Tournament socialization tends to stifle innovation and risk-taking and produces a homogeneous workforce with very similar norms.[115] Because tournament socialization tends to make employees more insecure and submissive to authority,[116] it tends to make the organization capable of only slow, incremental changes to its culture and way of doing business.[117]

Contest socialization treats each socialization stage as a "contest" in which participants build up a performance record over time. Failure is generally considered a learning experience and not grounds for punishment or termination.

Serial or Disjunctive.   During **serial socialization**, new hires are given access to supportive organizational members who serve as role models and mentors. Newcomers are generally expected to follow in the footsteps of their predecessors. **Disjunctive socialization** leaves newcomers alone to develop their own interpretations of the organization and the situations they observe. Serial socialization helps to maintain continuity and a sense of history. Under disjunctive socialization, newcomers develop their roles in isolation. Disjunctive socialization tends to happen when new employees replace the "old guard."

Investiture or Divestiture.   **Investiture socialization** builds newcomers' self-confidence and reflects senior employees' valuing of newcomers' knowledge and personal characteristics. Investiture tactics tell recruits that the company likes them just the way they are and that the organization wants to utilize their unique skills.

Divestiture socialization tries to deny and strip away certain personal characteristics by requiring newcomers to "pay their dues" before becoming full organizational members. Military boot camp is like this. Organizations use divestiture tactics to strip away existing behaviors and attitudes and introduce new ones desired by the organization. Divestiture socialization processes include an identity creating as well as an identity destroying process, and they are unethical and inappropriate in most work organizations.[118]

What to Include.   Effective socialization programs get new hires productive faster by teaching them about the company, its key strategic objectives, and work processes and help them continue to feel good about their choice to join the company. Communicating business goals and values helps employees understand their role in contributing to the company's success. Goldman Sachs has a Day One Orientation, followed by a series of e-mails sent during new employees' first 100 days with tips to help them to fit into the company's culture. Between six and 12 months after joining Goldman, newcomers attend a one-day symposium led by a top officer to give them an opportunity to discuss the firm's values of "teamwork, meritocracy, and integrity."[119]

Although socialization is most important for new organization members, regardless of the years of work experience they have, understanding the cultural aspects of one's workgroup and company are essential to functioning effectively in a new environment. Some of the information employees should learn through socialization includes information about:[120]

- *Culture*: Including company norms, values, behavior patterns, rituals, language, and traditions.
- *Politics*: Including information about formal and informal power structures and work relationships.
- *Organizational goals and policies*: Which include understanding the rules and the principles that maintain the culture of the organization.

Whom to Include.   Some companies recognize that an employee's entire family is affected by a member's employment and include families in the socialization process to facilitate their acclimation to the company and the community. Giving new hires' families information about the area, or even having a separate family orientation, can facilitate the entire family's transition and increase their commitment to the company.

The employees who will be important to the new hire's job success should play a role in the socialization process. Managers should be accountable for the successful socialization of their new hires. At many companies, top leaders also welcome new employees. Cisco CEO John Chambers hosts a "Chat with Chambers" for groups of new employees several months after they start with the company.[121] Socialization can also include coworkers essential to the new hire's job success.

How to Use Technology.   Automating part of the socialization process and using the company's intranet helps to coordinate and store the stream of paperwork and e-mail correspondence related to training, benefits programs, and contract approvals. Automated processes can give new hires e-mail addresses and network access, provide access to the employee handbook, and manage the training and administrative aspects of the onboarding and socialization process.[122] This helps to ensure legal compliance by tracking new hires' socialization activities against checklists, and it improves the quality of the socialization process by giving hiring managers timely reminders on how to assimilate and manage new employees.

IBM uses IBM@Play, a set of training tools that use video game technology and three-dimensional Internet environments, to facilitate new hire socialization. Some new IBM employees in India, China, and the United States use "avatars," or representations of themselves, in one of two Internet virtual worlds, PlaneShift or Second Life, to expedite orientation and improve mentoring relationships.

Internet-based socialization may not be best for all types of information. One study found that employees who went through a computer-based orientation reported lower levels of socialization in the areas of people, politics, organizational goals, and values compared with employees who attended an in-person orientation session.[123]

so what

Technology can help socialize employees more efficiently and effectively.

The Government Accountability Office uses an online system to notify appropriate departments in advance of a new hire's arrival so they can prepare equipment, establish necessary accounts, and prepare the office space.[124] At the Department of Homeland Security, automated processes allow new hires to complete all forms before reporting to work.[125]

Effective Socialization

An effective socialization program actively involves new employees, encourages them to ask questions, and clarifies their role in business strategy execution. Investing in acclimating new hires pays off in higher commitment, faster time to productivity, and higher performance.[126] Socialization is enhanced by a high-quality relationship between the new hire and his or her manager.[127] Research suggests that socializing new employees as a group, using formal activities and materials in a predetermined order within a specified time frame, giving newcomers access to role models or mentors, and providing social support enhance newcomer loyalty, reduce turnover, and increase commitment, job satisfaction, task mastery, and values congruence with the organization.[128]

Marriott created Voyage, a virtual learning environment, to increase the speed of new managers' onboarding and socialization. Each "voyager" is guided by a coach in completing the program before transitioning to a leadership role. Voyage is focused on the social aspects of communication, participation, and connection and includes social media, webcasting, and access to traditional learning management system features, including webcasts and e-learning coursework. Because Voyage can be accessed via mobile devices, employees can obtain training at any time and revisit it if they need a refresher.[129]

The HR department usually has overall responsibility for socialization planning and follow-up and should coordinate with the employee's supervisor to avoid the duplication or omission of important information. It is also important to solicit feedback from everyone involved in the process through discussions with new employees after their first year on the job or by giving questionnaires to all relevant individuals (e.g., managers or coworkers). Having a formal and systematic follow-up process not only helps evaluate the program's effectiveness, it can also identify areas for further improvement.[130]

The new hire's manager needs to be involved and committed to taking the time to get the new hire up to speed quickly. Pairing coworker mentors or "buddies" with new hires for a few days or weeks can facilitate their transition, help incorporate them into their workgroup, and familiarize them with other key employees. This can be particularly helpful if a new hire must wait a few weeks or months before the company's next formal orientation program begins.

Onboarding and socialization success can be measured using metrics of how many new hires have e-mail addresses ready by their first day of work and the percentage satisfied with their onboarding and socialization experience.[131] New hire attrition and performance are also relevant metrics for evaluating the success of these programs. This chapter's case study discusses how Facebook socializes its new engineers.

CASE STUDY: Socializing New Engineers at Facebook[131]

By their second day on the job, all new engineers at Facebook attend Facebook Bootcamp, six weeks in the trenches fixing software bugs. The primary goal of Bootcamp is to get new hires up to speed on all parts of Facebook's code base while developing good long-term habits, including fixing bugs as they are found rather than leaving them for future engineers. The immersive cultural indoctrination training includes one-on-one sessions with mentors and talks from senior engineers, showing them the ropes, and preparing them to quickly contribute to Facebook.

Because Facebook also believes that engineers are most effective when working on things they are passionate about, new hires interview all engineering teams during Bootcamp and choose which one they ultimately join.

Facebook credits Bootcamp with its ability to write code and add new features quickly when needed. Consistent with the social networking mission of the company, the friendships and the professional networks created during Bootcamp continue as the new hires disperse across the company. Its focus on training may also help Facebook compete with Google and other companies for engineering talent.

Questions:

1. How does spending the first six weeks at Facebook fixing software bugs help socialize new engineering hires?
2. How does letting new engineering hires choose which team they want to work on after Bootcamp motivate the teams?
3. How else can Facebook improve the networking of its new hires to enable them to help each other once Bootcamp ends?

The Trainee

The primary goal of training is to try to change employee behavior or teach new skills and behaviors to individuals or workgroups. One of the most important factors in whether or not training will be learned, transferred to the work environment, and impact organizational performance is the trainee. New skills and behaviors can only occur if they have been learned and if the trainee then chooses to use them in the work context. The trainee obviously has a large impact over both what is learned and what is applied back on the job.

Research clearly shows that people benefit differently from training and development experiences. Although some people learn new behaviors and perspectives easily from work, life, and formal courses, others do not.[133] **Learning agility** is the ability to learn from experience and to apply that knowledge to new and different situations. Adapting how we think and respond to a situation, and bringing what we have learned from past experiences to the current situation while remaining open and inquisitive, helps us to be most effective.[134] Agile learners have been shown to have more successful careers.[135] Curiosity, proactive skill-building, getting feedback on improvement opportunities, thinking through problems from a fresh perspective, and explaining one's thinking to others are all thought to be part of learning agility.[136]

A second important trainee characteristic is the desire to transfer learning back to the job to improve work outcomes or productivity. **Motivation to transfer** reflects the intention and the willingness to transfer any knowledge acquired in a training or development activity back to the work context.[137] Some employees view training as an opportunity to take a break from work rather than learn a different way of doing things on the job. Ensuring that trainees understand the importance of the training and of transferring the new skills and behaviors is essential in increasing their motivation to transfer them.

A third trainee characteristic relevant to training performance and transfer is self-regulation. **Self-regulation** refers to processes enabling an individual to guide his/her goal-directed activities over time, including modulation of thought, affect, behavior, or attention.[138] In self-guided training, as is common with e-learning technologies, self-regulatory processes are particularly important to success due to the low degree of structure and lack of external guidance.[139]

learning agility
the ability to learn from experiences and to apply that knowledge to new and different situations

motivation to transfer
the intention and the willingness to transfer any knowledge acquired in a training or development activity back to the work context

so what❓

The old adage, "You can lead a horse to water, but you can't make it drink" is reflected in the fact that trainees share the responsibility for learning and transferring training material to their jobs.

self-regulation
processes enabling an individual to guide his/her goal-directed activities over time

Develop Your Skills

Self-Regulation[140]

Respond to the items below using the scoring key provided. Be sure to answer honestly to gain the best insight into your self-regulation tendencies. Think about your current college courses in responding to the items.

Strongly Disagree	Disagree	Slightly Disagree	Neutral	Slightly Agree	Agree	Strongly Agree
(1)	(2)	(3)	(4)	(5)	(6)	(7)

\<-------|--------------|-------------|------------|------------------|------------|----------|------->

____ 1. I ask myself questions to make sure I know the material I have been studying.

____ 2. When work is hard, I either give up or study only the easy parts.

____ 3. I work on practice exercises and answer end of chapter questions even when I don't have to.

____ 4. Even when study materials are dull and uninteresting, I keep working until I finish.

____ 5. Before I begin studying, I think about the things I will need to do to learn.

____ 6. I often find that I have been reading for class but don't know what it is all about.

____ 7. I find that when the teacher is talking I think of other things and don't really listen to what is being said.

____ 8. When I'm reading, I stop once in a while and go over what I have read.

____ 9. I work hard to get a good grade even when I don't like a class.

Scoring

For items 2, 6, and 7 subtract your answer from 7. Replace your initial answer with this new score. Now add up your scores to all 9 items to calculate your self-regulation score.

If your score is *54 or greater*, you have strong self-regulation skills. These skills should help you perform well in training environments.

If your score is *in between 27 and 54*, your self-regulation skills are good, but at least a few could be improved further. Read over the nine items, and identify strategies to improve in your weak areas.

If your score is *27 or lower*, most of your self-regulation skills could be improved. Read over the nine items, and try to identify a few areas in which you can try to improve. Set goals for yourself, and try to identify specific strategies to help you improve in each area.

The better you are able to self-regulate during training, the easier it will be for you to learn and transfer the material to the job. This chapter's Develop Your Skills feature gives you the chance to evaluate your self-regulation tendencies.

Summary and Application

The success of any organization depends heavily on its ability to maximize the talents and the capabilities of its workforce. Training and development are essential for helping new hires adjust to the organization and become productive, improving employees' performance, and ensuring a pipeline of future leadership talent. Following the five-step training process enhances training effectiveness and helps to ensure that the training program has maximum business impact. Because people differ in their learning styles and other characteristics, it is helpful to take learner characteristics into account when designing training programs. Manager support and learner self-management strategies are essential if learned skills, attitudes, and behaviors are to be used back on the job.

Diversity training, global leadership training, and ethics training address specific organizational needs. Organizations also make many choices in establishing socialization programs, including how formal they are and whether to socialize new hires individually or as a group. By taking the time to plan a training program and evaluate its effectiveness, the benefits of training can be maximized.

Real World Response

How Training Drives Performance at McDonald's

Since 1961, McDonald's Hamburger University's class attendance has increased from an average of 10 students per week to more than 200. Professors from around the world deliver the training, using a combination of self-study, hands-on lab activities, and classroom and e-learning modules.[141] In addition to its main U.S. campus, Hamburger University also has campuses in Sydney, Munich, Tokyo, Brazil, and Hong Kong.[142]

Training is aligned with employees' career paths, including crew, restaurant managers, mid-managers, and executives.[143] Participants in the management training and education programs can even earn credit toward their two- or four-year degree.[144]

McDonald's uses technology to maximize the effectiveness of its training programs. In Japan, rather than shadowing instructors in stores, McDonald's now trains all part-time employees using the Nintendo DS handheld to teach tasks such as interacting with customers and frying potatoes. McDonald's estimates that using Nintendo cuts the necessary training time for these topics in half.[145]

McDonald's also uses its university to address its biggest challenge of recruiting and retaining skilled managers.[146] In China, the selection rate to get into Hamburger University as a management trainee is less than 1 percent, making it even harder to get into than Harvard University.[147] To date, over 275,000 franchisees, employees, and suppliers have graduated from Hamburger University and helped McDonald's execute its strategy and achieve its goals.[148]

Takeaway Points

1. The five steps to effective training are conduct a needs assessment, develop learning objectives, design the training program, implement the training, and evaluate the training.
2. The three types of learning objectives are cognitive, affective, and psychomotor. Cognitive objectives relate to knowledge. Affective objectives relate to attitudes, relationships, or appreciation, and psychomotor objectives relate to physical skills.
3. Training methods include classroom training, on-the-job training, virtual training, experiential training, and games.
4. Because learner characteristics can influence training outcomes, it is important to match training methods to learner needs. Learning style refers to how people process information differently when learning. By matching training methods to learners' learning styles, learning outcomes are enhanced.

5. Kirkpatrick's four levels of training evaluation are reaction, learning, behavior, and results. Reaction refers to whether learners liked the training. Learning refers to changes in learner knowledge, skills, behavior, or attitudes as a result of the training. Behavior reflects whether what was learned in training is used on the job, which is also called training transfer. Results indicates the business impact of the training outcomes.

6. Three common training programs are ethics, global leadership, and diversity training. Socialization and onboarding are other types of training done to assimilate new hires into the organization and help them reach full productivity as quickly as possible.

7. Socialization success is enhanced by top management support of the socialization program, socializing new employees as a group, giving participants access to role models or mentors, and using formal activities and materials in a predetermined order in a specified time frame.

Discussion Questions

1. What could happen if an organization did not conduct a needs analysis?
2. What could happen if an organization did not evaluate a training program?
3. How should people be selected to participate in a training program?
4. How can lifelong learning help an organization obtain a competitive advantage?
5. What types of problems can training not solve? Which would be better handled by other areas of HRM?
6. What types of problems can training best solve?
7. If your organization did not want to spend money evaluating training, how would you convince them to invest in doing so?
8. Can you teach people to be ethical? How?
9. What do you think are the biggest obstacles to transferring ethics training back to the job? How can an organization overcome these challenges?
10. Describe an ideal socialization experience. What would make this experience the most effective for you?

Personal Development Exercise: What Is Your Personal Learning Style?

Point your favorite browser to http://www.personal.psu.edu/bxb11/LSI/LSI.htm, and complete the learning styles inventory assessment. When you are finished, answer the following questions:

1. Do you agree with your assessment? Why or why not?
2. Given your assessed learning style preferences, what types of training programs would be the best fit for you?
3. How can this type of information help organizations improve the effectiveness of their training programs?

Strategic HRM Exercises

Exercise: Training at Apple Stores[149]

Apple prefers to hire people who are passionate about Apple products to work in its retail stores. Passionate employees who personally like and use its products help enhance the customer experience. Apple Store employees helped make it the fastest-growing U.S. retail chain in history to reach sales of $1 billion and consistently rank among the most profitable retailers.

Apple designed its stores by first creating mockups in a warehouse to ensure the ultimate stores were optimally engineered for what customers would need. Everything from the music to employees' interactions with customers is very well planned. Apple intensively controls customer interactions and forbids employees from prematurely acknowledging any glitches. Apple Store employees have no sales quotas and receive no commissions, although employees must sell service packages with devices, or they will be retrained or moved to another position.

Apple Stores rely on training to create very controlled and consistent employee interactions with customers. Extensive employee training includes a series of podcasts explaining to new hires that selling is all about the approach—helping customers solve problems rather than selling something. Employees are also trained by watching other employees get customers' permission to ask some questions to understand their needs, then probing to identify which products would be the best solutions. New hires also attend classes on Apple's customer service principles and learn how to work together because customers notice when employees aren't getting along. Technology support staff, called "Geniuses", are even trained to say, "as it turns out" instead of "unfortunately" to sound less negative.

1. How does Apple Stores' training help it achieve a competitive advantage?
2. What are the downsides to Apple Stores' training approach?
3. Are you a good fit with Apple Stores' approach to training? What do you like and dislike about it and why? What would make it a better match with your preferences?

Exercise: Gamified Training

Visit https://learning.elucidat.com/course/54e76dd05253f-54e76df8814d4, and work through the sample fraud protection course. Then answer the questions below and be prepared to share your insights with the class.

1. What elements of the training helped to keep you engaged?
2. Do you think you would have learned the material better if the course was presented as a trainer talking about the issues in a video? Why or why not?
3. What could help to increase the effectiveness of this training tool?

Exercise: Socializing for Strategic Impact

Divide the class into groups of three to five students. Each group will be assigned one of the three questions to address. Be prepared to share your answers with the class.

1. Imagine you are responsible for the onboarding and socialization of new hires for Starbucks. What type of socialization experience would you create and why? What would you avoid doing and why?
2. Imagine you are responsible for the onboarding and socialization of new hires for airport security screeners. What type of socialization experience would you create and why? What would you avoid doing and why?
3. Imagine you are responsible for the onboarding and socialization of new nursing hires for a hospital. What type of socialization experience would you create and why? What would you avoid doing and why?

Integrative Project

Describe the onboarding and socialization experience you would create for your new hires in the position you used in the previous chapter. Be sure to address all socialization options in Table 7.3. Be sure to explain your choices. Also identify three learning objectives for your new hire training program to help new hires contribute to business strategy execution.

Video Case

Imagine that a coworker at Happy Time Toys approached you for advice about how to improve the training transfer of a new training program. *What do you say or do?* Go to this book's video case, watch the challenge video for this chapter, and choose the best video response. Be sure to also view the outcomes of the two responses you didn't choose.

Discussion Questions

1. Which aspects of HRM discussed in this chapter are illustrated in these videos? Explain your answer.
2. How is ethics illustrated in these videos? Explain your answer.
3. As a manager, how else might you handle the situation? Explain your answer.

Endnotes

1. McDonald's. (2017). Hamburger University. Retrieved March 15, 2017, from http://corporate.mcdonalds.com/mcd/corporate _careers/training_and_development/hamburger_university.html
2. *Ibid.*
3. Building organizational capabilities: McKinsey global survey results. (2010, March). mckinseyquarterly.com. Retrieved March 17, 2017, from https://www.mckinseyquarterly.com /Putting_a_value_on_training_2634#footnote1
4. 2010 training industry report. (2011). *Training Magazine*, November/December, 18–31.
5. Training top 125. (2011). *Training Magazine*, January/February, 57.
6. See www.ad.org
7. Lawler, E. E., III, & Worley, C. G. (2011). *Management reset: Organizing for sustainable effectiveness*. San Francisco, CA: Jossey-Bass.
8. Wang, H. C., He, J., & Mahoney, J. T. (2009). Firm-specific knowledge resources and competitive advantage: The roles of economic- and relationship-based employee governance mechanisms. *Strategic Management Journal*, *30*, 1265–1285.
9. Gent, M. J., & Dell'Omo, G. G. (1989). The needs assessment solution. *Personnel Administrator*, July, 82–84.
10. Freifeld, L. (2017). 2017 training top 125 best practices and outstanding training initiatives. *Training Magazine*. Retrieved March 19, 2017, from https://trainingmag.com/trgmag-article/2017 -training-top-125-best-practices-and-outstanding-training-initiatives
11. Pruitt, L. (2011). Strategies for success. *Training Magazine*, March/April, 24–25.
12. Training top 125. (2011). *Training Magazine*, January/February, 55.
13. Anderson, L., & Krathwohl, D. (Eds.) (2001). *A taxonomy for learning, teaching, and assessing: A revision of Bloom's taxonomy of educational objectives*. New York: Longman.
14. Krathwohl, D. R., Bloom, B. S., & Masia, B. B. (1964). *Taxonomy of educational objectives, nook II: Affective domain*. New York: David McKay Company, Inc.
15. Based on Anderson, L., & Krathwohl, D. (Eds.) (2001). *A taxonomy for learning, teaching, and assessing: A revision of Bloom's taxonomy of educational objectives*, pp. 67–68. New York: Longman.
16. Based on Krathwohl, D. R., Bloom, B. S., & Masia, B. B. (1964). *Taxonomy of educational objectives, book II: Affective domain*. New York: David McKay Company, Inc.
17. Based on Dave, R. H. (1970). In R. J. Armstrong et al. (Eds.), *Developing and writing behavioral objectives*, Tucson, AZ: Educational Innovators Press; Harrow, A. J. (1972). *A taxonomy of the psychomotor domain*. New York: David McKay Co.; Simpson, E. (1972). *The classification of educational objectives in the psychomotor domain, Vol. 3*. Washington, DC: Gryphon House.
18. Training top 125. (2011). *Training Magazine*, January/February, 71.
19. Training top 125. (2011). *Training Magazine*, January/February, 75.
20. Kane, Y. I., & Sherr, I. (2011, June 15). Secrets from Apple's genius bar: Full loyalty, no negativity. *Wall Street Journal*. Retrieved March 14, 2017, from http://online.wsj.com /article/SB10001424052702304563104576364071955678908 .html
21. Training top 125. (2017). *Training Magazine*, January, 60–95.
22. 2010 training industry report. (2010). *Training Magazine*, November/December, 18–31.
23. Training top 125. (2011). *Training Magazine*, January/February, 59.
24. Training top 125. (2011). *Training Magazine*, January/February, 89.
25. Freifeld, L. (2017). 2017 training top 125 best practices and outstanding training initiatives. *Training Magazine*. Retrieved March 19, 2017, from https://trainingmag.com/trgmag-article /2017-training-top-125-best-practices-and-outstanding-training -initiatives
26. Frauenheim, E. (2007). IBM's people chief: A leader in leadership. *Workforce Management*, May 21, pp. 1, 20–23
27. 2010 training industry report. (2010). *Training Magazine*, November/December, 18–31.
28. Video games can be highly effective training tools, study shows: Employees learn more, forget less, master more skills. (2010, October 20). *ScienceDaily*. Retrieved March 16, 2017, from http: //www.sciencedaily.com/releases/2010/10/101019171854.htm
29. *Ibid.*
30. *Ibid.*
31. Sitzmann, T. (in press) A meta-analytic examination of the instructional effectiveness of computer-based simulation games. *Personnel Psychology*.
32. Video games can be highly effective training tools, study shows: Employees learn more, forget less, master more skills. (2010, October 20). *ScienceDaily*. Retrieved March 16, 2017, from http://www.sciencedaily.com/releases/2010/10/101019171854 .htm

33. Freifeld, L. (2017). 2017 training top 125 best practices and outstanding training initiatives. *Training Magazine*. Retrieved March 19, 2017, from https://trainingmag.com/trgmag-article/2017-training-top-125-best-practices-and-outstanding-training-initiatives

34. Best practices & outstanding initiatives. (2011). *Training Magazine*, January/February, 94–98.

35. Everson, K. (2015). Aon's strategic mind. *Chief Learning Officer*, September, 22–25.

36. Marquez, J. (2007). Goldman Sachs: Optimas award winner for general excellence. *Workforce Management*, March 26, 22.

37. Ibid.

38. The benefits of lifelong learning. (1997). *Journal of European Industrial Training*, February–March, 3.

39. Sternberg, R. J., & Zhang, L. (Eds.) (2001). *Perspectives on thinking, learning, and cognitive styles*. Mahwah, NJ: LEA.

40. Dunn, R., Ingham, J., & Deckinger, L. (1995). Effects of matching and mismatching corporate employees' perceptual preferences and instructional strategies on training achievement and attitudes. *Journal of Applied Business Research*, *11*, 30–37.

41. Freifeld, L. (2011). Farmers' premier position. *Training Magazine*, January/February, 26–33.

42. Bissell, J., White, S., & Zivin, G. (1971). Sensory modalities in children's learning. In G. S. Lesser (Ed.), *Psychology and educational practice,* pp. 130–155. Glenview, IL: Scott Foresman & Company.

43. Dunn, R. S., & Dunn, K. J. (1979). Learning styles/teaching styles: Should they . . . can they . . . be matched? *Educational Leadership*, *36*, 238–244.

44. Towler, A., & Dipboye, R. L. (2003). Development of a learning style orientation measure. *Organizational Research Methods*, *6*, 216–235.

45. Christensen, U. J. (2017, January 23). Adaptive learning methods could close the trained worker skills gap. *Chief Learning Officer*. Retrieved March 19, 2007, from http://www.clomedia.com/2017/01/23/adaptive-learning-methods-close-trained-worker-skills-gap/?utm_source=MyEmma&utm_medium=Email&utm_campaign=CLO%20Today

46. Sramek, J. (2014, March 17). Adaptive learning: A game-changer for corporate training? *Training Magazine*. Retrieved March 19, 2017, from https://trainingmag.com/adaptive-learning-game-changer-corporate-training

47. Shein, E. (2014, June 18). Adaptive learning creates more effective training. *Computerworld*. Retrieved March 19, 2017, from http://www.computerworld.com/article/2490380/it-skills-training/adaptive-learning-creates-more-effective-training.html

48. Sramek, J. (2014, March 17). Adaptive learning: A game-changer for corporate training? *Training Magazine*. Retrieved March 19, 2017, from https://trainingmag.com/adaptive-learning-game-changer-corporate-training

49. Training top 125. (2011). *Training Magazine*, January/February, 61.

50. Smith, A. (2011, May 6). E-mail training needed to avoid cyber battles. *Society for Human Resource Management*. Retrieved June 23, 2011, from http://www.shrm.org/LegalIssues/FederalResources/Pages/EMailTraining.aspx

51. Ibid.

52. Training top 10 hall of fame. (2011). *Training Magazine*, January/February, 52–53.

53. Everson, K. (2015). Aon's strategic mind. *Chief Learning Officer*, September, 22–25.

54. Kirkpatrick, D. L. (1998). *Evaluating training programs: The four levels*, 3rd ed. San Francisco, CA: Berrett-Koehler Publishers, Inc.; Kirkpatrick, D. L., & Kirkpatrick, J. D. (2005). *Transferring learning to behavior: Using the four levels to improve performance*. San Francisco, CA: Berrett-Koehler Publishers, Inc.

55. Pinchevsky, T. (2009). Brand training the McDonald's way. *Minyanville.com*. Retrieved March 15, 2017, from http://www.minyanville.com/businessmarkets/articles/mcdonalds-university-hamburger-minyanville-manual-franchise/9/14/2009/id/24481

56. Training top 125. (2011). *Training Magazine*, January/February, 55.

57. Training top 125. (2011). *Training Magazine*, January/February, 61.

58. Ibid.

59. Kraiger, K., Ford, J. K., & Salas, E. (1993). Application of cognitive, skill-based and affective theories of learning to new methods of training evaluation. *Journal of Applied Psychology*, *78*, 311–328.

60. McGeough, D. (2011). Measuring ROI. *Training Magazine*, March/April, 27.

61. Liu, X., & Batt, R. (2007). The economic pay-offs to informal training: Evidence from routine service work. *Industrial and Labor Relations Review*, *61*, 75–89.

62. Gamification. *TrainingIndustry.com*. Retrieved March 17, 2017, from https://www.trainingindustry.com/wiki/entries/gamification.aspx

63. Ibid.

64. McDonald's till training game case study. (2017). *Kineo*. Retrieved March 17, 2017, from http://www.kineo.com/case-studies/mcdonalds-till-training-game

65. Gale, S. F. (2017). Taking leadership in a new direction at Western Union. *Chief Learning Officer*, March, 54–55.

66. Penfold, S. (2016, January 26). 5 ways to use gamification in online training (that can't be done with traditional training). *Elucidat*. Retrieved March 17, 2017, from https://blog.elucidat.com/gamification-online-training/

67. Ibid.

68. Blume, B. D., Ford, J. K., Baldwin, T. T., & Huang, J. L. (2010). Transfer of training: A meta-analytic review. *Journal of Management*, *36*, 1065–1105.

69. Ibid.

70. Ibid.

71. Pattni, I., & Soutar, G. N. (2009). The effectiveness of self-management training in organisations from two culturally different countries. *Journal of Management Development*, *28*, 633–646; Frayne, C., & Geringer, J. M. (2000). Self-management training for improving job performance: A field experiment involving salespeople. *Journal of Applied Psychology*, *85*, 361–372.

72. Lee, K. (2011). Reinforce training. *Training Magazine*, May/June, 24.

73. Skinner, B. F. (1950). Are theories of learning necessary? *Psychological Review*, *57*, 193–216; Skinner, B. F. (1953). *Science and human behavior*. New York: Macmillan; Skinner, B. F. (1954). The science of learning and the art of teaching. *Harvard Educational Review*, *24*, 86–97.

74. MacDonald, C. (2015). Ethical practice: HR must champion a principled culture. *HR Magazine*, December, 40.

75. Schwartz, M. S. (2016). How to minimize corruption in business organizations: Developing and sustaining an ethical corporate culture. *Crime and Corruption in Organizations*, 273–296.

76. Russ-Eft, D. F. (2003). Corporate ethics: A learning and performance problem for leaders? *Human Resource Development Quarterly*, *14*, 1.

77. SHRM ® Legal Report, November–December 2002.

78. See Clark, M. M. (2004). New sentencing guidelines to reward ethical culture, compliance commitment. *HR Magazine*, *49*, 28.

79. Caligiuri, P. M., & DiSanto, V. (2001). Global competence: What is tt—and can it be developed through global assignments?

Human Resource Planning Journal, 24, 27–38; Conner, J. (2000). Developing the global leaders of tomorrow. *Human Resource Management*, 39, 147–157.

80. Developing successful global leaders. (2011). *Training Magazine*, May/June, 58–62.

81. Ajarimah, A. A. (2001). Major challenges of global leadership in the twenty-first century. *Human Resources Development International*, 4, 9–19.

82. Caligiuri, P. M. (2000). The big five personality characteristics as predictors of expatriate success. *Personnel Psychology*, 53, 67–88; Caligiuri, P. M. (2000). Selecting expatriates for personality characteristics: A moderating effect of personality on the relationship between host national contact and cross-cultural adjustment. *Management International Review*, 40, 61–80.

83. Caligiuri, P. M. (2000). Selecting expatriates for personality characteristics: A moderating effect of personality on the relationship between host national contact and cross-cultural adjustment. *Management International Review*, 40, 61–80.

84. Caligiuri, P. M. (2006). Developing global leaders. *Human Resource Management Review*, 16, 219–228.

85. Kalman, F. (2013). New brew: Anheuser-Busch InBev's Jim Brickey. *Talent Management*, November, 42–45.

86. Caligiuri, P. M., & Tarique, I. (2006). International assignee selection and cross-cultural training and development. Refereed book chapter in I. Björkman & G. Stahl (Eds.), *Handbook of research in international human resource management*. London: Edward Elgar Publishing.

87. *From Culture, Leadership, and Organizations: The GLOBE Study of 62 Societies*, by House, Robert J.; *Global Leadership and Organizational Behavior Effectiveness Research Program*. Reproduced with permission of Sage Publications, Inc. via Copyright Clearance Center.

88. Caligiuri, P. M. (2006). Developing global leaders. *Human Resource Management Review*, 16, 219–228.

89. Ibid.

90. Training top 125. (2011). *Training Magazine*, January/February, 57.

91. Bezrukova, K., Spell, C. S., Perry, J. L., & Jehn, K. A. (2016). A meta-analytical integration of over 40 years of research on diversity training evaluation. *Psychological Bulletin*, 1227–1274; McGuire, D., & Bagher, M. (2010). Diversity training in organisations: An introduction. *Journal of European Industrial Training*, 34, 493–505.

92. Das, A. S. (2010). Diversity is a necessary job skill, not an HR policy. *Vault.com*. Retrieved March 17, 2017, from http://www.vault.com/blog/in-good-company-vaults-csr-blog/diversity-is-a-necessary-job-skill-not-an-hr-policy

93. Rynes, S., & Rosen, B. (1995). A field survey of factors affecting the adoption and perceived success of diversity training. *Personnel Psychology*, 48(2), 247–270.

94. Hastings, R. R. (2011, February 24). Diversity training pitfalls to avoid. *Society for Human Resource Management*. Retrieved March 18, 2017, from https://sts.shrm.org/STS/default.aspx?wa=wsignin1.0&wtrealm=https%3a%2f%2fwww.shrm.org%2f_trust&wctx=https%3a%2f%2fwww.shrm.org%2f_layouts%2f15%2fauthenticate.aspx%3fsource%3d%252fresourcesandtools%252fhr-topics%252fbehavioral-competencies%252fglobal-and-cultural-effectiveness%252fpages%252fdiversitytrainingpitfallstoavoid.aspx

95. Moscato, D. (2005). Using technology to get employees on board. *HR Magazine*, April, 107–109.

96. Williams, R. (2003). *Mellon learning curve research study*. New York: Mellon Corp.

97. Training top 125. (2011). *Training Magazine*, January/February, 55.

98. Van Maanen, J., & Schein, E. H. (1979). Toward a theory of organizational socialization. *Research in Organizational Behavior*, 1, 209–264.

99. Noe, R. A. (2005). *Employee training and development*. New York: McGraw-Hill/Irwin.

100. Ibid.

101. Chao, G. T., O'Leary-Kelly, A, M., Wolf, S., Klein, H. J., & Gardner, P. D. (1994). Organizational socialization: Its content and consequences. *Journal of Applied Psychology*, 79, 730–743.

102. Van Maanen, J., & Schein, E. H. (1979). Toward of theory of organizational socialization. *Research in Organizational Behavior*, 1, 209–264.

103. Cascio, W. F. (2003). *Managing human resources*. New York: McGraw-Hill/Irwin.

104. Albrecht, S. L., Bakker, A. B., Gruman, J. A., Macey, W. H., & Saks, A. M. (2015). Employee engagement, human resource management practices and competitive advantage: An integrated approach. *Journal of Organizational Effectiveness: People and Performance*, 2, 7–35.

105. Noe, R. A. (2005). *Employee training and development*. New York: McGraw-Hill/Irwin.

106. Guynn, J. (2010, September 12). Facebook invests heavily in developing new engineers' talent. *Los Angeles Times*. Retrieved March 15, 2017, from http://www.tampabay.com/news/business/workinglife/article1120737.ece

107. Salopek, J. J. (2011). Onboarding program indoctrinates new workers at MACH speed. *Workforce Management*, June. Retrieved March 19, 2017, from http://www.workforce.com/2011/06/19/onboarding-program-indoctrinates-new-workers-at-mach-speed/

108. Johnson, L. K. (2006, September 1). Rapid onboarding at Capital One. *Harvard Management Update*, Article Reprint Number U0609C.

109. Van Maanen, J., & Schein, E. H. (1979). Toward a theory of organizational socialization. *Research in Organizational Behavior*, 1, 209–264; Allen, D. G. (2006). Do organizational socialization tactics influence newcomer embeddedness and turnover? *Journal of Management*, 32, 237–256.

110. Allen, D. G. (2006). Do organizational socialization tactics influence newcomer embeddedness and turnover? *Journal of Management*, 32, 237–256.

111. Van Maanen, J., & Schein, E.H. (1979). Toward of theory of organizational socialization. *Research in Organizational Behavior*, 1, 235.

112. Training top 125. (2011). *Training Magazine*, January/February, 93.

113. Gruman, J. A., Saks, A. M., & Zweig, D. I. (2006). Organizational socialization tactics and newcomer proactive behaviors: An integrative study. *Journal of Vocational Behavior*, 69, 90–104.

114. See Rosenbaum, J. E. (1979). Tournament mobility: Career patterns in a corporation. *Administrative Science Quarterly*, June 24, 220–241.

115. Van Maanen, J. (1978). People processing: Strategies of organizational socialization. *Organizational Dynamics*, 7, 29–30.

116. *Ibid.*

117. *Ibid.*

118. Van Maanen, J., & Schein, E. H. (1979). Toward a theory of organizational socialization. *Research in Organizational Behavior*, 1, 209–264.

119. Levering, R. (2006, January 10). Warmer welcomes, fatter profits. *Fortune*. Retrieved March 18, 2017, from http://money.cnn.com/2006/01/09/news/companies/bestcos_welcomerituals/index.htm

120. Based on Chao, G. T., O'Leary-Kelly, A. M., Wolf, S., Klein, H. J., & Gardner, P. D. (1995). Organizational socialization: Its content and consequences. *Journal of Applied Psychology*, 79, 730–743; Dubinsky, A. J., Howell, R. D., Ingram, T. N., & Bellenger, D. N. (1986). Salesforce socialization. *Journal of Marketing*, 50, 192–207; Fisher, C. D. (1986). Organizational socialization: An integrative review. *Research in Personnel and Human Resource Management*, 4, 101–145.

121. Levering, R. (2006, January 10). Warmer welcomes, fatter profits. *Fortune*. Retrieved March 18, 2017, from http://money.cnn.com /2006/01/09/news/companies/bestcos_welcomerituals/index.htm

122. Moscato, D. (2005). Using technology to get employees on board. *HR Magazine*, April, 107–109.

123. Wesson, M. J., & Gogus, C. I. (2005). Shaking hands with a computer: An examination of two methods of organizational newcomer orientation. *Journal of Applied Psychology*, *90*(5), 1018–1026.

124. Hansen, F. (2008, October 8). Onboarding for greater engagement. *Workforce Management*. Retrieved March 19, 2017, from http://www.workforce.com/2008/10/08/onboarding -for-greater-engagement/

125. *Ibid.*

126. *Ibid.*

127. Major, D. A., Kozlowski, S. W. J., Chao, F. T., & Gardner, P. D. (1995). A longitudinal investigation of newcomer expectations, early socialization outcomes, and the moderating effect of role development factors. *Journal of Applied Psychology*, *80*, 418–431.

128. Griffeth, R. W., & Hom, P. W. (2001). *Retaining valued employees*. Thousand Oaks, CA: SAGE; Allen, D. G. (2006). Do organizational socialization tactics influence newcomer embeddedness and turnover? *Journal of Management*, *32*, 237–256; Cooper-Thomas, H. D., & Anderson, N. (2005). Organizational socialization: A field study into socialization success and rate. *International Journal of Selection and Assessment*, *13*, 116–128.

129. Masotto, T. (2013). Careers become voyages at Marriott International. *Talent Management*, December, 44–47.

130. Cascio, W. F. (2003). *Managing human resources*. New York: McGraw-Hill/Irwin.

131. Hansen, F. (2008, October 8). Onboarding for greater engagement. *Workforce Management*. Retrieved March 19, 2017, from http://www .workforce.com/2008/10/08/onboarding-for-greater-engagement/

132. Based on Guynn, J. (2010, September 12). Facebook invests heavily in developing new engineers' talent. *Los Angeles Times*. Retrieved June 15, 2011, from http://www.tampabay.com /news/business/workinglife/article1120737.ece; Gertzfield, B. (2010, January 19). Bootcamp: Growing culture at Facebook. Facebook.com. Retrieved June 15, 2011, from http://www .facebook.com/notes/facebook-engineering/bootcamp-growing -culture-at-facebook/249415563919; Bosworth, A. B. (2009, November 19). Facebook engineering bootcamp. Facebook.com. Retrieved March 15, 2017, from http://www.facebook.com/notes /facebook-engineering/facebook-engineering-bootcamp /177577963919

133. McCall, M., Lombardo, M. M., & Morrison, A. (1988). *The lessons of experience*. Lexington, MA: Lexington Books.

134. Baldwin, T. T., & Ford, J. K. (1988). Transfer of training: A review and directions for future research. *Personnel Psychology*, *41*, 63–105; Mathieu, J. E., & Martineau, J. W. (1997). Individual and situational influences on training motivation. In J. K. Ford, S. W. J. Kozlowski, K. Kraiger, E. Salas, & M. S. Teachout (Eds.), *Improving training effectiveness in work organizations*, pp. 193–221. Mahwah, NJ: Erlbaum; Colquitt, J., LePine, J., & Noe, R. (2000). Toward an integrative theory of training motivation: A meta-analytic path analysis of 20 years of research. *Journal of Applied Psychology*, *85*, 678–707.

135. Dries, N., Vantilborgh, T., & Pepermans, R. (2012). The role of learning agility and career variety in the identification and development of high potential employees. *Personnel Review*, 41.

136. Lombardo, M. M., & Eichinger, R. W. (2000). High potentials as high learners. *Human Resource Management*, *39*, 321–329.

137. Noe, R. A. (1986). Trainee attributes and attitudes: Neglected influences on training effectiveness. *Academy of Management Review*, *11*, 736–749; Mathieu, J. E., & Martineau, J. W. (1997). Individual and situational influences on training motivation. In J. K. Ford, S. W. J. Kozlowski, K. Kraiger, E. Salas, & M. S. Teachout (Eds.), *Improving training effectiveness in work organizations*, 193–221. Mahwah, NJ.

138. Karoly, P. (1993). Mechanisms of self-regulation: A systems view. *Annual Review of Psychology*, *44*, 23–52.

139. Schmidt, A. M., & Ford, J. K. (2003). Learning within a learner control environment: The interactive effects of goal orientation and metacognitive instruction on learning outcomes. *Personnel Psychology*, *56*, 405–429.

140. Copyright © 1990 by *American Psychological Association*. Reproduced with permission from "*Motivational and Self-Regulated Learning Components of Classroom Academic Performance*," by P.R. Pintrich and E.V. DeGroot, *Journal of Educational Psychology*, 1990, 82: 33-40.

141. McDonald's. (2017). Our curriculum. Retrieved March 15, 2017, from http://corporate.mcdonalds.com/mcd/corporate _careers/training_and_development/hamburger_university /our_curriculum.html

142. Pinchevsky, T. (2009). Brand training the McDonald's way . Minyanville.com. Retrieved March 15, 2017, from http://www .minyanville.com/businessmarkets/articles/mcdonalds-university -hamburger-minyanville-manual-franchise/9/14/2009/id/24481

143. McDonald's. (2017). Our curriculum. Retrieved March 15, 2017, from http://corporate.mcdonalds.com/mcd/corporate_careers /training_and_development/hamburger_university/our _curriculum.html

144. McDonald's. (2017). Archways to opportunity. Retrieved March 15, 2017, from https://www.mcdonalds.com/us/en-us/careers /training-and-education.html

145. McDonald's to train staff with Nintendos. (2011, March 24). Foxnews.com. Retrieved March 15, 2017, from http://www.foxnews.com/scitech/2010/03/24/ mcdonalds-train-staff-with-nintendos/

146. Walters, N. (2015, January 26). McDonald's Hamburger University can be harder to get into than Harvard and is even cooler than you'd imagine. *Bloomberg News*. Retrieved March 15, 2017, from http://www.businessinsider.com /mcdonalds-hamburger-university-2333

147. *Ibid.*

148. *Ibid.*

149. Frankel, A. (2007, November 1). Magic shop. *Fast Company*. Retrieved March 14, 2017, from https://www.fastcompany .com/60838/magic-shop; Frankel, A. (2007). *Punching IN: The unauthorized adventures of a front-line employee*. New York: Collins; Kane, Y. I., & Sherr, I. (2011, June 15). Secrets from Apple's genius bar: Full loyalty, no negativity. *Wall Street Journal*. Retrieved March 14, 2017, from http://online.wsj. com/article/SB10001424052702304563104576364071955567 8908.html; Blodget, H. (2012, June 24). Check out how Apple brainwashes its store employees—turning them into clapping, smiling zealots. *Business Insider*. Retrieved March 12, 2017, from http://www.businessinsider.com/how-apple-trains-store -employees-2012-6; Smith, J. (2016, April 1). Here's what it's really like to work in an Apple store. *Business Insider*. Retrieved March 17, 2017, from http://www.businessinsider.com /what-its-like-to-work-at-an-apple-store-2016-4/#-1

chapter 8

Performance Management

Learning Objectives

AFTER STUDYING THIS CHAPTER, YOU SHOULD BE ABLE TO:

1 Describe the three main benefits of performance management.

2 Explain the balanced scorecard.

3 Describe how goal setting affects performance.

4 List the possible sources of performance information.

5 Describe the difference between performance measurement and performance ranking methods.

6 Explain why feedback is important to goal accomplishment.

7 Describe the steps in the progressive discipline process.

8 Describe three common obstacles to performance management effectiveness.

Real World Challenge

Managing Performance at GE

GE is a multinational conglomerate with over $123 billion in revenue in 2016.[1] The company wants to ensure that its employees collaborate, make fast and effective business decisions, and provide customers with superior products and services. GE has been using the same performance management system for a long time and believes it can do better to promote continuous coaching and shared accountability between managers and their direct reports. GE also wants a better way to support its culture of continuous improvement.[2]

GE managers also don't like reducing feedback into a score on a scale of 1 to 5 and want a way of focusing on the feedback conversation on employee development instead.[3] The company asks you for advice on how to create an effective and motivating performance management system that is consistent with its culture of collaboration and continuous improvement and its business strategy of providing the highest quality products and services. After reading this chapter, you should have some good ideas.

Globalization and a challenging economic environment have increased the importance of carefully choosing and executing business strategies. Everyone in an organization needs to do all that they can to ensure organizational performance and success. Most major U.S. corporations have invested in performance management systems to support their strategies of creating high-performance organizations. Almost every major Fortune 2000 company has used some form of a performance management system that annually evaluates employees on their goal attainment.[4]

Executives at global engineering giant Fluor Corporation are required to identify and mentor talented employees. Fluor's leadership development program continually tracks the top 10 percent of the company's 42,000 employees to keep tabs on its pipeline of high performers. The company relies on talent management software that enables learning and performance management, assessment tools, and skills and competency tracking.[5]

performance management
directs and motivates employees, workgroups, and business units to accomplish organizational goals by linking past performance with future needs, setting specific goals for future behavior and performance, providing feedback, and identifying and removing performance obstacles

Performance management is the system that directs and motivates employees, workgroups, and business units to accomplish organizational goals. By linking past performance with future needs and by setting specific goals for future behavior and performance, performance management helps align an organization's people and processes toward common goals that support the business strategy. Feedback on goal progress and the identification and removal of performance obstacles help to ensure maximum employee contribution to organizational objectives.

Because Sprint knows that feedback is the key to improving performance, it tries to give all its employees coaching as part of its ongoing performance management process. Managers assess employees on three to five criteria that each link to a strategic objective. Most employees are also able to go online to view their progress toward their individual performance objectives.[6]

Employees' performance management objectives are a little different from the organization's goals. The organization is usually interested in assessing employees' performance to ensure strategic execution and align goals across the organization, develop employees, and appropriately allocate rewards and punishments. Employees are usually interested in having their work assessed for the purposes of personal development, rewards, and the satisfaction of doing a good job. As a manager, remembering to communicate praise and appreciation during a performance management session is important in helping to meet the employee's goals.

Could you do your best work if you had no goals or feedback on how well you were doing? We know that we couldn't. Would you enjoy your job more if you had a clear understanding of what you were expected to do and received frequent feedback on your performance? We know that we would. The most effective performance management systems meet the goals of both employees and the organization. Because it influences employees' goals and motivation, performance management influences what employees *will* do.

In this chapter, we first discuss why performance management is important. We then explore the balanced scorecard and the steps in the performance management process. After turning our attention to goal setting, we discuss various performance information sources and measurement methods. We then explain how performance is improved through feedback and taking corrective action and discuss obstacles to effective performance management. The chapter concludes with a discussion of legal and ethical issues in performance management. After reading this chapter, you should have a good idea of how organizations manage the performance of individuals, teams, and business units.

Why Is Performance Management Important?

People often think of performance management as focusing on the performance of individual employees. However, performance management also focuses on:

1. The organization as a whole;
2. Organizational subunits (business units or departments);

3. Work teams or groups;
4. Work processes (purchasing, product development, and manufacturing); and
5. Projects (changing a manufacturing process or adopting a new technology).

The overall goal of performance management is to ensure that all parts of the organization and all its processes are optimally working together to achieve desired results. Performance management has three main benefits:

1. Aligns organizational goals with individual goals and organizational processes.
2. Gives employees clear goals and feedback.
3. Generates useful data.

Let's explore each of these benefits in greater detail.

Aligns Organizational Goals with Team and Individual Goals

Performance management identifies organizational goals, measures effectiveness and efficiency in obtaining those goals, and communicates this information to the relevant performer (organization, business unit, workgroup, or individual). It is important to remember that behaviors are not the same as results. A busy employee may not be contributing to the accomplishment of organizational goals, and getting something done does not guarantee that it was done in the most efficient, effective, or ethical manner. Done correctly, performance management helps to ensure that the right things are being done in the right way to achieve meaningful results. Aligning goals across all levels of the organization helps maximize efficiency and effectiveness.

If work is done as part of an interdependent team, it is also important to provide team-level in addition to individual-level goals and feedback. An employee who appears to be a strong individual performer might achieve that performance at the expense of the team as a whole. Providing feedback on team processes and team goal achievement helps to improve team effectiveness.

Understanding the behaviors and outcomes that impact an organization's strategic execution and competitive advantage gives insight into the goals that should be set for business units, teams, and individuals. This chapter's Strategic Impact feature describes how Google identified the behaviors that most impact its managers' effectiveness and used them in its performance management system.

so what?

Performance feedback should be provided at the individual and group level if employees work in teams.

 Strategic Impact

Developing Managers at Google

Google researched whether good managers matter and, if so, how. After identifying positive relationships between good management and employee retention and team performance, follow-up interviews revealed eight behaviors that make a good Google manager and five behaviors to avoid. The good behaviors include being results oriented, expressing interest in team members' success and well-being, and being a good coach. The undesirable behaviors include spending too little time managing and communicating and lacking a consistent approach to performance management and career development. These are now incorporated into the company's coaching sessions. Teams give managers feedback on these behaviors to help them understand what they're doing well and how they can improve. This process has helped the vast majority of Google's lower-rated managers to improve substantially.[7]

Gives Employees Clear Goals and Feedback

There is an old saying that "what gets measured gets done." One of the most important things performance management does is to let employees know what they should be doing and how they are doing. Without clear goals and feedback on whether they are meeting their goals, employees cannot know whether they should be doing their jobs differently. Goal setting and feedback are two of the most powerful motivational and performance tools available to managers, and it is well worth the investment of time and effort to provide both to employees.[8]

Employees typically want to know how they are doing, how they could improve in the future, how they could earn larger rewards, and how to better achieve their personal goals through their work. Most people want to do a good job, and goals and feedback help them know what to do and how well they are doing so that they can do their best. Employees also want to be treated with respect. Employees choose how much effort to put into their work and whether to stay with the organization. Accordingly, their needs and interests need to be met to maximize the effectiveness of the organization's talent.

Goal setting in the absence of feedback is ineffective.[9] Both goals and feedback are needed to affect performance, and often coaching helps as well. Goals direct and energize action, whereas feedback allows the tracking of progress in relation to the goal. Performance improvement is most likely when feedback indicates that change is necessary and the employee perceives a need to change his or her behavior. The employee must also react positively to the feedback and believe change is feasible, set appropriate goals to regulate his or her behavior, and takes actions that lead to skill and performance improvement.[10] Feedback in the form of praise by itself is insufficient to improve performance—feedback should be specific and task-related. Feedback is also most important for complex tasks in which the performer cannot easily judge his or her own performance.[11] WD-40 Co. created a performance management process in which employees received feedback to help them improve rather than a label such as "excellent" or "good." As a result, employee engagement scores increased dramatically, and the company's performance improved.[12]

Generates Useful Data

The data obtained from performance measurements are useful in many ways. They are used in benchmarking, or setting standards for comparison with best practices elsewhere in the organization or in other organizations. They reveal the results of change efforts, such as training and safety programs. Performance management data also helps the organization treat employees fairly and consistently based on their actual performance and contribution to organizational outcomes. In addition, performance management data is necessary to calculate the return on investment of new work processes, technologies, or training initiatives.

Balanced Scorecard

In the industrial age dominated by factories, most of an organization's assets were in property, plant, and equipment. In today's information age, much more of an organization's value is reflected in its talent, brands, customer relationships, and innovative processes. Because the financial accounting system is not as good at valuing these more intangible assets, Robert S. Kaplan and David P. Norton introduced the concept of the balanced scorecard.[13] The **balanced scorecard** is a performance measurement system that translates the organization's strategy into four perspectives:

1. *Learning and growth outcomes*: Including employee satisfaction, retention, and skills.
2. *Business process outcomes*: Including quality, cost, and quantity produced and the business processes of procurement, production, and order fulfillment.
3. *Customer outcomes*: Including customer satisfaction and retention and market share.
4. *Financial outcomes*: Including operating income, economic value added, and return on capital.

so what

Most employees want to do a good job, and goals and feedback are important to letting them know how to improve.

so what

Praise alone is not enough to improve performance—specific, task-related feedback is essential.

balanced scorecard

a performance measurement system that translates the organization's strategy into financial, business process, learning and growth, and customer outcomes

The four outcomes are sequential—learning and growth lead to improved business processes, which lead to better customer outcomes, which lead to improved financial performance. According to Kaplan and Norton, "The measurement system should be only a means to achieve an even more important goal—a strategic management system that helps executives implement and gain feedback about their strategy."[14] The balanced scorecard focuses on balancing:

1. Internal and external measures.
2. Performance results and the drivers of future results.
3. Objective and subjective performance measures.

> *"The measurement system should be only a means to achieve an even more important goal—a strategic management system that helps executives implement and gain feedback about their strategy."*
>
> **—Robert Kaplan and David Norton**

The Balanced Scorecard is shown in Figure 8.1.
Four factors are included for each of the four balanced scorecard perspectives:

1. *Objectives*: What are the major objectives to be achieved (e.g., profitable growth)?
2. *Measures*: What observable metrics will be used to measure progress toward the objective (e.g., net margin growth)?
3. *Targets*: What are the specific goals for each measure (e.g., 3 percent increase in net margin)?
4. *Initiatives*: What specific actions, resources, or programs will be provided to help meet the objective (e.g., sales force training)?

figure **8.1**

Kaplan and Norton's Balanced Scorecard[15]

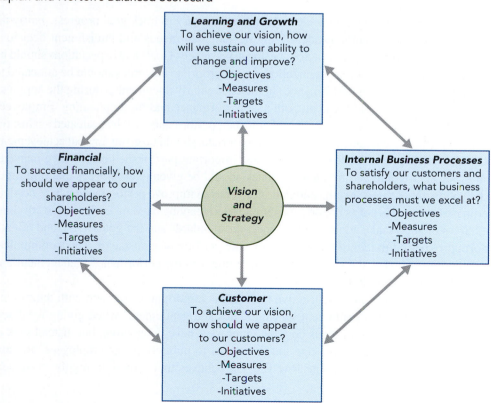

Kaiser Permanente's Northeast Division set up a balanced scorecard system that produces a report that accompanies employees' paychecks. Performance data are also available on the company's intranet. To ensure widespread use, data are periodically repackaged to keep the information fresh so that it continues to attract employees' attention.[16]

Steps in the Performance Management Process

There are nine steps in the performance management process:

1. Link short- and long-term organizational goals to the organization's mission and business strategy.
2. Identify subgoals for each business unit, department, workgroup, and individual based on these overall organizational goals and standards.
3. Communicate goals and expectations throughout the organization, and motivate employees to pursue them by connecting them to their personal goals.
4. Create work processes and assign resources to support the goals.
5. Measure progress on goal achievement.
6. Regularly assess individual, workgroup, and business unit performance relative to the goals.
7. Regularly give feedback on goal progress to improve performance and remove obstacles.
8. Identify and overcome obstacles to goal achievement.
9. Reward goal achievement.

Business strategies should include specific short- and long-term goals for the inputs, behaviors, and processes necessary to achieve the organization's goals. These short- and long-term goals should also be clearly linked to the overall organizational mission.[17] The goals are then prioritized, and subgoals and metrics are identified for each business unit, department, workgroup, and individual. These goals should be consistent with each other and decided jointly by the affected individual or group and management. Sensis, a leading Australian directory, advertising, and information provider, enables all its employees to develop objectives, identify needed competencies, create development plans, measure progress and performance, and plan for the future.[18]

Standards for assessing goal achievement are necessary to track goal progress. Fairly allocating rewards and accurately identifying development needs and punishment decisions require being able to differentiate across performance levels. Goals and expectations should be communicated throughout the organization, and appropriate resources should be allocated to support goal achievement. Performance should be regularly documented during the appraisal stage, and feedback should focus on both past performance and future planning. Employees need to know what is expected of them and how their performance will be evaluated against the standards. Rewards, and punishments when appropriate, should be given for goal achievement.

Goals, coaching, and feedback are the most important part of the performance management process. Ongoing and frequent feedback should be given to employees that reinforces the behaviors that achieve results and that intervenes to improve performance where needed. Interim performance is not as important as employees receiving ongoing feedback and coaching that allows them to make adjustments to meet the standards and the goals at the end of each performance period to identify and overcome any performance obstacles. This communication requirement makes the supervisor's commitment to the performance management and feedback process essential for its success.[19]

Giving both positive and constructive feedback is important. Consistent with their motto that they are "ladies and gentlemen serving ladies and gentlemen," when giving feedback, Ritz-Carlton managers don't focus on what employees have done wrong but instead seek to help them improve. Supervisors use staff meetings to publicly praise employees, and any criticism is done in private.[20] The Ritz-Carlton believes that providing regular feedback, sharing positive employee stories, and giving employees public recognition motivates the highest performance and increases employees' engagement.[21] Recognition is a powerful way of communicating to employees what behaviors the organization wants to see.

Setting Goals and Standards

Goal setting is the foundation of both personal and organizational success. A good performance goal is measurable, easily understandable, and results oriented. The easiest things to measure—the number of parts made or the number of people trained—are often not the things most important to strategic execution. As Albert Einstein said, "Not everything that can be counted counts, and not everything that counts can be counted." The Ritz-Carlton believes that, "If you can't define it, you can't control it, you can't measure it, and you can't improve it."[22]

> *"Not everything that can be counted counts, and not everything that counts can be counted."*
>
> —**Albert Einstein**

Organizational goals are usually established during the strategic planning process. These high-level goals are then translated into **results**, or the specific subgoals for each unit that will be the focus of the performance management process. Individual employees' performance goals and results should be based on a job analysis and tied to organizational strategies, values, and objectives.

results
the specific subgoals for each unit that will be the focus of the performance management process

To be measurable, results are described in terms of quantity, quality, cost, or timeliness, such as a percentage increase in sales or percentage decrease in resource usage. For example, an organizational goal may be to increase annual profit by 20 percent within one year. Two subgoals could be to increase the profit of the Internet sales department by 25 percent and decrease overhead costs by 10 percent within the year.

Performance goals should be challenging and SMART:

- *Specific*, clear and understandable (also stretching)
- *Measurable*, verifiable and results-oriented (also motivating and meaningful)
- *Achievable* (also acceptable and agreed upon)
- *Relevant* to the mission (also realistic, results-oriented, and rewarding)
- *Time-bound* with a deadline, schedule, and milestones (also tangible)

Because incentives tied to goal accomplishment have a strong effect on employees' behavior, it is critical to ensure that goals do not have unintended consequences. For example, when mortgage brokers and lending officers were given goals and incentives to make more mortgage loans, they began to compromise lending standards to meet these goals and earn bonuses. Of course, this practice is now recognized as one of the contributors to the 2008 crisis in the financial services industry.[23]

In addition to actual performance outcomes, which can be influenced by factors beyond employees' control, employees' task and interpersonal behaviors are also important to assess. Whether employees work collaboratively, ethically, and consistently with organizational policies and procedures is often as important to the organization as what they accomplish. Factors beyond employees' control should be identified and not used against them in evaluating their performance.

Standards specify what level of results will be considered acceptable. For example, a machine operator might meet expectations if he or she averaged 200 high-quality parts an hour over eight hours during the fiscal year. Averaging between 200 and 250 parts per hour exceeds expectations, over 250 reflects superior performance, and anything less than 200

standards
specify what level of results will be considered acceptable

does not meet expectations. Standards are typically linked to different levels of rewards and punishments, with remedial action taken when standards are not being met.

In setting goals and standards, it is important to identify what outcomes and measures mean the most to internal and external customers, stakeholders, and employees. Having stakeholders work together to create clear, easily understandable goals to address their needs helps to increase commitment to the process and its outcomes. Just having a goal is not enough—being committed to the goal is essential for it to motivate performance.[24] It is also helpful to recognize that if performance management needs change over time, goals and measures may need adjusting.

It is important to maintain an appropriate balance between financial and nonfinancial goals and limit the number of goals to a manageable amount. Having too many goals is distracting rather than performance enabling. Because its evaluation process revealed that its hotels do best when they focus their attention on just a few things, The Ritz-Carlton, featured in this chapter's opening Real World Challenge, makes sure every business unit has no more than three priorities at a time.[25] As one Ritz-Carlton vice president says, "Once you go beyond the top three priorities, you start to really diffuse your resources, your bandwidth."[26]

> *"Once you go beyond the top three priorities, you start to really diffuse your resources, your bandwidth."*
>
> **—Vice President, The Ritz-Carlton**

Hundreds of research studies have demonstrated the performance benefits of specific, challenging goals[27] for individuals,[28] groups,[29] organizational units,[30] and entire organizations.[31] By providing direction and a standard against which progress can be monitored, challenging goals can enable people to guide and refine their performance. Specific goals can boost motivation and performance by leading people to:

- Focus their attention on specific objectives;[32]
- Increase their effort to achieve these objectives;[33]
- Persist in the face of setbacks;[34] and
- Develop new strategies to better deal with complex challenges to goal attainment.[35]

Goals affect performance by affecting the direction of action, the degree of effort exerted, and persistence in pursuing the goal. Table 8.1 provides some guidelines for effective goal setting based on over 40 years of research.[36]

table **8.1**

Guidelines for Successful Goal Setting[37]

1. Goals that are both specific and difficult lead to highest performance.

2. Goal commitment is most important when goals are specific and difficult.

3. High goal commitment is achieved when:

   a. The performer is convinced that the goal is important.

   b. The performer is convinced that the goal is attainable.

4. In addition to directly influencing performance, self-efficacy influences:

   a. Goal difficulty;

   b. Goal commitment;

   c. The response to negative feedback or failure; and

   d. The choice of task strategies.

5. Goal setting is most effective when feedback shows progress in relation to the goal.

HR Flexibility

Learning Versus Performance Goals

In situations where the acquisition of knowledge and skills rather than an increase in effort and persistence is the primary objective, specific challenging learning goals are more appropriate than outcome goals. A learning goal draws attention away from the end result. The focus instead is on the discovery of effective strategies or processes to attain desired results.

PricewaterhouseCoopers incorporates both performance and learning goals into their coaching and performance management practices. PWC, like many organizations, hires for aptitude rather than existing skills. Mentors help new employees discover ways to develop their competencies within the company and assign them specific high learning rather than performance goals. Employees assigned specific challenging learning goals in the early stages of discovering how to execute the various aspects of their job typically outperform those who are immediately given specific high-performance goals.[38]

Another issue to be aware of when setting goals is whether the intention is to promote learning or to motivate high performance. Perhaps surprisingly, the optimal goals to set for each situation differ, as we describe in this chapter's HR Flexibility feature.

Goals should be reasonable and balanced with other organizational objectives and motivational tools. Overly ambitious goal setting can lead to risky or unethical behavior as employees try to reach them. Enron's sales incentive system, which was based solely on the volume of revenue that they generated and not whether the trades were sound, is blamed as a key factor in Enron's implosion.[39] In another case, Bausch & Lomb salespeople falsified sales reports to meet their performance quota.[40] Too strong a focus on goals can narrow employees' focus to the point that other important features (e.g., safety, cooperation, and ethics) are neglected. Goals tied to large rewards may also dampen employees' intrinsic motivation and decrease learning by focusing employees exclusively on goal attainment.[41]

Performance Information Sources

Because this is a textbook on human resource management, we will focus the rest of our discussion on managing individual and workgroup performance, although similar steps are relevant for performance management at higher organizational levels. Performance feedback can be obtained from one or from many sources. As shown in Figure 8.2, **multisource assessments** (sometimes called 360-degree assessments) involve the employee's supervisor as well as other sources that are familiar with an employee's job performance. The most common source of performance feedback is the supervisor, but feedback can involve multiple sources of ratings, including customers, peers, subordinates, and anyone aware of the employee's performance in a relevant area.[42] Ratings from nonsupervisors are generally used only for employee development and performance evaluations, and promotion and transfer decisions are usually informed by supervisor ratings. Global beverage giant AB InBev

multisource assessments performance feedback from the employee's supervisor as well as other sources that are familiar with an employee's job performance

Shcherbinator/Shutterstock

Acquiring thorough and accurate performance information is essential to effective performance management. Many organizations, including AB InBev, conduct annual multisource assessments of senior employees and spend time reviewing the feedback with each individual.

figure **8.2**

figure **8.2**

Multisource Assessment

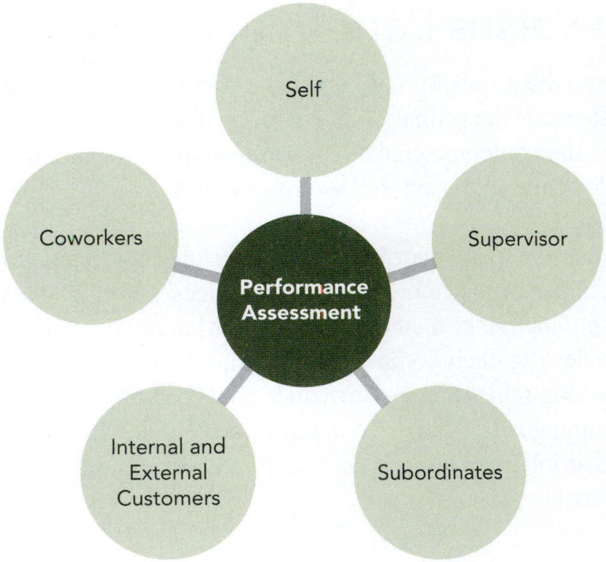

conducts an annual 360-degree assessment of its 800 or so senior employees that includes a 90-minute review session with each employee.[43]

For ratings to be effective, employees must accept the rating process and believe that it is fair.[44] Fairness perceptions are strongly related to the perceived accuracy of the ratings received.[45] Performance information sources should be selected and weighted based on their credibility and ability to observe and accurately rate the employee's behaviors. During the employee review process, United Airlines requires its managers to talk about other managers' employees first, motivating them to pay attention to all employees and reinforcing the goal of collaboration.[46]

We next discuss possible performance assessment sources in more detail.

Employees typically expect and prefer performance feedback from their supervisor, as the supervisor oversees their performance, and performance management is considered part of his or her job.[47] Supervisors can be asked to assess factors including job performance, development needs, promotion potential, and specific competencies. To identify promotion candidates who may have been overlooked or underestimated by their supervisor, WellPoint uses "challenge sessions" in which supervisors in a group scrutinize one another's evaluations.[48] The supervisor's boss should ensure that the supervisor has been diligent in conducting subordinates' performance assessments and should be involved in promotion assessments.

Asking employees to assess their own performance and capabilities is very important and often occurs at the beginning of a performance appraisal meeting. In addition to improving communication between the employee and the supervisor, a self-assessment helps to identify possible areas for additional coaching or development. Although employees are obviously in the best position to observe their own interpersonal and task behaviors, a limitation of self-assessments is the fact that people aren't always good judges of their own talents. Some high performers tend to rate themselves too low, and others rate themselves too high.[49] The key reasons to include self-evaluations are to allow employees to provide performance information that the supervisor or others don't have and to allow employees to convey their professional development goals and needs to the organization.

Although a supervisor is often most familiar with an employee's job performance outcomes, coworkers are often better able to see the employee's task and interpersonal behaviors on the job.[50] Think of someone who behaves differently when she or he knows the boss is around

?so what?

Asking employees to assess their own capabilities and performance is a great start to a performance appraisal meeting.

than when the boss is gone, and you'll understand what we mean. Peers are often the most knowledgeable about their coworkers' performance, particularly when work is done interdependently or in teams.

Task acquaintance, or the amount and type of work contact an evaluator has with the person being assessed,[51] is important as someone can only accurately rate those aspects of a person's work performance that they observe. Supervisors, peers, and subordinates often see different aspects of a person's work behaviors and performance.[52]

Although peers tend to get a good look at each others' task and interpersonal behaviors, they tend to rate each other more honestly when the ratings are used for developmental purposes rather than evaluative purposes to determine pay, promotion, or disciplinary outcomes. To reduce the influence of politics and friendships, coworkers must understand the goals and standards and be familiar with the job requirements for the position. Some organizations follow the lead of Olympic judges and eliminate the lowest and highest peer ratings and average the rest.[53]

Upward reviews in which the target employee is reviewed by one or more subordinates can also provide useful feedback. Subordinates may often see their supervisors' interpersonal and leadership behaviors, giving them a unique and important perspective on his or her strengths and limitations.

One limitation of subordinate feedback is that subordinates are often reluctant or even afraid to give their supervisors negative feedback, particularly if they fear retaliation. Rater anonymity is critical, but if subordinates believe that their responses might be identifiable (e.g., if the supervisor has only a few subordinates, or if only one subordinate knows of a particular incident), then their ratings are not likely to be accurate, if subordinates agree to participate at all. In our experience, a disproportionate number of unanswered questions on a survey about a supervisor often suggests a problem as much as do low ratings. Essentially, if they can't say something nice about their boss, many employees choose to say nothing at all.

Internal customers are users within the organization of any products or services supplied by the employee. External customers are those outside the company. Because both internal and external customers have an opportunity to observe employees' task and interpersonal behaviors, their feedback helps to incorporate the perspective of the company's stakeholders. Incorporating customer feedback can expand the variety of stakeholders employees seek to please and can improve customer service quality. Because external customers do not see or understand the work processes and rules that influence employees' task behaviors, they often cannot easily separate an employee's task behaviors from the regulations, policies, and resources that direct and constrain the employee's options.[54] As a result, it can be best to ask external customers to evaluate interpersonal behaviors.

It is important to recognize cultural constraints on performance management systems and feedback sources. A multisource feedback system, for example, requires a fairly egalitarian mindset and value system that does not exist in more hierarchical and paternal cultures.[55] Workers in India, which tends to place less value on others' opinions, would view it as culturally inappropriate to ask employees to evaluate their supervisor.[56]

Performance Measurement Methods

Identifying which performance measures to use is a critical part of the performance management process. It is important to choose measures that are appropriate to the organizational level and the desired results and to use measures that are valid and reliable. The measures should be practical, simple, and help to clearly distinguish between different performance levels. The two primary types of performance measurement methods are rating methods and ranking methods, which we discuss next.

Performance Rating Methods

There are a variety of performance measurement methods, with different strengths and limitations. **Performance rating methods** compare an employee's performance to a set of standards to identify a number or letter rating that represents the employee's performance level. Performance rating methods allow all employees to receive a high performance rating if they deserve it. Let's explore some of the most commonly used performance rating methods.

Essay Appraisal.   The **essay appraisal method** requires the assessor to write a brief essay providing an assessment of the strengths, weaknesses, and potential of the target employee. Although they give the rater broad latitude in what areas of performance are covered, because essay length and contents vary across assessors, essay appraisals are difficult to use in comparing employees.[57]

Critical Incident Appraisal Method.   With the **critical incident appraisal method**, an assessor discusses specific examples of the target employee's positive and negative behaviors with the employee. Although this technique helps communicate specific behavioral examples to the target employee during the performance appraisal interview, it is very time consuming for the supervisor to record the critical incidents when they occur. It is also less helpful to wait months to give an employee feedback on his or her excellent or deficient behavior, and the method cannot be easily used to compare employees. Critical incident appraisal is best when the rater's personal assessment and feedback are important, and it should only be used when the assessor has ample opportunity to observe the target employee's work behavior.

Graphic Rating Scale.   A **graphic rating scale** typically uses ratings of unsatisfactory, average, above average, and outstanding to evaluate either work quality or personal traits, including attitude and communication skills. Although graphic rating scales may seem simplistic, they are more reliable and easier to use to compare employees than are essay appraisals.[58]

Because the performance evaluation is summarized as a single number reflecting poor to good performance, there can be some disagreement between the employee and the rater over the appropriate rating. Culture can influence self-ratings on a graphic rating scale. U.S. employees tend to rate themselves very high, usually a 4 or 5 on a 5-point scale. In many European cultures, the highest rating might be a 3, and in Asian cultures, many employees would be resistant to rate themselves at all.[59]

The usefulness of graphic rating scales is enhanced when they are used in combination with essay appraisals and critical incidents highlighting specific behaviors and incidents reflecting the rating being given. An example of a graphic rating scale is in Figure 8.3.

United Airlines uses four rating levels: Outstanding performance, exceeds expected performance, valued performance, and performance expectations not met. An "outstanding" performance rating requires consistently and significantly exceeding performance expectations and setting the highest performance standards within the organization. The "exceeds expected performance" rating is given to employees consistently exceeding expectations and outperforming peer employees. The "valued performance" rating is given to employees consistently meeting and occasionally exceeding expectations. If a worker's performance does not consistently meet expectations or match peers' performance, a rating of "performance expectations not met is given."[60]

Behaviorally Anchored Rating Scales (BARS).   **Behaviorally anchored rating scales** (BARS) use a set of behavioral statements describing good or bad performance with respect to important work qualities, including organizing abilities, adaptability, and relationship building. These statements are developed from critical incidents collected both from the assessor and the subject. An example of a BARS is in Figure 8.4.

figure **8.3**

Example of a Graphic Rating Scale

	Unsatisfactory	Average	Above Average	Outstanding
Work quality: Neatness, accuracy, and thoroughness of work			X	
Work quantity: Volume of acceptable work		X		
Cooperation: Works effectively with others to accomplish organizational goals				X
Initiative: Originates or develops ideas and gets projects started			X	

figure **8.4**

Example of a Behaviorally Anchored Rating Scale for Initiative

Score	Performance	Behavior
5	Outstanding	Makes valuable suggestions for improvement; proactively identifies creative solutions to problems; anticipates customer needs.
4	Above Average	Keeps in touch with customers; proactively identifies solutions to problems; presents ideas for improvement.
3	Average	Handles day-to-day responsibilities on own; manages most problems presented as part of own job.
2	Below Average	Reactive to problems; relies on supervisor to solve job challenges.
1	Poor	Does only what is told; needs to be asked repeatedly before performing a task.

Behavioral Observation Scales (BOS). **Behavioral observation scales** (BOS) measure the frequency of desired behaviors.[61] BOS provide more feedback than do BARS, and they are better than more simple rating scales at informing employees how they need to adjust their behavior and the specific behaviors they need to do more or less of. An example of a behavioral observation scale is in Figure 8.5.

behavioral observation scales

measure the frequency of desired behaviors

figure **8.5**

Example of a Behavioral Observation Scale

Rating	Behavior
	Job Knowledge
4	1. Follows organizational procedures.
4	2. Follows machine operating procedures.
5	3. Follows proper machine shutdown procedures.
	Teamwork
3	1. Voluntarily helps others when own workload allows.
5	2. Builds camaraderie with teammates.
4	3. Praises teammates when they do well.
3	4. Gives constructive feedback to teammates when appropriate.

Rating scale:
5 = Employee engaged in this behavior 95 to 100% of the time.
4 = Employee engaged in this behavior 85 to 94% of the time.
3 = Employee engaged in this behavior 75 to 84% of the time.
2 = Employee engaged in this behavior 65 to 74% of the time.
1 = Employee engaged in this behavior less than 65% of the time.

forced-choice rating method
forces the assessor to choose the statement that best fits the target employee from a provided set of statements that are scored and weighted in advance

Forced-Choice Rating Method.   The **forced-choice rating method** forces the assessor to choose the statement that best fits the target employee from a provided set of statements that are scored and weighted in advance. The assessor does not know the scores or weights assigned to the individual statements. Although this helps prevent rater bias, evaluations can still be faked by the rater by merely thinking about a good employee when evaluating the lower performing target employee.[62]

Raters tend to dislike the forced-choice method because they feel they are not being trusted.[63] The need to keep the scoring key secret also makes communicating performance information to the target employee virtually impossible. Because the magnitude of the different behaviors is unknown, it is also difficult to compare employees. Figure 8.6 shows an example of a forced choice rating scale.

figure **8.6**

Example of a Forced-Choice Rating Scale for Leadership

Least Applicable		Most Applicable
	Tactful	
X	Easy to please	
	Collaborative	
	Delegative	
	Directive	X

Checklist Method. With the **checklist method**, the assessor uses a checklist of prescaled descriptions of behavior to evaluate the employee.[64] If the assessor believes that a checklist item describes the target employee, the item is checked. If not, it is left blank. Each checklist item can be weighted equally, or some may be given more weight than others in calculating the final score. The assessor does not know the weights of the behaviors on the checklist. A final rating is obtained by summing (after weighting, if appropriate) the scale values of the items that have been marked.

The checklist method is time consuming and expensive. Making employees aware of the checklist can help clarify what is expected of them, but too many items on the checklist can be distracting, and factors not on the checklist are not likely to be attended to. An example of a checklist is shown in Figure 8.7.

checklist method
the assessor uses a checklist of pre-scaled descriptions of behavior to evaluate the employee

figure **8.7**

Example of a Checklist

- ☐ Shows respect to coworkers
- ☐ Reports to work on time
- ☐ Produces high-quality work
- ☐ Puts full effort into the work
- ☐ Follows instructions as they are given

Work Standards. Using **work standards** involves comparing an employee's performance to output targets that reflect different levels of performance. For example, producing 30 acceptable parts an hour might be considered minimally acceptable, 40 acceptable parts per hour considered good, and 50 parts per hour considered outstanding performance. Because it requires precise measurement of performance to compare to the standards, this method is most appropriate for production-oriented employees.

work standards
comparing an employee's performance to output targets that reflect different levels of performance

Management By Objectives. **Management by objectives** requires the rater to evaluate the target employee against mutually set goals. Employees typically help set their performance goals to prevent a perception that the standards are unfairly high. Because performance objectives are clear and jointly set, employees' commitment to achieving them tends to be high, and the evaluation tends to be more objective. By focusing on the goals and letting employees decide how to accomplish them, subordinates can be better motivated. At Caterpillar, every manager regularly meets with each employee to set SMART goals and agree on performance standards. Managers then actively manage and support employees' performance throughout the year.[65]

management by objectives
the rater evaluates the target employee against mutually set goals

Performance Ranking Methods

Performance ranking methods compare employees to each other in some way, making it impossible for all employees to receive a high rating even if all employees are outstanding. We next discuss the three primary performance ranking methods.

performance ranking methods
compare employees to each other in some way

Forced Ranking. The **forced ranking method** ranks employees in order of best to worst performance. This method usually involves averaging the rating provided by multiple assessors. Although this is a simple method that helps reduce single-rater bias, it can be impractical for large groups. Yahoo! asks managers to rank their employees, allocating raises and bonuses accordingly.[66]

forced ranking method
employees are ranked in order of best to worst performance

Paired Comparison. **Paired comparison method** requires comparing every employee in a workgroup to the other group members. The paired comparison method systematizes ranking and enables better comparisons among the employees being rated. Every individual

paired comparison method
every employee in a work-group is compared to the other group members

in the group is compared with all others in the group. The evaluations received by each person in the group are counted and turned into percentage scores. The scores provide a fair idea as to how each individual in the group is judged by the assessor.

forced distribution method
the rater distributes performance ratings into a prespecified performance distribution

Forced distribution method.   The **forced distribution method** requires the rater to distribute performance ratings into a prespecified performance distribution. Forced-ranking systems typically use strict percentages (such as top 20 percent, vital 70 percent, and bottom 10 percent) to identify employees as either A (the best), B, or C players. A class graded on a curve uses the forced distribution method.

This method is based on the premise that an organization should identify its best and worst performers, then reward and nurture the former and rehabilitate and/or remove the latter.[67] Although this method can promote a competitive and achievement-based culture, it can also erode teamwork, decrease employees' desire to help each other, and encourage an "everyone for himself or herself" attitude. GE uses a 20/70/10 guideline (20 percent top performers, 70 percent middle performers, and 10 percent "less effectives"), although it has backed off rigid enforcement of these percentages.[68] Chemtura, a $3 billion specialty chemicals company, eliminated forced distributions because of the demotivating effect of having to give some excellent performers mediocre ratings.[69]

?so what

Because the forced distribution method promotes a competitive and achievement-based culture, it can undermine teamwork and employees' desire to help each other.

Ethical Issues.   An important ethical concern with the ranking methods involves the annual firing or giving poor evaluations to a set number of the lowest performers even if these employees are performing up to standard. If the HRM system is performing well and all employees are good performers, the forced ranking method could result in disciplinary action against the lowest rated but still successful employees. Although it is not a requirement that low-rated employees be terminated, many organizations including GE do terminate a set percentage of their lowest ranked employees if they do not improve their ranking within a set period of time. The legal ramifications of inappropriately using termination quota systems have led some organizations to abandon the use of forced ranking systems, and several class-action lawsuits have exclusively focused on the validity of forced-distribution appraisal systems.

?so what

If most or all employees are performing well, ranking methods will result in poor evaluations for some good performers.

Predicting Deviance

For some organizations, employee behaviors can create a tremendous liability for the company. Global banks are under pressure to improve their legal compliance following a wave of high-profile scandals and large financial penalties.[70] Companies including investment banks and commodities dealers also stand to benefit from the early identification of employees likely to commit unethical and unauthorized acts.

Beginning in 2016, senior managers in the United Kingdom can be held accountable for the actions of their subordinates and even serve jail sentences for their transgressions. Accordingly, finance companies often spend as much as 20 percent of their revenue on compliance, hiring experts to sift through employee communications and use artificial intelligence to scrutinize what employees do at work to flag employees who might deviate from the norm for their peer group. Shouting on the phone, logging into a work computer at odd hours, or visiting the restroom more than average could all trigger an investigation.[71]

HR has an ethical responsibility ensure that a fair performance management process becomes properly integrated in the organization's culture. One of the purposes of performance management is also to establish a culture in which individuals and groups take responsibility for continuous improvement of business processes, personal skills, behaviors, and contributions. Thus, HR can and should include an ethical dimension in performance management by ensuring that the performance management process is not solely driving efforts to extract more from people.[72] But performance management is often tied to monetary rewards, which can create ethical challenges for employees. When Wells Fargo wanted its employees to cross-sell more products and meet challenging sales goals, the company's ethics workshop clearly sent the message that the company did not want them creating fake bank accounts in the name of unsuspecting clients. Risk professionals were even deployed to deter and eliminate the illegal activity,[73] but this was not enough. Meeting the high sales goals was necessary to continue earning a paycheck, and that motivation overshadowed the ethical message.

Improving Performance Through Feedback and Rewards

Many supervisors dread the process of filling out performance appraisal forms and meeting with employees to discuss their ratings. Many supervisors rightly worry that they haven't spent sufficient time watching their employees' behavior, and their ratings might be proven wrong if questioned. If a supervisor feels that it isn't worth the time to fill out a form since his or her employees have been doing just fine, it suggests that he or she is viewing the rating, not the communication process, as the goal. Supervisors must understand that the most important part of the performance management process is the ongoing communication around the measurements that helps employees adjust what they're doing to better meet their goals.

In addition, performance reviews often influence the pay increase or bonus pay an employee receives and should be taken seriously to maximize the accuracy of these compensation decisions. The challenge with using performance management ratings for both compensation and employee development purposes is that it can force managers to choose between giving an employee accurate but lower feedback and giving them a raise or bonus. If they choose to give a low rating and the employee is not happy with the subsequent raise or bonus, their motivation and engagement is likely to suffer, and they may consider leaving the company. Recognizing this challenge, after merging with Continental Airlines in 2010, United Airlines decoupled employee performance ratings from its compensation decisions so that its managers no longer had to artificially rate people high in order to give them a raise or bonus.[74]

If performance management is done well throughout the year, the performance appraisal discussion should be a review of feedback that has already occurred and a discussion of future goals and development plans. As Vineet Nayar, CEO of HCL Technologies, says, "We have come to think very differently about performance reviews. Rather than see them as evaluations—or, worse, judgments—of the employee's work of the past year, we now think of them as opportunities to discuss development."[75] David McKay, President and CEO of RBC, Canada, adds, "We spend an enormous amount of time as a team talking about people's skill sets, how they have to evolve and what are the best roles for them to take on."[76] SAP, Adobe, Gap, GE, Accenture, and Microsoft have all eliminated annual performance reviews, replacing them with regular check-ins and continuous feedback and coaching.[77]

> *"We have come to think very differently about performance reviews. Rather than see them as evaluations—or, worse, judgments—of the employee's work of the past year, we now think of them as opportunities to discuss development."*
>
> **—Vineet Nayar, CEO, HCL Technologies**

Performance Review Process

A performance review typically follows three steps: Preparation, communication, and follow through. In the preparation step, the information needed for the evaluation is gathered from all relevant sources. Be sure to include employees in this process, asking them to evaluate themselves and explain any performance challenges or deficiencies. In the next step, the performance appraisal meeting is conducted. During the meeting, it is important to remember the importance of the performance review to the employee and that the employee is likely nervous. It is important to be positive, put the employee at ease, and listen to what she or he wants to say. The meeting should focus on identifying the employees' strengths, constructively identifying where and how the employee could improve, and setting and documenting mutual goals and objectives for the next year. In the follow-through stage, the supervisor gives the employee regular feedback and coaching to help him or her achieve these goals. Regular support and praise helps keep the employee motivated and focused on goal attainment.

Supervisors should be coached to not find and focus solely on negative feedback during performance review meetings. Identifying and leveraging employees' strengths is often more valuable than trying to identify areas of weakness and focusing solely on improving them. Sheryl Sandberg, COO of Facebook, says, "At Facebook, we try to be a strengths-based organization, which means we try to make jobs fit around people rather than make people fit around jobs. We focus on what people's natural strengths are and spend our management time trying to find ways for them to use those strengths every day."[78]

It may also be appropriate to ask employees who are meeting or exceeding their goals to identify additional skills or positions for which they would like to be considered or developed in the future. Feedback should always be constructive. Never attack the feedback recipient, but do point out the issues with any problem behavior, and give examples of how the behavior could be corrected.

Employees performing well should be praised, rewarded, and encouraged to continue their high performance. As one expert states, "One of the biggest complaints employees have is they are not sufficiently recognized by their organizations for the work that they do."[79] All employees should be shown respect during the performance appraisal process, and the positive contributions that they make should be acknowledged and appreciated. Nonmonetary rewards including praise for specific behaviors or accomplishments, hearing "thank you" for a great job, and feeling that what they do is recognized and appreciated can be very motivational. Margaret Thompson-Schulz, a district manager at Cengage Learning, thanks her sales representatives with baseball games, barbeques at her house, and other forms of appreciation and has one of the highest employee retention rates as a result.

One of the most important things to remember in communicating performance information is the importance of listening to the employee's input. Giving employees a chance to describe and explain their performance is related to greater satisfaction with the appraisal and more positive attitudes toward the manager.[80] Wouldn't you be more satisfied with the performance management process if you could describe your achievements or explain why you were recently unable to perform up to a standard? It is good practice to start any performance review meeting by asking the employee to describe their performance and identify and explain any obstacles they faced that they feel affected their ability to meet their goals. What you learn might change your understanding of the employee's performance and the causes of their performance.

Eric Broder Van Dyke/Shutterstock

Rewards do not need to be expensive to be effective. Nonmonetary rewards, including gift certificates, outings to baseball games, and other forms of appreciation can improve employee morale and retention.

table 8.2

Providing Effective Feedback[81]

To provide the most effective and impactful feedback:
• Focus on the specific behavior or performance rather than what you think the feedback indicates about the individual (e.g., their integrity or their character) to decrease defensiveness and focus the person on what they can do to be more effective.
• Provide feedback that frames the person's performance relative to his or her goals, past performance, or improvement rate and minimize comparisons to others. Be supportive.
• Be specific in describing the desired behavior or performance.
• Jointly set specific, relevant goals, or persuade the employee to accept the goals you provide.
• Provide limited, focused information and data to avoid overwhelming the employee or putting him or her on the defensive.

Giving negative feedback is something many people find uncomfortable. Positive feedback is easier to give and to accept. Negative feedback often meets with resistance unless it is objective, from a credible source, and given tactfully. Feedback should also be impersonal and objective if it is to have the desired effect of motivating the employee. Table 8.2 highlights five principles for providing effective feedback.

This chapter's Develop Your Skills feature gives you some strategies for effective performance review meetings.

 # Develop Your Skills

Performance Review Strategies

1. *Before the meeting, thoroughly and objectively review the employee's performance throughout the entire time period.* Complete the performance appraisal rating form, and document the reasons for your ratings. Avoid overrating a poor performer because that rating becomes a standard for what performance the organization is willing to accept in the future, and it could be used against the organization in a lawsuit.
2. *Identify and focus on no more than three areas for improvement.* Performance management is not micromanagement. Try to identify the potential improvement areas that would have the biggest impact on the employee's overall effectiveness. Because it is difficult to work on more than three issues at a time, focusing the employee's efforts should lead to greater improvements.
3. *Begin the performance review meeting in a friendly and respectful way.* Ask the employee to describe his or her performance over the rating period and any challenges faced in meeting the goals. Jointly solve any issues the employee communicates.
4. *Communicate the effect that the employee's positive and negative behavior or performance has had on other employees, customers, or the organization.* Be constructive and focus on the behavior, not the individual. Use positive verbal

Continued

and nonverbal behaviors (e.g., make frequent eye contact, don't raise your voice, and lean forward).

5. *Focus on what's in it for the employee to improve in the targeted areas.* Does the employee value a promotion? More effective interactions with coworkers? Tying your goals into your employee's goals should make the employee more receptive to your feedback and development efforts and increase their commitment to the new goals.

6. *Clearly communicate the performance goals and standards.* Take the time to ensure that the employee understands the goals and standards and what constitutes success. Discuss the importance of the alignment of the organization's strategic plan, the business unit's goals, and the individual employee's goals. This is a good time to reinforce the organization's values, mission, and business strategy and how the employee's work fits into the broader organization.

7. *After persuading the employee to be willing to act on the targeted areas of development, co-develop an action plan and set SMART goals to achieve them.* Work closely together to identify any coaching or development opportunities, identify specific improvement measures, and establish a timeline for feedback. Identify any potential performance constraints including insufficient resources (including time), conflicting goals, underperforming coworkers, and a lack of authority to get things done.

8. *End the meeting by making sure the employee feels respected, valued, and recognized for his or her contributions and effort.* Try to ensure that the employee feels fairly compensated and values the rewards that will come with high performance.

9. *Follow up within a month* to offer coaching or other assistance to help the employee stay focused on the improvement areas and to help overcome any obstacles.

10. *Recognize and reward improvement as well as goal accomplishment.* Praise and recognition can be very effective motivators in addition to financial rewards.

so what

The same performance message can be interpreted differently in different cultures.

Cultural differences can impact how feedback is received and interpreted. This chapter's Global Issues feature describes how culture can affect the interpretation of feedback.

🌐 Global Issues

Cultural Influences on the Interpretation of Feedback

The same feedback can be interpreted very differently based on the culture of the person receiving it. One study asked respondents in China, Korea, and the United States to interpret the performance feedback, "There is room for improvement, but overall, this is good." East Asian managers were more likely to perceive this message as feedback given for relatively poor performance, whereas the U.S. managers took the message more literally and inferred that it conveyed a relatively positive assessment.[82] Wording feedback to match the interpretational style of the employee will make you more effective at giving feedback.

Continuous Performance Management

Because they emphasize financial rewards and punishments and take place at the end of the year, annual performance reviews do a good job holding employees accountable for their past behavior, but they do not improve current performance or groom talent for the future, both of which are more critical for organizational adaptability and long-term performance.[83] The best performance management process is one that takes place throughout the year, not just at an annual performance review meeting. **Continuous performance management** is ongoing and involves the employee in evaluating his or her performance and setting performance goals and provides continuous coaching and feedback throughout the year.

Because it is more informal and requires managers to more regularly discuss development with their employees, continuous performance management requires a continuous feedback culture to succeed. Deloitte believes that its new model of frequent, informal manager check-ins with subordinates has led to more meaningful discussions and insights and greater employee satisfaction.[84]

Some organizations are removing numerical ratings from performance evaluations, focusing the conversation on qualitative judgments and coaching. Managers at Juniper Systems and Cargill were able to effectively allocate merit pay without the numerical ratings, and they felt that the merit pay decisions were more valid as a result of paying closer attention to employee performance throughout the year.[85] Adobe found that its continuous performance management system also reduced voluntary employee turnover 30 percent after introducing a frequent check-in program because employees were better monitored and coached. Involuntary departures rose 50 percent because managers are now required to regularly have tough discussions with struggling employees rather than putting them off until the next performance review cycle.[86] At one insurance company that eliminated formal performance ratings, merit pay amounts were shared by employees and interpreted as performance scores. When these "shadow ratings" started to affect other talent management decisions, the company went back to formal ratings, although it kept other changes, including quarterly feedback sessions, to maintain its new commitment to employee development.[87]

Although continuous performance management is a good fit for many organizations, in some industries and fields (e.g., sales and financial services), emphasizing accountability and financial rewards for individual performers still makes sense. When Intel conducted a two-year pilot program eliminating formal appraisal scores in favor of feedback, supervisors had no problem differentiating performance or distributing performance-based pay. Nonetheless, company leadership returned to using formal appraisal scores because it was felt that they created healthy competition and clear outcomes.[88]

> **continuous performance management**
> an ongoing performance appraisal process that involves the employee in evaluating his or her performance and setting performance goals and provides continuous coaching and feedback

Improvement and Development Plans

Performance management is not about punishment. The goal is to ensure that employees are performing at least to standard, if not to their full capacity. The primary goal of a performance appraisal discussion with an employee is to enable the employee to improve in ways that allow both the employee and the organization to succeed. The second objective is to create a performance record that can withstand legal scrutiny.[89]

If an employee meets or exceeds his or her goals, no corrective action is typically necessary. Nonetheless, the employee should be given positive feedback and asked to identify any performance obstacles and development opportunities that would be helpful in maintaining and further improving his or her performance. Monetary or nonmonetary rewards should be given for goal attainment, and the organization should try to learn what it can from successful employees to inform its future staffing, training, and coaching efforts.

If an employee's performance is below standard, corrective action should be taken to correct the performance or behavior problem. First determine if the problem is a performance

so what**?**

Praise and appreciation are as important as corrective feedback when it comes to motivating employees to meet their goals.

problem (employee has not been able to demonstrate mastery of skills/tasks) or a behavior problem (employee may perform the tasks but creates an environment that disrupts the workplace), then address it accordingly.

Improvement Plans

A **performance improvement plan** is a tool to monitor and measure an employee's deficient work products, processes, and/or behaviors to improve performance or modify behavior. It should constructively and clearly communicate how the inadequate performance determination was made, what corrective and/or disciplinary actions will be taken, by whom and when, and when and how the individual's performance will be reviewed again. A performance improvement plan should be created in partnership with the employee to help address the performance obstacles being faced and to increase the employee's commitment to the plan and to behavior change.

Table 8.3 illustrates what a performance improvement plan might look like.

The acronym FOSA+ can help you remember the steps to take to write an effective performance improvement plan to an employee who has broken a company rule or who is performing poorly. These same steps can also guide a meeting with an employee to discuss rule violation or performance issues. FOSA+ stands for:

F	Facts that define the problem, including the company's expectations.
O	Objectives that help the employee understand how to resolve the problem.
S	Solutions that can help the employee strategize how to reach the objectives.
A	Actions that will be taken if the problem is not corrected.
+	Plus your overall efforts and support to help the employee succeed.

When the focus is on making an employee's good performance even better rather than improving an employee's unacceptable performance, the improvement plan is usually called an **employee development plan**. Intercontinental Hotel Group managers work with each employee to create a personal development plan to help employees grow and advance in the company.[90] Intercontinental Hotel Group's "My Room to Grow" program tailors the performance review process to allow performance reviews to be conducted for different lengths of time for different positions to avoid interfering with a hotel's ability to provide high-quality

table **8.3**

Performance Improvement Plan

Employee Name: _____	Date: _____
Improvement Needs (responsibilities, skills, behaviors)	
Objectives and Expected Results (include metrics where possible)	
Actions Necessary to Meet Expectations (include both employee actions and supervisor resources and support to be provided)	
Timeframe (include dates for progress review as well as final improvement deadline)	
Employee Signature: _____ Supervisor Signature: _____	Date: _____ Date: _____

customer service. Performance ratings evaluate both employees' competencies and behaviors, and they are used to identify strong performers who can move between business functions and global regions.[91]

Progressive Discipline

Disciplinary action should not be taken without a legitimate reason or just cause. Most organizations apply some form of **progressive discipline**, or using increasingly severe measures when an employee fails to correct a deficiency after being given a reasonable opportunity to do so. The goal of progressive discipline is to alert an employee of the need to correct a problem using the least severe action necessary to stimulate change. The severity of the action is increased only if the problem is not corrected with the lower level of discipline.

progressive discipline
using increasingly severe measures when an employee fails to correct a deficiency after being given a reasonable opportunity to do so

The typical progressive discipline steps are:

1. *Counseling*: Bringing a problem to the employee's attention before it becomes serious enough to require a written warning placed in the employee's file. The counseling meeting does not need to be documented.
2. *Written warning*: A written letter or completed form specifying the problem's history, the employee's explanation, and the company's expectations for change along with the consequences for not improving in a specified period of time is given to the employee and placed in the employee's file. If the employee does not improve, this step may be repeated with a stronger statement of the consequences for not improving. The first written warning may state that failure to improve "may lead to further disciplinary action," and the second warning may state that "this is a final warning, and failure to correct the problem will result in suspension."
3. *Suspension without pay*: The length of the suspension is not as critical as the act of suspension. Most suspensions are for less than a week, and often last one to three days. After a discussion with the employee, a written record of the suspension specifying the reason, the start and end dates, and that it is a final warning is placed in the employee's file and given to the employee at the start of the suspension.
4. *Termination*: Termination is used when earlier steps have not produced the necessary results. The employee must be given an opportunity to provide an explanation, and the organization must fairly consider and investigate the provided information. A written notice of termination is prepared after the discussion and consideration of all available information.

There is no rigid set of steps nor is there an inflexible rule that all steps must be followed before terminating an employee. For example, some organizations may suspend an employee with pay before a suspension without pay. The organization's policies, the circumstances of each situation, and the supervisor's or human resource department's judgment as to the least severe action necessary to correct the situation help to determine which step to use. Serious offences including fighting, harassment, or drug use might warrant skipping the first step or two. The discipline process for smaller problems, including tardiness or substandard work performance, typically begins with the lowest step. For legal purposes, it can be helpful to have a witness or note taker attend progressive discipline meetings to document what is communicated during each meeting.

Frito-Lay's "Discipline Without Punishment" method of changing employee behavior is focused on changing behavior in a positive manner and making employees responsible for their improvement.[92] The process begins with an oral reminder, then a written reminder, and if necessary a day of suspension with pay called a "commitment to change." During the commitment to change step, the employee must write a letter defining what they are going to do

so what?

Terminations do not have to follow a set series of steps. If the employment relationship is at-will, termination can happen at any time.

to correct the problem. Failing to submit a written commitment to change is considered an automatic acceptance of the employee's resignation. If the employee does not live up to their commitment for the next year, the signed letter of commitment gives Frito-Lay the right to accept their resignation. Because the separation is an acceptance of a resignation rather than a discharge, the employee may not be eligible for unemployment benefits depending on the state's unemployment laws.[93]

At each progressive discipline meeting, the employee should be informed of his or her unacceptable behavior or performance and given specific work-related examples. Do not assume that the employee knows what the problem is. Acceptable behavior or performance standards should be explained, and the employee should be given an opportunity to explain why the problem exists in case it is not under his or her control (for example, resources may be insufficient, or coworkers may be interfering). Change expectations and the consequences of failing to comply within a specified time period should be clearly communicated in a nonthreatening way.

This chapter's case study explores how Intercontinental Hotels Group uses performance reviews to help it achieve its expansion and performance goals.

CASE STUDY: Improving Collaboration Through Performance Management

Prudential Financial in Newark, New Jersey, relies on employee collaboration to best address complex customer needs.[94] Being inclusive, collaborative, and consistently showing respect for each other is so important that it is included as one of the company's core values.[95] Prudential Financial values its collaborative culture so highly that collaboration is also included in employees' performance assessments.

To help avoid the emergence of a toxic culture, if there is a problem with an employee, the supervisor or HR manager involves the company's Incident Oversight Team, which includes someone from corporate HR, someone from the company's health and wellness unit, a member of the company's global security team, and a company lawyer. A meeting is then held with the employee, and a specific recounting of the problem behavior is given to the employee along with an explanation of how the behavior hurt other employees. The employee must then choose a specific improvement plan, which might include a book, a course, a counselor, or a life coach, and regular meetings are held with the Incident Oversight Team to check on the employees' progress. Because Prudential Financial understands that toxic employees can drive good employees out of the company, it also holds its supervisors accountable for properly managing them.[96]

Questions
1. How can performance management help collaboration in an organization?
2. How would you recommend that Prudential Financial identify potentially toxic employees?
3. What type of improvement plan do you think would be of the most help to an employee displaying negative behaviors in the area of collaborating effectively with coworkers?

Performance Management Obstacles

Let's turn our attention to three of the most common obstacles to effective performance management: Not communicating a performance plan, a lack of accountability, and human biases and errors.

Not Communicating a Performance Plan

A **performance plan** describes desired goals and results (typically in terms of quantity, quality, timeliness, and the process to be followed), how results will be measured and weighted, and what standards will be used to evaluate results. Performance plans typically cover one year but can be done for any appropriate time period (e.g., a six-month project should be covered by a six-month performance plan).

Performance plans are best developed in partnership with the employee to maximize employee commitment and help to ensure that the plan is fully understood. A timeline for discussing goal progress throughout the time period should be included in the performance plan to ensure that the employee receives appropriate feedback and coaching. Performance plans provide the input for employees' future performance reviews. Any planned training or development activities should also be included in the performance plan. Performance reviews periodically look at past performance relative to the performance plan. Coaching should occur more frequently, be forward-looking, and focus on reinforcing desired behaviors.

performance plan
describes desired goals and results, how results will be measured and weighted, and what standards will be used to evaluate results

A Lack of Accountability

Accountability means that an individual is expected to provide a regular accounting to a superior about the results of what she or he is doing and will be held responsible for the outcome. To encourage desired performance management behaviors, organizations must make managers accountable for providing regular and accurate feedback and reward them for doing a good job. Responsibility for the appraisal system as a whole should be located at a senior organizational level to ensure company-wide commitment and involvement.

Online performance management systems assist managers when they give job performance feedback to their employees.[97] For example, computers can recommend phrases for describing the employee's performance. Nonetheless, most online systems still require a face-to-face conversation with the employee. In fact, the primary objective of American conglomerate TRW's online system is to "support face-to-face discussion between employee and manager."[98]

accountability
an individual is expected to provide a regular accounting to a superior about the results of what she or he is doing and will be held responsible for the outcome

Human Biases and Errors

Some of the most common weaknesses in a performance management system involve the tendency of evaluators to be too lenient, too critical, or too subjective. It is difficult to observe others' behavior and accurately interpret its causes, effects, and desirability. Subjectivity and bias can also play a significant role in the appraisal process. This can be minimized through rater training, thorough performance documentation throughout the year, clearly communicating goals and expectations, and basing performance standards on observable behaviors and outcomes. We next discuss a variety of rating errors that can compromise objectivity and accuracy in performance measurement.

Personal Standards.   Categories such as below average, fair, good, and superior can mean different things to different people. Training raters to understand the behaviors and performance

so what?

Because factors other than an employee's performance can influence their performance evaluations of subordinates, it is important to train managers in recognizing and reducing the effects of their natural biases.

standards for each rating level is essential in ensuring consistent ratings across supervisors that can be used to accurately compare employees.

contrast effect
over- or under-rating someone due to a comparison with someone else

Contrast Effect.   The **contrast effect** occurs when a rating determination is made by comparing the target employee with someone else rather than with the performance standards. Justifying a high rating for a poorly performing employee by saying, "Rosa may not deserve an 'outstanding' rating, but she is doing much better than the other employees" is inappropriate. Ratings should be made by comparing performance to the goals and performance standards, evaluating actual performance to expected performance.

first impression bias
initial judgments influence later assessments

First Impression Bias.   **First impression bias** occurs when initial judgments influence later assessments. If a new employee gets off to a slow start but reaches a high-performance level, the impression of the employee's low initial performance should not dominate his or her performance assessment.

recency effect
allowing recent events and performance to have a disproportionately large influence on the rating

Recency Effect.   Performance ratings should also not be overly influenced by an employee's most recent performance. The **recency effect** occurs when recent events and performance are given a disproportionately large influence on the rating. Keeping notes on employees' performance and regularly recording employees' performance can make it easier to remember performance and behavior earlier in the performance rating time period.

high potential error
confusing potential with performance

High Potential Error.   **High potential error** occurs when potential is confused with performance. Just because an employee has the potential to be a high performer, perhaps due to high ratings as a job candidate or high training performance, unless that high performance is realized, he or she should not receive a high rating.

halo effect
letting one positive factor influence assessments of other areas of behavior or performance

Halo Effect.   The **halo effect** occurs when one positive factor influences assessments of other areas of behavior or performance, resulting in an inappropriately high overall performance rating. For example, if Leon is friendly and likable, it does not mean that he is also hard working or productive.

horns effect
letting one negative factor influence assessments of other areas of behavior or performance

Horns Effect.   The **horns effect** happens when one negative factor influences assessments of other areas of behavior or performance, resulting in an inappropriately low overall performance rating. Allowing one disfavored trait or work factor to overwhelm other, more positive performance elements results in an unfairly low overall performance rating. For example, if Pat tends to be frequently late to work, it does not necessarily mean that she is unproductive.

similar-to-me effect
giving high ratings to someone because she or he is perceived as being similar to the rater

Similar-to-Me Effect.   The **similar-to-me effect** occurs when high ratings are given to someone because they are perceived as being similar to the rater. Being alums of the same school, having similar hobbies, or having similar talents with the person being rated can lead to unconsciously awarding higher performance ratings than is appropriate.

leniency error
all employees are given high ratings regardless of performance

Leniency Error.   **Leniency error** occurs when high ratings are given to all employees regardless of their performance. Some raters do this to avoid conflict or even to make it look like they are good managers with high-performing staff.

central tendency
rating all employees in the middle of the scale regardless of performance

Central Tendency.   **Central tendency** is rating all employees in the middle of the scale regardless of their performance. Some managers inappropriately feel that to maintain motivation, no employee should be given the highest rating regardless of their performance.

Stereotyping.   A **stereotype** is a belief that everyone in a group shares certain characteristics or will behave in the same way. Raters need to avoid generalizing about members of a group and focus instead on individuals' performance. A restaurant manager who rates male servers lower than female servers because of a perception that men are not as good as women at customer service is showing stereotyping bias.

stereotype
believing that everyone in a particular group shares certain characteristics or abilities or will behave in the same way

Opportunity Bias.   **Opportunity bias** reflects the ignoring of factors beyond the employee's control that influence his or her performance (either positively or negatively). Rating an employee's performance low because a production machine broke due to a manufacturing defect is obviously unfair. Employees should be rewarded and punished for the results of their own efforts, not luck or misfortune.

opportunity bias
ignoring factors beyond the employee's control that influence his or her performance

Legal and Ethical Issues in Performance Management

A performance appraisal should be able to help the organization show just cause for termination and other disciplinary action. Poorly executed performance appraisals may actually harm a legal case. Performance appraisal-related litigation in federal courts shows that rater training and perceived fairness are both significant factors in determining the outcomes of lawsuits.[99] Rater training is essential for reducing bias and enhancing rating accuracy. Perceived fairness is higher when performance management discussions address issues considered to be relevant by the employee and the supervisor.[100] If rating systems are too subjective and do not help employees improve their performance, employees are likely to have concerns about the fairness of the process.[101] This is particularly true of lower-rated employees[102] or employees denied larger raises or bonuses as a result of their performance rating.

If a performance appraisal program disparately impacts a protected group, an age discrimination claim may be supported by Title VII. If members of a protected group disproportionately receive low performance ratings, courts may scrutinize the program's job relatedness and validity. If low performance ratings are given by a supervisor to "get back at" an employee for a non-job-related reason, retaliation charges may also be filed. For example, if an employee opposes any employment practice that is unlawful under Title VII or age discrimination, or reports the practice to the EEOC or appropriate state agency, employers are prohibited against retaliating.

A negative performance evaluation can also be interpreted under Title VII as an "adverse employment action" and support a hostile work environment/discrimination claim. Without sufficient evidence of poor performance, the employer is likely to have a hard time defending against this claim. An employee may also pursue a claim of negligence in conducting, or failure to conduct, a performance evaluation if the employee is not given a regularly scheduled evaluation. If it is reasonably foreseeable that the oversight would cause severe emotional distress, the employer may be liable for negligent performance appraisal if the employee can prove that the employer owed a duty of care to the employee, breached this duty, the employee suffered a reasonably foreseeable legally recognizable injury, and the employer's failure to act is what caused the injury.[103]

As we have stressed, it is important that there be a clear communication plan at the beginning of the performance management process before performance communication occurs throughout the year.[104] Documenting specific incidences of poor performance is also important in supporting low performance ratings. As one managerial guidebook describes the importance of preparation for the performance review meeting, "There should never be any surprises at a performance review."[105]

Table 8.4 summarizes some of the elements a performance management system should have to be legally compliant.

Having a clear communication plan and documenting poor performance incidences are important for legal defensibility.

table **8.4**

Tips for Establishing a Legally Defensible Performance Management System

Existing case law suggests that to reduce the risk of a lawsuit a performance management system should have the following characteristics:

- Performance appraisal content and criteria should be based on a job analysis and linked to actual job duties and responsibilities.
- Evaluation criteria should be objective rather than subjective whenever possible.
- Raters should have personal knowledge of the performance of the person being rated.
- Supervisors should be trained in conducting a performance appraisal.
- Poor performers should be given an opportunity to improve.
- The performance appraisals should not have disparate impact on any protected group.
- Specific examples of poor performance should be documented to support a low performance rating.

Summary and Application

Performance management is an important tool for aligning individual, team, business unit, and organizational goals. Goal setting, feedback, and coaching are at the core of effective performance management, with managers communicating performance feedback and helping to remove performance obstacles throughout the year. Performance information from peers, supervisors, coworkers, and internal and external customers can supplement an employee's self-ratings of performance. Feedback should be respectful, clear, and focused on both past and future performance.

Multiple performance measurement approaches can be used together, depending on the goals of the performance appraisal and the type of performance review desired. For example, combining the BARS or graphic rating scales with an essay form is simple, effective in identifying training and development needs, and facilitates other management decisions. To be fair and objective, performance assessments must be based solely on the employee's job-related behavior and results in comparison to the performance standards. A performance plan and progressive discipline can be used to improve an employee's performance. High performers should be recognized and rewarded.

A lack of accountability and a variety of biases and errors can interfere with effective performance management. Training raters can help to reduce these biases.

Real World Response

Managing Performance at GE

GE is often cited as a company that effectively develops its future leaders. GE credits its success not to forms, rankings, or technologies but to the intensity of the discussion it has with its employees about both performance and values.[106] Managers are expected to spend several hours thinking about and discussing each employee's performance, and top leaders do not hesitate to question a manager's appraisal if it does not do the employee justice.

Most of GE's leaders, including the chairman, spend a minimum of 30 percent of their time on talent-related issues, including development opportunities, succession, organization and talent strategy, and global talent.[107] GE's vice president of executive development and chief learning officer Raghu Krishnamoorthy says, "Effective talent review is an intensely human process that calls for extensive demands on a leadership's time. There are no formulas or equations. The power lies in giving people the attention, candid feedback, and mentoring they deserve through a company-wide commitment to human-capital development.[108]

GE recently reengineered its performance reviews to focus on continuous feedback and coaching.[109] Rather than a once-a-year meeting in which salaried employees receive one of five labels ranging from "role model" to "unsatisfactory," managers now coach and guide employees toward their goals through-out the year.[110] GE even rolled out an app called PD@GE to enable managers to deliver more regular feedback.[111] The app accepts voice and text inputs, attachments, and even handwritten notes[112] and then compiles the messages and forms a performance summary that is delivered to employees at the end of the year. Managers are also being trained to improve their feedback conversations with employees.[113]

Takeaway Points

1. The three main benefits of performance management are aligning organizational goals with individual goals and organizational processes, giving employees clear goals and feedback, and generating useful data

2. The balanced scorecard balances internal and external measures, performance results and the drivers of performance results, and objective and subjective performance measures.

3. Goals affect performance by affecting the direction of action, the degree of effort exerted, and persistence in pursuing the goal. Feedback on goal progress is essential for learning whether any changes are needed to accomplish the goal.

4. Performance information can come from the performer, his or her supervisor, coworkers, and internal and external customers. Task acquaintance determines the appropriateness of using a particular source to evaluate an employee's performance—people should only be asked to rate behaviors or performance that they actually observe.

5. Performance rating methods compare employee performance to a set of standards. Performance ranking methods compare each employee to other employees in some way, forcing some employees to receive the highest and lowest ratings.

6. Goals direct and energize action, whereas feedback allows the tracking of progress in relation to the goal. Feedback indicating that change is necessary is most impactful when the employee perceives a need to change his or her behavior, reacts positively to the feedback and believes change is feasible, sets appropriate goals to regulate their behavior, and takes actions that lead to skill and performance improvement.

7. The first step in the progressive discipline process is to bring the problem to the employee's attention through counseling. A written warning, suspension with pay, and ultimately termination may follow if the behavior or performance is not improved.

8. Three common obstacles to performance management effectiveness are not communicating a performance plan, a lack of accountability, and human biases and errors.

Discussion Questions

1. If you were not performing up to standard, what would you want your supervisor to do?
2. If a newly hired subordinate came to you with concerns about his being able to perform well on the job, what would you do? Why?

3. How should the performance of an assembly line worker making cars be evaluated? How should the performance of a marketing executive for the same company be evaluated? Why do your recommendations for each job differ?
4. Would you want your coworkers to evaluate your job performance to determine the amount of financial bonus you receive? Why or why not?
5. Would you want your subordinates to evaluate your job performance to determine the amount of financial bonus you receive? Why or why not?
6. How would you give feedback to a new employee struggling to learn his or her job?
7. How would you overcome the common obstacles to performance management?

Personal Development Exercise: Constructive Criticism Role Play

The more you practice giving feedback, the better you will get at it. This exercise gives you the opportunity to practice giving feedback to a subordinate. View the video "Delivering Feedback—Fixing Performance Problems" (7:52) and "How to Give Constructive Criticism" (2:35). Then watch the videos, "Coaching: The Power of Questions (6:19)" and "Employee Gets Fired and Flips Out" (2:05).

Now find a partner and role play the following constructive criticism situation in a retail store. When you have finished, the feedback receiver should give the constructive criticism sender feedback on how well he or she did and how he or she could improve. Switch partners and repeat the exercise in the other role, using the second scenario.

Scenario 1

Your partner's work has been getting sloppy. S/he typically turns in high-quality reports, but over the past month, you've had to put increasing time into revising them before being able to give them to your boss. You don't have time to do this and know s/he can do a lot better. You don't know why the quality of his or her work has been slipping, but you would like him/her to return to his or her previous level of quality and attention to detail. Be sure to include performance standards in your discussion.

Scenario 2

Your partner has been taking credit for your ideas in the last two team meetings with the boss. She or he never used to do this, and you think s/he is very talented and generally enjoy working together. However, when the boss praises a specific idea or section of a report that was yours alone, you would like your partner to stop claiming that it was his or hers.

Strategic HRM Exercises

Exercise: Goal Setting

Practice good goal-setting techniques by setting goals for your academic performance this year. Be sure to break your goals into subgoals, and make sure your goals are SMART. Identify metrics for assessing your performance toward your goals during the year to get feedback on how you are doing. Identify three of the biggest likely obstacles to reaching your goals, and devise strategies to overcome them.

Exercise: Your Feedback Seeking Behavior[114]

Your own feedback seeking behavior will influence your success in whatever profession you choose. To better understand how you seek feedback, use the following scale to respond honestly to the statements below. Score your answers using the provided scoring key, then answer the questions at the end of the exercise.

Strongly Disagree	Disagree	Slightly Disagree	Neutral	Slightly Agree	Agree	Strongly Agree
(1)	(2)	(3)	(4)	(5)	(6)	(7)

_____ 1. I would cheerfully greet my supervisor hoping that this would lead to a conversation about a task that I had effectively completed.

_____ 2. After performing poorly, I would show my supervisor that I was taking responsibility for my performance and taking corrective measures.

_____ 3. I would indirectly make reference to an assignment completed successfully when I saw my boss.

_____ 4. I would inform my boss that I wasn't able to complete my assignment on time but that I would stay late that night to finish it.

_____ 5. After successfully completing an assignment, I would show it to my coworker if I thought my boss would later ask him/her about my performance.

_____ 6. After performing poorly, I would try to schedule outside appointments to avoid my supervisor.

_____ 7. I would hide from my supervisor if I had performed poorly or had failed to complete an assignment on time.

_____ 8. After performing poorly, I would take one or more of my vacation days in order to avoid any interaction with my supervisor.

_____ 9. I would inform my supervisor immediately after performing poorly and tell/ guarantee/promise him or her that I would do an excellent job next time.

_____ 10. After performing poorly, I would try to avoid eye contact with my supervisor so that s/he didn't start a conversation with me about my performance.

_____ 11. I would display my excellent work for my coworkers and hope they might relay some positive remarks to my supervisor.

_____ 12. I would admit to my supervisor that I had performed poorly and tell him/ her that I learned from the experience and would not repeat the incident.

_____ 13. I would confess about my poor performance to my supervisor immediately but have several solutions prepared to show that I would not make the same mistake twice.

_____ 14. After performing poorly, I would go the other way when I saw my supervisor coming.

_____ 15. After performing poorly, I would pretend to be sick and stay home in order to avoid negative feedback from my boss.

_____ 16. After performing well, I would ask my supervisor about my performance to draw his/her attention to my success.

_____ 17. After performing poorly, I would tell my supervisor immediately before s/ he got angry and upset about it.

Scoring

The sum of your responses to items 1, 3, 5, 11, and 16 is your *feedback-seeking behavior* score: _____

The sum of your responses to items 6, 7, 8, 10, 14, and 15 is your *feedback-avoiding behavior* score: _____

The sum of your responses to items 2, 4, 9, 12, 13, and 17 is your *feedback-mitigating behavior* score: _____

Interpretation

Your *feedback-seeking* score indicates the degree to which you actively seek performance-related feedback information following high performance. Seeking feedback helps us understand how we are performing and get our supervisor to notice our high performance. Feedback-seeking scores range from 5 to 35, with higher scores reflecting more proactive feedback seeking.

Your *feedback-avoiding* score reflects the degree to which you avoid seeking feedback when you know you have underperformed. Actively avoiding feedback when we perform poorly deprives us of information that could help us to improve. Feedback-avoiding scores range from 6 to 42, with higher scores reflecting a greater avoidance of feedback after low performance.

Your *feedback-mitigating behavior* score indicates the impression management behaviors you tend to engage in after performing poorly. These strategies help mitigate the damage to your image following poor performance by changing the nature of the feedback interactions you subsequently have with your supervisor. These strategies include apologies, excuses, or short-circuiting by communicating information about the poor performance before the supervisor has the opportunity to show emotions such as anger. Feedback mitigation is often intended to influence the supervisor to make an external rather than an internal attribution for the low performance. This can reduce the negative ramifications of poor performance.

1. Do you agree with this feedback? Why or why not?
2. What do you think you can change about yourself given this feedback? What will be better for you if you make these changes?
3. How will you make these changes? Set specific goals, identify metrics, and create a timeline for making a positive change.

Exercise: Evaluating Evaluation Forms

Imagine that you are a manager at Motivation Maximizers, a management consulting company. Consultants are responsible for working in teams of three to five to help clients improve employee engagement and motivation. Each project generally lasts three to four months and involves employee interviews, an employee survey, written report, and presentation to the client's leadership team of the team's recommendations.

Consultants are currently evaluated annually to provide both developmental feedback and determine their raise and performance bonus. Each consultant's manager uses a single form to evaluate each of their subordinate's performance every February. Motivation Maximizers' leadership recognizes that its consultants are the heart of its business. Due to consultant feedback that the current appraisal system is unfair and does not provide sufficient feedback, the leadership team wants to modify the performance appraisal system to improve the perceived fairness and utility of the current system.

Working alone or in a small group, identify the strengths and potential problems with using the following evaluation form for consultants at Motivation Maximizers. Also create an evaluation form that you think would better meet the organization's objectives. Be prepared to share your ideas and evaluation form with the class.

	Unacceptable	Below Expectations	Above Expectations	Exceptional
Indicate your evaluation of the employee's performance by checking the relevant rating for each performance dimension.				
Leadership				
Ethics				
Communication				
Work Quality				
Meets Deadlines				

Exercise: Giving Feedback Using FOSA+

We would like to thank Professor Robert Mooney of Texas State University for this exercise idea.

View the video, "How to Discipline an Employee" (3:30). Then find a partner and decide who will play the role of manager and who will be the employee. Next, choose one of the following performance issues, and practice giving feedback using FOSA+. You may also create a performance improvement plan if you would like. Be sure to communicate specific performance standards if you are playing the role of the manager. Feel free to make up any facts you like in communicating your feedback. When you have finished, switch partners and roles and do the exercise again.

1. The employee has been late in turning in project spreadsheets for the past month, delaying the project.
2. The employee has been leaving work early for the past week, leaving others to pick up the slack.
3. The employee has been making negative comments about the team's project to others in the team, hurting morale.
4. The employee has been spending a lot of time on the phone with friends, distracting others working in the area.
5. The employee has been smoking inside the building instead of in the smoking area outside the office.

Exercise: What Went Wrong?

View the video, "Performance Appraisal Gone Bad!" (4:35). After watching the video, answer the following questions:

1. Describe what you think are the three biggest errors made by the supervisor during this performance appraisal meeting.
2. What could the employee have done to improve the quality of the performance appraisal meeting?
3. What could the organization do to prevent performance appraisal meetings like this from happening?

Integrative Project

Using the same job you chose for the previous chapter, describe the performance management system you would establish to best align the goals of employees in that job with organizational goals and values. Also create a performance appraisal form for the job, and explain why your choice is most appropriate given the goals of the appraisal.

Video Case

Imagine that you are a manager at Happy Time Toys about to have a performance management meeting with a subordinate. The subordinate's previously excellent performance has declined, and this is the second time you have had to meet with him to discuss his performance. *What do you say or do?* Go to this book's video case, watch the challenge video for this chapter, and choose the best video response. Be sure to also view the outcomes of the two responses you didn't choose.

Discussion Questions

1. Which aspects of HRM discussed in this chapter are illustrated in these videos? Explain your answer.
2. How do these videos illustrate effective and ineffective performance management? Explain your answer.
3. As a manager, what else would you do to handle this situation? Explain your answer.

Endnotes

1. Yahoo! Finance (2017). General Electric Company (GE). Retrieved February 11, 2017, from https://finance.yahoo.com /quote/GE/key-statistics?p=GE

2. Baldassarre, L., & Finken, B. (2015, August 12). GE's real-time performance development. *Harvard Business Review.* Retrieved March 11, 2017, from https://hbr.org/2015/08 /ges-real-time-performance-development

3. McGraw, M. (2016, July 27). Farewell to performance ratings at GE. *HRE Daily.* Retrieved March 11, 2017, from http://blog .hreonline.com/2016/07/27/farewell-to-performance-ratings -at-ge/

4. Ramachandran, R. (2007, September 12). Forced-ranking systems in performance management. *Talent Management.* Retrieved March 18, 2017, from http://talentmgt.com/articles /view/forcedranking_systems_in_performance_management

5. Gale, S. F. (2012, March 7). From Texas to Timbuktu—How Fluor tracks talent on a global scale. *Workforce.com.* Retrieved March 22, 2012, from http://www.workforce.com/2012/03/07 /from-texas-to-timbuktuhow-fluor-tracks-talent-on-a-global-scale/

6. Krell, E. (2011). All for incentives, incentives for all. *HR Magazine*, 56. Retrieved March 19, 2017, from http://www .shrm.org/Publications/hrmagazine/EditorialContent/2011/0111 /Pages/0111krell.aspx

7. Gardner, N., McGranahan, D. & Wolf, W. (2011). Question for your HR chief: Are we using our 'people data' to create value? *McKinsey Quarterly*, March. Retrieved March 19, 2017, from http://www.mckinsey.com/business

-functions/organization/our-insights/question-for-your-hr-chief -are-we-using-our-people-data-to-create-value

8. Wood, R. E., Mento, A. J., & Locke, E. A. (1987). Task complexity as a moderator of goal effects: A meta-analysis. *Journal of Applied Psychology*, 72, 416–425.

9. Erez, M. (1977). Feedback: A necessary condition for the goal setting-performance relationship. *Journal of Applied Psychology*, 62, 624–627; Locke, E. A., Shaw, K. N., Saari, L. M., & Latham, G. P. (1981). Goal setting and task performance: 1969–1980. *Psychological Bulletin*, 90, 125–152.

10. Smither, J. W., London, M., & Reilly, R. R. (2005). Does performance improve following multisource feedback? A theoretical model, meta-analysis, and review of empirical findings. *Personnel Psychology*, 58, 33–66.

11. Neubert, M. J. (1998). The value of feedback and goal setting over goal setting alone and potential moderators of this effect: A meta-analysis. *Human Performance*, 11, 321–335.

12. Blanchard, K. (2017). How to build a high trust workplace. *Chief Learning Officer*, March, 14.

13. Kaplan, R. S., & Norton, D. P. (1992). The balanced scorecard—measures that drive performance. *Harvard Business Review*, 70, 71–79; Kaplan, R. S., & Norton, D. P. (1996). *The balanced scorecard: Translating strategy into action.* Boston, MA: Harvard Business School Press.

14. Kaplan, R.S. & Norton, D.P. (1996). *The Balanced Scorecard: Translating Strategy into Action.* Boston: Harvard Business School Press, 272.

15. Reprinted by permission of *Harvard Business Review*. Exhibit from *"Using the Balanced Scorecard as a Strategic Management System,"* by R.S. Kaplan and D.P. Norton, January-February 1996. Copyright © 1996 by Harvard Business Publishing; all rights reserved.

16. Balancing measures: Best practices in performance management. (1999, August). National Partnership for Reinventing Government. Retrieved March 19, 2017, from http://govinfo .library.unt.edu/npr/library/papers/bkgrd/balmeasure.html

17. *Ibid.*

18. DDI World. (2007). Maximizing performance. Retrieved March 19, 2017, from http://www.ddiworld.com/DDIWorld /media/client-results/Au_sensis_MaxPerf_rr_ddi.pdf?ext=.pdf

19. Craig, S. E., Beatty, R. W., & Baird, L. S. (1986). Creating a performance management system. *Training and Development Journal*, April, 38–42.

20. Gallo, C. (2008, February 29). Employee motivation the Ritz-Carlton way. *Bloomberg*. Retrieved March 19, 2017, from https://www.bloomberg.com/news/articles/2008-02-29 /employee-motivation-the-ritz-carlton-waybusinessweek -business-news-stock-market-and-financial-advice

21. See http://www.ritzcarlton.com/en/about/gold-standards.

22. Robison, J. (2008, December 11). How the Ritz-Carlton manages the mystique. *GALLUP Management Journal*. Retrieved March 17, 2017, from http://gmj.gallup.com /content/112906/how-ritzcarlton-manages-mystique.aspx#1

23. Smith, K. (2009, April 28). Misaligned incentives and the economic crisis. *Bloomberg*. Retrieved March 20, 2017, from https://www.bloomberg.com/news/articles/2009-04-28 /misaligned-incentives-and-the-economic-crisis

24. Klein, H. J., Wesson, M. J., Hollenbeck, J. R., & Alge, B. J. (1999). Goal commitment and the goal-setting process: Conceptual clarification and empirical synthesis. *Journal of Applied Psychology*, 84, 885–896.

25. Robison, J. (2008, December 11). How the Ritz-Carlton manages the mystique. *GALLUP Management Journal*. Retrieved March 17, 2017, from http://gmj.gallup.com/ content/112906/how-ritzcarlton-manages-mystique.aspx#1

26. *Ibid.*

27. Locke, E. A., & Latham, G. P. (2002). Building a practically useful theory of goal setting and task motivation: A 35-year odyssey. *American Psychologist*, 57, 705–717.

28. Baum, J. R., & Locke, E. A. (2004). The relationship of entrepreneurial traits, skill, and motivation to subsequent venture. *Journal of Applied Psychology*, 89, 587–598.

29. O'Leary-Kelly, A. M., Martocchio, J. J., & Frink, D. D. (1994). A review of the influence of group goals on group performance. *Academy of Management Journal*, 37(5), 1285–1301.

30. Rogers, R., & Hunter, J. (1991). Impact of management by objectives on organizational productivity. *Journal of Applied Psychology*, 76, 322–336.

31. Baum, J. R., Locke, E., & Smith, K. (2001). A multi-dimensional model of venture growth. *Academy of Management Journal*, 44, 292–303.

32. Locke, E. A., & Bryan, J. (1969). The directing function of goals in task performance. *Organizational Behavior and Human Performance*, 4, 35–42.

33. Bandura, A., & Cervone, D. (1983). Self-evaluative and self-efficacy mechanisms governing the motivational effects of goal systems. *Journal of Personality and Social Psychology*, 45, 1017–1028.

34. Latham, G. P., & Locke, E. A. (1975). Increasing productivity with decreasing time limits: A field replication of Parkinson's law. *Journal of Applied Psychology*, 60, 524–526.

35. Wood, R. E., & Locke, E. A. (1990). Goal setting and strategy effects on complex tasks. In B. Staw & L. L. Cummings (Eds.), *Research in organizational behavior*. Vol. 12, pp. 73–109. Greenwich, CT: JAI Press.

36. Locke, E. A. (1996). Motivation through conscious goal setting. *Applied and Preventive Psychology*, 5, 117–124.

37. Adapted from Locke, E. A. (1996). Motivation through conscious goal setting. *Applied and Preventive Psychology*, 5, 117–124.

38. Seijts, G. H., & Latham, G. P. (2005). Learning versus performance goals: When should each be used? *Academy of Management Executive*, 19, 124–131.

39. Ordonez, L., Schweitzer, M. E., Galinsky, A., & Bazerman, M. (2009). Goals gone wild: How goals systematically harm individuals and organizations. *Academy of Management Perspectives*, 23, 6–16.

40. *Ibid.*

41. *Ibid.*

42. For a more thorough discussion of performance appraisal, see Murphy, K. R., & Cleveland, J. (1995). *Understanding performance appraisal: Social, organizational, and goal-based perspectives*. Thousand Oaks, CA: SAGE.

43. Kalman, F. (2013). New brew: Anheuser-Busch InBev's Jim Brickey. *Talent Management*, November, 42–45.

44. Reilly, R. R., & Chao, G. T. (1982). Validity and fairness of some alternative employee selection procedures. *Personnel Psychology*, 3,: 1–62.

45. Elicker, J. D., Levy, P. E., & Hall, R. J. (2006). The role of leader-member exchange in the performance appraisal process. *Journal of Management*, 32, 531–551.

46. Kuehner-Hebert, K. (2013). United Airlines: More collaborative performance reviews. *Talent Management*, June, 44–47.

47. Bernardin, H. J., & Beatty, R. W. (1984). *Performance appraisal: Assessing human behavior at work*. Boston, MA: Kent.

48. Kiger, P. J. (2002). Elements of WellPoint's succession-planning program. *Workforce*, April, 51.

49. Yammarino, F., & Atwater, L. (1993). Understanding self-perception accuracy: Implications for human resource management. *Human Resource Management*, 32, 231–247; John, O. P., & Robins, R. W. (1994). Accuracy and bias in self-perception: Individual differences in self-enhancement and the role of narcissism. *Journal of Personality and Social Psychology*, 66, 206–219; Furnham, A., & Stringfield, P. (1998). Congruence in job-performance ratings: A study of 360 feedback examining self, manager, peers, and consultant ratings. *Human Relations*, 51, 517–530.

50. Kane, J. S., & Lawler, E. E. (1979). Performance appraisal effectiveness: Its assessment and determinants. In B. Staw (Ed.), *Research in organizational behavior*, Vol. 1. Greenwich, CT: JAI Press.

51. Kingstrom, P. O., & Mainstone. L. E. (1985). An investigation of rater-ratee acquaintance and rater bias. *Academy of Management Journal*, 28, 641–653.

52. Borman, W. C. (1974). The rating of individuals in organizations: An alternative approach. *Organizational Behavior and Human Performance*, 12, 105–124.

53. U.S. Office of Personnel Management. (1997, September). 360-degree assessment: An overview. Retrieved March 21, 2017, from http://www.opm.gov/perform/wppdf/360asess.pdf

54. *Ibid.*

55. U.S. Office of Personnel Management. (1997, September). 360-degree assessment: An overview. Retrieved March 21, 2017, from http://www.opm.gov/perform/wppdf/360asess.pdf

56. *Ibid.*

57. Oberg, W. (1972). Make performance appraisal relevant. *Harvard Business Review*, January–February, 61–67.

58. *Ibid.*

59. Hastings, R. R. (2009, September 16). Customize performance management to fit global cultures. *Society for Human Resource Management*. Retrieved March 20, 2017, from https://www .shrm.org/resourcesandtools/hr-topics/employee-relations/pages /customizeperformance.aspx

60. Kuehner-Hebert, K. (2013). United Airlines: More collaborative performance reviews. *Talent Management*, June, 44–47.

61. Latham, G. P., & Wexley, K. N. (1977). Behavioral observation scales for performance appraisal purposes. *Personnel Psychology*, 30, 255–268.

62. Oberg, W. (1972). Make performance appraisal relevant. *Harvard Business Review*, January–February, 61–67.

63. *Ibid.*

64. Monga, M. L. (1983). *Management of performance appraisal*. Bombay, India: Himalaya Publishing House.

65. DDI World. (2007). Customized training. Retrieved March 20, 2017, from http://www.ddiworld.com/DDIWorld/media/client -results/caterpillar_rr_ddi.pdf?ext=.pdf

66. The struggle to measure performance. (2006, January 9). *Bloomberg Businessweek*. Retrieved July 22, 2011, from https://www.bloomberg.com/news/articles/2006-01-08 /the-struggle-to-measure-performance

67. Meisler, A. (2003). Dead man's curve. *Workface Management*, 81, 44.

68. The struggle to measure performance.(2006, January 9). *Bloomberg*. Retrieved March 22, 2017, from https: //www.bloomberg.com/news/articles/2006-01-08/the-struggle-to -measure-performance

69. *Ibid.*

70. Dillow, C. (2016, March 23). Palantir and Credit Suisse team up to track down rogue traders. *Fortune*. Retrieved February 10, 2017, from http://fortune.com/2016/03/23/palantir-to-track-down -rogue-traders/

71. Finch, G., & Robinson, E. (2017, January 23). Bad behavior database aims to stop rogue traders before they act. *Bloomberg Businessweek* 32–33.

72. Leigh, A. (2013, September 10). "Is your performance management doing good or harm?" *Ethical Leadership*. Retrieved March 21, 2017, from http://www.ethical-leadership .co.uk/human-resources-and-business-ethics-56/

73. Corkery, M., & Cowley, S. (2016, September 16). Wells Fargo warned workers against sham accounts, but 'they needed a paycheck.' *The New York Times*. Retrieved March 21, 2017, from https://www.nytimes.com/2016/09/17/business/dealbook /wells-fargo-warned-workers-against-fake-accounts-but-they -needed-a-paycheck.html

74. Christensen, S. T. (2015, October 2). 3 ways companies are changing the dreaded performance review. *Fast Company*. Retrieved February 29, 2017, from https://www.fastcompany .com/3051779/3-ways-companies-are-changing-the-dreaded -performance-review.

75. Hamel, G. (2010, August 24). HCL's CEO on its 'management makeover.' *The Wall Street Journal*. Retrieved July 23, 2011, from http://blogs.wsj.com/management/2010/08/24 /hcls-ceo-on-its-management-makeover/?KEYWORDS=HCL

76. Audrerie, J. B. (2016, January 25). 20 quotes about digital economy, talents, and skills. *Futurs Talents*. Retrieved January 17, 2017, from http://futurstalents.com/transformation-digitale /intelligence-digitale/20-quotes-about-digital-economy-talents- and-skills/9/

77. Wright, A. D. (2016). SAP ditches annual reviews. *HR Magazine*, October, 16.

78. *Ibid.*

79. More than job demands or personality, lack of organizational respect fuels employee burnout. (2006, November 15). *Knowledge@Wharton*. Retrieved March 21, 2017, from http: //knowledge.wharton.upenn.edu/article.cfm?articleid=1600

80. Korsgaard, M. A., & Roberson, L. (1995). Procedural justice in performance evaluation: The role of instrumental and non-instrumental voice in performance appraisal discussions. *Journal of Management*, 21, 657–669.

81. DeNisi, A. S., & Kluger, A. N. (2000). Feedback effectiveness: Can 360-degree appraisals be improved? *Academy of Management Executive*, 14, 129–139.

82. Sanchez-Burks, J., Lee, F., Choi, I., Nisbett, R. E., Zhao, S., & Jasook, K. (2003). Conversing across cultures: East-West communication styles in work and non-work contexts. *Journal of Personality and Social Psychology*, 85, 363–372.

83. Cappelli, P., & Tavis, A. (2016). The performance management revolution. *Harvard Business Review*, October. Retrieved February 11, 2017, from https://hbr.org/2016/10 /the-performance-management-revolution

84. *Ibid.*

85. *Ibid.*

86. Duggan, K. (2015, December 15). Six companies that are redefining performance management. *Fast Company*. Retrieved February 14, 2017, from https://www.fastcompany .com/3054547/six-companies-that-are-redefining-performance -management

87. Cappelli, P., & Tavis, A. (2016). The performance management revolution. *Harvard Business Review*, October. Retrieved February 11, 2017, from https://hbr.org/2016/10 /the-performance-management-revolution

88. *Ibid.*

89. Segal, J. (2016). That difficult conversation. *HR Magazine*, April, 74–75.

90. InterContinental Hotels Group. (2011, May 9). Career progression. Retrieved March 21, 2017, from http://careers.ihg .com/what-we-offer

91. Stevens, M. (2011, July 1). Performance reviews boost talent at InterContinental Hotels. *People Management*. Retrieved July 21, 2011, from http://www.peoplemanagement.co.uk /pm/articles/2011/07/performance-reviews-boost-talent-at -intercontinental-hotels.htm

92. Grote, D. (2006). *Discipline without punishment: The proven strategy that turns problem employees into superior performers*. New York: AMACOM.

93. *Ibid.*

94. Prudential. (2017). A focus on talent. Retrieved February 15, 2017, from http://jobs.prudential.com/talent.php

95. Prudential. (2017). Our mission, vision, core values. Retrieved February 15, 2017, from http://corporate.prudential.com/view /page/corp/31838

96. Milligan, S. (2015, August 14). When a toxic worker is well-liked by managers. *Society for Human Resource Management*. Retrieved February 15, 2017, from https://www.shrm.org /ResourcesAndTools/hr-topics/employee-relations/Pages/When -a-Toxic-Worker-Is-Well-Liked-by-Managers.aspx

97. Van Fleet, D. D., Peterson, T. O., & Van Fleet, E. W. (2005). Closing the performance feedback gap with expert systems. *Academy of Management Executive*, 19, 38–53.

98. Neary, D. B. (2002). Creating a company-wide, online, performance management system: A case study at TRW, Inc. *Human Resource Management*, 41, 493.

99. Werner, J. M., & Bolino, M. C. (1997). Explaining U.S. Court of Appeals decisions involving performance appraisal: Accuracy, fairness, and validation. *Personnel Psychology, 50*, 1–24.

100. Greenberg, J. (1986). Determinants of perceived fairness of performance evaluations. *Journal of Applied Psychology, 71*, 340–342.

101. Landy, F. J., Barnes-Farrell, J. L., & Cleveland, J. N. (1980). Perceived fairness and accuracy of performance evaluation: A follow-up. *Journal of Applied Psychology, 65*, 355–356.

102. Flint, D. (1999). The role of organizational justice in multisource performance appraisal: Theory-based applications and directions for research. *Human Resource Management Review, 9*, 1–20.

103. Van Bogaert, D. (2003). New legal battlegrounds for performance evaluations. Retrieved May 17, 2012, from http://myweb.lmu.edu/dbogaert/NewLegalBattlegroundsPEdvb.pdf

104. Gordon, M., & Miller, V. (2011). *Conversations about job performance: A communication perspective on the appraisal process.* J. M. Phillips & S.M. Gully (Eds.). New York: Business Expert Press; Drewes, G., & Runde, B. (2002). Performance appraisal. In S. Sonnentag (Ed.), *Psychological management of individual performance*, pp. 137–154. New York: Wiley.

105. London, S. I. (1998). *How to comply with federal employee laws,* pp. 173. Rochester, NY: The VIZIA Group.

106. Krishnamoorthy, R. (2014, April 17). The secret ingredient in GE's talent-review system. *Harvard Business Review*. Retrieved February 17, 2017, from https://hbr.org/2014/04/the-secret-ingredient-in-ges-talent-review-system

107. Krishnamoorthy, R. (2014, April 17). The secret ingredient in GE's talent-review system. *Harvard Business Review*. Retrieved February 17, 2017, from https://hbr.org/2014/04/the-secret-ingredient-in-ges-talent-review-system

108. Krishnamoorthy, R. (2014, April 17). The secret ingredient in GE's talent-review system. *Harvard Business Review*. Retrieved February 17, 2017, from https://hbr.org/2014/04/the-secret-ingredient-in-ges-talent-review-system

109. Silverman, R. E. (2016, June 8). GE re-engineers performance reviews, pay practices. *The Wall Street Journal*. Retrieved February 15, 2017, from https://www.wsj.com/articles/ge-re-engineers-performance-reviews-pay-practices-1465358463

110. McGraw, M. (2016, July 27). Farewell to performance ratings at GE. *HRE Daily*. Retrieved February 14, 2017, from http://blog.hreonline.com/2016/07/27/farewell-to-performance-ratings-at-ge/

111. Duggan, K. (2015, December 15). Six companies that are redefining performance management. *Fast Company*. Retrieved February 14, 2017, from https://www.fastcompany.com/3054547/the-future-of-work/six-companies-that-are-redefining-performance-management

112. Baldassarre, L., & Finken, B. (2015, August 12). GE's real-time performance development. *Harvard Business Review*. Retrieved February 11, 2017, from https://hbr.org/2015/08/ges-real-time-performance-development

113. McGraw, M. (2016, July 27). Farewell to performance ratings at GE. *HRE Daily*. Retrieved February 14, 2017, from http://blog.hreonline.com/2016/07/27/farewell-to-performance-ratings-at-ge/

114. Moss, S. E., Valenzi, E. R., & Taggart, W. (2003). Are you hiding from your boss? The development of a taxonomy and instrument to assess the feedback management behaviors of good and bad performers. *Journal of Management, 29*, 487–510. (Scales are on p. 499.)

PART 4

Managing Total Rewards

chapter 9

Base Compensation

Learning Objectives

AFTER STUDYING THIS CHAPTER, YOU SHOULD BE ABLE TO:

1 Describe the difference between financial and nonfinancial compensation.

2 Describe the four forces influencing direct financial compensation.

3 Describe how organizations can evaluate the worth of a job.

4 List the three methods most commonly used for job pricing.

5 List four special compensation issues facing organizations.

6 Describe the Fair Labor Standards Act, the Equal Pay Act, and workers' compensation.

Real World Challenge

Strategic Global Compensation at Johnson & Johnson

The Johnson & Johnson Family of Companies (J&J), headquartered in New Brunswick, New Jersey, has more than 250 operating companies operating in more than 60 countries worldwide. The company employs over 125,000 people in its pharmaceutical, consumer (e.g., Band-Aids, Splenda sweetener, and Aveeno skin care), and medical devices (e.g., hip implants, stents, and blood glucose monitors) divisions.[1] Because of its many acquisitions and due to compensation differences in the various countries it does business in, salaries and bonuses are inconsistent across the organization.

J&J wants to increase the consistency of its employees' compensation experiences throughout the company. This goal is made particularly challenging by the fact that similar-sounding jobs can be very different in each of its three divisions. For example, a pharmaceutical sales representative job is very different from a sales representative in the consumer products division.[2]

J&J also wants to standardize its compensation practices across its business units and global regions to increase employees' opportunities to move internationally[3] and improve its alignment with local labor market practices.[4] The company asks your advice in reaching its compensation goals. After reading this chapter, you should have some good ideas.

Compensation is the human resource management (HRM) activity that deals with the rewards that employees receive. Compensation policies influence business results, organizational capability, talent attraction and retention, employee motivation, and employee satisfaction.[5] Because compensation is a large percentage of most organizations' costs, it also influences financial performance.

Pay is also one of the primary reasons that many people even seek employment. In addition to filling psychological and financial needs, pay often indicates an individual's value to the organization. Poorly designed or executed compensation systems have the power to be divisive, deter cooperation, demotivate employees, or even push talented employees to seek better opportunities elsewhere. The primary goal of compensation is to maintain external competitiveness and internal fairness and control undesirable turnover while meeting the organization's need to control salary costs.

Even small organizations need to develop appropriate compensation structures. An effective compensation plan helps to ensure a company's competitiveness for new hires and helps retain current employees. It is also easier for employees to accept structured pay grades and compensation policies that have been in place from the company's beginning rather than trying to change individuals' idiosyncratic compensation deals as the company grows.

In this section of the book, "Managing Total Rewards," we turn our attention to the rewards and the benefits organizations give their employees. Most organizations cannot afford to give their employees the highest possible salary, the most generous health insurance, and other benefits. The decisions an organization makes about how to reward and incentivize employees has a large effect on its ability to recruit and retain employees and motivate them to perform their best. Understanding different types of compensation and how compensation is determined can help you make better employment decisions as well as pay your own employees appropriately for your company's goals. By influencing goals and motivation, compensation influences what employees *will* do in our book's overall model of HRM.

In this chapter, we discuss what compensation is, followed by how compensation can be strategic. We then turn our attention to the factors that influence compensation and how to evaluate the worth of a job to an organization. Job pricing is then explained, and methods of communicating compensation are discussed. Some current compensation issues are then described, followed by several laws and regulations affecting compensation. After reading this chapter, you should have a good idea of what compensation is and how organizations determine base pay levels.

What Is Compensation?

Employees and their employers have an exchange relationship in which employees apply their time and talents to create value for the organization in exchange for tangible and intangible rewards that employees value. Although money isn't the only reason people work, it is usually one of the main reasons. How organizations choose to compensate employees can make them more or less attractive as employers, motivate different behaviors, and affect financial outcomes.

There are many types of compensation. Employees exchange their labor for both financial and nonfinancial rewards. Financial compensation is both direct and indirect. **Direct financial compensation** consists of the pay an employee receives in the form of wages, salary, bonuses, and commissions. Direct financial compensation is the largest element of base compensation. **Indirect financial compensation** (benefits) consists of all the tangible and financially valued rewards that are not included in direct compensation, including free meals, vacation time, and health insurance. Incentive pay is a popular form of indirect compensation and will be the focus of the next chapter.

Nonfinancial compensation includes employee rewards and incentives that are not financial in nature. Flexible work schedules that give employees an alternative to an 8-to-5 work schedule, development opportunities, casual dress codes, and helping employees balance

---

direct financial compensation
compensation received in the form of salary, wages, commissions, stock options, or bonuses

indirect financial compensation
all the tangible and financially valued rewards that are not included in direct compensation, including free meals, vacation time, and health insurance

 so what

Employees value more than money as compensation for their talents and efforts.

nonfinancial compensation
rewards and incentives given to employees that are not financial in nature

work with the other demands in their life are all valuable to employees and can be considered a type of compensation.

To better understand the role of financial and nonfinancial compensation in employee motivation, consider the following conversation:

> Kim: I can't believe you left your job at Monkey Magnets. They have the highest pay around.
> Fred: That's true, but I worked so much I never saw my family. At my new job, I'm home by five, and I even have time for my hobbies. I've never been happier!

In this case, Kim is clearly motivated best by financial rewards, whereas Fred values work–life balance. Because different people are motivated by different things, it is important to be as flexible as possible in rewarding employees in the ways that they most value. Rewards work best when they are tailored to the individual employee the organization is trying to motivate. Would you be equally motivated by a $100 Amazon.com gift card, dinner with your boss, and a day off? Most people have a preference, and to motivate employees the most effectively, it is best to match the reward to what employees most value.

Base pay reflects the size and scope of an employee's responsibilities. Base pay is typically reviewed annually in light of an individual's performance and experience, competitive trends, and the geographic location of the job. Annual cost of living raises are often given to counter the effects of inflation on employees' purchasing power.

Severance pay is given to employees upon termination of their employment. The amount of severance pay a departing employee receives is typically based on their length of eligible employment with the company. There is no legal requirement to provide severance pay. When it is offered, many employers have the departing employee sign a release agreeing to not sue the organization in exchange for receiving the severance pay.

Total rewards include everything an employee perceives to be of value that results from the employment relationship. Total rewards include:

- Financial and nonfinancial compensation
- Benefits
- The physical work environment
- Organizational culture
- Professional development
- Performance management and recognition
- Work/life balance

Many companies, including Coca-Cola Enterprises, Rio Tinto, and Mercer, publish information about their total rewards packages on their website. Retailer Kohl's publishes its total rewards proposition on the careers page of its website. The company's total rewards proposition includes:[6]

- Pursuing good health so you can do the things you love at home and on the job
- Planning for your financial future with increased confidence
- Being active and engaged in your community
- Growing and achieving greatness through the work you do every day
- Developing positive relationships with those around you

For many employees, recognition, praise, and appreciation are an important type of reward. As leadership trainer Dale Carnegie said, "People work for money but go the extra mile for recognition, praise and rewards."[7] Two great things about recognizing and praising employees is that it is easy to do and inexpensive.

> *"People work for money but go the extra mile for recognition, praise and rewards."*
>
> **—Dale Carnegie, Leadership Trainer**

base pay
reflects the size and scope of an employee's responsibilities

severance pay
given to employees upon termination of their employment

total rewards
everything an employee perceives to be of value that results from the employment relationship

Strategic Compensation

Early compensation policies focused on enabling an organization to recruit and retain employees while complying with relevant legal requirements. Pay was primarily determined by the employee's tenure with the organization and hierarchical position. Increasingly, however, compensation is seen as an important tool in acquiring a competitive advantage. Compensation is most strategic and effective when viewed as an investment and used to enhance organizational performance.

Compensation policies can reduce labor cost per unit of output and motivate employees to perform better and develop their skills. The goal of a strategic compensation system is to:

- Attract and retain qualified employees;
- Reflect the relative value of each job;
- Be externally competitive and internally consistent and fair;
- Motivate individual performance and employees' contribution to organizational goal achievement;
- Foster employee engagement and productive work relationships; and
- Comply with all state and federal laws and regulations.

A strategic perspective on compensation focuses on tailoring a firm's compensation system to reinforce the firm's business strategy.[8] Because a good fit or alignment between a firm's business strategy and its human resource management system leads to better firm performance, a company's business strategy should be a key determinant of its compensation system.[9]

For example, unlike **fixed pay** that pays employees a set amount regardless of performance, **variable pay** bases some or all an employee's compensation on employee, team, or organizational performance. Variable pay reinforces the competitive advantage of cost efficiency because the pay system helps to control labor costs.[10] To maximize motivation, variable pay is usually based on performance, over which the employee has some degree of control. Diversified firms are more likely to link employee pay with business unit performance, whereas less diversified firms are more likely to link employee pay with corporate performance.[11]

Strategic compensation requires managing both pay structure and pay mix. **Pay structure** is an organization's array of pay rates for different skills or work,[12] including the difference in pay among employees in different job families.[13] Deciding how much more to pay executives than entry-level hires or how much to pay marketing employees compared to manufacturing employees are pay structure decisions. Pay structures can be designed to price jobs at the prevailing market rate or to preserve internal pay equity by compensating each job consistently with the positions above and below it in the company hierarchy. Figure 9.1 illustrates the pay structure in a hypothetical IT department.

fixed pay
pays employees a set amount regardless of performance

variable pay
bases some or all an employee's compensation on employee, team, or organizational performance

pay structure
the array of pay rates for different work or skills within a single organization

figure **9.1**

Pay Structure

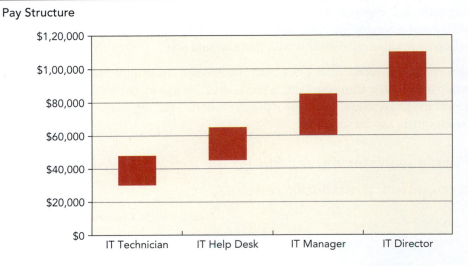

Pay mix is the relative emphasis given to different compensation components.[14] Because different combinations of compensation components motivate different behaviors and focus employees on different goals, pay mix is an important dimension of compensation strategy.[15] Some forms of compensation are based on short-term results (e.g., merit pay or annual bonus), whereas others are based on long-term performance (e.g., stock options). Compensation criteria emphasizing long-term pay will better align employees' interest in achieving long-term performance goals than will short-term incentives.[16] For example, given the longer time frame required for innovation, an innovation strategy may require a focus on long-term performance based compensation.[17]

pay mix
the relative emphasis given to different compensation components

so what?

Compensation can best motivate employees when it focuses on short-term as well as long-term goals.

What Influences Direct Financial Compensation?

Direct financial compensation is influenced by many factors. The organization, the job, the specific employee, and external factors can all influence how much pay an individual receives. Let's explore each of these in greater detail.

The Influence of the Organization on Direct Financial Compensation

Different industries and different organizations within an industry pay differently based on their profitability and resources. For example, Goldman Sachs is able to pay employees more than a typical local bank. One consideration in your own career is what industry to work in as well as what career to pursue. Some industries are able to pay more than others due to greater growth, profitability, and resources. If money and career advancement are important to you, growing industries with high profit margins and valuable resources may be able to offer you greater rewards and career advancement than declining industries with low or shrinking profit margins.

It is important to remember that although a financially successful organization may be able to pay above market salaries, it may not choose to do so as other factors affect compensation decisions for different jobs. Some organizations have a compensation policy of being a **pay leader** and seek to give employees greater rewards than do their competitors. Companies with an innovation or customer service business strategy, including Starbucks, SAS, and Google, use this strategy to attract and retain higher quality employees that are critical to their success. Although factors other than pay influence motivation and retention, employees do tend to be more motivated[18] and turnover is often lower[19] when rewards are greater.

Other organization\s, including Wal-Mart, are **pay followers** and seek to pay their front-line employees as little as possible to support their low-cost business strategy. Pay followers often pay below the market average wage rate due to an inability to pay more or a belief that these employees are easily replaceable. Although a pay-follower policy does reduce salary expenses, pay followers often experience high turnover and lower employee performance, which can make employee costs higher than if the organization just paid a higher wage rate. If below-market pay rates fail to generate and retain sufficient numbers of acceptable hires, raising pay to at least market rates is often necessary. Organizations may be pay leaders in areas essential to their competitive advantage and pay followers in less strategic areas.

so what?

To maximize your own compensation, carefully choose your industry as well as your career.

pay leader
organization with a compensation policy of giving employees greater rewards than competitors

pay followers
pay their front-line employees as little as possible

Sorbis/Shutterstock

Some organizations, including Starbucks, choose to give their employees greater rewards than do their competitors. This allows the company to hire higher-performing employees and also increases the length of time employees spend with the employer. When training costs are high or if long-term customer relationships are critical this can be a particularly effective strategy.

The Influence of the Job on Direct Financial Compensation

For both ethical and legal reasons, it is important to have a clear plan to meaningfully distinguish between jobs and employees for pay purposes. Organizations should ensure that pay differences across employees are based upon variations in job requirements, including skill, effort, working conditions, job responsibility, and mental and physical requirements rather than bias. A job should be established to be worth a certain wage rate to the organization and a person hired to fill it at that rate. Exceptions are sometimes made for high-level jobs for which the incumbent may expand or reduce the scope of the job depending upon his or her ability and interests or for particularly high performers at risk of leaving the organization.

resource dependence theory
proposes that organizational decisions are influenced by both internal and external agents who control critical resources

Resource dependence theory[20] argues that organizational decisions are influenced by both internal and external agents who control critical resources. According to this theory, an organization must acquire resources (e.g., money, technology, or accreditation from regulatory agencies) to survive, and it interacts with other actors who control such resources. Whoever controls these critical resources (e.g., technology or money) has considerable influence over the organization. Because positions that secure valuable resources are more important than those that do not, employees holding such positions are typically paid more.[21]

For example, employees in private academic institutions who successfully raise money (e.g., chief development officer or admissions director) are paid comparatively more than their counterparts in public academic institutions for which fundraising is less critical.[22] In addition, the relative pay level of research and development (R&D) executives increases as their firms allocate more resources to R&D.[23] The most important resource in a high-technology company pursuing a competitive advantage through innovation is the ability to produce innovative products or solutions. This means that R&D employees have the potential to make the greatest contribution to the firm's success, and they are usually paid more than are other employee groups to attract top talent.

The Influence of the Employee on Direct Financial Compensation

If equity is more important to an organization than equality, then individual differences in ability and contribution should be recognized. **Wage differentials** are differences in wages between workers, groups of workers, or workers within a career field. For example, the highest performing employee in a workgroup might be paid more than his or her coworkers even though they all hold the same job.

wage differentials
differences in wages between various workers, groups of workers, or workers within a career field

Seniority and merit are two of the largest influences on wage differentials among people holding the same job in an organization. Additional worker characteristics commonly considered to justify wage differentials include experience, education, competencies, skills, performance, and tenure with the employer.

To maximize motivation, individual differences in ability and contribution should be equitably recognized. To prevent a sense of inequity on the part of lower paid employees, wage differentials should be identified, explained, and documented. Job titles can help to differentiate the reasons some workers are more highly paid—for example, physician assistant I and physician assistant, II.

Wage differentials across individuals sometimes result from in-group bias and demographic similarity to those making pay allocation decisions. Research has found that people tend to give less favorable treatment to individuals with dissimilar demographic characteristics. One study found that the gender gap in executive pay (male executives tend to earn more than female executives) is smaller when a greater number of women sit on the compensation committee.[24]

Employees' preferences for compensation characteristics can also influence compensation policy. In one year, Convergys, a company that manages accounting, payroll, and benefits for organizations in over 40 countries, had such a high turnover rate that they had to recruit 50,000 new people to maintain a staffing level of 35,000. To reduce attrition, Convergys tried some "silver bullet" approaches such as across-the-board pay raises, but these had limited success. Finally, they used a data-driven approach to determine the specific HR practices that would be most likely to enhance retention. Convergys learned that employees were more likely to stay with the company if they received half their annual pay raises every six months instead of receiving the entire amount once a year. This change cost almost nothing, but it enhanced retention.[25]

This chapter's HR Flexibility feature discusses the role of compensation in the current home healthcare worker shortage in the United States.

Motivation is maximized if employees' compensation preferences are reflected in the compensation policy.

HR Flexibility

The Role of Pay in the Home Healthcare Worker Shortage

Home healthcare aides, a job filled primarily by women and minorities, are one of the fastest-growing occupations in the United States. Over the past decade, the number of home healthcare workers increased from 700,000 to more than 1.4 million, rising to over 2 million if the independent caregivers employed by clients through public programs are included.[26]

It has always been hard to keep workers in these important but difficult jobs, and the annual turnover rate is currently 40 to 60 percent.[27] Demand for them continues to grow, with people saying overwhelmingly that they want to remain at home as they age. For that to happen, the United States will need an additional 633,000 home healthcare workers by 2024.[28] Caregiver shortages were the top industry threat in 2016, with 70 percent of respondents stating it was one of their top three concerns.[29] In addition to the cost of replacing them, turnover causes losses in productivity and morale, as well as increased stress among the workers who stay.[30]

Decreasing home healthcare worker turnover is essential for stabilizing the industry. In 2013, the Labor Department finally gave home healthcare workers minimum wage and overtime rights under the federal Fair Labor Standards Act. Since then, because most states have not boosted Medicaid funding to help agencies cope with the increased wage rates, healthcare employers have struggled to maintain profits.[31] The Healthcare Association of New York (HANY) estimated the cost of a $15 minimum hourly wage to home care agencies would reach $1.7 billion annually.[32]

Nonetheless, low wages are a major reason for the home healthcare worker shortage. Workers in this field average $11 per hour, or about $22,450 annually. In comparison, at the end of 2016, McDonald's employees made more than $10 per hour. Home healthcare workers often drive long distances to clients' homes, often without reimbursement, and perform physically and emotionally demanding tasks. Even the ones with a passion for the work are likely to burn out.[33] Because of the low wages and mostly part-time work (although many would prefer full-time hours), these caregivers often sink into poverty. Approximately a third receive food stamps, and 28 percent rely on Medicaid for health insurance.[34]

The Influence of External Forces on Direct Financial Compensation

labor market
all of the potential employees located within a geographic area from which the organization might be able to hire

The Labor Market.   The **labor market** for a position consists of all of the potential employees located within a geographic area from which the organization might be able to hire. If fast food cashiers in an area tend to be paid about $8 per hour, a new fast food restaurant is likely to set its cashier pay at that level. Many organizations try to set compensation at a level consistent with the prevailing rate in the relevant labor market.

The labor market differs for different positions. How far do you think an employee would be willing to drive to work as a cashier for an Exxon gas station? Would people be likely to relocate to be able to accept the position? Assuming that most people would not be willing to relocate for such a low-paying job, and that most people would be willing to drive up to 5 miles to get there, the qualified people in a 5-mile driving radius would constitute that gas station's labor market for the cashier position, and the wage rates for other cashier jobs in that area would determine what that gas station would be willing to pay its own cashiers.

The labor market expands as positions are located higher in the organization. Now think about the labor market for the job of vice president for Exxon. Many executives would be willing to relocate for that position, making the labor market national or even international in nature. Executive level salaries are thus affected by the salaries paid to other industry executives in the country or even globally.

Different geographic labor markets often have different compensation levels. One U.S. corrugated cardboard manufacturer learned that the different turnover and performance rates across its plants were due in part to its compensation system. It paid the same rate for production employees in all of its plants across the country. Those rates were at or above market in some areas but below market in others. Turnover was higher and performance was lower in the plants in which pay was below the local market rate, and the organization lost many good employees to higher-paying local manufacturers in those areas.

?so what

Employees in the same job may be paid differently if the labor market for the position differed at the time each was hired.

The labor market during the time of an employee's hire can result in differing pay for employees in the same job. The starting pay of an employee hired during a tight labor market when talent is hard to find may be a bit higher than the starting pay of an employee hired when talent is plentiful.

Economic Factors.   Economic factors can influence compensation policy by increasing or decreasing the organization's ability to pay and the supply of workers available. When an economy contracts, the increase in the labor supply tends to decrease the market rate for labor. In a strong economy, the labor market tightens, and employers must pay more to acquire needed talent. Sometimes shortages or surpluses arise for some specialty skills, such as nurses, software engineers, or machine operators. A recent construction skills shortage in the U.K. prompted a 5 percent pay increase for skilled construction workers in just three months.[35]

Labor Unions.   Labor unions influence compensation through the process of collective bargaining. Hours, wages, and other terms and conditions of employment are areas of mandatory collective bargaining between management and unions under the Wagner Act. The terms and conditions of one company's collective bargaining contract can influence the compensation policies of nonunionized companies who compete for the same talent. If a nonunionized company wants to be competitive in the labor market, it often must at least match the terms of the local union contract. **Cost-of-living allowances** are "escalator clauses" in union contracts that automatically increase wages based on the U.S. Bureau of Labor Statistics' annual cost of living index to offset the effects of inflation on employees' purchasing power.

cost-of-living allowances
clauses in union contracts that automatically increase wages based on the U.S. Bureau of Labor Statistics' cost of living index

Legislation.   Federal and state laws can influence compensation decisions. In the U.S., the Equal Pay Act prohibits paying employees differently on the basis of gender. A variety of equal employment legislation, including the Americans with Disabilities Act and the Age Discrimination in Employment Act, also prohibit discrimination against protected groups in employment matters, which includes compensation. In Indonesia, the government's Ministry of Manpower and Transmigration mandates the payment of a religious holiday allowance called the Tunjangan Hari Raya, also known as thirteenth month compensation.[36]

State laws can also influence compensation policy. This chapter's case study explores the impact of state law on compensation at a not-for-profit corporation. Legal issues in compensation will be covered in more detail later in this chapter.

Global Issues.   Setting compensation rates in local markets around the world can create wide variability in pay. For example, market pay for an engineer in the United States might be $75,000, but in India, the same position might warrant only the equivalent of $12,000. Decisions must be made regarding how to balance compensation in the local currency and market with the company's average pay for that position. Employees in different countries also differently value different types of compensation. Although the United States tends to emphasize bonuses and incentives, areas including Asia put more weight on salary than bonuses.

so what?

Because people in different countries prefer different compensation structures, it is important to attend to global differences when making compensation decisions.

CASE STUDY: "Reasonable" Compensation at a Not-for-Profit Organization

Richard Grasso successfully ran the New York Stock Exchange (NYSE) during a time of increasing global competition. During his time as the Chairman and CEO of the NYSE, the organization earned record profits. A lawsuit was brought against Grasso claiming that the compensation he received as chairman of the nonprofit NYSE violated New York's not-for-profit corporation law requiring that the compensation of officers of nonprofit corporations be reasonable.[37] Grasso's retirement plan grew to more than $139 million during his 36-year tenure at the organization, and over the next four years, he was due to receive $48 million in deferred pay.[38]

The NYSE's compensation committee set the CEO's compensation based on an assessment of the NYSE's performance and the median compensation of a group of peer CEOs. The court found that Grasso had failed to adequately disclose the size of his large compensation package to the exchange's board of directors.[39] In addition, many of the comparison CEOs' companies were not of comparable size, revenue, or complexity.[40] It was also alleged that Grasso had personally chosen the members of the compensation committee, many of whose companies were listed on the NYSE. Grasso was ordered to return tens of millions of dollars in retirement pay. To help shareholders better evaluate executives, the Securities and Exchange Commission changed the compensation-reporting rules and added disclosure rules about pensions and postretirement perks.[41]

Questions

1. What do you think is "reasonable" compensation for a not-for-profit organization?
2. Whose responsibility is it to inform a company's board of directors of the CEO's total compensation details?
3. Do you think that it is possible for a CEO to be paid too much? How would you determine an appropriate amount? Why?

Evaluating the Worth of a Job

Let's turn our attention to a variety of methods used to evaluate jobs to determining compensation levels.

Market Pricing

market pricing
uses external sources of information about how others are compensating a certain position to assign value to a company's similar job

Market pricing uses external sources of information about how others are compensating a certain position to assign value to a company's similar job. Market pricing identifies the economic worth of a job on the open labor market based on what is needed to attract and retain qualified individuals. If entry-level accountants in the area are paid $60,000, then an organization wishing to hire a good entry-level accountant should expect to have to pay at least this much. Most organizations target salary levels at or above the market—paying between the 60th to 75th percentiles and 40th to 60th percentiles are the most common competitive targets.[42] Market pricing is particularly important when an organization believes that it must pay competitively in the open market to attract sufficient numbers of appropriately qualified talent.[43]

The usefulness of the market pricing method depends on the accuracy of the job analysis used to define the job, the ability to find similar jobs in the labor market, and the quality and comprehensiveness of the market pricing data available for those jobs. Because it can be difficult to identify comparable jobs and obtain accurate market rate information, particularly for specialized jobs in which companies tend to develop their own talent, market pricing can be difficult to use. For example, a consulting company that puts new hires through extensive training to learn its proprietary methods and technology will find it difficult to obtain useful market pricing information because those skills do not exist in other organizations.

For management positions, hotelier Four Seasons closely monitors competitors' room rates and pay scales. The goal is to charge the most per room in a given market and pay salaries between the 75th and 90th percentile—the magic ratio that executives believe attracts the right people and maximizes profits.[44]

Table 9.1 lists some Internet resources that can be useful in determining market compensation levels. Although this information can help identify appropriate market-based salary ranges, the organization must still decide what it wants a position's starting salary range and average to be. To maintain fairness and consistency, formal starting pay policies should be developed to address extending different starting pay offers to different finalists.

The resources in Table 9.1 can also help you research salary levels for different occupations in different areas of the United States when you are looking for a job. Talent shortages or surpluses in different labor markets can mean sizeable differences in pay for the same job.

table **9.1**

Determining Market Compensation Levels

O*NET Online: www.onetonline.org
Salaries Review: www.salariesreview.com
Salary.com: www.salary.com
Salary Expert: www.salaryexpert.com
America's Career InfoNet: www.acinet.org
College Grad Job Hunter: www.collegegrad.com
JobStar: http://jobstar.org
The Riley Guide: www.rileyguide.com

If money is important to you, and if you are flexible about where you live, a little research could help you earn a higher salary for the same work. Because money alone does not ensure happiness, be sure to factor in the cost of living and local amenities before deciding where your quality of life will be higher.

Compensation surveys are surveys of other organizations conducted to learn what they are paying for specific jobs or job classes. These surveys may be conducted by the organization with targeted labor market competitors, outsourced to a consulting firm, or purchased. It is often possible to purchase market pricing information from a variety of sources on the Internet or even find it for free at sites including Salary.com and PayScale.com. When buying market pricing data via the Internet, "free and cheap are not always the best value, and the job you're trying to price may not have a counterpart on even the most expensive lists, anyway."[45]

When a company places a different value on a job than does the local labor market, which happens for an estimated 10 to 20 percent of jobs, external labor market pricing will be insufficient.[46] For example, a company pursuing a customer service strategy may value cashiers more highly than a local competitor pursuing a low-cost strategy because employees in this customer-facing position are key to executing the business strategy. Additionally, if market rates are depressed due to gender or other types of bias, then this bias will also be reflected in the organization's pay structure.[47]

One compensation expert says, "The rule of thumb I like to use, and it will vary from company to company, but I think it's fairly accurate, is that for 80 to 90 percent of the jobs in your company, the internal value and the external value will be the same. So the value your firm places on, for example, an accountant is going to be the same as it is in your area's labor market. But for some jobs, it doesn't match, and that's where you need to use a combination of approaches."[48]

Benchmark jobs are jobs that tend to exist across departments and across diverse organizations, allowing them to be used as a basis for compensation comparisons. A benchmark job may have slightly different job titles across organizations, but it has enough consistency that it can be used as a basis for comparison.

Smaller organizations must often find ways to compete successfully for top talent without being able to pay top salaries. 2tor, a rapidly growing organization that develops technology platforms to enable universities to effectively deliver their curricula online, depends on top talent to maintain its competitive advantage and high growth rate, but it only pays at market levels. In addition to offering a full suite of benefits including a 401(k) plan, tuition reimbursement, and paid parental leave, 2tor focuses on creating a fun work environment and hiring people passionate about the company's goal of revolutionizing education by bringing great universities online.[49] A teamwork culture, free food, and fun parties keep employees feeling recognized, engaged, and rewarded.

Job Evaluation Methods

Job evaluation is a systematic process that uses expert judgment to assess differences in value between jobs. Job evaluation does not address employees, their performance, or their pay—only the relative size and value of a job compared to the others in the organization. Consistency and fairness are maximized by consistently assessing all organizational jobs using a common framework. A common job evaluation methodology translates all organization jobs into some kind of number, grade, or point total that can be used to put a dollar value on the worth of the job to the organization. We next discuss several of the most common job evaluation techniques.

Ranking Method.   The nonquantitative **ranking method** of job evaluation compares jobs to each other based on their overall worth to the organization or their relative difficulty to rank them from most to least valuable. The ranking is based on subjective judgments of

compensation surveys
surveys of other organizations conducted to learn what they are paying for specific jobs or job classes

benchmark jobs
jobs that tend to exist across departments and across diverse organizations, allowing them to be used as a basis for compensation comparisons

job evaluation
a systematic process that uses expert judgment to assess differences in value between jobs

ranking method
subjectively compares jobs to each other based on their overall worth to the organization

figure 9.2

The Ranking Method of Job Evaluation

Job Rank	Monthly Salary
1. Accountant	$8,000
2. Accountant assistant	$5,500
3. Receptionist	$4,000
4. Filing clerk	$3,000
5. Data Entry Specialist	$2,250

characteristics, including skill, the mental and physical effort required, responsibility, and working conditions. Because of the number of comparisons required, the ranking method is best for smaller organizations with less than 30 jobs to be evaluated.

The determination of pay level for each job is also subjective and depends on the nature of each job compared to those ranked above and below it. An example of the results of the ranking method for a small accounting business is shown in Figure 9.2.

job classification method
subjectively classifies jobs into an existing hierarchy of grades or categories

Job Classification Method. The **job classification method** of job analysis subjectively classifies jobs into an existing hierarchy of grades or categories. Each level in a grade or category has a description and list of associated job titles, and each job is subjectively assigned to the grade or category that is the closest match with the entire job. A common set of job grading standards developed for an occupation that distinguish different levels of work are used to ensure equity in assigning jobs to a grade or category.

Jobs of similar status are sometimes combined into a single category even when the requirements of the jobs differ. This can make it difficult to write comprehensive descriptions of each class, and it can oversimplify differences between jobs and classes. If the job grading standards have any built-in biases, protected groups might be negatively impacted. An example of the results of the job classification method of job analysis is shown in Figure 9.3.

point factor method
uses a set of compensable factors to determine a job's value

compensable factor
any characteristic used to provide a basis for judging a job's value

Point Factor Method. The **point factor method** of job evaluation uses a set of compensable factors to determine the value of each job. A **compensable factor** is any characteristic used to provide a basis for judging a job's value. After prioritizing each compensable factor in order of importance, each factor is subdivided into levels, which are assigned points. The compensable factors must be clearly and carefully established, and the levels of each factor must mean the same to all pay rates. Weights are then established for each compensable factor to calculate an overall point score for a job.

In applying the point factor method, benchmark jobs are selected based on their having equitable pay (neither overpaid nor underpaid) and representing a wide range of the

figure 9.3

The Job Classification Method of Job Evaluation

Class	Description
1	*Executives*: Including department manager and office manager.
2	*Skilled workers*: Including accountant, purchasing specialist, and trainer.
3	*Semiskilled workers*: Including machine operators and data entry specialists.
4	*Semiskilled workers*: Including cashiers and janitors.

compensable factors (e.g., some jobs would be at the low end of each factor and others at the high end). These benchmark jobs are rated on each factor, and the resulting points are summed to produce a total point score for each job. The benchmark jobs are then grouped by their total point scores and assigned to pay grades with similarly rated jobs with the total pay for each job divided into pay for each factor. Any necessary adjustments are then made to ensure equitable valuing of each factor. The remaining jobs in the organization are compared with the benchmark jobs, and the pay rates for each factor are summed to identify their pay rates. Point scores are often grouped into a single pay level. For example, jobs with point totals from 200 to 250 may all be paid $55,000.

It is best to use only a few compensable factors, which typically include four categories:

1. *Skill*: Including experience, ability, and education.
2. *Responsibilities*: Including both fiscal and supervisory duties.
3. *Effort*: Both mental and physical.
4. *Working conditions*: Including location, hazards, environmental extremes (e.g., working in a freezer or near a furnace).

Figure 9.4 shows an example of the results of the point factor method.

By considering core aspects of content and context that are common to all jobs, the point factor method provides a clear, understandable, and systematic method for defining and comparing the requirements for all types of jobs at all levels. Although this method can be used for a wide range of jobs, including newly created jobs, the judgments are subjective and biases can adversely affect protected groups of employees (e.g., minorities, older workers, or women). The method is also complex and time consuming to develop and use, and work that is complex, novel, or varied may be difficult to express in precise point values.

figure 9.4

The Point Factor Method of Job Evaluation

1. Point Values for Each Compensable Factor

Compensable Factor	Point Values for Each Level					Total
	1	2	3	4	5	
Skill	11	22	33	44	55	165
Responsibilities	10	20	30	40	50	150
Effort	6	12	18	24	30	90
Working Conditions	7	14	21	28	35	105
Maximum total points for all factors based on their importance to the job						510

2. Converting Points into Pay Level

Job	Hourly Pay	Hourly Pay for Skill	Hourly Pay for Responsibilities	Hourly Pay for Effort	Hourly Pay for Working Conditions
Office Manager	$21.50	$9.50	$6.50	$5.00	$ .50
Payroll Specialist	$17.00	$7.50	$5.00	$4.00	$ .50
Data Entry Specialist	$12.50	$6.00	$2.50	$2.50	$1.50
Receptionist	$10.00	$5.00	$2.00	$2.00	$1.00

Hay Group Guide Chart–Profile Method
a point–factor system is used to produce both a profile and a point score for each position

Hay Group Guide Chart–Profile Method.   The **Hay Group Guide Chart–Profile Method** of job evaluation extends the point factor method. The Hay Group method dates to the 1950s and is used extensively to evaluate executive, managerial, supervisory, and professional white- and blue-collar jobs.[50] For each job, a point–factor system is used to produce a profile in which the weight and relationship of the factors reflects the size and nature of the job. For example, problem solving is weighted more heavily than accountability for research jobs, but the reverse is true for production line jobs.[51]

The Hay Group method analyzes jobs based on four main factors:[52]

1. *Know-how*: The level of knowledge, skills, and experience necessary for fully acceptable job performance.
2. *Problem solving*: The span, complexity, and level of analytical, evaluative, and innovative thought required by the job.
3. *Accountability*: The job holder's discretion to direct resources or to influence or determine the course of events, and his/her accountability for the consequences of his/her decisions and actions.
4. *Working conditions*: The working environment, mental stress, physical risks, and sensory attention and physical effort needed. Working conditions is typically used for nonexempt jobs and excluded for managerial positions.

One weakness of the Hay Guide Chart is that it may have a gender bias. The choice of factors is skewed towards traditional management values, consistently valuing male-dominated management functions more highly than the nonmanagement functions more likely to be performed by women.[53] This can be an issue if the organization must legally defend a gender-based pay disparity. In the European Union, using a job evaluation can provide a legal defense for equal pay claims, but care must be taken to ensure that the method used does not have a gender bias.[54]

Position Analysis Questionnaire

Position Analysis Questionnaire
a structured job evaluation questionnaire that is statistically analyzed to calculate pay rates based on how the labor market is valuing worker characteristics

The **Position Analysis Questionnaire** (PAQ) is a job analysis technique that is also useful in evaluating jobs for compensation purposes. Rather than using subjective judgments of jobs' compensable factors, the PAQ uses statistical determinations of how the labor market is actually valuing worker characteristics. The PAQ is a structured job analysis questionnaire that is subdivided into six sections covering 187 job elements. For example, one section uses 35 job elements to assess the types of information sources that a worker must perceive.

The publisher controls all aspects of the PAQ's use from its acquisition through its processing and statistical analysis.[55] The job evaluation equation used to score the PAQ is proprietary but is empirically derived from the labor market. The job evaluator enters ratings of the 187 job elements into a computer that generates the job evaluation point total for the job. The factors and their weights can be tailored for an organization.

Job Pricing

Job evaluations typically result in either a ranking of jobs in terms of their value to the organization or the assignment of a point total to each job based on its relative value to the organization. **Job pricing** is the generation of salary structures and pay levels for each job based on the job evaluation data. The three most common job pricing systems are the single-rate system, pay grades, and broadbanding, which we discuss next.

job pricing
the generation of salary structures and pay levels for each job based on the job evaluation data

Single-Rate System

Under a single-rate pay system, a single market-determined rate is paid for the job. All employees performing the job are paid the same rate. A single-rate system is appropriate when the job doesn't allow for a significant performance difference across employees and when the employee is paid for time on the job or for simply completing the job as directed. For example, lower-level service jobs that allow employees little discretion in how they do the work or assembly line jobs that must be performed a certain way are good candidates for a single-rate pay system. Unions often like single-rate pay systems because judgment-based pay differences are eliminated.

Pay Grades

Many organizations, including the military, base their compensation plans on pay grades or pay scales. A **pay grade** is the range of possible pay for a group of jobs. A pay grade is derived from factors including necessary education, tasks performed, and required skills and abilities. New hires typically start at the minimum pay rate and work their way up the pay grade.

A pay grade clarifies compensation by communicating what an employee's base compensation will be based on how long they hold the job. Although this method does not work for some positions, including CEO or sales, it is effective for most positions. Figure 9.5 illustrates a hypothetical pay grade structure for four different pay grades.

A pay grade's salary maximum does not have to be higher than the minimum of the next higher grade, although it can be. The salary range in a pay grade is typically plus or minus 15 to 25 percent of the midpoint. The midpoint of a pay grade is usually 20 to 30 percent higher than the midpoint of the preceding pay grade. When employees have reached or are above their pay range maximums, approximately half of companies use lump-sum bonuses to continue to reward and incentivize them.[56]

Organizations usually design pay grades by looking at the positions in their company and identifying basic factors including education needed, tasks involved, and skills and abilities required. The military's pay grade structure compensates its people based on their rank and their time in service at that rank. This type of approach works well because employees know from the time of enlisting what their base income is, as well as what it will be after a certain length of time. Although this method of delineating and communicating compensation grades works for most positions, it doesn't work as well for positions such as CEO or sales representative.

Broadbanding

Broadbanding is the use of very wide pay grades (for example, salary ranges of plus or minus 30 to 60 percent of the salary midpoint) to increase pay flexibility. Looking at Figure 9.5, pay grades 1 and 2 might be consolidated into band A and grades 3 and 4 into band B. Broadbanding was popularized in the 1990s to support flatter, faster, de-bureaucratized organizational cultures and to empower managers to make compensation decisions. The cost-control mechanisms of narrower bands are sacrificed under broadbanding, which increases the potential for employees to float to the top of their pay bands and become overpaid relative to the market. The successful adoption of broadbanding requires managers to be trained in the approach as this method puts them in charge of the majority of pay decisions.

pay grade
(or pay scale) the range of possible pay for a group of jobs

broadbanding
using very wide pay grades to increase pay flexibility

figure **9.5**

Pay Grade Structure

Grade	Salary Minimum	Salary Midpoint	Salary Maximum
1	$12,000	$15,000	$18,000
2	$14,500	$19,000	$23,500
3	$18,000	$23,000	$28,000
4	$22,000	$29,000	$36,000

Communicating Compensation

Pay is important to employees because it's more than a number—it's an emotional measure of how valued an employee feels. This feeling of one's value plays a large role in how engaged we are in our work. Unfortunately, perceptions about pay often don't reflect reality, even if the employer pays above average rates. In fact, two-thirds of surveyed people who were being paid the market rate believed that they were actually *underpaid*, representing a huge discrepancy and unnecessarily decreasing their engagement.[57]

How well employees understand the organization's compensation plan and philosophy also influences the effectiveness of the compensation system in meeting its goals. Even if an organization pays well, if employees believe that it does not, then the compensation plan is unlikely to have maximum impact. Clearly communicating compensation plans is worth the effort and can lead to harder-working, more engaged, and more productive employees.[58]

? so what

Clearly communicating compensation plans can increase perceptions of fairness and improve motivation and retention.

Compensation plans can be difficult to explain because of the many factors that go into developing them. Nonetheless, compensation plans should be explained to employees in as simple and understandable a way as possible. In addition to pay level, it is important to communicate salary advancement potential and timing. A below-market starting pay level might be more acceptable if a recruit or employee knows that there is a lot of room for salary and career advancement over a reasonable period of time with high performance or additional skill development.

Accounting and consulting giant PricewaterhouseCoopers (PwC) launched an initiative to better communicate to employees how it determines the compensation ranges for all of its service and nonpartner levels. PwC now communicates to each employee the PwC salary midpoint and average and the market midpoint and average for their position. The new communication system tells employees where they are relative to their peers and creates an open dialogue in the performance review process about why they are earning what they are and what they need to do to earn more.[59]

Supervisors and supporting HRM professionals should be readily available to explain compensation plans to employees and to answer any questions. This can improve fairness perceptions as employees better understand differing pay rates across their unit and the company. Open communication can also provide an opportunity for HRM to receive feedback about compensation issues that may arise if market rates change.

PwC lets every employee know both the midpoint and average salary levels for their position for both PwC and the external labor market. This helps to create an open dialog about why employees are earning what they are, and what they need to do to increase their salary.

Compensation Issues

Getting compensation policy right is essential to organizational performance. Organizations strive to balance salary costs with fairness, and most try to treat employees as equitably as possible. To minimize compensation-related lawsuits, organizations should establish a procedure for hearing and adjusting wage complaints. Wages should be sufficient to provide a reasonable standard of living and not exploit employees. In addition, wages should be paid promptly and correctly. To help manage ethical issues, checks and balances should be put in place to prevent financial abuse.

efficiency wages
above-market wages raise labor productivity and/or decrease employer costs enough to pay for the cost of the higher wages

When Wal-Mart, a retailer known for reducing costs by treating wages as an expense to be minimized, wanted to reduce a slide in store performance and counter increasing threats from other retailers, it decided to try paying its workers more.[60] **Efficiency wages** is the economics term for the idea that above-market wages raise labor productivity and/or decrease employer costs enough to pay for the cost of the higher wages. The gains from the higher wages might include greater productivity, lower turnover, less shirking, higher-quality hires, and healthier workers resulting from their higher incomes.[61] Wal-Mart also improved employees' schedules and work hours and began providing more training to provide a clearer path for hourly employees wanting to get into higher-paying management jobs. The effort seems to be working, with customer survey scores rising for 90 consecutive weeks and sales up more than the average for its competitors. Employee spending at Wal-Mart has also risen, offsetting some of the cost of the pay increase.[62]

Organizations must also manage issues related to pay equity and team, executive, and global compensation. We discuss these next, in addition to ethical compensation issues.

Equity

As we discussed earlier, organizations pay people for what they do—their jobs. Doing this effectively both attracts and retains appropriate talent and preserves feelings of fairness among employees who are paid differently. Two of the most often cited fairness principles underlying compensation systems are:

1. Equal pay for equal work
2. Higher pay for more important work.

Compensation equity is evaluated both internally and externally. **Internal equity** exists when employees perceive their pay to be fair relative to the pay of other jobs in the organization. Most people would find it inequitable if a lower level position is paid more than their job. **Employee equity** refers to the perceived fairness of the relative pay between employees performing similar jobs for the same organization. If a new employee with less experience and lower skills is paid more than a higher performing, experienced employee, then the experienced employee is likely to perceive unfairness. **External equity** exists when an organization's employees believe that their pay is fair when compared to what other employers pay their employees who perform similar jobs. If a local competitor pays employees 20 percent more than their employer pays them, they probably don't feel that this is fair.

Because employees who feel unfairly paid are less motivated and more likely to leave, it is important to attend to equity perceptions when developing or evaluating a compensation system. Two of the most common equity issues in compensation are comparable worth and wage rate compression.

Comparable Worth.   The idea of **comparable worth** is that if two jobs have equal difficulty requirements, the pay should be the same, regardless of who fills them. The issue is not whether women and men should be paid the same for doing the same job, but that jobs that tend to be held by women (e.g., housekeeper or secretary) tend to be paid less than those that tend to be held by men (e.g., mechanic or truck driver) even though the jobs contribute equally to organizational performance.

The reasons why the gender pay gap exists are still unclear, although factors including discrimination against women, women staying out of the workforce for extended periods due to family responsibilities, and job evaluation techniques that undervalue female occupations are all thought to contribute to the issue.

Wage Rate Compression.   **Wage rate compression** happens when starting salaries for new hires exceed the salaries paid to experienced employees. Wage rate compression is an internal equity issue that can create morale problems and increase turnover of highly skilled and experienced employees as they seek higher salaries elsewhere. The primary cause of

---

internal equity
when employees perceive their pay to be fair relative to the pay of other jobs in the organization

employee equity
the perceived fairness of the relative pay between employees performing similar jobs for the same organization

so what?

Employees evaluate the fairness of their pay based on comparisons with coworkers and with what other employers pay similar employees.

external equity
when an organization's employees believe that their pay is fair when compared to what other employers pay their employees who perform similar jobs

comparable worth
if two jobs have equal difficulty requirements, the pay should be the same, regardless of who fills them

wage rate compression
starting salaries exceed the salaries paid to experienced employees

wage rate compression is increasing market rates for skills that are in short supply. Some ways organizations can address wage compression are to:

- Increase the pay of experienced employees the organization would like to retain by giving them equity adjustments;
- Develop experienced employees for promotion to higher-paying positions; and
- Introduce pay-for-performance plans that give high-performing employees the opportunity to earn higher pay.

Team Compensation

? so what

If work is performed in interdependent teams, rewarding "star" performers can undermine team effectiveness.

Team rewards motivate effective teamwork behaviors. Tying team rewards to team performance motivates team members to pursue team goals rather than individual goals.[63] Interdependent work teams require organizations to shift the emphasis of their compensation and rewards programs from individual to team rewards. Any remaining individual rewards should acknowledge employees who are effective team players—people who freely share their expertise, help when needed, and improve their teams. A "star" system that rewards only individual performance undermines team effectiveness. Some individual rewards may be appropriate for rewarding particularly critical individual contributions to the team, but the bulk of rewards, typically at least 80 percent, need to be made at the team level.

The focus of effective team-based reward and recognition systems is promoting teamwork and accomplishing the team's goals while meeting individual members' needs. Southwest Airlines is an example of a company that relies heavily on collective rewards such as profit sharing and stock ownership to promote teamwork. Unlike other airlines, Southwest also allows flight crews to check the box "team delay" to avoid wasting time assessing and placing blame for problems instead of solving them.[64]

This chapter's Develop Your Skills feature gives you the chance to identify whether you are likely to enjoy working in a team based work system.

Develop Your Skills

Would You Enjoy Working in a Team-Based Work System?[65]

Many organizations have adopted team-based work systems, and it is likely that you will work in a team at some point in your career. Performing your best and maximally enjoying your job depends in part on finding a work-and-rewards environment that fits your work style and motivational preferences. This self-assessment gives you the opportunity to identify your attitude toward teamwork and receiving rewards based on the performance of your team rather than working alone and receiving individually based rewards. Understanding your attitudes toward teamwork and team-based pay will help you identify the work environment that will best motivate you.

Use the following scale to respond to the statements below. Please answer honestly—there are no right or wrong answers. When you are finished, follow the scoring instructions below.

Strongly Disagree	Disagree	Slightly Disagree	Neutral	Slightly Agree	Agree	Strongly Agree
(1)	(2)	(3)	(4)	(5)	(6)	(7)

Continued

_____1. I generally prefer to work as part of a team.

_____2. Teams perform better when all team members get the same rewards.

_____3. I find that working as a member of a team increases my ability to perform effectively.

_____4. It makes sense to give rewards to team members based primarily on the overall performance of the team.

_____5. I feel that, if given a choice, I would prefer to work in a team rather than work alone.

_____6. I like to be rewarded based solely on my performance, not my team's performance.

Scoring

For statements 2 and 6, subtract your response from 8, and replace your initial response with this new number. Add up your responses to the six statements, using the new number for these two statements and your original response for the other four statements to calculate your preference for team-based work score.

Interpretation

If your score is 36 or higher, you have a preference for team-based work and may enjoy working in a team setting. If your score is 12 or lower, you have a preference for individual rather than team based work and rewards and may not enjoy working in team-based environments. If your score is in between 13 and 35, you do not have a strong preference for team-based or individual work.

Executive Compensation

Executive compensation deserves special attention. Not only are the base salaries of executives higher than those of low-level-managers or operative personnel, executives frequently operate under bonus and stock option plans that can dramatically increase their total financial rewards. Senior executives at IBM, General Electric, or Merck may earn multiple millions of dollars in addition to base salary and special benefits such as golden parachutes that other employees do not receive. A **golden parachute** refers to lucrative benefits including bonuses and stock options given to executives in the event a company is taken over. Alan Fishman led Washington Mutual for 17 days before it failed and left with $19 million in signing bonuses and severance pay thanks to his golden parachute.[66]

golden parachute
lucrative benefits given to executives in the event the company is taken over

Does it matter if the CEO receives a generous compensation package? Although the research is inconclusive, a greater pay differential between executives and lower-level employees has been found to be related to lower product quality[67] and employee feelings of inequity. Many shareholder activists and even CEOs are calling for corporate boards of directors to implement internal pay equity policies, keeping CEO pay to a reasonable multiple of the company's most senior managers. Not only would such policies reduce excess spending and unnecessarily high CEO compensation expenditures, but it would also address inequities and a growing disconnect between the CEO and his or her senior management team.[68] GE CEO Jeffrey Immelt said, "To motivate staff and avoid excesses, chief executives' pay should remain within a small multiple of the pay of their 25 most senior managers. The key relationship is the one between the CEO and the top 25 managers in the company because that is the key team. Should the CEO make five times, three times, or twice what this group make? That is debatable, but 20 times is lunacy."[69]

so what

Paying top executives too much more than lower-level employees can decrease perceptions of fairness and company performance.

"To motivate staff and avoid excesses, chief executives' pay should remain within a small multiple of the pay of their 25 most senior managers."

—**Jeffrey Immelt, CEO, GE**

Motivated by perceived inequities in executive compensation, the 2010 Dodd–Frank Wall Street Reform and Consumer Protection Act mandates periodic shareholder approval of executive compensation. Some organizations are taking steps to better align executives' pay with their performance and risk strategies. In the aftermath of the subprime mortgage crisis, Credit Suisse gave executives some of the toxic assets as part of their compensation plans.[70]

Dodd-Frank also included a requirement that publicly traded companies publish, in addition to CEO pay figures, both median worker pay and the ratio between CEO and median worker pay. The requirement was created amid claims that executive pay incentives fueled excessive risk before the 2008 financial crisis and is supported by unions and worker advocacy groups who say it is a helpful metric in keeping track of excessive CEO pay.[71]

Executive compensation can also be a strong signal of what a company values. When executives reduce their own salaries in tough economic times, this can make it easier for employees to also accept pay cuts and stay engaged. This chapter's Strategic Impact feature highlights the impact that executive compensation can have during challenging economic times.

Global Compensation

Compensation becomes even more complex when organizations must pay employees in multiple parts of the world. Not only do laws differ in different countries, tax policies, inflation rates, currency exchange rates, and the cost of living must also be addressed. To manage these issues, organizations often turn to these policies:

- *Cost-of-living adjustments*: Pay increases to account for a higher cost of living in one country versus another.
- *Housing allowance*: Payments to subsidize or cover housing and related costs (such as utilities) in high-cost areas.
- *Hardship premiums*: Increased salary for living in an area with a lower quality of life or less safety (often necessary for employees assigned to third-world countries).
- *Tax equalization payments*: Increased salary to make up for higher taxes that reduce take-home pay and decrease employees' purchasing power; some countries have no income tax, whereas others have income tax rates exceeding 50 percent; and some U.S. states have no income tax, whereas others have income tax rates that can exceed 10 percent.
- *Inflation adjustments*: Larger and/or more frequent raises to maintain employees' purchasing power in the face of inflation.

Strategic Impact Feature

Executive Pay Cuts to Prevent Layoffs

During the recession in 2009, Rob Katz, CEO of Vail Resorts in Colorado, cut his $840,000 annual salary to $0 before asking his employees to take pay cuts as well to help employees save their jobs. To save more than $10 million, the board of directors took a pay cut of 20 percent, executives 10 percent, and seasonal workers 2.5 percent, and only 50 of the resort's 15,000 employees had to be laid off.[72]

This chapter's Global Issues feature explores the importance of global compensation norms to multinational corporations.

Global Issues

Global Compensation Issues at Johnson & Johnson

Multinational organizations that conduct business globally must constantly deal with international compensation issues. For example, Johnson & Johnson, featured in this chapter's opening Real World Challenge, is sensitive to global differences in compensation norms. To keep up with hyperinflation, its businesses in Venezuela and Argentina perform frequent salary reviews. J&J businesses in China and Indonesia are also less transparent than J&J businesses in other global regions about salary levels due to national sensitivities.[73]

Compensation Laws and Regulations

Numerous federal and state laws and regulations influence compensation. The three most important federal laws affecting compensation are the Fair Labor Standards Act, the Equal Pay Act, and workers' compensation.

The Fair Labor Standards Act

The **Fair Labor Standards Act (FLSA)** was passed in 1938 to stimulate economic recovery from the Great Depression. The FLSA is a federal law that sets standards for minimum wages, overtime pay, and equal pay (added under the 1963 Equal Pay Act) for men and women performing the same jobs. Employers may not fire or discriminate in any other manner against an employee for filing a complaint or participating in a legal proceeding under FLSA.

The FLSA applies to organizations with employees who engage in interstate commerce, produce goods for interstate commerce, or handle, sell, or work on goods or materials that have been moved in or produced for interstate commerce. The FLSA also covers domestic service workers, such as housekeepers, cooks, and full-time babysitters, who receive at least $1,400 in cash wages from one employer in a calendar year, or if they work a total of more than eight hours a week for one or more employers. Let's explore the implications of the FLSA on overtime pay and minimum wage in more detail.

Overtime Pay. **Exempt employees** are employees who meet one of the FLSA exemption tests, are paid a fixed salary, and are not entitled to overtime. **Nonexempt employees** (not exempt from coverage) are employees who do not meet any one of the FLSA exemption tests and are paid on an hourly basis and covered by wage and hour laws regarding minimum wage, overtime pay, and hours worked. Limited exceptions apply to doctors, lawyers, teachers, and outside sales employees. Under the FLSA, all employees are considered nonexempt unless the employee's position meets specific exemption criteria or unless the regulations specifically allow an exemption that the employer has opted to use.

Fair Labor Standards Act (FLSA)
a federal law that sets standards for minimum wages, overtime pay, and equal pay for men and women performing the same jobs

exempt employees
meet one of the FLSA exemption tests, are paid on a fixed-salary basis, and are not entitled to overtime

nonexempt employees
do not meet any one of the FLSA exemption tests and are paid on an hourly basis and covered by wage and hour laws regarding minimum wage, overtime pay, and hours worked

An employee who meets the salary and job duties criteria may be exempt from FLSA minimum wage and overtime pay requirements under various exemptions. Exemptions include:

- *Executives* whose primary duty is managing the company or a department.
- *Administrators* performing office or nonmanual work directly related to running the company.
- *Creative professionals* including composers, singers, and professionals whose primary duty consists of performing work requiring advanced knowledge (beyond high school) that is primarily intellectual in character and includes the exercise of discretion and independent judgment.

When state overtime laws differ from federal requirements, the employee is entitled to overtime pay for the actual time worked based on the higher standard. Time paid for but not actually worked (vacation, sick leave, holidays, and other paid leave) is excluded. Private employers cannot provide compensatory time off in lieu of overtime pay, although with employee agreement, state and local government employers may provide compensatory time off. If an employee works unauthorized overtime, it must be paid—unauthorized overtime is a disciplinary issue, not a compensation issue. Compensable time for covered, nonexempt employees may include:

- Travel
- Meetings
- Training
- Rest and meal periods
- On-call duty
- Changing clothes and preparing for work

Minimum Wage. A primary goal of the FLSA was to ensure a maximum number of jobs paying at least a minimum livable wage. Right now, the federal minimum wage is $7.25 per hour. When violations of wage and hour laws are found, Department of Labor investigators may recommend changes in employment practices to establish compliance. Employers who willfully or repeatedly violate the minimum wage or overtime pay requirements are subject to a civil money penalty of up to $1,100 for each violation.

State laws often affect minimum wage rates for different industries. When an employee is covered by both state and federal minimum wage laws, the employee is entitled to the higher wage rate.

The Equal Pay Act

The basic provisions of the Equal Pay Act are prohibitions against gender-based wage discrimination. Employees in the same company who are performing work that requires equal skill, effort, and responsibility and who are performing under similar working conditions must *not* be paid differently based on gender. Pay differentials are permissible if based on factors other than gender such as seniority, education, and experience and may also be paid for shift work, dissimilar working conditions, and additional job duties or for additional skills.

The Equal Employment Opportunity Commission (EEOC) administers and enforces the Equal Pay Act. The penalties for violations are the recovery of:

- *Compensatory damages* for intentional discrimination.
- *Punitive damages* for discrimination that is intentional and engaged in with malice or reckless indifference to the federally protected rights of the employee.

Caps on the amount of compensatory and punitive damages are determined by the size of the employer.

Employees ordinarily bear the burden of proof under FLSA, but the employer can be obligated to give employees access to work records so that they can attempt to prove claims. If the employer has not adequately maintained records, the court may accept the employee's claim and require the employer to disprove the allegations.

Workers' Compensation

Workers' compensation is a type of insurance that replaces wages and medical benefits for employees injured on the job in exchange for relinquishing the employee's right to sue the employer for negligence. Payments can include weekly payments to replace wages, compensation for past and future economic loss, payment or reimbursement of medical expenses, and dependent benefits if the worker is killed during employment.

In the United States, most employees injured on the job have an absolute right to medical care for any injury and often monetary payments to compensate for any resulting disabilities. Most employers must obtain workers' compensation insurance or risk financial penalties. Commercial insurance companies offer these policies, and if the employer is deemed an excessive risk to insure at market rates, it can obtain coverage through an assigned-risk program.

Workers' compensation is administered on a state-by-state basis and overseen by a state governing board. Many states have established public uninsured employer funds to pay benefits to workers whose employers illegally fail to purchase insurance.

workers' compensation
a type of insurance that replaces wages and medical benefits for employees injured on the job in exchange for relinquishing the employee's right to sue the employer for negligence

so what?

Workers' compensation insurance is mandatory for most employers.

Summary and Application

Compensation is a critical HRM activity due to its influence on employee motivation and behavior as well as its cost to the organization. Strategic compensation policies can reduce labor cost per unit of output and motivate employees to perform better and develop their skills. What an individual is paid is affected by the organization, job, employee, and various external forces. Market pricing, various job evaluation methods, and the Position Analysis Questionnaire are some of the methods used to evaluate jobs to determine their relative worth to the organization. Job pricing then converts this information into salary structures and pay levels for each job.

Organizations must also manage challenges including ethical issues, pay equity, and team, executive, and global compensation. Numerous federal and state laws affect compensation, including the Fair Labor Standards Act, the Equal Pay Act, and workers' compensation. Although all managers must be familiar with compensation policies and legislation, because there is so much to know about compensation, it is also a specialty area within the field of HRM.

Real World Response

Strategic Global Compensation at Johnson & Johnson

Johnson & Johnson (J&J) wanted to standardize its compensation practices across its business units and global regions to increase employees' opportunities to move internationally and create a more consistent employee experience throughout the company.[74] To do this, it conducted a job evaluation to establish job frameworks, using varying levels of rigor at different organizational levels. Global compensation and executive teams performed job evaluations for J&J's 500 top executives, and local HR and regional compensation teams mapped the jobs of 22,000 managers and 98,000 other staff.[75]

J&J then standardized compensation across its various businesses and regions, making it easier for its workers to move around within the company. The company gave businesses two years to move everyone into the new pay ranges, and no employee's pay was decreased during the change.[76] Performance bonus targets increased for 27 percent of employees, stayed the same for 35 percent, and decreased for 38 percent. Starting in 2011, employees with salaries above their pay grade received lump-sum payments instead of raises until their salary fell within the appropriate pay grade.[77]

Although the cost savings from the changes were minimal, this wasn't the goal. The new global compensation system is intended to be more consistent and equitable for employees across the company. The changes have allowed J&J to develop single career models across its businesses, improve succession planning, more easily integrate newly acquired companies, and allow The Johnson and Johnson Family of Companies to present a more uniform face at graduate recruitment fairs.[78]

Takeaway Points

1. Financial compensation is the pay an employee receives in the form of wages, salary, bonuses, and commissions. Nonfinancial compensation are the rewards received that are not financial in nature, including free meals, a casual dress code, and skill development.

2. The organization, job, individual employee, and external forces all influence direct financial compensation. Organizations can choose to be pay leaders or pay followers, and they may not have the ability to pay high wages even if they would like to. Different jobs have different values to the organization. Individuals who make larger contributions to organizational performance often receive higher pay than those who do not. The labor market, economic factors, labor unions, and legislation also influence direct financial compensation.

3. Market pricing is the use of external sources of information about how others are compensating a certain position to assign value to a company's similar job. Job evaluation is a more systematic process that uses expert judgment to assess jobs' relative value. Ranking subjectively compares jobs to each other. Job classification subjectively classifies jobs into an existing hierarchy of grades or categories. The point factor method uses a set of compensable factors to determine a job's value. The Hay Group Guide Chart–Profile Method uses the point–factor method to produce a profile and point score for each position. The Position Analysis Questionnaire is a structured job evaluation questionnaire that is statistically analyzed to calculate pay raises based on how the labor market is valuing worker characteristics.

4. The single-rate system, pay grades, and broadbanding are most commonly used for job pricing.

5. Equity, compensating teams, global compensation, and executive compensation are special issues facing many organizations.

6. The Fair Labor Standards Act covers minimum wages and overtime requirements. The Equal Pay Act prohibits gender-based wage discrimination. Workers' compensation is a type of insurance that replaces wages and medical benefits for employees injured on the job.

Discussion Questions

1. When should an organization be a pay leader, and when should it be a pay follower?
2. Why would nurses in one state be paid more than nurses in another state for doing the same job?
3. What do you think is the maximum appropriate difference between the CEO and the organization's lowest paid employee? Why?

4. Would you work for below-market wages? Why or why not? Is there any time when you would consider accepting below-market pay?

5. If you were experiencing wage compression and found yourself being paid less than new hires, what would you do?

6. Do you think that executives should receive golden parachutes when they leave a company? Why or why not?

Personal Development Exercise: Negotiate a Pay Raise

In this exercise, you will negotiate a pay raise with a partner.

Role for Employee

Imagine that you have been working as a consultant for two years and have not received a pay raise despite being one of your work group's best performers. The organization has frozen salaries over this time due to a weak economic environment, but recently business has picked up, and you've heard rumors of some employees in other departments getting raises again. You currently make $60,000, but if raises hadn't been frozen, you figure you would be earning at least $70,000 by now.

You feel that you might need to look for other jobs if your pay doesn't increase soon. You believe you could get at least $68,000 at another company, plus future raises that are still frozen at your current employer. You decide to approach your supervisor to ask for a raise. Call your partner by his/her real name, and do your best to persuade him or her to give you a raise.

Role for Supervisor

Your organization has survived a tough two years. As consultants, your business suffers the ups and down of the economy. Fortunately, the pay freeze your company established two years ago helped save enough money that layoffs were avoided. Although the organization has seen an increase in business lately, management is not convinced that a recovery is sustainable and has asked supervisors like you to remain frugal to help prevent future layoffs if the downturn continues.

An employee is about to approach you to ask for a raise. This employee is currently making $60,000, which is the average for the employee's workgroup. Like the rest of your employees, this employee has not received a pay raise for two years. This person is one of your best performers.

You do have some discretion over your subordinates' salaries, and you have heard of other managers giving modest increases to top performers with other job offers. All your team members are performing well, and you would hate to have to let any of them go. Hear the employee out, and use his/her real name.

Strategic HRM Exercises

Exercise: Compensation Decisions

Imagine that you own a small clothing store specializing in men's suits. Your business strategy is to be a low-cost provider of quality suits. You have a staff of five people, all of whom receive an annual salary:

- One buyer responsible for choosing and acquiring the store's merchandise
- Two salespeople (salary only, no commission)

- One cashier
- One store manager

1. How would you allocate your $200,000 salary budget across these four positions to best align your pay structure with your business strategy? Explain your decisions.

Now imagine that you own a small clothing store specializing in men's suits, but your business strategy is to provide high-quality customer service. You have a staff of five people, all of whom receive an annual salary:

- One buyer responsible for choosing and acquiring the store's merchandise
- Two salespeople (salary only, no commission)
- One cashier
- One store manager

2. How would you allocate your $200,000 salary budget across these four positions to best align your pay structure with your business strategy? Explain your decisions.

Exercise: How Much Are You Likely to Earn?

Using any three of the online resources listed in Table 9.1, "Determining Market Compensation Levels," identify the salary range you could expect to earn in a position you are considering in an area of the United States in which you are considering living. Then answer the following questions:

1. Do the sources you chose tend to provide similar salary estimates?
2. Is the salary range what you expected? Why or why not?
3. How can tools like these be useful to HRM professionals as well as job seekers?

Exercise: Designing Compensation Packages

We would like to thank Professor Robert T. Mooney at Texas State University for this exercise idea.

Using online resources including BLS.gov and O*NET, design a financial compensation package for the same job in two different states. Assume that each location is free to pay prevailing local wages. You are free to choose the states and the job that interest you. One suggestion is to choose a job you are considering pursuing and two states in which you would consider living.

Exercise: Workers' Compensation: Should Heroism at Work Be Covered?

View the video, "News Report; Regarding Workers Comp Lawsuit" (2:59). After watching the video, answer the following questions:

1. Do you think that the employee's injuries should be covered by workers' compensation? Why or why not?
2. Why do you think the claim was denied? What might be the risk of approving the employee's workers' compensation claim?
3. How could McDonald's prevent this issue from happening again?

Integrative Project

Using the same job you used for the previous chapter, describe the base compensation you would establish for this position in the U.S. city of your choice. Be sure to describe the process you used in making your decision. Use at least three of the Web resources in Table 9.1 in completing this assignment.

Video Case

Imagine that a subordinate who has worked for Happy Time Toys for a year asks to speak with you. She just learned that a newly hired coworker is making $1/hour more than her, and she feels that this is unfair. *What do you say or do?* Go to this book's video case, watch the challenge video for this chapter, and choose the best video response. Be sure to also view the outcomes of the two responses you didn't choose.

Discussion Questions

1. Which aspects of HRM discussed in this chapter are illustrated in this video? Explain your answer.
2. What ethical issues are illustrated in this video? Explain your answer.
3. As a manager at Happy Time Toys, what else might you do to handle this situation? Explain your answer.

Endnotes

1. Johnson & Johnson. (2017). About Johnson & Johnson. Retrieved March 20, 2017, from https://www.jnj.com/about-jnj

2. O'Donovan, D. (2011, June 6). Johnson and Johnson rolls out global compensation strategy. *Jobsbody.* Retrieved March 20, 2017, from http://jobsbody.blogspot.com/2011/06/johnson-and-johnson-rolls-out-global.html

3. Rockoff, J. D. (2010, February 17). J&J to cut bonus targets for some. *The Wall Street Journal.* Retrieved March 20, 2017, from http://online.wsj.com/article/SB10001424052748704398804575071720286022184.html

4. O'Donovan, D. (2011, June 6). Johnson and Johnson rolls out global compensation strategy. *Jobsbody.* Retrieved July 30, 2011, from http://jobsbody.blogspot.com/2011/06/johnson-and-johnson-rolls-out-global.html

5. Gerhart, B., & Milkovich, G. T. (1990). Organizational differences in managerial compensation and financial performance. *Academy of Management Journal, 4,* 663–691.

6. Kohls. (2017). Our total rewards. Retrieved March 20, 2017, from http://kohlscareers.com/our-total-rewards/

7. Top 10 quotes about rewards and recognition. (2014, November 10). *Awards Network.* Retrieved May 7, 2017, from http://blog.awardsnetwork.com/top-10-quotes-rewards-recognition

8. Milkovich, G. T., & Newman, J. (2002). *Compensation,* 7th ed. Homewood, IL: Irwin.

9. Gomez-Mejia, L. R., & Balkin, D. B. (1992). *Compensation, organizational strategy, and firm performance.* Cincinnati, OH: South-Western; Montemayor, E. F. (1996). Congruence between pay policy and competitive strategy in high performing firms. *Journal of Management, 22,* 889–908.

10. Milkovich, G. T., & Newman, J. (2002). *Compensation,* 7th ed. Homewood, IL: Irwin.

11. Pitts, R. A. (1976). Diversification strategies and organizational policies of large diversified firms. *Journal of Economics and Business, 8,* 181–188.

12. Milkovich, G. T., & Newman, J. (2002). *Compensation,* 7th ed. Homewood, IL: Irwin.

13. Pfeffer, J., & Davis-Blake, A. (1987). Understanding organizational wage structures: A resource dependence approach. *Academy of Management Journal, 30,* 437–455.

14. Milkovich, G. T., & Newman, J. (2002). *Compensation,* 7th ed., pp. 664 Homewood, IL: Irwin.

15. Gerhart, B. (2000). Compensation strategy and organizational performance. In S. Rynes & B. Gerhart (Eds.), *Compensation in organizations.* San Francisco, CA. Jossey-Bass.

16. Gerhart, B., & Milkovich, G. T. (1990). Organizational differences in managerial compensation and financial performance. *Academy of Management Journal, 4,* 663–691.

17. Eisenhardt, K. M. (1988). Agency- and institutional-theory explanations: The case of retail sales compensation. *Academy of Management Journal, 31,* 488–511; Jensen, M., & Meckling, W. H. (1976). Theory of the firm: Managerial behavior, agency costs and ownership structure. *Journal of Financial Economics, 4,* 305–360; Vroom, V. (1964). *Work and motivation.* New York: Wiley.

18. David, P., Hitt, M. H., & Gimeno, J. (2001). The influence of activism by institutional investors on R&D. *Academy of Management Journal, 44,* 144–158.

19. Igalens, J., & Roussel, P. (1999). A study of the relationships between compensation package, work motivation, and job satisfaction. *Journal of Organizational Behavior, 20,* 1103–1025.

20. Peterson, S. J., & Luthans, F. (2006). The impact of financial and nonfinancial incentives on business–unit outcomes over time. *Journal of Applied Psychology, 91,* 156–165.

21. Pfeffer, J., & Salancik, G. R. (1978). *The external control of organizations: A resource dependence perspective.* Maple Press.

22. Pfeffer, J., & Davis-Blake, A. (1987). Understanding organizational wage structures: A resource dependence approach. *Academy of Management Journal, 30,* 437–455.

23. Pfeffer, J., Davis-Blake, A., & Julius, D. J. (1995). AA officer salaries and managerial diversity: Efficiency wage or status? *Industrial Relations, 34,* 73–94.

24. Pfeffer, J., & Davis-Blake, A. (1987). Understanding organizational wage structures: A resource dependence approach. *Academy of Management Journal, 30,* 437–455.

25. Carpenter, M. A., & Wade, J. B. (2002). Micro level opportunity structures as determinants of non-CEO executive pay. *Academy of Management*, *45*, 1085–1103.

26. Shin, T. (2012). The gender gap in executive compensation: The role of female directors and chief executive officers. *The ANNALS of the American Academy of Political and Social Science, 639*(1), 258–278.

27. Mullich, J. (2005). Attacking attrition at Convergys. *Workforce Management*, March, 46–47; Harris, J. G., Craig, E., & Light, D. A. (2010). The new generation of human capital analytics. *Accenture, Institute for High Performance Research Report*, July.

28. Span, P. (2016, September 23). Wages for home care aides lag as demand grows. *The New York Times*. Retrieved March 21, 2017, from https://www.nytimes.com/2016/09/27/health/home-care-aides-wages.html

29. Span, P. (2016, September 23). Wages for home care aides lag as demand grows. *The New York Times*. Retrieved March 21, 2017, from https://www.nytimes.com/2016/09/27/health/home-care-aides-wages.html

30. Span, P. (2016, September 23). Wages for home care aides lag as demand grows. *The New York Times*. Retrieved March 21, 2017, from https://www.nytimes.com/2016/09/27/health/home-care-aides-wages.html

31. Baxter, A. (2016, May 24). Wages, caregiver shortages top list of home health threats. *Home Health Care News*. Retrieved March 21, 2017, from http://homehealthcarenews.com/2016/05/wages-caregiver-shortages-top-list-of-home-health-threats/

32. McPherson, B. (2016). Preventing caregiver turnover. *Home Care*, February. Retrieved March 21, 2017, from http://www.homecaremag.com/operations-management/february-2016/preventing-caregiver-turnover

33. Dickson, V., & Schencker, L. (2016, June 27). CMS proposes $180 million pay cut for home health. *Modern Healthcare*. Retrieved March 21, 2017, from http://www.modernhealthcare.com/article/20160627/NEWS/160629911

34. Baxter, A. (2016, May 24). Wages, caregiver shortages top list of home health threats. *Home Health Care News*. Retrieved March 21, 2017, from http://homehealthcarenews.com/2016/05/wages-caregiver-shortages-top-list-of-home-health-threats/

35. McPherson, B. (2016). Preventing caregiver turnover. *Home Care*, February. Retrieved March 21, 2017, from http://www.homecaremag.com/operations-management/february-2016/preventing-caregiver-turnover

36. Span, P. (2016, September 23). Wages for home care aides lag as demand grows. *The New York Times*. Retrieved March 21, 2017, from https://www.nytimes.com/2016/09/27/health/home-care-aides-wages.html

37. Skills shortage drives up construction pay by 5 percent. (2015, August 7). *RAC*. Retrieved March 20, 2017, from https://www.racplus.com/news/skills-shortage-drives-up-construction-pay-by-5/8687341.article

38. Does Indonesia require us to pay workers a '13th month' allowance? (2011). *Bloomberg BNA*. Retrieved March 21, 2017, from http://hr.bna.com/hrrc/2129/split_display.adp?fedfid=23699087&vname=idsnref100&fn=23699087&jd=a0c9t6a5y0&split=0

39. New York's not-for-profit law empowers Attorney General Spitzer to pursue former NYSE Chairman Richard Grasso for excessive compensation. (2006, March 22). Retrieved March 20, 2017, from https://www.nixonpeabody.com/en/ideas/articles/2006/03/22/new-yorks-not-for-profit-law-empowers-attorney-general-spitzer-to-pursue-former-nyse-ch

40. Executive compensation case studies: A supplement to the WorldatWork executive rewards questionary. (2009). *WorldatWork*. Retrieved March 20, 2017, from http://www.worldatwork.org/waw/adimLink?id=36434

41. Lucchetti, A., & Lublin, J. S. (2006, October 20). Grasso is ordered to repay millions in compensation. *The Wall Street Journal Online*. Retrieved March 20, 2017, from https://www.wsj.com/articles/SB116128286185197983

42. Executive compensation case studies: A supplement to the WorldatWork executive rewards questionary. (2009). *WorldatWork*. Retrieved August 1, 2011, from http://www.worldatwork.org/waw/adimLink?id=36434

43. Thurm, S. (2010, March 6). For CEO pay, a single number never tells the whole story. *The Wall Street Journal*. Retrieved August 1, 2011, from http://online.wsj.com/article/SB10001424052748703862704575099491419050822.html

44. WorldatWork. (2009). *Job evaluation and market-pricing practices*. Scottsdale, AZ: WorldatWork.

45. Armstrong, M., & Barron, A. (1995). *The job evaluation handbook*. London: IPD.

46. O'Brien, J. M. (2008, February 1). A perfect season. *Fortune*. Retrieved November 22, 2010, from http://money.cnn.com/2008/01/18/news/companies/fourseasons.fortune/index.htm?postversion=2008020111

47. Market pricing versus job evaluation: Why not both? (2010, December 3). Compensation.BLR.com. Retrieved August 3, 2011, from http://compensation.blr.com/whitepapers/Compensation/Compensation-Administration/Market-Pricing-Versus-Job-Evaluation-Why-Not-Both/

48. *Ibid.*

49. Armstrong, M., & Barron, A. (1995). *The job evaluation handbook*. London: IPD.

50. Market pricing versus job evaluation: Why not both? (2010, December 3). Compensation.BLR.com. Retrieved August 3, 2011, from http://compensation.blr.com/whitepapers/Compensation/Compensation-Administration/Market-Pricing-Versus-Job-Evaluation-Why-Not-Both/

51. 2tor. (2017). Careers. Retrieved March 201, 2017, from https://careers-2u.icims.com/jobs/search?ss=1&hashed=-435744538&mobile=false&width=1212&height=500&bga=true&needsRedirect=false&jan1offset=-300&jun1offset=-240

52. The Hay Group guide chart-profile method of job evaluation. (2010). Hay Group. Retrieved June 22, 2017, from https://www.haygroup.com/downloads/au/Guide_Chart-Profile_Method_of_Job_Evaluation_Brochure_web.pdf

53. WorldatWork. (2007). *The WorldatWork handbook of compensation, benefits & total rewards: A comprehensive guide for HR professionals*. New York: Wiley.

54. See http://www.haygroup.com/en/our-library/videos/hay-group-job-evaluation/ for more information about this method.

55. Steinburg, R. J. (1992). Gendered instructions—Cultural lag and gender bias in the Hay system of job evaluation. *Work and Occupations*, *19*, 387–423.

56. Gilbert, K. (2005). The role of job evaluation in determining equal value in tribunals—Tool, weapon, or cloaking device? *Employee Relations*, *27*, 7–19.

57. For more information, see http://www.paq.com/?FuseAction=Main.PAQProgram

58. Miller, S. (2017). Budget item: Retention. *HR Magazine*, February, 15.

59. Smith, D. (2015). Most people have no idea whether they're paid fairly. *Harvard Business Review*, December. Retrieved January 23, 2017, from https://hbr.org/2015/10/most-people-have-no-idea-whether-theyre-paid-fairly

60. Nickels, D. (2010, January 26). How to explain employees' total compensation. *Compensation Today*. Retrieved March 20, 2017, from http://www.payscale.com/compensation-today/2010/01/how-to-explain-employees-total-compensation

61. Newquist, C. (2011, May 13). PwC unveils changes to compensation structure. *Going Concern*. Retrieved August 15, 2011, from http://goingconcern.com/2011/05/pwc-unveils-changes-to-compensation-structure/

62. Nassauer, S. (2016, January 20). Wal-Mart to boost wages for most U.S. store workers. *The Wall Street Journal*. Retrieved February 25, 2017, from https://www.wsj.com/articles/wal-mart-to-increase-wages-for-most-u-s-store-workers-1453315937

63. Weiss, A. (2014). *Efficiency wages: Models of unemployment, layoffs, and wage dispersion*. Princeton University Press.

64. Irwin, N. (2016, October 15). How did Wal-Mart get cleaner stores and higher sales? It paid its people more. *The New York Times*. Retrieved February 24, 2017, from https://www.nytimes.com/2016/10/16/upshot/how-did-walmart-get-cleaner-stores-and-higher-sales-it-paid-its-people-more.html?rref=collection%2Fsectioncollection%2Fupshot&action=click&contentCollection=upshot&region=rank&module=package&version=highlights&contentPlacement=1&pgtype=sectionfront

65. Parker, G., McAdams, J., & Zielinski, D. (2000). *Rewarding teams: Lessons from the trenches*. San Francisco, CA: Jossey-Bass.

66. Sinton, P. (2000, February 23). Teamwork the name of the game for Ideo. *San Francisco Chronicle*. Retrieved August 22, 2011, from http://www.sfgate.com/cgi-bin/article.cgi?file=/chronicle/archive/2000/02/23/BU39355.DTL

67. Adapted from Shaw, J. D., Duffy, M. K., & Stark, E. M. (2001). Team reward attitude: Construct development and initial validation. *Journal of Organizational Behavior*, *22*, 903–917; Kirkman, B. L., & Shapiro. D. L. (2001). The impact of cultural values on job satisfaction and organizational commitment in self-managing work teams: The mediating role of employee resistance. *Academy of Management Journal*, *44*, 557–569; and Campion, M.A., Medsker. G. J., & Higgs. C. (1993). Relations between work group characteristics and effectiveness: Implications for designing effective work groups. *Personnel Psychology*, *46*, 823–850.

68. Golden parachutes: How the bankers went down. (2009, February 24). Mint.com. Retrieved August 11, 2011, from http://www.mint.com/blog/trends/golden-parachutes-how-the-bankers-went-down/

69. Cowherd, D. M., & Levine, D. I. (1992). Product quality and pay equity between lower-level employees and top management: An investigation of distributive justice theory. *Administrative Science Quarterly*, *37*, 302–320.

70. Internal pay equity methodologies. (2011). Compensationstandards.com. Retrieved from http://www.compensationstandards.com/nonMember/files/IntPay.htm

71. *Ibid.*

72. Lagorio, J., & Jucca, L. (2009, October 20). Credit Suisse changes executive pay structure. *Reuters*. Retrieved March 21, 2017, from http://www.reuters.com/article/us-creditsuisse-compensation-idUSTRE59J4N420091020

73. Lynch, S. N. (2017, February 6). Acting SEC chair takes aim at Dodd-Frank CEO pay ratio rule. *Fox Business*. Retrieved March 21, 2017, from http://www.foxbusiness.com/markets/2017/02/06/acting-sec-chair-takes-aim-at-dodd-frank-ceo-pay-ratio-rule.html

74. Pepitone, J. (2009, November 23). Heroes of the economy: Where are they now? *CNNMoney*. Retrieved July 26, 2011, from http://money.cnn.com/galleries/2009/news/0911/gallery.economy_heroes/index.html

75. O'Donovan, D. (2011, June 6). Johnson and Johnson rolls out global compensation strategy. *Jobsbody*. Retrieved July 30, 2011, from http://jobsbody.blogspot.com/2011/06/johnson-and-johnson-rolls-out-global.html

76. Rockoff, J. D. (2010, February 17). J&J to cut bonus targets for some. *The Wall Street Journal*. Retrieved July 30, 2011, from http://online.wsj.com/article/SB10001424052748704398804575071720286022184.html

77. O'Donovan, D. (2011, June 6). Johnson and Johnson rolls out global compensation strategy. *Jobsbody*. Retrieved July 30, 2011, from http://jobsbody.blogspot.com/2011/06/johnson-and-johnson-rolls-out-global.html

78. *Ibid.*

79. Rockoff, J. D. (2010, February 17). J&J to cut bonus targets for some. *The Wall Street Journal*. Retrieved July 30, 2011, from http://online.wsj.com/article/SB10001424052748704398804575071720286022184.html

80. O'Donovan, D. (2011, June 6). Johnson and Johnson rolls out global compensation strategy. *Jobsbody*. Retrieved July 30, 2011, from http://jobsbody.blogspot.com/2011/06/johnson-and-johnson-rolls-out-global.html

chapter 10

Incentives

Learning Objectives

AFTER STUDYING THIS CHAPTER, YOU SHOULD BE ABLE TO:

1 Explain why organizations might choose to tie pay to performance.

2 Describe when it is appropriate to have a high level of reward differentiation across employees.

3 Describe some of the criticisms of stock options as an incentive tool.

4 Explain how pay for performance improves employee motivation and performance.

5 Describe the golden rule of pay for performance plans.

6 Explain the difference between errors of commission and errors of omission in incentive pay and their impact on organizations.

Real World Challenge

Incentive Compensation at Sprint

When Dan Hesse became CEO of telecommunications giant Sprint, he wanted to eliminate any confusion in employees' minds about what the company would be focused on and what would be important for strategic execution. Hesse identified three strategic pillars of Sprint's corporate strategy:[1]

- Improve the customer experience
- Strengthen Sprint's brand
- Generate cash and increase profits.

Sprint wants to ensure that its performance management and pay for performance systems support these three strategic pillars and each other. The company wants its incentive pay to be linked to employees' performance, but it also wants to be fair during the volatile economy. The company asks for your advice in creating a compensation system that consistently ties employee rewards to the key pillars of its corporate strategy. After reading this chapter, you should have some good ideas.

Incentives can give organizations a competitive advantage by aligning employees' goals and behaviors with the company's strategy and goals. Rewards are also one of the most powerful motivational tools managers have at their disposal. The rewards offered by a job not only determine whether someone is willing to accept a job offer but also how much effort he or she is willing to put forth. **Fixed rewards** are all types of pre-determined compensation including salary and benefits. **Variable rewards**, also called incentives, link rewards to factors identified as valuable, including performance, skills, competence, and contribution. Variable rewards are "at risk," meaning that they are not guaranteed like base salary, but they have to be earned by reaching set behavior or performance targets. When Meg Whitman became CEO of Hewlett-Packard, she received an annual salary of just $1 but could earn over $8 million if the company hits certain performance goals.[2]

Although surveys often find that employees identify base pay as the most important element of their employment arrangement, research has found that contingent pay has a stronger influence on an organization's financial performance.[3] When it comes to motivating employees, famed investor Charlie Munger, vice chairman of Berkshire Hathaway, once said, "Never, ever think about something else when you should be thinking about the power of incentives." Some form of variable pay is used by most Fortune 1000 companies[4] and by most European organizations.[5]

> *"Never, ever think about something else when you should be thinking about the power of incentives."*
>
> —**Charlie Munger, vice chairman, Berkshire Hathaway**

The clearing of the island of Penang illustrates the motivational power of incentives. Before 1786, Penang was covered with thick jungle and infested with malaria. When English captain Francis Light of the East India Company chose Penang as a new harbor for ships on their way to China to get fresh food and water, he needed his soldiers to clear the jungle. Understandably, his soldiers were not very excited about the job. To motivate them, Light loaded the ship's guns with silver dollars and fired them into the jungle. The work was rapidly finished, and Fort Cornwallis quickly established.

Motivating and rewarding high performance improves organizational performance and helps to retain top talent. By influencing goals and motivation, incentives influence what employees *will* do in our model of human resource management (HRM). This chapter begins with a discussion of issues to consider when designing incentive plans. The chapter then discusses various types of incentive pay and how to effectively use it to motivate desired individual, team, and organizational outcomes. Issues related to incenting executives, salespeople, and innovation are discussed as well as issues unique to rewarding teams. After reading this chapter, you should have a good understanding of how incentives are used to motivate different behaviors and outcomes.

fixed rewards
pre-determined compensation (salary and benefits)

variable rewards
link rewards to factors determined as valuable, including performance, skills, competence, and contribution (incentives)

so what

Incentives cannot remedy a negative work environment.

Designing Incentive Plans

No incentive package can fix a negative work environment, but incentives can help motivate employees to engage in supportive and desirable behaviors. Incentive pay plans should be designed not only to reward desired performance but also to minimize conflict and unfairness. Many incentive plans fail because they are a poor fit with the setting or because they are poorly implemented. Employees can also have negative reactions to new compensation plans that threaten their incomes. When Korean bank Standard Chartered tried to base employee pay on performance to improve competitiveness, it triggered an extended strike that hurt the bank's business.[6]

The top four reasons organizations give for tying pay to performance are to:[7]

- Recognize and reward high performers;
- Increase the likelihood of achieving corporate goals;
- Improve productivity; and
- Move away from an entitlement culture.

Before designing an incentive pay plan to motivate performance, it is important to consider the:

- Preference of individual employees;
- Size of the rewards for high performance;
- Method of motivating individual job performance; and
- Objectivity of the evaluation process that determines the rewards.

Employees differ in how they value different types of rewards. Do you equally value $50, a preferred parking space, and an "employee of the week" certificate? It is important to ensure that the incentive being offered is something valued by the employees it is intended to motivate. Cultural issues affect the desirability of different types of rewards to different employees. This chapter's Global Issues feature discusses different reward preferences in different countries.

 # Global Issues

Global Recognition Programs[8]

To be most effective, organizational rewards must be consistent with employees' cultural values about work.[9] Here are some examples of how appropriate forms of recognition differ across countries:[10]

- Nonmaterial rewards are valued in China where employees consider face/reputation to be more important than financial possessions. Nonmaterial rewards such as public praise make Chinese employees feel acknowledged by their organizations, reinforcing their face/reputation.
- In India, certificates and awards containing the company's logo are highly valued.
- Clocks and watches are taboo in Asian countries because timepieces are reminders of mortality.
- French workers tend to scoff at effusive gratitude and view thank you notes with skepticism.
- Avoid giving Chinese employee anything green, as the color is associated with an adulterous spouse.
- In South Korea, employees often find public recognition awkward.
- In India, where wages are low, household items including toasters and microwaves are highly valued.
- Gift certificates or gift cards for merchandise or services are among the most common incentive programs for U.S. companies.

Identify Goals for the Incentive Plan

It is better to have no bonus system at all than to have a bad one. A bad incentive plan encourages people to do the wrong things in the wrong way, and it often leads to cynicism, anger, and indifference.[11] The first and most important step when considering setting up a bonus system is to identify what the organization really wants people to do or accomplish as a result of the

so what?

A poorly designed incentive plan can motivate the wrong behaviors and create anger and indifference.

incentive. As former GE executive Steven Kerr said, there is no point in rewarding A if what you want is B.[12] Table 10.1 summarizes some of the many behaviors and outcomes that can be influenced by incentive programs.

table **10.1**

What Can Incentive Plans Influence?

- Individual performance
- Team performance
- Organizational performance
- Customer service
- Production quality
- Production quantity
- Teamwork
- Attendance
- Safety
- Revenue growth
- Increase in market share
- Cost reductions
- Productivity improvements

This chapter's HR Flexibility feature illustrates how different incentive plans can help to motivate different employee behaviors. Each of the incentive plans will be discussed in more detail later in the chapter.

 HR Flexibility

Motivating Different Behaviors Through Incentives

Goal	Incentive
Fewer accidents	Give awards to employees seen using proper safety techniques.
Decreased production costs	A Scanlon gainsharing program that rewards employee groups for their ideas that reduce the cost of production; profit sharing.
Long-term organizational performance	Stock options that vest in a few years; profit sharing.
Improved productivity this month	A pay for performance plan that awards employees with up to 25 percent of their base salary for meeting performance goals.
Improved cooperation	Team-based pay for performance awards; spot awards; recognition awards.
Improved customer service	Recognition awards; spot awards for high-quality customer service interactions.
Employees becoming proficient at additional skills	Skill- (or competency-) based pay.

?so what

Rewards are less effective at motivating performance if all employees receive the same reward.

Budgeting

Setting a budget for an incentive pay program is important to ensure that it motivates employees while also creating a positive return on investment for the organization. Too little incentive fails to maximize employees' motivation, yet too much unnecessarily decreases the company's earnings. "Our reward and recognition program recognizes the value employees bring to the table, and, therefore, it would be the last thing cut from the budget," says Shannon Murray, compensation specialist at railroad company CSX Corp.[13]

> *"Our reward and recognition program recognizes the value employees bring to the table, and, therefore, it would be the last thing cut from the budget."*
>
> **—Shannon Murray, CSX Corp.**

Employers fund variable pay programs in many ways. The most common are through:

- Company performance
- Reduced merit increases
- Reductions in head count
- Reduced benefits
- Pay freezes

During the economic downturn, data storage provider NetApp lowered incentive payout targets to make sure everyone got their bonus. When business improved, the incentive payout leaped to 171 percent, and employees received $146.7 million in bonuses, or about 8 percent of the company's operating budget.[14] Nonprofit research and development firm MITRE opted not to grant pay raises in 2010 due to the soft economy, and instead it gave lump-sum merit payments to everyone in the company. Some managers skipped their own payments to allow more money to be budgeted for others in their divisions.[15]

reward differentiation
differentiating rewards based on performance rather than giving all employees the same reward

Differentiating Rewards

How would you feel if you worked for weeks on a high-quality course paper only to earn the same grade as a student who turned in a lower quality paper written the night before? If all employees receive the same reward regardless of their individual performance, the incentive program is not as motivating as it would be if higher performers received higher rewards. This is the idea behind **reward differentiation**, or differentiating rewards based on performance rather than giving all employees the same reward. Differentiating rewards allows the organization to communicate the message to the majority of employees that "your performance was good, and you are getting the target rewards." The smaller group of high performers receive the message, "your performance was outstanding, and your rewards are above target."[16]

Table 10.2 summarizes some of the outcomes that differentiated rewards based on performance can influence.

The appropriate level of reward differentiation is influenced in part by the organization's culture and teamwork norms. If the norm in a high-performance culture organization is

Differentiating rewards and giving top performers something extra rather than giving all employees the same reward can help send the right message to the highest performing employees. By giving just a few employees recognition awards such as an "employee of the month" parking space helps them to know that the organization recognizes and appreciates their performance even if they choose to park in their regular parking space.

table **10.2**

What Differentiated Rewards Can Influence[17]

- Aligning pay with performance and organizational values
- Promoting the retention of top performers
- Promoting the performance improvement (or attrition) of low performers
- Supporting the business strategy
- Providing evidence that certain employees create more value than others
- Making the best use of scarce reward resources

to set high individual performance standards and have a very small percentage of employees defined as high performers, only 5 to 10 percent of employees might receive the highest rewards. This creates a more competitive work environment than would an incentive system in which more employees receive higher awards.

If work is done interdependently, or if it is difficult to identify employees' relative contribution to a project or outcome, differentiation can undermine cooperation and teamwork. Imagine working on an interdependent team that exceeded its goals, but only one team member (not you) receives a reward for the team's performance. Most people would not be motivated by an incentive system that failed to also recognize their good performance and contributions to the successful team. In an independent sales environment, however, most people would find it appropriate and motivating to have high performers recognized with greater rewards than lower performers. High and low performers should be treated differently, but be careful not to alienate or demotivate anyone in the process.

so what

Differentiated rewards undermine cooperation and teamwork.

Setting Goals and Identifying Performance Measures

One of the most important elements of a successful variable pay system is the defining of desired performance. If desired performance is not what the organization really needs, or if the variable pay system focuses employees on only part of what is important to organizational performance, unintended negative consequences often result. When Albuquerque, New Mexico, wanted to reduce the overtime being paid to its garbage collectors, it offered them bonuses for completing their routes during an eight-hour shift. The program motivated drivers to speed during their routes, skip pickups, and dangerously overload their trucks to reduce the number of trips they had to make to the dump.[18] This was obviously not the intent of the incentive program, but it was a logical outcome given what was being rewarded and how performance was defined.

If an incentive system unintentionally encourages employees to compete too much, undermining, bullying, or other inappropriate and unethical behavior can result.[19] Another good example is the New Orleans Saints professional football team's incentive program that offered thousands of dollars to players for big hits that knocked opponents out of games.

The most effective variable rewards programs are transparent and understood by all employees. The focus should be on assessing outcomes related to business strategy execution and business performance. Rewards should be fair and based on multiple measures that capture employees' actual contributions to organizational success.[20] In addition to performance review scores, variable pay can be based on competencies, supporting coworkers, hard work, and other role-specific factors.[21] Some companies use incentive pay to reward specific behaviors. Employees at Chesapeake Energy can earn a $1,500 bonus by completing health screenings, working toward or maintaining a healthy weight, and exercising three or more days a week.[22]

To motivate performance, employees must be able to impact the outcomes linked to their bonus. Rewarding someone based on something they can't control is more of a lottery ticket than an incentive plan. Lower level employees' incentives should be most strongly linked to how the individual employee performs. Nonetheless, linking at least some incentive pay to organizational performance helps to keep employees' goals aligned with those of the organization and promotes collaboration and teamwork. This chapter's Strategic Impact feature describes how lubricant maker WD-40 linked its incentive pay to factors employees could control.

so what?

If employees cannot impact the outcomes linked to a reward, the reward is not motivational to them.

Strategic Impact

Success Through Incentives at WD-40

When an employee survey found that employees at lubricant maker WD-40 wanted their incentive compensation to be better linked to measures within their control, the company listened. The roughly 50-50 mix of global and country bonus was changed to be weighted more heavily on country performance. The HR team now works with the finance department to give every employee quarterly reports on earnings and sales performance so that they know where they stand and what they need to do. In the first year of the new program, every employee earned a bonus, and the company had the best year in its over 60-year history. WD-40 credited the redesigned incentive plan as a major factor in its success.[23]

Incenting Short- and Long-Term Performance

Different types of incentives target different employee behaviors and outcomes. Focusing employees on both long-term and short-term goals best aligns employees' goals with organizational objectives.

Short-term incentives.   **Short-term incentives** are one-time variable rewards used to motivate short-term employee behavior and performance (typically one year or less). Commonly used short-term incentives include bonuses and profit sharing. **Profit sharing** distributes organizational profits to all employees. Profit sharing only rewards employees when the organization is profitable, providing financial flexibility. During difficult economic times, however, poor profit sharing distributions can be demotivating. Because employees are not directly responsible for the organization's profits, the motivational effect of profit-sharing plans can be less than individual incentive plans through which employees have greater control over earning rewards.

Short-term incentive pay is one of the most frequently used forms of incentive compensation to motivate specific goals including:

- Attendance
- Customer service
- Safety behaviors
- Production quality
- Production quantity

Adobe provides a $20 monthly subsidy for commuting to work via bicycle, and its Seattle employees are given $30 vouchers for kayaking to work. The company provides all U.S. employees with a $100-per-month subsidy for using public transit to commute to work.[24]

short-term incentives
one-time variable rewards used to motivate short-term employee behavior and performance (typically one year or less)

profit sharing
organizational profits are distributed to all employees

Long-term incentives.   **Long-term incentives** are intended to motivate employee behaviors and performance that support company value (e.g., share price) and long-term organizational health. Long-term incentives are usually based on cycles of at least one year. Performance goals can be objective (e.g., 50 percent growth in sales), measured against an industry peer group (e.g., obtaining 40 percent market share), or something else. Awards are typically based on a predetermined multiple of base salary.

The most frequently used long-term performance incentives are stock options. **Stock options** give an employee the right to buy shares of the company's stock at a certain price (the exercise price) during some future period of time. If the market value of the stock is higher than the exercise price, the employee can sell the shares for a profit. If the stock price is below this price, the options are "underwater" and are worthless, although organizations have the option of repricing the options to restore their value and motivating potential. **Vesting**, or the point at which employees can sell or transfer the stock option, can occur on the date of grant, but it more commonly occurs gradually over a period of months or years. When an employee leaves the company, typically all vested options are forfeited if not exercised within 90 days. Although stock options are often used to incentivize executives because they are responsible for factors influencing the organization's long-term performance, they can be used for all employees. Startup companies often use the potential rewards offered by stock options to entice top talent to work for them despite lower base pay. By giving employees a tangible stake in the organization's longer-term performance, stock options help to focus employees on more than making short-term performance numbers.[25]

Critics of stock option plans believe that they compensate employees for reasons unrelated to employee performance. Such variations could cause undesirable effects, as employees receive different results for options awarded in different years. When Google's stock price fell and many of its employees' options were under water, meaning that they were worth less than the exercise price, Google exchanged them for options with lower exercise prices to keep its employees motivated.[26]

Critics also believe that stock options can motivate executives to manage the company for the short term rather than the long term. Another issue is that stock prices often are not directly under the control of managers, creating reinforcement problems or potentially reinforcing the wrong behaviors. For example, options can motivate executives to engage in unethical behaviors including inflating earnings to maximize the value of their stock options, as we discussed earlier. Nonetheless, they can be good performance motivators if properly managed. Movie streaming service Netflix grants options monthly rather than annually to smooth the effects of the stock's volatility. This allows employees to worry less about underwater options and focus on enhancing Netflix's performance.[27]

Pay Mix

Pay mix is the proportion of pay that is fixed versus variable. Basing too much pay on meeting certain performance measures can undermine organizational effectiveness. The bulk of many investment bankers' total pay used to be an annual bonus linked to performance, which led many to take outsize risks trying to hit a home run. This risk taking led to serious problems for many big banks, which have now shifted away from the large bonus toward base salary and long-term incentives.[28]

As one incentive expert stated, "Do rewards motivate people? Absolutely. They motivate people to get rewards."[29] To prevent competition or a narrow focus on earning incentives from undermining organizational performance, it is essential to balance the mix of individual, group, and team rewards. Organizations can incentivize individual, work group, or organizational performance in a variety of ways, as we discuss next.

Individual Incentive Plans

Individual incentive plans are most likely to succeed when employees work at least somewhat independently and the contributions of individual employees can be accurately identified. Because they focus employees on maximizing their own performance, individual incentive plans are more appropriate when competition among employees is acceptable or desirable than when cooperation is essential for effective performance. The most common incentive plans for individual employees are pay for performance plans, skill-based pay, recognition awards, and alternative rewards.

Pay for Performance

Although people are differentially motivated by money, pay can be a powerful motivator because it determines the degree to which people will be able to satisfy many of their needs and wants. In addition to base pay, employees can be rewarded for their individual performance as well as the performance of their work group or even the entire organization. **Pay-for-performance programs**, also called merit pay, reward employees based on some specific measure of their individual performance. If the amount employees produce or sell determines their pay, then they make more money when they perform better. Seeing a clear link between effort, job performance, and the reward enhances motivation. Atlanta-based law firm Alston & Bird regularly provides employees with merit bonuses up to 10 percent of their base pay, and that payout has gone as high as 25 percent when budget goals are exceeded.[30] Data storage and management company NetApp gives patent bonuses ranging from $4,000 to $12,000 to employees who patent a new idea, employee referral bonuses of up to $2,500, and on-the-spot cash bonuses for outstanding achievements.[31]

Some companies establish formal incentive programs to motivate employees and improve performance by providing positive reinforcement for engaging in certain behaviors or reaching specific goals. For example, payroll processor Paychex gives employees rewards of $100 to $300 each year for healthy activities including getting flu shots and dental checkups, attending yoga or aerobics classes, biking to work, and running a 5K race.[32]

Variable pay plans. **Variable pay plans** are pay for performance plans that put a small amount of base pay at risk, in exchange for the opportunity to earn additional pay if performance meets or exceeds a standard. For example, all employees of Chicago-based Ameritech Corp. are compensated using a variable-pay approach. Every Ameritech employee has a set of target incentives ranging from 5 to 35 percent of pay. A portion of the incentive amount is based on the performance of the employee's business unit (about 60 percent), with the remainder based on individual performance (about 40 percent).[33]

Spot awards. **Spot awards** are given immediately, or "on the spot," as soon as a desired behavior is seen.[34] Effective spot reward programs depend on discretion, timely acknowledgements, and obvious links between employee actions and recognition. Giving small rewards more frequently can affect employee motivation and satisfaction more than a larger annual reward and better support camaraderie.[35] Recognizing customer service behaviors weekly with a gift card or other recognition better reinforces them than would an annual award.

Sunnyvale, California, systems engineering consulting firm Scitor's Be Our Guest program is a good example of a spot award. Employees award Be Our Guest bonuses, usually ranging from $100 to $300, to coworkers who go beyond the call of duty at work. If someone feels a coworker has done something worthy, the giver fills out a card indicating the amount of the

pay-for-performance program (merit pay)
rewards employees based on some specific measure of their performance

so what

Motivation is maximized when employees see a clear link between their effort and the reward.

variable pay plan
pay for performance plans that put a small amount of base pay at risk, in exchange for the opportunity to earn additional pay if performance meets or exceeds a standard

spot awards
awards given immediately when a desired behavior is seen

so what

Smaller, more frequent rewards can be more motivating than a single larger reward.

bonus, and the recipient can spend it as he or she likes through his or her expense account.[36] Managers and peers at Brocade Communications Systems award spot bonuses of up to $2,000 to high-performing employees.[37] At San Francisco-based hotel chain Kimpton, managers give employees special tokens to reward them for delivering "Kimpton Moments" that deliver outstanding customer service. A $10,000 prize is given to the employee with the best "moment" of the year.[38]

extrinsic motivation
motivation that comes from outside the individual, including performance bonuses

intrinsic motivation
derived from an interest in or enjoyment from doing a task

Individual differences.   As Vineet Nayar, CEO of IT and software development company HCL Technologies, says, "I believe that you can divide employees into two groups: Those motivated by what they receive from their employer, and those motivated by what they are allowed to do by their employer."[39] **Extrinsic motivation** comes from outside the individual, including performance bonuses. When we are motivated to do a task because doing so will lead to a valued reward, we are extrinsically motivated. **Intrinsic motivation** comes from an interest in or enjoyment from doing a task. When we are motivated by what we do rather than by tangible external rewards for doing it, as when we engage in a hobby, we are experiencing intrinsic motivation.

> *"I believe that you can divide employees into two groups: Those motivated by what they receive from their employer, and those motivated by what they are allowed to do by their employer."*
>
> —Vineet Nayar, CEO, HCL Technologies

When employees are motivated by the work itself, extrinsic motivation and incentives may be detrimental to performance.[40] When famed baseball manager Joe Torre was offered a new contract at the Yankees, the organization offered reduced pay but more incentives based on the team's performance. Torre says, "I was insulted that they thought I needed to be motivated financially to go out there and do a better job. That's when I walked away."[41]

> *"I was insulted that they thought I needed to be motivated financially to go out there and do a better job. That's when I walked away."*
>
> —Joe Torres, former manager of the New York Yankees

This chapter's case study explores Hewlett-Packard's experience in introducing extrinsic rewards in a very intrinsically motivating workplace.

CASE STUDY: Motivation Through Incentives at Hewlett-Packard

In its early days, Hewlett-Packard did not regard money as a motivator and had no bonus system. HP has a high-commitment workplace that empowers employees and offers them challenging careers. When 13 managers asked to adopt a pay-for-performance program tying 10 to 20 percent of their employees' pay to their team's performance to increase productivity and focus employees on team rather than individual performance, the organization agreed.

Continued

Managers set a series of production goals for several teams and based their members' pay on three levels of rewards. Managers believed that 90 percent of the teams could reach Level 1 goals, 50 percent would reach Level 2, and only 10 to 15 percent could reach the highest Level 3 goals.[42]

But the managers were wrong. For the first six months, almost all teams reached the two highest reward levels. Because this required paying employees more than expected, managers raised the goal levels. This new focus on high performance and rewards led high-performing teams to prevent less experienced workers from joining them. Less employee movement across teams meant that less knowledge was shared or transferred among employees.[43]

As more workers complained and employees began to focus on doing what they needed to do to earn the rewards rather than on the many other things that would help the company, managers tried redesigning the system. Troubles continued to mount for three years until HP scrapped the entire experiment. When it did, relieved workers threw management a party.[44] As one expert said, "The HP experience shows the more you focus people on monetary incentives, the more you use money as a goal and a driver, the more dysfunction you have. We've seen the same thing on Wall Street."[45]

Questions

1. What do you think were the biggest factors in the failure of the incentive program at HP?
2. Why might employees prefer to have only fixed pay and no incentive pay if the incentive pay system meant that they could earn more money?
3. What would you recommend that HP try instead of pay for performance to accomplish their initial goals of increasing productivity and focusing employees on team rather than individual performance?

How you view money can influence how motivated you will be by monetary incentive programs. Some people place a great importance on money and view it as a symbol of success. For others, money represents the freedom to do whatever they want to do. Still others view money as unimportant or even shameful.[46] This chapter's Develop Your Skills feature will help you to better understand how you view money and how money motivates you. The point is to remember to match the nature of a reward to the values and the needs of the person you are trying to motivate with the incentive.

Develop Your Skills

Are You Motivated by Money?[47]

What does money mean to you? Money obviously impacts people's motivation and work-related behavior in organizations,[48] but money means different things to different people. The better you understand how you view money, the better you will understand how strongly money motivates you at this point in your life (it may change over time).

This self-assessment gives you the opportunity to better understand your attitudes toward money. Place your response on the line to the left of each question using the scale below and then follow the scoring instructions. Be honest—there are no right or wrong answers.

Continued

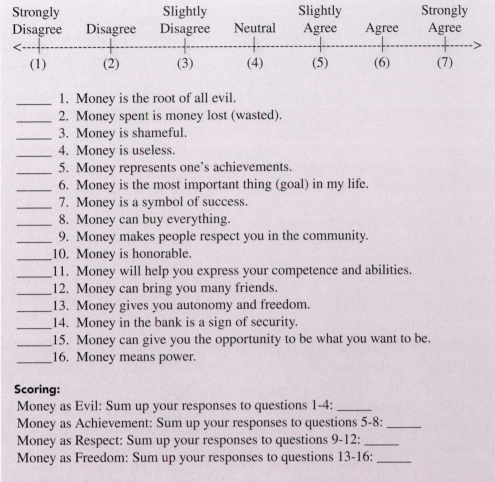

Strongly Disagree	Disagree	Slightly Disagree	Neutral	Slightly Agree	Agree	Strongly Agree
(1)	(2)	(3)	(4)	(5)	(6)	(7)

_____ 1. Money is the root of all evil.
_____ 2. Money spent is money lost (wasted).
_____ 3. Money is shameful.
_____ 4. Money is useless.
_____ 5. Money represents one's achievements.
_____ 6. Money is the most important thing (goal) in my life.
_____ 7. Money is a symbol of success.
_____ 8. Money can buy everything.
_____ 9. Money makes people respect you in the community.
_____10. Money is honorable.
_____11. Money will help you express your competence and abilities.
_____12. Money can bring you many friends.
_____13. Money gives you autonomy and freedom.
_____14. Money in the bank is a sign of security.
_____15. Money can give you the opportunity to be what you want to be.
_____16. Money means power.

Scoring:
Money as Evil: Sum up your responses to questions 1-4: _____
Money as Achievement: Sum up your responses to questions 5-8: _____
Money as Respect: Sum up your responses to questions 9-12: _____
Money as Freedom: Sum up your responses to questions 13-16: _____

Interpretation:
Money as Evil: If your score is 16 or lower, you do not view money as being evil. Scores of 17 or above reflect a stronger view that money is evil. People who view money as evil are less motivated by incentive programs.

Money as Achievement: If your score is 12 or lower, you do not view money as reflecting your achievements. Scores of 13 or above reflect a stronger view that money does reflect your achievements. Research has found that high-income people tend to think that money reflects one's achievement and is less evil.[49] People who more highly value money as achievement tend to be more highly motivated by incentive programs.

Money as Respect: If your score is 14 or lower, you do not view money as being a means of gaining others' respect. Scores of 15 or above reflect a stronger view that money is a means of attaining others' respect. People who view money as a means to gain respect tend to be more highly motivated by incentive programs.

Money as Freedom: If your score is 19 or lower, you do not view money as being a source of freedom. Scores of 20 or above reflect a stronger view that money is a source of freedom. Viewing money as a source of freedom can increase the motivational effects of incentive programs.

The golden rule with pay-for-performance plans is that you get what you reward. Be sure to think through the possible unintended consequences of incentive programs, and evaluate the effects they have on employee behaviors and other outcomes. Tying traders' pay to the number of loans made or to the revenue they generated without sufficiently considering the risks associated with those activities contributed to the recent financial crisis.[50] Problems often arise when compensation practices are designed such that employees can benefit from the upside without being exposed to sufficient risk of loss on the downside.

so what?

Because you get what you reward, be sure to identify the possible unintended consequences of an incentive plan before implementing it.

Skill-Based Pay

Rather than paying employees for job performance, **skill-based pay** rewards employees for the range and/or depth of their knowledge and skills.[51] Broader skills make workers more flexible and enable them to contribute to the organization in a greater number of ways. Skill depth is related to deeper levels of expertise. When work is organized in teams, skill-based pay can encourage all team members to develop the skills needed to help the team be flexible and perform at its best.

An example of skill-based pay is when a General Mills plant implemented a plan that paid employees in several types of jobs based on their attained skill levels for their job.[52] Workers could attain three levels of skill in their job:

1. *Limited ability* (ability to perform simple tasks without direction);
2. *Partial proficiency* (ability to apply more advanced principles on the job); and
3. *Full competence* (ability to analyze and solve problems associated with that job).

General Mills periodically tested workers to see if they had earned certification at the next higher skill level on their job. If they had, they received higher pay even though they kept the same job. The program increased employees' overall skill levels, and it increased managers' ability to move employees from job to job as needed.

Skill-based pay plans are found predominantly in blue-collar environments because of the relative ease of understanding what skills are important to job performance. **Competency-based pay** is used to evaluate the skills and knowledge of professional workers. Using salespeople as an example, the employer first learns what its best salespeople do well. It might be locating sales leads, tailoring the sales pitch to the client, or strong customer relationship management. Once the elements that predict sales success are identified, all sales employees would be compensated based on how well they show those competencies.[53]

The United States has seen a strong trend toward **multicrafting**, in which employees gain proficiency in two or more trades.[54] Multicrafting rewards a balance between employee flexibility through skill breadth (by making it possible for employees to do different jobs) and high-quality work through skill depth. Although this type of system is most common in manufacturing, it is appropriate for other types of organizations that require high levels of employee skill and high employee involvement (e.g., call centers and specialized retail stores).[55]

Skill-based pay is common in many countries, including Japan. In many Japanese companies, all employees are covered under the same pay grade schedule. An employee's job grade is based on all the jobs and responsibilities the employee can do, not what he or she is actually doing. Reflecting the Japanese emphasis on cross-training, job rotation, and understanding the needs of the company as a whole, the three roughly equal factors used to determine pay are:[56]

1. Knowledge and skill
2. Effort
3. Cooperation with supervisors

The return on investment for skill-based pay systems is minimal for low-skill jobs. Skill-based pay is most appropriate when there is a wide range (in depth and or breadth) of

skill-based pay
rewards employees for the range and depth of their knowledge and skills

competency-based pay
skill-based pay for professional jobs

multicrafting
employees gain proficiency in two or more trades

so what

Skill-based pay is most appropriate when a wide range of skill depth or breadth, knowledge, or competencies is required.

skills, knowledge, or competencies that employees need to acquire and use in their jobs. This tends to make skill-based pay most effective in settings such as manufacturing, where the skills, knowledge, and competencies are relatively concrete and easy to assess. Skill-based pay is also appropriate for high involvement or lean organizations because both require a high level of employee skill and flexibility, leading to a positive return on investment.[57] Although training and administrative costs are higher, companies using skill-based pay tend to have fewer, more highly paid, and more productive employees.[58]

Recognition Awards

recognition awards
rewards for specific achievements such as tenure with the organization, helping a coworker, or attendance

Recognition awards are often used to reward specific achievements such as tenure with the organization, helping a coworker, and safety or wellness behaviors. The railroad company CSX started a recognition program after employee feedback that they were working hard, and their paycheck wasn't enough. The company first launched a product-based program that wasn't widely used. CSX now uses a computer-based system that allows employees to recognize and reward their peers' contributions. A company representative says, "Our employees in the field have tough jobs, and they need to know they are valued—by their supervisors and peers. This program is aligned with our core mission and values, and the results have been terrific. . . . People are asking that these recognitions be included in our newsletters. They want to see how other employees are impacting the company."[59] Smaller companies can easily offer recognition awards as well. Colorado-based digital marketing agency Bluetent hosts a "Great Work" lunch once a month, where a peer-nominated coworker is honored with a $100 prize.[60]

Alternative Rewards

For most compensation systems, cash is king. However, many organizations effectively use creative noncash awards, incentives, and recognition programs to supplement pay and improve their total rewards programs. Alternative rewards include a personal thank-you note, a preferred parking space, a unique award, and management doing something personal such as dressing in a crazy outfit or spending the day on the roof if employees meet sales targets.

Although their low cost makes alternative rewards particularly useful for firms following a low-cost business strategy, they can be effective in all organizations. Retailer Ann Taylor gives its more productive salespeople more favorable hours, which improves sales, rewards high-performing employees, and motivates all sales employees to perform their best.[61] One study found that although financial incentives initially had a greater effect on profit and customer service, over time, financial and nonfinancial incentives had an equally significant impact.[62] Low-cost recognition methods include a positive letter put in the employee's file, a preferred parking space, public praise (e.g., in the company newsletter), or a unique award.

 so what

Rewards do not have to be monetary or expensive to be motivational.

Sometimes simple gestures can get great results. AT&T Universal Card Services in Jacksonville, Florida, uses the World of Thanks award as one of more than 40 recognition and reward programs. A pad of colored papers shaped like a globe with "Thank You" written all over it in different languages can be used by anyone in the company to send a message of thanks to someone else. The program has been extremely popular—in four years, employees used more than 130,000 of the notes.[63]

In addition to motivating higher performance, alternative rewards may also promote ethical work behavior. One survey found that 91 percent of employed adults agreed that workers are more likely to behave ethically when they have a good work–life balance.[64] Employees have lives outside of work, and facilitating work–life balance can reward and motivate employees. Offering a *compressed workweek* allows employees to work a 40-hour week in less than five days. *Job sharing*, which allows two or more people to split a single job, is another option. One person might perform the job on Mondays and Tuesdays, the other person on Thursdays and Fridays, and both people might work on Wednesdays. Alternatively, one employee could work in the mornings and the other in the afternoons. This option requires finding compatible pairs of employees who can successfully share the responsibilities of one job but can help motivate and retain skilled workers—for example retirees and parents with young children.

Flextime is another scheduling option that lets employees decide when to go to work, within certain parameters. Companies typically establish a core set of work hours, say 9:00 a.m. to 3:00 p.m., during which time all employees need to be at work. Employees have flexibility to schedule their other two hours of work either before or after this core period. Flextime can reward high-performing employees by helping them better match their work schedule to their personal needs and preferences.

Telecommuting is another way employers can reward high-performing employees and facilitate their work–life balance. Telecommuting allows employees to work from home and

Letting high-performing employees work some hours from home if they continue to perform well can reward those employees and motivate them to continue to do a good job because they do not want to lose the valued privilege.

link to the company's offices via computer. This eliminates commuting time for employees, increases their ability to meet family demands, and can save the company money by reducing the company's need for office space.[65] Although not limited to incentive use, telecommuting is seen by many employees as an effective incentive to sustain high performance.

Effective managers often find ways to reward employees even if the organization lacks a formal incentive program. A Westinghouse sales manager agreed to pay for and cook lunch for all 16 of his direct reports if they met their sales quotas. They subsequently outdid their goals in 18 out of 19 months. Corporate higher-ups volunteered to foot the bill for the luncheons, but the manager refused, saying that the incentive worked because he personally went to the supermarket to buy the steaks with his own money and because employees got a kick out of seeing the boss become a cook and a waiter.[66]

An increasing number of employers are linking incentives with flexible benefits by rewarding employees with additional points or funds to spend on additional benefits, including health insurance, vacation days, and other perks. Flexible benefit points can also be awarded to staff in challenging economic times when pay is frozen to boost morale and loyalty. The value and flexibility of allotting additional points for flexible benefits helps employees maximize the value of the company's expenditure. When giving employees additional points to use in a flexible benefits program, it is important to clearly communicate if it is a one-time award or something the organization tends to regularly do. Morale could be negatively affected if the points become expected and are then discontinued.[67]

Group Incentive Plans

The goal of incentive plans for workgroups and teams is to motivate teams to accomplish group goals and align the group's objectives with organizational goals. As with individual incentives, group incentives can put a portion of group members' pay at risk in exchange for the opportunity to earn additional pay if the group's performance meets or exceeds a certain goal. Recognition awards are also appropriate for motivating and rewarding groups. Group incentives are most appropriate when employees work interdependently and it is difficult to identify the contributions of individual group or team members.

One popular type of group incentive plan is gainsharing. Under a **gainsharing** plan, the organization shares the value of productivity gains with employees. Gainsharing can increase teamwork and cooperation by focusing employees' attention on lowering cost and improving productivity. The two most common types of gainsharing programs are Scanlon plans and Improshare systems.

gainsharing
the firm shares the value of productivity gains with employees

Scanlon plans
gainsharing programs based on implementing employee suggestions for lowering the cost per unit produced

Improshare
a gainsharing plan based on a mathematical formula that compares a performance baseline with actual productivity during a given period with the goal of reducing production time

Scanlon plans are gainsharing programs based on implementing employee suggestions for lowering the cost per unit produced. Any savings per unit of output are shared between the employees and the company. Because all employees receive an equal bonus, the reward may not reflect the actual contribution of all employees to the performance improvement.

An **Improshare** gainsharing plan is based on a mathematical formula that compares a work team's baseline performance with its actual productivity during a given period with the goal of reducing production time. When the team's actual productivity is greater than the baseline, the savings is shared equally with the team members. "Improshare" means improved productivity through sharing, and it focuses on reducing production time. This clear link between performance and rewards can be a strong productivity motivator, since high performance will lead to financial rewards.

Whole Foods Market has an effective Improshare program. When department teams in a store finish a four-week period under their payroll budget, the surplus gets handed down to the employees whose efficiency created the savings. Every four weeks, managers divide any payroll budget surplus by the hours logged by employees and add the resulting "gainshare" to the employees' hourly wages. The company claims the incentive not only motivates workers to step it up a notch but also aids in recruiting. Newcomers need a two-thirds vote from colleagues to be hired permanently, and team members are careful to screen out people whose low performance might jeopardize their future gainsharing awards.[68]

? so what

Because gainsharing programs are self-funding, the financial risks are minimal.

By sharing profits with employees, group incentive plans such as profit sharing and gainsharing only reward groups when the company's performance is good and it can afford it. As a result, gainsharing programs are self-funding. By sharing the risk and rewards of company performance with employees, these incentive systems help to focus employees on company issues and help align individual and organizational goals. Chrysler uses a formula of sharing with employees $800 for every 1 percent in profit margin on its North American sales. Southwest Airlines has engaged in profit sharing for over 40 years and shared $586 million, an average of 13 percent of salary, with its 54,000 employees in 2017.[69]

As with all incentive plans, care must be taken to avoid conflict across different incentive plans. For example, offering a team reward that conflicts with an individual reward undermines the effectiveness of the incentive scheme.

Organizational Incentive Plans

Organizational incentive plans are designed to align employee goals with organizational goals by rewarding employees for organizational-level performance. Variable pay and profit sharing plans are popular self-funding forms of organizational incentives. At Kimpton Hotels, customer raves can earn the entire staff gift certificates, cash, or other prizes.[70]

Although stock options are often awarded for individual performance, because their value depends on organizational performance, they are also a type of organizational incentive. **Employee stock ownership plans** are tax-exempt employer-established employee trusts that hold company stock for employees. The amount of stock an employee receives can be based on a percent of pay and/or time with the company. Employees are regularly informed of the value of their accounts, and they can sell their stock back to the organization or on the open market when they leave or retire. ESOPs are often a key part of employees' retirement plans, and the employer can receive tax benefits if the ESOP qualifies. The value of an ESOP is not guaranteed by any government agency, however, and employees can lose their retirement income if the company fails or if the value of the stock declines significantly.

employee stock ownership plans (ESOPs)
tax-exempt employer-established employee trusts that hold company stock for employees

Incentive Plans for Special Situations

There are many special situations that call for specific types of incentive plans. We next give particular attention to executive incentives, sales incentives, and innovation incentives.

Executive Incentives

Organizations design special incentive plans for their executives to better attract, motivate, and retain top managerial talent and to align executives' goals with organizational and stakeholder goals. Although often focused on company financial performance, outcomes including organizational culture and environmental performance are often rewarded as well. The most common executive incentive plans are profit sharing, short- and long-term incentives, supplemental benefits, and deferred compensation. Stock and stock options are particularly popular among publicly traded companies because company ownership helps to align long-term executive and company interests. As one expert says, "You want senior leaders to have most of their incentives driven by how the company performs because they are the people who can have the greatest impact on that."[71]

Executives often receive a low base salary and a high percentage bonus tied to overall company and individual performance. Executive bonuses typically range from 50 to 75 percent of base salary for smaller companies to 75 to 150 percent for larger companies.

One of the key challenges in creating executive incentive plans is deterring executives from engaging in unethical behavior and from taking too much or too little risk.[72] Research has found that CEOs were more likely to manipulate firm earnings when they had more out-of-the-money options (options with a strike price above the current stock price and therefore worthless) and lower stock ownership.[73] The 2010 Dodd-Frank Act implemented new regulations regarding executive compensation, including more open disclosure of executive pay and incentive compensation.[74]

so what?

Out-of-the-money options can motivate CEOs to take unacceptable risks and engage in unethical behaviors.

Sales Incentives

Sales incentives can focus strictly on the value of sales made by an employee or sales group or on the broader customer relationship management process. Customer relationship management involves finding and attracting new customers, retaining existing customers, enticing former clients back, and reducing the costs of servicing existing clients. Many of these activities do not result in a direct sale but contribute to the organization's long-term sales performance. Global pharmaceutical company GlaxoSmithKline changed its sales incentive plan from individual achievement of sales targets to one based on customer feedback and adherence to company policy, only to simplify it four years later due to complaints and frustration at the program's complexity.[75]

Payments processor Heartland Payment Systems gives new sales hires a choice of two compensation plans. The most aggressive plan, chosen by about 75 percent of new hires because of the high potential upside, pays employees on a commission-only basis. The other plan is a hybrid that pays employees for completing each of four levels in the sales process regardless of whether a sale is ultimately made. Employees who select the hybrid plan typically change to the commission-only plan after three to six months when they gain confidence. Heartland's sales professionals earn a commission on every sale they make plus a monthly residual percentage as long as they retain the customer. When sales professionals reach a certain performance level, they can earn stock options through promotions and incentive programs. Heartland regularly has more than a dozen salespeople earn more than the CEO.[76]

Table 10.3 highlights some of the decisions that must be made when designing a sales incentive program.

table **10.3**

Sales Incentive Program Decisions

Sales incentive programs need to:
• Define who is eligible for the incentive plan (are retail store cashiers eligible or only floor salespeople?).
• Identify the salary/incentive mix that supports the targeted total compensation level for sales people.
• Identify the incentive formula that translates performance into incentive pay.
• Define when a sale counts and how co-sales will be credited.
• Define the length of the sales cycle.

Incenting Innovation

Innovation has a large impact on organizations' survival and successes, helping them better respond to market changes.[77] Innovative organizations can better create and exploit new opportunities, get new products to market faster, and better capture first-mover advantage. Incentives can motivate employees by inspiring enthusiasm and can compensate employees for the risks and inevitable failures involved in developing innovations. When there is a lot of uncertainty, as is the case when pursuing a radical innovation, overemphasizing external and objective performance reduces the necessary intrinsic incentive and curiosity. Because innovation typically requires failure, incentives rewarding the desired innovation process and following corporate and ethical guidelines can be more appropriate than pay-for-performance plans that reward employees only for successful innovations.

 so what

Because short-term extrinsic rewards can undermine innovation, it is best to use long-term incentives such as stock options.

A series of studies indicate that extrinsic rewards including bonuses, pay increases, and awards are detrimental to innovation.[78] Material rewards can prompt employees to focus on pursuing more incremental, smaller innovations that are easy to accomplish rather than the more difficult yet more impactful radical innovations. Research has found that long-term incentives including stock options are associated with more heavily cited patents, more patent filings, and patents of greater originality. Short-term incentives appear to be unrelated to innovation.[79]

Managing Incentive Systems

Incentive systems must be carefully managed to ensure that they provide an adequate return on investment to the organization and do not result in any unintended consequences such as unethical behavior. Three important issues in managing incentive systems are the accuracy of the performance measurements and the feedback given to employees, the use of technology, and return on the investment in the incentive plan.

Accurate Performance Measurement and Feedback

One of the most important elements of a successful incentive program is that it provides accurate and timely performance feedback so that employees know if they need to change their strategies to meet their goals and earn the incentive. At Novo Nordisk's manufacturing facility in Clayton, NC, hourly workers are eligible for a 10 percent bonus each quarter. To inspire them, posters hang throughout the facility showing the running tally of how much they would receive if the bonus were paid today. Top salespeople receive a five-day trip for two to destinations such as Monte Carlo, Maui, or the Bahamas; top performers for five years straight get a $5,000 bonus, a company car upgrade, and other perks.[80]

figure **10.1**

Incentive Errors

	Does Not Receive Award	Receives Award
Does Not Deserve Award	Accurate Decision	Error of Commission
Deserves Award	Error of Omission	Accurate Decision

There are two possible types of errors in awarding incentives. **Errors of commission** occur when an employee receives an undeserved reward, either because the performance measurement system inaccurately identified him or her as a deserving employee or due to some other reason. Giving an undeserving employee an award can undermine the motivation of his or her coworkers, particularly the higher performing employees who did deserve it.

Errors of omission occur when an employee who deserves a reward does not receive one. If a performance measurement system does not thoroughly or accurately evaluate all employees' performance, it is easy to miss a high-performing employee who deserves to receive the incentive award. Errors of omission can damage the motivation of high-performing employees by failing to recognize their contributions. Whenever implementing an incentive program, it is important to be able to accurately and thoroughly assess employees on their relevant performance to minimize the occurrence of both types of errors. Figure 10.1 illustrates these two types of errors.

Technology

Incentive compensation management technologies are used by organizations of all sizes to automate calculations and incentive payment processes. Technology can greatly reduce the time, cost, and risk involved with implementing incentive compensation plans. Technology also facilitates the delivery of timely and accurate performance feedback to employees. "Having access, literally, 24 hours a day to see how they're progressing is important," says one expert, because they can say, 'I'm doing great' or, 'I need to step it up because I'm really behind.'"[81] Technology can also give managers the compensation and the performance metrics they need to better understand and drive employee behavior and performance. IT, the Internet, and corporate intranets can all improve the effectiveness of incentive and reward programs.

Online incentive and recognition programs can be very effective in motivating employees. Program information can be quickly communicated through intranet sites or e-mail, and the speed at which rewards are received strongly reinforces desired behaviors. Many Internet incentive sites exist, including maritz.com, hinda.com, and loyaltyworks.com. Many incentive sites are point-based and work like airline frequent flier programs. Employees earn points for reaching certain goals or for doing certain things over a set period of time, and they can cash the points in for a variety of merchandise, trips, and other awards. In many cases, employees can choose the reward they want, adapting the rewards to be those most motivating to each employee.

An important requirement for online incentive programs is that employees must have Internet access. This is challenging for companies with employees who do not have regular access to company computers. Many online vendors will provide supplemental paper materials for these employees, but other companies find ways to give all employees computer access. One company saved enough money by putting its incentive program online that it installed computer kiosks so that all employees had access and scheduled time on the computer as part of the workday. Incentive programs should be well promoted and made an integral part of the job.

error of commission
an employee receives an undeserved reward

error of omission
an employee who deserves a reward does not receive one

Motivation can be undermined by not give deserving employees rewards as well as by giving rewards to undeserving employees.

Letting employees choose their own rewards enhances motivation.

Evaluating the Effectiveness of an Incentive Program

An incentive program cannot be declared a success until the final results have been evaluated. Feedback from participants and program administrators on the program's clarity, motivational appeal, and success at incentivizing the intended behaviors is important in understanding the strengths and weaknesses of the program. This feedback is also useful in improving the program. Gathering as much objective, quantitative evidence as possible on the impacts of the program will help identify what worked and what did not. Reflecting on any unintended consequences attributable to the incentive program is also important. An honest evaluation of whether the program's goals were met is also essential in evaluating and improving the program if it is intended to be used again in the future.

Return on Investment

It is important to evaluate the return on investment of any incentive program. An incentive program should generate greater value in terms of improved performance, improved customer service, or reduced turnover than it costs to implement. Simple charting can be used as well as more sophisticated statistical analyses to identify unintended consequences, problems, and optimal incentive levels.

Figure 10.2 illustrates the relationship between incentive bonuses and customer service quality. In the figure, bonus payout amount is along the bottom, and customer service quality is up the side. In this organization, lower incentive bonuses improve customer service quality, but higher bonuses lead to lower customer service quality. Clearly, the incentive program is having some unintended consequences that deserve further investigation.

figure **10.2**

Customer Service Quality by Bonus Payout Level

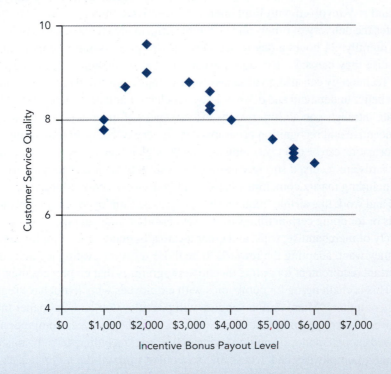

Summary and Application

Incentives are a powerful motivational tool. Used improperly, however, they can undermine cooperation, teamwork, and organizational performance. A variety of incentives are available to motivate individual, team, and organizational outcomes. To maximize the motivational power of the incentive program, it is important to match the incentives to what the employee values.

Real World Response

Incentive Compensation at Sprint

Although Sprint links base pay to median market values, it ensures that everyone is committed to the company's success through targeted success metrics and/or through sales goal incentive programs. The three strategic pillars of Sprint's corporate strategy are:[82]

- Improve the customer experience
- Strengthen Sprint's brand
- Generate cash and increase profits

To fairly link incentive pay to employees' performance and to their support of these three strategic pillars, performance objectives are set based on internal and market conditions. To ensure that performance-related bonuses stay fair during the ups and downs of a volatile economy, Sprint changed the performance period for employees' goals to six months instead of a year. Bonus payouts are still made once a year, but they are based on their goal achievements during two separate six-month periods. This allows Sprint to adjust performance targets if its forecast changes dramatically during the year.

Sprint also regularly changes the mix of targets in its executives' compensation plans. Goals are set for performance in areas including net service revenue, subscriber growth, and new device sales.[83] The amount of at-risk compensation increases as employees move up in the company.[84] Stan Sword, Sprint's vice president of total rewards, states, "Incentives remain only part of compensation. An effective compensation system should focus employees on what really matters to the organization while helping employees reach their full potential."[85]

Takeaway Points

1. Organizations typically tie pay to performance to recognize and reward high performers, increase the likelihood of achieving corporate goals, improve productivity, and move away from an entitlement culture.
2. When work is done interdependently or when it is difficult to identify employees' relative contribution to results, it is less appropriate to have a high reward differentiation. When work is done independently, the organization wants to set very high individual performance standards, and competition among employees is acceptable or desirable, then high reward differentiation is appropriate.
3. Stock options can help to align individual goals with organizational objectives, but they can also punish or compensate employees for factors beyond their control. Stock options can also motivate executives to engage in unethical behavior to maximize the value of their stock options.
4. Linking pay to specific goal accomplishment helps employees to see a clear link between their effort, job performance, and the reward, which enhances motivation.

5. The golden rule with pay-for-performance plans is that you get what you reward. Incentives can have unintended effects on employee motivation and behaviors, and it is important to consider the range of behaviors that an incentive is motivating.

6. Errors of commission occur when undeserving employees receive an incentive award. Giving an undeserving employee an award can undermine the motivation of his or her coworkers, particularly the higher performing employees who did deserve it. Errors of omission occur when deserving employees do not receive an incentive award. Errors of omission can damage the motivation of high-performing employees by failing to recognize their contributions. It is important to accurately and thoroughly assess employees on their relevant performance to minimize the occurrence of both types of errors.

Discussion Questions

1. What would better motivate you, a collaborative work culture or a lucrative pay-for-performance system? What would be your ideal pay mix?
2. What behaviors or outcomes do you think incentive plans best motivate?
3. What behaviors or outcomes do you think incentive plans are the weakest at motivating?
4. What incentives would you recommend to motivate a product development team responsible for creating new toys?
5. Should executives be rewarded differently from regular employees? Why or why not?
6. What incentive plans do you think would be most effective at motivating attendance?
7. What incentive plans do you think would be most effective at motivating customer service?

Personal Development Exercise: What Motivates You?

You can develop your capabilities as a manager by better understanding different ways of motivating and rewarding employees. You can also better prepare for your own career by better understanding the employment factors that are important to you.

Using the following scale, honestly rate the importance of each of the following types of incentives.

Unimportant			Neutral			Critical
(1)	(2)	(3)	(4)	(5)	(6)	(7)

_____ 1. Respect
_____ 2. Recognition
_____ 3. Work–life balance
_____ 4. Collegial work environment
_____ 5. Doing work you love
_____ 6. Stock options
_____ 7. Spot rewards for good performance
_____ 8. Profit sharing
_____ 9. Skill-based pay
_____ 10. Employee stock ownership plan (ESOP)

Scoring Instructions

Add up your responses to items 1 to 5. This is your intrinsic reward preference score. Scores on this scale can range from 5 to 35, with higher numbers reflecting a stronger preference for intrinsic rewards. Scores above 25 reflect a strong preference for intrinsic motivation and rewards.

Now add up your responses to items 6 to 10. This is your extrinsic reward preference score. Scores on this scale can range from 5 to 35, with higher numbers reflecting a stronger preference for extrinsic rewards. Scores above 25 reflect a strong preference for extrinsic motivation and rewards.

Interpretation

Think about the scale with your higher score, and think about the types of jobs and organizations that will offer what is most important to you. Consider the scale with your lower score, and think about the types of jobs and organizations that will be less attractive to you. Also consider the specific reward types that you rated highest to identify the rewards you most value, and identify whether they are short- or long-term incentives. Now consider what you can do as a job seeker to maximize your fit with the rewards of your future job and what you can do as a manager to generate the highest motivation among all your employees.

Strategic HRM Exercises

Exercise: Aligning Incentives with Business Strategy

Form groups of three to five students. Each group will be assigned one of the following situations and will be given 15 minutes to identify an appropriate incentive plan to support the described employees' performance in that organization.

1. French fry cooks at McDonald's
2. Salespeople at luxury retailer Tiffany's
3. Building code inspectors
4. Research scientists at a biotechnology company
5. The CEO of Apple Computer
6. A team manufacturing employees responsible for assembling specialty motors

Exercise: Flexible Incentive Pans

We would like to thank Professor Kathy Broneck of Pima Community College for this exercise idea.

Using the list of behaviors and outcomes that incentive plans can influence in Table 10-1, identify at least one specific behavior or performance goal for each as well as an appropriate reward for reaching that goal. You may use any job you choose. Be prepared to share your answers with the class.

Exercise: Incentives at Potash, Inc.

Point your favorite web browser to http://www.potashcorp.com/proxy_circular/2013/compensation/discussion-and-analysis/incentive-plan/ and read about fertilizer company Potash Corporation's incentive compensation. When you have finished, answer the following questions:

1. In what key ways has Potash aligned the interests of its executive officers and shareholders?

2. How does Potash focus employees' attention on short-, middle-, and long-term performance objectives?
3. What elements of Potash's incentive compensation system appeal the most to you? If you were a manager at the company, what would you be the most motivated by?

Exercise: Motivation Through Incentives

View the humorous video, "Employee Motivation Comedy Sketch," (2:39). After watching the video, answer the following questions:

1. Do you think that constant incentives for every task completed would be an effective incentive system? Why or why not?
2. Do you think that smaller but more frequent rewards are more motivational than larger, longer-term rewards? Why or why not?
3. What do you think would be the ideal pay mix for a managerial job? Why?

Integrative Project

Using the same job you used for the previous chapter, describe the incentive pay system you would establish for this position. Be sure to explain your objectives for the incentive system and why your recommendations are likely to be effective in meeting these objectives. Also describe the pay mix you would establish for the job and how differentiated the rewards would be.

Video Case

Imagine that you are meeting with other Happy Time Toys managers to decide how to best incent toy developers to develop more innovative new product lines. *What do you say or do?* Go to this book's video case, watch the challenge video for this chapter, and choose the best video response. Be sure to also view the outcomes of the two responses you didn't choose.

Discussion Questions

1. What concepts from the chapter are illustrated in these videos? Explain your answer.
2. What ethical issues are illustrated in these videos? Explain your answer.
3. How else might you handle this situation? Explain your answer.

Endnotes

1. Krell, E. (2011). All for incentives, incentives for all. *HR Magazine*, 56. Retrieved March 22, 2017, from https://www .shrm.org/hr-today/news/hr-magazine/pages/0111krell.aspx
2. Pepitone, J. (2011, September 30). HP CEO Meg Whitman's salary: $1. *CNN Money*. Retrieved September 30, 2011, from http://money.cnn.com/2011/09/30/technology/meg_whitman_ salary/index.htm?iid=HP_LN
3. Gerhart, B., & Milkovich, G. T. (1990). Organizational differences in managerial compensation and financial performance. *Academy of Management Journal, 33*, 663–691.
4. Luthans, F., & Stajkovic, A. D. (1999). Reinforce for performance: The need to go beyond pay and even rewards. *Academy of Management Executive, 13*, 49–57.
5. Miller, S. (2010, March 1). Companies worldwide rewarding performance with variable pay. *Society for Human Resource Management*. Retrieved March 21, 2017, from https://www .shrm.org/resourcesandtools/hr-topics/compensation/pages/ variableworld.aspx
6. Cha, S. (2011, September 12–18). Foreign investors steer clear of Korean banks. *Bloomberg Businessweek*, 50–51.

7. Miller, S. (2011, September 14). Study: Pay for performance pays off. *Society for Human Resource Management*. Retrieved March 22, 2017, from https://www.shrm.org/resourcesandtools/hr-topics/compensation/pages/paysoff.aspx

8. Culture shock! 10 tips for creating global incentive and recognition programs. (2011). Maritz.com. Retrieved September 14, 2011, from http://www.maritz.com/News-Events-and-Insights/Press-Center/Press-Kits/~/media/Files/MaritzDotCom/News%20Events%20and%20Insights/Media%20Kit/Press%20Kit/Travel-Insight-Global-Incentives-Whitepaper.ashx; Pyrillis, R. (2011, August). Avoid culture shock when rewarding international employees. *Workforce Management Online*. Retrieved September 14, 2011, from http://www.workforce.com/archive/feature/benefits-compensation/avoid-culture-shock-rewarding-international-employees/index.php

9. Awasthi, V. N., Chow, C. W., & Wu, A. (2001). Cross-cultural differences in the behavioral consequences of imposing performance evaluation and reward systems: An experimental investigation. *The International Journal of Accounting*, *36*, 291–309.

10. Awasthi, V. N., Chow, C. W., & Wu, A. (2001). Cross-cultural differences in the behavioral consequences of imposing performance evaluation and reward systems: An experimental investigation. *The International Journal of Accounting*, *36*, 291–309; Pyrillis, R. (2011, September 21). Avoid culture shock when rewarding international employees. Workforce.com. Retrieved March 22, 2017, from http://www.workforce.com/2011/08/23/avoid-culture-shock-when-rewarding-international-employees/; Malone, S. (2010, May 10). A tale of adultery and green tractors. *Reuters*. Retrieved March 22, 2017, from http://uk.reuters.com/article/2010/05/10/us-manufacturing-summit-quirks-idUKTRE6496LT20100510

11. Locke, E. (2004). Linking goals to monetary incentives. *Academy of Management Executive*, *18*, 130–133.

12. Kerr, S. (1995). On the folly of rewarding A, while hoping for B. *Academy of Management Executive*, *9*, 7–14.

13. Beyer, L. (2011, May). Top performers look for a little love outside of pay. *Workforce Management Online*. Retrieved March 21, 2017, from http://www.workforce.com/2011/05/01/top-performers-look-for-a-little-love-outside-of-pay/

14. 25 top-paying companies: NetApp. (2011). *CNN Money*. Retrieved September 9, 2011, from http://money.cnn.com/galleries/2011/pf/jobs/1101/gallery.best_companies_top_paying.fortune/11.html

15. *Ibid.*

16. Kochanski, J., & Kegerise, R. (2011, June 21). How to use 'carve-outs' to truly pay for performance. SHRM Online. Retrieved March 22, 2017, from https://www.shrm.org/resourcesandtools/hr-topics/compensation/pages/carve-outs.aspx

17. Fuller, J. J., & Tinkham, R. (2002). Making the most of scarce reward dollars. *Employee Benefits Journal*, *27*, 3–8.

18. Pfeffer, J., & Sutton, R. I. (2006). *Hard facts, dangerous half-truths, and total nonsense: Profiting from evidence-based management*. Boston, MA: Harvard Business Press.

19. Werbel, J., & Balkin, D. B. (2010). Are human resource practices linked to employee misconduct?: A rational choice perspective. *Human Resource Management Review, 20*(4), 317–326.

20. Ovsyannikov, M. (2010, May). Pay to perform vs. pay to fail. *Talent Management Magazine*, 16–19.

21. Gray, K. (2009, September 21). How not to do incentive pay. *BNET*. Retrieved September 14, 2011, from http://www.bnet.com/article/how-not-to-do-incentive-pay/344828

22. Flint, J. (2011, May 16–22). Alternative energy. *Bloomberg BusinessWeek*, 76.

23. Krell, E. (2011). All for incentives, incentives for all. *HR Magazine*, 56. Retrieved March 21, 2017, from https://www.shrm.org/hr-today/news/hr-magazine/pages/0111krell.aspx

24. 25 top-paying companies: Adobe Systems. (2011). *CNN Money*. Retrieved March 19, 2017, from http://money.cnn.com/galleries/2011/pf/jobs/1101/gallery.best_companies_top_paying.fortune/19.html

25. Brandes, P., Dharwadkar, R., Lemesis, G. V., & Heisler, W. J. (2003, February). Effective employee stock option design: Reconciling stakeholder, strategic, and motivational factors. *Academy of Management Executive*, *17*, 77–93; Caldbeck, J. (2013, October). How to hire the best. *INC*, 86; Rafter, M. V. (2004, September). As the age of options wanes, companies settle on new incentive plans. *Workforce Management*, *83*, 64–67.

26. Carlson, N. (2009, March 11). Google bails out employees, socks it to shareholders. *Business Insider*. Retrieved March 25, 2017, from http://www.businessinsider.com/google-options-repricing-bails-out-15642-employees-2009-3

27. Goldfarb, J., & Holding, R. (2011, May 8). Incentives play role in success of Netflix. *The New York Times*. Retrieved March 17, 2017, from http://www.nytimes.com/2011/05/09/business/09views.html?_r=2&src=twr

28. Whitney, K. (2010). Are incentives dangerous? *Talent Management Magazine*, July, 44–47.

29. Kohn, A. (1993). Why incentive plans cannot work. *Harvard Business Review*, September–October, 54–63.

30. 25 top-paying companies: Alston & Bird. (2011). *CNN Money*. Retrieved March 21, 2017, from http://money.cnn.com/galleries/2011/pf/jobs/1101/gallery.best_companies_top_paying.fortune/3.html

31. Gupta, S. (2015, March 5). The 10 top-paying companies. *Fortune*. Retrieved March 21, 2017, from http://fortune.com/2015/03/05/top-paying-best-companies/

32. Unusual perks: Paychex. (2010, January 21). *Fortune online*. Retrieved March 21, 2017, from http://money.cnn.com/galleries/2010/fortune/1001/gallery.bestcompanies_unusual_perks.fortune/9.html

33. Caudron, S. (1993). Master the compensation maze. *Personnel Journal*, June. *2*, 64.

34. Nelson, B. (1994). *1001 ways to reward employees,* p. 19. New York: Workmen Publishing.

35. Demos, T. (2010, April 5). Motivate without spending millions. *CNN Money*. Retrieved March 21, 2017, from http://money.cnn.com/2010/04/05/news/economy/job_motivate.fortune/index.htm

36. Daniels, C. (1999, November 22). Thank you is nice, but this is better. *Fortune*, p. 370.

37. 25 top-paying companies: Brocade Communications Systems. (2011). *CNN Money*. Retrieved March 21, 2017, from http://money.cnn.com/galleries/2011/pf/jobs/1101/gallery.best_companies_top_paying.fortune/9.html

38. 25 top-paying companies: Kimpton Hotels & Restaurants. (2011). *CNN Money*. Retrieved March 21, 2017, from http://money.cnn.com/galleries/2011/pf/jobs/1101/gallery.best_companies_top_paying.fortune/15.html

39. Hamel, G. (2010, November 18). HCL's CEO on its 'management makeover.' *The Wall Street Journal*. Retrieved March 21, 2017, from http://blogs.wsj.com/management/2010/08/24/hcls-ceo-on-its-management-makeover/?KEYWORDS=HCL

40. Deci, E. L., Koestner, R., & Ryan, R. M. (1999). A meta-analytic review of experiments examining the effects of intrinsic vs. extrinsic motivation. *Psychological Bulletin*, *125*, 627–688.

41. Brady, D. (2010). Joe Torre. *Bloomberg Businessweek*, June 21–27, 96.

42. Gray, K. (2009, September 21). How not to do incentive pay. *BNET*. Retrieved March 21, 2017, from http://www.bnet.com/article/how-not-to-do-incentive-pay/344828

43. Lagace, M. (2003, April 14). Pay for performance doesn't always pay off. *Harvard Business School Working Knowledge*. Retrieved March 21, 2017, from http://hbswk.hbs.edu/item/3424.html

44. Beer, M., & Cannon, M. D. (2004). Promise and peril in implementing pay-for-performance. *Human Resource Management*, *43*, 3–48.

45. Gray, K. (2009, September 21). How not to do incentive pay. *BNET*. Retrieved March 21, 2017, from http://www.bnet.com/article/how-not-to-do-incentive-pay/344828

46. Tang, T. L. P. (1992). The meaning of money revisited. *Journal of Organizational Behavior*, *13*, 197–202.

47. From "The Meaning of Money Revisited," by Tang, T.L.P., *Journal of Organizational Behavior*, 1992, 13: 197-202. Reprinted with permission of John Wiley & Sons, Inc.

48. Lawler, E. E. (1981). *Pay and organization development*. Reading, MA: Addison-Wesley Publishing Co.; Tang, T. L. P. (1992). The meaning of money revisited. *Journal of Organizational Behavior*, *13*, 197–202.

49. Tang, T. L. P. (1992). The meaning of money revisited. *Journal of Organizational Behavior*, *13*, 197–202.

50. Levine, M. (2016, April 21). Regulators don't want bankers to be paid for taking risk. *Bloomberg View*. Retrieved March 22, 2017, from https://www.bloomberg.com/view/articles/2016-04-21/regulators-don-t-want-bankers-to-be-paid-for-risk

51. Ledford, G., Jr. (1991). Three case studies on skill-based pay: An overview. *Compensation & Benefits Review*, March–April, 11–23.

52. Ledford, G., Jr., & Bergel, G. (1991). Skill-based pay case no. 1: General Mills. *Compensation & Benefits Review*, March–April, 24–38.

53. Caudron, S. (1993). Master the compensation maze. *Personnel Journal*, June, *2*, 64.

54. Ledford, G. E., Jr., & Heneman, H. G., III. (2011). Skill-based pay. *Society for Human Resource Management and the Society for Industrial and Organizational Psychology*, June. Retrieved March 21, 2017, from http://www.ledfordconsultingnetwork.com/sites/default/files/SIOP-SHRM%20-%20Skill-Based%20Pay,%20FINAL.pdf

55. *Ibid.*

56. *Ibid.*

57. *Ibid.*

58. Murray, B., & Gerhart, B. (1998). An empirical analysis of a skill-based pay program and plant performance outcomes. *Academy of Management Journal*, *41*, 68–78; Ledford, G. E., Jr., & Heneman, H. G., III. (2011). Skill-based pay. *Society for Human Resource Management and the Society for Industrial and Organizational Psychology*, June. Retrieved March 21, 2017, from http://www.ledfordconsultingnetwork.com/sites/default/files/SIOP-SHRM%20-%20Skill-Based%20Pay,%20FINAL.pdf

59. Beyer, L. (2011, May). Top performers look for a little love outside of pay. *Workforce Management Online*. Retrieved March 21, 2017, from http://www.workforce.com/2011/05/01/top-performers-look-for-a-little-love-outside-of-pay/

60. The best places to work: 2016. (2016, November 15). *Outside*. Retrieved March 22, 2017, from https://www.outsideonline.com/2134736/best-places-work-2016

61. O'Connell, V. (2008, September 10). Retailers reprogram workers in efficiency push. *The Wall Street Journal*, A1.

62. Peterson, S. J., & Luthans, F. (2006). The impact of financial and nonfinancial incentives on business–unit outcomes over time. *Journal of Applied Psychology*, *91*, 156–165.

63. Nelson, B. (2011). Secrets of successful employee recognition. Quality Digest, August. Retrieved March 22, 2017, from http://www.qualitydigest.com/aug/nelson.html

64. Worthington, B. (2007, May 3). Work/life balance influences workplace ethics. *Human Resource Executive Online*. Retrieved September 14, 2011, from http://www.hreonline.com/HRE/story.jsp?storyId=12614425

65. Time to take another look at telecommuting. (2002, May). *HR Focus*, 8.

66. Byrne, J. A. (2003). How to lead now: Getting extraordinary performance when you can't pay for it. *Fast Company*, *73*, 62.

67. Flexible benefits: Linking flex with incentive schemes. (2010, September 1). Employeebenefits.co.uk. Retrieved March 21, 2017, from https://www.employeebenefits.co.uk/issues/september-2010/flexible-benefits-linking-flex-with-incentive-schemes/

68. Kaihla, P. (2006, March 23). Best-kept secrets of the world's best companies. *Business 2.0 Magazine*. Retrieved March 21, 2017, from http://money.cnn.com/2006/03/23/magazines/business2/business2_bestkeptsecrets/index.htm

69. Blasi, J. (2017, March 20). How Southwest Airlines and others are creating a new breed of capitalism. *Fortune*. Retrieved March 20, 2017, from http://fortune.com/2017/03/20/southwest-airlines-profit-sharing/

70. 25 top-paying companies: Kimpton Hotels & Restaurants. (2011). *CNN Money*. Retrieved March 21, 2017, from http://money.cnn.com/galleries/2011/pf/jobs/1101/gallery.best_companies_top_paying.fortune/15.html

71. Whitney, K. (2010). Are incentives dangerous? *Talent Management Magazine*, July, 44–47.

72. Sepe, S. M. (2010). Making sense of executive compensation. *Delaware Journal of Corporate Law*, 36.

73. Zhang, X., Bartol, K. M., Smith, K. G., Pfarrer, M. D., & Khanin, D. M. (2008). CEOs on the edge: Earnings manipulation and stock-based incentive misalignment. *Academy of Management Journal*, *51*, 241–258.

74. See http://www.sec.gov/about/laws/wallstreetreform-cpa.pdf for the Dodd-Frank Act.

75. Silverman, E. (2015, April 13). Glaxo to change its compensation program for U.S. sales reps. *The Wall Street Journal*. Retrieved March 22, 2017, from http://blogs.wsj.com/pharmalot/2015/04/13/glaxo-to-change-its-compensation-program-for-u-s-sales-reps/

76. Hansen, F. (2010). Inside Heartland Payment Systems' successful sales recruiting machine. *Workforce Management Online*, October. Retrieved March 21, 2017, from http://www.workforce.com/2010/10/12/inside-heartland-payment-systems-successful-sales-recruiting-machine/

77. Dougherty, D., & Hardy, C. (1996). Sustained product innovation in large, mature organizations: Overcoming innovation-to-organization problems. *Academy of Management Journal*, *39*, 1120–1154; Li, Y., Li, D., Li, H., & Zhao, Y. (2006). The effect of organizational reward and control on firm performance in Chinese technology firms. In H. Li (Ed.), *Growth of new technology ventures in China's emerging market*, pp. 196–218. Northampton, MA: Edward Elgar Publishing Ltd.

78. Amabile, T. M. (1983). *The social psychology of creativity*. New York: Springer-Verlag; Amabile, T. M., Hennessey, B. A., & Grossman, B. S. (1986). Social influences on creativity: The effects of contracted-for-reward. *Journal of Personality and*

Social Psychology, 50, 14–23; Hennessey, B. A., & Amabile, T. M. (1998). Reward, intrinsic incentive, and creativity. *American Psychologist, 53*, 674–675.

79. Lerner, J., & Wulf, J. (2007). Innovation and incentives: Evidence from corporate R&D. *The Review of Economics and Statistics, 89*, 634–644.

80. 25 top-paying companies: Novo Nordisk. (2011). *CNN Money*. Retrieved September 9, 2011, from http://money.cnn.com/galleries/2011/pf/jobs/1101/gallery.best_companies_top_paying.fortune/25.html

81. Hein, K. (2006, February 1) Anatomy of an online sales incentive program. *Incentive Magazine*. Retrieved March 21, 2017, from http://www.incentivemag.com/Strategy/Consumer/Anatomy-of-an-Online-Incentive-Program/

82. Krell, E. (2011). All for incentives, incentives for all. *HR Magazine, 56*. Retrieved March 21, 2017, from https://www.shrm.org/hr-today/news/hr-magazine/pages/0111krell.aspx

83. Campos, A. (2013, October 8). How Sprint is planning a great turnaround. *The Motley Fool*. Retrieved March 22, 2017, from https://www.fool.com/investing/general/2013/10/08/how-sprint-is-planning-a-great-turnaround.aspx

84. Davis, M. (2016, July 29). Sprint updates executives' pay, showing big stock deals. *The Kansas City Star*. Retrieved March 22, 2017, from http://www.kansascity.com/news/business/technology/article92674502.html

85. Krell, E. (2011). All for incentives, incentives for all. *HR Magazine, 56*. Retrieved March 21, 2017, from https://www.shrm.org/hr-today/news/hr-magazine/pages/0111krell.aspx

chapter 11

Benefits

Learning Objectives

AFTER STUDYING THIS CHAPTER, YOU SHOULD BE ABLE TO:

1 Why do organizations offer employee benefits?

2 What are mandatory benefits, and why do organizations offer them?

3 What are customary benefits, and why do organizations offer them?

4 What are optional benefits, and why do organizations offer them?

5 What are some of the challenges in communicating benefits information to employees?

6 What influences an organization's benefit choices?

Real World Challenge

Using Benefits Strategically at SAS

Business software company SAS Institute Inc. pursues a competitive advantage based on the theory that happy employees lead to happy customers. To support its high-involvement culture, SAS created a warm, supportive atmosphere and a human resource strategy focused on employee retention. Its employee retention goal drives its benefits policy and is credited with being a big reason that SAS's turnover is consistently low.[1]

SAS's motto is, "Treat employees as if they make a difference to the company, and they will."[2] SAS is willing to provide employees with generous benefits that help them be productive and remain committed to the organization. Kristen Vosburgh, senior director of compensation and benefits says, "Even where the ROI is hard to determine, we get support from the CEO, as long as the benefit makes sense for our employees and the business."[3]

Imagine that SAS asks you for advice about what benefits to offer its employees to enhance its competitive advantage and retain its valued employees. After reading this chapter you should have some good ideas.

employee benefits
nonwage compensation
or rewards given to
employees (indirect
compensation)

total compensation
(total rewards)
the combined value of
direct (pay and bonuses)
and indirect (nonwage)
compensation

Employee benefits are nonwage compensation or rewards given to employees. Benefits are sometimes referred to as indirect compensation in contrast to pay, which is considered direct compensation. The combined value of direct and indirect compensation is an employee's **total compensation** or total rewards. Additional nonmonetary benefits, including a collegial work environment and doing meaningful work, are also valued by employees. Many people are willing to accept lower pay in exchange for valued benefits.

Benefits include medical insurance, tuition reimbursement, sick and vacation leave, retirement savings plans, product discounts, and free food. Companies use benefits to attract and retain employees and sometimes to compensate for offering lower pay than competitors.

Because of their effects on an organization's ability to attract and retain talent and enable employees to perform better at work, corporate executives in the United States overwhelmingly view benefits as important for creating a competitive advantage. In 2016, private U.S. organizations spent an average of 30.3 percent of an employee's annual salary on benefits. The cost of legally required benefits, including workers' compensation and Social Security costs, averaged 7.8 percent; the cost of health benefits averaged 7.6 percent; paid leave costs averaged 6.9 percent; and retirement and savings costs averaged 4 percent. Larger organizations spend more on voluntary benefits than do companies with fewer employees.[4] Salesforce.com's benefits include up to $510 per month for commuting and parking expenses; up to $5,250 per year in tuition reimbursement for pre-approved, job-related courses; up to $100 per month reimbursement for fitness activities and weight-management programs; and up to seven days of paid time off to volunteer in the community.[5]

Although they can help organizations in various ways, the high and rising cost of benefits, particularly rapidly increasing healthcare costs, has placed benefits costs on the list of the three most important factors affecting companies' finances. Nonetheless, because employee benefits have been shown to be positively related to firm productivity[6] and employee satisfaction, research suggests that benefits expenses should be viewed as an investment rather than as expense.[7] As SAS CEO Jim Goodnight, featured in this chapter's opening Real World Challenge, said, "Knowledge-based companies need knowledge workers. Looking at... services that keep employees motivated, loyal, and doing their best work as merely an expense and not an investment is, I think, a little shortsighted."[8] Diamond Pet Foods provides its employees a benefits package that includes free health insurance, unquestioned time off to handle family emergencies, bonuses, and profit sharing because the return on its investment has been well worth it. Turnover is only 3 percent, compared to an industry average of 11 percent, and the benefits increase employee morale, well-being, and productivity.[9]

"Knowledge-based companies need knowledge workers. Looking at... services that keep employees motivated, loyal, and doing their best work as merely an expense and not an investment is, I think, a little shortsighted."

—Jim Goodnight, CEO, SAS

Effectively using benefits to maximize both their value to employees and the return on investment for the company improves organizational effectiveness. Understanding the benefits you value the most can also help you better evaluate prospective employers. The focus of this chapter is on the purpose and strategic use of employee benefits. Different types of benefits are described, as well as methods of benefits management. By influencing motivation, benefits influence what employees *will* do in our book's overall model of HRM.

What Is the Purpose of Benefits?

When salary budgets are tight, or when the hiring market is competitive, providing better benefits than competitors can help organizations attract and retain top employees. Because benefits help to create a positive employee experience, they can also boost employee performance, satisfaction, commitment, and retention.[10] Additional reasons organizations offer employee benefits are to promote employee health, provide financial protection, and improve employees' work/life balance.[11] Although some organizations may pursue these goals for moral reasons, many do it for economic and productivity reasons. One survey found that technology companies tend to use benefits to attract highly skilled talent, whereas nontechnology companies often use them to control healthcare costs.[12]

When asked to explain Google's approach to employee benefits, Executive Chairman Eric Schmidt says,

Google's approach to employee benefits is to provide things that make it easier for employees to be and stay productive and focused on work. In addition to enjoying quality food and having access to gyms and laundry rooms, employees can easily get a haircut, get their cars washed, and have their dry cleaning done.

> "The goal is to strip away everything that gets in our employees' way. We provide a standard package of fringe benefits but on top of that are first-class dining facilities, gyms, laundry rooms, massage rooms, haircuts, carwashes, dry cleaning, commuting buses—just about anything a hardworking employee might want."[13]

💬 HR flexibility

Goal-Directed Benefits

Goal	Benefits
Attracting recruits	Housing, relocation, and transportation allowances; health, dental, and life insurance; flextime and telecommuting.
Decreasing absenteeism	Wellness program; flextime; personal days; onsite daycare for kids and elders.
Increasing financial security	Health, life, workers' compensation, and disability insurance; prescription drug coverage; financial planning seminars; retirement plan.
Increasing retirement security	Greater 401(k) match; financial planning seminars; long-term-care insurance.
Decreasing healthcare claims	Wellness program; fitness center; health coaches; free healthy lunches and snacks; stress management program.
Decreasing employee stress	Flextime; fitness center; financial and retirement planning; onsite daycare for kids and elders; personal days.
Improving employee skills	Tuition reimbursement; paid sabbaticals.
Improving retention	Flextime; 401(k); health, dental, and life insurance benefits; improving the employee experience (onsite oil changes, dry cleaning, food, massages, and health care).

Employee stress costs organizations more than $300 billion annually in productivity, absenteeism, and turnover as well as higher medical, legal, and insurance expenses.[14] Organizations can help their employees relieve their stressors by providing services such as:

- Employee assistance programs to provide stress management
- Wellness programs
- Financial and legal counseling
- Professional financial advice to decrease financial stress and improve employees' financial security
- Schedule flexibility to help employees meet both work and life demands.

Different benefits meet different objectives. This chapter's HR Flexibility feature links some common goals of employee benefits with appropriate benefit options to achieve that goal.

? so what

Stress isn't just unpleasant; it also increases absenteeism, turnover, medical and legal expenses, and decreases productivity.

Types of Benefits

Some benefits are required by law, whereas others are at the discretion of the employer. Table 11.1 summarizes the various mandatory, customary, and optional benefits employers offer.

table 11.1

Types of Benefits

Mandatory Benefits	Customary Benefits	Optional Benefits
Social Security	Life insurance	Work/life benefits
Unemployment insurance	Disability insurance	Free food
Workers' compensation	Health insurance	Workout facility
Family Medical Leave Act (FMLA)	Retirement plan	Domestic partner benefits
COBRA health coverage		Flexible spending account
		Nonfinancial benefits
		Creative benefits

Mandatory Benefits

By law, organizations with a certain number of employees must offer Social Security, unemployment insurance, workers' compensation, FMLA leave, and COBRA health coverage. We next discuss each of these benefits in more detail.

Social Security.   The Social Security Act of 1935 provides retirement income to qualified workers and their spouses after working a certain number of hours. Employees and the employer both make mandatory contributions to the **Social Security** system. Benefits can be claimed beginning at age 62, although starting to collect benefits at a later age increases the amount received. A worker's earnings history determines his or her benefits level. Higher earnings generate a greater monthly benefit based on a progressive formula. Benefits increase over time based on a cost-of-living index. Social Security can supplement a retiree's income, but it is usually insufficient to fund a comfortable retirement on its own.

Although the amount varies widely across individuals based on their earnings history and the length of time worked, Social Security replaces an average of 40 percent of an individual's

Social Security

provides retirement income to qualified workers and their spouses after working a certain number of hours preretirement income. The structure of the benefits formula replaces a larger percentage of earnings for lower earners than for higher earners. Social Security taxes are withheld by the employer as a payroll tax on pay below a certain level.[15]

Although Social Security continues to assure basic income to the elderly, disabled, and survivors, it has been in the news a lot lately because of a projected funding gap and overall budget deficits. It seems clear that some adjustments in Social Security benefits and financing are needed, but large-scale changes would be disruptive.[16] Many experts are advising younger workers not to count on Social Security and to save and invest their own money to provide for a comfortable retirement.

so what?

Because experts have warned about the long-term stability of the Social Security system, it is wise to save and invest independently to ensure a comfortable retirement.

Unemployment insurance.   The Social Security Act of 1935 also established **unemployment insurance** to provide temporary income during periods of involuntary unemployment. Unemployment benefits are based on a percentage of the individual's earnings over a recent 52-week period and allow workers to maintain their consumption of basic goods and services during economic recessions. The goal of unemployment insurance is to preserve many other jobs that could be lost if these workers lost their income and spending power.

Unemployment insurance benefits are given to workers who become unemployed through no fault of their own. An employee who voluntarily quits or is terminated for cause is not eligible for benefits, nor is a self-employed person or someone who refuses a comparable job offer. In most states, employees who participate in a strike are also not covered unless the striking worker is permanently replaced. Unemployment benefits are required by law, although eligibility, benefit amounts, and the duration of benefits vary by state.[17]

unemployment insurance
provides temporary income during periods of involuntary unemployment

Workers' compensation.   **Workers' compensation insurance** pays for medical costs and sometimes time off if an employee suffers a job-related sickness or accident and survivor benefits in the case of an employee's death. Most states require that employers provide workers' compensation insurance benefits, which typically cover the following in the event of an employee's illness or death:

1. Any reasonable and necessary medical expenses (e.g., hospital bills and medication);
2. Disability income benefits to cover lost wages when the employee is unable to work;
3. Rehabilitation benefits to help the employee recover; and
4. Survivor death benefits if the employee died because of the work injury.

The cost of workers' compensation insurance depends on three factors:

1. The risk of injury for the particular occupation.
2. The company's injury experience rating, influenced by the frequency and severity of the injuries sustained by the company's employees.
3. The level of benefits provided in the state in which the company is located.

workers' compensation insurance
pays for medical costs and sometimes time off if an employee suffers a job-related sickness or accident and survivor benefits in the case of an employee's death

A better company safety record decreases the workers' compensation payroll tax rate, saving the company money. Designing jobs to minimize the risk of injuries and making safety a priority can help contain workers' compensation insurance costs. Some states allow companies, typically in the same industry, to organize self-insurance pools to help contain workers' compensation insurance costs. Members share each other's risk, and losses are paid from premiums and investment returns.

so what?

Designing jobs to maximize safety not only decreases injuries, it can also decrease the cost of workers' compensation insurance.

The Family and Medical Leave Act of 1993.   The **Family and Medical Leave Act (FMLA)** of 1993 (amended in 2008) requires most employers to provide employees up to 12 weeks of unpaid leave for the following reasons:[18]

1. The birth and care of the eligible employee's child, or placement for adoption or foster care of a child with the employee;

Family and Medical Leave Act
requires most employers to provide employees up to 12 weeks of unpaid leave to care for family members

2. The care of an immediate family member (spouse, child, or parent) who has a serious health condition; and

3. The care of the employee's own serious health condition.

The FMLA also requires that employee's group health benefits be maintained during the leave. The Family and Medical Leave Act and National Defense Authorization Act of 2008 amends the FMLA to permit a family member to take up to 26 workweeks of leave to care for a member of the armed forces, National Guard, or Reserves with a serious injury or illness.

The FMLA is administered by the Employment Standards Administration's Wage and Hour Division within the U.S. Department of Labor, and it applies to employers with at least 50 employees within a 75-mile radius. The employer must give employees returning from FMLA leave the same job or a job equivalent to the one they held before taking the leave, and health insurance and other employee benefits must be maintained during the leave.

This chapter's Strategic Impact feature describes how Patagonia uses family oriented benefits to improve employee retention.

 # Strategic Impact

Using Benefits to Retain Employees at Patagonia

Attracting and retaining both men and women can be easier if employees' work–life balance is attended to and if employees' childcare needs are better met. Although most parents in the United States do not have a right to any paid time off with a baby, much less affordable child care, many organizations are realizing the benefits of offering family benefits beyond what is required by law.

Patagonia, which has 100 percent retention of its female employees once they become mothers, offers new mothers 16 weeks of fully paid maternity leave. Both fathers and adoptive mothers get 12 weeks of fully paid leave, and the high-quality on-site child care is run by well-trained teachers. All employees get 12 weeks of full pay for any serious medical condition or a serious medical condition of a spouse, domestic partner, child or parent. Twelve weeks of leave are given for an employee's active military duty, and 12 weeks are given to care for a member of the military. Parents who need to travel for work can even bring a nanny or a partner paid for by Patagonia. If a partner can't come on the trip, one of the teachers will. Mothers have full access to their infants during the day and can nurse in meetings, although many women opt to just go next door and do it.[19]

Consolidated Omnibus Budget Reconciliation Act
provides a continuation of group health coverage for employees and qualified beneficiaries that might otherwise be terminated when an employee experiences a qualifying event

COBRA.   The **Consolidated Omnibus Budget Reconciliation Act** health benefit provision (COBRA) was passed by Congress in 1986. COBRA provides a continuation of group health coverage for employees and qualified beneficiaries that might otherwise be terminated when an employee experiences a qualifying event. Qualifying events include termination for reasons other than gross misconduct, a reduction in work hours, divorce or legal separation, and death of the covered employee.

The provided health coverage must generally be the same that the qualified beneficiary had immediately prior to the qualifying event. Beneficiaries may be required to pay up to 102 percent of the employer's cost of the plan (the cost of the plan plus 2 percent for administrative costs). Employers with at least 20 employees are required by law to offer COBRA coverage.[20]

Customary Benefits

Customary benefits are those that are so commonly provided that employees view them as an entitlement. For example, sick leave and vacation days have come to be expected by most employees.

Insurance.   Health, life, and disability insurance are the three most common types of insurance offered as employee benefits. **Life insurance** pays a beneficiary a sum of money after the death of an insured individual. **Disability insurance** supplements workers' compensation insurance to provide continued income if an employee becomes disabled.

Although employers are not responsible for their employees' health choices, healthier employees are more productive, use fewer sick days, have fewer workers' compensation claims, and have cheaper health insurance premiums.[21] **Health insurance** provides healthcare and sometimes dental insurance coverage for employees and their dependents. Because the cost of health insurance for individuals is much higher than that of employer-sponsored plans, many people would be unable to afford it if they did not receive it as an employee benefit. Microsoft's healthcare policy pays 100 percent of premiums for employees and their dependents, with no deductible or payroll contributions, and it covers everything from weight management to autism therapy.[22] Healthcare benefits are the most common benefit used for recruiting employees at all levels of the organization.[23]

Prior to World War II, few workers had health insurance coverage. During the war, employers began circumventing government wage controls by offering health insurance coverage to better attract scarce recruits, and the practice continued when the war ended. The United States is now the only industrialized nation tying health insurance to employment—most other countries have government-run universal healthcare systems. Employer-provided health insurance has come to be highly valued and expected by many employees in the United States—one survey found that for 91 percent of respondents getting health benefits through work was just as important as getting a salary.[24] Countries such as China that do not tie health insurance to employment often experience greater competitiveness due to lower labor costs.

The increasing cost of providing employee health insurance is of growing concern to many employers. In 2016, the average annual premium was $6,435 for single coverage and $18,142 for family coverage.[25] Starbucks spends more on employee health care than it does on coffee.[26] To help control rising health insurance costs, a current trend is to share the cost of health insurance with employees.[27] Although this increases employees' costs, it allows them to maintain health insurance coverage more cheaply than they would be able to do independently. Some large organizations self-insure by funding their own health insurance plans to avoid state insurance regulations, which gives them greater control over costs. Organizations that self-insure typically purchase employer stop-loss coverage to protect against high utilization or catastrophic claims. To help control its healthcare costs, U-Haul educates its employees about what to ask doctors when prescribed medications and when to get a second opinion, and it offers courses for employees and spouses on navigating their healthcare options.[28] Because it can easily cost over $10,000 for a hospital visit, if even a few visits can be prevented through health and wellness initiatives, it is a win for both the employees and the company.[29]

Because health insurance benefits can differ across companies, it is a good idea to analyze the cost of health plans offered by different employers as well as what they

When organizations expand into other countries it is important to understand the local culture and how it is likely to affect the implementation of the company's human resource management practices. To be most effective, it is usually necessary to balance some of the best HRM practices from the organization's home country with some HRM practices that better fit the local culture.

Rob Marmion/Shutterstock

cover when deciding where to work. For example, if job offer A is for $35,000 plus health insurance benefits, and job offer B is for $38,000 with health insurance benefits, it would be a mistake to assume that the second offer is worth more. Assume that job A covers the full monthly health insurance premium and has an annual deductible (the amount you need to cover before insurance coverage kicks in) of $500. If you needed to spend the entire deductible on medical expenses, your net salary for job A would fall $500 to $34,500.

Now suppose that job B requires you to pay 20 percent of the cost of your monthly health insurance premium ($250 per month) and has an annual deductible of $1,000. Paying the required $250 for 12 months would reduce your salary by $3,000 ($250 × 12 months), making your net salary at job B $35,000. If you had to spend the full deductible on medical costs, the net salary at job B would fall an additional $1,000 to $34,000. If reimbursable medical expenses are capped at $500,000 at job B but at $1,000,000 for job A, the relative value of the better medical coverage at job A rises even further.

Retirement plans.   Financially confident employees are less stressed. If employees have financial challenges, the risk of unethical behavior including fraud, theft, exaggerated workers' compensation claims, and other behaviors also increases.[30] Employees who are financially unprepared for retirement can harm productivity and profitability. If employees continue to work because they have to, not because they want to, it can create **presenteeism** when an employee physically comes to work but does not function at his or her full potential.

The two broad types of retirement plans are defined benefit plans and defined contribution plans. **Defined benefit retirement plans** promise participants a monthly benefit at retirement, either a specific amount (such as $2,000 per month) or an amount determined by a formula that considers salary and tenure. For example, the benefit formula might be:

2 percent × years of service × average financial compensation (AFC)

In this case, an employee with 35 years of service and a monthly AFC of $4,000 would receive up to a $2,800 monthly pension. Defined benefit retirement plans, or pensions, are declining in popularity due to their high cost to the employer.

Defined contribution retirement plans do not promise a specific benefit level at retirement. In a defined contribution plan, the employer, the employee, or both contribute to the employee's individual account, and the tax-deferred contributions are invested on the participant's behalf. Often the employer will match employee contributions up to a certain percentage of salary (e.g., for every dollar the employee puts in, the employer will match it up to 5 percent of the employee's base salary). In retirement, participants receive the balance in their account, which depends on contributions plus or minus the performance of the investments. Defined contribution plans include 401(k) plans, 403(b) plans, profit-sharing plans, and employee stock ownership plans.

Nonprofit research and development firm MITRE helps its employees save enough to replace 80 to 100 percent of their salaries during retirement. The company matches up to 12 percent of employees' retirement contributions with immediate vesting. The employee participation rate is 99 percent.[31] In 401(k) plans, investments in any publicly traded securities, mutual funds, and options are allowed. In 403(b) plans, investments are limited to annuity contracts, mutual funds, and money-market funds.

Traditional 401(k) plans are funded with pre-tax dollars. Income taxes are then paid on both 401(k) earnings and contributions at the time of their withdrawal. Roth 401(k) plans allow employees to contribute post-tax dollars to a retirement account. The earnings on Roth contributions can be withdrawn tax free as long as the distribution occurs at least five years after the first Roth contribution and the individual is at least 59-1/2 years old. Employers' contributions cannot receive Roth tax treatment, and there are limits to how much can be contributed annually to either type of 401(k).

presenteeism
an employee physically comes to work but does not function at his or her full potential.

defined benefit retirement plan:
promise participants a monthly benefit at retirement

defined contribution retirement plan
the employer, the employee, or both contribute to the employee's individual account, and the contributions are invested on the participant's behalf

Employees always have a nonforfeitable right to their own retirement plan contributions, but they are only entitled to employer contributions once they are vested. **Vesting** is the point at which an employee earns a nonforfeitable right to benefits funded by employer contributions. Vesting is used to promote employee retention. There are two basic vesting schedules, although plans may vest faster:[32]

- Under the three-year schedule, workers are 100 percent vested after three years of service.
- Under the six-year graduated schedule, workers become 20 percent vested after two years and 20 percent more each following year, becoming 100 percent vested after six years of service.

What you do with your money now will affect how you live when you are older. To help you understand the importance of saving as much as you can and starting as soon as you can, this chapter's Develop Your Skills feature illustrates the effect of saving different amounts of money for different time periods at two different interest rates. Notice how large the difference in the total amount saved is if you start saving early because of the effects of compounding where your earned interest earns its own interest! We strongly recommend saving as much as you can afford starting now (if you haven't started already) and putting a large amount of your future raises into your savings or retirement account to increase your financial wealth and retirement security. If you don't get used to having and spending a larger salary, it is much easier to save it. It is also important to always have some savings as you move throughout your career to give you the financial resources to acquire new skills, look for a better job, or focus on your family.

If your employer offers to match your retirement contributions, try to contribute enough to at least receive the greatest possible employer contribution. Also factor in the value of employer retirement contributions when evaluating job offers. If job X offers a $50,000 salary and lets you contribute up to $5,000 per year toward retirement with a 100 percent match, your net salary would be $55,000 ($50,000 + the $5,000 employer match) if you contributed the maximum amount to your retirement account. If job Y offers a $52,000 salary and only

vesting
the point at which an employee earns a nonforfeitable right to benefits funded by employer contributions

so what**?**

Saving as much as you can starting as soon as you can increases your financial wealth, retirement security, and financial resources to choose to switch jobs or careers or work less in the future.

 # Develop Your Skills

Understanding the Effects of Saving Over Time

Monthly Savings Amount	Interest Rate	Amount Saved in 10 Years	Amount Saved in 20 Years	Amount Saved in 30 Years	Amount Saved in 40 Years
$ 100	4%	$ 14,725	$ 36,677	$ 69,405	$ 118,196
$ 500	4%	$ 73,625	$183,387	$ 347,025	$ 590,981
$1,000	4%	$147,250	$366,775	$ 694,049	$1,181,961
$2,000	4%	$294,500	$733,549	$1,388,099	$2,363,923
$ 100	6%	$ 16,388	$ 46,204	$ 100,452	$ 199,149
$ 500	6%	$ 81,940	$231,020	$ 502,258	$ 995,745
$1,000	6%	$163,879	$462,041	$1,004,515	$1,991,491
$2,000	6%	$327,759	$924,082	$2,009,030	$3,982,981

table 11.2

Promoting Retirement Readiness[35]

1. ***Evaluate employees' retirement readiness.*** Track employees' participation in the organization's retirement plan, contribution rates, investment diversification, and account balances to assess whether employees are on the right track to a comfortable retirement. Performing these analyses for employee groups with five, 10, and 20 or more years to go until retirement and for different demographic subgroups can make it easier to understand what action plans are needed to improve employees' retirement readiness.

2. ***Understand your workforce and design a retirement plan to match their needs.*** A 25-year-old employee has different retirement planning needs than does a 55-year-old employee.[36] Providing greater incentives for saving more, such as automatic annual deferral increases and a different employer match, can help employees save more. Because many employees defer only enough to earn the full company match, rather than matching 50 percent of the first 4 percent of an employee's deferred salary contribution, which would lead to an 8 percent retirement saving rate, consider matching 25 percent of the first 8 percent, which would lead to a 10 percent saving rate at no additional cost to the company.

3. ***Use targeted communications for different employee groups.*** Response and action rates increase when retirement plan messages target different demographics and make action easy, such as e-mails with one-click responses. Many employees also need more than just information; they need guidance in evaluating their options and understanding the right choices for them.

4. ***Enhance employees' financial literacy.*** Financial literacy tends to be lower among employees under age 35 and less educated workers. Helping employees understand the effects of inflation and compound interest rates and the importance of financial planning enhances their ability to make good financial decisions.

a 50 percent match on contributions up to $5,000, your net salary would be only $54,500 [$52,000 + (0.5 × $5,000)].

It is important for employers to encourage employees to set high retirement plan contribution levels. Unless an employee is contributing at least 9 to 12 percent of pay to a defined contribution plan over their full career, they are unlikely to reach the retirement goal of replacing most of their pre-retirement income. Research has found that nearly half of baby boomers are at risk of not having enough retirement resources to pay for basic expenses and uninsured medical costs.[33] Setting as high a contribution match as possible can help, as research has shown that participants are likely to defer as much as necessary to receive the full matching contribution.[34] Table 11.2 highlights steps organizations can take to promote greater retirement readiness for employees.

The **Employee Retirement Income Security Act of 1974 (ERISA)** is a federal law that protects employees' retirement benefits from mismanagement. ERISA sets minimum standards for most voluntarily established health and retirement plans in private industry and requires plans to regularly provide participants with information about plan features and funding, vesting, and benefit accrual. It also gives participants the right to sue for benefits and breaches of fiduciary duty.[37]

Optional Benefits

Optional benefits include free food, exercise facilities, telecommuting, and other things that are at the discretion of the organization. These benefits are typically targeted at specific organizational goals or employee needs, including reinforcing the organization's culture and retaining employees.

Employee Retirement Income Security Act of 1974 (ERISA)
a federal law that protects employees' retirement benefits from mismanagement

? so what

Optional benefits are not given altruistically—they are linked to business goals and are intended to enhance employee attraction, performance, and retention.

Work–life benefits.   Longer commutes and longer workdays have made it more difficult for many employees to meet life responsibilities or pursue outside hobbies and interests. At the same time, many organizations have realized that what employees accomplish is more important than how much face time they spend in the office. Workplace flexibility is a tool being used by organizations of all sizes to help employees achieve greater work/life balance while meeting business needs. Flexible work arrangements allow employees to work a nontraditional workday. Some employees may come to work earlier or stay later than others. For example, instead of working from 8 to 5, flextime employees might work from 6 to 3 or from 10 to 7. Employees might work four 10-hour days instead of five eight-hour days, or employees might share a job, each working half-time. Job sharing can work well as long as tasks, roles, and responsibilities are coordinated.

Telecommuting allows employees to work at home some or all the time. To keep telecommuting employees engaged and integrated into the work unit, it can be helpful to have them attend regular weekly or monthly meetings in person. Telecommuting may require employees to work set hours, as is the case with telecommuting customer service representatives, but it can also allow flexibility in when employees get their work done. Telecommuting benefits have tripled over the past 30 years, from 20 percent in 1996 to 60 percent in 2016.[38]

About 95 percent of Cisco's employees use flextime, and 85 percent telecommute using the company's video conferencing and virtual meeting technologies.[39] Southwest Michigan First, an economic development advising agency, created a staff position for the sole purpose of ensuring that every employee uses their flextime and maintains a healthy balance between working and cheering at their kids' sporting events or engaging in favorite hobbies.[40]

Stress, obesity, and depression are key factors influencing employee health and performance, and all three are likely to increase when work and life are poorly integrated. Flexibility increases employees' ability to take advantage of wellness services including health screenings and physician visits.[41] Flexible work arrangements also enable employees to perform child or elder care, teach or take classes, avoid wasting time sitting in traffic, and better balance work and life responsibilities. When offered at least moderate degrees of workplace flexibility, both lower- and higher-wage employees reported greater job satisfaction and engagement.[42] For flexibility to work, the organization's culture must support its use. If employees feel that using flexibility could hurt their career advancement potential, they are less likely to use it even if it would benefit them.

Companies named to *Fortune* magazine's annual World's Most Admired Companies list are more likely to treat work/life issues as a top priority. Mel Stark, vice president at Hay Group, says that, "The world's most admired companies understand that money is not always what matters most to employees. . . . They have focused on fostering work/life balance for employees while increasing productivity and decreasing the likelihood that work tasks will crowd out personal time."[43]

so what?

Failing to effectively integrate your work and family lives can increase your stress level and harm your health.

"The world's most admired companies understand that money is not always what matters most to employees . . . . They have focused on fostering work/life balance for employees while increasing productivity and decreasing the likelihood that work tasks will crowd out personal time."

—**Mel Stark, vice president, Hay Group**

domestic partners

two people who are not married but are in a same-sex or opposite-sex arrangement similar to marriage

Domestic partner benefits.   **Domestic partners** are two people who are not married but are in a same-sex or opposite-sex arrangement similar to marriage. Some of the benefits that require a legal marriage include workers' compensation survivor benefits, Social Security survivor benefits, FMLA and ERISA coverage, and eligibility for COBRA health benefits coverage. These benefits are not available to domestic partners.

Many organizations have grappled with the question of whether or not to treat domestic partners the same as legal spouses when it comes to benefits. Although country and state laws can help organizations answer that question, it is often the company's choice. Providing domestic partner benefits can promote a more diverse workforce, enhance a company's reputation as an employer, or just promote employv e equity. Domestic partner benefits can be expensive, however, and the benefits of offering them must be weighed against their cost. A 2011 SHRM survey found that 35 percent of organizations provided healthcare coverage to same-sex domestic partners, and 32 percent provided this coverage to opposite-sex domestic partners.[44]

flexible spending account

an employer-sponsored benefit that allows you to pay for eligible medical expenses on a pre-tax basis

Flexible spending accounts.   A **flexible spending account** (FSA) is an employer-sponsored benefit that allows you to pay for eligible medical expenses on a pre-tax basis (similar accounts exist for dependent and child-care expenses). A FSA helps reduce the cost of medical expenses that are not covered by the company's health insurance plan.

Nonfinancial benefits.   Companies are recognizing that nonfinancial benefits can play an important part in employee engagement. Hay Group research representing about 4 million employees worldwide found that five of the seven most common reasons employees leave an organization are nonfinancial:[45]

- Lack of career development opportunities
- Poor work climate
- Lack of challenging work
- Direction of the organization
- Lack of recognition.

? so what

Because people differently value different rewards, it is important to offer nonfinancial rewards that are valued by different employee groups.

Because the relative importance of nonfinancial rewards can vary considerably across employees, it is important to identify what most appeals to different employee groups. For example, employees in an entrepreneurial business unit might focus on a positive and engaging work environment, and employees in a slower-growing unit might be more interested in career development. As one expert says, "What motivates, retains, and energizes a research and development group is likely to be very different than what works for employees in a sales organization. Breaking down the employee population into logical segments can make a lot of sense as the organization determines what engages employees."[46]

Creative Benefits

Some organizations try to differentiate themselves as employers by offering creative benefits, including sabbaticals, free or discounted products, free food, onsite massages, bringing pets to work, and paid internships with nonprofit groups. Table 11.3 lists some organizations' more unique benefits.

An organization's culture and values typically influence the level and mix of benefits it provides. Creative benefits should also be viewed as an investment like any other benefit. Discounts on company products increase external brand awareness and enable employees to serve as brand ambassadors as they use the product. Free healthy food can boost employees' energy levels and decrease healthcare costs. Financial counseling helps employees better manage their budgets and reduce financial stress. Letting employees take paid leave to volunteer with a nonprofit organization can both increases employees' skills and reinforce the company's values and mission. IBM sends groups of employees to developing countries to partner with

table **11.3**

Creative Benefits[47]

> **World Wildlife Fund:** Every other Friday off.
>
> **New Belgium Brewing:** Employees get free beer every week, a free cruiser bicycle during their first year, a free brewery-hopping trip to Belgium in their fifth year, and a four-week sabbatical and tree planted in their name in the campus orchard after 10 years.
>
> **Cranium:** A family-inclusive culture with parties at every major holiday and free take-home games for employees.
>
> **Clif Bar:** Dogs can come to work with their owners, 2.5 hours of paid workout time per week, and a $6,500 incentive for the purchase of a hybrid or biodiesel car.
>
> **Electronic Arts:** Free EA games, education assistance, free onsite gym, onsite restaurant.
>
> **Morningstar:** Six-week paid sabbatical every four years.
>
> **Cisco:** Brings a car care company to the office twice a week for oil changes.
>
> **Patagonia:** After one year of service, employees can apply for two-month internships with environmental not-for-profits (during which time they're still paid by Patagonia); new parents get two months paid paternity or maternity leave.
>
> **Kimpton Hotels & Restaurants:** Hotel staff can bring their pets to work and leave them with onsite pet care specialists.
>
> **Nike:** Climbing wall, pool, sports bar, basketball court, personal trainer, tennis coach, and a discount store for Nike gear.
>
> **Mattel:** Employees only work a half day every Friday.
>
> **Atlantic Health:** Its onsite childcare is available for its employees' children and grandchildren.
>
> **Boxed Wholesale:** Will pay up to $20,000 for an employee's wedding.
>
> **PricewaterhouseCoopers (PwC):** Provides associates and senior associates $1,200 per year toward their student loans for up to six years.
>
> **BCF Agency:** Horror movie Mondays, Easter egg hunts, office derby races, pumpkin carving contests, and piñata parties.

local nonprofits, startups, and government officials to address issues including health care, education, and economic development.[48] Smaller companies can promote employee volunteerism as well. SSPR, a Chicago-based public relations firm, gives all employees eight paid hours off for group volunteer projects and 16 hours for individual projects.[49]

This chapter's case study highlights employee benefits at PwC.

CASE STUDY: Benefits at PwC[50]

Global professional services giant PricewaterhouseCoopers (PwC) provides core, flexible, and voluntary benefits to its employees to help them meet their personal health and well-being needs and goals. PwC's core benefits provide a fixed level of coverage, although employees can choose to increase this coverage. Provided core benefits include life insurance, income protection insurance, and private medical insurance.

Reflecting its philosophy of shared responsibility, PwC offers extensive flexible benefits through its PwC's Choices program to meet the needs of its diverse workforce. PwC's flexible

Continued

benefits include a defined contribution pension, health screenings, childcare vouchers, and bicycles for work. Employees can also trade up to five of their 25 holiday days per year for additional benefits or trade other benefits for up to five additional vacation days.

PwC's voluntary benefits include discounted gym memberships, retail and service discounts, and a concierge service that can arrange vacations or book theater tickets. Employees can request changes to their benefits package annually to ensure that the benefits are most valued by and appropriate for each employee.

Questions

1. What are the advantages of offering core benefits? Why not let employees choose all of their benefits?
2. How might offering such a variety of benefits create a competitive advantage for PwC?
3. Which benefits have the most appeal to you? Are there any benefits that you would require before accepting a job? Why?

Many organizations are addressing employee career development needs and their own skills gaps with education benefits. In addition to tuition reimbursement, some companies including the law firm Cooley reimburse employees up to $3,000 a year for boosting their knowledge through seminars and courses.[51]

? so what

As with all HRM activities, benefits should be matched to local cultures and preferences.

Global Benefits

The value of a benefit can vary in different cultures. For example, one study found that Canadians gave higher priority to work/life balance than did employees in the United Kingdom or Hong Kong.[52] This chapter's Global Issues feature highlights employees' varying financial concerns in different cultures and reinforces the point that it is important to match human resource management (HRM) practices, including benefits, to local cultures and preferences.

 # Global Issues

Employees' Top Three Financial Concerns Across Different Cultures[53]

	#1	#2	#3
India	Health insurance	Job security	Enough money to live on
Mexico	Job security	Paying bills during sudden income loss	Health insurance
Australia	Enough money	Paying bills during sudden income loss	Job security
United Kingdom	Job security	Enough money to live on	More time to spend with family
United States	Paying bills during sudden income loss	Enough money to live on	Health insurance

Another issue with global benefits is the existence of "vested rights." In many countries other than the United States, any benefit or incentive that is offered for a minimum period of time becomes an acquired employee right. An acquired employee right cannot be withdrawn by the employer unless it is clearly communicated when the benefit is offered that it is offered at the will of the employer. These issues make it even more important to think through the expected return on an employee benefit and to clearly communicate that it may be withdrawn in the future if that is the organization's desire.

Communicating Benefits Information

Although benefits frequently account for 30 to 40 percent of an employee's total compensation,[54] a disconnect exists between what organizations spend on benefits and employees' perception of their value.[55] Benefits workshops, employee meetings, and social networking tools can help ensure that the benefits program is valued, understood, and best utilized by employees.[56] Employees also better understand the value of their benefits when they contribute to their cost.[57]

Communicating benefits information can be challenging. Employees are not likely to read and fully understand lengthy benefits booklets, benefit plans and options can be complex, and many people do not have much interest in learning about their benefits until they need to use them. Clearly communicating benefits information in understandable language, communicating frequently about benefits in ways employees are likely to respond to, and communicating benefits information to the employee's spouse and family as well as the employee can improve the effectiveness of benefits communications. It can also be helpful to review benefits information again a year or so after employees begin working for an organization. When people first join an organization, their attention is frequently focused on the new job, not on the details of their benefits.

Total Compensation Statement

Communicating total compensation to employees via an annual **total compensation statement** can more clearly communicate an employee's salary, bonus, and the value of the benefits. Table 11.4 shows a sample total compensation statement.

total compensation statement
communicating total compensation in detail through a written summary of employee direct and indirect compensation

table 11.4

Sample Total Compensation Statement

TOTAL COMPENSATION STATEMENT		
Liam Jones 101 Main Street Hometown, CA 90096		
Title: Manager II		Date of Birth: 05/12/88
Salary Grade: 04		
Form of Compensation	**Company Contribution**	**Your Contribution**
Salary Paid	$ 59,100	
Social Security	$ 3,311	$ 3,311
Medicare	$ 841	$ 841
Medical Plan	$ 6,722	$ 1,500
Prescription Drug Plan	$ 2,475	
Retirement Plan	$ 4,729	$ 2,364
Paid Time Off	$ 1,818	
Daycare	$ 11,000	
Total Contribution	**$89,996**	**$8,016**
Employer Paid Benefits	**$30,896**	

Video game maker Zynga, known for elaborate employee benefits and perks including pet insurance and free meals, gives employees an annual compensation report itemizing each perk and providing an estimate of how much each employee saves.[58]

Benefits Communication Tools

 so what

To maximize the effectiveness of a benefit program, communication and implementation are as important as the actual benefits offered.

The most effective benefit programs are often not the most generous or elegantly designed but those that are communicated and implemented most effectively.[59] Benefits should be marketed to employees in a way that gives them the sense that they are valued as individuals, rather than that the organization is providing the benefit out of a legal or competitive obligation. The best benefits messages convey a genuine commitment to employees and their families. As one expert says, "a 'B-rated' benefits plan with the right motive could very well take a company farther than an 'A+' plan that employees perceive to be there for obligatory motives."[60]

Fewer than half of Americans with employer-based health coverage know their medical plan's annual deductible or when their company holds open enrollment, and most spend less than 30 minutes reviewing their benefits options.[61] To increase employees' benefits awareness, it is best to use a variety of tactics to communicate benefit information throughout the year, including:[62]

- Regular mail
- E-mail
- Text messages
- Benefits website
- QR codes
- Face-to-face communication.

The best benefit plans collaborate with and educate employees to help them maximize the value of their benefits. If employees are involved in choosing their benefit options, they are likely to know more about them.

Managing Benefits

Many employers choose to outsource the administration of their benefits because it requires specialized knowledge. The choice of what benefits to offer and at what level to best meet the organization's goals should be made strategically by the organization. Actively engaging employees in shaping benefit programs through employee surveys, focus groups, and employee committees helps to understand and best meet their needs and wants.[63] The effectiveness of the organization's benefits in meeting the organization's benefit goals and employee needs should also be tracked.

Benefits Level

so what

To avoid misalignment, benefit costs need to be considered when setting total compensation rates at, below, or above the market.

The choice of how much to invest in employee benefits is influenced by:

- The organization's competition for talent
- The organization's compensation strategy
- The organization's culture
- Characteristics of the organization's workforce.

If an organization needs to hire top talent and its competitors offer generous benefits, it may need to match those benefits to be competitive as an employer. The cost of the total compensation package should be monitored against the industry average to ensure consistency with the organization's intention of paying below, at, or above-market compensation.

When deciding what benefits to offer to employees, it is important to consider employees' preferences, which often change over time. Younger employees may initially put greater value on tuition reimbursement and recreation facilities and then transform to prioritize daycare and a 401(k) match as their lives change. It is a good idea to track employees' use of different benefits and regularly survey current and prospective employees to understand the value they place on different benefits. The top five employee benefits in 2016 were:[64]

1. Employer-paid health insurance
2. Vacation/paid time off
3. Performance bonus
4. Paid sick days
5. 401(k) plan, retirement plan, and/or pension.

Flexible Benefit Plans

Flexible benefits plans, also called cafeteria plans, give employees a budget to allocate among allowed benefit options (e.g., retirement benefits, health insurance, disability insurance, and daycare). Flexible benefits plans were established by the Revenue Act of 1978 and are regulated by Internal Revenue Code Section 125. An annual open enrollment period allows employees to change their allocations to meet their current needs and preferences. Employees are increasingly using electronic submissions to make their open enrollment choices over the Internet.[65]

A flexible benefits plan can be funded by the employer, the employee, or both. Flexible benefits plans enable employers to provide employees greater benefits while reducing both the employer's and the employees' tax bills. They also help organizations manage their benefits costs by controlling the dollars allocated to each employee and by sharing increased benefits costs with employees.

Flexible benefits plans have been gaining in popularity with increasing health and child care costs. Small businesses, unable to capitalize on the economies of scale used by larger companies, are even more affected by increasing benefits costs. Flexible benefits plans have helped organizations of all sizes retain a competitive benefits package that maximizes the value of the benefits to each employee. Employer contributions to cafeteria plans are tax deductible for the employer and are not subject to income tax for the employee. Flexible benefits plans have been found to improve employees' understanding of and satisfaction with their benefits.[66]

Since flexible benefit plans are monitored by the IRS, record keeping and benefit payments must be accurate and timely. Many companies hire an outside firm to manage their plan, which increases the cost. Some insurance companies also provide administrative services for flexible plans, and software can enable even a small business to manage a flexible benefit plan.

To ensure that flexible benefits plans are fair to all employees, the IRS does not let employees carry over unused credits or benefits to the next year. In addition, no more than 25 percent of the tax-favored benefits go to highly compensated employees, officers earning above a certain salary range, or those who own greater than 1 percent of the company (if they earn over $150,000) or greater than 5 percent (for others).[67]

so what

Flexible benefits plans maximize the value of the benefits received by each employee and increase employees' understanding of their total compensation package.

Best Practices

Employees indicate their top barriers to engaging and participating in employer-sponsored benefits and health-related programs include:[68]

- *Trust*: Employees must trust the employer's intentions, believe the benefits are credible, and trust that the employer and the benefits manager will keep their information confidential.
- *Time*: Employees are busy, and finding extra time to take advantage of benefit offerings such as financial planners and fitness facilities can be difficult.
- *Money*: If contributing to a co-payment or allocating salary dollars to a benefit could hurt employees' ability to meet their basic needs, they are less likely to participate in the benefit (e.g., a retirement plan).
- *Stress*: Change can be difficult for busy people or for people who perceive a lifestyle change as a burden.

To support employee participation in employer benefit programs, it can be helpful to:[69]

- Align benefits with company culture, and implement trust-building strategies to increase participation in wellness programs and financial counseling.
- Include spouses, dependents, and family members in company communication efforts to provide support for everyday activities and change efforts (e.g., smoking cessation programs or health improvement initiatives).
- Communicate benefits information throughout the year, not just during open enrollment.
- Provide summary benefits resources that include cost and benefit comparisons of different choices, the actual cost of benefits including health care, and information about any upcoming benefit or coverage changes as well as anything that could increase employees' out-of-pocket benefit costs.
- Provide stress management information and resources to both help employees manage the demands of their work and home life and to enable them to take better advantage of the employer's other benefit offerings.

Summary and Application

Although some benefits must be offered by law, organizations have a great deal of choice when it comes to employee benefits. Although benefits can be expensive, they should be viewed as an investment and used to accomplish organizational objectives. Well-developed and well-communicated benefits can improve recruiting, retention, and employee performance outcomes.

The cost of benefits programs makes it important to regularly assess the utility of an organization's benefit offerings. Balancing the desire to offer employees appropriate benefits with financial responsibility requires being proactive in benefits evaluation. External benchmarking and surveying new hires to learn what competitors are offering can help an organization maintain its desired benefits strategy. Surveying employees to identify how well they understand and utilize available benefits can also be insightful. Unless employees understand their benefits choices, the full value of their benefits, and how best to utilize the organization's benefits, the benefits program will not live up to its full potential in meeting its goals.

Real World Response

Using Benefits Strategically at SAS

The first employee benefits offered by business software company SAS were free M&Ms every Wednesday (they now go through 22 tons of M&Ms every year).[70] Since then, SAS's benefits have grown to include a retirement plan, free on-site medical care, unlimited sick days, a 50,000-square-foot fitness center, inexpensive gourmet cafeterias, and heavily subsidized daycare for employees' children.[71] SAS also encourages employees to adhere to a 35-hour workweek. SAS's work/life" department is staffed by a team of social workers charged with relieving employees' life problems ranging from finding the best nursing home for aging parents to getting their kids into the right college.[72]

Why does SAS provide so many benefits? Generosity has nothing to do with it. The variety of benefits help employees stay healthy, stay happy, and stay at SAS. They help reinforce a culture that attracts, motivates, and retains talented people, minimizing the cost of turnover. The 17 percent difference between SAS's average annual 3 percent turnover and the industry average saves SAS as much as $80 million in annual recruiting and training costs.[73] "You can pay the money to employees in the form of benefits, or you can pay headhunters and corporate trainers to fund the revolving door of people coming in and out; to me, it's a no-brainer," says CEO Jim Goodnight.[74] Given the advanced skills required of most SAS employees and the difficulty of finding them in a tight talent market for PhD-level talent, it is strategic for SAS to focus on retaining the high-quality talent it currently employs.

The strategic use of employee benefits has helped make SAS a leader in the business software market. SAS's 9,000 employees are happy and experienced at their jobs, which keeps customers coming back year after year.[75] Goodnight says, "95 percent of my assets drive out the front gate every evening. It's my job to bring them back. I think our history has shown that taking care of our employees has made the difference in how our employees take care of our customers. With that as our vision, the rest takes care of itself."[76]

Takeaway Points

1. Some employee benefits are required by law. Others are offered to promote employee health, provide financial protection, and improve employees' work/life balance. Improved employee performance, satisfaction, commitment, and retention are also common goals of employee benefits.

2. By law, organizations with a certain number of employees must offer Social Security, unemployment insurance, workers' compensation, FMLA leave, and COBRA.

3. Customary benefits are benefits employees tend to expect. For example, sick leave and vacation days have come to be expected by most employees.

4. Optional benefits are offered at the discretion of the organization and are typically targeted at specific organizational goals or employee needs, including reinforcing the organization's culture and retaining employees.

5. Employees often do not read or fully understand lengthy benefits booklets, benefit options can be complex, and many people only have an interest in learning about their benefits when they need to use them.

6. Employee benefits offerings are influenced by the organization's competition for talent, its compensation strategy, its culture, and characteristics of its workforce.

Discussion Questions

1. When looking for a job, how important are benefits to you?
2. Are there any benefits that an employer unable to pay a market-competitive salary could offer that could overcome the lower pay?
3. What employer benefits do you feel are most important to provide? Why?
4. Because employers in other countries do not have this cost, health insurance increases the cost of U.S.-made goods and decreases the cost competitiveness of many U.S. companies. Do you feel that employers should provide health insurance to their employees? Explain your answer.
5. How can employers simultaneously meet the benefit needs of diverse employees with different needs?
6. Do you consider the value of the total compensation you would be paid or only look at the salary when choosing between jobs?
7. How can employers do a better job communicating the total value of what they give employees through both direct and indirect compensation?

Personal Development Exercise: Your Personal Benefits Preferences

Make a list of the five to 10 employment benefits you would like to have right now. Then prioritize these benefits to identify those most and least important to you. Now think about what benefits you might want to have in 20 years, and prioritize this list.

Your two lists are probably different. Write a two-page paper describing how organizations can best meet the needs of employees with both sets of benefits preferences.

Strategic HRM Exercises

Exercise: Using Benefits Strategically

Working alone or in a small group of four to six people, imagine that you are in charge of employee benefits for a clothing retailer (e.g., Gap or Abercrombie & Fitch). A recent customer and employee survey has identified a variety of organizational needs. You have been asked to brainstorm possible benefit offerings to meet the following organizational goals and identify metrics to assess the effectiveness of each:

1. Reinforce the organization's customer service strategy.
2. Recruit high quality talent.
3. Retain current high-quality employees.
4. Improve employee performance.

Prepare to share your ideas with the rest of the class.

Exercise: Changing the Daycare Benefit at Google[77]

Google prides itself on offering great employee benefits. Its generous benefits are one of the reasons Google is frequently named to *Fortune's* Best Companies to Work For list. As its young employees started becoming parents, Google added world-class on-site daycare to its benefits offerings, subsidizing $37,000 of the cost for each child.

As growing Google watched the wait list for its in-house daycare facilities increase to 700, it decided to address the issue by modifying the cost for employees' children. Parents with two children in Google's daycare would now have to pay more than $57,000 a year rather than the current $33,000. The change meant that many parents would have to find less expensive daycare elsewhere.

Although Google parents complained and some even cried, Google implemented the change. The hike was slightly smaller than initially proposed, and the cost hikes were phased in for currently enrolled children. Class sizes increased, and coverage hours decreased. Google also started charging people $250 just to stay on the daycare waiting list. As a result, the waiting list decreased by over half.

After the changes, Google stopped marketing the daycare to potential recruits as a benefit of working at Google.

Form a small group of three to five people and discuss the following questions. Be prepared to share your answers with the class.

Questions

1. Google leaders viewed the daycare challenge as a supply-and-demand imbalance, and that price could be used to ration child care to those who really wanted it. Although this is an economically rational perspective, do you feel that it is fair to employees?
2. What can this situation tell us about the consequences of changing a valued employee benefit?
3. As organizations grow and their benefits needs change, how can they best decrease or discontinue a benefit that has become too expensive even if it is still valued by some employees?

Exercise: Retirement Planning

Use your favorite search engine to find a retirement calculator. Set a retirement goal, and use online calculator to determine how much to save now and how much you would need to save if you started in five or 10 years. Then create an action plan to identify how you can best reach your goal. Be realistic—it may not be possible to save much while still in school, but it can be very helpful to create a plan now for what you will need to do once you graduate and get a job.

Exercise: Employee Benefits at Smaller Companies

View the video, "Low Cost, High Impact Staff Retention Tools–Richard Lloyd Accounting Recruitment (4:47)." After watching the video, answer the following questions:

1. What low-cost benefits would most appeal to you as an employee?
2. How could some of these benefits help to create a competitive advantage for a small employer?
3. What other ideas do you have for low-cost employee retention interventions for any size employer?

Integrative Project

Using the same job you used for the previous chapter, describe the employee benefits package you would offer for this position. Be sure to explain your objectives for your employee benefits and why your recommendations are likely to be effective in meeting these objectives. Will the benefits be the same for everyone, or will employees be able to choose some of their benefits? Don't forget to consider the cost of the benefits in your decision making.

Video Case

Imagine that a coworker tells you about a conversation he just had with some employees who feel that other local employers compensate their employees more fairly than does Happy Time Toys. This is surprising because you know that Happy Time Toys' pay and benefits are above average for the area. *What do you say or do?* Go to this book's video case, watch the challenge video for this chapter, and choose the best video response. Be sure to also view the outcomes of the two responses you didn't choose.

Discussion Questions

1. What HRM concepts from the chapter are illustrated in these videos? Explain your answer.
2. What ethical issues are illustrated in these videos? Explain your answer.
3. How else might you handle this situation? Explain your answer.

Endnotes

1. Costigan, J. (2011). Benefits: The hidden tool of strategic growth. *Forbescustom.com*. Retrieved March 21, 2017, from http://www.forbescustom.com/HCMPgs/HCMBenefitsP1.html

2. Flint, J. (2011). Analyze this. *Bloomberg Businessweek*, February 21–27, 82–83.

3. Costigan, J. (2011). Benefits: The hidden tool of strategic growth. *Forbescustom.com*. Retrieved March 21, 2017, from http://www.forbescustom.com/HCMPgs/HCMBenefitsP1.html

4. Miller, S. (2011, June 27). Employee benefits 2011: Fewer guarantees. *Society for Human Resource Management*. Retrieved March 22, 2017, from https://www.shrm.org/resourcesandtools/hr-topics/benefits/pages/benefits2011.aspx

5. Time off and leaves. (2017). *Salesforce.com*. Retrieved May 5, 2017, from http://www.getsalesforcebenefits.com/your-benefits/work-life/time-off-and-leaves#Sabbatical; Perks. (2017). *Salesforce.com*. Retrieved May 5, 2017, from http://www.getsalesforcebenefits.com/your-benefits/work-life/perks

6. Tsai, K. H., Yu, K. D., & Fu, S. Y. (2005). Do employee benefits really offer no advantage on firm productivity? An examination of Taiwan's shipping industry. *Journal of the Eastern Asia Society for Transportation Studies, 6,* 838–850.

7. Barber, A. E., Dunham, R. B., & Formisano, R.A. (1992). The impact of flexible benefits on employee satisfaction: A field study. *Personnel Psychology, 45,* 55–74.

8. Levoy, R. P., & Levoy, B. (2007). *222 secrets of hiring, managing, and retaining great employees in healthcare practices*, pp. 37. Boston, MA: Jones and Bartlett.

9. Leibs, S. (2013). You can buy employee happiness. (But should you?). *INC,* December, 109–112.

10. Williams, M. L., Malos, S. B., & Palmer, D. K. (2002). Benefit system and benefit level satisfaction: An expanded model of antecedents and consequences. *Journal of Management*, 28, 195–215; Tremblay, M., Sire, B., & Balkin, D. B. (2000). The role of organizational justice in pay and employee benefits satisfaction, and its effects on work attitudes. *Group and Organization Management*, 25, 269–290.

11. Dulebohn, J. H., Molloy, J. C., Pichler, S. M., & Murray, B. (2009). Employee benefits: Literature review and emerging issues. *Human Resource Management Review*, 19, 86–103.

12. Schramm, J. (2016). Give the people what they want. *HR Magazine*, October, 66.

13. Levin-Epstein, A. (2011, March 22). Google job perks: Top 10 reasons we want to work there. *CBS Money Watch*. Retrieved March 22, 2017, from http://www.cbsnews.com/news/google-job-perks-top-10-reasons-we-want-to-work-there/

14. American Psychological Association. (2017). Coping with stress at work. Retrieved March 22, 2017, from http://www.apa.org/helpcenter/work-stress.aspx

15. Longley, R. (2011). Applying for Social Security retirement benefits. About.com. Retrieved March 22, 2017, from http://usgovinfo.about.com/od/socialsecurity/a/socsecapply.htm

16. Aaron, H. J. (2011). Social Security reconsidered. *National Tax Journal*, 64, 385–414.

17. U.S. Department of Labor. (2010, January 13). State unemployment insurance benefits. Retrieved March 22, 2017, from http://workforcesecurity.doleta.gov/unemploy/uifactsheet.asp

18. U.S. Department of Labor. (2011). The Family and Medical Leave Act (FMLA). Retrieved March 22, 2017, from https://www.dol.gov/whd/fmla/

19. Olsen, E. (2016, October 16). This is what work–life balance looks like at a company with 100% retention of moms. *Quartz*. Retrieved February 23, 2017, from https://qz.com/806516/

the-secret-to-patagonias-success-keeping-moms-and-onsite-child-care-and-paid-parental-leave/

20. U.S. Department of Labor. (2012). COBRA continuation health coverage FAQs. Retrieved March 22, 2017, from https://www.dol.gov/agencies/ebsa/about-ebsa/our-activities/resource-center/faqs/cobra-continuation-health-coverage-compliance

21. Miller, S. (2011, January 11). Employees' retirement readiness is employer priority. *Society for Human Resource Management.* Retrieved March 22, 2017, from https://www.shrm.org/resourcesandtools/hr-topics/benefits/pages/readiness.aspx

22. 25 top-paying companies: Microsoft. (2011). *CNN Money.* Retrieved March 22, 2017, from http://money.cnn.com/galleries/2011/pf/jobs/1101/gallery.best_companies_top_paying.fortune/20.html

23. Schramm, J. (2015). Targeting top talent. *HR Magazine*, April, 61.

24. Beyer, L. (2011, October 26). Heightened awareness of benefits plays a pivotal role within employee experience. *Workforce.* Retrieved March 22, 2017, from http://www.workforce.com/2011/10/26/heightened-awareness-of-benefits-plays-pivotal-role-in-employee-experience/

25. The Henry J. Kaiser Family Foundation. (2016, September 14). 2016 employer health benefits survey. *KFF.org.* Retrieved February 12, 2017, from http://kff.org/report-section/ehbs-2016-section-one-cost-of-health-insurance/

26. Kowitt, B. (2010, June 7). Starbucks CEO: 'We spend more on health care than coffee.' *CNNMoney.* Retrieved March 21, 2017, from http://money.cnn.com/2010/06/07/news/companies/starbucks_schultz_healthcare.fortune/index.htm?section=money_topstories&utm_source=feedburner&utm_medium=feed&utm_campaign=Feed%3A+rss%2Fmoney_topstories+%28Top+Stories%29

27. Mudumba, R. (2011, November 10). Will employer sponsored insurance erode over time? *Self Funding Magazine.* Retrieved March 21, 2017, from http://www.selffundingmagazine.com/article/will-employer-sponsored-insurance-erode-over-time-.html

28. Lytle, T. (2014). Choosing HR for the long haul. *HR Magazine*, April, 46–47.

29. Bates, S. (2015). An analytical approach to benefits. *HR Magazine*, September, 47–51.

30. Unser, R. (2011, November 28). Viewpoint: Six steps to put employees on the retirement readiness path. *Society for Human Resource Management.* Retrieved March 21, 2017, from https://www.shrm.org/resourcesandtools/hr-topics/benefits/pages/readinesspath.aspx

31. 25 top-paying companies: MITRE. (2011). *CNN Money.* Retrieved March 22, 2017, from http://money.cnn.com/galleries/2011/pf/jobs/1101/gallery.best_companies_top_paying.fortune/17.html

32. U.S. Department of Labor. (2011). Frequently asked questions about pension plans and ERISA. Retrieved March 22, 2017, from https://www.dol.gov/agencies/ebsa/about-ebsa/our-activities/resource-center/faqs/retirement-plans-and-erisa-consumer

33. VanDerhei, J., & Copeland, C. (2010). The EBRI retirement readiness rating: Retirement income preparation and future prospects. *Employee Benefit Research Institute*, July. Retrieved March 23, 2017, from http://www.ebri.org/pdf/briefspdf/EBRI_IB_07-2010_No344_RRR-RSPM1.pdf

34. Lucas, L. (2010, October 8). 401(k) fatigue a common complaint among employees. *Workforce Management.* Retrieved March 23, 2017, from http://www.workforce.com/2010/10/08/401k-fatigue-a-common-complaint-among-employees/

35. Unser, R. (2011, November 28). Viewpoint: Six steps to put employees on the retirement readiness path. *Society for*

Human Resource Management. Retrieved March 22, 2017, from https://www.shrm.org/resourcesandtools/hr-topics/benefits/pages/readinesspath.aspx; 3 questions that predict your retirement readiness. (2011, June 10). *U.S. News Money.* Retrieved March 22, 2017, from http://money.usnews.com/money/blogs/planning-to-retire/2011/06/10/3-questions-that-predict-your-retirement-readiness; Miller, S. (2011, January 11). Employees' retirement readiness is employer priority. *Society for Human Resource Management.* Retrieved March 22, 2017, from https://www.shrm.org/resourcesandtools/hr-topics/benefits/pages/readiness.aspx

36. Wang, M., & Schultz, K. S. (2010). Employee retirement: A review and recommendations for future investigation. *Journal of Management*, 36, 172–206.

37. U.S. Department of Labor. (2011). Employee Retirement Income Security Act—ERISA. Retrieved March 23, 2017, from http://www.dol.gov/dol/topic/health-plans/erisa.htm

38. 2016 employee benefits: Looking back at 20 years of employee benefits offerings in the U.S. (2016, June 20). *Society for Human Resource Management.* Retrieved July 2, 2017, from https://www.shrm.org/hr-today/trends-and-forecasting/research-and-surveys/pages/2016-employee-benefits.aspx.

39. 25 top-paying companies: Cisco. (2011). *CNN Money.* Retrieved March 22, 2017, from http://money.cnn.com/galleries/2011/pf/jobs/1101/gallery.best_companies_top_paying.fortune/14.html

40. The best places to work: 2016. (2016, November 15). *Outside.* Retrieved March 22, 2017, from https://www.outsideonline.com/2134736/best-places-work-2016

41. van Steenbergen, E. F., & Ellemers, N. (2009). Is managing the work–family interface worthwhile? Benefits for employee health and performance. *Journal of Organizational Behavior, 30,* 617–642.

42. Workplace flexibility in the United States: A status report. (2011). *Families and Work Institute and the Society for Human Resource Management.* Retrieved March 23, 2017, from http://familiesandwork.org/downloads/WorkplaceFlexibilityinUS.pdf

43. Miller, S. (2011, March 11). 'Most admired' tie rewards to performance, address work/life. *Society for Human Resource Management.* Retrieved March 23, 2017, from https://www.shrm.org/resourcesandtools/hr-topics/benefits/pages/mostadmired.aspx

44. 2011 employee benefits: A research report by the Society for Human Resource Management. (n.d.). Retrieved March 23, 2017, from https://www.shrm.org/ResourcesAndTools/hr-topics/benefits/Documents/2011_Emp_Benefits_Report.pdf

45. Sammer, J. (2011, September 1). Nonfinancial rewards: Finding new ways to engage. *Society for Human Resource Management.* Retrieved March 23, 2017, from https://www.shrm.org/resourcesandtools/hr-topics/benefits/pages/nonfinancialrewards.aspx

46. *Ibid.*

47. Agovino, T. (2017). Tinkering with time. *HR Magazine*, February, 46; Milligan, S. (2016). Your wish is our benefit. (2016). *HR Magazine*, September, 33; Bailey, S. (2011). Benefits on tap. *Bloomberg Businessweek*, March 21–27, 96–97; Watson, K. W. (2011, January 24). Balancing 'ACTS': Help employees understand and reduce stress. *Society for Human Resource Management.* Retrieved March 22, 2017, from https://www.shrm.org/resourcesandtools/hr-topics/benefits/pages/balancingacts.aspx; Flint, J. (2010). Inside the swoosh. *Bloomberg Businessweek*, November 29–December 5, 98–99; Hanel, M. (2011). Garage mahal. *Bloomberg Businessweek*, November 21–27, 104–105; Unusual perks. (2011, January 20).

CNN Money. Retrieved March 23, 2017, from http://money. cnn.com/galleries/2011/news/companies/1101/gallery. bestcompanies_unusual_perks.fortune/2.html; Heneman, T. (2011, November 5). Patagonia fills payroll with people who are passionate. *Workforce*. Retrieved July 2, 2017 from http://www .workforce.com/2011/11/05/patagonia-fills-with-people-who-are-passionate/; EA Jobs. (2011). Benefits. Retrieved March 23, 2017, from http://careers.ea.com/benefits; The best places to work: 2016. (2016, November 15). *Outside*. Retrieved March 22, 2017, from https://www.outsideonline.com/2134736/best-places-work-2016

48. Agovino, T. (2016). The giving generation. *HR Magazine*, September, 37–43

49. Agovino, T. (2016). The giving generation. *HR Magazine*, September, 37–43

50. PwC. (2017). Pay and benefits. Retrieved March 23, 2017, from http://www.pwc.co.uk/careers/experienced-jobs/aboutpwc/reward.html; Barton, T. (2010, November 29). Case study: PricewaterhouseCoopers offers flexible and voluntary perks. *Employee Benefits*. Retrieved March 23, 2017, from https://www.employeebenefits.co.uk/issues/december-2010/case-study-pricewaterhousecoopers-offers-flexible-and-voluntary-perks/; PwC. (2017). Benefits. Retrieved March 23, 2017, from http://www.pwc.com/us/en/careers/campus/why-pwc/employee-benefits.html

51. Chew, J. (2016, March 8). These 10 great companies offer high pay. *Fortune*. Retrieved March 21, 2017, from http://fortune.com/2016/03/08/top-paying-companies-salary/

52. Chiang, F. F. T., & Birtch, T. (2007). The transferability of management practices: Examining cross-national differences in reward preferences. *Human Relations*, 60, 1293–1330.

53. MetLife. (2007). Study of international employee benefits trends. New York: Metropolitan Life Insurance Company. Retrieved March 22, 2017, from http://www.whymetlife.com/international/downloads/iEBTS.pdf

54. Benefits statements can spotlight hidden value. (2011, April 8). *Society for Human Resource Management*. Retrieved March 22, 2017, from https://www.shrm.org/ResourcesAndTools/hr-topics/benefits/Pages/BenefitsStatements.aspx

55. Gilligan, T. (2010). Exploding the benefits education myth. *Compensation Benefits Review, 42,* 52–57.

56. Miller, S. (2011). Employee benefits 2011: Fewer guarantees. *Society for Human Resource Management*, June. Retrieved March 22, 2017, from https://www.shrm.org/resourcesandtools/hr-topics/benefits/pages/benefits2011.aspx

57. Wilson, M., Northcraft, G. B., & Neale, M. A. (1985). The perceived value of fringe benefits. *Personnel Psychology, 38,* 309–320.

58. Mangalindan, J. P. (2012, April 13). What it's really like to work at Zynga. *Fortune*. Retrieved March 24, 2017, from http://fortune.com/2012/04/13/what-its-really-like-to-work-at-zynga/

59. Sammer, J. (2011, September 1). Nonfinancial rewards: Finding new ways to engage. *Society for Human Resource Management*. Retrieved March 23, 2017, from https://www.shrm.org/resourcesandtools/hr-topics/benefits/pages/nonfinancialrewards.aspx

60. McGhee, J. B. (2011, July 8). Tight salary budgets? Benefits can be a major retention tool. *Society for Human Resource Management*. Retrieved March 21, 2017, from https://www.shrm.org/resourcesandtools/hr-topics/benefits/pages/retentiontool.aspx

61. Beyer, L. (2011, October 26). Heightened awareness of benefits plays pivotal role in employee experience. *Workforce*

.com. Retrieved March 23, 2017, from http://www.workforce.com/2011/10/26/heightened-awareness-of-benefits-plays-pivotal-role-in-employee-experience/

62. Miller, S. (2011, August 1). Most U.S. employers opt for 'passive' open enrollment. *Society for Human Resource Management*. Retrieved March 22, 2017, from https://www.shrm.org/resourcesandtools/hr-topics/benefits/pages/passiveenrollment.aspx; Beyer, L. (2011, October 26). Heightened awareness of benefits plays pivotal role in employee experience. *Workforce.com*. Retrieved March 23, 2017, from http://www.workforce.com/2011/10/26/heightened-awareness-of-benefits-plays-pivotal-role-in-employee-experience/

63. 'Best companies' take collaborative approach to benefits. (2011, September 1). *Society for Human Resource Management*. Retrieved March 23, 2017, from https://www.shrm.org/resourcesandtools/hr-topics/benefits/pages/collaborativeapproach.aspx

64. Dishman, L. (2016, February 3). These are the best employee benefits and perks. *Fast Company*. Retrieved March 21, 2017, from https://www.fastcompany.com/3056205/these-are-the-best-employee-benefits-and-perks

65. Miller, S. (2011, August 1). Most U.S. employers opt for 'passive' open enrollment. *Society for Human Resource Management*. Retrieved March 22, 2017, from https://www.shrm.org/resourcesandtools/hr-topics/benefits/pages/passiveenrollment.aspx

66. Barber, A. E., Dunham, R. B., & Formisano, R. A. (2006). The impact of flexible benefits on employee satisfaction: A field study. *Personnel Psychology*, 45, 55–74.

67. IRS. (2011). Publication 15-B – main content. Retrieved March 22, 2017, from https://www.irs.gov/publications/p15b/ar02.html

68. Midwest Business Group on Health. (2011, November). Employee health engagement: Identifying the triggers and barriers to engaging employees in their health benefits and wellness programs. Retrieved March 22, 2017, from http://www.tcyh.org/lifestyle/resources/MBGH%20Engagement%20White%20Paper.pdf

69. *Ibid.*

70. Inc. (2011). No doubt about it. September, 104–110.

71. SAS (2011). Benefit Programs. https://www.sas.com/en_ca/company-information/employee-retiree-services/on-boarding/benefits.html (accessed October 24, 2011).

72. Hampton, S. (2010, April 12). The world's best employer. *Your International Business*. Retrieved October 24, 2011, from http://yourinternationalbusiness.blogspot.com/2009/12/worlds-best-employer.html

73. Inc. (2011). No doubt about it. September, 104–110.

74. Hampton, S. (2010, April 12). The world's best employer. *Your International Business*. Retrieved October 24, 2011, from http://yourinternationalbusiness.blogspot.com/2009/12/worlds-best-employer.html

75. *Ibid.*

76. *Ibid.*

77. Nocera, J. (2008, July 5). On daycare, Google makes a rare fumble. *The New York Times*, A1, A12. Retrieved December 7, 2011, from http://www.nytimes.com/2008/07/05/business/05nocera.html; 'Don't touch my perks': Companies that eliminate them risk employee backlash. (2008, July 23). *Knowledge@Wharton*. Retrieved March 23, 2017, from http://knowledge.wharton.upenn.edu/article.cfm?articleid=2019; Nocera, J. (2008, July 5). On daycare, Google makes a rare fumble. *The New York Times*. Retrieved March 23, 2017, from http://www.nytimes.com/2008/07/05/business/05nocera.html

PART 5

Managing the Work Environment and Increasing Employee Engagement

chapter 12

Creating a Healthy Work Environment

Learning Objectives

AFTER STUDYING THIS CHAPTER, YOU SHOULD BE ABLE TO:

1 Describe what is meant by a culture of safety, and explain why it is important.

2 Describe ergonomics, and explain why it helps improve workplace safety and health.

3 Explain what OSHA is, and describe its primary goal.

4 Explain how employee wellness programs benefit employers.

5 Describe the difference between functional and dysfunctional stress.

6 Describe the three forms of bullying at work.

7 Explain how organizations can protect employees and others in the workplace from workplace violence.

Real World Challenge

Wellvolution at Blue Shield of California

Insurer Blue Shield of California is a $13.4 billion nonprofit health plan providing insurance to over 4 million people.[1] The company's Lodi call center was known for its daily potlucks of chips, dips, candy, and other unhealthy foods. Two-thirds of its employees were overweight, and half of those were obese.[2]

The company wanted to reduce its rising health insurance premiums and change the company culture to be one of wellness. It knows that changing its culture and getting employees to permanently change their behaviors will be a challenge. Assume the company asks you for ideas on changing its culture and promoting healthier employee behaviors. After reading this chapter, you should have some good ideas.

Many of us take today's workplace focus on safety for granted. Sophisticated tests are run on equipment before it is put into service on assembly lines or elsewhere, and working conditions are continually monitored by high-tech sensors. We have certainly come a long way in the last 100 years, and injuries and deaths continue to decline in many occupations.[3]

Organizations of all sizes and in all lines of work need to be concerned about employee safety and security for ethical as well as business-related reasons. Tripping, slipping, and falling can happen anywhere. Repetitive motion injuries are a risk to computer users, grocery checkers, assembly line workers, and people in other physically repetitive jobs.[4] As Edmund F. Kelly, chairman, president, and CEO of Boston-based Liberty Mutual Insurance Co. said, "Safety is an investment and not an expense because, apart from any moral or ethical considerations, a safer workplace is more efficient and more economical. As an insurer, we see firsthand the immediate cost of a lack of safety."[5] Providing safe working conditions, adequately training all staff, conducting regular safety checks, and ensuring that adequate policies and procedures are in place and enforced all help to reduce the risk of environmental accidents as well as personal injury or death.

> *"Safety is an investment and not an expense because, apart from any moral or ethical considerations, a safer workplace is more efficient and more economical. As an insurer, we see firsthand the immediate cost of a lack of safety."*
>
> **—Edmund F. Kelly, chairman, president, and CEO, Liberty Mutual Insurance Co.**

It should not be surprising that healthier employees boost a company's bottom line. Healthier employees are more productive, take fewer sick and disability days, and are at a lower risk for many serious health problems. Employee health and wellness are of increasing importance to employers around the world. Although it is the individual employee who ultimately makes choices about whether or not to lead a healthy lifestyle, factors including work stress and a lack of time can make it difficult for employees to make healthy choices.

Employee wellness programs help create an environment in which healthy behaviors become the norm. Because a substantial amount of employers' healthcare costs and productivity losses are related to stress and employee lifestyle choices, some companies have experienced a $6 or more return for every dollar spent on employee wellness initiatives, including smoking cessation, healthy eating, stress management, and exercise programs.[6] Over a four-year period, IBM invested $79 million in various wellness programs that saved the company about $191 million in lower health costs for participants.[7]

In this final section of the book, "Managing the Work Environment and Increasing Employee Engagement," we turn our attention to creating an environment in which employees can excel. Efforts invested in improving employee safety and health, creating positive labor–management relations, and managing employee engagement and turnover can pay large dividends for both organizations and their employees. In this chapter, we discuss how organizations can positively impact employee safety, wellness, and security. Better understanding how to create a healthy work environment can help you be healthier and more productive and help you maximize the health and effectiveness of your subordinates as well. By improving employee health and safety, creating a healthy work environment influences what employees *can* and *will* do in our book's overall model of human resource management (HRM).

Employee Safety

Forty years ago, 14,000 U.S. workers were killed on the job every year. That number is now closer to 5,000.[8] Nonetheless, there were 2.9 million nonfatal injuries in 2016 alone.[9] Minimizing workplace injuries and accidents is of interest to both employees and their employers. As Senior Vice President Ed Galante of Texas-based ExxonMobil, the global oil and gas industry leader in most measures of worker safety, said, "Safety performance is a critical leading indicator of the overall quality and competence of an organization. It has been our experience that a disciplined approach to improving safety performance benefits all aspects of our operations. Our focus on safety has also helped us achieve lower costs, better reliability, and higher plant utilization, all contributing to the bottom line."[10]

> *"It has been our experience that a disciplined approach to improving safety performance benefits all aspects of our operations."*
>
> **—Ed Galante, Senior Vice President, ExxonMobil**

The important role of HRM in safety often becomes clear following serious accidents. BP's rapid growth and numerous acquisitions over the previous 15 years coupled with BP CEO John Browne's focus on numbers made shareholder value the ultimate goal, often to the detriment of safety. Investigations concluded that numerous failings in equipment, risk management, safety management, working culture at the site, maintenance and inspection, and general health and safety assessments combined to cause the catastrophe. As John Hofmeister, retired president of Houston-based Shell Oil Co. and former group human resource director of the Shell Group, puts it: "Unfortunately, in the hydrocarbon industry, if you don't take the HR profession seriously, people die."[11]

> *"Unfortunately, in the hydrocarbon industry, if you don't take the HR profession seriously, people die."*
>
> **—John Hofmeister, retired president of Houston-based Shell Oil Co.**

Why Is Employee Safety Important?

U.S. Secretary of Labor Hilda Solis said, "Every day in America, 12 people go to work and never come home. Every year in America, 3.3 million people suffer a workplace injury from which they may never recover. These are preventable tragedies that disable our workers, devastate our families, and damage our economy."[12] Workplace fatalities, injuries, and illnesses result in estimated economic losses of to 4 to 5 percent of gross domestic product.[13] Improving workplace safety pays tremendous dividends in terms of lower workers' compensation and insurance costs and improved employee productivity, morale, and retention.

Injuries related to lifting, pulling, pushing, holding, carrying, or throwing objects are the top cause of disabling injury in the United States and cost employers over $15 billion in 2016, nearly 25 percent of total injury costs. Next common are falls on the same or a lower level and being struck by an object or equipment.[14]

One organization reduced accidents by using text analysis of e-mail, performance management data, and employee comments to identify accident risks and understand the causes of high-risk behavior.[15] In addition to the obvious moral and ethical reasons to keep employees safe, investigating the causes of accidents can lead to easy solutions that have large financial and safety benefits, as this chapter's Strategic Impact feature illustrates.

♟ Strategic Impact

The Business Case for Safety

A global manufacturing company discovered that when overtime for operators, maintenance, and skilled trade workers exceeds 12.5 hours for three weeks, accidents increased by 105 percent. When the company added additional employees to reduce the need for overtime, the company saved $370 million from fewer accidents in just six months.[16]

The role of HRM in safety is to not only hire and train the right people but also to build a strong safety culture. Professor Wayne Cascio believes that the chief human resources officer "has to be the conscience of the company, has to say things to the CEO that others don't want to say about effective safety management."[17] Because of its role in hiring, training, evaluating performance and giving feedback, providing incentives, and separating employees HRM plays a key role in the creation and maintenance of any type of culture, including a safety culture.

A Culture of Safety

safety culture

the shared safety attitudes, beliefs, and practices that shape employees' safety behavior

A **safety culture** is the set of shared safety attitudes, beliefs, and practices that shape employees' safety behavior. Because developing a strong safety culture has a large impact on accident reduction,[18] developing a safety culture should be a top priority for all managers.[19] In a strong safety culture, all employees feel a responsibility for safety and pursue it every day. Employees are willing to identify unsafe behaviors and conditions and take steps to correct them.

An organization's safety culture is influenced by:[20]

- Management and employee attitudes;
- Supervisor priorities, accountability, and responsibilities;
- Management and employee norms, beliefs, and assumptions;
- Employee safety training and motivation;
- Manager and employee involvement and commitment;
- Production and financial pressures;
- Actions employees take (or do not take) to correct unsafe behaviors and situations.

so what

Creating a culture of safety is one of the most important things an organization can do to protect employees' health and safety.

Building a culture of safety brings together employees across all organizational levels. Perhaps the most important element in creating a culture of safety is a CEO who makes a culture of safety a core value that permeates every aspect of their organization.[21] Without management commitment, safety is likely to lose the frequent battle with production and profitability. Showing the direct and indirect costs of accidents, including higher workers' compensation premiums, lost productivity, turnover, and lack of trust, can help secure managers' commitment. Training all employees in safety and health, communication, and hazard recognition can help strengthen a safety culture. Recognizing employees for doing the right things and communicating and celebrating successes are also important.[22]

Having a clear safety vision and mission can also help create a strong culture of safety. Creating and communicating a clear safety policy is also important.[23] One study found that across multiple industries a supportive work environment was strongly related to improved safety outcomes.[24] In 2010, the deadliest U. S. mining disaster in over 40 years caused the deaths of 29 miners. The disaster was attributed to a workplace culture that valued production over safety.[25] The deadly explosion at Transocean's Deepwater Horizon drilling rig and resulting offshore oil spill was attributed in part to a poor safety culture.[26] Tokyo Electric has also been criticized for the lax safety culture that developed in the years leading up to the Fukushima Daiichi plant nuclear disaster following the tsunami.[27]

Coca-Cola, DuPont, Nabisco, and Kraft Foods have also used incentive programs to reinforce the importance of safety and keep safety on everyone's minds. By giving employees small prizes or the chance to receive larger prizes, organizations create a positive buzz for good safety performance, reinforcing a culture of safety. However, care must be taken to ensure that a safety incentive program does not discourage employees from reporting accidents or injuries because they want to receive the reward. OSHA has called for increased attention to whether a safety incentive is great enough to dissuade reasonable workers from reporting injuries. If so, an OSHA recordkeeping rule is being violated,[28] and OSHA investigators and compliance officers have been instructed to launch a recordkeeping investigation.[29]

Although positive reinforcement for safe work practices and proactive safety measures including reporting near misses and reducing hazards are important, reducing the presence of hazards should be the priority of any safety program. Reducing dangers in the work environment and creating a more ergonomic workflow can greatly reduce the opportunity for injury. Focusing on injury and illness prevention programs reduce accidents and help develop a culture of safety. Conducting periodic safety risk assessments is a great way to reduce workplace hazards, increase employees' awareness of hazards and risks, and improve the current safety management system. A safety risk assessment involves taking a thorough look at the workplace to identify hazards, analyze or evaluate the risks associated with each hazard, and determine appropriate ways to eliminate or control the hazard.

Although it can be effective to use progressive discipline to reinforce safety procedures and safe behaviors, a focus on punishing employees for accidents and injuries can undermine a culture of safety. Accurate reporting of accidents and injuries is critical to diagnosing why people are getting hurt, and zero accident tolerance policies and other injury discipline programs can encourage employees to lie about injuries. One study of employees in five industries found an average of 2.48 unreported accidents for every accident that was reported to the organization. Underreporting was higher when safety climates were poorer or where supervisor safety enforcement was inconsistent.[30] A program that only disciplines an employee for lack of safety when someone is injured rather than when any unsafe behavior occurs is an anti-injury reporting program, not a safety program.[31]

When Paul O'Neill became CEO of aluminum giant Alcoa, he made worker safety a priority for business as well as safety reasons. Whenever an employee got hurt, O'Neill required the senior members of the department to deliver a plan showing how the injury would never happen again. To do this, the executives had to become intimately involved with the manufacturing process, leading to conversations with frontline employees about their ideas. This led to streamlining operations, lower costs, higher quality, and improved productivity. Not only did employee safety improve, Alcoa's profits quintupled in just 13 years.[32]

Ergonomics

A comfortable work environment could mean the difference between an average performer and a superstar.[33] **Ergonomics** involves designing the work environment to reduce the physical and psychological demands placed on employees. Factors including lighting, furniture, equipment layout, lifting or moving objects, vibration, and temperature are studied and improved to maximize employee comfort and performance. The goal of ergonomics is improved employee performance and reduced injuries and errors. Improving comfort and reducing environmental distractions improves productivity and reduces the risk of accidents and injuries.

Workplace injuries resulting from repetitive motions, including typing and playing an instrument, are the most common occupational hazards. Repeated motions and vibrations can

so what?

Incentive programs can reinforce safety, but they can also discourage employees from reporting accidents or injuries.

so what?

Reducing workplace hazards and not punishing employees for accidents and injuries enhance workplace safety.

ergonomics
designing the work environment to reduce the physical and psychological demands placed on employees

The goal of ergonomics is to reduce injuries and improve performance. Properly using ergonomic office chairs and keeping the keyboard at the correct height can reduce the risk of wrist, back, and neck pain and help employees work more comfortably.

cumulative trauma disorder

skeletal and muscle injuries that occur when the same muscles are used to perform tasks repetitively

overwork muscles, tendons, and nerves, and place excessive stress on hands, wrists, arms, and shoulders. **Cumulative trauma disorders** are the skeletal and muscle injuries that occur when the same muscles are used to perform tasks repetitively.

One type of cumulative trauma disorder is *carpal tunnel syndrome*, a hand and wrist injury common to teachers, secretaries, chefs, and assembly line workers. Educating workers on the safest ways to work as well as redesigning tools, workstations, or the job can help prevent carpal tunnel syndrome. The goal of training is to inform employees and managers about risk factors contributing to carpal tunnel syndrome and reducing awkward wrist postures and the number of repetitive motions. Adjustable workstations should be provided that accommodate the majority of employees who work in that area to prevent awkward wrist positions and minimize the stressful effects of repetitive motions. Ergonomic job design for repetitive tasks includes:[34]

- Analyzing the task sequence to allow changes in body position;
- A regular work–rest schedule to relieve muscles from mechanical stress;
- Regular work breaks to avoid monotonous and repetitive work patterns; and
- Rotating tasks to move workers from one job to another.

The Occupational Safety and Health Administration (OSHA)

Occupational Safety and Health Administration (OSHA)

created by the Occupational Safety and Health Act to set and enforce protective workplace safety and health standards

In 1970, the Occupational Safety and Health Act (OSH Act) was passed to prevent workers from being seriously injured or killed at work. The OSH Act states that "Each employer shall furnish to each of his employees' employment and a place of employment that are free from recognized hazards that are causing or likely to cause death or serious physical harm to his employees,"[35] and it holds employers with at least one employee responsible for providing a safe workplace. The OSH Act created the **Occupational Safety and Health Administration (OSHA)** to set and enforce protective workplace safety and health standards. OSHA also provides information, training, and assistance to workers in the area of worker safety and health.[36] OSHA covers most private sector workers and employers either directly through federal OSHA or through a state program that is OSHA-approved and at least as effective as the federal OSHA program.

Employers and employees both have responsibilities under OSHA. Employers must:[37]

- Follow all relevant OSHA safety and health standards.
- Find and correct safety and health hazards.
- Inform employees about chemical hazards through training, labels, alarms, color-coded systems, chemical information sheets, and other methods.
- Notify OSHA within 8 hours of a workplace fatality or when three or more workers are hospitalized.
- Provide requested personal protective equipment at no cost to workers.
- Keep accurate records of work-related injuries and illnesses.
- Post OSHA citations injury and illness summary data, and the OSHA "Job Safety and Health – It's the Law" poster (shown in Figure 12.1) in the workplace where workers will see them.
- Not discriminate or retaliate against any worker for using their rights under the law.

Marcin Balcerzak/Shutterstock

figure 12.1

The OSHA "Job Safety and Health – It's the Law" Poster[38]

All workers have the right to:

- A safe workplace.
- Raise a safety or health concern with your employer or OSHA, or report a work-related injury or illness, without being retaliated against.
- Receive information and training on job hazards, including all hazardous substances in your workplace.
- Request an OSHA inspection of your workplace if you believe there are unsafe or unhealthy conditions. OSHA will keep your name confidential. You have the right to have a representative contact OSHA on your behalf.
- Participate (or have your representative participate) in an OSHA inspection and speak in private to the inspector.
- File a complaint with OSHA within 30 days (by phone, online or by mail) if you have been retaliated against for using your rights.
- See any OSHA citations issued to your employer.
- Request copies of your medical records, tests that measure hazards in the workplace, and the workplace injury and illness log.

This poster is available free from OSHA.

Contact OSHA. We can help.

Employers must:

- Provide employees a workplace free from recognized hazards. It is illegal to retaliate against an employee for using any of their rights under the law, including raising a health and safety concern with you or with OSHA, or reporting a work-related injury or illness.
- Comply with all applicable OSHA standards.
- Report to OSHA all work-related fatalities within 8 hours, and all inpatient hospitalizations, amputations and losses of an eye within 24 hours.
- Provide required training to all workers in a language and vocabulary they can understand.
- Prominently display this poster in the workplace.
- Post OSHA citations at or near the place of the alleged violations.

FREE ASSISTANCE to identify and correct hazards is available to small and medium-sized employers, without citation or penalty, through OSHA-supported consultation programs in every state.

1-800-321-OSHA (6742) • TTY 1-877-889-5627 • www.osha.gov

Employees have the right to:[39]

- Working conditions that do not pose a risk of serious harm.
- Receive information and training (in a language workers can understand) about chemical and other hazards, methods to prevent harm, and OSHA standards that apply to their workplace.
- Review records of work-related injuries and illnesses.
- Get copies of test results done to find and measure hazards in the workplace.

- File a complaint asking OSHA to inspect their workplace if they believe there is a serious hazard or that their employer is not following OSHA rules; when requested, OSHA will keep all identities confidential.
- Use their rights under the law without retaliation or discrimination. Any type of discrimination complaint including demotion and transfer must be filed within 30 days of the alleged discrimination.

OSHA Log of Work-Related Injuries and Illnesses.   OSHA's Log of Work-Related Injuries and Illnesses (Form 300) is used to record work-related injuries and illnesses as well as the severity of each case. The form is used to record specific details about when and how a work-related incident happened. An illness or an injury is considered work related if an event in the work environment contributed to or caused the condition or significantly aggravated a preexisting condition. Work-related injuries and illnesses must be recorded within seven calendar days if they result in:

- Loss of consciousness
- Death
- Restricted work activity or job transfer
- Medical treatment beyond first aid
- Formal diagnosis by a physician or other licensed health care professional, including a chronic irreversible disease, a punctured eardrum, and a fractured or cracked bone.

Form 300 must be kept for each site or location expected to be in operation for at least one year. Employees have the right to review their employer's injury and illness records. The purpose of Form 300 is to collect better information about the incidence of occupational injuries and illnesses and improve employees' awareness of and involvement in the recording and reporting of work-related injuries and illnesses.

OSHA standards
rules describing the methods employers must legally follow to protect their workers from hazards

so what

Even if there is no specific OSHA standard for a workplace hazard, the General Duty Clause requiring employers to keep their workplaces free of serious recognized hazards may still apply.

OSHA Standards.   **OSHA standards** are rules describing the methods employers must legally follow to protect their workers from hazards.[40] Before issuing a standard, OSHA goes through a very extensive process that includes substantial public engagement, notice, and comment. A significant risk to workers must be shown to exist, and feasible measures employers can take to protect their workers must be identified. Construction, general industry, maritime, and agriculture standards limit the amount of hazardous chemicals to which workers can be exposed, require the use of specific safe practices and equipment, and require employers to monitor certain workplace hazards.[41]

Examples of OSHA standards include requirements to provide slip-and-fall protection, prevent exposure to some infectious diseases, ensure the safety of workers who enter confined spaces, prevent exposure to harmful substances including asbestos and lead, put guards on machines, provide respirators and safety glasses or other personal protective equipment, and provide training for certain dangerous jobs. There are also standards for exposure to human immunodeficiency virus (HIV), hepatitis B virus (HBV), and other blood-borne pathogens to protect employees regularly exposed to blood and other bodily fluids. The General Duty Clause of the OSH Act requiring employers to keep their workplaces free of serious recognized hazards is generally cited when no specific OSHA standard applies to a hazard.[42]

Exposure to hazardous chemicals is a serious workplace safety issue. OSHA's Hazard Communication Standard requires that information about the identities and the hazards of chemicals must be available and understandable to workers. Chemical manufacturers and importers must evaluate the hazards of the chemicals they produce or import and prepare labels and safety data sheets to convey the hazard to customers and users of the chemicals. Labels and safety data sheets must be available for all exposed workers, and workers must be trained to handle the chemicals appropriately.[43] The top OSHA violations tend to include fall protection, hazard communication, scaffolding, and respiratory protection.[44]

OSHA Inspections.   OSHA inspections are conducted onsite or via telephone by highly trained compliance officers and initiated without advance notice. Because OSHA cannot inspect all 7 million workplaces it covers each year, the agency focuses its resources on the most hazardous workplaces in the following order of priority:[45]

1. *Imminent danger situations:* Hazards that could cause death or serious physical harm receive top priority. Compliance officers ask employers to correct these hazards immediately or remove endangered employees.
2. *Fatalities and catastrophes:* Incidents that involve a death or the hospitalization of three or more employees are the second priority. Employers must report such events to OSHA within 8 hours.
3. *Complaints:* Employee allegations of hazards or violations also receive high priority. Employees may request anonymity when filing complaints.
4. *Referrals of hazard information from other federal, state or local agencies, individuals, organizations or the media* receive the next priority.
5. *Follow-ups:* Checks for addressing violations cited during previous inspections are also conducted in certain circumstances.
6. *Planned or programmed investigations:* Inspections aimed at specific high-hazard industries or individual workplaces that have experienced high rates of injuries and illnesses are also given priority.

When OSHA issues a citation to an employer, the employer is given an opportunity for an informal conference with the OSHA area director to discuss citations, penalties, fines, abatement dates, and other relevant information. A citation includes methods an employer may use to fix the problem and the date by when the corrective actions must be completed. Employers have the right to contest any part of the citation, including whether a violation actually exists. Workers may only challenge the deadline for when a problem must be resolved. Appeals of citations are heard by the independent Occupational Safety and Health Review Commission.[46] The agency and the employer may work out a settlement agreement to resolve the matter and eliminate the hazard.

OSHA's primary goal is correcting hazards and maintaining compliance rather than issuing citations or collecting fines.[47] One study found that OSHA workplace safety inspections decreased injury rates by 9.4 percent and workplace injury costs by 26 percent with no loss to sales, employment, or firm survival. Following an inspection, an employer saved an average of $355,000 due to lower workers' compensation insurance and medical costs.[48]

OSHA Information and Training.   OSHA offers several programs and services to help employers identify and correct job hazards as well as improve their injury and illness prevention programs. OSHA provides a free onsite consultation service for small businesses with fewer than 250 workers at any single site and no more than 500 employees nationwide. Onsite consultation services do not result in penalties or citations. Each year, OSHA makes more than 30,000 consultation visits to small businesses to provide free compliance assistance. OSHA also has compliance assistance specialists throughout the nation who can provide general information about OSHA standards and compliance assistance.[49] In addition, OSHA offers a variety of cooperative programs to help prevent fatalities, injuries, and illnesses in the workplace.[50]

OSHA Training Institute (OTI) Education Centers are a national network of nonprofit organizations authorized by OSHA to deliver occupational safety and health training to private sector workers, supervisors, and employers.[51] OSHA also has a variety of educational materials and electronic tools available on its website.[52] These include safety and health topics pages, safety fact sheets, expert adviser software, copies of regulations and compliance directives, videos, and other information for employers and workers. OSHA's software programs and e-tools walk employers through safety and health issues and common problems to find the best solutions for their workplaces. OSHA's extensive publications help explain OSHA standards, job hazards, and mitigation strategies, and it provide assistance in developing effective safety and health programs.[53]

so what?

OSHA helps employers create and maintain safe workplaces as well as enforces the Occupational Safety and Health Act.

Employee Wellness

Employee wellness programs are initiatives designed to increase company performance or employee performance or morale through improved employee health. Companies are increasingly investing in wellness programs to improve their bottom lines while building a great workplace.[54] When implemented correctly using company-specific research and planning, wellness programs can have big benefits for both the employer and the employees. Wellness programs benefit employers by:[55]

- Reducing injuries
- Lowering healthcare costs
- Reducing absenteeism
- Improving employee morale and loyalty
- Improving employee productivity
- Reducing workers' compensation and disability related costs.

Because they both help to control an organization's healthcare expenses and promote employee satisfaction and productivity, organizations are increasingly implementing and promoting preventive employee wellness programs. In 2016, 72 percent of organizations were providing wellness resources and information to employees, up 18 percent from 1996.[56] North Carolina–based N2 Publishing hired a full-time nutritionist and sports therapist and started a wellness program full of fitness challenges including "Can you really cut out the sugar?" The company's bare-bones office motto "function over flash" reflects the company's preference to spend money on things that matter instead of office furniture, allowing it to donate $2 million to fight human trafficking in a single year.[57]

so what

Because many wellness initiatives do not require a lot of space or expense, smaller organizations can also implement wellness programs.

Smaller organizations are also implementing wellness programs. Encouraging employees to avoid sending nonessential e-mails at night and on the weekend, facilitating lunchtime fitness activities, making healthy snacks available even if from a vending machine, and facilitating friendly wellness competitions don't cost a lot but can positively change employees' health behaviors.[58]

Wellness programs can address factors including healthy eating, smoking cessation, weight management, physical activity, and stress management. Novartis Pharmaceuticals offers all employees a "buy-four-get-one-free" card as an incentive to choose the healthier options in the cafeteria, and an on-site nutritionist consults with employees one-on-one.[59] Smoking cessation initiatives helped Johnson & Johnson reduce its percentage of smokers, and GlaxoSmithKline offers an on-site fitness center, walking trails, and fitness-focused lunch-and-learns.[60] Because the biggest reason employees cite for not participating in wellness programs is often a lack of time during the workday,[61] creating a culture of wellness in which healthy lifestyle choices are the norm and are supported by managers and coworkers can help employees maintain their new behaviors.

Wellness programs often begin with a health assessment questionnaire that allows for immediate follow-up and engagement in health-promoting programs. The health assessment itself can help to engage employees in personal health improvement programs by having them reflect on their healthy habits and lifestyle. Because health assessment data allows wellness programs to be customized to best meet the needs of each individual, research has demonstrated a positive impact on population health and financial outcomes for well-designed programs that incorporate a health assessment with follow-up feedback.[62]

Technology is enhancing the reach and the effectiveness of wellness programs. Employers are increasingly using mobile technology including smart phones to support employee wellness initiatives.[63] Online health portals can customize content, tools, and guidance to the individual's health risks, health conditions, and readiness to change. Employees can be steered into program components best suited to improving their health based on their self-efficacy, barriers to change, and other data collected in the health assessment.[64]

Some organizations adopt competitive fitness challenges and social network sites similar to Facebook to share results and let employees support each other. Clinton Hospital entered

HR Flexibility

Wellness Initiatives for Organizations of All Sizes

Larger Organizations Can:

Provide an onsite fitness center

Offer onsite medical care for sick or well visits

Provide an onsite cafeteria offering healthy meals and snacks

Provide extensive employee training on wellness topics, including bullying prevention and stress management

Provide onsite smoking cessation and weight loss programs

Smaller Organizations Can Instead:

Provide employee discounts for local fitness centers

Grant employees extra wellness days to enable medical visits and relaxation

Provide free or subsidized healthy snacks

Create a strong culture of respect and wellness

Offer online smoking cessation and weight loss programs

---

a 100-day countywide fitness challenge in which teams of six employees competed against other local businesses to see who could walk the most, eat the healthiest, or lose the most weight. Participants logged onto a private social network to share results and support each other. The competitive challenge, online camaraderie, and the cash prizes for the winning team and the individual who lost the most weight attracted 37 percent of Clinton Hospital's staff to participate in the program.[65]

Organizations of all sizes can implement wellness programs to meet employees' needs and realize meaningful financial benefits. If a wellness program preempts 25 unnecessary emergency department visits, the company can easily save $50,000, and preventing four inpatient hospital stays can save at least $100,000. For a 2,000-employee company, these numbers are not unrealistic.[66] Although larger organizations can obviously dedicate greater resources to wellness, many initiatives exist that do not cost a lot of money or require onsite space. When Google started putting bottled water at eye level in the cooler and moved soda to the bottom, water intake increased by 47 percent, and calories employees consumed at work from drinks fell 7 percent.[67] This chapter's HR Flexibility feature highlights some common wellness initiatives used by both larger and smaller organizations.

Many organizations are finding that their wellness programs are accomplishing their goals. Alcon, a global eye care provider, found that more than half of its employees at high risk for high cholesterol or high blood pressure moved to moderate or low risk within two years because of its customized health enhancement plan that identifies employees' health characteristics and risk factors, and it verifies and rewards positive change with various incentives. The program is partially credited with saving Alcon $1.5 million in medical and pharmacy claims in a single year.[68]

Wellness Incentives

Used effectively, **wellness incentives** that reward employees for engaging in healthy behavior or for participating in wellness programs can improve the likelihood that employees will adopt healthier behaviors. Payroll processor Paychex awards employees $100 to $300 every year for healthy activities including dental check-ups, getting flu shots, biking to work, and attending aerobics or yoga classes.[69]

wellness incentives rewards for engaging in healthy behavior or participating in wellness programs

 so what?

Although good health should be motivational on its own, many employees also respond well to incentives for healthy behaviors.

Behavioral economics research suggests that the same decision errors that contribute to poor health-related behaviors can be used to "supercharge" incentive programs to more effectively motivate behavior change.[70] For example, people place more weight on the present than the future when making decisions and are more attracted to immediate than delayed benefits. We are also more deterred by immediate than delayed costs. Many behavioral patterns that undermine wellness involve immediate benefits and delayed costs. For example, eating a tasty snack provides immediate gratification but may cause later obesity. Many wellness interventions also involve immediate costs (such as the inconvenience of exercising) with delayed and possibly uncertain health improvement months or years later. From this perspective, annual health insurance premium adjustments are unlikely to be maximally effective in motivating behavior change because the consequences are delayed. Ideally, incentives should provide small but tangible and frequent positive feedback or rewards. An exercise promotion program offering a year-end rebate for gym attendance or a small annual health insurance premium reduction is far less likely to succeed than one offering incentives at every visit. The same concepts apply to most health-related behaviors, such as smoking cessation or medication adherence, for which incentives might prompt immediate attention to otherwise delayed benefits.[71]

The best wellness incentive programs inspire long-term lifestyle changes so that the healthy behaviors continue when the incentives are reduced or removed. The Health Insurance Portability and Accountability Act (HIPAA) of 1996 requires that programs providing incentives based on health status factors (e.g., cholesterol below 200) meet several conditions, including a limit on the size of the incentive offered (generally 20 percent of the total health insurance premium). Programs that provide incentives based on standards that do not involve health status factors (e.g., completing a health risk assessment) can provide unlimited incentives as long as the incentive is equally available to all participants.[72]

Engaging wellness programs often offer interactive websites, online health risk assessments, and personalized wellness plans. Integrating them with social networking sites and mobile applications also gives employees flexibility in when, where, and how they access wellness resources and thus makes it easier to do so. It is also important to remember that even small incentives can be effective at changing employees' behaviors, particularly if awarded frequently. Incentives of just $100 have been shown to boost participation in weight management and smoking cessation programs.[73] Here are one expert's tips for effective health incentives:[74]

- They should be as low as possible to get results.
- Choose incentives that help sustain positive "buzz" and generate the highest participation.
- If the honor system is used for reporting wellness activities, communicate the company's expectations clearly, and ask employees to sign a registration form promising honest reporting.
- Incentives should be consistent with what employees are being asked to do—completing an online health self-assessment questionnaire might warrant a lower reward than a biometric check of cholesterol, blood pressure, and body fat.

so what

Even small incentives can be effective at changing employees' behaviors, particularly if awarded frequently.

Issues with perceived fairness can complicate the use of wellness incentives. One large organization's trial smoking cessation program offering a pilot group a $750 incentive to quit smoking tripled smoking cessation rates from 5 percent to 14.7 percent after nine to 12 months, but when the company decided to offer the program to all employees, feedback from nonsmoking employees resulted in a change from the $750 reward to a $625 penalty for smokers. Nonsmokers did not like the company rewarding their coworkers for something they did themselves without a reward.[75]

This chapter's Case Study highlights how Johnson & Johnson uses incentives as part of its wellness programs.

CASE STUDY: Johnson & Johnson's Wellness Programs

Johnson & Johnson has long been committed to employee wellness, launching its first employee health initiative in 1978. Its wellness program called "Live for Life" includes a health risk assessment, biometric screenings, free health counseling for high-risk employees, and even a financial incentive for participating. The incentives are the same for all employees. Employees get a $500 discount on their healthcare premiums for taking the confidential health risk assessment[76] that identifies health and lifestyle risks, including tobacco use, cholesterol, blood pressure, and inactivity.[77] Healthy employees continue to receive the discount, as do employees found to have some of the risk factors and who participate in the risk management program.[78]

J&J created "Healthy Future" goals to challenge employees to be more health conscious, and it centralized employee health management through its One Health Organization.[79] J&J's leaders estimate that its wellness programs have saved the company over $250 million in just 10 years, returning a value of almost three times what was invested in employee wellness.[80] In just five years, the percentage of J&J employees who smoke fell by more than two-thirds, and the number with high blood pressure or who were physically inactive declined by more than half.[81]

Questions

1. How does J&J create a culture of health?
2. What do you think are some of the most important elements of J&J's wellness program?
3. What are some downsides to using incentives as part of a wellness program?

Some wellness programs may violate state laws protecting employees' off-duty conduct. Some states including New York have "smokers' rights" laws protecting individuals from discrimination on the basis of their lawful use of tobacco products outside of the workplace. California has broader coverage that includes any lawful activity off the employer's premises during nonworking hours. It is important to review state laws to ensure that a wellness program complies with state requirements.[82]

Stress

Stress is not always bad, and the lack of stress is not always good.[83] The small amount of adrenaline generated by mild stress makes action more likely and even increases the brain's ability to form new memories.[84] Good stress is also called **functional stress**.[85] Functional stress is the experience of a manageable level of stress that generates positive emotions including satisfaction, excitement, and enjoyment. A challenging project is an example of functional stress. Functional stress can lead to positive outcomes including job satisfaction, but if the resulting anxiety is unmanaged, it can lead to counterproductive behaviors.[86]

Dysfunctional stress refers to either under- or over-arousal stemming from too few or too many demands continuing for too long. Factors including conflicting goals and a harsh boss can interfere with job performance and lead to dysfunctional stress.

functional stress
manageable levels of stress that generate positive emotions including satisfaction, excitement, and enjoyment

so what?

It is important to review state laws to ensure that a wellness program does not violate state laws protecting employees' off-duty conduct.

so what?

Not all stress is bad—functional stress can generate positive outcomes as long as it is properly managed.

dysfunctional stress
an overload of stress resulting from a situation of under- or over-arousal continuing for too long

Andrey_Popov/Shutterstock

Some of the ways experts recommend managing dysfunctional stress are to take regular breaks, exercise, and meditate. Some offices now supply exercise equipment such as yoga balls and treadmill desks to make it easier for employees to engage in wellness activities during the workday.

Although both functional and dysfunctional stress can lead to negative outcomes including emotional exhaustion, dysfunctional stress is also related to withdrawal and turnover. Stress due to working long hours was cited as the reason Pfizer Chairman and CEO Jeffrey Kindler retired.[87] Stress, depression, anxiety, and poor social support can undermine employees' performance and wellness efforts. Stress also increases employees' use of healthcare and disability benefits and employee assistance programs.

Undergoing any level of stress for too long can cause health problems, including elevated blood pressure and high cholesterol. Workplace stress triggers include a heavy workload, lack of clarity about responsibilities, and low perceived meaningfulness of the work.[88] Stress is also due to excessive work hours, lack of work–life balance, and job insecurity. Fortunately, human resource management strategies can address many of these causes of stress. One of the most important stress management approaches is to allow employees greater control over their own work patterns and schedules. A positive organizational culture, open communication between managers and employees, and letting employees participate in decision-making also help to decrease employee stress.[89]

It is important to address stress factors as part of employee wellness initiatives. The most effective corporate wellness programs focus on emotional as well as physical factors, including counseling to address underlying issues.[90] One of the best approaches to reducing job stress is asking managers to encourage and lead employees in stress relief activities such as walking, laughing, eating healthier, and even meditating.[91] As a reminder of the importance of regularly stepping away from their desks, Kaiser Permanente employees can have stretch break reminders sent to their computers that suggest a variety of stretches throughout the day.[92]

problem-focused coping strategies
deal directly with the cause of stress

emotion-focused coping strategies
focus on the emotions brought on by the stressor

Problem-focused coping strategies that deal directly with the cause of stress are more effective than **emotion-focused coping strategies** that focus on the emotions brought on by the stressor.[93] Actively promoting positive employee attitudes, moods, and emotions fights stress and burnout and improves employees' performance and job satisfaction. Stress can be managed through various coping strategies that focus on:

1. Changing the situation through direct action (e.g., quitting the job or hiring an assistant)
2. Changing the way we think about the situation through cognitive reappraisal (e.g., focusing on the developmental aspects of a challenging assignment)
3. Focusing on managing the stress reaction symptoms (e.g., working out or meditating).

so what

Positive stress management strategies are important for all employees.

Positive stress management strategies include social support, music, humor, meditation, exercising, maintaining a positive outlook, and getting enough rest. Other symptom-focused coping strategies can be harmful, including drinking, drug use, and overeating. One of the best ways to reduce stress on the job is to make moderate exercise part of a regular routine.[94] It is important to remember that removing the source of stress is more effective than managing stress symptoms.[95] This chapter's Develop Your Skills feature gives you some tips on how to manage your stress.

 # Develop Your Skills

Managing Your Stress

Although it is impossible to avoid all stress, these suggestions are useful in reducing the number of stressors in your life:

- *Avoid the things that cause you stress:* If heavy traffic raises your stress level, try to arrange work hours to avoid the traffic, find a different and less popular route, or see if you can telecommute to work sometimes; if rushing home from work to prepare dinner is a stressor, try to prepare multiple meals on the weekend that can be reheated quickly during the work week.
- *Just say "no":* No one can do everything—establish limits and stick to them.
- *Exercise:* Go for a walk or run, take the stairs, or spend some time at the gym.
- *Prioritize:* If you can't get everything done, identify what is most important, and eliminate tasks that are not truly necessary.
- *Proactively relax:* Techniques including exercise, yoga, meditation, massages, and power naps can help you relax and manage your stress; taking a brief break to review our accomplishments, relax, and prioritize the remaining tasks can be rejuvenating and help us spend our time doing the right things.
- *Make time for yourself:* If you have hobbies and interests that are important to you, be sure to allot some time to the activities you enjoy every day even when you are busy to help you relax and feel in control; also ensure that you get sufficient sleep.
- *Adjust your standards:* If your best quality work isn't necessary, settle for a little less, and turn your attention to getting other tasks done.
- *Stay positive:* Reflect on all that is positive in your life and all things of which you are appreciative.
- *Reframe stressful situations:* Look at challenges and stressful situations as opportunities for growth and self-improvement.
- *Focus on what you can control:* Focus on the things you have influence over, such as how you react to stressful situations, rather than dwelling on the things you cannot control.

Giving positive feedback and assigning employees to tasks and projects that utilize their strengths energizes employees to put their full effort into their jobs. Receiving negative feedback often leads people to focus more on their weaknesses than their strengths. As management expert Peter Cappelli says, "Cranking up negative consequences, which seems to be the dominant view of motivation, is not really good for people's mental health."[96] Negative feedback such as, "You really messed up that project," increases stress during times that are already stressful.

> *"Cranking up negative consequences, which seems to be the dominant view of motivation, is not really good for people's mental health."*
>
> **—Peter Cappelli, management expert**

A big source of stress for many employees is financial pressures.[97] A CNN poll found that money worries were the largest source of stress for people around the world.[98] A research study also found that 72 percent of Americans lose sleep over their finances.[99] Given that 49 percent of one survey's respondents are living paycheck to paycheck, and 61 percent do not have enough money in an emergency fund to cover six months of expenses,[100] it is easy to understand why employees are distracted by and stressed about money. Compounded with a fear of losing their jobs in a challenging economy, it is not surprising that over 75 percent of doctor visits are related to stress.[101] In addition to insomnia, people with high levels of financial stress suffer from a variety of stress-related illnesses, including ulcers, migraines, anxiety, depression, and heart attacks.[102] Many organizations are incorporating financial management, retirement, and budgeting programs into their wellness and stress management plans to help employees deal with this serious stressor and realizing a return of over 300 percent on this investment.[103]

Too often, job stress is treated with medication or counseling rather than by making appropriate changes in the workplace and to workloads. Leaders at Merck, the global pharmaceutical company based in Whitehouse Station, New Jersey, listened to employee complaints about problems including overwork, inadequate training, and lack of communication and created employee teams to address them. Work was analyzed and reorganized to give workers more control over their workloads and schedules. In payroll, for example, the company learned that most employees' work was most critical early in the week. To reduce the amount of overtime payroll employees had to put in, they were allowed to telecommute more often and to work compressed work weeks. These changes reduced overtime costs, absenteeism, and turnover.[104]

Some companies realize that helping employees balance work and life demands can reduce employees' stress. Management consultant Booz Allen Hamilton Inc. has employees identify their life responsibilities, and then work is arranged around those commitments.[105] Some companies, including research and development firm Draper Laboratory in Cambridge, Massachusetts, even refuse to buy smart phones or other communication devices for employees to prevent them from being "on call" 24 hours a day, giving them time to decompress.[106]

For most people, occasional stress is a part of work life. Successful managers handle stress well, proactively reduce their employees' stress, and help their employees manage their stressors. To help your employees manage their stress:[107]

so what

As a manager, you can help employees manage their stress by helping them balance their work and life demands.

- Ensure that workloads match employees' capabilities and resources.
- Teach employees time management skills.
- Design jobs to provide meaning, stimulation, and opportunities for employees to use their skills.
- Clearly define employee roles and responsibilities.
- Give employees the opportunity to participate in decisions and actions affecting their jobs.
- Improve communication and reduce uncertainty about career development and future employment prospects.
- Provide opportunities for social interaction among employees.
- Establish work schedules that are compatible with demands and responsibilities outside the job.
- Facilitate regular stress breaks.

workplace bullying
repeated incidents or a pattern of behavior that is intended to intimidate, offend, degrade, or humiliate a particular person or group of people

Bullying

Workplace bullying is a repeated incidents or a pattern of behavior that is intended to intimidate, offend, degrade, or humiliate a particular person or group of people.[108] Additional bullying behaviors include ignoring, making unreasonable or menial work assignments, teasing, gossiping, or holding the target to a different performance standard.[109]

Approximately 27 percent of employees report having felt bullied at some point in their working lives.[110] Bullying affects employers through higher workers' compensation costs and higher disability insurance rates, not to mention a reputation as a difficult place in which to work.

Both targets of bullying and observers of bullying report psychological problems such as distress, humiliation, anger, anxiety, discouragement, depression, lower job satisfaction, eroded attachment to the job and organization, and greater intention to leave.[111] Twenty percent of victims

so what

Bullying is a serious workplace problem and should not be ignored.

leave their jobs.[112] Many bullying targets report stress-related health problems, and targeted individuals suffer debilitating anxiety, panic attacks, clinical depression, and even post-traumatic stress.[113] Research suggests that psychological well-being is impaired more through psychologically abusive behavior than physically abusive behavior.[114] Research also suggests that as much as 71 percent of bullies are in management positions, and 29 percent are peers and subordinates.[115]

Many companies view bullying as a type of harassment and include bullying in their workplace harassment policies. Recognizing the negative effects on employee safety as well as the organization as a whole, many organizations have also begun implementing specific anti-bullying policies.

In the United States, workplace bullying has been found to be four times more common than sexual harassment,[116] but the issue affects all countries, professions, and workers. One poll of over 16,000 people worldwide found that:[117]

- 83 percent of European respondents reported having been physically or emotionally bullied;
- 65 percent in the Americas; and
- 55 percent in Asia.

The lowest reported rates of bullying were in Belgium (38 percent) and China (40 percent). One Norwegian study found that subordinates of less conscientious and more neurotic supervisors who were under stress reported greater exposure to workplace bullying. In addition, subordinates who perceived their supervisor as being introverted and low in agreeableness reported significantly more workplace bullying.[118] This chapter's Global Issues feature describes how bullying perceptions differ around the world. Table 12.1 provides tips on creating a bully-free workplace.

 # Global Issues

Bullying Perceptions Differ Around the World

Countries differ in how they deal with workplace bullies. Some cultures view bullying as a workplace safety issue, whereas others see it as a violation of personal rights. In other countries, particularly in those in which employment is not at-will and employees are difficult to terminate, bullying is used as a tactic to force targeted employees to quit. In 2013, South Africa passed laws to combat harassment in the workplace, allowing employees to obtain a protection order against an abusive colleague or employer. In Australia, harassed or bullied employees are encouraged to first try to resolve the issue through the organization's harassment policy before escalating the issue to the Fair Work Commission. The police are also able to handle complaints, and bullies can be prosecuted for harassment or assault.[119]

In the United Kingdom, conduct that creates an environment harmful to someone's dignity could constitute harassment even if the complaint is made by someone other than the employee affected. In France, bullying is referred to as "moral harassment," defined as "repeated acts leading to a deterioration of the working conditions that are likely to harm the dignity, physical, or psychological health of the victim or his/her career" and is outlawed. French laws allow for both civil and criminal action against a bully, with maximum penalties as high as two years in prison and a fine of 30,000 Euros.[120]

Among the first European countries to enact workplace bullying laws were Sweden and France. Countries including Denmark, Norway, and the Netherlands have followed suit.[121] Some countries, including Poland, now address harassment at work in their formal labor codes.[122]

table **12.1**

Creating a Bully-Free Workplace[123]

- **Foster a supportive culture** and encourage open communication across all organizational levels.

- **Introduce a specific zero-tolerance bullying policy** developed in partnership with employees from all organizational levels to increase general awareness of appropriate work behavior. The policy should cover the definition of what bullying is and what it is not, as well as the consequences of breaching the organization's standards. It should also clarify who to report to and clearly explain the procedure for making and investigating all complaints.

- **Include anti-bullying training during new manager training, and monitor newly promoted people for inappropriate behavior.** Because bullying often emerges when people are promoted and gain power, anything done to increase new managers' leadership competence and understanding of bullying is critical. Emphasize that treating all employees with respect is the way to make the company productive.

- **Repeatedly communicate both the definition of workplace bullying and your organization's policy at all levels** so that situations can be identified and managed early. Increasing awareness may also encourage more employees to feel empowered to combat bullying by refusing to take part or refusing to silently watch it happen.

- **Increase the perceived cost to the perpetrator** to deter potential bullies from taking action by communicating and enforcing negative consequences for bullying.

- **Try to screen out people who are abusive during the hiring process** using structured interview questions and assessments of past behavior. If a mistake is made, terminate the bully.

Substance Abuse

The Ford Motor Company initiated some of the first workplace sobriety programs as early as 1914.[124] Since then, employer-sponsored substance abuse programs have taken many shapes and forms. Ronald Reagan's signing into law Executive Order 12564 in 1986 banning the use of drugs for both on and off duty federal employees introduced the concept of a drug-free workplace. The Drug-Free Workplace Act of 1988 requires some federal contractors and all federal grantees to agree to provide drug-free workplaces as a precondition of receiving a federal contract or grant.[125]

In a drug-free workplace, the employer has enacted policies and procedures to ensure that employees, customers, and vendors are not:[126]

- Taking or using alcohol or illegal drugs
- Selling drugs
- Affected by the after effects of alcohol or illegal drugs outside of the workplace during nonwork time (i.e., hangovers).

More than 70 percent of substance abusers are employed,[127] and when they come to work, they don't leave their problems at home. As many as 20 percent of U.S. workers who die on the job test positive for alcohol or other drugs. Drug or alcohol impairment constitutes an avoidable workplace hazard that increases accident risks, lowers productivity, reduces profits, increases absenteeism, and increases insurance costs. Drug-free workplace programs can help improve worker safety and health as well as business performance.

There are five components to a comprehensive drug-free workplace program:[128]

1. *A written policy* supported by top management and understood by employees that is consistently enforced; a good example of such a policy is available online at http://www.ialr.org/index.php?option=com_content&view=article&id=242&Itemid=143.

2. *Supervisor and manager training* in identifying and dealing with substance abuse.
3. *Employee education* focusing on the dangers of drug and alcohol use and the availability of counseling and treatment.
4. *An Employee Assistance Program (EAP)* that provides confidential counseling for employees and their family members on a wide range of problems including substance abuse; an EAP can be established in-house or contracted from professional counseling service firms.
5. *Drug testing* for the early identification and referral to treatment for employees with substance abuse problems.

Some employees object to the random drug testing that is a part of many drug-free workplace programs. Failing a drug test does not mean that the employee was impaired at work, only that a substance was used during the time period covered by the test. Because most employees feel that drug testing is intrusive and reflects a lack of employer trust, it is essential that the testing be done with dignity and respect, honoring employees' privacy. The drug testing policy should specify the frequency of the drug testing, the type of testing used, and the substances for which employees will be tested. Employees should be selected for drug testing in a fair and consistent manner, and the selection process should be clearly explained in the drug testing policy.[129] Because drug testing is not allowed in every state, it is important to check with a state's department of labor to understand current laws.

Many workers with substance abuse problems can return safely to the workplace if given access to appropriate treatment, continuing care, and supportive services.[130] Although OSHA does not require them, drug-free workplace programs are complements to other initiatives that help keep workplaces safe.

Drug testing can deter workers from reporting injuries and accidents if doing so might trigger a mandatory drug test that could test positive for illegal substances. Testing injured workers for drugs before they are sent to a hospital sends the message to drug-using employees that injuries should not be reported, which is detrimental to workplace safety. Nonetheless, OSHA considers workplace drug use a huge problem and believes that its dangers outweigh any disincentives to reporting injuries drug testing might pose. Using drugs on the job puts other people at risk and must be taken seriously.[131]

Although small companies are less likely to have programs in place to combat substance abuse, they are often the employer of choice for illegal drug users. Workers who know that they will not be able to comply with a drug-free workplace policy seek jobs at organizations that don't have one. Given that the cost of a single accident can devastate a small business, it is particularly important for small businesses to implement drug-free workplace programs.

so what?

Although it can deter drug use, drug testing can also dissuade employees from reporting injuries and accidents that might trigger a mandatory drug test.

Security Issues

According to the U.S. Department of Justice, the workplace is the most dangerous place to be in the United States.[132] Acts of violence can be committed in a workplace by a current or a former employee, someone in an outside relationship with an employee, or someone with a legitimate reason for being on the premises, such as a customer. Workplace violence, including sabotage, results in injuries and death, post-incident counseling, legal actions and fees, court awards, poor morale, increased absenteeism, productivity loss, turnover, and bad publicity.[133] A safer and more secure work environment is a healthier work environment.

Workplace Violence

Workplace violence is any act or threat of physical violence, harassment, intimidation, or other threatening disruptive behavior that occurs at the workplace.[134] It can affect and involve employees, clients, customers and visitors. Every year nearly 2 million U.S. workers report

workplace violence
any act or threat of physical violence, harassment, intimidation, or other threatening disruptive behavior that occurs at the workplace

having been victims of acts of workplace violence,[135] and more than 800 die as a result of it.[136] Organizations have both a moral and a financial obligation to protect their workforce. The annual cost of workplace violence to U.S. companies is estimated to be as high as $121 billion.[137]

Factors that may increase the risk of violence for some workers at certain worksites include:[138]

- Exchanging money with the public
- Working with volatile, unstable people
- Working alone or in isolated areas
- Providing services and care
- Working where alcohol is served
- Working late at night or in areas with high crime rates.

? so what

A zero-tolerance policy toward workplace violence and training in workplace aggression and its prevention improves workplace safety.

Delivery drivers, healthcare professionals, law enforcement personnel, and those who work alone are at increased risk for workplace violence.[139] When risk factors can be identified, the risk of violence can be greatly reduced if employers take appropriate precautions. One of the best protections is a zero-tolerance policy toward workplace violence that covers all workers, patients, clients, visitors, contractors, and anyone else who may come in contact with employees.[140] The most effective organizations develop a multidisciplinary and proactive approach, including training at all levels of the workforce. Treating employees fairly and courteously also helps to decrease workplace aggression.[141]

Table 12.2 describes a variety of proactive approaches for developing a workplace violence prevention program.

By regularly assessing their worksites, employers can identify methods for reducing the likelihood of incidents occurring. OSHA believes that a well-written and implemented workplace violence prevention program can reduce the incidence of workplace violence in all

table **12.2**

Proactive Approaches for Developing a Workplace Violence Prevention Program[142]

1. Adopt a zero-tolerance policy toward workplace violence, including threats and harassment.

2. Review company policies and the emergency action plan at least annually.

3. Provide physical protective measures when possible; consider using keycard access systems at main entrances, and arrange office space such that unescorted visitors are easily noticed.

4. Train supervisors to avoid negligent hiring and retention.

5. Train all supervisors and managers in identifying and dealing with early workplace violence warning signs and potential safety problems.

6. Train employees in CPR and first aid.

7. Install silent, concealed alarms at reception desks and closed-circuit television to monitor activity from a central security office.

8. Ensure that temporary employee providers appropriately screen their workers for potential workplace violence issues.

9. Offer and publicize an employee assistance program (EAP), and educate the employees regarding its services.

10. Conduct regular security audits and risk assessments of each company facility, and have a crisis management plan in place for each one, including an action plan for securing the premises if violence occurs.

workplaces.[143] A workplace violence prevention program can be independent or part of the organization's broader injury and illness prevention program, employee handbook, or manual of standard operating procedures. It is critical that all workers know the policy and understand that all workplace violence claims will be investigated and remedied promptly. Not disciplining employees for inappropriate behavior only encourages more of it. OSHA also encourages employers to develop additional methods as necessary to protect employees in high-risk industries.

No organization is immune to the wide range of threatening and violent conduct that is workplace violence. For both humanitarian and legal reasons, all organizations must protect employees and others in the workplace by taking preventive measures, making efforts to detect potential threats as quickly as possible, effectively intervening, and managing the consequences should workplace violence take place. The responsibility and capabilities to design, implement, and manage a workplace violence prevention program spans multiple organizational units, and it begins with a firm commitment from top management for a respectful and safe work environment.

Zero-tolerance workplace violence policies are important. As one expert said, "It really doesn't make sense for an employer not to have a zero-tolerance policy in place. By investigating reports of threats and harassing behavior, employers send an important message that this type of behavior is not tolerated, and also it can help keep situations in check and from spiraling out of control."[144]

> *"By investigating reports of threats and harassing behavior, employers send an important message that this type of behavior is not tolerated, and also it can help keep situations in check and from spiraling out of control."*

so what**?**

Because most workplace violence occurs because of an unresolved conflict or domestic issues, employee assistance programs and supportive supervisors can help decrease the risk of violence.

There are numerous benefits of proactively managing the potential for workplace violence. In addition to avoiding costly incidents in terms of financial liability and corporate reputation, organizations can improve employee productivity, morale, and their public image for responsibility and safety by communicating that they take safety seriously. Most workplace violence incidents happen when there is an unresolved conflict or when an employee or employee's spouse feels that they have lost control of their lives. Employee assistance programs help, as well as a supervisor just showing that he or she cares about the employee. Providing a way for employees to anonymously vent their frustrations and problems can also be helpful.

Under the Occupational Safety and Health Administration's General Duty Clause, employers are required to furnish employees with a work environment that is free from recognized hazards "that are causing or are likely to cause death or serious physical harm to [its] employees." That means that an employer has a duty to get involved when an employee talks about suicide or threatens or harms another person, making a culture of awareness important.

ASIS International, the preeminent organization for security professionals, and the Society for Human Resource Management developed a standard (available online) to serve as a resource and tool that organizations of all sizes can use to develop, evaluate, and implement policies, practices, and structures related to workplace violence.[145]

Disaster Preparedness and Response

Many organizations proactively prepare for the threat of emergencies, including natural disasters, acts of terrorism, the spread of disease, and technological accidents. When employees and their organizations are impacted by a crisis, disaster plans are critical for effectively minimizing damage and resuming operations as quickly as possible. The American Red Cross recommends that disaster plans cover three subjects:[146]

1. Human resources
2. Physical resources
3. Business continuity

A disaster planning team of representatives from relevant areas including HRM, operations, information technology, and security typically conducts an organizational assessment of how different types of disasters would affect the organization and its employees and determines how each should be handled. A written disaster plan is then developed that describes how the organization will respond to various situations if they were to occur. Factors including how employees will be accounted for, how backup databases will be accessed, how key employees will get their work done, and who will assume various duties and responsibilities are described. Training is then conducted to practice coordinating and executing the disaster recovery plan. The training can also serve as a test of the effectiveness of the disaster plan and identify areas that need improving. After an incident happens, the organization's employee assistance program can help employees recover.

The Red Cross advises keeping employee contact information current and designating one remote phone number on which messages can be recorded for employees. Emergency lights should automatically turn on when power is lost, and computer data should be frequently backed up in an offsite location. Emergency supplies including a first aid kit, tools, flashlights with extra batteries, and food and water should also be kept handy. A minimum supply of the materials needed for business continuity should also be kept on hand in case of supply disruptions.[147] OSHA has also created a variety of standards pertaining to emergency preparedness and response.[148]

Summary and Application

Creating a healthy work environment pays huge dividends for both employees and organizations. Helping employees make healthy lifestyle choices, manage stress, and work in a respectful and safe work environment improves performance and reduces health insurance and workers' compensation costs. It is also the right thing to do for ethical and legal reasons. Creating a culture of safety and attending to ergonomic design can benefit everyone.

Wellness programs help employees lead healthier lives and manage stress. Preventing bullying and creating a safe work environment helps keep employees engaged and productive. Managing the potential for workplace violence and helping prevent employee substance abuse also keeps employees safe and productive. Disaster preparedness plans help organizations protect their human and physical resources and maintain business continuity should a disaster strike. Creating a healthy work environment by improving employee health and safety is an important responsibility of HRM as well as other areas of the organization.

Real World Response

Wellvolution at Blue Shield of California

Blue Shield of California wanted to improve employees' health, control rising health insurance premiums, and engage employees in a new culture of wellness. To do this, it launched a companywide program called "Wellvolution" starting with its leadership team. A three-day retreat for all employees who manage others across the state of California showed management the value of "wellvolutionizing" employee health and gained their commitment to and involvement in the program.[149]

The focus of the program is on fun and on keeping employees engaged. Now, instead of junk food potlucks, employees enjoy potlucks with fruit and other healthy options. Some cubicles are now equipped with treadmills with integrated phones and computers to let employees work as they work out. Programs including Weight Watchers and freedom from smoking programs help meet a variety of employee wellness needs. Employee stress buster groups now take short breaks to trade jokes and play games. Tai chi, on-site massages, and a money management program also help employees manage their stress.[150]

Cafeterias were redesigned to make healthy food more abundant and easier to get. The healthiest food options are now labeled, and nutritional information is clearly displayed. Healthy offerings are priced low enough to attract budget-minded employees. Special vending machines help users navigate selections based on individual nutritional specifications such as organic food, calorie count, or fat content. As an added incentive to healthier eating, some of the vending machine proceeds are donated to local charities.[151]

Blue Shield created a daily challenge to encourage employees to engage in a variety of healthy behaviors[152] and also offers a variety of incentives for participating in Wellvolution. Participating in activities such as free wellness assessments and biometric screenings earns employees discounts on their medical plan premiums or a health day off to use to relax and rejuvenate.[153] To help employees take care of their emotional health, Blue Shield offers webinars, desktop yoga exercises and video clips, chair and table massages at several locations, and stress-buster activities every Wednesday, including Wii games, yoga, and imagery CDs, to encourage stress breaks and team building.[154]

Blue Shield of California has won numerous awards for its Wellvolution program.[155] Its employees have also experienced a 22 percent increase in physical activity and a 22 percent decrease in smoking in just three years. The impressive 70 percent employee participation rate suggests that the benefits will continue to mount for Blue Shield and its employees.[156]

Takeaway Points

1. A culture of safety is the set of shared safety attitudes, beliefs, and practices that shape employees' safety behavior. It is important because it focuses employees on behaving safely and can reduce the number and cost of accidents and injuries.

2. Ergonomics involves designing the work environment to manage the psychological and the physical demands placed on employees. The goal of ergonomics is improved employee performance and reduced injuries and errors. Improving comfort and reducing environmental distractions improves productivity and reduces the risk of accidents and injuries.

3. OSHA is the Occupational Safety and Health Administration. OSHA standards are rules describing the methods employers must legally follow to protect their workers from hazards. OSHA also conducts inspections and provides information and training to help employers identify and correct job hazards. OSHA's primary goal is correcting hazards and maintaining compliance rather than issuing citations or collecting fines.

4. Healthier employees are more productive, take fewer sick and disability days, and are at a lower risk for many serious health problems. Wellness programs can help to improve productivity and morale and reduce injuries, absenteeism, and health care costs.

5. Functional stress is the experience of a manageable level of stress that generates positive emotions, including satisfaction, excitement, and enjoyment. Dysfunctional stress is an overload of stress resulting from a situation of under- or over-arousal

continuing for too long. Prolonged dysfunctional stress can result in health problems, withdrawal, turnover, and burnout.

6. Bullying at work can involve verbal abuse; offensive, threatening, humiliating, or intimidating verbal or nonverbal behaviors; and work interference or sabotage that prevents work from getting done.

7. Organizations can protect employees and others in the workplace by taking preventive measures, making efforts to detect potential threats as quickly as possible, effectively intervening, and managing the consequences should workplace violence take place.

Discussion Questions

1. Should employers get involved in their employees' healthy lifestyle choices? Why or why not?
2. Do you think that it is appropriate for an employer to punish employees, say by docking a small amount of pay, when they do not follow or meet certain wellness goals? Why or why not?
3. Do you think that it is appropriate for an employer to offer incentives for employees to follow or meet certain wellness goals? Why or why not?
4. What are some of the best ways you have found to control your own stress?
5. How do you think organizations can weed out potential bullies during the hiring process?
6. How do you think organizations can best prevent employee substance abuse?
7. What role do you think supervisors and coworkers play in preventing workplace violence?

Personal Development Exercise: Substance Abuse Case Study

This exercise will give you the chance to think about how to best handle a subordinate you suspected might be abusing an illegal substance. Read the scenario "Issue: Drug Abuse in the Workplace" at: https://www.bloomberg.com/news/articles/2008-09-16/issue-drug-abuse -in-the-workplacebusinessweek-business-news-stock-market-and-financial-advice, and then answer the following questions.

1. What do you think Liz did well, and what could she have done better in dealing with Amber's changing behavior and performance?
2. At what point do you think Amber should have been approached about the possibility of substance abuse?
3. How would you deal with this situation?

Strategic HRM Exercises

Exercise: Fun and Games Improve Safety Performance

One popular program that can help to enhance organization's safety culture awards scratch-off game cards based on employees' weekly safety performance. Employees win points that can be redeemed for merchandise, trade and collect the cards to win more points, or enter quarterly drawings for even larger cash prizes. After implementing the Safety Jackpot game card program, Ampco Parking Systems decreased the number of lost time accidents by 48 percent and decreased its workers' compensation costs by 62 percent.[157]

This type of program works best when tied to proactive and behavior-based objectives. For instance, employees might earn game cards by:[158]

- Being in compliance with all safety policies
- Suggesting a safety initiative
- Having a successful safety audit
- Attending a training program
- Reporting a "near miss" incident
- Going above and beyond in the area of safety.

Working alone or with a small group, answer the following questions. Be prepared to present your ideas to the class.

1. How do you think awarding game cards to employees after weekly safety goals are met influences employees' behavior?
2. How would you best structure this type of game to maximize results?
3. If you were an employee, what would best motivate you to make safety a top priority even when you are feeling pressured to put productivity over safety to meet a deadline?

Exercise: Recognizing Bullying

Watch the videos, "10 Signs You Work for a Bully Boss" (6:29) and "Lateral Violence in the Workplace" (7:36). After watching the videos, answer the following questions:

1. How can bullying hurt organizations as well as the targets of the bullying?
2. If you suspect a subordinate of yours is bullying his or her staff, what would you do?
3. How can the HR department help prevent bullying and deal with it if it happens?

Exercise: Culture of Wellness at Blue Shield of California

View the video, "Bryce Williams, Director, Wellvolution, Blue Shield of California, Talks Effective Wellness Programs" (5:05). After watching the video, answer the following questions:

1. Why do you think the Wellvolution program has been so successful?
2. How can organizations such as Blue Shield get employees to participate in this type of program when it requires such a dramatic behavior and culture change?
3. How would you persuade top management to support a program like Wellvolution?

Exercise: Stress Management

View the video, "Stress in the Workplace" (4:58). After watching the video, answer the following questions:

1. What are some of the primary sources of stress in the workplace?
2. How can HRM tools be used to help reduce this stress?
3. If you were a manager, what would you do to help reduce your employees' stress?

Exercise: Calculating the Cost of Workplace Injuries

Point your favorite browser to the Safety Management Group's injury cost calculator at http://www.safetymanagementgroup.com/injury-cost-calculator.aspx. Enter different values as the cost of a workplace injury (line A of the spreadsheet), and enter different profit margins (line

D of the spreadsheet) to learn the indirect cost of the injury as well as the amount of revenue the company required to offset the loss. Then answer the following questions:

1. Economically speaking, how much money would it be worth investing in workplace safety to prevent a single workplace injury with a direct cost of $1,000?
2. If a company has a lower profit margin, does it need to earn more or less revenue to offset the total cost of an injury compared to a company with a higher profit margin?
3. After using this calculator, what advice would you give a company deciding whether or not to invest in upgrading its safety program?

Integrative Project

Using the same job you used for the previous chapter, describe what you would do to create a healthy work environment for employees in this position. Be sure to explain your objectives and why your recommendations are likely to be effective in meeting these objectives. Don't forget to consider the cost of your recommendations in your decision-making.

Video Case

Imagine that you are meeting with coworkers to discuss the poor safety record of the packaging department at Happy Time Toys. Accidents have been increasing lately, and you are very concerned. *What do you say or do?* Go to this book's video case, watch the challenge video for this chapter, and choose the best video response. Be sure to also view the outcomes of the two responses you didn't choose.

Discussion Questions

1. What concepts from the chapter are illustrated in this video? Explain your answer.
2. How are the effects of rewards and punishments illustrated in this video? Explain your answer.
3. How else might you handle this situation? Explain your answer.

Endnotes

1. Fast facts. (2017). Blue Shield of California. Retrieved March 23, 2017, from https://www.blueshieldca.com/bsca/about -blue-shield/corporate/fast-facts.sp
2. Walsh, J. (2011). Special report: Creating a culture of wellness helps companies tighten their belts. *Workforce Management*, April, 26–28, 30.
3. Greengard, S. (2012, January 4). Playing it safe: A look at workplace safety during the Roaring '20s and now. *Workforce*. Retrieved March 23, 2017, from http://www.workforce. com/2012/01/04/playing-it-safe-a-look-at-workplace-safety-during -the-roaring-20s-and-now/
4. Repetitive stress injuries in the workplace. (2017). NOLO. Retrieved March 23, 2017, from http://www.nolo.com/legal -encyclopedia/repetitive-stress-injuries-workplace-32281.html#
5. Ibid.
6. Berry, L. L., Mirabito, A. M., & Baun, W. B. (2010). What's the hard return on employee wellness programs? *Harvard Business Review*, 88, 104–112, 142.
7. Wells, S. (2010). Getting paid for staying well. *HR Magazine*, February, 59–61.
8. VanderMey, A. (2017, January 25). Construction worker deaths hit highest level since recession. *Fortune*. Retrieved March 27, 2017, from http://fortune.com/2017/01/25/occupational-safety -workplace-accidents/
9. Ibid.
10. Safety and health programs: Can you make *your* company safer? (2017). GROCO. Retrieved March 11, 2017, from http://www.groco.com/readingroom/bus_safetyprograms.aspx
11. Ciccarelli, M. C. (2011, March 1). BP's bubbling cauldron. *Human Resource Executive Online*. Retrieved March 25, 2017,

from http://www.hreonline.com/HRE/view/story
.jhtml?id=533332933

12. Solis, H. (2011, April 28). One is too many. U.S. Department of Labor. Retrieved January 17, 2012, from http://social.dol.gov /blog/one-is-too-many/

13. World Heath Organization. (2017). Safety and health at work. Retrieved March 23, 2017, from http://www.ilo.org/global /topics/safety-and-health-at-work/lang--de/index.htm

14. Liberty Mutual. (2016). 2016 Liberty Mutual workplace safety index. Retrieved March 24, 2017, from https://www .libertymutualgroup.com/about-liberty-mutual-site/research -institute-site/Documents/2016%20WSI.pdf

15. Deloitte Consulting, LLP. (2016). *Bersin by Deloitte*. New York: Deloitte Consulting LLP.

16. Zappe, J. (2009, July 23). A 'killer' app that puts the science in recruiting. Ere.net. Retrieved March 24, 2017, from http://www .ere.net/2009/07/23/a-killer-app-that-puts-the-science-in-recruiting/

17. Ciccarelli, M. C. (2011, March 1). BP's bubbling cauldron. *Human Resource Executive Online*. Retrieved January 25, 2017, from http://www.hreonline.com/HRE/view/story .jhtml?id=533332933

18. Hofmann, D. A.., Burke, M. J. & Zohar, D. (2017) 100 years of occupational safety research: From basic protections and work analysis to a multilevel view of workplace safety and risk. *Journal of Applied Psychology*, *102*(3), 375–388.

19. OSHA. (2012). Creating a safety culture. Retrieved January 17, 2012, from http://www.osha.gov/SLTC/etools/safetyhealth /mod4_factsheets_culture.html

20. *Ibid.*

21. Tucker, S., Ogunfowora, B., & Her, D. (2016). Safety in the C-suite: How chief executive officers influence organizational safety climate and employee injuries. *Journal of Applied* Psychology, *101*(9), 1228–1239; Dollard, M. F., & Bakker, A. B. (2010). Psychosocial safety climate as a precursor to conducive work environments, psychological health problems, and employee engagement. *Journal of Occupational and Organizational Psychology*, *83*, 579–599; Colford, J. (2005). The ROI of safety. BusinessWeek. Retrieved January 11, 2012, from http://www.businessweek.com/adsections/2005 /pdf/0534_roi.pdf

22. Occupational Safety and Health Administration. (2012). Creating a safety culture. Retrieved January 17, 2012, from http://www.osha.gov/SLTC/etools/safetyhealth/mod4 _factsheets_culture.html

23. Zohar, D. (2010). Thirty years of safety climate research: Reflections and future directions. *Accident Analysis & Prevention*, *42*, 1517–1522.

24. Nahrgang, J. D., Morgeson, F. P., & Hofmann, D. A. (2011). Safety at work: A meta-analytic investigation of the link between job demands, job resources, burnout, engagement, and safety outcomes. *Journal of Applied Psychology*, *96*, 71–94.

25. Maher, K. (2011, December 7). Feds blame owner of West Virginia mine. *The Wall Street Journal*. Retrieved January 4, 2012, from http://online.wsj.com/article /SB10001424052970204770404577082341518182150. html?mod=djem_jiewr_HR_domainid

26. The Associated Press. (2011, April 22). Deepwater Horizon owner Transocean had poor safety culture, says Coast Guard. Retrieved January 24, 2012, from http://blog.al.com /wire/2011/04/deepwater_horizon_owner_transo.html

27. Krolicki, K., & Fujioka, C. (2011, June 24). Special report: Japan's 'throwaway' nuclear workers. *Reuters*. Retrieved March 26, 2017, from http://www.reuters.com/article/2011/06/24 /us-japan-nuclear-idUSTRE75N18A20110624?feedType =RSS&feedName=topNews&utm_source=feedburner&utm _medium=feed&utm_campaign=Feed%3A+reuters %2FtopNews+%28News+%2F+US+%2F+Top+News%29&utm _content=Google+Feedfetcher

28. Occupational Safety and Health Administration. (2011). Part 1904—Recording and reporting occupational injuries and illnesses. Retrieved March 25, 2017, from http://www.gpo.gov /fdsys/pkg/CFR-2011-title29-vol5/pdf/CFR-2011-title29-vol5 -part1904.pdf

29. Rolfsen, B. (2012). New OSHA enforcement memo targets safety incentive programs, retaliation. *Bloomberg BNA: Occupational Safety & Health Reporter*. Retrieved March 28, 2017, from http://news.bna.com/osln/OSLNWB/split_display .adp?fedfid=24845673&vname=oshnotallissues&jd =a0d1e0a0p8&split=0

30. Probst, T. M., & Estrada, A. X. (2010). Accident under-reporting among employees: Testing the moderating influence of psychological safety climate and supervisor enforcement of safety programs. *Accident Analysis & Prevention*, *42*, 1438–1444.

31. Hellman, G. (2010, May 20). Recordkeeping: Michaels discusses safety incentive programs, urges focus on culture of safety. *Bloomberg BNA Occupational Safety & Health Reporter*. Retrieved January 12, 2017, from http://news.bna .com/osln/OSLNWB/split_display.adp?fedfid=17197601& vname=oshnotallissues&fn=17197601&jd=a0c3d9b0h3& split=0

32. Duhigg, C. (2012). *The power of habit: Why we do what we do and how to change it*. New York: Random House.

33. Baron, L. (2006). The economics of ergonomics. *Journal of Accountancy*, December. Retrieved March 24, 2017, from http://www.journalofaccountancy.com/Issues/2006/Dec /TheEconomicsOfErgonomics.htm

34. Canadian Centre for Occupational Health and Safety. (2012). Carpal tunnel syndrome. Retrieved March 24, 2017, from http://www.ccohs.ca/oshanswers/diseases/carpal .html

35. U.S. Department of Labor. (1970). OSH Act of 1970. Retrieved March 21, 2017, from https://www.osha.gov/pls /oshaweb/owadisp.show_document?p_table=OSHACT&p _id=3359

36. Occupational Safety and Health Administration. (2011). At-a-glance OSHA. Retrieved March 21, 2017, from http://www.osha .gov/Publications/3439at-a-glance.pdf

37. *Ibid.*

38. From http://www.osha.gov/Publications/osha3165.pdf

39. Occupational Safety and Health Administration. (2011). At-a-glance OSHA. Retrieved March 21, 2017, from http://www.osha.gov/Publications/3439at-a -glance.pdf

40. *Ibid.*

41. Occupational Safety and Health Administration. (2012). At-a-glance OSHA. Retrieved March 21, 2017, from http://www.osha .gov/Publications/3439at-a-glance.pdf

42. *Ibid.*

43. U.S. Department of Labor (2012). Hazard communication. Retrieved March 24, 2017, from http://www.osha.gov/dsg /hazcom/index.html

44. Mihelich, M. (2013). OSHA's most-cited workplace safety violations. *Workforce*, November, 12.

45. Occupational Safety and Health Administration. (2012). OSHA fact sheet. Retrieved March 24, 2012, from http://www.osha.gov/OshDoc/data_General_Facts/factsheet-inspections.pdf

46. Occupational Safety and Health Administration. (2012). At-a-glance OSHA. Retrieved March 24, 2017, from http://www.osha.gov/Publications/3439at-a-glance.pdf

47. Occupational Safety and Health Administration. (2012). OSHA fact sheet. Retrieved March 24, 2017, from http://www.osha.gov/OshDoc/data_General_Facts/factsheet-inspections.pdf

48. Levine, D. I., Toffel, M. W., & Johnson, M. S. (2012). Randomized government safety inspections reduce worker injuries with no detectable job loss. *Science, 336*(6083), 907–911.

49. Occupational Safety and Health Administration. (2012). At-a-glance OSHA. Retrieved January 17, 2012, from http://www.osha.gov/Publications/3439at-a-glance.pdf

50. *Ibid.*

51. *Ibid.*

52. For a listing of free publications, visit OSHA's website at https://www.osha.gov/pls/publications/publication.html

53. Occupational Safety and Health Administration. (2012). At-a-glance OSHA. Retrieved March 25, 2017, from http://www.osha.gov/Publications/3439at-a-glance.pdf

54. Pyrillis, R. (2014). All is not well. *Workforce*, February, 24–27.

55. Wellness programs: What are the general steps for implementing a wellness program, and how can a wellness program benefit employers? (2015, March 25). *Society for Human Resource Management.* Retrieved March 23, 2017, from https://www.shrm.org/resourcesandtools/tools-and-samples/hr-qa/pages/wellnessprogramscontributingtotheemployer%E2%80%99sbottomline.asp

56. Society for Human Resource Management. (2016). *2016 employee benefits.* Alexandria, VA: SHRM.

57. The best places to work: 2016. (2016, November 15). *Outside.* Retrieved March 22, 2017, from https://www.outsideonline.com/2134736/best-places-work-2016

58. Lucas, S. (2013, May 6). Wellness programs that work for small businesses. *Inc..* Retrieved March 26, 2017, from http://www.inc.com/suzanne-lucas/wellness-programs-that-work-for-small-businesses.html

59. Zook, T. (2006, April 24). The ROI of wellness. *Forbes.com.* Retrieved January 17, 2012, from http://www.forbes.com/2006/04/21/wellness-programs-gold-standards-cx_tz_0424wellness.html

60. *Ibid.*

61. Ball, T. J., Heath, E. M., Waite, P. J., Fargo, J., & Bates, S. C. (2010). Selected barriers and incentives for participation in a university wellness program. *Medicine & Science in Sports & Exercise, 42*, 39.

62. Noyce, J., Crighton, A., Anderson, D., & Pronk, N. (2011, July 28). Uncommon knowledge: The value of health assessment data. *Society for Human Resource Management.* Retrieved March 23, 2017, from https://www.shrm.org/resourcesandtools/hr-topics/benefits/pages/assessmentdata.aspx

63. Miller, S. (2011, January 10). U.S. businesses spend more on wellness programs. *Society for Human Resource Management.* Retrieved January 12, 2012, from http://www.shrm.org/hrdisciplines/benefits/Articles/Pages/WellnessSpend.aspx

64. Noyce, J., Crighton, A., Anderson, D., & Pronk, N. (2011, July 28). Uncommon knowledge: The value of health assessment data. *Society for Human Resource Management.* Retrieved March 23,

2017, from https://www.shrm.org/resourcesandtools/hr-topics/benefits/pages/assessmentdata.aspx

65. Rafter, M. V. (2012). Can social media produce wellness results? *Workforce Management,* June, 36–40.

66. Purcell, J. (2016, April 20). Meet the wellness programs that save companies money. *Harvard Business Review.* Retrieved March 26, 2017, from https://hbr.org/2016/04/meet-the-wellness-programs-that-save-companies-money

67. Kuang, C. (2012). The Google diet. *Fast Company*, April, 48.

68. Saperstein, J. (2013). Bet on employee wellness programs. *Talent Management Magazine*, July, 42–43.

69. Unusual perks: Paychex. (2010, January 21). *CNNMoney.com.* Retrieved March 25, 2017, from http://money.cnn.com/galleries/2010/fortune/1001/gallery.bestcompanies_unusual_perks.fortune/9.html

70. Volpp, K. G., Pauly, M. V., Loewenstein, G., & Bangsberg, D. (2009). P4P4P: An agenda for research on pay for performance for patients. *Health Affairs, 28*(1), 206–214.

71. Volpp, K. G., Asch, D. A., Galvin, R., & Loewenstein, G. (2011). Redesigning employee health incentives—Lessons from behavioral economics. *The New England Journal of Medicine, 365*, 388–390.

72. U.S. Department of Labor. (2012). The HIPAA nondiscrimination requirements. Retrieved March 25, 2017, from http://www.dol.gov/ebsa/faqs/faq_hipaa_ND.html

73. Wells, S. (2010). Getting paid for staying well. *HR Magazine*, February, 59–61.

74. *Ibid.*

75. Volpp K. G. et al. (2009). A randomized, controlled trial of financial incentives for smoking cessation. *The New England Journal of Medicine, 360*, 699–709.

76. Johnson & Johnson: A wellness success story. (2009, November 10). *Corporate Wellness Insights.* Retrieved January 16, 2012, from http://www.corporatewellnessinsights.com/2009/11/johnson-johnson-wellness-success-story.html

77. Healthy People. (2012). JNJ.com. Retrieved January 12, 2012, from http://www.jnj.com/wps/wcm/connect/042752004f5563709db4bd1bb31559c7/healthy-people.pdf?MOD=AJPERES

78. Johnson & Johnson: A wellness success story. (2009, November 10). *Corporate Wellness Insights.* Retrieved January 16, 2012, from http://www.corporatewellnessinsights.com/2009/11/johnson-johnson-wellness-success-story.html

79. Johnson & Johnson (2017). Culture of health. Retrieved March 27, 2017, from https://www.jnj.com/caring/citizenship-sustainability/culture-of-health

80. Berry, L. L., Mirabito, A. M., & Baun, W. B. (2010). What's the hard return on employee wellness programs? *Harvard Business Review*, December. Retrieved March 24, 2017, from http://hbr.org/2010/12/whats-the-hard-return-on-employee-wellness-programs/ar/1

81. *Ibid.*

82. Bruce, S. (2012, May 17). GINA, state statues, and your wellness program. *HR Daily Advisor.* Retrieved March 25, 2017, from http://hrdailyadvisor.blr.com/archive/2012/05/17/HR_Policies_Procedures_Wellness_Lawsuits_GINA.aspx?source=HAC&effort=23

83. Meurs, J. A., & Perrewe, P. L. (2011). Cognitive activation theory of stress: An integrative theoretical approach to work stress. *Journal of Management, 37*, 1043–1068.

84. McGaugh, J. L. (2000). Memory: A century of consolidation. *Science, 287*, 248–251.

85. Selye, H. (1956). *The stress of life.* New York: McGraw-Hill.

86. Rodell, J. B., & Judge, T. A. (2009). Can 'good' stressors spark 'bad' behaviors? The mediating role of emotions in links of challenge and hindrance stressors with citizenship and counterproductive behaviors. *Journal of Applied Psychology, 94,* 1438–1451.

87. Lublin, J. S., & Rockoff, J. D. (2010, December 7). CEO's stress worried Pfizer. *The Wall Street Journal.* Retrieved March 25, 2017, from http://online.wsj.com/article /SB10001424052748703471904576003712155819784 .html?mod=djem_jiewr_HR_domainid

88. Schramm, J. (2009). Stress as a workplace health risk. *HR Magazine,* May, 108.

89. *Ibid.*

90. Poor emotional wellbeing is obstacle to wellness efforts. (2011, August 22). *Society for Human Resource Management.* Retrieved March 24, 2017, from https://www.shrm.org/resourcesandtools /hr-topics/benefits/pages/wellbeingandwellness.aspx

91. Ray, A. (2011, December 20). To promote wellness, help employees reduce workplace stress. *Society for Human Resource Management.* Retrieved March 24, 2017, from https://www.shrm .org/resourcesandtools/hr-topics/benefits/pages/reducestress.aspx

92. *Ibid.*

93. Callan, V. J. (1993). Individual and organizational strategies for coping with organizational change. *Work and Stress, 7,* 63–75; Folkman, S., Lazarus, R. S., Gruen, R. J., & DeLongis, A. (1986). Appraisal, coping, health status, and psychological symptoms. *Journal of Personality and Social Psychology, 50,* 571–579.

94. Ray, A. (2011, December 20). To promote wellness, help employees reduce workplace stress. *Society for Human Resource Management.* Retrieved March 24, 2017, from https: //www.shrm.org/resourcesandtools/hr-topics/benefits/pages /reducestress.aspx

95. Cooper, C. L., & Cartwright, S. (1994). Healthy mind; healthy organization—A proactive approach to occupational stress. *Human Relations, 47,* 455–472.

96. Goudreau, J. (2007, August 6). Dispatches from the war on stress. *BusinessWeek,* 74–75.

97. Miller, S. (2016, April 29). Employees' financial issues affect their job performance. *Society for Human Resource Management.* Retrieved March 27, 2017, from https://www .shrm.org/resourcesandtools/hr-topics/benefits/pages/employees -financial-issues-affect-their-job-performance.aspx

98. Poll: Money worries world's greatest cause of stress. (2009, September 30). *CNN.* Retrieved January 25, 2012, from http://articles.cnn.com/2009-09-30/world/stress.survey .money_1_stress-worry-men-and-women?_s=PM:WORLD

99. Don't lose sleep over finances. (2016, July 28). Better Business Bureau. Retrieved March 26, 2017, from http://www.bbb.org /acadiana/news-events/news-releases/2016/07/dont-lose-sleep -over-finances/

100. Bloom, E. (2017, June 29). Here's how many Americans are living paycheck-to-paycheck. *CNBC.* Retrieved July 2, 2017, from http://www.cnbc.com/2017/06/29/heres-how-many -americans-are-living-paycheck-to-paycheck.html

101. Goldberg, J. (2016, June 12). The effects of stress on your body. *Webmd.com.* Retrieved March 26, 2017, from http://www .webmd.com/balance/stress-management/effects-of-stress -on-your-body

102. Soong, J. (2012, January 25). The debt-stress connection. *WebMD.* Retrieved March 25, 2017, from http://www.webmd .com/balance/features/the-debt-stress-connection

103. Larocque, J. (2010, June 11). The cure for employee stress: Financial wellness. *Corporate Wellness Magazine.* Retrieved January 20, 2012, from http://www.corporatewellnessmagazine .com/article/cure-for-employee.html

104. Laabs, J. (1999). Workforce overload. *Work Force,* 30–37.

105. Goudreau, J. (2007, August 6). Dispatches from the war on stress. *BusinessWeek,* 74–75.

106. *Ibid.*

107. Coping with stress at work. (n.d.). *American Psychological Association.* Retrieved March 26, 2017, from http://www.apa .org/helpcenter/work-stress.aspx; Ray, A. (2011, December 20). To promote wellness, help employees reduce workplace stress. *Society for Human Resource Management.* Retrieved March 26, 2017, from https://www.shrm.org/resourcesandtools /hr-topics/benefits/pages/reducestress.aspx; How to change the organization to prevent job stress.(1999). NIOSH Publication No. 99-101. Retrieved March 24, 2017, from http://www .cdc.gov/niosh/docs/99-101/; Mayo Clinic. (2012). Stress management. Retrieved March 24, 2017, from http://www .mayoclinic.com/health/coping-with-stress/SR00030 /NSECTIONGROUP=2

108. OSH answers fact sheets. (2017). Canadian Centre for Occupational Health and Safety. Retrieved March 27, 2017, from https://www.ccohs.ca/oshanswers/psychosocial/bullying.html

109. Workplace Bullying Institute. (2012). The WBI definition of workplace bullying. Retrieved March 23, 2017, from http: //www.workplacebullying.org/individuals/problem/definition/

110. Namie, G. (2014). 2014 WBI U.S. workplace bullying survey. *Workplace Bullying Institute,* February. Retrieved March 26, 2017, from http://www.workplacebullying.org/wbiresearch /wbi-2014-us-survey/

111. Ashforth, B. E. (1994). Petty tyranny in organizations: A preliminary examination of antecedents and consequences. *Human Relations, 47,* 755–778; Ashforth, B. E. (1997). *Canadian Journal of Administrative Sciences, 14,* 126–140; Infante, D. A., & Gordon, W. I. (1986). Superiors' argumentativeness and verbal aggressiveness as predictors of subordinates' satisfaction. *Human Communication Research, 12,* 117–125; Rayner, C., Hoel, H., & Cooper, C. L. (2002). *Workplace bullying: What we know, who is to blame, and what can we do?* New York: Taylor & Francis; Rayner, C., & Keashly, L. (2005). Bullying at work: A perspective from Britain and North America. In S. Fox & P. E. Spector (Eds.), *Counterproductive work behavior: Investigations of actors and targets,* pp. 271–296. Washington, DC: American Psychological Association; Tepper, B. J. (2000). Consequences of abusive supervision. *Academy of Management Journal, 43,* 178–190.

112. Rayner, C. (1997). The incidence of workplace bullying. *Journal of Community & Applied Social Psychology, 7,* 199–208.

113. WBI survey: Workplace bullying health impact. (2012, August 9). *Workplace Bullying Institute.* Retrieved March 27, 2017, from http://www.workplacebullying.org/2012-d/

114. Dailey, R., Lee, C., & Spitzberg, B. H. (2007). Psychological abuse and communicative aggression. In B. H. Spitzberg & W. R. Cupach (Eds.), *The dark side of interpersonal communication,* 2nd ed., pp. 297–326. Mahwah, NJ: Lawrence Erlbaum Associates.

115. Rayner, C. (1997). The incidence of workplace bullying. *Journal of Community & Applied Social Psychology, 7,* 199–208.

116. Namie, G., & Namie, R. (2000). Workplace bullying: Silent epidemic. *Employee Rights Quarterly,* Autumn.

117. Monster global poll reveals workplace bullying is endemic. (2011, June 10). Retrieved March 24, 2017, from http://www.onrec.com/news/news-archive/monster-global-poll-reveals-workplace-bullying-is-endemic

118. Mathisen, G. E., Einarsen, S., & Mykletun, R. (2011). The relationship between supervisor personality, supervisors' perceived stress and workplace bullying. *Journal of Business Ethics*, *99*, 637–651.

119. Henry Carus Associates. (2017). A guide to worldwide bullying laws. Retrieved March 25, 2017, from https://www.hcalawyers.com.au/blog/bullying-laws-around-the-world/

120. *Ibid.*

121. Cobb, E. (2011, July 8). Workplace bullying: A global overview. *Management-Issues*. Retrieved March 23, 2012, from http://www.management-issues.com/opinion/6235/workplace-bullying-a-global-overview/

122. Proskauer. (2017). Bullying, harassment, and stress in the workplace—A European perspective. Retrieved March 25, 2017, from http://www.internationallaborlaw.com/files/2013/01/Bullying-Harassment-and-Stress-in-the-workplace-A-European-Perspective.pdf

123. Klein, K. E. (2008, May 7). Employers can't ignore workplace bullies. *Bloomberg Businessweek*. https://www.bloomberg.com/news/articles/2008-05-07/employers-cant-ignore-workplace-bulliesbusinessweek-business-news-stock-market-and-financial-advice; Sutton, R. I. (2010). *The no asshole rule: Building a civilized workplace and surviving one that isn't*. New York: Business Plus; Office bullying plagues workers across races, job levels, and educational attainment, according to CareerBuilder's new study. (2011, April 20). CareerBuilder. Retrieved March 25, 2017, from http://www.careerbuilder.com/share/aboutus/pressreleasesdetail.aspx?sd=9%2F18%2F2014&id=pr842&ed=12%2F31%2F2014

124. Heathfield, S. M. (2016). Developing a drug-free workplace. The Balance. Retrieved March 24, 2017, from https://www.thebalance.com/developing-a-drug-free-workplace-1918311

125. U.S. Department of Labor. (2017). Drug-Free Workplace Act of 1988 requirements. Retrieved March 25, 2017, from http://www.dol.gov/elaws/asp/drugfree/screenr.htm

126. Heathfield, S. M. (2016). Developing a drug-free workplace. The Balance. Retrieved March 24, 2017, from https://www.thebalance.com/developing-a-drug-free-workplace-1918311

127. Reilly, J. (2011). Why worry about drugs and alcohol in the workplace? USA Mobile Drug Testing. Retrieved March 25, 2017, from http://usamdt.com/blog/why-worry-about-drugs-and-alcohol-in-the-workplace/

128. Occupational Safety and Health Administration. (2012). Workplace substance abuse. Retrieved January 20, 2012, from http://www.osha.gov/SLTC/substanceabuse/

129. Heathfield, S. M. (2016). Developing a drug-free workplace. The Balance. Retrieved March 24, 2017, from https://www.thebalance.com/developing-a-drug-free-workplace-1918311

130. Occupational Safety and Health Administration. (2012). Workplace substance abuse. Retrieved January 20, 2012, from http://www.osha.gov/SLTC/substanceabuse/

131. Hellman, G. (2010, May 20). Recordkeeping: Michaels discusses safety incentive programs, urges focus on culture of safety. *Bloomberg BNA Occupational Safety & Health Reporter*. Retrieved January 12, 2012, from http://news.bna.com/osln/OSLNWB/split_display.adp?fedfid=17197601&vname=oshnotallissues&fn=17197601&jd=a0c3d9b0h3&split=0

132. Anfuso, D. (1994). Deflecting workplace violence. *Personnel Journal*, *73*(10), 66–77.

133. Gurchiek, K. (2009, December 4). Experts: Lay foundation to prevent workplace violence. *Society for Human Resource Management*. Retrieved March 23, 2017, from https://www.shrm.org/hr-today/news/hr-news/pages/layfoundation.aspx

134. Occupational Safety & Health Administration. (2017). Workplace violence. Retrieved March 24, 2017, from http://www.osha.gov/SLTC/workplaceviolence/

135. Occupational Safety & Health Administration. (2017). Workplace violence. Retrieved January 21, 2012, from http://www.osha.gov/SLTC/workplaceviolence/

136. Ellington, A. (2016, January 19). Workplace violence prevention. *BLR.com*. Retrieved March 26, 2017, from http://safety.blr.com/workplace-safety-news/emergency-planning-and-response/violence-in-workplace/Workplace-violence-prevention/

137. *Ibid.*

138. Occupational Safety & Health Administration. (2017). Retrieved March 25, 2017, from http://www.osha.gov/SLTC/workplaceviolence/

139. *Ibid.*

140. *Ibid.*

141. Kennedy, D. B., Homant, R. J., & Homant, M. R. (2004). Perception of injustice as a predictor of support for workplace aggression. *Journal of Business and Psychology*, *18*, 323–336.

142. Smith, S. J. (2002). Workplace violence. *Professional Safety*, *47*, 11, 34–44; Gurchiek, K. (2009, December 4). Experts: Lay foundation to prevent workplace violence. *Society for Human Resource Management*. Retrieved March 23, 2017, from https://www.shrm.org/hr-today/news/hr-news/pages/layfoundation.aspx; USDA Physical Security Program. (2017). Security in the workplace—Informational material. Retrieved January 23, 2017, from http://www.dm.usda.gov/physicalsecurity/workplace.htm

143. Occupational Safety & Health Administration. (2017). Workplace violence. Retrieved March 25, 2017, from http://www.osha.gov/SLTC/workplaceviolence/

144. Leonard, B. (2010). Complacency presents challenge for preventing workplace violence. *Society for Human Resource Management*. Retrieved March 25, 2017, from https://www.shrm.org/hr-today/news/hr-news/pages/complacencypresentschallengeforpreventingworkplaceviolence.aspx

145. *ASIS/SHRM WVP.1-2011*. (2011). Retrieved March 25, 2017, from http://webstore.ansi.org/RecordDetail.aspx?sku=ASIS%2fSHRM+WVP.1-2011

146. American Red Cross. (2017). American Red Cross ready rating. Retrieved March 24, 2017, from http://www.readyrating.org/

147. *Ibid.*

148. Occupational Safety & Health Administration. (2017). Emergency preparedness and response. Retrieved January 24, 2017, from http://www.osha.gov/SLTC/emergencypreparedness/

149. Walsh, J. (2011). Special report: Creating a culture of wellness helps companies tighten their belts. *Workforce Management*, April, 26–28, 30.

150. *Ibid.*

151. *Ibid.*

152. How is your well-being? (2017). *Wellvolution*. Retrieved March 27, 2017, from https://wellbeingtracker.meyouhealth.com/learn/wellvolution?utm_source=Facebook&utm_medium=Post&utm_campaign=DC1

153. Blue Shield of California. (2017). Incentives and programs. Retrieved March 27, 2017, from https://www.blueshieldca.com /bsca/about-blue-shield/careers/wellvolution/incentives.sp

154. Blue Shield of California. (2017). Emotional well-being. Retrieved March 27, 2017, from https://www.blueshieldca.com /bsca/about-blue-shield/careers/wellvolution/well-being.sp

155. Blue Shield of California. (2012). Wellness awards and press. Retrieved March 27, 2017, from https://www.blueshieldca.com /bsca/about-blue-shield/careers/wellvolution/awards-press.sp

156. Walsh, J. (2011). Special report: Creating a culture of wellness helps companies tighten their belts. *Workforce Management*, April, 26–28, 30.

157. It's a proven success! (2012). Safetyjackpot.com. Retrieved March 26, 2017, from http://morail.org/mainstreet/documents /SafetyJackpotProgramOverview.pdf

158. It's a proven success! (2012). Safetyjackpot.com. Retrieved March 26, 2017, from http://morail.org/mainstreet/documents /SafetyJackpotProgramOverview.pdf

chapter 13

Creating Positive Employee-Management Relations

Learning Objectives

AFTER STUDYING THIS CHAPTER, YOU SHOULD BE ABLE TO:

1 List some of the arguments supporting unions.

2 List some of the arguments against unions.

3 Describe what is meant by collective bargaining.

4 Describe what is meant by management rights.

5 Explain the difference between distributive and integrative negotiation.

6 Describe what can happen when negotiations break down.

7 Explain the three labor relations strategies.

8 Describe how unions impact human resource management.

Real World Challenge

The Labor Management Partnership at Kaiser Permanente

Kaiser Permanente is currently the leading nonprofit integrated health plan in the United States, serving more than 10.6 million members. In a single year, Kaiser may schedule over 40 million outpatient visits, perform over 224,000 inpatient surgeries, deliver over 100,000 babies, and fill over 80 million prescriptions.[1]

In 1995, Kaiser Permanente (KP) was losing more than $250 million a year and was being advised by a management consultant to break itself up to better match the cost structures of competing health maintenance organizations, but CEO Dr. David Lawrence knew that doing this would mean abandoning Kaiser's historic commitment to being an integrated healthcare insurer and provider as well as its valued and hard-earned reputation as an employee union-friendly employer.

Labor–management relations at Kaiser had been growing more hostile, with Kaiser pursuing wage and benefit reductions to stay competitive and the unions responding with strikes.[2] To better coordinate bargaining strategy, 26 local unions representing KP workers had joined together in the Coalition of Kaiser Permanente Unions.[3] Neither side wanted to compromise patient care. Both parties wanted to redefine their relationship to meet the needs of both the company and its unions. Imagine that they approached you for advice. What would you have told them? After reading this chapter, you should have some good ideas.

labor union
an organization of workers formed for the purpose of advancing its members' interests in respect to wages, benefits, and working conditions

A **labor union** is "an organization of workers formed for the purpose of advancing its members' interests in respect to wages, benefits, and working conditions."[4] Unions are democratic institutions whose members elect national, regional, and local leadership. Unions are guided by constitutions that are drafted and ratified by their members. The constitutions formalize policies to govern how a union operates, detailing everything from leadership compensation to processes for settling internal disagreements.[5] The goal of a union is typically to further the social, safety, and economic interests of its members.

Unions are important for any manager or human resource professional to understand. Unions have the potential to influence everything from an organization's business strategy to its structure and management of its employees.[6] The employee relations role can also be very different in unionized compared to nonunionized companies. In addition, the quality of an organization's employee–management relations can influence the economic health of the community.

Unions have both supporters and detractors.[7] Detractors claim that unions are bad for the economy because they result in higher prices, are not focused on business goals including higher quality and efficiency, or are no longer needed now that so many laws exist to protect worker safety and interests. Some also feel that union demands are often unreasonable and not aligned with the strategic goals of the business. For example, when French newspaper *Le Monde* introduced computers in the early 1990s to improve efficiency and lower costs, they had to negotiate with the trade union that controls the printing of French national newspapers. The union successfully demanded that for each new computer *Le Monde* had to pay for one print worker to type on the keyboard and another to simultaneously watch the screen.[8] This clearly reduced the savings *Le Monde* was hoping for from the increased efficiency.

collective bargaining
when the employer and the union negotiate in good faith on wages, benefits, work hours, and other employment terms and conditions

Despite examples like this in which unionization hurt organizational productivity, unions and **collective bargaining** do tend to protect everyday workers, reduce job stress,[9] and can improve company productivity.[10] Union workers often have higher professional standards because the unions increase opportunities for worker training. Many unions even offer their own training.[11] Some of the most successful U.S. companies have a unionized workforce, including Southwest Airlines, AT&T, Costco, and UPS.

In this chapter, we describe the origins of labor relations and collective bargaining. We discuss the role of labor unions and discuss methods of establishing positive employee–management relations. Understanding the role of unions can help you better decide if you would like to join one and will help you manage employees more effectively in a unionized environment. Unfair labor practices and employee rights and discipline are also covered. Creating positive employee–management relations influences *effective work processes* in our book's overall model of human resource management (HRM).

Why Do Workers Join Unions?

? so what

Unionized workers typically earn higher pay and benefits than non-unionized workers.

Although there is more to the decision to unionize than just pay, one of the selling points unions use to attract members or to organize employees into unions is the fact that union members earn better wages and benefits than nonunionized workers. As American social activist Robert Alan Silverstein said, "Today, although there are still sweatshops and other inhumane working conditions for many workers around the world, the labor movement has won numerous victories that many of us take for granted, such as the five-day work week, 8-hour workday, paid holidays, and the end of child labor."[12]

"Today, although there are still sweatshops and other inhumane working conditions for many workers around the world, the labor movement has won

*numerous victories that many of us take for granted,
such as the five-day work week, 8-hour workday, paid
holidays, and the end of child labor."*

—Robert Alan Silverstein

Reducing employment uncertainty and increasing fairness have strong influences on employees' decision to unionize. One study found that employees' belief that company rules or policies were unfair or administered to their detriment were more likely to turn to strong unions for assistance. Dissatisfaction with management alone was not enough—employees were more likely to unionize when they also perceived that the union was effective in negotiating both better wages and benefits and protecting employees against unfair dismissals.[13] Union membership is also related to employees' perceptions of job security, ideology, and job satisfaction. Poor worker–management relationships are also associated with greater union membership.[14]

Many employees choose not to unionize, and unionization rates have fallen for the last few decades. Barry T. Hirsch, a labor economist at Georgia State University, explains, "Unionized companies obviously raise wages and benefits for their workers, and while they often raise productivity, typically they're at a cost disadvantage, and unionized companies haven't fared as well. In addition, in an increasingly globalized, very fast-moving world, unionized companies may not be able to adjust as quickly."[15] Companies have also become more ideologically opposed to unions and more aggressive about resisting union organizing drives.[16] In addition, the deregulation of key industries and the shift in employment from the industrial to the service sector and from the historical union strongholds of the Midwest and Northeast to the Sunbelt states has decreased union influence.

Labor Relations and Collective Bargaining

The organized labor movement in the United States has a long history. There are thousands of unions in the United States, and in 2016, 10.7 percent of the employed population in the United States was a member of a union.[17] In 2017, 34.4 percent of public sector workers were unionized compared to 6.4 percent of private sector workers.[18] In 2016, New York had the highest rate of union membership among all workers at 23.6 percent, and South Carolina had the lowest rate of union membership at 1.6 percent.[19]

National Labor Relations Act of 1935 (Wagner Act) guarantees the right of nonmanagerial employees of firms engaged in interstate commerce to join unions and bargain collectively

The three types of unions are:

1. *Industrial unions*: Composed primarily of semiskilled employees in manufacturing industries.
2. *Trade unions*: Composed primarily of skilled employees in a single trade (e.g., plumbers, carpenters, and machinists).
3. *Employee associations*: Professional employees (e.g., healthcare workers, clerical workers, and teachers).

Let's turn our attention to the history of labor relations in the United States.

Labor Relations

Congress approved the **National Labor Relations Act of 1935**[20], also called the Wagner Act, to encourage a healthy relationship between private-sector workers and

Industrial unions represent semiskilled employees in manufacturing industries, including garment manufacturing workers as shown in the photo.

their employers. A key provision of the Wagner Act guarantees the right of nonmanagerial employees of firms engaged in interstate commerce to join unions and bargain collectively. The Wagner Act was intended to curb the work stoppages, strikes, and general labor conflict that had become common. It extends a variety of rights to workers wishing to form, join, or support unions or labor organizations; to workers already represented by unions; and to groups of at least two nonunionized employees who seek to modify their working conditions or wages. The Wagner Act also prohibits discriminating against pro-union applicants. The National Labor Relations Board (NLRB) was established to administer the Wagner Act and regulate labor–management relations at the national level.

The Wagner Act governs union organizing and collective bargaining for most of the private sector. The **Railway Labor Act** governs employment relations for airlines and railroads and is enforced by the National Mediation Board.[21] Because of the economic importance of airlines and railroads, the Railway Labor Act tries to substitute bargaining, arbitration, and mediation for strikes in resolving labor disputes. Public sector collective bargaining is regulated by various state statutes for state and local government workers and federal statutes for federal workers.

The Wagner Act protects workers' rights to join labor unions that represent their interests and/or to take other collective action to defend their workplace rights. The act clearly states the rights of American workers:[22]

> Employees shall have the right to self-organization; to form, join, or assist labor organizations; to bargain collectively through representatives of their own choosing; and to engage in other concerted activities for the purpose of collective bargaining or other mutual aid or protection. . . .

The Wagner Act officially recognizes that under modern economic conditions workers must be free to organize collectively. Before the Wagner Act, employers could spy on, punish, interrogate, and terminate union members without just cause. As a declared national policy, the Wagner Act encourages collective bargaining and defines the rights of both employees and employers in this process. It is now illegal for any employer to ban employee discussion about unions or to retaliate against an employee for union organization efforts. As long as production is not disrupted, workers have the right to talk about organizing and to pass out union membership cards anywhere in the workplace. Handing out informational leaflets about unionizing is also legally protected provided it is done on a worker's own time and in nonwork areas such as the cafeteria, a locker room, or the parking lot. An employer cannot threaten or intimidate employees or try to bribe them with special benefits or pay increases to discourage unionization.

The Wagner Act prohibits "unfair labor practices" on the part of employers. Employers cannot fire workers for joining unions, cannot refuse to bargain with a union representing a majority of workers, and cannot establish company unions. Examples of unfair labor practices are presented in Table 13.1.

The National Labor Relations Act of 1947, also called the Taft-Hartley Act, amended the Wagner Act to clarify what are considered unfair labor practices by unions and employees to extend the Wagner Act's protections. The Taft-Hartley Act amended the section granting workers the right to self-organization by adding that employees "shall also have the right to refrain from any or all such activities." This legalized state **right-to-work laws** that prohibit **union shops** in which all workers in a unionized workplace are forced to join the union and pay dues.

Labor organizations oppose right-to-work laws and argue that since a union acting as a bargaining agent is compelled to represent all the workers in question, not just those belonging to the union, it is only fair that all employees should pay their share for the benefits of union representation by being dues-paying union members. Union shops are legal in states that have not adopted right to work laws. Figure 13.1 shows which states are currently right-to-work states.

Railway Labor Act
governs employment relations for airlines and railroads

 so what

Because employers used to spy on, punish, interrogate, and fire union members without just cause, the Wagner Act was passed to protect workers' rights.

The National Labor Relations Act of 1947
(also called the Taft-Hartley Act) amended the Wagner Act to clarify what are considered unfair labor practices by unions and employees

right-to-work laws
state laws that prohibit union shops in which all workers in a unionized workplace must join the union and pay dues

union shop
all workers in a unionized workplace are forced to join the union and pay dues

 so what

In right-to-work states, workers in a unionized workplace cannot be required to join the union and pay dues. In union states, all workers in a unionized workplace must join the union and pay dues.

table **13.1**

Unfair Labor Practices

By the employer:

- Discouraging membership support for union negotiators by using promises, threats, punishment, or discrimination

- Assigning difficult or dangerous work duties to discourage union participation

- Refusing to abide by the negotiation ground rules agreed to by both sides

- Refusing to supply information requested by the union in order to bargain intelligently

- Engaging in surface bargaining by acting as if the company is negotiating but taking positions which could not be the basis of give-and-take bargaining

- Observing, listening to, or interfering with employees when they are meeting with union organizers or when they are discussing union matters with coworkers

By the union:

- Using bribes, threats, or coercion to influence employees' decision to vote for a union

- Threatening nonunion supporters with loss of work if the union is elected

- Refusing to process the grievance of an employee who has criticized the union or its officials

- Punishing or firing workers for giving up their union membership

figure **13.1**

2017 Right-to-Work States[23]

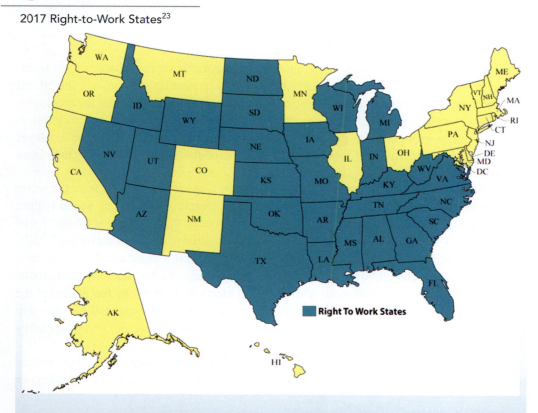

Right To Work States

In addition to union shops, U.S. companies can operate under several different union models:

closed shop
exclusively employs people who are already union members

- **Closed shop**: Exclusively employs people who are already union members. An example is a compulsory hiring hall, where the employer must recruit directly from the union. In 1947, the Taft-Hartley Labor Act declared the closed shop illegal. Although the Wagner Act permits construction employers to enter into pre-hire agreements to draw their workforces exclusively from a pool of employees dispatched by the union, construction employers are under no legal obligation to enter into such agreements.

agency shop
requires nonunion workers to pay a fee to the union for its services in negotiating their contracts

- **Agency shop**: Requires nonunion workers to pay a fee to the union for its services in negotiating their contracts.
- **Open shop**: Does not discriminate based on union membership in employing or keeping workers. Some workers benefit from a union or the collective bargaining process despite not contributing to the union.

open shop
does not discriminate based on union membership in employing or keeping workers

In response to the McClellan Committee's findings of widespread union corruption in the late 1950s, the **Labor Management Reporting and Disclosure Act of 1959**, also known as the Landrum-Griffin Act, outlined a bill of rights for union members and established procedures for union elections, discipline, and financial reporting. The act requires unions to annually file a detailed disclosure form with the U.S. Department of Labor showing how member dues were spent, including the salaries of union officers and staff.[24] The Landrum-Griffin Act applies to all members of unions in the private sector and to those federal, state, or local government employees who belong to unions representing both public and private employees.

Labor Management Reporting and Disclosure Act of 1959
(the Landrum-Griffin Act) outlined a bill of rights for union members and sets up procedures for union elections, discipline, and financial reporting

The Landrum-Griffin Act guarantees all union members a voice in union affairs. Employees can express their views, arguments, or opinions at union functions without punishment. A union member may hand out leaflets to other union members as long as the union member doesn't advocate supporting a rival union or breaking the contract with the employer. Freedom of assembly is also protected, allowing union members to meet outside of regular union meetings and discuss union affairs without fear of reprisals from union officials.

How Do Unions Organize?

Currently, the method for workers to unionize in a particular workplace involves first obtaining the signatures of at least 30 percent of employees requesting a union, and the NLRB then verifying the signatures and ordering a secret ballot election. If over half the employees sign a paper or electronic authorization card requesting a union, the employer can choose to waive the secret ballot election process and voluntarily recognize the union. The employer never sees the authorization cards or any other information that could identify how individual employees voted.

card check
employees sign a card of support if they are in favor of unionization; if a majority of workers (over 50 percent) sign a union authorization card, the NRLB requires the employer to recognize the union without a secret ballot election

The Employee Free Choice Act being considered by Congress would eliminate the secret ballot in union organizing efforts by allowing a **card check**. A card check would require employees sign an authorization card if they are in favor of unionization. If a majority of workers (over 50 percent) sign a card and they are submitted to and verified by the NLRB, the NRLB would require the employer to recognize the union without a secret ballot election. If over 30 percent but 50 percent or fewer employees sign a union authorization card or petition, the NLRB would still order a secret ballot election. Technology has increased the efficiency of union organization drives. Unions can now set up informational websites and e-mail announcements to collective bargaining unit members and use online signup rather than paper cards.

It is important to note that unions can go too far in their organizing efforts. For the first time in U.S. labor law history, in 2016 a jury found that a union defamed and disparaged an employer during a bitter organizing campaign. A local branch of the Service Employees International Union (SEIU) used a coordinated campaign including fliers, newsletters, e-mails, websites, rallies, and protests and routinely published information describing nonexistent wage violations and labor law abuses at the company.[25] Because the union directed this information to the employer's customers, at least 12 businesses severed their relationship with the company,[26] with one customer describing at trial how she decided to fire the company after union protestors stormed into her building and occupied her conference rooms to protest her relationship with the firm.[27] The verdict cost the union at least $7.8 million in compensatory damages and interest, driving the union into bankruptcy.[28]

How Are Unions Decertified?

The Wagner Act entitles employees who no longer want a union to represent them to get rid of their union through a **decertification election**. Although decertification elections are not uncommon, negotiating the Wagner Act takes careful planning. Only employees or other labor unions may request a decertification election—not employers. To request a decertification election, employees must file a decertification petition signed by at least 30 percent of the employees in the bargaining unit asserting that the currently certified union no longer represents the employees.

Decertification petitions may be filed any time a contract is not in effect, provided the union has had at least one year to represent the employees. Because the Wagner Act requires that all decertification efforts be free of any coercive management influence, petition signatures must be collected on nonwork time and in nonwork areas. Employer resources may not be used in gathering signatures, and the names of the union and the employer must be filled in on the petition before any signatures are collected. Once the NLRB receives and validates the decertification petition, a decertification election date is scheduled (typically in approximately 60 days). Prior to the election, both the union and the employer may campaign to influence the vote. The NLRB will decertify the union if a simple majority of voting employees vote against it.[29]

decertification election
an election to determine if a majority of employees want to no longer be represented by a union

so what?

Unions can be removed through a decertification election if a majority of employees vote to no longer be represented by the union.

Worker Centers

Worker centers are usually 501(c)(3) nonprofit community organizations that offer services to their members including worker advocacy, lobbying, training, and legal advice. They often serve immigrant populations and workers in low-wage industries including farming, retail, fast food, and home health care. Worker centers typically focus on a specific type of worker, including taxi drivers, janitors, or domestic workers, who are unable to join unions because they are independent contractors. The primary goal of a worker center is to help members achieve economic justice and to improve working conditions and safety. Most worker centers are not subject to the National Labor Relations Act or the Labor–Management Reporting and Disclosure Act, freeing them to engage in corporate campaigns including boycotting one business to pressure another business (called a secondary boycott) and picketing by activists not directly affected by the employer. They are not bound by the same collective bargaining rules that unions are, and they are not required to disclose as much as unions about their internal workings and sources of funding.[30]

Unions are using worker centers to forge new ways of organizing workers in situations that fall outside the reach of the traditional model of collective bargaining. Because worker centers are often backed by unions,[31] however, they are facing a backlash from some businesses who believe that they should be subject to labor laws governing the unionization of new groups of workers.[32]

Collective Bargaining

Collective bargaining occurs when the employer and the union negotiate in good faith on employment terms and conditions to generate a written contract. In addition to wages and benefits, labor unions bargain over virtually all aspects of the employment relationship, including working conditions, work locations, staffing levels, job descriptions and classifications, promotion and transfer policies, layoff and termination policies, employment discrimination protections, grievance procedures, and seniority provisions.

Unions are the only vehicle through which workers can have a collective bargaining agreement. Without a collective bargaining agreement, employees' workplace rights are more limited, and employers have greater latitude to make up work rules and disciplinary procedures. Under employment at will, for example, nonunion employers can usually dismiss an employee without cause. Unions often negotiate fairer and worker-friendly discharge procedures that set clear expectations for employees.

The only legislative requirement regarding collective bargaining is that both parties bargain in good faith with intent on reaching an agreement. Taking a strong position on an issue, called **hard bargaining**, is acceptable, but **surface bargaining**, or merely going through the motions of negotiations with no intent of reaching an agreement, would constitute "bad-faith bargaining" and violate the law. Refusing to meet, adopting a "take-it-or-leave-it" approach, delaying meetings, or failing to give the chief negotiator sufficient authority to make agreements are also examples of bad-faith bargaining and could prompt an unfair labor practice charge.[33]

A **collective bargaining agreement** is a legal written contract between organized labor and an employer that is enforceable through the negotiated grievance and arbitration procedure. Collective bargaining agreements are the result of negotiations regarding hours, wages, and employment terms and conditions. The inability of management and the union to reach an agreement may culminate in either a labor strike or a management lockout. A union can strike, or the employer can lock out workers only when a contract is not in effect.

Collective bargaining agreements typically contain a "just cause" clause requiring an employer to show a provable, legitimate reason for disciplining or terminating an employee. The just cause clause helps to deter workplace practices that are unlawful, discriminatory, or arbitrary and gives workers rights to a hearing and arbitration before being fired. To reduce employment uncertainty, collective bargaining agreements often describe employee protections if the company is restructured, merged with, or bought out by another company. Others contain specific provisions that restrict the amount of work employers can outsource, helping to protect union members' jobs.[34]

The three categories that are part of a collective bargaining agreement are mandatory, permissive, and illegal subjects. Mandatory bargaining subjects are those required by the National Labor Relations Board and by law. Permissive subjects, such as employee rights, may be negotiated but do not have to be. Illegal subjects, including rights protected under federal or state law, may not be negotiated. For example, closed shop clauses that require all employees to be union members before being hired are illegal in some states under the 1947 Taft-Hartley Act. Table 13.2 highlights some of the mandatory, permissive, and illegal bargaining subjects.

hard bargaining
taking a strong position on an issue

surface bargaining
going through the motions of negotiations with no intent of reaching an agreement

collective bargaining agreement
a legal written contract between organized labor and an employer that is enforceable through the negotiated grievance and arbitration procedure

Worker Rights

The NLRB requires most private-sector employers to notify workers of their rights guaranteed under the Wagner Act. Under the rule, most private-sector employers (including labor unions) must post a notice of employee rights where other workplace notices are normally displayed. The notification requirement applies to all businesses that are subject to the Wagner Act, which excludes agricultural, railroad, and airline employers.[35] The required employee rights poster is shown in Figure 13.2.

figure **13.2**

Employee Rights Poster[36]

Employee Rights
Under the National Labor Relations Act

The National Labor Relations Act (NLRA) guarantees the right of employees to organize and bargain collectively with their employers, and to engage in other protected concerted activity or to refrain from engaging in any of the above activity. Employees covered by the NLRA* are protected from certain types of employer and union misconduct. This Notice gives you general information about your rights, and about the obligations of employers and unions under the NLRA. Contact the National Labor Relations Board (NLRB), the Federal agency that investigates and resolves complaints under the NLRA, using the contact information supplied below, if you have any questions about specific rights that may apply in your particular workplace.

Under the NLRA, you have the right to:

- Organize a union to negotiate with your employer concerning your wages, hours, and other terms and conditions of employment.
- Form, join or assist a union.
- Bargain collectively through representatives of employees' own choosing for a contract with your employer setting your wages, benefits, hours, and other working conditions.
- Discuss your wages and benefits and other terms and conditions of employment or union organizing with your co-workers or a union.
- Take action with one or more co-workers to improve your working conditions by, among other means, raising work-related complaints directly with your employer or with a government agency, and seeking help from a union.
- Strike and picket, depending on the purpose or means of the strike or the picketing.
- Choose not to do any of these activities, including joining or remaining a member of a union.

Under the NLRA, it is illegal for your employer to:

- Prohibit you from talking about or soliciting for a union during non-work time, such as before or after work or during break times; or from distributing union literature during non-work time, in non-work areas, such as parking lots or break rooms.
- Question you about your union support or activities in a manner that discourages you from engaging in that activity.
- Fire, demote, or transfer you, or reduce your hours or change your shift, or otherwise take adverse action against you, or threaten to take any of these actions, because you join or support a union, or because you engage in concerted activity for mutual aid and protection, or because you choose not to engage in any such activity.
- Threaten to close your workplace if workers choose a union to represent them.
- Promise or grant promotions, pay raises, or other benefits to discourage or encourage union support.
- Prohibit you from wearing union hats, buttons, t-shirts, and pins in the workplace except under special circumstances.
- Spy on or videotape peaceful union activities and gatherings or pretend to do so.

Under the NLRA, it is illegal for a union or for the union that represents you in bargaining with your employer to:

- Threaten or coerce you in order to gain your support for the union.
- Refuse to process a grievance because you have criticized union officials or because you are not a member of the union.
- Use or maintain discriminatory standards or procedures in making job referrals from a hiring hall.
- Cause or attempt to cause an employer to discriminate against you because of your union-related activity.
- Take adverse action against you because you have not joined or do not support the union.

If you and your co-workers select a union to act as your collective bargaining representative, your employer and the union are required to bargain in good faith in a genuine effort to reach a written, binding agreement setting your terms and conditions of employment. The union is required to fairly represent you in bargaining and enforcing the agreement.

Illegal conduct will not be permitted. If you believe your rights or the rights of others have been violated, you should contact the NLRB promptly to protect your rights, generally within six months of the unlawful activity. You may inquire about possible violations without your employer or anyone else being informed of the inquiry. Charges may be filed by any person and need not be filed by the employee directly affected by the violation. The NLRB may order an employer to rehire a worker fired in violation of the law and to pay lost wages and benefits, and may order an employer or union to cease violating the law. Employees should seek assistance from the nearest regional NLRB office, which can be found on the Agency's Web site: **http://www.nlrb.gov.**

You can also contact the NLRB by calling toll-free: **1-866-667-NLRB (6572)** or (TTY) **1-866-315-NLRB (1-866-315-6572)** for hearing impaired.

If you do not speak or understand English well, you may obtain a translation of this notice from the NLRB's Web site or by calling the toll-free numbers listed above.

*The National Labor Relations Act covers most private-sector employers. Excluded from coverage under the NLRA are public-sector employees, agricultural and domestic workers, independent contractors, workers employed by a parent or spouse, employees of air and rail carriers covered by the Railway Labor Act, and supervisors (although supervisors that have been discriminated against for refusing to violate the NLRA may be covered).

This is an official Government Notice and must not be defaced by anyone.

SEPTEMBER 2011

table 13.2

Mandatory, Permissive, and Illegal Bargaining Subjects

Mandatory Subjects	Permissive Subjects	Illegal Subjects
Wages	Definition of the bargaining unit	Proposals to discriminate against people based on a protected characteristic
Overtime	Retiree health insurance or pension benefits	Union-shop clauses in right-to-work states
Seniority	Ground rules	Closed-shop clauses (in some states)
Grievance procedures	Settlement of pending grievances or unfair labor practices charges	Allowing workers to refuse to handle goods produced by nonunion companies
Safety and work practices	Pre-employment drug testing	
Procedures for layoff, recall, discharge, and discipline	Whether the employer will use the union's label on its products	

Management Rights

The labor agreement negotiated through collective bargaining often identifies the rights of management. If a management rights section is not included in the contract, management may reason that it has all rights except those restricted by law or by contract with the union.

Management rights typically cover three areas:

1. The right to identify the business objectives of the company
2. The right to determine the uses to which the company's material assets will be devoted
3. The right to take disciplinary action against an employee for cause.

Negotiating

Negotiation is a process in which two or more parties make offers, counteroffers, and concessions in order to reach an agreement. In addition to being a core component of collective bargaining, most managers do a lot of negotiating as part of their jobs. In addition to job offers and contracts with customers and suppliers, negotiations are also conducted to secure resources and make deals with bosses and subordinates.

There are two types of negotiation: Distributive and integrative. **Distributive negotiation** occurs under zero-sum conditions where any gain to one party is offset by an equivalent loss to the other party.[37] Distributive negotiation essentially distributes resources among the parties involved. Because distributive negotiation structures the conflict in a win–lose way, it tends to be competitive and adversarial as the parties negotiate who is going to get how much. For example, every dollar management gives to the union in the form of more expensive health-care coverage is a dollar the company cannot invest in marketing or product development.

Integrative negotiation is a win–win negotiation in which the agreement involves no loss to either party.[38] In general, integrative bargaining is better than distributive bargaining because neither party feels that they have lost when it is over. Integrative bargaining helps to build good long-term relationships and minimizes bad feelings between the parties. Because management and workers must work together once the negotiations are finished, this is particularly beneficial in collective bargaining.

negotiation
is a process in which two or more parties make offers, counteroffers, and concessions in order to reach an agreement

distributive negotiation
occurs under zero-sum conditions where any gain to one party is offset by an equivalent loss to the other party

so what

Managers often do a lot of negotiating in areas including collective bargaining, job offers, and contracts with suppliers and customers.

integrative negotiation
a win–win negotiation in which the agreement involves no loss to either party

The classic example of integrative negotiation during a dispute over an orange will help illustrate the idea. Tyler and Ryan take the position that they want the whole orange. The dispute moderator gives each of them one half of the orange. However, a different, win–win outcome existed that could have been identified if the parties' interests were more thoroughly considered. Ryan wanted to eat the meat of the orange, but Tyler just wanted the peel to use in baking some cookies. If the mediator had understood their interests, they could have both gotten all of what they wanted, rather than just half.[39]

The four fundamental principles of integrative negotiation are:[40]

- *Separate the people from the problem.* Separate relationship issues (emotions, misperceptions, or communication issues) from substantive issues, and deal with them independently.
- *Focus on interests, not positions.* Negotiate over what people really want and need, not what they say that want or need.
- *Create options for mutual gain.* Look for new solutions to the problem that will allow both sides to win, not just focus on the original positions that assume that for one side to win the other side must lose. What can be added to the agreement to make concessions in some areas acceptable?
- *Insist on objective criteria.* If they exist, outside, objective fairness criteria for the negotiated agreement are helpful in establishing reasonable positions (such as the terms of another company's union–management contract).

This chapter's case study highlights the results of integrative negotiation at General Motors' (GM) Tonawanda plant.

CASE STUDY: Union/Management Cooperation at General Motors' Tonawanda Plant[41]

A few years ago, the future of one of the largest engine plants in the world, General Motors' Tonawanda engine plant in Buffalo, New York, was in jeopardy during the financial crisis. Workers and management came together to try to make the plant more efficient. They agreed to several changes, including introducing an alternative work schedule with 10-hour shifts Monday through Thursday rather than a five-day-a-week schedule.

To prepare the plant for producing the new Ecotec engine, both contractors and United Auto Workers members made infrastructure improvements for new equipment. Both hourly and salaried workers visited equipment suppliers to test production of the new engine and provide feedback on the equipment, allowing improvements to be made before the equipment was delivered.

Union representatives and company officials also worked together to convince GM to open a logistical optimization center at one end of the 1.1-million-square-foot building to produce "kits" of raw parts used by assembly line workers. Management and union leaders lauded a cooperative spirit for helping convince top GM leaders that the center would be worthwhile. The process in which the kits are now produced is unique among GM's 54 U.S. plants and could serve as a model for others across the country. With a company commitment for $900 million in work producing three new engines at the facility, managers and labor officials added new jobs in addition to recalling almost 100 laid-off workers. In 2016, the Tonawanda plant was one of three GM plants in western New York chosen for a collective $334 million upgrade, due in large part by the strong work ethic at the plant.

Continued

Questions:

1. How was what happened at the Tonawanda plant an example of integrative negotiation?
2. Why do you think both management and the union were willing to adopt an integrative negotiation strategy?
3. What do you think would help maintain the cooperative spirit between management and the union at the Tonawanda plant?

When negotiating, it is helpful to research and understand the individual(s) with whom you will be negotiating. Try to begin with a positive exchange, create an open and trusting environment, and emphasize win–win situations. Be sure to prepare well, listen actively, and think through your alternatives. The more options you feel you have, the

table **13.3**

Negotiation Tips

Here are some suggestions for being an effective negotiator:[42]

- *Identify what you can and cannot part with.* Identify the things most important to you and the things that are less important. Act like everything is important, and grudgingly concede ground on the things that matter less to you. Be careful not to show too much desire for something, or your bargaining power will be reduced. If the other side can tell that you emotionally want something, this will weaken your bargaining power.

- *Try to identify and use sources of leverage.* Leverage is anything that can help or hinder a party in a bargaining situation. For example, a seller who must sell is at a disadvantage, and if the other party needs to move quickly, you might be able to make a tougher offer.

- *Show the other side that you understand their position.* Help the other side see you as an ally by mirroring their emotions. If the other person appears frustrated, let him or her know that you recognize he or she is frustrated. They may respond with, "You're right. I'm frustrated!" but now you're agreeing on something. By empathizing with the other party, you stand a better chance of preserving a cordial and productive atmosphere.

- *Suppress your emotions.* Negotiations can stir emotions, especially anger. Constantly reminding yourself of your goal can help you remain an appropriate level of detachment and continue to see the issues clearly. Stay rationally focused on the issue being negotiated, and take a break if emotions start to flare up. Avoid arguing vigorously for your own opinion, refusing to consider changing your position, and trying to win regardless of the interpersonal costs.

- *Know your BATNA.* BATNA is an acronym for "best alternative to a negotiated agreement." It is what you could have done had no negotiation taken place, or what you will do if you can't reach an agreement with the other party. Having acceptable alternatives to the contract (e.g., closing a plant or adopting robotic technology to replace workers) can also increase one party's leverage over the other. If negotiations stall, letting the other side know that you're prepared to proceed with your backup plan can also help to get the process started up again.

- *Try perspective taking:* Put yourself in the other person's position, and try to understand their point of view; avoid ridiculing the other's ideas and using sarcasm.

- *Create solutions:* Brainstorm with the other person, ask questions, and try to create new solutions to the problem; negotiating is about compromise, not an either/or proposition.

- *Reach out:* Reach out to the other person, make the first move, and try to make amends if something goes wrong.

?so what

To negotiate most effectively, be sure to understand both the issues being negotiated as well as the individual with whom you will be negotiating.

better the negotiating position you will be in. Table 13.3 gives you some tips on being an effective negotiator.

Negotiation Breakdowns

Sometimes the contract negotiation process breaks down despite the desire of both sides to reach agreement. When a negotiation impasse occurs, there are several methods of getting the negotiation process restarted.

Third-party assistance.   **Mediation** is one of the two basic types of third-party intervention in a negotiation. Mediation uses a neutral third party to attempt to resolve the dispute through facilitation. The mediator's objective is to persuade both parties to resume negotiations and work toward a settlement. The mediator cannot impose a settlement, only help identify solutions, make recommendations, and restore blocked communication channels. Tact, patience, and diplomacy are essential mediation skills.

Arbitration is when an impartial third party acts as both judge and jury in imposing a binding decision on both negotiating parties. **Rights arbitration** covers disputes over the interpretation of an existing contract and is often used in settling grievances. **Interest arbitration** resolves disputes over the terms of a collective bargaining agreement currently being negotiated. Arbitration is only possible when an arbitration clause is in the contract binding both parties to it.

Union strategies for overcoming a negotiating impasse.   When a union feels that extreme pressure is needed to get management to agree to important bargaining demands, it can utilize strikes and boycotts. **Strikes** occur when union members refuse to work, halting production or services. The union hopes that the lost business and revenue will force management to agree to its terms. A five-day general strike in Israel over the employment conditions of workers contracted through employment agencies crippled Israel's transportation, banking, and other sectors.[43]

Strikes are most effective when a company's business is thriving and the company has not built up a large inventory of products it can distribute during the strike. Because workers have little income during a strike and the risk that union members will lose their jobs to replacements, union members are usually very reluctant to strike.

An employee's right to strike is a critical component of the right to organize under the Wagner Act, but not all strikes are protected. The main types of strikes the Wagner Act covers are:

- *Unfair labor practice strikes*: Protest illegal employer activities.
- *Economic strikes*: Disputes over wages or benefits.
- *Recognition strikes*: Strikes intended to force employers to recognize unions.
- *Jurisdictional strikes*: Affirm members' right to certain job assignments and protest the work assignments to another union or to unorganized employees.

Employers can legally hire replacement workers during unfair labor practice and economic strikes. If replacements are hired when a union goes on an economic strike, the company does not have to lay off the replacement workers when the strike ends. At the end of an unfair labor practice strike, strikers must be reinstated to their former positions provided they have not participated in any misconduct.

If union members engage in strikes considered unlawful under the Wagner Act (e.g., sit-down strikes or strikes that endanger employers' property), they lose Wagner Act protection. The right to strike also may be limited by agreements to submit disputes to arbitration for a specified period of time before striking. Because many states have strike-related legislation, it is important to be familiar with relevant state laws.

A **boycott** involves union members' refusing to use or buy the firm's products to exert economic pressure on management. Unions once encouraged third parties such as customers and suppliers to stop doing business with the company in a **secondary boycott**. The Taft-Hartley Act made secondary boycotts illegal.

---

mediation
using a neutral third party to attempt to resolve the dispute through facilitation

arbitration
an impartial third party acts as both judge and jury in imposing a binding decision on both negotiating parties

rights arbitration
covers disputes over the interpretation of an existing contract and is often used in settling grievances

interest arbitration
resolves disputes over the terms of a collective bargaining agreement currently being negotiated

strike
union members refuse to work, halting production or services

boycott
union members refuse to use or buy the firm's products to exert economic pressure on management

secondary boycott
when a union encourages third parties such as customers and suppliers to stop doing business with the company

lockout
management keeps employees away from the workplace and uses management staff or replacements to run the business

Management strategies for overcoming a negotiating impasse. Management sometimes believes that extreme pressure is warranted to get a union to lower or drop a demand. The primary methods management can use to do this are lockouts and replacing striking workers. In a **lockout**, management keeps employees away from the workplace and uses management staff or replacements to run the business. Employees do not get paid during a lockout, making the strategy most effective when the union treasury is low (preventing the union from supporting locked out members) or when the business has sufficient inventories of finished products to supply customers for a while. When members of United Auto Workers Local 1887 were locked out for six weeks, hundreds of supervisors and managers worked 12-hour shifts to keep the plant running.[44]

Harley-Davidson threatened to move its manufacturing jobs from York, Pennsylvania, to a new plant in Kentucky if the union rejected its demands. Employees at Harley-Davidson Inc.'s largest factory subsequently agreed to job cuts of nearly 50 percent, more work-rule flexibility, and a seven-year labor deal in exchange for the company's commitment to invest $90 million in the York, Pennsylvania, plant.[45]

dysfunctional conflict
conflict that focuses on emotions and differences between both parties (e.g., personality conflict)

Hiring replacement workers either temporarily or permanently is legal during an economic strike that is part of a collective bargaining dispute. However, doing so risks the animosity and bitterness of employees after the strike, which could adversely impact the company's performance long after the strike ends.

functional conflict
conflict that balances both parties' interests to maximize mutual gains (e.g., task conflict)

Conflict management strategies. Conflict can be **dysfunctional** and focus on emotions and differences between both parties (e.g., personality conflict) or **functional** and balance both parties' interests to accomplish mutual goals and maximize mutual gains (e.g., task conflict). The five conflict management strategies are:[46]

collaborating
attempting to work with the other person to find some solution that fully satisfies the concerns of both parties

1. **Collaborating**: Attempting to work with the other person to find some solution that fully satisfies both parties' concerns. Collaborating might take the form of exploring a disagreement to learn from each other's insights, concluding to resolve some condition that would otherwise have them competing for resources, or trying to find a creative solution to an interpersonal problem.

compromising
trying to find some expedient, mutually acceptable middle ground solution that partially satisfies both parties

2. **Compromising**: Trying to find some expedient, mutually acceptable middle ground solution that partially satisfies both parties. Compromising gives up more than competing but less than accommodating, and it does not explore the issue in as much depth as collaborating. Compromising might mean splitting the difference, exchanging concessions, or seeking a quick middle-ground position.

3. **Accommodating**: Neglecting one's own concerns to satisfy the concerns of the other person. Accommodating might take the form of selfless generosity or yielding to another's point of view.

accommodating
neglecting one's own concerns to satisfy the concerns of the other person

4. **Competing**: Pursuing one's own concerns at the other person's expense. This is a power-oriented mode in which the goal is to win; competing might mean standing up for your rights, defending a position which you believe is correct, or simply trying to win.

competing
pursuing one's own concerns at the other person's expense

5. **Avoiding**: Not immediately pursuing one's own concerns or those of the other person and not addressing the conflict. Avoiding might take the form of diplomatically sidestepping an issue, postponing the issue until later, or simply withdrawing.

avoiding
not immediately pursuing one's own concerns or those of the other person and not addressing the conflict

This chapter's HR Flexibility feature will help you understand when to adopt each of these conflict management strategies when negotiating.

A key negotiating skill is the ability to influence others. This chapter's Develop Your Skills feature helps you develop your influence skills.

HR Flexibility

When to Use Different Conflict Management Strategies

Although collaborating tends to be the best overall conflict management strategy, each of the five strategies can be effective in different situations. Here is an overview of the best uses for each strategy.

1. *Collaborating*: Best used when the goal is to satisfy both sides; a good choice when the interests of both sides are too important to be compromised, the relationship will be ongoing, and mutual trust is important.
2. *Compromising*: Best used when the issue is of modest importance, and each side is committed to his or her position, but goal attainment is not worth the potential conflict of using a more power-oriented competing strategy; also useful to achieve temporary agreements or reach acceptable solutions under time pressure.
3. *Accommodating*: A good choice when the issue is of low importance to you, and you want to show that you are reasonable or to create goodwill or keep the peace.
4. *Competing*: A good choice when fast action is necessary (e.g., emergencies), unpopular decisions must be made, or the relationship will not be ongoing; this style risks decreasing the other party's engagement, commitment, and empowerment.
5. *Avoiding*: Appropriate when the issue is of low importance, additional time or information is needed, or tensions need to be reduced.

Develop Your Skills

Influence Tactics

Being able to persuade and influence others is a skill that will help you in both your personal and professional lives. Influencing others is also an important skill in negotiating. These are some commonly used influence tactics that will help you flexibly adapt your influence approach to the person and situation to help you be more effective.

1. **Legitimating tactics**: Enhancing one's formal authority to make a request by referring to precedents, rules, contracts, or other official documents.
2. **Personal appeals**: Asking someone to do something as a personal favor or "because we're friends."
3. **Assertiveness**: Using pressure, coercion, or persistent follow-up to gain compliance.
4. **Ingratiation**: Using flattery or praise to put the other person in a good mood and make them more likely to help.
5. **Inspirational appeals**: Appealing to the other person's values, aspirations, or ideals to gain his or her commitment.
6. **Rational persuasion**: Using facts and logic to persuade the other person.
7. **Upward appeals**: Obtaining or merely referring to the support of higher-ups.
8. **Coalition tactics**: Engaging the help of others to persuade someone to do something.
9. **Exchange**: Offering to exchange something of value now or in the future for someone's cooperation.

legitimating tactics
enhancing one's formal authority to make a request by referring to precedents, rules, contracts, or other official documents

personal appeals
asking someone to do something as a personal favor or "because we're friends"

assertiveness
using pressure, coercion, or persistent follow-up to gain compliance

ingratiation
using flattery or praise to put the other person in a good mood and make them more likely to help

inspirational appeals
appealing to the other person's values, aspirations, or ideals to gain his or her commitment

rational persuasion
using facts and logic to persuade the other person

upward appeals
obtaining or referring to the support of higher-ups

coalition tactics
engaging the help of others to persuade someone to do something

exchange
offering to exchange something of value now or in the future for someone's cooperation

Strategic Labor Relations

As in any relationship, both labor and management choose how to interact with the other party and what goals to pursue. A labor relations strategy helps both the organization and the union proactively focus on the best ways to accomplish their goals. Often the difference between labor and management is not what the ultimate goal should be, but how each party believes that goal should be accomplished. Once shared goals are identified, it can be easier to develop a shared strategy to reach them.[47] Developing a labor relations strategic plan and strategy helps each side stay focused on its goals.

Labor Relations Strategic Plan

labor relations strategic plan
identifies the labor relations goals desired individually or jointly by labor and management, determines the best strategy to reach those goals, and develops and executes the actions needed to implement that strategy

Labor relations are too often reactive, involving minimal planning. Management and labor spend more time reacting to each other than trying to develop effective approaches to achieve their mutual goals. A **labor relations strategic plan** identifies the labor relations goals desired individually or jointly by labor and management, determines the best strategy to both reach those goals and comply with labor law, and develops and executes the actions needed to implement that strategy.[48] A labor relations strategic plan provides a foundation for better communication and a constructive approach to the conduct of labor relations.[49]

Labor Relations Strategies

compliance labor relations strategy
relies heavily on the application of labor law to enforce the rights and the obligations created by statute and by contract

There are three primary labor relations strategies:[50]

1. **Compliance strategy**: Relies heavily on the application of labor law to enforce the rights and the obligations created by statute and by contract; this is the predominant strategy used in the federal and private sectors, and its effectiveness depends on forcing the other party to do what the contract or the law requires it to do.

collaboration labor relations strategy
relies heavily on labor relations to pursue an interest-based approach to problem solving

2. **Collaboration strategy**: Relies heavily on labor relations to pursue an interest-based approach to problem solving; requires a high degree of trust and commitment as well as both parties acknowledging that the other brings value to the relationship. It is also possible to combine the compliance and collaboration strategies.

avoidance labor relations strategy
management engages in lawful or unlawful efforts to prevent a union from forming or seeks the decertification of an existing union

3. **Avoidance strategy**: Management engages in lawful or unlawful efforts to prevent a union from forming or seeks the decertification of an existing union.

In a collaboration labor relations strategy, effective communication processes and true collaboration enable both parties to work together to solve problems and take advantage of opportunities. Collaboration does not mean co-management or joint decision-making. Rather, the union is involved early in the decision-making process, and management makes the final decisions. This arrangement preserves management's decision-making rights and prevents the union from becoming a part of management.[51] Table 13.4 summarizes the advantages and the disadvantages of pursuing a collaboration labor relations strategy.

Employers' perceptions of the contributions that trade unions make to their businesses are associated with the type of interaction employers have with them.[52] When both sides are committed to a collaborative relationship, positive outcomes can result. Labor and management at Kaiser Permanente, featured in this chapter's opening Real World Challenge, have successfully used a collaboration labor relations strategy and engaged in interest-based negotiations for three sets of negotiations between 2000 and 2010.[53]

The International Specialty Products Corporation had issues with poor quality, high costs, and low employee morale. Making process changes and formalizing improved methodologies improved performance, but these changes could not have been made without first changing the adversarial relationship that the union and management had for many years.[54] Canadian company Molson Breweries credits improved labor–management relations with its success in achieving growth in productivity, quality, innovation, customer satisfaction, and time to market.[55]

table **13.4**

Advantages and Disadvantages of a Collaboration Labor Relations Strategy

Advantages:
• Interest-based bargaining is used to resolve disputes, which focuses attention on the problem not the parties.
• Decision-making quality can be improved.
• Implementing decisions can be easier.
• Better communication can result.
• Trust can be strengthened.
Disadvantages:
• Union membership may not support the relationship and suspect union leaders of pursuing their personal interests rather than the union membership's interests.
• Lower-level management may believe that upper management has "sold out" to the union.
• Change can take longer because interest-based bargaining can take longer than traditional bargaining.
• The new skills needed by both sides require changes in attitudes toward and approaches to the other party.

How Unions Impact Human Resource Management

Unions promote and protect the interests of all employees regardless of whether they pay union dues, and even those workers who may never even be represented by a union. Small businesses that are not unionized are also impacted by labor unions. When local unions negotiate contracts with other companies, the wage, benefit, and other outcomes can influence what other employers need to offer in order to be competitive for talent. Research has found that that a large union presence in an industry or region can affect wages and working conditions even for nonunion workers.[56]

Once a union contract is in place, it governs many aspects of human resource management. One employee relations lawyer believes that when it comes to unions, "The issue is one of facing the harsh truth that whenever you get the union in your business, you're outsourcing your human resources, as near as I can tell."[57] He elaborates that in a unionized organization, rather than doing those things that make a company succeed, the HR department's time and resources are spent administering and dealing with the intricacies of the collective bargaining contract.[58] Let's turn our attention to how unions can impact the different functional areas of HRM.

> *"The issue is one of facing the harsh truth that whenever you get the union in your business, you're outsourcing your human resources, as near as I can tell."*
>
> —**Employee relations lawyer**

so what?

Even if a company is not unionized, a large union presence in the industry or region can influence the wages and working conditions it offers its own employees.

so what?

Because union contracts cover so many aspects of HRM, they often limit the organization's ability to adopt many HRM initiatives until the next contract is negotiated.

How do Unions Impact Staffing?

Unions generally negotiate for job opportunities to be granted based on **seniority**, or the length of time the employee has worked for the employer. Not only are job assignments and shift preferences given based on seniority, layoffs can also be determined by negotiated last in, first out rules that lay off the newest employees first. This is obviously not the best way to

seniority
the length of time the employee has worked for the employer

staff strategically, as job fit and merit are not even considered. It also decreases supervisors' influence over workers by denying them the ability to incentivize and reward employees with preferred work schedules, shifts, and job assignments.

Some unions are involved in candidate assessment and hiring. The workforce readiness assessment program of Building Futures screens candidates in Providence, Rhode Island, for construction jobs. Building Futures is a labor–management partnership that promotes the benefits of using union contractors and their skilled union workers, representing the interests of both contractors and building trades unions in Rhode Island. It also helps candidates who do well on the workforce readiness assessment secure building trade apprenticeships.[59]

A collective bargaining agreement specifying that promotions will be based on seniority rather than merit influences the types of competencies the firm should hire. Seniority-based promotions make leadership competencies critical hiring criteria for lower-level positions because as they gain seniority, lower-level hires will advance in the organization. Even in nonunion companies, the effects from competitors' union agreements can occur as the nonunion companies adjust their pay, benefits, and terms and conditions of employment to successfully compete for new hires and prevent current employees from leaving to work for a competitor.

How Do Unions Impact Performance Management?

The union contract gives employees specific rights in filing grievances and settling disputes. When negotiating dispute resolution systems, it is important to consider the conflict-related motivations and behaviors of both management and workers, as well as the likely consequences of the design choice on both parties' future motivations and behaviors.[60]

A 1975 U.S. Supreme Court decision granted employees **Weingarten rights**[61] that guarantee employees the right to union representation during investigatory interviews by the employer. If an interview could lead to the employee being disciplined or terminated, or affect his or her working conditions, the employee can request that a union representative or officer be present at the meeting. Without representation, the employee may refuse to answer any questions. A union cannot force a worker to use the union grievance procedure, although it may have a representative present at the grievance meeting. A worker may choose to try to settle a problem directly with the employer unless specifically prohibited by the bargaining agreement.

Performance appraisal is often not used as a basis for making compensation and staffing decisions in unionized companies because many unions do not like the fact that the appraisal generally comes from the supervisor, who may be biased. Unions tend to be more receptive to performance information given for feedback purposes. This is quite different from nonunionized organizations where performance appraisal data are used to determine job assignments, pay raises, promotions, development needs, and termination and layoff decisions.

How Do Unions Impact Employee Training and Development?

Because turnover tends to be lower at unionized organizations,[62] investments in training are often greater than in nonunionized companies because there is a higher return on the training investment. In addition, many unions are involved in member training and development.

Unions can be instrumental in the identification of worker training needs because members understand the working environment. In some cases, union members are the training providers with training occurring at union learning centers or on the job. One advantage to having unions provide training is their access to on-the-ground skills and experience among their members. Moreover, they understand how the skills they are teaching are used in the workplace. With their direct access to workers, they can help to identify the skills and the competencies needed to keep workers and businesses competitive. This is one goal of Denver's newly formed SkillBuild Colorado and, in particular, of one of its members, the Constructors and Designers Alliance.[63] One expert believes that the future of nanotechnology, "green jobs," and other emerging technologies might be a good fit for unions to pool resources to create a value for both members and employers.[64]

Weingarten rights
guarantee employees the right to union representation during investigatory interviews by the employer

 so what

Because turnover tends to be lower in unionized organizations, the return on investments in training are often greater than in nonunionized organizations.

This chapter's Strategic Impact feature describes how one union has partnered with employers to provide skills training for union members and non-members.

 ## Strategic Impact

The District 1199C Training and Upgrading Fund[65]

The District 1199C Training and Upgrading Fund is a partnership of the National Union of Hospital & Health Care Workers; American Federation of State, County, and Municipal Employees; and 50 contributing healthcare employers in the Philadelphia area. The fund's mission includes building coalitions with employers, government agencies, area school districts, community agencies, and area schools of nursing and allied health. The fund serves 18,000 Philadelphia area union members and community residents, providing access to information, counseling, academic remediation, and on-site skills training for individuals wanting to work or advance within a variety of healthcare and human services careers.

The fund works closely with area employers to provide customized educational programs that address employees' literacy needs as well as skills upgrading. Fund staff work closely with employers in growing their own high skilled workers from among their entry-level workforce. The fund also works with employers to address their recruitment and retention needs.

The fund was created to assist members and the community in upgrading out of dead-end jobs and keeping pace with increasing technological demands. The Training and Upgrading Fund's Learning Center in Center City, Philadelphia provides basic and job skills training to over 2,000 students per year. About half the students are union members, and half are community residents, including laid-off workers and welfare recipients. The Training Fund enjoys a national reputation as a model joint labor–management partnership in education.

How Do Unions Impact Compensation and Benefits?

Unionized employees tend to increase total compensation costs for the employer. On average, unionized employees earn approximately 17 percent higher wages than comparable nonunionized employees.[66]

Unions usually negotiate pay raise policies that avoid merit pay in favor of **cost-of-living adjustments** tied to inflation indicators such as the Consumer Price Index. Unions are often suspicious of managerial favoritism in merit pay decisions and also believe that union solidarity is undermined when employees must compete against each other for raises. Nonunionized organizations tend to prefer merit pay and bonuses to recognize top performers and motivate all employees. Unions are likely to be more favorable toward group incentives such as profit sharing or gainsharing plans that tend to reinforce group cohesion.[67]

Unions often negotiate more valuable benefits for employees. In addition to receiving more benefits than nonunionized workers, unionized workers tend to pay less for the benefits they receive. Nonunionized workers often share benefits costs with their employer.[68] Retirement benefits are often more secure for unionized workers because unions tend to negotiate for defined benefit plans that provide a fixed amount of income to retirees. Nonunionized workers

cost-of-living adjustment
tied to inflation indicators rather than merit

are more likely to have a defined contribution plan such as a 401(k) that requires only that the employer set aside a certain amount of the employee's monthly income in a plan that meets Employee Retirement Income Security Act (ERISA) standards. Defined contribution plans have more uncertainty regarding what a worker's retirement income will be. While only 14 percent of nonunion workers have guaranteed pensions, 68 percent of union workers do. More than 97 percent of union workers have jobs that provide health insurance benefits, but only 85 percent of nonunion workers do.[69]

Establishing Positive Labor–Management Relations

Kzenon/Shutterstock

Trust, respect, and open communication are the foundation of effective labor-management relations. To create a partnership mindset, workers must see themselves as part of the larger organization and not just a member of a union.

Research suggests that relational factors including conflict and workplace culture are more important determinants of organizational performance than are the structural factors of unionization and shared governance.[70] Trust, respect, and open communication are at the core of positive labor–management relations. One expert notes that Kaiser Permanente and its unions, featured in this chapter's opening real world challenge, "are attempting to build an innovative model of management—a relationship of mutual respect."[71] Unions can be contributing partners in organizational development and systemic improvement, but workers must think of themselves as part of the larger organization, not just as members of unions. Management can help facilitate this partnership mindset.

Developing proactive employee relations strategies for remaining union-free is a goal of many nonunionized employers. Employee surveys, exit interviews, focus groups, and staff meetings are great ways to assess the organizational climate, promote two-way communication, and stay informed of workers' concerns. Establishing a positive work environment through special events, monetary and nonmonetary recognition programs, and diversity and inclusion programs also helps keep labor–management relations positive.

Establishing and communicating consistently used and fair workplace policies and procedures through employee handbooks and intranet sites also promotes positive employee-management relations. It is also important to develop and implement grievance, discipline, and termination policies based on the organizational code of conduct.

In both unionized and nonunionized organizations, labor–management committees often focus on joint problem-solving and building mutual trust. These committees can effectively deal with issues including work hours, training, personnel issues, and workplace safety and health. Labor–management committees often focus on less controversial issues such as safety at first and move to more complex issues as trust is established. When they function well, these committees can prevent the need to bring unnecessary issues to the bargaining table, simplifying the collective bargaining process. The trust established through the committee meetings and joint problem solving can also decrease the combative relationship between management and labor at the bargaining table.

Employee participation does have limits. Some decisions, such as corporate financial planning, must be made by management alone. In fact, most of the participation that takes place involves the employee's immediate workplace environment. Management may also resist cooperative structures. Managers often believe that workers will bypass and inhibit middle management and slow the decision-making process. Labor–management committees

? so what

Establishing trust between workers and management improves the quality of the labor-management partnership and decreases the likelihood of a combative relationship.

can help to reduce absenteeism, accidents, and grievances and improve collective bargaining relationships and overall job satisfaction.[72]

Global Labor Relations

Although the influence of labor unions has declined significantly in some sectors of the U.S. economy, this is not the case abroad. In many countries, collective labor enjoys a strong presence. In some countries, collective representation differs radically from the United States in that collective agreements often legally apply to an entire industry sector, making even nonunion workers covered by the agreements. For example, in Brazil, all workers must be in unions. Labor unions in Europe tend to operate at the industry rather than company level.[73]

Multinational organizations must address the challenge of reconciling the labor policies and practices of the home country with those of each host country. Whether the host country is a developing or an advanced economy can create very different challenges. For example, most other advanced economic democracies have universal health insurance and do not recognize employment at will.[74]

Multinational organizations with European operations need to become familiar with legislation requiring **works councils**, or councils of elected workers that participate in shared workplace governance.[75] Works councils provide workers with input on workplace issues. In Germany, works councils cooperate with management over scheduling, safety standards, dispute resolution, efficiency improvements, and shop floor conditions.[76] If management fails to comply with local laws on works councils and labor unions, a company's actions can be declared void or business plans significantly delayed. Indonesia also requires works councils that provide workers a level of representatives beyond their unions.

Some European countries require **codetermination**, or worker representation on the company's board of directors (e.g., Germany).[77] Although not common in the United States, worker representation on the board ensures that worker interests be considered at the strategic level of the firm (e.g., which factory will be closed or where will the company expand its facilities).

A current issue in global labor relations concerns the disparities between home and host country labor standards and practices when companies outsource production to companies in other countries. Apple has received considerable media attention over the poor working

works councils
councils of elected workers that participate in shared workplace governance

codetermination
worker representation on the company's board of directors

so what**?**

Some countries require worker representation on the company's board of directors to ensure that worker interests are considered at the strategic level.

🌐 Global Issues

Collective Bargaining Coverage and Union Participation in Europe[80]

	Proportion of Employees in Unions	Collective Bargaining Coverage
Belgium	50%	96%
Finland	74%	91%
France	8%	98%
Germany	18%	62%
Ireland	31%	44%
Spain	19%	70%
Switzerland	21%	51%
United Kingdom	26%	29%

conditions for employees in Chinese subcontractor Foxconn's facilities where products including the iPad are made.[78] After considerable consumer and social backlash, companies including Nike, Starbucks, Disney, and Wal-Mart are increasingly recognizing the importance of monitoring the labor conditions under which their products are manufactured. The AFL-CIO filed what is known as a Section 301 petition asking the U.S. government to take action against China over persistent violations of labor rights, charging that China had systematically failed to adhere to such basic international requirements as barring child labor, permitting free association, and enforcing minimum wages, working hours, and occupational health and safety standards.[79]

This chapter's Global Issues feature summarizes the proportion of employees in unions and the collective bargaining coverage in several European countries.

Summary and Application

A positive labor–management relationship is beneficial to both workers and management. A labor relations strategy helps move the parties' labor–management relationship from being something that just happens to a planned, well thought-out approach to effective dealings in labor–management relations.[81] Because of the impact union contracts have on the strategic use of HRM, it is beneficial to maintain a trusting and collaborative relationship with workers regardless of whether or not they are unionized. Numerous state and federal laws exist governing both employer and worker rights in the unionization and collective bargaining process.

Real World Response

The Labor Management Partnership at Kaiser Permanente

Kaiser Permanente's over 250,000 physicians, nurses, and employees share the common goal of making lives better.[82] After a crucial labor–management meeting in 1995, the most ambitious and complex labor–management partnership in U.S. history was launched in response to competitive pressures within the healthcare industry. Kaiser Permanente and the Union Coalition created the Labor Management Partnership to transform their relationship and improve the organization's ability to best serve its members.[83]

The partnership is anchored by employee involvement at work, interest-based problem solving in contract negotiations, and broad-based consultation on issues such as how to best use electronic medical records technologies. A labor–management strategy group oversees the partnership and works together on issues including marketing, designing, and planning new facilities, and planning how to expand services to the uninsured in the context of changing national healthcare policies.[84] Workers, managers, and physicians use joint decision-making and a common interest-based problem-solving process, and employees work in collaborative work groups that continually improve performance.[85] The partnership inspires ongoing communication, innovation, and high performance.[86]

The partnership brings frontline managers, workers, and physicians together to make full use of everyone's expertise and perspectives to identify and implement solutions that best address systemic issues. The frontline employees who do the job every day are able to offer innovative solutions. Stewards and union team co-leads are becoming work unit leaders. Managers are doing less directing work and more coaching and mentoring. Physicians are now supported by all staff in providing high-quality, compassionate, patient-centered care, improving the entire care experience.[87]

Many experts consider Kaiser's labor–management partnership a model. Jeffrey Pfeffer, a professor at Stanford University's Graduate School of Business says, "Kaiser Permanente is one of the only organizations I know of that is trying to build a genuine partnership between its unions and management."[88] Kaiser is now a national leader in introducing and using electronic medical records technologies, organizing healthcare delivery via frontline "unit-based" teams.[89] The partnership has been credited not only with improving patient care and satisfaction but in making Kaiser Permanente a better place to work.[90] Kaiser has turned around its finances and experienced positive operating margins under the partnership.[91]

Takeaway Points

1. Union supporters argue that unions protect workers, reduce job stress, and can improve organizational productivity. Union workers' professional standards are often higher than those of nonunion workers, and unions can improve members' skills through a variety of training programs. Workers join unions because they tend to increase workers' pay and benefits and reduce job uncertainty.

2. Union detractors claim that unions are bad for the economy because they result in higher prices, are not focused on business goals, or are no longer needed in the presence of the extensive legislation that now exists. Union demands can also be unreasonable and nonstrategic to the organization.

3. Collective bargaining occurs when the employer and the union negotiate in good faith on employment terms and conditions to generate a written collective bargaining agreement. Both parties must bargain in good faith with intent on reaching an agreement. Different bargaining subjects can be required by law, optional, or illegal to negotiate.

4. Management rights typically cover three areas: The right to identify the business objectives of the company, the right to determine the uses to which the company's material assets will be devoted, and the right to take disciplinary action against an employee for cause.

5. Distributive negotiation is a win–lose negotiation in that any gain to one party is a loss to the other side. Integrative negotiation is a win–win negotiation in which the agreement results in no loss to either party. Integrative bargaining helps to build good long-term relationships, and minimizes bad feelings between the parties.

6. When a negotiation impasse occurs, third-party assistance of mediation or arbitration can help. Unions may call for strikes or boycotts to pressure management to make concessions. Management may resort to lockouts to pressure the union to return to the bargaining table.

7. A compliance labor relations strategy relies heavily on the application of labor law to enforce the rights and the obligations created by statute and by contract. A collaboration labor relations strategy relies heavily on labor relations to pursue an interest-based approach to problem solving. In an avoidance strategy management engages in lawful or unlawful efforts to prevent a union from forming or seeks the decertification of an existing union.

8. Unions influence HRM because once a union contract is in place, it governs many aspects of human resource management. Staffing, training, termination, performance management, and compensation practices may all be determined by the negotiated contract, leaving little discretion to strategically apply HRM and reducing managers' discretion in hiring, motivating, and managing their employees.

Discussion Questions

1. Do you feel that the employment relationship is more legal and contractual or a fundamental human relationship involving more fundamental human rights? Explain your answer.
2. Is a management policy of trying to suppress union formation ethical?
3. As a worker, would you prefer to be represented by a labor union? Why or why not?
4. As a company, would you prefer your employees to be unionized? Why or why not?
5. If both sides are stuck in negotiating a labor contract, what are the best actions to take to move the negotiation process forward?
6. If you were an HR manager and learned that union representatives have begun approaching your employees to encourage them to sign union authorization cards, what would you do in your role as HR manager?
7. What influence tactics do you tend to use the most? How can you become more comfortable with the other tactics to improve your ability to influence others?

Personal Development Exercises

Exercise: Managing Conflict

View the video, "Work Scenarios with Coworkers" (1:29) and answer the following questions.

1. What did each employee do wrong in the video? What were the consequences?
2. What did each employee do right in the video? Why were these behaviors more effective at reducing the conflict?
3. What can you do to ensure that your behavior is closer to the second video?

Exercise: Influencing Others

View the video "Killer Attitude Covert Influence Tactics" (7:57) to learn some strategies for influencing others. Then review the conflict management and influence strategies you learned in this chapter.

Working with a partner, role play Scenario A in which an HR manager needs to influence a store manager to promote a new voluntary leadership skills training program. The person role playing the store manager should give the HR manager a realistic hard time, pushing the HR manager to use a variety of conflict management and influence tactics. Don't make it easy on the HR manager! When you have finished, switch both roles and partners with other groups finishing the exercise at the same time and role play Scenario B, playing the other role with a different partner. Be sure that the store manager gives the HR manager feedback about what was effective and ineffective in the effort to influence the store manager.

Scenario A – Influencer (HR Manager)

Your company's HR team wants all store managers to promote a new voluntary leadership skills training program among floor sales associates. HR feels that this program will strengthen both customer service skills and increase the promotability of associates. One of your store managers feels that the training won't be helpful and will take floor time away from already busy associates. Not seeing the benefits being worth the costs in time to a very busy workforce, the store HR manager agrees with the store manager and isn't promoting the training. Your role is to influence the store HR manager to support the training initiative and boost enrollments in the course.

Scenario A – Influence Target (Store Manager)

Your HR team wants all store managers to promote a new voluntary leadership skills training program among floor sales associates. HR feels that this program will strengthen both customer service skills and increase the promotability of associates. You feel that the training won't be helpful and will take floor time away from already busy associates. Not seeing the benefits as being worth the costs in time to a very busy workforce, you aren't promoting the training.

Your role is to act as you believe the store manager would in the situation. Be realistic, and be challenging—you want to push your partner to apply new skills! Be sure to give feedback about what your partner did well to influence your behavior and how he or she could improve further.

Scenario B – Influencer (HR Manager)

During a trip around your store, you overhear an employee telling some ethnic and racial jokes in the store lunch room. You recognize the employee and see that she or he is sitting with some friends who also like to get together after work. At another table nearby, you see a group of African-American and Latino employees. You are not sure whether these employees overheard the jokes. You are concerned about the potential for harassment complaints and the creation of an inappropriate climate for diversity in this store. Your role is to intervene to stop this behavior.

Scenario B – Influence Target (Store HR Manager)

Racial, gender, and sexual-orientation jokes are common at your store and seem to be told by all employees. You feel that it's just another way store employees socialize at work and bond with each other—you don't think they really mean to insult other employees. It's so widespread that you feel that it doesn't really hurt anyone. You also believe that what you say and do with your friends on break is none of the organization's business and want the company to respect your freedom to say and do whatever you want with your friends while on break.

Your role is to act as you believe the store HR manager would in the situation. Be realistic, and be challenging—you want to push your partner to apply new skills! Be sure to give feedback about what your partner did well to influence your behavior and how he or she could improve further.

Strategic HRM Exercises

Exercise: Are Unions Good or Bad?

Watch the two videos: "A Brief History of Unions" (1:31) and "2/13/10 Unions Bad News for Americans" (4:24). When you have finished, answer the following questions.

1. Why do you think unions are good for the United States?
2. Why do you think unions are bad for the United States?
3. If you were starting a company, would you want your employees to be unionized? Why or why not?

Exercise: The Benefits of Being Either a Union or a Right-to-Work State

We would like to thank Professor Kathy Broneck of Pima Community College for this exercise idea.

As you learned in this chapter, in right-to-work states, workers in a unionized workplace cannot be required to join the union and pay dues. In union states, all workers in a unionized workplace must join the union and pay dues.

In this activity, the class will be divided into groups of three to five students. Each group will be assigned a role of either being in a right-to-work state or a union state. The groups assigned the role of right-to-work state will discuss the advantages of changing to a union state. The groups assigned the role of union state will discuss the advantages of changing to a right-to-work state. Take notes and be prepared to share your ideas with the class after 15 minutes.

Exercise: Collective Bargaining

View the video "What is Collective Bargaining?" (2:23). After watching the video and considering what you learned in this chapter, answer the following questions:

1. What do you think are the strongest benefits of collective bargaining for companies and employees?
2. What do you think are the biggest weaknesses of collective bargaining for companies and employees?
3. Do you think that collective bargaining should be protected by law? Why or why not?

Integrative Project

Develop a strategy to promote positive labor–management relations at your organization. Determine if you want to encourage unionization or try to prevent it, and identify strategies to accomplish your goal. How will you ensure that workers and management pursue a collaborative partnership and prevent adversarial relationships from developing?

Video Case

Imagine that both you and another manager at Happy Time Toys need extra help to meet your holiday deadlines. You just learned that only one of your two temporary help position requisitions were approved, not both. *What do you say or do?* Go to this book's video case, watch the challenge video for this chapter, and choose the best video response. Be sure to also view the outcomes of the two responses you didn't choose.

Discussion Questions

1. What influence tactics are illustrated in this video? Explain your answer.
2. What conflict management strategies are illustrated in this video? Explain your answer.
3. How else might you handle this situation? Explain your answer.

Endnotes

1. Kaiser Permanente. (2017). Who we are. Retrieved March 25, 2017, from http://www.kaiserpermanentejobs.org/who-we-are.aspx
2. Kochan, T., Eaton, A., McKersie, R., & Adler, P. (2009). *Healing together: The labor-management partnership at Kaiser Permanente*. Ithaca: Cornell University/ILR Press.
3. Kaiser Permanente. (2017). History of the LMP. Retrieved March 25, 2017, from http://www.lmpartnership.org/what-is-partnership/history-partnership
4. Labor union. (2017). *Merriam-Webster*. Retrieved March 26, 2017, from https://www.merriam-webster.com/dictionary/labor%20union
5. Katz, H. C., Kochan, T. A., & Colvin, A. J. S. (2008). *An introduction to collective bargaining & industrial relations,* 3rd ed. New York: McGraw-Hill.
6. Kaufman, B. (2004). What unions do: Insights in economic theory. *Journal of Labor Research, 25,* 351–382.

7. Kleinhenz, J., & Smith, R. (2011). Regional competitiveness: Labor–management relations, workplace practices, and workforce quality. *Business Economics*, *46*, 111–124.

8. The revolution at Le Monde. (2011, July 30). *The Economist*, 57–58.

9. Baugher, J. E., & Roberts, J. T. (2004). Workplace hazards, unions, and coping styles. *Labor Studies Journal*, *29*, 83–106.

10. Doucouliagos, C., & Laroche, P. (2003). What do unions do to productivity? A meta-analysis. *Industrial Relations: A Journal of Economy and Society*, *42*, 650–691; Hirsch, B. T. (2004). What do unions do for economic performance? *Journal of Labor Research*, *25*, 415–455.

11. Belman, D. (1992). Unions, the quality of labor relations, and firm performance. In L. Mishel & P. B. Voos, (Eds.), *Unions and economic competitiveness.* Armonk, NY: M.E. Sharpe.

12. Silverstein, R. A. (2012). DoOneThing.org. Retrieved March 25, 2017, from http://www.betterworldheroes.com/pages-a/alan-quotes.htm

13. Buttigieg, D. M., Deery, S. J., & Iverson, R.D. (2007). An event history analysis of union joining and leaving. *Journal of Applied Psychology*, *92*, 829–839; Tetrick, L. E., Shore, L. M., McClurg, L. N., & Vandenberg, R. J. (2007). A model of union participation: The impact of perceived union support, union instrumentality, and union loyalty. *Journal of Applied Psychology*, *92*, 820–828.

14. Shulruf, B., Yee, B., Lineham, B., Fawthorpe, L., Johri, R., & Blumenfeld, S. (2010). Perceptions, conceptions, and misconceptions of organized employment. *The Journal of Industrial Relations*, *52*, 236–241.

15. Greenhouse, S. (2011, January 21). Union membership in U.S. fell to a 70-year low last year. *The New York Times*. Retrieved March 25, 2017, from http://www.nytimes.com/2011/01/22/business/22union.html

16. *Ibid.*

17. Bureau of Labor Statistics. (2017, January 26). Union members summary. Retrieved February 6, 2017, from https://www.bls.gov/news.release/union2.nr0.htm

18. *Ibid.*

19. *Ibid.*

20. See www.nlrb.gov and https://www.nlrb.gov/national-labor-relations-act for more information.

21. See https://www.fra.dot.gov/eLib/Details/L03014 for more information on the Railroad Labor Act.

22. National Labor Relations Board. (1935). National Labor Relations Act. Retrieved March 25, 2017, from https://www.nlrb.gov/national-labor-relations-act

23. Copyright © 2017 The National Right to Work Committee. Used with permission.

24. Office of Labor-Management Standards (OLMS). (2010, February 25). Labor Management Reporting and Disclosure Act. Retrieved March 26, 2017, from https://www.dol.gov/olms/regs/compliance/lmrda-factsheet.htm

25. Employer wins $5 million from bullying union. (2016, October 3). Fisher Phillips. Retrieved March 26, 2017, from https://www.fisherphillips.com/resources-newsletters-article-employer-wins-5-million-from-bullying-union

26. Schappel, C. (2016, October 12). $5.3M verdict gives employers blueprint to sue bullying unions. *HRMorning.com*. Retrieved February 22, 2017, from http://www.hrmorning.com/verdict-gives-employers-blueprint-to-sue-bullying-unions/

27. Employer wins $5 million from bullying union. (2016, October 3). Fisher Phillips. Retrieved March 26, 2017, from https://www.fisherphillips.com/resources-newsletters-article-employer-wins-5-million-from-bullying-union

28. Walsh, T., Bloom, H. M., & Rosen, P. B. (2016, December 14). Defamation verdict drives union into bankruptcy. *Jackson Lewis*. Retrieved February 22, 2017, from http://www.laborandcollectivebargaining.com/2016/12/articles/unions-and-organizing/defamation-verdict-drives-union-into-bankruptcy/

29. Decertification election. (2017). *National Labor Relations Board*. Retrieved March 26, 2017, from https://www.nlrb.gov/rights-we-protect/whats-law/employees/i-am-represented-union/decertification-election

30. Grossman, R. J. (2013). Leading from behind? *HR Magazine*, December, 37–41.

31. AFL-CIO. (2017). Worker center partnerships. AFL-CIO. Retrieved February 12, 2017, from http://www.aflcio.org/About/Worker-Center-Partnerships

32. Maher, K. (2013, July 24). Worker centers offer a backdoor approach to union organizing. *The Wall Street Journal*. Retrieved February 13, 2017, from https://www.wsj.com/articles/SB10001424127887324144304578622050818960988

33. Employer/union rights and obligations. (2017). National Labor Relations Board. Retrieved March 26, 2017, from https://www.nlrb.gov/rights-we-protect/employerunion-rights-and-obligations

34. Snell & Wilmer, L.L.P. (2004). Outsourcing and the duty to bargain. *The Workplace Word,* September. Retrieved March 26, 2017, from http://www.swlaw.com/assets/pdf/publications/2004/09/01/Sept_04_WPW.pdf

35. Leonard, B. (2011, August 25). NLRB mandates notification of union organizing rights. *Society for Human Resource Management*. Retrieved March 26, 2017, from http://ri.shrm.org/files/NLRB%20Mandates%20Notification%20of%20Union%20Organizing%20Rights%208%2011.pdf

36. National Labor Relations Board (2017). Employee Rights Under the National Labor Relations Act. https://www.nlrb.gov/sites/default/files/documents/1562/employeerightsposter-8-5x11.pdf (accessed March 25, 2017).

37. Crump, L. (2005). For the sake of the team: Unity and disunity in a multiparty Major League Baseball negotiation. *Negotiation Journal*, *21*, 317–342.

38. Fisher, R., & Ury, W. (1983). *Getting to yes*. New York: Penguin Books; Fisher, R., Ury, W., & Patton, B. (1992). *Getting to yes: Negotiating agreement without giving in*, 2nd ed. New York: Houghton Mifflin.

39. De Dreu, C. K. W. (2005, June). A PACT against conflict escalation in negotiation and dispute resolution. *Current Directions in Psychological Science 14*, 149.

40. Fisher, R., & Ury, W. (1983). *Getting to yes*. New York: Penguin Books; Choi, D. (2010). Shared metacognition in integrative negotiation. *International Journal of Conflict Management*, *21*, 309–333; Shapiro, D. L. (2006). Teaching students how to use emotions as they negotiate. *Negotiation Journal*, January, 105 109; Lewicki, R. J., Barry, B., Saunders, D. M., & John, M. W. (2003). *Negotiation*, 4th ed. Boston, MA: McGraw-Hill/Irwin.

41. Gulley, N. (2012, February 9). GM gearing up. TonawandaNews.com. Retrieved February 21, 2012, from http://tonawanda-news.com/local/x2063986517/GM-gearing-up; Fink, J. (2016, December 14). Tonawanda plant to build new GM engine; $334 million investment in 3 WNY plants; Cuomo credited. *Buffalo Business First*. Retrieved March 25, 2017, from http://buffalonews.com/1996/08/07/labor-management-relations-wins-work-for-plant/; Pye, D. (2010, February 19). Town of Tonawanda: New engine line slated for GM powertrain. *Lockport Union-Sun & Journal*. Retrieved March 25, 2017, from http://www.lockportjournal.com/news/local_news/town

-of-tonawanda-new-engine-line-slated-for-gm-powertrain/article_86791921-c363-54ed-a432-8afb2a628499.html

42. Adapted from Kaplan, M. (2005, May). How to negotiate anything. *Money, 34,* 116–119; Delahoussaye, M. (2002, June). Don't get mad, get promoted. *Training, 39,* 20; Fisher, R., Ury, W. L., & Patton, B. (1991). *Getting to yes: Negotiating agreement without giving in.* New York: Penguin.

43. David, J. (2012, February 17). Israel: General strike ends in compromise on contracted workers. *Bloomberg BNA.* Retrieved February 21, 2012, from http://hr.bna.com/hrrc/2129/split_display.adp?fedfid=24655984&vname=idsnnot&fn=24655984&jd=a0d0u1u0m6&split=0

44. Melcer, R. (2006). Mallinckrodt workers set to return. *St. Louis Post-Dispatch,* April 21.

45. Maher, K. (2009, December 3). Harley-Davidson union makes concessions. *The Wall Street Journal.* Retrieved March 25, 2017, from http://online.wsj.com/article/SB100014240527487037350045745722235665660450.html?mod=djem_jie_360

46. Thomas, K. W. (1976). Conflict and conflict management. In M. D. Dunnette (Ed.), *Handbook of industrial and organizational psychology,* pp. 889–935. Chicago, IL: Rand McNally.

47. Federal Labor Relations Authority. (2012). Guidance on developing a labor relations strategic plan. Retrieved March 25, 2017, from https://webcache.googleusercontent.com/search?q=cache:MG2ZBXYJvUQJ:https://www.flra.gov/system/files/webfm/OGC/Guidances/FLRA%2520GC%2520Guidance%2520on%2520Developing%2520a%2520Labor%2520Relations%2520Strategic%2520Plan%2520--%2520FLRAgc.doc+&cd=1&hl=en&ct=clnk&gl=us

48. *Ibid.*

49. *Ibid.*

50. Walton, R. E., Cutcher-Gershenfeld, J., & McKersie, R. (1994). *Strategic negotiations—A theory of change in labor-management relations.* Boston, MA: Harvard Business School Press; Cooke, W. N., & Meyer, D. G. (1990). Structural and market predictors of corporate labor relations strategies. *Industrial and Labor Relations Review, 43,* 280–293; Nissen, B. (2003). Alternative strategic directions for the U.S. labor movement: Recent scholarship. *Labor Studies Journal, 28,* 133–155.

51. Federal Labor Relations Authority. (2012). Guidance on developing a labor relations strategic plan. Retrieved March 25, 2017, from https://webcache.googleusercontent.com/search?q=cache:MG2ZBXYJvUQJ:https://www.flra.gov/system/files/webfm/OGC/Guidances/FLRA%2520GC%2520Guidance%2520on%2520Developing%2520a%2520Labor%2520Relations%2520Strategic%2520Plan%2520--%2520FLRAgc.doc+&cd=1&hl=en&ct=clnk&gl=us

52. Shulruf, B., Yee, B., Lineham, B., Fawthorpe, L., Johri, R., & Blumenfeld, S. (2010). Perceptions, conceptions, and misconceptions of organized employment. *The Journal of Industrial Relations, 52,* 236–241.

53. Kochan, T., Eaton, A., McKersie, R., & Adler, P. (2009). *Healing together: The labor-management partnership at The Kaiser Permanente.* Ithaca, NY: Cornell University/ILR Press; McKersie, R. B., Sharpe, T., Kochan, T., Eaton, A., Strauss, G., & Morgenstern, M. (2008). Bargaining theory meets interest-based negotiations: A case study. *Industrial Relations, 47,* 66–96.

54. Ostrowsky, J. (2005). *Union-management cooperation: Can a company move from an adversarial relationship to a cooperative relationship and is interest-based bargaining a necessary condition to do so?* Schmidt Labor Research Center Seminar Research Series, University of Rhode Island.

55. *Ibid.*

56. Katz, H. C., Kochan, T. A., & Colvin, A. J. S. (2008). *An introduction to collective bargaining & industrial relations,* 3rd ed. New York: McGraw-Hill.

57. Lane. R. (2011, February 28). With membership bottoming out, what does the future hold for unions? *Bloomberg BNA.* Retrieved December 12, 2011, from http://hr.bna.com/hrrc/2130/split_display.adp?fedfid=19692028&vname=hrrnotallissues&fn=19692028&jd=a0c6j3r3t2&split=0

58. *Ibid.*

59. Wagner, S. (2010). Unions as partners: Expanding the role of organized labor in workforce development. *National Fund for Workforce Solutions,* November. Retrieved March 25, 2017, from http://www.jff.org/publications/unions-partners-expanding-role-organized-labor-workforce-development

60. Nabatchi, T., & Bingham, L. B. (2010). From postal to peaceful: Dispute systems design in the USPS REDRESS® program. *Review of Public Personnel Administration, 30,* 211–234.

61. See http://caselaw.lp.findlaw.com/scripts/getcase.pl?court=US&vol=420&invol=251 for the U.S. Supreme Court decision.

62. Cotton, J. L., & Tuttle, J. M. (1986). Employee turnover: A meta-analysis and review with implications for research. *The Academy of Management Review, 11,* 55–70.

63. Wagner, S. (2010). Unions as partners: Expanding the role of organized labor in workforce development. *National Fund for Workforce Solutions,* November. Retrieved March 25, 2017, from http://www.jff.org/publications/unions-partners-expanding-role-organized-labor-workforce-development

64. Lane. R. (2011, February 28). With membership bottoming out, what does the future hold for unions? *Bloomberg BNA.* Retrieved December 12, 2011, from http://hr.bna.com/hrrc/2130/split_display.adp?fedfid=19692028&vname=hrrnotallissues&fn=19692028&jd=a0c6j3r3t2&split=0

65. Wagner, S. (2010). Unions as partners: Expanding the role of organized labor in workforce development. *National Fund for Workforce Solutions,* November. Retrieved March 25, 2017, from http://www.jff.org/publications/unions-partners-expanding-role-organized-labor-workforce-development; District 1199C Training & Upgrading Fund. (2012). Retrieved March 25, 2017, from http://www.1199ctraining.org/; 1199C Member Benefits. (2017). District 1199C Training & Upgrading Fund. Retrieved March 25, 2017, from http://www.1199ctraining.org/1199c-member-benefits

66. Hirsch, B. T., & Macpherson, D. A. (2003). *Union membership and earnings data book: Compilations from the current population survey.* Bureau of National Affairs.

67. Western, B., & Rosenfeld, J. (2011). Unions, norms, and the rise in U.S. wage inequality. *American Sociological Review, 76,* 513–537.

68. Fronstin, P. (2011, July 1). The impact of the recession on employment-based health benefits: The case of union membership. EBRI Notes, *32*(7).

69. Pennsylvania AFL-CIO. (2017). Why you need a union. Retrieved March 25, 2017, from http://www.paaflcio.org/?page_id=298; Benefits of union membership. (2017). *Union Plus.* Retrieved March 25, 2017, from https://www.unionplus.org/page/benefits-union-membership

70. Gittell, J. H., von Nordenflycht, A., & Kochan, T. A. (2004). Mutual gains or zero sum? Labor relations and firm performance in the airline industry. *Industrial & Labor Relations Review, 57,* 163–179.

71. Kaiser Permanente. (2017). History of the LMP. Retrieved March 25, 2017, from http://www.lmpartnership.org/about/how-partnership-works/history-lmp

72. Blumner, N. (1998). The role of cooperative structures in workplace transformation. Cornell University. Retrieved March 25, 2017, from http://www.mildredwarner.org/gov-restructuring/special-projects/cooperative

73. Association of Corporate Council. (2012). Works councils in the European Union (EU). Retrieved February 21, 2017, from http://www.acc.com/legalresources/quickcounsel/wciteu.cfm

74. *Ibid.*

75. *Ibid.*

76. Volkswagen's lasting lesson for labor. (2014, February 20). *Bloomberg*, 8.

77. Gimmy, M. A. (2016). A new model for corporate governance? *Labor Law Magazine*, March. Retrieved March 27, 2017, from http://www.laborlaw-magazine.com/2016/12/05/a-new-model-for-corporate-governance/

78. Duhigg, C., & Barboza, D. (2012, January 25). In China, human costs are built into an iPad. *The New York Times*. Retrieved March 25, 2017, from http://www.nytimes.com/2012/01/26/business/ieconomy-apples-ipad-and-the-human-costs-for-workers-in-china.html?pagewanted=all

79. Alden, E. (2012, January 27). Apple, China, labor rights, and U.S. workers. *Council on Foreign Relations*. Retrieved March 25, 2017, from http://blogs.cfr.org/renewing-america/2012/01/27/apple-china-labor-rights-and-u-s-workers/

80. Data from compare countries. (2012). Worker-Participation.eu. Retrieved March 25, 2017, from http://www.worker-participation.eu/National-Industrial-Relations/Compare-Countries?countries%5B%5D=157&countries%5B%5D=290&countries%5B%5D=357&countries%5B%5D=273&countries%5B%5D=346&countries%5B%5D=613&countries%5B%5D=379&countries%5B%5D=302&countries%5B%5D=335&countries%5B%5D=2638&countries%5B%5D=525&countries%5B%5D=313&countries%5B%5D=324&countries%5B%5D=368&countries%5B%5D=2649&countries%5B%5D=602&fields%5B%5D=2&fields%5B%5D=4

81. Federal Labor Relations Authority. (2012). Guidance on developing a labor relations strategic plan. Retrieved March 26, 2017, from https://webcache.googleusercontent.com/search?q=cache:MG2ZBXYJvUQJ:https://www.flra.gov/system/files/webfm/OGC/Guidances/FLRA%2520GC%2520Guidance%2520on%2520Developing%2520a%2520Labor%2520Relations%2520Strategic%2520Plan%2520--%2520FLRAgc.doc+&cd=1&hl=en&ct=clnk&gl=us

82. Kaiser Permanente. (2017). Fast facts about Kaiser Permanente. Retrieved March 25, 2017, from https://share.kaiserpermanente.org/article/fast-facts-about-kaiser-permanente/

83. Kaiser Permanente. (2017). History of partnership. Retrieved March 25, 2017, from http://www.lmpartnership.org/what-is-partnership/history-partnership

84. Kochan, T., Eaton, A., McKersie, R., & Adler, P. (2009). *Healing together: The labor-management partnership at Kaiser Permanente*. Ithaca, NY: Cornell University/ILR Press.

85. Kaiser Permanente. (2017). About our labor management partnership. Retrieved March 25, 2017, from http://www.lmpartnership.org/about-lmp

86. Kaiser Permanente. (2017). How the largest labor management partnership in the nation succeeds in tumultuous times. Retrieved March 25, 2017, from https://share.kaiserpermanente.org/article/labor-day-perspective-largest-labor-management-partnership-nation-succeeds-tumultuous-times/

87. Kaiser Permanente. (2017). About our labor management partnership. Retrieved March 25, 2017, from http://www.lmpartnership.org/about-lmp

88. *Ibid.*

89. Kochan, T., Eaton, A., McKersie, R., & Adler, P. (2009). *Healing together: The labor-management partnership at Kaiser Permanente*. Ithaca, NY: Cornell University/ILR Press.

90. Kaiser Permanente. (2017). About our labor management partnership. Retrieved March 25, 2017, from http://www.lmpartnership.org/about-lmp

91. Kochan, T., Eaton, A., McKersie, R., & Adler, P. (2009). *Healing together: The labor-management partnership at Kaiser Permanente*. Ithaca, NY: Cornell University/ILR Press.

chapter 14

Managing Engagement and Turnover

Learning Objectives

AFTER STUDYING THIS CHAPTER, YOU SHOULD BE ABLE TO:

1 Describe employee engagement, and explain why it is important to organizations.

2 Explain the three types of organizational commitment.

3 Describe the six types of turnover.

4 Describe the three types of involuntary separations.

5 Explain how voluntary turnover can be reduced.

6 Explain why succession management is important.

7 Describe workforce redeployment.

Real World Challenge

Engaging Employees at Allstate

Allstate Insurance Company's execution of its business strategy and ability to achieve its goals rely on its engaged employees. The company depends on employees' skill, dedication, and caring to reinforce its reputation and to best serve its customers.[1] Allstate knows that employee engagement is also critical to the innovation and continuous improvement required to succeed in its challenging industry.

As one of the largest U.S. insurance companies, Allstate employees often help people during their most difficult times. Allstate employees are engaged by their work that gives them the opportunity to help others, but the company wants to do more to keep its employees engaged and to align its employees' goals with company objectives. Assume that Allstate asks for your advice on how to keep its employees engaged and focused on the company's goals. What advice would you give them? After reading this chapter, you should have some good ideas.

employee engagement
when employees are committed to, involved with, enthusiastic, and passionate about their work

One of the main goals of human resource management (HRM) is to manage employee engagement, commitment, and turnover. High **employee engagement** occurs when employees are committed to, involved with, and enthusiastic about their work.[2] Employees who are dissatisfied, disengaged, and uncommitted cost their organizations in lower productivity, lost business opportunities, and higher turnover. Mike George, president and CEO of QVC, believes that establishing a workplace culture in which positive values including teamwork and open, honest communication are reinforced enhances employee engagement.[3] A culture of trust is one of the most important drivers of employee engagement, commitment, and retention. Employees in organizations with stronger cultures of trust collaborate better with coworkers, have more energy at work, are more productive, suffer less chronic stress, and stay with their employers longer.[4]

By building trust, managers can give employees the direction and the energy to get their jobs done with extraordinary results. Douglas R. Conant, CEO of Campbell Soup Company, said, "I strongly believe that you can't win in the marketplace unless you win first in the workplace. If you don't have a winning culture inside, it's hard to compete in the very tough world outside . . . You can't ask employees to achieve extraotrdinary results if they're not fully engaged."[5] Conant tracks only two things at the highest level in the company and reports them every year in Campbell's annual report: Total three-year shareowner return and employee engagement.[6] Every employee who participates in the performance management process must include a specific objective regarding engagement.[7]

> *"I strongly believe that you can't win in the marketplace unless you win first in the workplace. If you don't have a winning culture inside, it's hard to compete in the very tough world outside . . . You can't ask employees to achieve extraordinary results if they're not fully engaged."*
>
> **—Douglas R. Conant, CEO of Campbell Soup**

There are many types of employee turnover, some of which can actually benefit an organization. Dysfunctional employee turnover can hurt organizational performance if top performers leave and replacement costs increase. Turnover is influenced by employee engagement as well as other factors. When one retailer with over 50,000 employees wanted to reduce its 30 percent annual turnover rate, it created profiles of employees who were both top performers and most likely to remain with the retailer. When new programs were created to attract and retain more people with this profile, the financial gain from the initiative exceeded $10 million.[8]

The Ritz-Carlton has an extraordinary number of engaged workers and extremely low turnover for the luxury hotel industry—a mere 18 percent compared to the industry average of 158 percent for line-level workers, 136 percent for supervisors, and 129 percent for managers. John Timmerman, The Ritz-Carlton's vice president of operations says, "We like turnover to be between 15 and 18 percent because fresh voices are valuable too."[9]

> *"We like turnover to be between 15 and 18 percent because fresh voices are valuable too."*
>
> **—John Timmerman, vice president of operations, The Ritz Carlton**

Employee engagement, commitment, and turnover are influenced by employees' career advancement in the organization. Because succession planning is important to not only getting the right people in the right jobs but also to reducing turnover and increasing engagement, we discuss it in this chapter.

Understanding how to increase employee engagement and commitment will help you to maximize the performance and contribution of your employees. This chapter describes how to use HRM to increase employee engagement and commitment. The pros and cons of different types of turnover are introduced, as well as common causes of turnover. Methods of analyzing the causes of turnover are discussed as well as a variety of retention strategies. Ways of managing involuntary turnover through layoffs, hiring freezes, and early retirement plans as well as through a sound succession management strategy will also be covered. Managing employee engagement, commitment, and turnover influence *effective work processes* in our book's overall model of HRM.

Employee Engagement

Satisfied employees stay longer and are more productive than are unhappy employees. Job satisfaction positively influences job performance even more for employees in complex, professional jobs.[10] Satisfied employees also benefit organizations because job satisfaction increases employees' **organizational citizenship behaviors**, or discretionary behaviors such as helping others that benefit the organization but are not formally rewarded or required as part of the job.[11]

Job dissatisfaction is related to higher absenteeism and turnover, as well as to other withdrawal behaviors including lateness, drug abuse, and grievances.[12] Because of the negative financial and productivity impact of these employee behaviors, improving employees' job satisfaction can be a very good investment.

A satisfied worker is not the same as an engaged worker and may or may not be contributing to his or her full potential. Engagement goes beyond satisfaction to include enthusiasm, passion, and commitment. Scott Irgang, director of labor relations for Pitney Bowes believes that engaged employees "take an active interest in the vision, the productivity and the future growth of the company. They understand how their piece fits in the whole puzzle. They speak well of us, and they mean it."[13]

> *"[Engaged employees] take an active interest in the vision, the productivity and the future growth of the company. They understand how their piece fits in the whole puzzle. They speak well of us, and they mean it."*
>
> —**Scott Irgang, director of labor relations for Pitney Bowes**

If you don't like your coworkers, your boss is mean, and you don't have the resources you need to get your job done, how would you feel? Would you put 100 percent into your work? Feeling respected and seeing how our work matters to the company and to others makes us feel more enthusiastic and engaged. Engaged employees give their full effort to their jobs, often going beyond what is required because they are passionate about the firm and about doing their jobs well. Disengaged workers do not perform at their optimal level because they lack the emotional and motivational connections to their employer that drive discretionary effort. Because disengaged workers feel they *have* to do the work rather than *wanting* to do the work, they generally do only the minimum required to keep their jobs.

A 2017 Gallup survey found that 87 percent of employees are not engaged.[14] This is particularly troubling given that high employee engagement is related to superior business performance. A different survey found that work units in the top quarter of employee engagement outperformed those in the bottom quarter by 10 percent on customer ratings, 22 percent in profitability, and 21 percent in productivity.[15] Work units in the top quarter also experienced lower turnover (25 percent in high-turnover organizations, 65 percent in low-turnover organizations), absenteeism (37 percent), safety incidents (48 percent), and quality defects (41 percent).[16]

Job resources including knowledge, autonomy, and a supportive environment are positively related to engagement.[17] Opportunities for development and personal growth also increase employee engagement.[18] As a manager, it is important to remember that the drivers of

organizational citizenship behaviors discretionary behaviors that benefit the organization but are not formally rewarded or required

so what**?**

Feeling respected and believing that our work matters increases our engagement.

table **14.1**

The Top Drivers of Employee Attraction, Retention, and Engagement[19]

Top Drivers of Attraction	Top Drivers of Retention	Top Drivers of Engagement
Competitive base pay	Base pay/salary	Leadership takes sincere interest in employees' well-being, behaves consistently with organization's core values, and is effective at growing the business.
Job security	Excellent career advancement opportunities	Understanding organization's goals and objectives and how one's job contributes to organizational goal attainment.
Career advancement opportunities	Trust/confidence in senior leadership	Reasonable workload and healthy work/life balance.

employee engagement can differ from the drivers of employee attraction and retention—what attracts people to join an organization is not always the same as what keeps them engaged and keeps them from leaving. Table 14.1 summarizes the different drivers of employee attraction, retention, and engagement.

Engaged employees help to engage customers, which increases a company's financial performance. Engagement expert Benjamin Schneider says, "The effects of employee engagement are seen most quickly in interactions with outsiders. The impact is quicker on customer satisfaction than on longer-term consequences like profits and market share."[20] This chapter's Strategic Impact feature highlights the link between employee and customer engagement.

 # Strategic Impact

Employee and Customer Engagement

Employee and customer engagement ultimately interact to influence financial outcomes.[21] Gallup research shows that companies that score above the 50th percentile on either employee or customer engagement tend to deliver 70 percent higher financial results than companies that score poorly on both measures, but companies scoring above the 50th percentile on *both* employee and customer engagement measures outperform companies below the 50th percentile on both measures by 240 percent.[22]

Rather than simply using employee engagement surveys to take employees' temperature, Starwood Hotels and Resorts Worldwide links employee engagement metrics with customer satisfaction and financial outcomes to understand how employee engagement impacts the guest experience. Better understanding how engaged employees affect customer engagement allows Starwood to prioritize its employee initiatives and maximize its business performance.[23]

"The effects of employee engagement are seen most quickly in interactions with outsiders. The impact is quicker on customer satisfaction than on longer-term consequences like profits and market share."

—**Benjamin Schneider, engagement expert**

Employee engagement is important at all levels in the company. There is a thin line between high potential and high performance. Poor managers can easily demotivate and derail an organization's future leaders and star performers through their own disengagement. As one expert put it, "Without competent managers, everything else falls apart. You have to have managers who are engaged."[24]

Engagement can be improved through adopting workplace practices that address supervisory communication, job design, resource support, working conditions, corporate culture, and leadership style.[25] Some of the best ways to enhance employee engagement include:[26]

- Having a quality onboarding experience
- Painting a compelling picture of the future
- Letting employees use their talents
- Ensuring that employees can see that they are making a difference
- Offering clear lines of sight and alignment between what an employee does and the organization's goals
- Enabling frequent and open feedback and communication
- Creating a feeling of community and support
- Treating employees fairly
- Making sure employee feel safe in speaking up
- Providing opportunities for job advancement.

The CEO of Campbell Soup writes personal, handwritten letters to thank and motivate employees every day.[27] Alcoa uses goal setting, feedback, bonuses, and recognition to keep its 60,000 employees engaged. An engagement index measured employees' satisfaction, company pride, intent to stay, and likeliness to refer a friend or a family member to work for the company. Although scores vary across the company's 200 locations in 31 countries, the goal is 81 percent engagement overall.[28]

This chapter's case study describes how REI views the link between employee engagement and organizational performance.

REI understands the important role its employees play in the company's success, and it invests in keeping them engaged, healthy, and happy. At this REI location, employees have a Friday off to enjoy an outdoor pursuit.

Mark Van Scyoc/Shutterstock

CASE STUDY: Engaging Employees at REI

U.S. retail and outdoor recreation services company Recreational Equipment Inc. (REI) has over 12,000 employees, sales over $2.5 billion, and donates nearly 70 percent of its profits back to the outdoor community.[29] REI believes that when its employees feel connected to its core purpose of inspiring, educating, and outfitting people for a lifetime of outdoor adventure and stewardship[30] they stay engaged and more authentically represent REI to the company's customers and communities.[31]

Because employees keep REI's business thriving, the company invests in keeping them engaged, happy, and healthy. REI has an inclusive, welcoming workplace and supports employees with comprehensive pay and benefits, including a retirement plan that doesn't require individual contributions, health care, gear discounts and free gear rentals, and an incentive pay program. REI also rewards employees with Yay Days twice a year—a paid day off for an outdoor pursuit or a stewardship project.[32]

To provide a meaningful, fun, and fulfilling workplace, REI also uses social media to build a positive relationship with its employees. Its online "company campfire" gives employees a voice in the company by allowing employees at all levels to share their thoughts and participate in debates and discussions. Almost half of its employees logged in just the first year it was launched.[33]

The company also hires an independent firm to conduct an annual employee engagement survey that asks for employee feedback on topics including commitment, supervision, customer focus, operational and leadership effectiveness, and communication. In 2015, the survey found that 86 percent of respondents were engaged.[34] Not surprisingly, REI's turnover is well below its industry average, and the company has been voted a Fortune "best company to work for" for 19 consecutive years.[35]

Questions

1. Why might engaged employees improve the customer experience at REI?
2. What can REI managers do to further improve employees' engagement?
3. Do you feel that employee engagement influences your own impressions of stores or your shopping behaviors as a customer? If so, how?

Although some factors are related to engagement in every culture,[36] the drivers of employee engagement can differ across countries. This chapter's Global Issues feature highlights the importance of matching engagement initiatives to local engagement drivers.

 Global Issues

Global Engagement Drivers[37]

Autonomy, feeling valued, trust in leadership, effective communication, career development, and good coworker and manager relationships influence engagement for employees around the world. Nonetheless, global organizations often cannot improve companywide engagement by focusing on a single set of engagement drivers. Although the same factors tend to influence employee engagement in

Continued

all countries, it is important to understand the drivers of engagement at different geographical units and locations to best match engagement initiatives to the most important engagement factors. Different business units, functions, and supervisors create different engagement challenges for employees in different locations.

In addition to the job and the company, national culture can also play a role in employee engagement. The table below compares the top engagement drivers in North America, Latin America, and Asia. Career opportunities is the strongest engagement driver in all three regions. This is not surprising as most employees want to keep their jobs fresh and interesting by learning new skills and advancing their careers. This suggests that organizations around the world can improve employee engagement by building a learning culture and allowing employees to learn new skills and take on new responsibilities when possible.

so what?

Although the same factors tend to influence engagement in all countries, because different engagement factors are most important, it is important to be flexible in the approaches taken to maximize engagement in different locations.

Top Drivers of Engagement in North America	Top Drivers of Engagement in Latin America	Top Drivers of Engagement in Asia
Career opportunities	Career opportunities	Career opportunities
Performance management	Recognition	Employer value proposition
Reputation	Pay	Recognition

Organizational Commitment

Organizational commitment is the extent to which an employee identifies with the organization and its goals and wants to stay.[38] Employees can feel committed to an employer in three ways:

1. **Affective commitment**: A positive emotional attachment to the organization and strong identification with its values and goals. Employees of an animal shelter may be affectively committed to the organization because of its goal of finding good homes for all pets. Affectively committed employees stay with an organization *because they want to*.
2. **Normative commitment**: Feeling obliged to stay with an organization for moral or ethical reasons. An employee whose expensive surgery was just enabled by an employer's health plan and work leave policy might feel a moral obligation to stay with the employer for at least a few years to repay the debt. Normatively committed employees stay with an organization *because they feel they should*.
3. **Continuance commitment**: Staying with an organization because of perceived high economic (leaving would mean losing valuable stock options) and/or social costs (coworker friendships) involved with leaving. Continuance commitment leads employees to stay with an organization *because they feel that they have to*.

These three types of organizational commitment are not mutually exclusive. It is possible to be committed to an organization in affective, normative, and continuance ways at the same time, to different degrees. Every employee has a "commitment profile" that reflects high or low levels of all three types of organizational commitment at a specific time.[39] Different profiles have different effects on workplace behavior such as job performance, absenteeism, and the likelihood of quitting.[40]

organizational commitment
the extent to which an employee identifies with the organization and its goals and wants to stay with the organization

affective commitment
a positive emotional attachment to the organization and strong identification with its values and goals

normative commitment
feeling obliged to stay with an organization for moral or ethical reasons

continuance commitment
staying with an organization because of perceived high economic and/or social costs involved with leaving

Burnout

so what

Taking regular vacations and maintaining work–life balance can help prevent burnout.

The opposite of engagement might be thought of as employee burnout.[41] **Burnout** refers to "exhaustion of physical or emotional strength or motivation usually as a result of prolonged stress or frustration."[42] Some organizations stay vigilant for the signs of possible employee burnout and take proactive steps to prevent it. Boston Consulting Group tries to identify employees who may be putting in so many hours that they are at risk of burning out. Managers help these team members better balance their workload, prioritize goals, and stay focused on delivering to the client rather than working long hours.[43] Because one thing that burned-out executives usually have in common is that they never took vacation,[44] PricewaterhouseCoopers tracks employees who have not taken enough vacation, sending them and their supervisor reminders that they should do so.[45]

Job demands including safety risks and complexity impair employees' health and positively relate to burnout.[46] Employees' perceptions of organizational respect can also influence burnout. If employees perceive that they or other employees are not treated with respect or dignity, burnout can occur through demoralization.[47] If disrespected employees need to mask their emotional reaction regarding how their organization treats them while they assist clients, this masking and suppressing could increase emotional exhaustion, a major component of burnout. Employees who feel respected by their organizations are more likely to expend genuine effort on the company's behalf and be less likely to experience burnout.[48]

To best help yourself and your employees, it is a good idea to learn to recognize the symptoms of burnout. Frequently canceling social activities because of work, rarely taking a vacation, rarely engaging in any hobbies or activities you used to enjoy, and constantly checking your smartphone are signs that you are on the road to burnout.[49] Table 14.2 describes some of the physical and behavioral signs of burnout as well as some of the effects burnout has on work performance.

Learning to recognize the signs of burnout and how to take proactive steps to prevent it can help you be a more effective employee and manager. Fatigue, headaches, and irritability are all signs that an employee is at a high risk for burnout.

One of the best ways of reducing the risk of employee burnout is to create a supportive organizational environment. This also helps all employees manage the negative aspects of stress. In addition, delegating, setting clear priorities and goals for both work and life activities, and taking vacations or even days off work to rejuvenate can help you stay engaged in your job.

table **14.2**

Burnout Symptoms

Burnout symptoms tend to fall into the three categories of physical symptoms, behavioral changes, and work performance.		
Physical Symptoms	**Behavioral Changes**	**Work Performance**
Fatigue	Emotional outbursts	Lower performance
Weight loss or gain	Irritability	Decreased initiative
Low energy	Sarcasm	Indifference
Headaches	Depersonalization	

table **14.3**

Turnover Benefits and Costs

Turnover Benefits	Turnover Costs
Creating promotion or transfer opportunities for other employees	Managing the employee's transition (supervisor's and HR representative's time)
Savings from not replacing the departing employee	Recruiting, hiring, and training a replacement worker
Better performance or customer service	Loss of clients
Acquiring new skills and competencies	Teamwork disruptions
Acquiring a better team player and corporate citizen	Lower production or work quality until a replacement is hired and up to speed
	Lower employee morale

Turnover

Employee turnover has both costs and benefits, as summarized in Table 14.3. The organization experiences direct costs due to managing the employee's transition and recruiting, hiring, and training a replacement worker. In 2016, the average cost to hire, orient, and train a new employee was $4,129.[50] Indirect costs may also occur, including a loss of clients, teamwork disruptions, diminished production or work quality until a replacement is hired and up to speed, and lowered employee morale. The average time it took to fill an open position in 2016 was 42 days.[51] Possible benefits of employee turnover include the creation of a promotion or a transfer opportunity for another employee, savings from not replacing the departing employee, better performance or customer service, the acquisition of new skills and competencies from hiring a replacement worker, and the acquisition of a better team player and corporate citizen.[52]

In addition to internal promotions and transfers, which also create vacancies, there are six primary ways of classifying turnover.[53] **Voluntary turnover** occurs when an employee chooses to leave the organization for personal or professional reasons. Voluntary turnover methods include a written or verbal resignation, not reporting for work as assigned, or retiring. External factors including high unemployment rates can influence voluntary turnover. If it is difficult to find another job, employees are less likely to leave. In 2016, the average employee tenure was eight years, and the average annual voluntary turnover rate was 11 percent.[54] **Involuntary turnover** occurs when the organization asks an employee to leave due to factors including poor performance, restructuring, downsizing, or a merger or acquisition.

Functional turnover is the departure of poor performers. **Dysfunctional turnover** is the departure of effective performers the company would have liked to retain.

Avoidable turnover is turnover that the employer could have prevented by addressing the cause of the turnover. Causes of avoidable turnover include low pay, job stress, and poor work–life balance. **Unavoidable turnover** is turnover that could not have been prevented by the employer, such as resignations due to family needs, serious illness, or death. Organizations generally try to minimize turnover that is voluntary, dysfunctional, and avoidable. Table 14.4 summarizes the different turnover types.

Optimal Turnover

Optimal turnover is not necessarily no turnover. Rather, it is the turnover level producing the highest long-term levels of productivity and business improvement.[55] Achieving optimal turnover means understanding both the financial gains and costs of different types of turnover

involuntary turnover
the separation is due to the organization asking the employee to leave

voluntary turnover
the separation is due to the employee's choice

 so what**?**

Not all turnover is bad—the turnover of low performers can benefit the organization.

functional turnover
the departure of poor performers

dysfunctional turnover
the departure of effective performers

avoidable turnover
turnover that the employer could have prevented

unavoidable turnover
turnover that the employer could not have prevented

optimal turnover
the turnover level producing the highest long-term levels of productivity and business improvement

table **14.4**

The Six Types of Turnover

Type of Turnover	Description
Voluntary	The employee chooses to leave for personal or professional reasons.
Involuntary	The employer discharges the employee due to poor performance, misconduct, or reorganization.
Functional	The departure of a poor performer that could benefit the organization.
Dysfunctional	The departure of a successful employee who the company would have liked to retain.
Avoidable	Preventable turnover (e.g., turnover due to a lack of promotion opportunities).
Unavoidable	Unpreventable turnover (e.g., turnover due to the relocation of the employee's spouse).

and controlling who stays and who leaves. Losing a high-performing employee could cost substantial lost revenue and future leadership talent, but losing a low-potential, poor performer creates the opportunity for a higher performing replacement. Employees and customers feel the effects of dysfunctional turnover on a daily basis in the form of inexperienced coworkers, more accidents, and lower quality and productivity.[56] Turnover consequences can only be understood by comparing the cost and productivity of the former employee with the cost and productivity of the replacement employee.[57]

?so what

Because most turnover occurs during the first few months on the job, socialization and early support can improve retention.

Because most turnover occurs during the first few months on the job, helping new employees adjust to the company and to their job can increase retention.[58] Because organizations have little opportunity to recover their investment in new employees who quit, newcomer turnover is problematic and expensive. Retention has become a strategic issue for many companies because it is their biggest constraint to growth.[59]

Although many managers are satisfied with simply minimizing turnover and measuring it against broad industry benchmarks, others have mastered turnover as a tool for achieving a maximum return on their investment in their workforce. Applebee's restaurant chain recognizes that not all turnover has the same value. Instead of rewarding managers for keeping overall turnover low, managers are rewarded for keeping turnover low among top-performing employees. Applebee's divides its hourly employees into the top 20 percent, the middle 60 percent, and the bottom 20 percent of performers. Applebee's knows that the loss of a top 20 percent hourly employee costs the company an average of $2,500, the loss of a middle 60 percent employee costs $1,000, and the loss of a bottom 20 percent employee actually *makes* the company $500. Accordingly, the company doesn't set retention goals for the bottom 20 percent. Applebee's developed its own Web-based software program that lets everyone from top executives to individual store managers identify their best employees and determine how well managers are doing at retaining them.[60]

Tracking turnover by tenure is also useful. For many companies, new hire turnover is much lower once employees make it past the two-year mark. Many high-performing sales companies find that salesperson turnover in the first year or two serves as a natural filter for low performers because new hires who are unable to meet aggressive sales goals actually self-select out of the organization. The sales professionals who remain are likely to have high productivity and long-term success with the company.[61] The appropriate timeframe for tracking new-hire turnover varies by job and by industry. In high-turnover industries such as retailing, one month might be an appropriate time for assessing new hire length of service. Healthcare organizations often use a 90-day period, and other industries use six-month or one-year measures.[62]

Misconceptions about voluntary turnover can lead managers and organizations to utilize ineffective retention strategies or strategies that retain the wrong employees while chasing out the best talent. It is important to remember that people tend to quit because they are dissatisfied with their jobs rather than because they are unhappy with their pay; managers can influence turnover through their behaviors as well as through training, rewards, and better hiring practices; and no single retention strategy is most effective in all situations.[63] Analyzing the causes for and types of turnover taking place enable more targeted and effective retention strategies. Table 14.5 summarizes what we have learned from research on turnover.

table **14.5**

Five Common Misperceptions About Voluntary Employee Turnover[64]

	Turnover Misconceptions	Evidence-Based Perspective
#1	All turnover is the same, and it's all bad.	• There are different types of turnover. • Some turnover is functional. • Turnover costs vary.
#2	People quit because of pay.	• Pay level and pay satisfaction are relatively weak predictors of individual turnover decisions. • Turnover intentions and job search are among the strongest predictors of turnover decisions. • Key attitudes such as job satisfaction and organizational commitment are relatively strong predictors. • Management/supervision, work design, and relationships with others are also consistent predictors.
#3	People quit because they are dissatisfied with their jobs.	• Job dissatisfaction is the driving force in fewer than half of individual turnover decisions. • There are multiple paths to turnover decisions. • Different paths have different retention implications. • It is also important to consider why people stay.
#4	There is little managers can do to directly influence turnover decisions.	• There are evidence-based human resource practices associated with turnover. • Recruitment, selection, and socialization practices during organizational entry affect subsequent retention. • Managers can influence the work environment and turnover decisions through training, rewards, and supervisory practices.
#5	A simple one-size-fits-all retention strategy is most effective.	• Context-specific evidence-based strategies are more effective. • Turnover analysis helps diagnose the extent to which turnover is problematic. • Organizational context matters for interpreting turnover data. • Multiple data collection strategies enable more targeted and effective retention strategies.

Involuntary Employee Separations

Not all employees work out, creating a need for involuntary employee separations. Downsizing, layoffs, and terminations are the most common reasons for involuntary employee separations.

downsizing
a permanent reduction of multiple employees intended to improve the efficiency or effectiveness of the firm

Downsizing.   **Downsizing** is a permanent reduction of multiple employees intended to improve the efficiency or the effectiveness of the firm.[65] Downsizing can improve a firm's financial standing by reducing and changing the workforce structure in a way that improves operational results.[66] Downsizing is usually done in response to a merger or acquisition, revenue or market share loss, technological and industrial change, new organizational structures, or inaccurate labor demand forecasting. Private sector employers often downsize to reduce costs, maximize shareholder returns, and remain competitive in an increasingly global economy. Public sector downsizings are typically driven by budget reductions and technology improvements that allow fewer workers to do the same amount of work.[67]

When used as a component of an overall reengineering or restructuring strategy, downsizing can be effective. However, downsizing does not always achieve its intended goals. One survey of restructuring practices among 531 large companies revealed that although well over half the companies surveyed achieved their goal of reducing costs and expenses, less than half achieved their goals of increased profitability, productivity, and customer satisfaction.[68] In one case of which we are aware, a unionized technology services company intending to pursue a low-cost strategy emerged from a downsizing with a significantly above-market labor cost due to the retention of many longer-term, higher-paid employees because of the union contract. Its higher labor cost interfered with its ability to execute its strategy of offering the lowest price. During the two years following a merger or acquisition, employees of both the acquired and acquiring companies are more likely to leave their positions than employees not affected by such an event. One study of 32,000 employees identified a 46 percent chance of departure for employees of an acquired company and 39 percent for the workforce of the acquirer.[69]

If the choice of which employees to downsize is not constrained by a collective bargaining agreement (which usually mandate the retention of the longest tenured employees), there are several ways to choose who to target in a downsizing, summarized in Table 14.6.

? so what

If not done strategically, downsizing can hurt an organization's competitiveness.

table **14.6**

Downsizing Targeting Methods

Targeting Method	Description
Across the board	Employees are reduced by the same percentage in all units.
Geographic	Specific locations are targeted for downsizing.
Business based	Only some segments of the business are targeted (e.g., one product line).
Position based	Specific jobs are targeted (e.g., middle managers).
Function based	Specific functions are targeted (e.g., marketing is downsized), usually during an organizational redesign.
Performance based	Poor performers are targeted.
Seniority based	The last people hired are the first downsized.
Salary based	The most highly paid employees are targeted.
Competency based	Employees with the competencies the company expects to need in the future are retained, and employees without those competencies are targeted.
Self-selection	Employees are allowed to self-select out of the company and given inducements including buyouts or early retirement packages to leave.

Workforce planning is an essential part of effective downsizing.[70] Some firms suffer downsizing only to have to upsize a few years later due to nonstrategic decisions, poor forecasting, or new employee competency requirements. Downsizing should begin only after establishing the need for downsizing and creating strategic goals for the reduction. During downsizing, it is important to keep everyone focused on the business strategy by consistently reminding employees that restructuring activities are part of a larger plan to improve the organization's performance. Sharing growth plans and renewal strategies with employees can also decrease anxiety and ease employees' post-downsizing transition.

Downsizing does not always lead to long-term, superior organizational performance or enhanced shareholder value.[71] Fully planning the downsizing and showing consideration for employees' morale and welfare are important to reduce the negative consequences the downsizing has on employees and the company.[72] Unintended outcomes of a downsizing include:

- Increased costs from voluntary turnover, training, and outside consultants
- Reduced shareholder value
- Decreased efficiency due to the loss of expertise
- Reduced morale and motivation (waves of downsizing are the worst)
- Increased absenteeism and turnover of desirable employees due to stress and uncertainty
- A damaged employer reputation.

In addition, when a company's employees take advantage of unemployment insurance, the company's future premiums rise. Companies often have to pay more to attract top talent after downsizing.[73] Given that downsizing is a traumatic event for all employees, the process should be carried out in the most expedient manner possible. Companies often make the mistake of spreading out the downsizing over a period of months and even years. A common yet particularly harmful practice is repeated large-scale downsizing.[74]

Companies often need to address **survivor syndrome**, or the emotional effects downsizing has on surviving employees both during and after a downsizing. The emotional aftereffects of downsizing include fear, anger, frustration, anxiety, and mistrust, which can threaten the organization's survival. Rather than focusing on job performance and business strategy execution, survivors often are preoccupied with whether additional layoffs will occur and feel guilty about retaining their jobs while downsized coworkers are struggling.[75] Employees who survive initial workforce reductions offer suffer job insecurity,[76] leading to a variety of adverse effects including higher turnover,[77] lower commitment and loyalty, and less flexibility among surviving employees.[78] Evidence regarding the effects of layoffs on survivors' productivity is mixed. Although some studies suggest that "survivor's guilt" leads to increased effort,[79] other studies suggest that job insecurity reduces productivity.[80]

Employer assistance during a downsizing takes many forms, including job placement services, career coaching, and skills training.[81] Many large organizations help employees find employment elsewhere in the organization through central processing points that bring together displaced employees and vacant positions. Employers frequently provide résumé coaching, job fairs, and access to office equipment to facilitate employee transitions out of the company.

Layoffs.   A **layoff**, also known as a reduction in force, is a temporary reduction of employees. Unlike downsizing, which is a permanent separation of employees, the company intends to rehire laid off employees when business picks back up. Employers tend to dislike layoffs compared to other downsizing methods, in part because they are forced by law (in the case of most public sector employees) or by bargaining agreements to employ seniority-based criteria in deciding which employees to separate during layoffs. Retaining the longest-tenured employees does not guarantee that the right competencies will remain in the company to allow it to execute its business strategy and emerge from the downsizing in a more competitive position, and it often means the retention of the most expensive employees.

survivor syndrome
the emotional effects of downsizing on surviving employees both during and after a downsizing

so what?

Downsizing is difficult for both the separated employees and the survivors.

layoff
temporary reduction of employees

Layoffs are also difficult on survivors and have been found to increase employee health problems and withdrawal behaviors.[82] Layoffs often have a negative impact on employee diversity because seniority-based layoff policies disproportionately affect women and minorities. During a layoff, career transition assistance is usually provided to employees along with job placement and training assistance, severance pay, and continuation of benefits such as health insurance for a certain period.

The negative effect of layoffs on a firm's reputation is significantly stronger for younger firms.[83] A layoff should not discriminate against any protected group (e.g., the layoff should not have an adverse impact based on age, sex, or race). In addition to EEOC compliance, the Age Discrimination in Employment Act applies to layoffs as does the Worker Adjustment and Retraining Notification Act (or WARN Act). The WARN Act is a federal law requiring employers of 100 or more full-time workers to give employees 60 days advance notice of closing or major layoffs.[84]

Rather than layoffs, it is sometimes possible to *redeploy* targeted employees to other parts of the company or to other jobs the company needs filled. Redeploying workers from an area in which they are no longer needed to an area that is experiencing a talent shortage can reduce the need to downsize any employees. *Cross training* employees in different skills and jobs can better enable their redeployment.

Additional ways to avoid the need for layoffs include *reducing work hours*, *reducing pay* so that all employees share the pain but no one loses a job, *sharing ownership* by reducing employees' pay but giving them company stock, and relying on *temporary employment* and *contract employment* arrangements so that core employees' jobs are protected and the temporary and contract workers are hired and let go as needed. Companies including Wegmans Food Markets, The Container Store, Scripps Health, and Aflac have never conducted a layoff.[85]

Ethical Downsizing and Layoffs.   For ethical reasons, companies should always have a working plan of how to conduct downsizing in a way that is consistent with the company's values and business strategy in case this becomes necessary on short notice. One expert believes that "A downsizing plan should be included in the strategic management plan of all organizations, regardless of whether they plan to downsize or not. By including such a plan, the organization will be better prepared to begin the staff-reduction process should it be forced to do so in response to environmental changes"[86] Having clear policies and procedures set up in advance makes it easier to do the right thing when downsizing is imminent.

Given the traumatic nature of downsizing, every communication and action should be consistent with the firm's values. If showing employees respect and communicating openly are important values, these become particularly important during downsizing. What and how the company communicates with separated employees sends a strong message about how it will treat the people who are staying and how it will treat outside stakeholders as well. In addition to the increased workload for survivors, a layoff or downsizing risks damaging an organization's reputation as a company and as an employer. It can take years to build a strong reputation that a single layoff can quickly damage. When downsizing is used as a strategic intervention as part of a broader strategic plan, it is generally perceived as a legitimate business practice. Nonetheless, a tarnished corporate reputation can produce dramatic effects throughout an organization's stakeholders, eventually decreasing an organization's market share and profitability.[87]

Perceptions of fairness are important during any type of downsizing. When people feel personally mistreated or underappreciated during a layoff, they tend to view the layoff as unfair even if they receive a favorable outcome such as a large severance package. As Professor Laurie Barclay said, "When people feel disrespected, it doesn't matter what outcome you give them — they are still going to experience anger and hostility."[88] When Intel cut 11 percent of its U.S. workforce, it gave many of them a minimum of six weeks' pay, up to 48 weeks of severance pay based on years of service, additional health insurance coverage, and six months of career transition service if they agreed to sign a separation agreement.[89]

so what

To minimize negative consequences, perceptions of fairness should be maximized during a downsizing.

"When people feel disrespected, it doesn't matter what outcome you give them — they are still going to experience anger and hostility."

—**Professor Laurie Barclay**

Table 14.7 summarizes some best practices in downsizing.

Terminations.   Rather than separating multiple employees as happens with downsizing or layoffs, **termination** is the permanent separation of a single employee. Although not a favorite part of the job for most managers, it is an essential part of HRM and organizational effectiveness. Discharging may happen immediately after a policy violation or other job misconduct (e.g., a safety violation or failure to report to work), or after a long pattern of poor performance. Most organizations use some form of progressive discipline for poor performers to give them a chance to improve. The typical progression of steps in progressive discipline is:

termination
the permanent separation of a single employee

1. Verbal warning
2. Written warning
3. Suspension
4. Discharge

table **14.7**

Best Practices in Conducting a Downsizing

Here is a summary of some of the best ways to conduct a downsizing:

- *Avoid harming your employer brand:* Treat departing employees respectfully.

- *Enable two-way communication:* Employees want honest and open communication of what is happening to the organization during downsizing. Management should listen to employees and communicate with them as frequently as possible.

- *Involve the right people in downsizing planning:* Senior leadership, human resource executives, and labor representatives all play key roles in strategic downsizing planning.

- *Identify and eliminate any work processes that will not be needed:* This helps protect those processes that are key to the organization's future.

- *Utilize incentives such as early retirement and buyouts:* Early retirement incentives allow employees to retire with either full or reduced pension benefits earlier than normal; buyouts provide a lump-sum payment to employees in exchange for their leaving the organization voluntarily. Both are popular with employees.

- *Try to retain the top talent the organization will need in the future:* Try to ensure the departure of only low-performing employees whose skills will not be critical to the organization in the future.

- *Provide career transition assistance:* Assistance can include career counseling, personal counseling, career/skill and career transition training, relocation assistance, outplacement assistance, résumé writing assistance, access to office equipment, paid time off, child care, financial counseling, and access to job fairs and Internet job placement sites.

- *Monitor progress:* Periodically review procedures, learn from mistakes and successes, and incorporate what is learned into downsizing procedures to allow the process to be completed more effectively.

- *Attend to the survivors:* The success or the failure of a downsized organization depends on the surviving workforce. A well-planned and managed downsizing process, which survivors perceive as having been fairly and respectfully administered, promotes trust and a belief in the future of the organization and empowers survivors.

separation agreement
a legal agreement between an employer and employee that specifies the terms of any employment termination

It is important to document the discharge and keep thorough and accurate records regarding the cause.[90] Having discharged (or downsized) employees sign a **separation agreement** that includes a release stating that the departing employee gives up some or all rights to sue can reduce the risk of future litigation. A separation agreement is a legal agreement between an employer and an employee that specifies the terms of any employment termination.[91] Separation agreements are not required by law and are used most often when a company does not have proper documentation to fire an employee but wants to end the employment relationship and reduce the possibility of a lawsuit or when the company wants to protect confidential information.[92] Legal counsel should be involved in writing any separation agreement. To be most effective:

- The agreement should include some sort of consideration, usually money beyond any standard severance agreement.
- The employee needs to be given appropriate time to consider the offer and even change his or her mind after signing it.
- The employee should be able to negotiate some of its contents to show that it was willingly signed.

so what

Avoid making a termination decision during an argument.

As is the case with downsizing, discharge decisions should be well thought out (rather than made emotionally in the heat of an argument). To reduce negative employee reactions, provide opportunities for employees to correct problems prior to taking action whenever possible, and clearly communicate and document job expectations and company policies. Asking employees to sign that they have read and understand important company policies is also helpful.

 # Develop Your Skills

Discharging Tips

Like it or not, at some point you will probably have to discharge someone. Your main task during a termination meeting is to be clear in letting the employee know they are being terminated and reduce the employee's desire to pursue any lawsuit against the company. Here are some tips to help you conduct a discharging meeting professionally and effectively:

- Remain respectful, impartial, and in control of the conversation at all times.
- Listen to employee requests for severance terms, but make final decisions later; being heard and considered will increase the employee's perceptions of fairness.
- Do not send mixed messages.
- The shock of being fired can prevent the employee from listening to all of what you are saying; be clear and repeat yourself if you feel your message is not being heard.
- If the person is being terminated, do not say "laid off" because it implies the possibility of return.
- Hold the meeting in a private, neutral location.
- Be empathetic, but do not apologize or say that a mistake is being made.
- Discuss the effective termination date and any severance package; have the details of the termination and any severance package in writing so the employee can take them with him or her.
- Be aware of legal compliance issues.
- Write up an accurate record of the termination interview, and provide a copy to the employee.
- Notify all relevant parties after discharge that the employee has been terminated.

When an employee is being told that he or she is being discharged, the goal is to be respectful but clear in letting him or her know that he or she has been terminated and why. Respect and fairness are critical to how the employee reacts to the news. One study found that of those who felt they had been treated with dignity during termination, less than 0.4 percent filed wrongful termination claims. Of those who felt they were treated "very unfairly," over 15 percent filed claims.[93]

All relevant facts about the employee's dismissal should be described. Explain how the employee failed to meet job requirements or violated company policy, and review past opportunities to address these problems. Give the employee a written letter outlining the date of discharge, any contractual obligations owed to the employee (e.g., severance package or continuing benefits), and the name of the manager who approved the discharge. Send copies of this letter to the discharged employee's immediate supervisor, payroll and benefits department, compliance officers, any labor organization to which the employee belongs, and the employee.

Some common discharging errors include doing it publicly, writing a positive letter of reference after a termination for cause (this opens the company to charges of negligent referral), trying to document a discharge for a just cause case that doesn't exist, firing an employee after a merit raise or favorable performance review, and stating that the person conducting the discharge meeting disagrees with the discharge. This chapter's Develop Your Skills feature provides some tips for effectively discharging an employee.

Termination checklists can help to ensure that the many details involved in an employee separation are completed efficiently. A sample termination checklist is shown in Figure 14.1.

figure **14.1**

Termination Checklist

Employee Name:	Employee Number:
Date of Separation:	

For an Involuntary Termination

[   ] Documentation of performance issues and any disciplinary actions are in the employee's file.

Prior to Employee's Last Day

[ ] Calculate any severance pay and pay owed for unused sick time or vacation days	[ ] Prepare the termination letter
[ ] Prepare final paycheck	[ ] Prepare COBRA letter
[ ] Schedule exit interview	[ ] Cancel stock options
[ ] Schedule e-mail and voicemail cancellation for end of employee's last day; forward both to another account for monitoring	[ ] Pay final expense report
[ ] Schedule cancellation of employee ID and parking access card for end of employee's last day	[ ] Cancel corporate credit card and check final statement

On Employee's Last Day

[ ] Present and explain COBRA letter	[ ] Obtain signed nondisclosure and/ or noncompete agreements
[ ] Collect keys, ID cards, company smartphone, computer, and other company property	[ ] Present last paycheck [ ] Mail last paycheck (date mailed: _____)
[ ] Exit interview (or date performed by phone: _____)	[ ] Verify address
[ ] Retrieve any company documents	[ ] Remove access to internal and external company databases and systems

Continued

| [ ] Communicate departure to relevant employees | [ ] Update status in the HRIS system |
| [ ] Execute retirement account transfer or mail payout check as requested by departing employee | [ ] Ensure the removal of all of the departing employee's personal belongings |

After the Employee Separates

| [ ] Check next company credit card statement for any charges | [ ] Mail final pay stub |
| [ ] Stop benefits coverage | [ ] Monitor e-mail and voicemail messages and route to appropriate staff |

Reason for leaving:

Separation date:

Employment at Will

Employment at will is an employment relationship in which the employment relationship can be legally terminated by either party at any time for just cause, no cause, or even a cause that is morally wrong as long as it is not illegal. Employment at will also allows an employee to quit for any reason. In most states, if an employment relationship is not covered by a formal contract, then it is governed by employment at will.

Although the courts generally have upheld companies' right to terminate at will, it is best not to terminate an employee without giving a reason or without following normal policies and procedures. Following formal discipline and termination procedures whenever possible helps to avoid discrimination and wrongful termination claims and protect employee morale. How would you feel coming to work at a company that seemed to fire employees on a whim? Employment at will is best used as a legal defense when it is not in a company's interests to follow their own policies inflexibly.[94] For example, if an employee is strongly suspected of stealing from or even harming clients, it is often best to dismiss her immediately using employment at will. Case law establishing when or if firms can rely on the at-will nature of the relationship varies from state to state.

so what

A union worker is protected by a just-cause provision in the union contract, which supersedes any state-granted employment-at-will employer termination rights.

Employment at will does not give an employer total protection for all employee discharges. Written employment contracts override employment-at-will provisions. Union contracts' "just cause" clauses also protect most unionized workers from arbitrary terminations and prohibit employers from firing workers unless they can show that a person should reasonably (due to "a just cause") be terminated. Some federal laws, including the National Labor Relations Act, also protect employees from being retaliated against—fired or disciplined, for example—for engaging in a protected activity such as opposing unlawful employer practices, or filing a valid workers' compensation claim, regardless of an employee's at-will status.

Certain state laws also limit employment-at-will provisions. Most states recognize that an implied employment contract exists between employers and employees that creates an exception to at-will employment. An implied employment contract occurs when an employer's personnel policies, handbooks, or other materials indicate that it will only fire an employee for good cause or specify a procedural process for firing. If an employee is fired in violation of an implied employment contract, the employer may be found liable for breach of contract.

The best way to ensure that an employment-at-will message has been adequately communicated to employees is by publishing the policy on something employees sign. Signing an employment application or to acknowledge reading an employee handbook produces a written record that an employee has read and understood the policy.

Employee Retention

Reducing voluntary turnover among the best employees improves organizational effectiveness and efficiency. Understanding why desirable employees are leaving can help an organization best target its retention efforts.

Understanding Why Employees Leave

There are many reasons people choose to leave organizations, including the desirability and ease of leaving.[95] Poorly defined job duties and unrealistic performance goals are also related to turnover, as are job characteristics associated with satisfaction, motivation, and job involvement.[96] In addition to being lured by other opportunities that provide more challenge or career development, people also leave jobs due to low pay and benefits, a lack of recognition, not having their voice heard, perceiving unfairness, and not being given professional growth opportunities.[97] Although some studies have shown that poor performers are more likely to quit than good performers,[98] other research has found that the best performers may be more likely to leave because they have better opportunities to pursue.[99]

After reducing employee benefits during the recent recession, many organizations are increasingly recognizing the importance of employee recognition and rewarding employees for their achievements.[100] Recognition for performance achievements, peer-to-peer recognition, and above-and-beyond performance recognition are increasingly common. Employee recognition can be as simple as a certificate or e-card or more formal manager recognition or award. As a nonprofit, the San Diego Zoo managed costs by trading zoo tickets for goods and services from local businesses that resonated with its employees.[101]

One key factor in voluntary turnover is the economic climate. Although top performers are usually at risk of being courted by other companies, if the economy is good and jobs are plentiful, retaining all employees is more difficult. When the economy is softer and fewer organizations are hiring, it is harder for employees to leave, and turnover rates are usually lower.

Voluntary turnover is difficult to reduce unless we know what is causing it. Because it is not uncommon for employers to focus their retention efforts on things that are less important to employees,[102] it is important for organizations to make an effort to understand why desirable employees are leaving. Because there are so many reasons why people quit their jobs, it can be helpful to conduct **exit interviews** to ask former employees why they left. These interviews can be used to improve conditions for current employees and reduce future turnover.

Technology can facilitate the exit interview process. Departing employees can be e-mailed and asked to take an online exit interview survey. The software allows managers to check exit survey data in real time via a website that tells managers how many surveys have been completed, participation rates, monthly exit statistics, and the top reasons for leaving. The system also allows managers to explore the reasons for leaving, including accessing detailed comments written by former or exiting employees.

It is sometimes beneficial to wait before conducting exit interviews. When Johnson & Johnson interviewed people whose loss it identified as dysfunctional to get insight as to why they left their jobs, it learned that people felt much freer in responding honestly when more time had passed. J&J learned that many of those former employees' poor communication with their supervisors did not allow them to understand how valued they were within the company. As a result of those discussions, J&J rehired a lot of its former employees.[103]

Research suggests that the former bosses of departing employees should not conduct exit interviews, especially if they are untrained in conducting them. Employees may be reluctant to discuss poor supervision as a reason for their departure, and supervisors may selectively interpret responses or not hear honest information about reasons for leaving.[104]

Employee satisfaction surveys can help to identify problems and areas of job dissatisfaction that can be addressed and hopefully prevent additional turnover. PricewaterhouseCoopers (PwC)

exit interview
asking separated employees why they left to acquire information that can be used to improve conditions for current employees

so what?

Exit interviews can be more informative if conducted a few weeks or months after an employee leaves.

conducts a comprehensive annual global survey covering individual team, leadership, flexibility, and compensation that is meant to go into every aspect of employees' work lives. After being broken down to the 100-person team level, the results are published and disseminated across the company.[105]

Retention Strategies

Retaining or losing an organization's best employees can influence its strategic ability to maintain a competitive advantage and maintain smoothly running operations.[106] Developing a retention plan that addresses the causes of turnover can improve the retention of critical employees and employees in key positions. In Table 14.8, we summarize some common retention strategies and next discuss them in more detail.

Honesty in Recruiting.   Giving potential employees realistic job previews that communicate potentially undesirable as well as positive aspects of the job and organization (e.g., a need for occasional travel or late hours) during the recruiting process reflects honesty and fairness. Research has found that the effects of a realistic preview on voluntary turnover reduction occur through trust.[107] Because unmet expectations about the job and the organization can lead to dissatisfaction which leads to turnover,[108] realistic job previews increase the likelihood that expectations will be met and can thus reduce subsequent turnover.[109]

Job Challenge.   To successfully compete in the semiconductor industry, Texas Instruments needs the best and brightest employees, but top engineers are hard to find. To maximize employee retention, the company's managers receive training in engaging employees to make sure they feel challenged and appreciated. Managers also regularly consider assignment changes that make the best use of their direct reports' skills, and they continually "re-recruit" their best people, regularly checking to ensure they are being challenged, helping them develop in their jobs, and exposing them to other opportunities that might better use their skills. Nurturing and keeping top employees is even a component of managers' performance reviews. Cross-training programs for employees can also support professional development while reducing turnover.

table **14.8**

Retention Strategies

Honesty in recruiting: Realistic job previews give applicants an honest picture of the job and company, improving trust, and decreasing the interest of people for whom the position would be a poor fit.

Job challenge: Being challenged and learning new things can keep employees engaged.

Higher-quality supervisors: Fair and trusted managers can improve retention.

Flexible work: Work flexibility enables employees to better balance work and life demands.

Location: Locating the company in a desirable area can boost retention.

Pay and benefits: Competitive pay and benefits helps improve retention.

Create accountability: Hold managers accountable for retaining top performers and for challenging and developing their subordinates.

Provide support: Stay in touch with new hires and help them overcome obstacles to performing well and staying with the company.

Create mobility barriers: Embedding employees in the company in such a way that their value is greater inside than outside the firm due to firm specific knowledge decreases the chance that they will leave.

Strengthen the culture: Creating a strong and positive culture can enhance employees' commitment to the company.

Higher Quality Supervisors.   One of the best retention management strategies can be the hiring and development of better bosses. Supervisors have a considerable impact on subordinates' turnover. Creating a climate of respect, fairness, and trust can positively affect employee retention, morale, and even employment liability by reducing stress, increasing commitment to the organization and to their supervisor, and improving performance.[110]

Flexible Work.   Work flexibility can also improve retention. Alternative job arrangements can give employees greater flexibility and help them to balance life and work. Flextime, telecommuting, and letting employees work a compressed work week can help employees better balance work and life responsibilities and make it possible for them to continue working. In 2014, 86 percent of the 2014 Best Companies to Work For offered employees some type of flexible schedule, including working from home at least one day a week. Another 78 percent of the top-ranked companies allowed employees to work a compressed work week, for example four 10-hour days rather than five eight-hour days. Another 51 percent of the 2014 Best Companies offered job sharing arrangements, letting two employees share a single position.[111]

Location.   Locating near companies that employ similar talent can also be strategic. A technology company in Silicon Valley might be able to acquire needed talent easily, and the ease with which employees can switch employers can help it keep its ideas fresh. However, the same risk of high turnover could compromise a research and development company that needs employees to stay with projects for a long time. Establishing a separate long-term research facility in a location where the skills of the team are not in as high demand, such as a rural community, can increase employee retention rates, although initial candidate attraction may be more challenging. Turnover at an Intersil semiconductor facility in rural Pennsylvania averaged only 2 percent, 18 percent lower than the industry average.[112]

Identifying a company location where desired talent is already available or recruiting from areas where desired talent is likely to find relocation to the company's location desirable can both improve staffing effectiveness. When GE had trouble finding people willing to move to "Dreary Erie, Pennsylvania," it began sourcing junior military officers. Previously used to sitting in mud holes, these recruits found the location to be fine. The program was so successful GE soon expanded it throughout the company.[113] Strategically locating a company in an area desirable to employees can also improve retention.

Pay and Benefits.   Competitive pay and benefits help attract and retain employees. However, even if a company has good benefits, if employees don't understand, value, or appreciate them, they are unlikely to influence retention. Consulting firm Watson Wyatt found that companies that offer rich benefits but have poor communication practices had an average 17 percent turnover rate for top-performing employees. Companies that offered less costly benefits but successfully communicated them had an average top talent turnover rate of 12 percent. The best situation, combining rich benefits with effective communication, was associated with an even lower 8 percent turnover rate for top performers.[114] A pay-for-performance plan can also help reduce turnover among top performers and improve the company's return on what it pays employees.[115]

Create Accountability.   Holding managers accountable for retaining top performers and ensuring that their subordinates have a clear and consistently monitored professional growth plan increases the chances that managers will engage in these employee retention behaviors. Evaluating and rewarding managers for meeting retention goals increases their commitment to doing so.

Provide Support.   Helping employees balance work and life and overcome obstacles to employment and job success can promote retention. Asiawide Refreshments Corporation, the Philippine licensed bottler of RC Cola, developed a formal program to acclimate new hires throughout their first 100 days on the job. A "First 100 Days Performance Plan" supports new employees from probation through the first 100 days.[116]

mobility barriers
factors that make it harder to leave an organization

Create Mobility Barriers.   **Mobility barriers** are factors that make it harder for an employee to leave an organization. Mobility barriers can include stock options that vest in the future, requiring employees to stay with the company to receive their full financial value; extensive training in a company's processes and procedures that are unique to that company; or desirable work attributes that competing employers lack.

Mobility barriers other than financial incentives to stay, which can sometimes be matched by other organizations, embed employees in the company in such a way that their value is greater inside than outside the firm due to firm specific knowledge. If the perceived cost of leaving is greater than the expected gain of joining a different organization due to commitment to one's workgroup, team, or company, turnover is less likely.[117]

Strengthen the Culture.   A strong, positive organizational culture may also help retain valued employees, and it is something competitors cannot easily imitate. Companies such as outdoor clothing and equipment company Patagonia, whose goal is to produce the highest-quality products while doing the least possible harm to the environment, have developed values-based companies with mission statements that appeal to recruits and employees alike. The appeal of the corporate culture helps retain employees with similar values.[118] In one survey, 3 out of 5 organizations said that their employee recognition program is also tied to the organization's core values.[119]

 # HR Flexibility

Retaining Employees of Different Generations[120]

	Traditionalists (1900–1945)	*Baby Boomers* (1946–1964)	*Generation X* (1965–1980)	*Generation Y* (1981–2000)
What they value at work:	Loyalty Hard work	Knowledge Years of service	Efficiency Ingenuity	Contribution Uniqueness
Best retention incentives:	Let them utilize their vast expertise and knowledge	Promote based on seniority Make them feel valued for their experience	Development Autonomy Flexible work hours	Development Feedback Appreciation
Overcoming obstacles:	Ask for input Communicate about change Ensure they are in roles that interest them	Have them mentor Generation Y employees to respect and leverage their institutional knowledge Ensure they are in roles that interest them	Encourage work–life balance Offer flexibility Communicate about their expectations and career growth	Provide clear goals and expectations Provide opportunities for development Give opportunities to be involved in other areas of the organization

Organizations must be flexible in the strategies they utilize to retain different employees. For example, as this chapter's HR Flexibility feature illustrates, different approaches tend to work best for different generations.

Managing Succession

Succession management is an ongoing process of systematically identifying, assessing, and developing organizational leadership to enhance performance. Succession management involves ongoing strategic talent planning, retirement and retention planning, and talent assessment and development. **Succession management plans** are written policies that guide the succession management process. Succession management can ensure leadership continuity, prevent key positions from remaining vacant after the incumbent leaves, prevent transition problems, and reduce incidents of premature promotion.

Succession management helps an organization best deploy talent to meet its business goals. In response to changing organizational and employee needs, succession management can identify the current or potential availability of internal organization replacements for key positions.[121] Succession management plans should be put in place before they are needed and can be very good investments. Research consistently finds that chief executives hired from outside the company are paid more than those promoted from within, often substantially more.

Although succession management can expedite the process of replacing a departing employee, employees identified by succession management as candidates for an open position should not be the only employees considered for the job. Information about an opening should generally be disseminated to all employees to give them the opportunity to apply in case some talent is being overlooked. It is obviously not ideal for an employee who would have been interested in a job to not learn of the vacancy and miss the opportunity.

Succession management requires much more than simply identifying which employees might be able to assume a particular position should an opening occur. Effective succession management builds a series of feeder groups up and down the entire leadership pipeline.[122] In contrast, **replacement planning** is narrowly focused on identifying specific back-up candidates for specific positions and does little to improve leadership readiness. Succession management is a key driver of employee retention, and it sends a signal to the firm's stakeholders that the firm's leadership is preparing for the future.[123] Replacement planning is helpful for quickly identifying a possible successor when a position unexpectedly opens.

Succession management should integrate talent management with the organization's strategic plan. Companies must identify and meet talent goals that support the organization's long-term direction, growth, and planned change. Replacements may need different competencies, values, and experiences than incumbents. Strategically managing succession should enable an organization to have the right people in the right place at the right time to execute the business strategy. With the impending retirement of baby boomers and increased demands for diversity, many organizations are building systems that provide talented high performers opportunities to grow.

United Airlines considers feedback from peers, subordinates, and supervisors as well as performance and competency ratings, personal goals, and career aspirations in its succession management system. Potential permanent and interim successors for every leadership position are identified, ensuring no essential job is vacant for long. Employees' competency gaps are addressed with development plans to ensure a broad and diverse pool of future leaders.[124] BIC, a global maker of products including razors, pens, and lighters, believes it is important for its managers to have real-time online access to information on each high-potential employee's development history, goals, and progress to maximize their feedback and development.[125]

If done strategically, succession management can help ensure that at least one internal candidate is able to quickly assume a key position should it become vacant. This can save the

succession management
an ongoing process of systematically identifying, assessing, and developing organizational leadership to enhance performance

succession management plans
written policies that guide the succession management process

replacement planning
identifying specific back-up candidates for specific senior management positions

so what**?**

Succession management should integrate talent management with the organization's business strategy to ensure the availability of the right skills.

organization considerable lost productivity while the position is vacant and the expense of identifying and possibly training a replacement. Succession management also helps retain talented employees who might otherwise leave to pursue higher-level positions at other organizations. Because succession management plans need to be revised as jobs and employees change, it can be a time-consuming process and is typically done only for key positions in the organization.

Best Practices for Succession Management

Fairness and communication openness are critical components of succession management. The process should be impartial, open, and backed by top management. Employees should be able to express an interest in being considered for positions that appeal to them and should not be coerced into pursuing positions in which they are not interested. Not everyone wants to be in a leadership position, and employees pressured into jobs they do not truly want are more likely to leave the organization. Feedback from as many sources as is reasonable (e.g., objective, multirater assessments) should be used in evaluating an employee's skills and candidacy for another position as objectively as possible. Incorporating feedback and creating "buy in" among key constituencies are also important cornerstones of successful succession management systems.

skills inventory
tracks employees'
competencies and
work experiences in a
searchable database

Maintaining **skills inventories** that track employees' competencies and work experiences in a searchable database and nominating employees for consideration for open positions rely on the cooperation and the participation of supervisors who are not always highly motivated to lose their best employees to other positions in the organization. Some managers perceive greater personal rewards for keeping their best people and not nominating them for opportunities elsewhere in the organization. If a manager continually invests time in developing her best subordinates for positions elsewhere in the organization and encourages them to pursue the positions they are interested in, this creates more work for the manager and compromises the performance of her own workgroup by continually cycling out the best-performing members. Some managers may even believe that they are grooming their own successors and hastening their own departure from the organization. Other managers derive intrinsic rewards from developing and mentoring employees to move up in an organization.

Managers' involvement and commitment is critical to the success of the succession management process because their skills assessments, promotability ratings, and development activities are central to succession management. Incentives for managers to do a good job identifying and developing high-potential talent can help secure their commitment. It is important that managers perceive greater rewards in identifying and developing their best talent for other positions in the organization than in keeping them on their own teams.

When Warner-Lambert's human resources senior leadership team prepared a set of principles as part of a redesign of its practices, the first principle stated, "Talent across the company is managed for the larger interests of the company. Our divisions are the stewards of that talent, and company-wide interests prevail."[126] Communicating and reinforcing strong, clear statements of this nature to managers throughout the company improves understanding and buy-in to the idea of talent being the company's rather than a manager's asset. Including succession management in all managers' performance appraisals and tying their development of future leadership talent to financial rewards and promotions also helps align managers' goals with those of the organization.

The succession management process should also align with other human resource processes, including recruitment, selection, rewards, training, and performance management. For example, if the current succession plan for a position indicates that the organization lacks depth in a particular talent, adjustments to the recruitment and selection system can bring more of that talent into the organization. Performance management systems can be modified to assess employees on the competencies they need to be qualified for other positions as well as on their performance in their current jobs. Succession management can help an organization deal with diversity issues and changing demographics by making promotion opportunities more available to a greater number of people in the organization. The best succession plans bridge the gap between individual career development opportunities and long-term business strategy. Because organizations constantly change, succession plans and the succession management process should be continuously reviewed and modified when necessary. The process should be designed to be ongoing, fluid, and adaptable to shifting and emerging contexts.

Some firms prefer to call employees targeted for accelerated development through succession management and career development programs "acceleration pools" rather than "high-potential pools" because the latter term implies that employees not in the pool are not high potential.[127] Because the definition of "high potential" can change as business requirements and goals change, and to avoid alienating employees not labeled "high potential," Internet company Yahoo! avoids calling any employees high potential. The firm's executive training program is offered not only to individuals identified as promotion candidates but to other employees as well. Nonetheless, Yahoo! pays special attention to its stars and focuses on the training and career development of select employees to reduce the chances that these key employees will leave. Leadership potential is also identified through performance reviews and at an annual session held by senior executives.[128]

Continually evaluating the success of a succession management program is important in ensuring its effectiveness at meeting the organization's succession goals. One large organization boasted about its succession management process, but after analyzing the data, it realized that virtually no senior managers ever came out of it. Clearly, some other subjective criteria were being used to determine promotions, which risks demoralizing good employees and increasing their turnover.[129]

Company executives need to both model effective succession management behaviors and hold line managers responsible for developing their subordinates' skills and knowledge (e.g., by including talent development in annual evaluations). However, data suggests that many companies fail to do this. One survey found that nearly half of respondents felt their organization's senior leadership does not align talent management strategies with business strategies and that senior managers do not spend enough time on talent management. Fifty-two percent of the respondents identified line managers' insufficient commitment to developing talent as a critical barrier to effective succession management. Furthermore, 50 percent observed that line managers were unwilling to categorize their people as top, average, or underperforming, and 45 percent felt that line managers failed to deal with chronic underperformance by employees.[130] Many well-designed succession management systems fail to live up to their potential because of a lack of commitment on the part of executives and line managers. Table 14.9 provides some best practices for effective succession management.

Mobility policies specify the rules by which people move between jobs within an organization. A mobility policy should clearly state both employees' and supervisors' responsibilities for employee development. For example, employees may be responsible for identifying the training programs they need to complete to qualify for a desired promotion and requesting from their supervisors the necessary time away from their jobs to complete this training. Supervisors may be responsible for helping their subordinates use and further develop the new skills back on the job, providing accurate assessments of subordinates' readiness for training and promotion opportunities, and for regularly coaching and providing feedback to subordinates.

Mobility policies also clearly document the rules for opening notification, eligibility qualification, compensation and advancement, and benefit changes related to advancement. Mobility policies should be well developed, clearly communicated, and perceived as fair by employees. Not every employee who desires a promotion or wishes to transfer

so what?

Calling participants in accelerated development programs "high potentials" risks alienating employees not in the program.

mobility policies
specify the rules by which people move between jobs within an organization

table **14.9**

Best Succession Management Practices

Here are some experts' recommendations for creating and maintaining an effective succession management system:

- *Keep the process simple.* Make the process logical and simple so that busy line managers do not feel that the process is burdensome.[131]

- *Use technology to support the process.* Technology enables the timely monitoring and updating of developmental needs and activities.[132]

- *Align succession management with overall business strategy.* Top executives and line managers will be more supportive of a system that clearly reinforces corporate goals and objectives.[133]

- *Focus on development.* Succession management must be flexible and oriented toward developmental activities rather than merely a list of high-potential employees and future positions they might fill.[134]

- *Model effective succession management behaviors at the top.* Company executives need to both model effective succession management behaviors and hold line managers responsible for developing their subordinates' skills and knowledge.[135]

- *Approach succession management as a key business activity.* Because of its key role in enabling long-term business strategy execution, succession management should be incorporated into hiring and developing employees as well as assigning them to projects, training, and other development activities.

 so what

Clear and well-communicated mobility policies increase employees' perceptions of promotion fairness.

to a different position will be able to do so, but if the process used to determine eligibility for these opportunities is perceived as fair, employees who do not get promoted are less likely to feel animosity toward the organization and may be more likely to stay with the company.

Redeploying Talent

workforce redeployment
the movement of employees to other parts of the company or to other jobs the company needs filled to match its workforce with its talent needs

Workforce redeployment is the movement of employees to other parts of the company or to other jobs the company needs filled to match the workforce with the organization's talent needs. Companies such as information technology (IT) service firms pursuing a customer intimacy strategy need to have optimal knowledge of their employees' skills and abilities to best match their employees with clients' needs. Software and analytical tools including PeopleSoft and SAS help organizations match their talent to specific business needs in the most profitable way. Software can shorten IT project completion times by using a database of employee competencies to generate staffing solutions to meet current demand and to anticipate priorities and needs for new projects. The deployment of this type of technology by one firm reduced project completion times by 10 to 40 percent and reduced overall resource requirements by 25 to 40 percent.[136]

IBM's Workforce Management Initiative borrows many of the same concepts of supply-chain management, such as capacity planning, supply and demand planning, and sourcing. To manage 100,000 global employees and about as many subcontractors in its IBM Global Services division, it built a structure that outlines internal and external skills and provides a real-time view of IBM's labor-supply-chain activities. The system catalogs skills, creating common descriptors around what people do, what their competencies are, and what experiences and references they have.[137] One global pharmaceutical company uses a labor–supply chain to better catalog its own employees' talents to help it make better decisions about when to use its own employees and when to call in contractors.[138]

Summary and Application

Retaining the right employees and keeping them engaged enhances organizational performance and efficiency. Understanding the different types of turnover and having a variety of retention strategies to deploy as appropriate can keep employees engaged and productive. When separations are necessary, conducting them fairly and attending to the needs of both the departing and surviving employees is important.

Succession management and workforce redeployment help to get the right people in the right place at the right time to execute the organization's business strategy. Both employees and their managers need to be actively involved in succession management. Fair and clearly communicated policies and processes as well as open communication help facilitate employee moves through and out of an organization.

Real World Response

Engaging Employees at Allstate

Allstate takes employee engagement seriously. Allstate's Good Work. Good Life. Good Hands program regularly identifies the linkages between what its employees value and what the company offers in exchange for their work. The company's Employee Life Cycle Survey Program is used to identify how well its various initiatives, programs, and efforts are supporting employee morale. The program includes checking in with new hires after 90 days to assess their integration into Allstate; an annual employee VOICE survey that measures employee engagement, satisfaction, and supervisor effectiveness; and a Good Work Pulse survey conducted several times every year to collect timely data to assess changing employee attitudes and evaluate the success of new initiatives to allow the company to take immediate corrective action when needed. When an employee leaves Allstate, an exit survey is done to determine what the employee found most compelling about Allstate's employee value proposition and why he or she is leaving.[139]

Allstate offers college tuition reimbursement, and its retirement programs also give employees a solid financial foundation.[140] To tie employees' goals to those of Allstate, the company also participates in profit sharing and rewards employees for their performance on customer satisfaction and retention metrics to ensure that customers' needs are put first.[141] Employee recognition programs are also used to enhance engagement. Annual employee excellence awards recognize employees who live up to Allstate's mission and vision, with company leaders presenting the awards on stage in front of spouses or partners.[142]

To enable work–life balance, Allstate offers employees generous paid time off, job sharing and work-at-home programs, and time-saving onsite services including oil changes, ATMs, and a barber shop.[143] Allstate also enhances employee engagement by making its training programs engaging. It revised its standard video training on ethics into a game in which each worker assumes a superhero identity while fighting a data-stealing villain named Data Gator.[144]

Allstate's initiatives are working. The company has received numerous awards and recognition, including being one of the "50 Happiest Companies in America" in 2014 and the "World's Most Ethical Company" in both 2015 and 2016.[145] Allstate Insurance Company of Canada has also been recognized for multiple years as having one of the top employee engagement scores in Canada.[146]

Takeaway Points

1. Employee engagement occurs when employees are committed to, involved with, and enthusiastic about their work. Engaged employees are more productive, enthusiastic, and likely to stay with the organization.

2. Affective commitment is a positive emotional attachment to the organization. Affectively committed employees identify with the organization's values and goals and stay with the organization because they want to. Normative commitment occurs when employees feel that they should stay with an organization for moral or ethical reasons. Continuance commitment occurs when employees stay with an organization because they feel that they have to. If an employee feels that the economic or social costs of leaving the organization would be too high, they are experiencing continuance commitment.

3. With voluntary turnover, the separation is due to the employee's choice. With involuntary turnover, the employee asks the employee to leave. Functional turnover is the departure of poor performers, whereas dysfunctional turnover is the departure of good performers the organization would have liked to retain. Avoidable turnover could have been prevented by the company, whereas unavoidable turnover could not have been prevented. Optimal turnover is the turnover level that produces the highest long-term levels of productivity and business improvement

4. Downsizing is a permanent reduction of multiple employees with the goal of improving organizational efficiency or effectiveness. Layoffs are a temporary reduction of employees. A termination is the permanent separation of a single employee.

5. Voluntary turnover can be reduced by understanding what causes it. Honesty in recruiting, job challenge, quality supervision, flexible work, support, mobility barriers, and a positive culture can all help improve employee retention.

6. If done strategically, succession management can help ensure that at least one internal candidate is able to quickly assume a key position should it become vacant. This can improve productivity and decrease the expense of having the job vacant and identifying and possibly training a replacement. Succession management also helps retain talented employees who might otherwise leave to pursue higher-level positions at other organizations.

7. Workforce redeployment is the movement of employees to other jobs or other parts of the company as needed to best match the workforce to the organization's talent needs.

Discussion Questions

1. Describe a job in which you've felt disengaged. What about the job or organization made you feel this way?

2. Describe a job in which you've felt engaged. What about the job or organization made you feel this way?

3. How do you think the different types of organizational commitment would influence employee motivation, performance, and retention? Which of the four would you most want to enhance in your subordinates, and how would you do it?

4. If you suspected that a coworker was experiencing the early signs of burnout, what could you do?

5. If an organization had to fire you because of low job performance, how would you like to be treated?

6. If you were classified as a middle-tier employee and saw the higher-tier receiving extra training and performance bonus awards, how would you feel? What effect might this have on your own motivation, commitment, and performance? What are the implications of your answer for how organizations should treat their employees?

7. If you were looking for a job, how might you find credible information about what working at different organizations would really be like?

8. How can supervisors enhance the effectiveness of an organization's succession management practices?

Personal Development Exercise: Termination Practice

This exercise will allow you to practice your termination meeting skills. First watch the two videos "How to Negotiate a Severance Package" (2:07) and "Firing—Supervisor Training: First Line of Defense" (2:28).

Now find a partner and decide who will first play the role of the sales employee being fired and who will play the role of the manager doing the firing. Imagine the employee has been working for the manager for five years and despite a strong first couple of years has had declining performance over the past two. The manager has sent the employee for training to try to improve his or her sales skills and assigned him or her a mentor to try to help, but the employee has not improved, and it is time to terminate him or her. The organization's financial performance has declined in the challenging economy and tries to discourage severance packages, although it has paid as much as $5,000 per year of service in the past. The employee currently makes a base salary of $45,000 per year and has two weeks of earned vacation time. Both partners can create reasonable additional details as needed to complete the exercise.

The manager should take the time to think of what to say to the employee being fired and write down anything he or she is willing to offer in a severance package. The employee should think about what he or she would like to negotiate for as a severance package in case attempts at retaining the job fail. Call each other by your first name, and try to be realistic yet don't make it too easy on the manager! When you are done, the employee should give the manager feedback on what was done well and what could be improved. Then switch roles and partners so that you do not repeat the exercise with the same partner. Both partners can create reasonable additional details as needed to complete the exercise.

Strategic HRM Exercises

Exercise: Strategically Managing Retention

Imagine that you work for Lucky Duck, a chain of convenience stores. You have been put in charge of creating your organization's retention policy. The company wants to focus on retaining top cashiers and facilitating the turnover of lower performing cashiers to improve efficiency and customer service. Working alone or in a small group, create a policy that would accomplish this goal. As part of your discussion, identify three exit interview questions, and be ready to explain to the class how you would use this information into a retention strategy for current or future employees.

Exercise: Flying Fish![147]

When John Yokoyama took over Seattle's Pike Place Fish Market, the previous owner's fear-based management style had led to low engagement, high turnover, and bad employee attitudes. To revive the business, he empowered employees to pursue his vision of being world famous. Yokoyama gave his employees permission to have fun with their jobs and to perform their best by bringing their whole selves to work every day. Together, Yokoyama and his employees developed four guiding principles:

1. *Choose Your Attitude.* We may have no control over what job you have, but we do control how we approach our job.
2. *Make Their Day.* Engage and delight customers and coworkers; don't grudgingly do the bare minimum.
3. *Be Present.* Don't dwell on where you aren't; instead, make the most of where you are. When talking to customers and coworkers, look them in the eye, and give them your full attention.
4. *Play.* Have as much fun as you can at whatever you're doing to cultivate a spirit of innovation and creativity.

View the video, "Management by Inspiration—Seattle's World Famous Pike Place Fish Market" (14:46). After watching the video, answer the following questions:

1. How do the employees at Pike Place Fish help each other stay engaged at work?
2. How can an organization use HRM to enact Yokoyama's four principles?
3. With what types of jobs would this approach work best? With what types of jobs would this approach not work well? Why?

Exercise: The Stan Problem

View the video, "The Stan Problem" (2:14). After watching the video, answer the following questions.

1. What was "The Stan Problem"?
2. As Stan's manager, what could have been done to prevent Stan's performance decline?
3. What can you do as Stan's manager to reengage him?

Integrative Project

Using the same job you used for the previous chapter, create a retention plan for employees based on their job performance. Be sure to address if and how you will manage different performance levels differently and what actions you will take to maximize employee engagement.

Video Case

Imagine that you are discussing Happy Time Toys' increasing turnover rates with some coworkers. This is a critical period for the company, and continued high turnover will adversely affect the company's ability to get the new product lines ready for holiday shipping. *What do you say or do?* Go to this book's video case, watch the challenge video for this chapter, and choose the best video response. Be sure to also view the outcomes of the two responses you didn't choose.

Discussion Questions

1. What HRM concepts from the chapter are illustrated in this video? Explain your answer.
2. What types of organizational commitment are illustrated in this video? Explain your answer.
3. How else might you handle the situation?

Endnotes

1. Talent management. (2017). Allstate. Retrieved March 27, 2017, from http://corporateresponsibility.allstate.com/workforce/talent-management

2. Attridge, M. (2009). Measuring and managing employee work engagement: A review of the research and business literature. *Journal of Workplace Behavioral Health, 24,* 383–398.

3. Hartley, D. (2012, May 29). Values are priceless at QVC. *Talent Management*. Retrieved June 5, 2012, from http://talentmgt.com/articles/view/values-are-non-negotiable-at-qvc/3

4. Zak, P. J. (2017). The neuroscience of trust. *Harvard Business Review*, January. Retrieved February 13, 2017, from https://hbr.org/2017/01/the-neuroscience-of-trust?utm_campaign=hbr&utm_source=twitter&utm_medium=social

5. *Ibid.*

6. *Ibid.*

7. When Campbell was in the soup. (2010, March 4). *Gallup Management Journal*. Retrieved January 23, 2012, from http://gmj.gallup.com/content/126278/Campbell-Soup.aspx#2

8. Silverstone, Y., & Harris, J. (2010). Put data to work. *Talent Management Magazine*, April, 32–35.

9. Robison, J. (2008, December 11). How the Ritz-Carlton manages the mystique. *GALLUP Management Journal*. Retrieved March 27, 2017, from http://gmj.gallup.com/content/112906/how-ritzcarlton-manages-mystique.aspx#1

10. Judge, T. A., Thoresen, C. J., Bono, J. E., & Patton, G. K. (2001). The job satisfaction-job performance relationship: A qualitative and quantitative review. *Psychological Bulletin, 127,* 376–407.

11. Organ, D. W. (1988). *Organizational citizenship behavior: The good soldier syndrome,* 1st ed.. Lexington, MA/Toronto: D.C. Heath and Company; Smith, C. A., Organ, D. W., & Near, J. P. (1983). Organizational citizenship behavior: Its nature and antecedents. *Journal of Applied Psychology, 68,* 653–663; Williams, L. J., & Anderson, S. E. (1991). Job satisfaction and organizational commitment as predictors of organizational citizenship and in-role behaviors. *Journal of Management, 17,* 601–617; LePine, J. A., Erez, A., & Johnson, D. E. (2002). The nature and dimensionality of organizational citizenship behavior: A critical review and meta-analysis. *Journal of Applied Psychology, 87,* 52–65.

12. Hulin, C. L., Roznowski, M., & Hachiya, D. (1985). Alternative opportunities and withdrawal decisions: Empirical and theoretical discrepancies and an integration. *Psychological Bulletin, 97,* 233–250; Kohler, S. S., & Mathieu, J. E. (1993). An examination of the relationship between affective reactions, work perceptions, individual resource characteristics, and multiple absence criteria. *Journal of Organizational Behavior, 14,* 515–530.

13. Kranz, G. (2011, July 21). Special report on employee engagement losing lifeblood. *Workforce*, 24–26, 28.

14. Gallup. (2017). The engaged workplace. Gallup.com. Retrieved February 12, 2017, from http://www.gallup.com/services/190118/engaged-workplace.aspx

15. Sorenson, S. (2013, June 20). How employee engagement drives growth. *Gallup*. Retrieved March 27, 2017, from http://www.gallup.com/businessjournal/163130/employee-engagement-drives-growth.aspx

16. Sorenson, S. (2013, June 20). How employee engagement drives growth. *Gallup*. Retrieved March 27, 2017, from http://www.gallup.com/businessjournal/163130/employee-engagement-drives-growth.aspx

17. Nahrgang, J. D., Morgeson, F. P., & Hofmann, D. A. (2011). Safety at work: A meta-analytic investigation of the link between job demands, job resources, burnout, engagement, and safety outcomes. *Journal of Applied Psychology, 96,* 71–94.

18. Crawford, E. R., LePine, J. A., & Rich, B. L. (2010). Linking job demands and resources to employee engagement and burnout: wA theoretical extension and meta-analytic test. *Journal of Applied Psychology, 95,* 834–848.

19. From "*What are the Top Drivers of Employee Attraction, Retention, and Sustainable Engagement?*" https://www.towerswatson.com/en/Insights/Newsletters/Europe/HR-matters/2014/12/What-are-the-top-drivers-of-employee-attraction-retention-and-sustainable-engagement. © 2014 Willis Towers Watson. Used with permission.

20. Tyler, K. (2011, March 1). Prepare for impact. *HR Magazine*. Retrieved March 25, 2017, from https://www.shrm.org/hr-today/news/hr-magazine/pages/0311tyler.aspx

21. Fleming, J. H., & Asplund, J. (2007, December 13). How employee and customer engagement interact. *Gallup Management Journal*. Retrieved March 27, 2017, from http://gmj.gallup.com/content/103081/How-Employee-Customer-Engagement-Interact.aspx

22. Robison, J. (2008, December 11). How the Ritz-Carlton manages the mystique. *Gallup Management Journal*. Retrieved March 27, 2017, from http://gmj.gallup.com/content/112906/how-ritzcarlton-manages-mystique.aspx.

23. Tyler, K. (2011, March 1). Prepare for impact. *HR Magazine*. Retrieved March 25, 2017, from https://www.shrm.org/hr-today/news/hr-magazine/pages/0311tyler.aspx

24. Rothschild, R. (2011, April 13). Employers seek more satisfaction with an engaged workforce. *Workforce*. Retrieved March 27, 2017, from http://www.workforce.com/2011/04/13/employers-seek-more-satisfaction-with-an-engaged-workforce/

25. Attridge, M. (2009). Measuring and managing employee work engagement: A review of the research and business literature. *Journal of Workplace Behavioral Health, 24,* 383–398.

26. Saks, A. M. (2006). Antecedents and consequences of employee engagement. *Journal of Managerial Psychology, 21,* 600–619; Rothschild, R. (2011, April 13). Employers seek more satisfaction with an engaged workforce. *Workforce*. Retrieved March 27, 2017, from http://www.workforce.com/2011/04/13/employers-seek-more-satisfaction-with-an-engaged-workforce/; Hastings, R. R. (2011, October 26). Study explores mysteries of employee engagement. *Society for Human Resource Management*. Retrieved March 27, 2017, from https://www.shrm.org/resourcesandtools/hr-topics/employee-relations/pages/mysteriesofemployeeengagement.aspx

27. When Campbell was in the soup. (2010, March 4). *Gallup Management Journal*. Retrieved March 26, 2017, from http://gmj.gallup.com/content/126278/Campbell-Soup.aspx#2

28. Tucker, M. A. (2010). Make managers responsible. *HR Magazine*, March, 75–78.

29. Vorhauser-Smith, S. (2013, August 14). How the best places to work are nailing employee engagement. *Forbes*. Retrieved March 27, 2017, from https://www.forbes.com/sites/sylviavorhausersmith/2013/08/14/how-the-best-places-to-work-are-nailing-employee-engagement/#1d2121fa5cc7

30. REI overview. (2017). REI. Retrieved March 27, 2017, from https://www.rei.com/about-rei/business.html

31. 2015 stewardship report. (2015). REI Co-Op. Retrieved March 27, 2017, from https://www.rei

.com/content/dam/documents/pdf/Stewardship%20
Reports/2015StewardshipReport.pdf

32. 2015 stewardship report. (2015). REI Co-Op. Retrieved
March 27, 2017, from https://www.rei.com/content/dam
/documents/pdf/Stewardship%20
Reports/2015StewardshipReport.pdf

33. Vorhauser-Smith, S. (2013, August 14). How the best places
to work are nailing employee engagement. *Forbes*. Retrieved
March 27, 2017, from https://www.forbes.com/sites
/sylviavorhausersmith/2013/08/14/how-the-best-places-to-work
-are-nailing-employee-engagement/#1d2121fa5cc7

34. 2015 stewardship report. (2015). REI Co-Op. Retrieved
March 27, 2017, from https://www.rei.com/content/dam
/documents/pdf/Stewardship%20Reports
/2015StewardshipReport.pdf

35. Vorhauser-Smith, S. (2013, August 14). How the best places
to work are nailing employee engagement. *Forbes*. Retrieved
March 27, 2017, from https://www.forbes.com/sites
/sylviavorhausersmith/2013/08/14/how-the-best-places-to-work
-are-nailing-employee-engagement/#1d2121fa5cc7

36. Gagné, M., & Bhave, D. (2011). Autonomy in the workplace:
An essential ingredient to employee engagement and well-being
in every culture. *Human Autonomy in Cross-Cultural Context*,
1(2), 163–187.

37. Development Dimensions International, Inc. (2015). Employee
engagement: The key to realizing a competitive Advantage.
Retrieved March 27, 2017, from http://www.ddiworld.com/ddi
/media/monographs/employeeengagement_mg_ddi.pdf?ext
=.pdf; Aon Hewitt. (2015). 2015 trends in global employee
engagement. Retrieved March 27, 2017, from http://www.aon
.com/attachments/human-capital-consulting/2015-Trends-in
-Global-Employee-Engagement-Report.pdf; Lundby, K. (2010).
*Going global: Practical applications and recommendations for
HR and OD professionals in the global workplace*. New York:
John Wiley and Sons.

38. Blau G. J., & Boal K. R. (1987). Conceptualizing how job
involvement and organizational commitment affect turnover and
absenteeism. *Academy of Management Review*, *12*, 288–300.

39. Meyer, J. P., & Allen, N. J. (1997). *Commitment in the
workplace: Theory, research, and application*. Thousand Oaks,
CA: Sage.

40. Meyer, J. P., & Herscovitch, L. (2001). Commitment in
the workplace: Toward a general model. *Human Resource
Management Review*, *11*, 299–326; Meyer, J., Stanley, D.,
Herscovich, L., & Topolnytsky, L. (2002). Affective,
continuance, and normative commitment to the organization:
A meta-analysis of antecedents, correlates, and consequences.
Journal of Vocational Behavior, *61*, 20–52; Klein, H., Becker, T.,
& Meyer, J. (2009). *Commitment in organizations: Accumulated
wisdom and new directions*. New York: Taylor & Francis.

41. Cole, M. S., Walter, F., Bedeian, A. G., & O'Boyle, E. H.
(2011). Job burnout and employee engagement: A meta-analytic
examination of construct proliferation. *Journal of Management,
38*, 1550-1581.

42. Merriam-Webster's Collegiate Dictionary. (2017). Retrieved
March 25, 2017, from http://www.merriam-webster.com
/dictionary/burnout

43. Goudreau, J. (2007, August 6). Dispatches from the war on
stress. *BusinessWeek*, 74–75.

44. Conlin, M. (2007, May 21). Do us a favor, take a vacation.
BusinessWeek, 88–89.

45. *Ibid*.

46. Nahrgang, J. D., Morgeson, F. P., & Hofmann, D. A. (2011).
Safety at work: A meta-analytic investigation of the link between
job demands, job resources, burnout, engagement, and safety
outcomes. *Journal of Applied Psychology*, *96*, 71–94.

47. More than job demands or personality, lack of organizational
respect fuels employee burnout. (2006, November 15).
Knowledge@Wharton Retrieved March 27, 2017, from http:
//knowledge.wharton.upenn.edu/article.cfm?articleid=1600

48. *Ibid*.

49. Silverstein, R. (2008, October 13). How to avoid occupational
burnout. *Entrepreneur*. Retrieved March 26, 2017, from http:
//www.entrepreneur.com/article/197744

50. Society for Human Resource Management. (2016, August 3).
Average cost-per-hire for companies is $4,129, SHRM survey
finds. *SHRM.org*. Retrieved February 14, 2017, from https:
//www.shrm.org/about-shrm/press-room/press-releases/pages
/human-capital-benchmarking-report.aspx

51. Society for Human Resource Management. (2016, August 3).
Average cost-per-hire for companies is $4,129, SHRM survey
finds. *SHRM.org*. Retrieved February 14, 2017, from https:
//www.shrm.org/about-shrm/press-room/press-releases/pages
/human-capital-benchmarking-report.aspx

52. Allen, D. G., & Bryant, P. C. (2012). Managing employee
turnover: Dispelling myths and fostering evidence-based
retention strategies, J. M. Phillips and S.M. Gully, (Eds.),
New York: Business Expert Press.

53. See Griffeth, R. W., & Hom, P. W. (2001). *Retaining valued
employees*. Thousand Oaks, CA: Sage for a more detailed
discussion of the types of turnover.

54. Society for Human Resource Management. (2016, August 3).
Average cost-per-hire for companies is $4,129, SHRM survey
finds. *SHRM.org*. Retrieved February 14, 2017, from https:
//www.shrm.org/about-shrm/press-room/press-releases/pages
/human-capital-benchmarking-report.aspx

55. The turnover myth. (2005, June). *Workforce Management*, 34–40.

56. Shaw, J. D. (2011). Turnover rates and organizational
performance: Review, critique, and research agenda.
Organizational Psychology Review, *1*(3), 187–213.

57. Boudreau, J. W., & Berger, C. J. (1985) Decision-theoretic
utility analysis applied to employee separations and acquisitions.
Journal of Applied Psychology, *70*, 581–612.

58. Cascio, W. F. (2003). *Managing human resources*. New York:
McGraw-Hill/Irwin.

59. Martin, C. (2002). *Managing for the short term: The new rules for
running a business in a day-to-day world*. New York: Doubleday.

60. Dalton, A. (2005). Applebee's turnover recipe. *Workforce
Management Online*, May. Retrieved January 2, 2012,
from http://www.workforce.com/article/20050526
/NEWS02/305269991

61. Hansen, F. (2007). Overhauling the recruiting process at CDW
Corp. *Workforce Management Online*, April. Retrieved March
27, 2017, from http://www.workforce.com/2007/04/11
/overhauling-the-recruiting-process-at-cdw-corp/

62. *Ibid*.

63. Allen, D. G., Bryant, P. C., & Vardaman, J. M. (2010). Retaining
talent: Replacing misconceptions with evidence-based strategies.
Academy of Management Perspectives, *24*, 48–64.

64. From "Retaining Talent: Replacing Misconceptions with
Evidence-Based Strategies," by Allen, D.G., Bryant, P.C., and
Vardaman, J.M., 2010, The Academy of Management Perspectives
by Academy of Management. Reproduced with permission of
Academy of Management via Copyright Clearance Center.

65. Freeman, S., & Cameron, K. S. (1993). Organizational downsizing: A convergence and reorientation framework. *Organization Science, 4*, 10–29.

66. Appelbaum, S. H., & Donia, M. (2001). The realistic downsizing preview: A multiple case study, part II: Analyses of RDP model; results of data collected and proposed new model. *Career Development International, 6*, 193–211.

67. Serving the American public: Best practices in downsizing. (1997, September). *National Performance Review*. Retrieved March 27, 2017, from http://govinfo.library.unt.edu/npr/library/papers/benchmrk/downsize.html#section_7

68. *Ibid.*

69. Cianni, M. (2013, June). How to retain top talent through an M&A. *Talent Management*, 42–43, 48.

70. See Cascio, W. F., & Wynn, P. (2004). Managing a downsizing process. *Human Resources Management, 43*, 425–436.

71. Cascio, W. F., Young, C. E. & Morris, J. R. (1997). Financial consequences of employment-change decisions in major U.S. corporations. *Academy of Management Journal, 40*, 1175–1189. De Meuse, K. P., Bergmann, T. J., Vanderheiden, P. A., & Roraff, C. E. (2004). New evidence regarding organizational downsizing and a firm's financial performance: A long-term analysis. *Journal of Managerial Issues, 16*, 155–177; Zyglidopoulos, S. C. (2004). The impact of downsizing on the corporate reputation for social performance. *Journal of Public Affairs, 4*, 11–25.

72. Iverson, R. D., & Zatzick, C. D. (2011). The effects of downsizing on labor productivity: The value of showing consideration for employees' morale and welfare in high-performing work systems. *Human Resource Management, 50*, 29–44.

73. Kucynski, S. (2000). Sweetening the pot. *HR Magazine*, March, 60–64.

74. Boroson, W., & Burgess, L. (1992). Survivors' syndrome. *Across the Board, 29*(11), 41–45.

75. Muirhead, S. (2004). Compassionate downsizing: Making the business case for education and training services. *The Conference Board/Across the Board*, January/February.

76. Brockner, J., Davy, J., & Carter, C. (1985). Layoffs, self-esteem, and survivor guilt: Motivational, attitudinal, and affective consequences. *Organizational Behavior and Human Decision Processes, 36*, 229–244; Greenhalgh, L., & Rosenblatt, Z. (1984). Job insecurity: Toward conceptual clarity. *Academy of Management Review, 9*, 438–448.

77. Greenhalgh, L., & Jick, T. D. (1979). The relationship between job insecurity and turnover, and its differential effects on employee quality level. Paper presented at the annual meeting of the Academy of Management, Atlanta; Sutton, R. I. (1983). Managing organizational death. *Human Resource Management, 22*, 391–412.

78. Staw, B. M., Sandelands, L. E., & Dutton, J. E. (1981). Threat-rigidity effects in organizational behavior: A multilevel analysis. *Administrative Science Quarterly, 26*, 501–524.

79. Brockner, J., Davy, J., & Carter, C. (1985). Layoffs, self-esteem, and survivor guilt: Motivational, attitudinal, and affective consequences. *Organizational Behavior and Human Decision Processes, 36*, 229–244; Brockner, J., Greenberg, J., Brockner, A., Bortz, J., Davy, J., & Carter, C. (1986). Layoffs, equity theory, and work motivation: Further evidence for the impact of survivor guilt. *Academy of Management Journal, 29*, 373–384.

80. Greenhalgh, L. (1982). Maintaining organizational effectiveness during organizational retrenchment. *Journal of Applied Behavioral Science, 18*, 155–170.

81. DeMeuse, K. P., Marks, M. L., & Dai. G. (2011). Organizational downsizing, mergers and acquisitions, and strategic alliances: Using theory and research to enhance practice. In S. Zedeck (Ed.), *APA handbook of industrial and organizational psychology, vol. 3: Maintaining, expanding, and contracting the organization*, pp. 729–768. Washington, DC: American Psychological Association.

82. Grunberg, L., Moore, S., & Greenberg, E. S. (2006). Managers' reactions to implementing layoffs: Relationship to health problems and withdrawal behaviors. *Human Resource Management, 45*, 159–178.

83. Flanagan, D. J., & O'Shaughnessy, K. C. (2005). The effect of layoffs on firm reputation. *Journal of Management, 31*, 445–463.

84. The Worker Adjustment and Retraining Notification Act. (n.d.). U.S. Department of Labor Employment and Training Administration fact sheet. Retrieved March 27, 2017, from http://www.doleta.gov/programs/factsht/warn.htm

85. Keating, C. (2012, January 20). No layoffs—ever! *CNN Money*. Retrieved March 27, 2017, from http://money.cnn.com/galleries/2012/pf/jobs/1201/gallery.best-companies-no-layoffs.fortune/?iid=HP_LN

86. Davis, J. A. (2003). Organizational downsizing: A review of literature for planning and research. *Journal of Healthcare Management, 48*, 181–199.

87. Muirhead, S. (2004). Compassionate downsizing: Making the business case for education and training services. *The Conference Board/Across the Board*, January/February.

88. Greer, M. (2005). Gut feelings drive fairness perceptions during layoffs. *Monitor on Psychology, 36*(7), 13.

89. Pressman, A. (2016, May 11). Intel offering health benefits to laid off workers. *Fortune*. Retrieved March 27, 2017, from http://fortune.com/2016/05/11/intel-health-benefits-to-laid-off-workers/

90. Panaro, J. (2003). Avoiding litigation in hiring and termination situations. *Association Management*, August. Retrieved October 12, 2011, from http://www.asaecenter.org/PublicationsResources/AMMagSidebarDetail.cfm?ItemNumber=9505; Larson, A. (2003). Wrongful termination of at-will employment." *ExpertLaw*, September. Retrieved December 12, 2011, from http://www.expertlaw.com/library/employment/at_will.html

91. The U.S. Equal Employment Opportunity Commission. (2012). Understanding waivers of discrimination claims in employee severance agreements. Retrieved March 28, 2017, from http://www.eeoc.gov/policy/docs/qanda_severance-agreements.html

92. Bowers, T. (2017, February 2). Everything you need to know about employment separation agreements. *The Balance*. Retrieved March 27, 2017, from https://www.thebalance.com/employment-separation-agreements-4046602; Bernstein, M. E. (2016, April 12). Drafting separation agreements for employers: A quick guide. *Law 360*. Retrieved March 27, 2017, from https://www.law360.com/articles/782043/drafting-separation-agreements-for-employers-a-quick-guide; Maya, J. C. (2017). What you need to know about severance packages. *Maya Murphy*. Retrieved March 27, 2017, from http://www.mayalaw.com/2013/05/09/what-you-need-to-know-about-severance-packages/

93. Lind, E. A. (1997). Litigation and claiming in organizations: Antisocial behavior or quest for justice? In R. A. Giacalone & J. Greenberg (Eds), *Antisocial behavior in organizations*, pp. 150–171. Thousand Oaks, CA: Sage.

94. Personnel Policy Service, Inc. (2004). Use at-will to defend your policies, not as a reason to terminate. Retrieved January 9, 2011, from www.ppspublishers.com/articles/gl/atwill_terminate.htm

95. March, J. G., & Simon, H. A. (1958). *Organizations*. New York: Wiley; Griffeth, R. W., & Hom, P. W. (2001). *Retaining valued employees*. Thousand Oaks, cA: Sage; see also Mitchell, T. R., Holtom, B. C., Lee, T. W., & Graske, T. (2001). How to keep your best employees: Developing an effective retention policy. *The Academy of Management Executive, 15*, 96.

96. Campion, M. A. & Mitchell, M. M. (1986). "Management Turnover: Experiential Differences Between Former and Current Managers," *Personnel Psychology*, 39: 57–69.

97. Boyens, J. (2006, September 22). Turnover revolves around rewards, respect, and requirements. *Nashville Business Journal*. Retrieved March 28, 2017, from http://nashville.bizjournals .com/nashville/stories/2006/09/25/smallb5.html

98. McEvoy, G. M., & Cascio, W. F. (1987). Do good or poor performers leave? A meta-analysis of the relationship between performance and turnover. *The Academy of Management Journal, 30*, 744–762.

99. Griffeth, R. W., Hom, P. W., & Gaertner, S. (2000). A meta-analysis of antecedents and correlates of employee turnover: Update, moderator tests, and research implications for the next millennium. *Journal of Management, 26*, 463–488.

100. Ladika, S. (2013). Companies recognizing importance of recognition. *Workforce*, December, 52.

101. Chandler, D. M. (2016). Taming the savage culture. *HR Magazine*, October, 26–27.

102. Two views on talent. (2015). *HR Magazine*, April, 54.

103. Marquez, J. (2006, October 23). Business first. *Workforce Management*, 23.

104. Giacalone, R. A., & Duhon, D. (1991). Assessing intended employee behavior in exit interviews. *The Journal of Psychology, 125*, 83–90; Griffeth, R. W., & Hom, P. W. (2001). *Retaining valued employees*. Thousand Oaks, CA: Sage.

105. Feffer, M. (2015, June 1). What makes a great employer? *HR Magazine*, 37–44.

106. Cardy, R. L., & Lengnick-Hall, M. L. (2011). Will they stay or will they go? Exploring a customer-oriented approach to employee retention. *Journal of Business and Psychology, 26*, 213–217.

107. Earnest, D. R., Allen, D. G., & Landis, R. S. (2011). Mechanism linking realistic job previews with turnover: A meta-analytic path analysis. *Personnel Psychology, 64*, 865–897.

108. Porter, L. W., & Steers, R. M. (1973). Organizational, work, and personal factors in employee turnover and absenteeism. *Psychological Bulletin, 80*, 161–176.

109. Phillips, J. M. (1998). Effects of realistic job previews on multiple organizational outcomes: A meta-analysis. *Academy of Management Journal, 41*, 673–690.

110. See Whitener, E. M., Brodt, S. E., Korsgaard, M. A., & Werner, J. M. (1998). Managers as initiators of trust: An exchange relationship framework for understanding managerial trustworthy behavior. *Academy of Management Review, 23*, 513–530.

111. Rafter, M. V. (2014, January 22). Best companies offer employees more flexible work options. *Great Place to Work*. Retrieved March 27, 2017, from http://reviews.greatplacetowork .com/blog/best-companies-offer-employees-more-flexible -work-options

112. Cappelli, P. (2001). A market-driven approach to retaining talent. In *Harvard Business Review, Harvard Business Review on finding and keeping the best people*, pp. 27–50. Boston, MA: Harvard Business School Publishing.

113. Grow, B. (2006, March 6). Renovating Home Depot. *BusinessWeek*, 50–58.

114. Poor health benefits communication hurts retention. (2005, March). *Employee Benefit News*, 18.

115. Sturman, M. C., Trevor, C. O., Boudreau, J. W., & Gerhart, B. (2003). Is it worth it to win in the talent war? Evaluating the utility of performance-based pay. *Personnel Psychology, 56*, 997–1035.

116. Villapaña, R. D. (2011, September 26). First 100 days: Cola firm's winning formula. PhilStar.com. Retrieved March 27, 2017, from http://www.philstar.com:8080 /business-usual/730567/first-100-days-cola-firms -winning-formula

117. Purcell, J. (2005). Business strategies and human resource management: Uneasy bedfellows or strategic partners? University of Bath Working Paper Series, #2005,16.

118. Hamm, S. (2006). A passion for the plan. *BusinessWeek*, August 21/28, 92–94.

119. Schramm, J. (2017). Not feeling the love? *HR Magazine*, February, 65.

120. Dodd, J., Saggers, S., & Wildy, H. (2009). Retention in the Allied Health workforce: Boomers, Generation X, and Generation Y. *Journal of Allied Health, 38*(4), 215; Talent edge 2020: Blueprints for the new normal. Deloitte, December. Retrieved March 27, 2017, from https://dupress.deloitte.com /content/dam/dup-us-en/articles/talent-edge-2020-blueprints -for-financial-services-companies/DUP102_TalentEdge2020 _Perspectives_Financial_Services.pdf; Kovary, G. (2013, January 24). Retaining your top talent from across the generations. *N-Gen Performance*. Retrieved March 27, 2017, from http://www.ngenperformance.com/blog/hr-training /retaining-your-top-talent-from-across-the-generations

121. Pope, B. (1992). *Workforce management: How today's companies are meeting business and employee needs*. Homewood, IL: Business One Irwin.

122. Charan, R., Drotter, S., & Noel, J. (2001). *The leadership pipeline*. San Francisco, CA: Jossey-Bass.

123. Aitchison, C. (2004). Succession planning at the Dixons Group. *Strategic HR Review, 3*(5), 24–27.

124. Ederle, K. (2012). How flexible is your succession plan? *Diversity Executive*, March/April, 18–21.

125. *Ibid.*

126. Kesler, G. C. (2002). Why the leadership bench never gets deeper: Ten insights about executive talent development. *HR Planning Society Journal, 25*(1), 32–44.

127. Wells, S. J. (2003). Who's next? *HR Magazine*, November, 45–50.

128. Frauenheim, E. (2006, November 15). Firms walk fine line with 'high-potential' programs. *Workforce Management*. Retrieved March 28, 2017, from http://www.workforce.com/2006/10/15 /firms-walk-fine-line-with-high-potential-programs/

129. Feeney, S. (2003). Irreplaceable you. *Workforce Management*, August, 36–40.

130. Guthridge, M., Komm, A. B., & Lawson, E. (2006). The people problem in talent management. *The McKinsey Quarterly, 2*, 6–8.

131. Fulmer, R. M. (2002). Choose tomorrow's leaders today. *Graziadio Business Report*, Winter. Retrieved March 29, 2017, from http://gbr.pepperdine.edu/021/succession.html

132. *Ibid.*

133. *Ibid.*

134. Conger, J. A., & Fulmer, R. M. (2003). Developing your leadership pipeline. *Harvard Business Review*, December, 76–84.

135. Guthridge, M., Komm, A. B., & Lawson, E. (2006). The people problem in talent management. *The McKinsey Quarterly, 2*, 6–8.

136. Agrawal, V., Manyika, J. M., & Richards, J. E. (2003). Matching people to jobs. *The McKinsey Quarterly*, *2*, 70–79.

137. Malykhina, E. (2005, March 21). Supplying labor to meet demand. *InformationWeek*. Retrieved March 28, 2017, from http://www.informationweek.com/supplying-labor-to-meet-demand/d/d-id/1031192

138. *Ibid.*

139. Talent management. (2017). Allstate. Retrieved March 27, 2017, from http://corporateresponsibility.allstate.com/workforce/talent-management

140. Allstate Insurance. (2017). Great place to work. Retrieved March 27, 2017, from http://reviews.greatplacetowork.com/allstate

141. Hogg, B. (2016, July 22). Let's talk leadership: John O'Donnell, CEO Allstate Insurance—Part 4. *Customer Think*. Retrieved March 27, 2017, from http://customerthink.com/letrs-talk-leadership-john-odonnell-ceo-allstate-insurance-part-4/

142. Hogg, B. (2016, July 22). Let's talk leadership: John O'Donnell, CEO Allstate Insurance—Part 4. *Customer Think*. Retrieved

March 27, 2017, from http://customerthink.com/letrs-talk-leadership-john-odonnell-ceo-allstate-insurance-part-4/

143. Allstate Insurance. (2017). Great place to work. Retrieved March 27, 2017, from http://reviews.greatplacetowork.com/allstate

144. Kuo, I. (2015, April 16). How Allstate's games-based training boosts employee engagement. *Gamification.co*. Retrieved March 27, 2017, from http://www.gamification.co/2015/04/16/how-allstates-games-based-training-boosts-employee-engagement/

145. Awards & recognition. (2017). Allstate. Retrieved March 27, 2017, from https://www.allstatenewsroom.com/about-allstate/awards/

146. Corporate. (2013). Allstate. Retrieved March 27, 2017, from http://www.allstate.ca/webpages/about/newsroom-corporate.aspx?article=best-2014

147. Christensen, J. (2003). First person: Gone fishin'. *Sales and Marketing Management*, *155*(4), 53; Hein, K. (2002). Hooked on employee morale. *Incentive*, *176*(8), 56–57; Lundin, S. C., Paul, H., & Christensen, J. (2000). *Fish! A remarkable way to boost morale and improve results*. New York: Hyperion; Yerkes, L. (2007). *Fun works: Creating places where people love to work*. San Francisco, CA: Berrett-Koehler.

Glossary

A

ability a stable and enduring capability to perform a variety of tasks (e.g., verbal or mechanical ability

accommodating neglecting one's own concerns to satisfy the concerns of the other person

accountability an individual is expected to provide a regular accounting to a superior about the results of what she or he is doing and will be held responsible for the outcome

action plan a strategy for proactively addressing an expected talent shortage or surplus

active job seeker someone actively looking for information about job opportunities

adverse impact (also called disparate impact) an employment practice has a disproportionate effect on a protected group, regardless of its intent

affective commitment a positive emotional attachment to the organization and strong identification with its values and goals

affirmative action plan describes in detail the actions to be taken, procedures to be followed, and standards to be met when establishing an affirmative action program

affirmative action proactive efforts to eliminate discrimination and its past effects

agency shop requires nonunion workers to pay a fee to the union for its services in negotiating their contracts

applicant tracking system software that helps manage the recruiting process

aptitude-treatment interaction the concept that some training strategies are more or less effective depending on a learner's particular abilities, personality traits, and other characteristics

arbitration an impartial third party acts as both judge and jury in imposing a binding decision on both negotiating parties

assertiveness using pressure, coercion, or persistent follow-up to gain compliance

assessment center puts candidates through a variety of simulations and assessments to evaluate their potential fit with and ability to do the job

avoidable turnover turnover that the employer could have prevented

avoidance labor relations strategy management engages in lawful or unlawful efforts to prevent a union from forming or seeks the decertification of an existing union

avoiding not immediately pursuing one's own concerns or those of the other person and not addressing the conflict

B

background checks assess factors including personal and credit characteristics, character, lifestyle, criminal history, and reputation

balanced scorecard a performance measurement system that translates the organization's strategy into financial, business process, learning and growth, and customer outcomes

base pay reflects the size and scope of an employee's responsibilities

behavioral interviews uses information about what the applicant has done in the past to predict future behaviors

behavioral observation scales measure the frequency of desired behaviors

behaviorally anchored rating scales use a set of behavioral statements relating to qualities important for performance

benchmark jobs jobs that tend to exist across departments and across diverse organizations, allowing them to be used as a basis for compensation comparisons

bona fide occupational qualification (BFOQ) a characteristic that is essential to the successful performance of a relevant job function

boycott union members refuse to use or buy the firm's products to exert economic pressure on management

brand a symbolic picture of all the information connected to a company or a product, including its image

broadbanding using very wide pay grades to increase pay flexibility

burnout exhaustion of physical or emotional strength or motivation usually as a result of prolonged stress or frustration

business process reengineering a more radical rethinking and redesign of workflow and business processes to achieve large improvements in speed, service, cost, or quality

business strategy defines how the firm will compete in its marketplace

business strategy how an organization will compete in a particular market

C

card check employees sign a card of support if they are in favor of unionization; if a majority of workers (over 50 percent) sign a union authorization card, the NRLB requires the employer to recognize the union without a secret ballot election

careers site the area of an organization's website devoted to jobs and careers with the company

case interview the candidate is given a business situation, challenge, or problem and asked to present a well thought out solution

central tendency rating all employees in the middle of the scale regardless of performance

centralized organizations concentrate power and decision-making authority at higher levels of the organization

checklist method the assessor uses a checklist of pre-scaled descriptions of behavior to evaluate the employee

closed shop exclusively employs people who are already union members

closed skills skills performed similarly or exactly like they are taught in training

coalition tactics engaging the help of others to persuade someone to do something

code of conduct specifies expected and prohibited actions in the workplace and gives examples of appropriate behavior

code of ethics a decision-making guide that describes the highest values to which an organization aspires

codetermination worker representation on the company's board of directors

cognitive ability tests assess general mental abilities including reasoning, logic, and perceptual abilities

collaborating attempting to work with the other person to find some solution that fully satisfies the concerns of both parties

collaboration labor relations strategy relies heavily on labor relations to pursue an interest-based approach to problem solving

collective bargaining agreement a legal written contract between organized labor and an employer that is enforceable through the negotiated grievance and arbitration procedure

collective bargaining when the employer and the union negotiate in good faith on wages, benefits, work hours, and other employment terms and conditions

collective socialization newcomers go through a common set of experiences as a group

common good standard the ethical action shows respect and compassion for all others, especially the most vulnerable

common law the body of case-by-case court decisions that determines what is legal and what remedies are appropriate

comparable worth if two jobs have equal difficulty requirements, the pay should be the same, regardless of who fills them

compensable factor any characteristic used to provide a basis for judging a job's value

compensation surveys surveys of other organizations conducted to learn what they are paying for specific jobs or job classes

compensatory approach high scores on some assessments can compensate for low scores on other assessments

competencies broad worker characteristics that underlie successful job performance

competency modeling identifies the worker competencies characteristic of high performance

competency-based pay skill-based pay for professional jobs

competing pursuing one's own concerns at the other person's expense

competitive advantage doing something differently from the competition that leads to outperformance and success

compliance labor relations strategy relies heavily on the application of labor law to enforce the rights and the obligations created by statute and by contract

compromising trying to find some expedient, mutually acceptable middle ground solution that partially satisfies both parties

Consolidated Omnibus Budget Reconciliation Act provides a continuation of group health coverage for employees and qualified beneficiaries that might otherwise be terminated when an employee experiences a qualifying event

contest socialization each socialization stage is a "contest" in which one builds up a performance record

contingent assessment methods a job offer is made contingent on passing the assessment

continuance commitment staying with an organization because of perceived high economic and/or social costs involved with leaving

continuous performance management an ongoing performance appraisal process that involves the employee in evaluating his or her performance and setting performance goals and provides continuous coaching and feedback

contrast effect over- or under-rating someone due to a comparison with someone else

core values the enduring beliefs and principles that guide an organization's decisions and goals

corporate social responsibility businesses showing concern for the common good and valuing human dignity

cost-of-living adjustment tied to inflation indicators rather than merit

cost-of-living allowances clauses in union contracts that automatically increase wages based on the U.S. Bureau of Labor Statistics' cost of living index

critical incident appraisal method an assessor discusses specific examples of the target employee's positive and negative behaviors with the employee

critical incidents job analysis technique job experts describe stories of good and poor performance to identify desirable and undesirable competencies or behaviors

cross-training training employees in more than one job or in multiple skills to enable them to do different jobs

cumulative trauma disorder skeletal and muscle injuries that occur when the same muscles are used to perform tasks repetitively

customary benefits commonly provided benefits that are viewed as an entitlement by employees

cut score a minimum assessment score that must be met or exceeded to advance to the next assessment phase or to be eligible to receive a job offer

D

decertification election an election to determine if a majority of employees want to no longer be represented by a union

defined benefit retirement plan: promise participants a monthly benefit at retirement

defined contribution retirement plan the employer, the employee, or both contribute to the employee's individual account, and the contributions are invested on the participant's behalf

desirable criteria job holder characteristics that may enhance job success but are not essential to adequate job performance

development focuses on developing competencies that an employee or a workgroup is expected to need in the future

direct financial compensation compensation received in the form of salary, wages, commissions, stock options, or bonuses

direct financial compensation compensation received in the form of salary, wages, commissions, stock options, or bonuses

disability insurance supplements workers' compensation insurance to provide continued income in the event of an employee becoming disabled

disjunctive socialization newcomers are left alone to develop their own interpretations of the organization and situations they observe

disparate treatment intentional discrimination based on a person's protected characteristic

distributive fairness the perceived fairness of the outcomes received

distributive negotiation occurs under zero-sum conditions where any gain to one party is offset by an equivalent loss to the other party

divestiture socialization tries to deny and strip away certain personal characteristics

division of labor the degree to which employees specialize

domestic partners two people who are not married but are in a same-sex or opposite-sex arrangement similar to marriage

downsizing a permanent reduction of multiple employees intended to improve the efficiency or effectiveness of the firm

dysfunctional conflict conflict that focuses on emotions and differences between both parties (e.g., personality conflict)

dysfunctional stress an overload of stress resulting from a situation of under- or over-arousal continuing for too long

dysfunctional turnover the departure of effective performers

E

efficiency wages above-market wages raise labor productivity and/or decrease employer costs enough to pay for the cost of the higher wages

efficiency-oriented recruiting metrics track how efficiently a firm is hiring

emotion-focused coping strategies focus on the emotions brought on by the stressor

employee benefits nonwage compensation or rewards given to employees (indirect compensation)

employee development plan an improvement plan with the goal making an employee's good performance even better

employee engagement when employees are committed to, involved with, enthusiastic, and passionate about their work

employee equity the perceived fairness of the relative pay between employees performing similar jobs for the same organization

employee handbooks print or online materials that document the organization's HRM policies and procedures

Employee Retirement Income Security Act of 1974 (ERISA) a federal law that protects employees' retirement benefits from mismanagement

employee stock ownership plans (ESOPs) tax-exempt employer-established employee trusts that hold company stock for employees

employee wellness program any initiative designed to increase company performance or employee performance or morale through improved employee health

employer brand summary of what an employer offers to employees

employer image an organization's reputation as an employer

employment at will an employment relationship in which either party can legally terminate the employment relationship at any time for just cause, no cause, or even a cause that is morally wrong as long as it is not illegal

equal employment opportunity a firm's employment practices must be designed and used in a manner that treats employees and applicants consistently regardless of their protected characteristics, such as their sex and race

ergonomics designing the work environment to reduce the physical and psychological demands placed on employees

error of commission an employee receives an undeserved reward

error of omission an employee who deserves a reward does not receive one

essay appraisal method the assessor writes a brief essay providing an assessment of the strengths, weaknesses, and potential of the target employee

essential criteria job holder characteristics that are vital to job performance

ethics the standards of moral behavior that define socially accepted behaviors that are right as opposed to wrong

evaluative assessment methods evaluate job candidates to identify whom to hire

exchange offering to exchange something of value now or in the future for someone's cooperation

exempt employees meet one of the FLSA exemption tests, are paid on a fixed-salary basis, and are not entitled to overtime

exit interview asking separated employees why they left to acquire information that can be used to improve conditions for current employees

explicit employment contract a written or verbal employment contract

external equity when an organization's employees believe that their pay is fair when compared to what other employers pay their employees who perform similar jobs

external recruiting source targets people outside the organization

extrinsic motivation motivation that comes from outside the individual, including performance bonuses

extrinsic rewards rewards with monetary value

F

fair discrimination when only objective, merit-based, and job-related characteristics are used to determine employment related decisions

Fair Labor Standards Act (FLSA) a federal law that sets standards for minimum wages, overtime pay, and equal pay for men and women performing the same jobs

fairness standard the ethical action treats all people equally, or at least fairly, based on some defensible standard

Family and Medical Leave Act requires most employers to provide employees up to 12 weeks of unpaid leave to care for family members

first impression bias initial judgments influence later assessments

fixed pay pays employees a set amount regardless of performance

fixed rewards pre-determined compensation (salary and benefits)

fixed socialization new hires are informed in advance when their probationary status will end

flexible benefits plans flexible benefits plan: give employees a set amount of credits or dollars to allocate among different benefits options provided by the employer

flexible spending account an employer-sponsored benefit that allows you to pay for eligible medical expenses on a pre-tax basis

forced distribution method the rater distributes performance ratings into a prespecified performance distribution

forced ranking method employees are ranked in order of best to worst performance

forced-choice rating method forces the assessor to choose the statement that best fits the target employee from a provided set of statements that are scored and weighted in advance

formal socialization structured socialization using specifically designed activities and materials that is done away from the work setting

formalization the degree to which organizational rules, procedures, and communications are documented

fraudulent recruitment (or truth in hiring) misrepresenting the job or organization to a recruit

functional conflict conflict that balances both parties' interests to maximize mutual gains (e.g., task conflict)

functional stress manageable levels of stress that generate positive emotions including satisfaction, excitement, and enjoyment

functional turnover the departure of poor performers

G

gainsharing the firm shares the value of productivity gains with employees

gap analysis comparing labor supply and demand forecasts to identify future talent needs

global mindset a set of individual attributes that enable you to influence individuals, groups, and organizations from diverse socio/cultural/institutional systems

golden parachute lucrative benefits given to executives in the event the company is taken over

graphic rating scale uses ratings of unsatisfactory, average, above average, and outstanding to evaluate either work quality or personal traits

H

halo effect letting one positive factor influence assessments of other areas of behavior or performance

hard bargaining taking a strong position on an issue

Hay Group Guide Chart–Profile Method a point–factor system is used to produce both a profile and a point score for each position

health insurance provides healthcare coverage for employees and their dependents

hierarchy the degree to which some employees have formal authority over others

high performance work systems high involvement or high commitment organizations

high potential error confusing potential with performance

horns effect letting one negative factor influence assessments of other areas of behavior or performance

hostile environment harassment unwanted verbal or physical conduct of a sexual nature creates a hostile, intimidating, or otherwise offensive working environment

human resource management the organizational function responsible for attracting, hiring, developing, rewarding, and retaining talent

human resource planning aligning the organization's human resources to effectively and efficiently accomplish the organization's strategic goals

human resource strategy links the entire human resource function with the firm's business strategy

I

implicit employment contract: an understanding that is not part of a written or verbal contract

Improshare a gainsharing plan based on a mathematical formula that compares a performance baseline with actual productivity during a given period with the goal of reducing production time

Inclusion everyone feels respected and listened to, and everyone contributes to their fullest potential

independent contractor an individual or business that provides services to another individual or business that controls or directs only the *result* of the work

indirect financial compensation all the tangible and financially valued rewards that are not included in direct compensation, including free meals, vacation time, and health insurance

indirect financial compensation all the tangible and financially valued rewards that are not included in direct compensation, including free meals, vacation time, and health insurance

individual socialization newcomers are socialized individually as in an apprenticeship

individualism the strength of the ties people have with others in their community—high individualism reflects looser ties with others

informal socialization unstructured, on-the-job socialization done by coworkers

ingratiation using flattery or praise to put the other person in a good mood and make them more likely to help

inspirational appeals appealing to the other person's values, aspirations, or ideals to gain his or her commitment

integrative negotiation a win–win negotiation in which the agreement involves no loss to either party

integrity tests assess attitudes and experiences related to reliability, trustworthiness, honesty, and moral character

interactional fairness the degree of respect and the quality of the interpersonal treatment received during the decision-making process

interest arbitration resolves disputes over the terms of a collective bargaining agreement currently being negotiated

internal equity when employees perceive their pay to be fair relative to the pay of other jobs in the organization

internal job posting systems communicate information about internal job openings to employees

internal recruiting source locates talent currently working for the company that would be a good fit with another position

Internet data mining proactively searching the internet to locate semipassive and passive job seekers with the characteristics and the qualifications needed for a position

intrinsic motivation derived from an interest in or enjoyment from doing a task

intrinsic rewards are nonmonetary and derived from the work itself

investiture socialization builds newcomers' self-confidence and reflects senior employees' valuing of newcomers' knowledge and personal characteristics

involuntary turnover the separation is due to the organization asking the employee to leave

J

job analysis a systematic process used to identify and describe the important aspects of a job and the characteristics a worker needs to perform the job well

job applications written information about skills and education, job experiences, and other job relevant information

job characteristics model objective job characteristics including skill variety, task identity, task significance, autonomy, and task feedback, lead to job satisfaction for people with a high growth need strength

job classification method subjectively classifies jobs into an existing hierarchy of grades or categories

job description written descriptions of the duties and the responsibilities of the job itself

job elements job analysis method expert brainstorming sessions identify the characteristics of successful workers

job enlargement adding more tasks at the same level of responsibility and skill related to an employee's current position

job enrichment a job design approach that increases a job's complexity to give workers greater responsibility and opportunities to feel a sense of achievement

job evaluation a systematic process that uses expert judgment to assess differences in value between jobs

job fairs a place where multiple employers and recruits meet to discuss employment opportunities

job knowledge tests measure the knowledge (often technical) required by a job

job pricing the generation of salary structures and pay levels for each job based on the job evaluation data

job rewards analysis job analysis technique that identifies the intrinsic and extrinsic rewards of a job

job rotation workers are moved through a variety of jobs to increase their interest and motivation]]

job task an observable unit of work with a beginning and an end

judgmental forecasting relies on managers' expertise to predict a firm's future employment needs

K

knowledge organized factual or procedural information that can be applied to perform a task

L

Labor Management Reporting and Disclosure Act of 1959 (the Landrum-Griffin Act) outlined a bill of rights for union members and sets up procedures for union elections, discipline, and financial reporting

labor market all of the potential employees located within a geographic area from which the organization might be able to hire

labor relations strategic plan identifies the labor relations goals desired individually or jointly by labor and management, determines the best strategy to reach those goals, and develops and executes the actions needed to implement that strategy

labor union an organization of workers formed for the purpose of advancing its members' interests in respect to wages, benefits, and working conditions

layoff temporary reduction of employees

learning agility the ability to learn from experiences and to apply that knowledge to new and different situations

learning objectives identify desired learning outcomes

learning style how people differ in how we process information when problem solving or learning

legitimating tactics enhancing one's formal authority to make a request by referring to precedents, rules, contracts, or other official documents

leniency error all employees are given high ratings regardless of performance

life insurance pays a beneficiary a sum of money to the beneficiary or beneficiaries after the death of an insured individual

lifelong learning a formal commitment to ensuring that employees have and develop the skill they need to be effective in their jobs today and in the future

lockout management keeps employees away from the workplace and uses management staff or replacements to run the business

long-term incentives motivate behaviors and performance that support company value and long-term organizational health

long-term orientation reflects a focus on long term planning, delivering on social obligations, and avoiding "losing face"

M

management by objectives the rater evaluates the target employee against mutually set goals

market pricing uses external sources of information about how others are compensating a certain position to assign value to a company's similar job

masculinity the degree to which a society values and exhibits traditional male and female roles—in highly masculine cultures, men are expected to be more assertive and to be the sole provider for the family

mediation using a neutral third party to attempt to resolve the dispute through facilitation

mission the organization's basic purpose and the scope of its operations

mobility barriers factors that make it harder to leave an organization

mobility policies specify the rules by which people move between jobs within an organization

motivation to transfer the intention and the willingness to transfer any knowledge acquired in a training or development activity back to the work context

multicrafting employees gain proficiency in two or more trades

multiple hurdles candidates must receive a passing score on an assessment before being allowed to continue in the selection process

multisource assessments performance feedback from the employee's supervisor as well as other sources that are familiar with an employee's job performance

N

National Labor Relations Act of 1935 (Wagner Act) guarantees the right of nonmanagerial employees of firms engaged in interstate commerce to join unions and bargain collectively

needs assessment the process of identifying any gaps between what exists and what is needed in the future in terms of employee performance, competencies, and behaviors

negligent hiring a company is considered responsible for the damaging actions of its employees if it failed to exercise reasonable care in hiring the employee who caused the harm

negotiation is a process in which two or more parties make offers, counteroffers, and concessions in order to reach an agreement

nonexempt employees do not meet any one of the FLSA exemption tests and are paid on an hourly basis and covered by wage and hour laws regarding minimum wage, overtime pay, and hours worked

nonfinancial compensation rewards and incentives given to employees that are not financial in nature including intrinsic rewards received from the job itself or from the work environment

nonfinancial compensation rewards and incentives given to employees that are not financial in nature

normative commitment feeling obliged to stay with an organization for moral or ethical reasons

O

observation watching people working in similar jobs for other companies to evaluate their potential fit with your organization

Occupational Safety and Health Administration (OSHA) created by the Occupational Safety and Health Act to set and enforce protective workplace safety and health standards

offshoring opening a location in another country or outsourcing work to an existing company abroad

online job board an Internet site that helps job seekers and employers find one another

open shop does not discriminate based on union membership in employing or keeping workers

open skills sets of principles that can be applied in many different ways

opportunity bias ignoring factors beyond the employee's control that influence his or her performance

optimal turnover the turnover level producing the highest long-term levels of productivity and business improvement

organizational citizenship behaviors discretionary behaviors that benefit the organization but are not formally rewarded or required

organizational chart diagram illustrating the chain of command and reporting relationships in a company

organizational commitment the extent to which an employee identifies with the organization and its goals and wants to stay with the organization

organizational culture The norms, values, and assumptions of organizational members that guide members' attitudes and behaviors.

organizational design selecting and managing aspects of organizational structure to facilitate organizational goal accomplishment

organizational image people's general impression of an organization based on both feelings and facts

organizational needs analysis identifies where in the organization development or improvement opportunities exist

organizational structure the organization's formal system of task, power, and reporting relationships

orientation training activities to help new hires fit in as organizational members

OSHA standards rules describing the methods employers must legally follow to protect their workers from hazards

other characteristics a miscellaneous category for worker characteristics that are not knowledges, skills, or abilities, including personality traits, values, and work styles

outsourcing hiring an external vendor to do work rather than doing it internally

P

paired comparison method every employee in a workgroup is compared to the other group members

passive job seeker someone not actively looking for a new job but who could be tempted by the right opportunity

pay followers pay their front-line employees as little as possible

pay grade (or pay scale) the range of possible pay for a group of jobs

pay leader organization with a compensation policy of giving employees greater rewards than competitors

pay mix the relative emphasis given to different compensation components

pay structure the array of pay rates for different work or skills within a single organization

pay-for-performance program (merit pay) rewards employees based on some specific measure of their performance

performance culture focuses on hiring, retaining, developing, motivating, and making work assignments based on performance data and results

performance improvement plan a tool to monitor and measure an employee's deficient work products, processes, and/or behaviors to improve performance or modify behavior

performance management directs and motivates employees, workgroups, and business units to accomplish organizational goals by linking past performance with future needs, setting specific goals for future behavior and performance, providing feedback, and identifying and removing performance obstacles

performance plan describes desired goals and results, how results will be measured and weighted, and what standards will be used to evaluate results

performance ranking methods compare employees to each other in some way

performance rating method compares employee performance to a set of standards to identify a number or letter rating that represents the employee's performance level

person needs analysis evaluates how individual employees are doing in the training area and determines who needs what type of training

person specification summarizes the characteristics of someone able to perform the job

personal appeals asking someone to do something as a personal favor or "because we're friends"

person-group fit match between an individual and his or her workgroup and supervisor

person-job fit the fit between a person's abilities and the job's demands and the fit between a person's desires and motivations and the job's attributes and rewards

person-organization fit fit between an individual's values, attitudes, and personality and the organization's values, norms, and culture

point factor method uses a set of compensable factors to determine a job's value

Position Analysis Questionnaire a copyrighted, standardized structured job analysis questionnaire

Position Analysis Questionnaire a structured job evaluation questionnaire that is statistically analyzed to calculate pay rates based on how the labor market is valuing worker characteristics

power distance how much inequality exists and is accepted among people with and without power

preferential treatment employment preference given to a member of a protected group

presenteeism an employee physically comes to work but does not function at his or her full potential.

problem-focused coping strategies deal directly with the cause of stress

procedural fairness the perceived fairness of the policies and the procedures used to determine the outcome

professional employer organization a company that leases employees to companies that need them

profit sharing organizational profits are distributed to all employees

progressive discipline using increasingly severe measures when an employee fails to correct a deficiency after being given a reasonable opportunity to do so

protected classes groups underrepresented in employment

psychomotor tests assess strength, physical dexterity, and coordination

Q

quid pro quo harassment unwanted verbal or physical conduct of a sexual nature made as a term or condition of employment or as a basis for employment and/or advancement decisions

R

race norming comparing an applicant's scores only to members of his or her own racial subgroup and setting separate passing or cutoff scores for each subgroup

Railway Labor Act governs employment relations for airlines and railroads

random socialization socialization steps are ambiguous or changing

ranking method subjectively compares jobs to each other based on their overall worth to the organization

rational persuasion using facts and logic to persuade the other person

realistic job preview presenting both positive and potentially negative information about a job in an objective way

reasonable accommodation an employer is required to take reasonable steps to accommodate a disability unless it would cause the employer undue hardship

recency effect allowing recent events and performance to have a disproportionately large influence on the rating

recognition awards rewards for specific achievements such as tenure with the organization, helping a coworker, or attendance

recruiting activities that affect either the number or the type of people willing to apply for and accept job offers

recruiting the set of practices and decisions that affect either the number or the types of individuals willing to apply for and accept job offers

recruitment spillover effects the positive or negative unintended consequences of recruiting activities

reinforcers anything that makes a behavior more likely to happen again

reliability how consistently a measure assesses a particular characteristic

replacement char graphically shows current jobholders, possible successors, and each successor's readiness to assume the job

replacement planning identifying specific back-up candidates for specific senior management positions

resource dependence theory proposes that organiza-tional decisions are influ-enced by both internal and external agents who con-trol critical resources

results the specific subgoals for each unit that will be the focus of the performance management process

résumé database a searchable database of prescreened résumés

reward differentiation differentiating rewards based on performance rather than giving all employees the same reward

rights arbitration covers disputes over the interpretation of an existing contract and is often used in settling grievances

rights standard the ethical action is the one that best respects and protects the moral rights of everyone affected by the action

right-to-work laws state laws that prohibit union shops in which all workers in a unionized workplace must join the union and pay dues

risk assessment identifying, analyzing, and prioritizing risks

risk control risk management planning and monitoring and resolving risks

risk management identifying, assessing, and resolving risks before they become serious threats

S

safety culture the shared safety attitudes, beliefs, and practices that shape employees' safety behavior

Scanlon plans gainsharing programs based on implementing employee suggestions for lowering the cost per unit produced

scientific management breaks work down into its simplest elements and then systematically improves the worker's performance of each element

screening assessment methods reduce the pool of job applicants to a group of job candidates

search firm an independent company that specializes in the recruitment of particular types of talent

secondary boycott when a union encourages third parties such as customers and suppliers to stop doing business with the company

selection the process of gathering and evaluating the information used for deciding which applicants will be hired

self-management strategies efforts to control one's motivation, emotions, and decision-making to enhance the application of learned capabilities to the job

self-regulation processes enabling an individual to guide his/her goal-directed activities over time

semipassive job seeker someone at least somewhat interested in finding a new job, but who inconsistently looks for one

seniority the length of time the employee has worked for the employer

sensory modality a system that interacts with the environment through one of the basic senses

sensory tests assess visual, auditory, and speech perception

separation agreement a legal agreement between an employer and employee that specifies the terms of any employment termination

sequential socialization the degree to which socialization follows a specific sequence of steps

serial socialization accessible and supportive organizational members serve as role models and mentors

severance pay given to employees upon termination of their employment

sexual harassment unwelcome sexual advances, requests for favors, and other verbal or physical conduct of a sexual nature

shared service center centralizes routine, transaction-based HRM activities

short-term incentives one-time variable rewards used to motivate short-term employee behavior and performance (typically one year or less)

similar-to-me effect giving high ratings to someone because she or he is perceived as being similar to the rater

simulation a type of work sample that gives candidates an actual job task to perform or simulates critical events that might occur to assess how well a candidate handles them

situational interview asks how the candidate might react to hypothetical situations

skill the ability to use some sort of knowledge in performing a physical task; often refers to psychomotor activities

skill-based pay rewards employees for the range and depth of their knowledge and skills

skills inventory tracks employees' competencies and work experiences in a searchable database

Social Security provides retirement income to qualified workers and their spouses after working a certain number of hours

socialization a long-term process of planned and unplanned, formal and informal activities and experiences through which an individual acquires the attitudes, behaviors, and knowledge needed to successfully participate as an organizational member

sourcing identifying qualified individuals and labor markets from which to recruit

span of control the number of people reporting directly to an individual

spot awards awards given immediately when a desired behavior is seen

staffing ratio indexing headcount with a business metric

stakeholder perspective considering the interests and opinions of all people, groups, organizations, or systems that affect or could be affected by the organization's actions

standards specify what level of results will be considered acceptable

stereotype believing that everyone in a particular group shares certain characteristics or abilities or will behave in the same way

stereotype believing that everyone in a particular group shares certain characteristics or abilities or will behave in the same way

stock options give an employee the right to buy shares of the company's stock at a certain price (the exercise price) during some future period of time

strategic planning a process for making decisions about an organization's long-term goals and how they are to be achieved

strategic recruiting metrics recruiting metrics that track recruiting processes and outcomes that influence the organization's performance, competitive advantage, or strategic execution

strike union members refuse to work, halting production or services

structured interview technique job experts provide information about the job during a structured interview

structured interview uses consistent, job-related questions with predetermined scoring keys

structured job analysis questionnaire a list of pre-identified questions designed to analyze a job

succession management plans written policies that guide the succession management process

succession management an ongoing process of systematically identifying, assessing, and developing organizational leadership to enhance performance

succession management the ongoing process of preparing employees to assume other positions in the organization

succession management the process of identifying critical jobs too important to be left vacant and creating a strategic plan to quickly fill them when they become available

succession planning identifying, developing, and tracking employees to enable them to eventually assume higher level positions

surface bargaining going through the motions of negotiations with no intent of reaching an agreement

survivor syndrome the emotional effects of downsizing on surviving employees both during and after a downsizing

T

talent inventories worksheets or databases summarizing each employee's competencies, qualifications, and anything else that can help the company understand how the employee can contribute

talent inventory manual or computerized records of employees' relevant characteristics, experiences, and competencies

talent philosophy a system of beliefs about how its employees should be treated

task acquaintance the amount and type of work contact an evaluator has with the person being assessed

task inventory approach job experts generate a list of 50 to 200 tasks that are grouped in categories capturing major work functions

task needs analysis focuses on identifying which jobs, competencies, abilities, and behaviors the training effort should focus on

task statements identify in specific behavioral terms the regular duties and responsibilities of a position

termination the permanent separation of a single employee

The National Labor Relations Act of 1947 (also called the Taft-Hartley Act) amended the Wagner Act to clarify what are considered unfair labor practices by unions and employees

total compensation statement communicating total compensation in detail through a written summary of employee direct and indirect compensation

total compensation (total rewards) the combined value of direct (pay and bonuses) and indirect (nonwage) compensation

total rewards everything an employee perceives to be of value that results from the employment relationship

total rewards the combined intrinsic and extrinsic rewards of a job

total rewards the sum of all of the rewards employees receive in exchange for their time, efforts, and performance

tournament socialization each stage of socialization is an "elimination round," and a new hire is out of the organization if he or she fails to pass

training evaluation systematically collecting the information necessary to make effective decisions about adopting, improving, valuing, and continuing an instructional activity or set of activities

training gamification applying gaming designs and concepts to training to make it more engaging for the learner and increase learning and performance outcomes

training transfer effectively using what is learned in training back on the job

training formal and informal activities to improve competencies relevant to an employee's or a workgroup's current job

trend analysis using past employment patterns to predict a firm's future labor needs

U

unavoidable turnover turnover that the employer could not have prevented

uncertainty avoidance the degree of anxiety felt in uncertain or unfamiliar situations

unemployment insurance provides temporary income during periods of involuntary unemployment

unfair discrimination when employment decisions and actions are not job-related, objective, or merit-based

union shop all workers in a unionized workplace are forced to join the union and pay dues

unlawful employment practices violate a federal, state, or local employment law

unstructured interview varying questions are asked across interviews, and there are usually no standards for evaluating answers

upward appeals obtaining or referring to the support of higher-ups

upward reviews the target employee is reviewed by one or more subordinates

utilitarian standard the ethical action best balances good over harm

V

validity how well a measure assesses a given construct and the degree to which you can make specific conclusions or predictions based on observed scores

variable pay plan pay for performance plans that put a small amount of base pay at risk, in exchange for the opportunity to earn additional pay if performance meets or exceeds a standard

variable pay bases some or all an employee's compensation on employee, team, or organizational performance

variable rewards link rewards to factors determined as valuable, including performance, skills, competence, and contribution (incentives)

variable socialization employees do not know when to expect to pass to a different status level, and the timeline may be different across employees

vesting the point at which an employee earns a nonforfeitable right to benefits funded by employer contributions

vesting the point at which employees can sell or transfer the stock option

virtue standard the ethical action is consistent with certain ideal virtues including civility, compassion, benevolence, etc.

vision long-term goals regarding what the organization wants to become and accomplish, describing its image of an ideal future

voluntary turnover the separation is due to the employee's choice

W

wage differentials differences in wages between various workers, groups of workers, or workers within a career field

wage rate compression starting salaries exceed the salaries paid to experienced employees

walk-ins people who apply for a job based on a sign on company property

weingarten rights guarantee employees the right to union representation during investigatory interviews by the employer

wellness incentives rewards for engaging in healthy behavior or participating in wellness programs

work samples evaluate the performance of actual or simulated work tasks

work standards comparing an employee's performance to output targets that reflect different levels of performance

workers' compensation insurance pays for medical costs and sometimes time off if an employee suffers a job-related sickness or accident and survivor benefits in the case of an employee's death

workers' compensation a type of insurance that replaces wages and medical benefits for employees injured on the job in exchange for relinquishing the employee's right to sue the employer for negligence

workflow analysis investigates how work moves through an organization to identify changes to increase efficiency and better meet customers' needs

workflow how work is organized to meet the organization's goals

workforce redeployment the movement of employees to other parts of the company or to other jobs the company needs filled to match its workforce with its talent needs

workplace bullying repeated incidents or a pattern of behavior that is intended to intimidate, offend, degrade, or humiliate a particular person or group of people

workplace tort a civil wrong in which an employer violates a duty owed to its customers or employees

workplace violence any act or threat of physical violence, harassment, intimidation, or other threatening disruptive behavior that occurs at the workplace

works councils councils of elected workers that participate in shared workplace governance

Name Index

Subject Index